THE PLACE OF STONE MONUMENTS

THE PLACE OF STONE MONUMENTS

Context, Use, and Meaning
in Mesoamerica's Preclassic Transition

JULIA GUERNSEY, JOHN E. CLARK, AND BARBARA ARROYO

Editors

DUMBARTON OAKS RESEARCH LIBRARY AND COLLECTION
WASHINGTON, D.C.

14 13 12 11 10   1 2 3 4 5

Library of Congress Cataloging-in-Publication Data

The place of stone monuments : context, use, and meaning in Mesoamerica's preclassic transition /
Julia Guernsey, John E. Clark, and Barbara Arroyo, editors.

p. cm. — (Dumbarton Oaks pre-Columbian symposia and colloquia)

Includes bibliographical references and index.

ISBN 978-0-88402-364-7 (hardcover : alk. paper)

1. Indians of Mexico—Antiquities—Congresses. 2. Indians of Central America—Antiquities—Congresses.
3. Monuments—Social aspects—Mexico—History—Congresses. 4. Monuments—Social aspects—Central
America—History—Congresses. 5. Monuments—Political aspects—Mexico—History—Congresses.
6. Monuments—Political aspects—Central America—History—Congresses. 7. Stele (Archaeology)—
Mexico—Congresses. 8. Stele (Archaeology)—Central America—Congresses. 9. Indian sculpture—Mexico—
Congresses. 10. Indian sculpture—Central America—Congresses. I. Guernsey, Julia, 1964– II. Clark, John E.
III. Arroyo, Barbara.

F1219.P685 2010

972'.01—dc22

2010006591

General Editor: Joanne Pillsbury

Managing Editor: Sara Taylor

Art Director: Kathleen Sparkes

Design and Composition: Melissa Tandysh

Volume based on papers presented at the symposium "The Place of Sculpture in Mesoamerica's Preclassic
Transition: Context, Use, and Meaning," organized by the Pre-Columbian Studies program at Dumbarton
Oaks. The symposium was held in Antigua, Guatemala, on October 5–6, 2007.

www.doaks.org/publications

CONTENTS

FIGURES

TABLES

FOREWORD

In 1967 Dumbarton Oaks held its first conference in the field of Pre-Columbian studies. The topic of the gathering was the Olmec, a culture that flourished in the Gulf Coast region of Mexico in the first millennium BC. A number of spectacular sculptures known as colossal heads had been discovered in the area over the course of the previous century, and this zone of Mesoamerica had become the focus of several innovative and important archaeological projects focusing on regional and interregional developments in the period known as the Preclassic. The 1967 conference was an opportunity to assess the state of the field in Olmec scholarship, which at the time was still a very young field. The papers from the conference were gathered and published in 1968 (Benson 1968).

Forty years and forty conferences later, the annual Pre-Columbian Studies symposium returned again to the subject of the Preclassic. The 2007 symposium, organized with the assistance of Barbara Arroyo, John E. Clark, and Julia Guernsey, focused on the place of stone monuments in the middle and later part of the Preclassic, the period between the precocious appearance of monumental sculpture at San Lorenzo ca 1000 BC and the rise of the Classic polities in the Maya region and Central Mexico. The editors of this volume refer to this period as the "Preclassic Transition," mindful of the 1,200-year spread included under the rubric. But as the editors point out, chronological phase names are

never perfectly compatible with archaeological data. The long-entrenched tripartite division of Mesoamerican prehistory into Preclassic, Classic, and Postclassic has always carried with it implications of a biological metaphor of development, florescence, and decline, even though there is nothing tentative about the colossal heads of the Preclassic, and the achievements of the Postclassic Aztecs are nothing less than exuberant florescence. Rather, the editors—supported elegantly by the authors in this volume—remind us of the complexities of this pivotal period, for which easy assumptions are often belied by new, finer-grained archaeological data.

Indeed, the traditional divisions of our neat schemata are challenged by these new data. The present volume illuminates the stylistic diversity of Preclassic sculpture, rich in regional variations but often sharing intriguing commonalities. A particular focus of attention in this volume is the context of these works, both within a site and against the backdrop of the broader region. What can the placement of sculpture within a site tell us about the meaning and function of the particular work, or even the site itself? How does later reuse of a sculpture affect our interpretations? What can the patterns of distribution of a sculptural type across a region tell us about social and political organization? How do we interpret a growing preference for relief carving over fully three-dimensional sculpture by the Late Preclassic? The chapters in this volume present abundant new data and new ways of thinking about Preclassic sculpture and society.

Over the past forty years we have seen a dramatic increase in research concerning the Preclassic, and this volume reflects the wealth of new data that have become available for the study of this period. Not surprisingly, new research has extended the traditional geographical and chronological boundaries of what have been considered Preclassic cultures. The term "Olmec" continues to be used, but the name does not fit comfortably for many of the polities discussed in the present volume. The chapters herein also call into question the traditional dividing line between Preclassic and what are thought of as Classic cultures, such as Maya. The examination of the life histories of sculptures and their contexts in this volume provides us with a fruitful way of rethinking the beginnings of Mesoamerican civilization.

It is often said that the creation of the Pre-Columbian Studies Program at Dumbarton Oaks owes its existence to a chance encounter Robert Woods Bliss had with a Middle Preclassic jadeite sculpture in Paris at the beginning of the twentieth century (Taube 2004:67–73). Entranced by the figure (then identified as Aztec but now known to be Olmec), Bliss began a lifelong engagement with Pre-Columbian art that ultimately led to the creation of the program of scholarly meetings at Dumbarton Oaks. At the time of his purchase of the sculpture, the Olmec had yet to be identified archaeologically—indeed it is a striking, but not uncommon, phenomenon that one of the earliest great cultures was one of the last to be identified. By the time Bliss died in 1962, great strides had been made in understanding the Olmec in particular and Preclassic cultures in general. A richer history of the culture that produced the striking jadeite sculpture was becoming apparent. In the past forty years, the focus at Dumbarton Oaks shifted away from the acquisition of objects to the support of research in the form of fellowships, field grants, conferences, and publications. The Preclassic has been the focus of many Dumbarton Oaks fellowship projects and publications since 1967, and we are pleased to have supported research on this topic over the years, including the 1993 symposium on social patterns in Preclassic Mesoamerica (Grove and Joyce 1999), and to be continuing the tradition with the present volume.

The chapters in this volume were originally presented at the Casa Santo Domingo in Antigua, Guatemala, on 5–6 October 2007. At that time, Dumbarton Oaks was in the midst of a renovation of the Main House, including the splendid Music Room, where symposia are normally held. The renovation at Dumbarton Oaks presented an opportunity for us to hold our scholarly gatherings elsewhere. In the early planning stages of the topic, Barbara Arroyo, John Clark, and Julia Guernsey suggested Antigua as a venue for the symposium. I am grateful to Edward Keenan, then director of Dumbarton Oaks, and the board of senior fellows, an advisory group including Elizabeth Boone, Warwick Bray, Clark Erickson, Virginia Fields, Louise Iseult Paradis, and David Webster, for their help and advice in the organization of this meeting. We were joined in Antigua by Jan Ziolkowski, who had assumed responsibilities as director of Dumbarton Oaks only a few months earlier. We are grateful for his participation in Antigua and for his support of the resulting publication. The symposium would not have been possible without the outstanding contributions of Emily Gulick, who coordinated the practical matters of this gathering. Her flawless planning ensured a productive and enjoyable meeting for the hundred-some attendees of the symposium. At the gathering itself, Emily was ably assisted by Mónica Antillón, Margarita Cossich Vielman, Adriana Linares Palma, and Lorena Paíz. We are also grateful for the assistance of numerous others who helped in various ways with both the symposium and the publication, including Miriam Doutriaux, Diego Gamboa, Bridget Gazzo, Gerardo Gutiérrez, Enrique Hurtado, Juan Antonio Murro, and Mary E. Pye. We are also grateful for the contributions of two anonymous reviewers, whose thoughtful comments on an initial draft of the manuscript were most helpful in the preparation of the final version of the volume. Two papers presented at the Antigua symposium, those by Vida Prater and Richard Hansen, were not available for publication in the present volume. The publication was prepared with the kind assistance of Arlene Colman of the New World Archaeological Foundation, with additional help from Emily Gulick and Emily Kline. The production of the volume was overseen by Kathy Sparkes, publications manager at Dumbarton Oaks, and Sara M. Taylor, art and archaeology editor. I offer everyone hearty thanks for their roles in seeing the symposium come to proper fruition as a publication.

Finally, I thank Barbara Arroyo, John Clark, and Julia Guernsey for their inspiration and hard work. They identified a topic of great potential—a topic ripe with new data and new ideas, but one in need of rigorous examination. The symposium transformed our understanding of the place of sculpture in the Preclassic, in the multiple senses of "place," as so elegantly argued by the editors in their preface. As is true of any good conference, the gathering may have prompted as many questions as it resolved, but the field is much richer for the efforts of the editors and authors of this volume.

Joanne Pillsbury
Director of Studies,
Pre-Columbian Program
Dumbarton Oaks

PREFACE

This book addresses the early development and spread of Mesoamerican civilization and the role(s) of stone monuments in that process. Book chapters grew from papers presented and discussed at the Dumbarton Oaks conference on early Mesoamerican sculpture held in Antigua, Guatemala, in October 2007, titled "The Place of Sculpture in Mesoamerica's Preclassic Transition: Context, Use, and Meaning." Conference participants considered the functions, uses, and meanings of stone monuments as they related to the growth and spread of Mesoamerican civilization. As with all Dumbarton Oaks conferences, focused and achievable goals were proposed for discussion, and participation was limited to a handful of invited presenters and an informed audience of listeners who engaged speakers in lively debate over a three-day period. The fruits of this creative dialogue are apparent in the following chapters, all of which were extensively revised and improved following the conference. Even the title for this book was adjusted based on discussions there. We replaced "sculpture" with "stone monuments" because many special, deliberately placed stones in early Mesoamerica were natural boulders rather than carved sculptures, a point explored in the final chapter of this book.

The conference focused on the interval bracketed by the twilight of Mesoamerica's first civilization, San Lorenzo (1000 BC), and the dawn of its first empire, Teotihuacan (AD 200). This prolonged, 1,200-year transition witnessed the development of civilization as plurality and diversity. Our goal at the conference was to illuminate this transformative epoch through a systematic study of its stone sculpture. In this temporal framework, it was not possible or feasible to discuss all the important centers of the Middle/Late Preclassic period. This deficiency, in itself, is testimony of the proliferation of cities and stone monuments by Late Preclassic times. For the conference we chose archaeological cases, among those realistically available, that filled gaps in current knowledge. The aim was to build on the strengths of previous research and to redress weaknesses. Thus we privileged case studies and data that are poorly known or inadequately published in English.

We did not consider stone monuments as ends in themselves but rather as aids to understanding how Mesoamerican civilization grew and spread. Presenters at the conference considered stone monuments in their sociohistorical contexts and settings as a means of recovering their ancient uses and meanings. Sculptural programs were evaluated against the backdrop of created centers, sacred landscapes, and "spatial experience" (Smith 2003:5). Participants were encouraged to go beyond common considerations of sacred space and to focus on monuments as dynamic objects deployed in elite claims to power and authority—claims that also included buildings, plazas, natural features of the landscape, and human constructions that mimicked natural features, such as pyramids qua mountains. We believed that examination of specific sites in terms of their sculptural programs, built environments, and associated artifacts would provide a better understanding of the changing nature of authority and of social and political organization during the Preclassic period. It would also highlight public representations as dynamic forces in the construction and manipulation of such authority.

The approaches to the analysis of stone monuments presented in the following chapters blend the best aspects of political economy, semiotics, and phenomenology. We are just as interested in how and why monuments were made as in what they meant at different times and places to different observers. The time and labor required to quarry, haul, and carve a monument were as important to its meaning as the images carved on it. Likewise, it made a significant difference where the monument was placed, what was beside it, who got to see it, and on what occasions. These are all issues of individual monument biography and context.

Most studies of stone monuments are necessarily limited to the final use and/or abuse of the monuments, and this is true for the contributions in this book. There are inherent limitations on possible analyses of function and meaning that derive from different histories of monument discovery and the conditions of their preservation. Conference participants focused on context at the most specific level that the monuments available for study allowed. For some sites, data are available on the final placement and uses of monuments in plazas and next to buildings and offerings. For others, detailed archaeological data are lacking, so context is approached in terms of broader chronological or stylistic patterns. At some sites, the monument program consisted of putting up a single sculpture. By itself, one data point may appear unimpressive

or uninformative, but viewed in regional and interregional contexts these singular instances constitute significant distributional data. As discussed in the first chapter, part of understanding the uses and meanings of Preclassic monuments is to identify when and where they did *not* occur.

Conference participants examined the sculptural programs of many Preclassic sites representative of different cultural groups to help interpret the rise of civilization instead of viewing sculpture solely as a product of civilization. This focus represents a shift in perspective from traditional studies, which consider Mesoamerican sculptures as the result of increasing social and political complexity, to the more dynamic view that these sculptures were a means through which these social and political forces were articulated and defined. Stone monuments in Preclassic Mesoamerica were more than the manifestation of artistic achievement. Their creation and deployment were integral to the initial rise and spread of civilization.

Although all participants subscribed to the same goals, differences in the nature of available data sets fostered fundamental differences in the approaches taken for reconstructing the functions and meanings of Preclassic stone monuments for individual sites and regions. Of the original thirteen presentations at the conference, eleven are published here. Two scholars invited to the conference could not come, and two participants could not accommodate Dumbarton Oaks's publication deadlines. Hence, the desired detailed treatments for Chalcatzingo, Tiltepec, Kaminaljuyu, and the Mirador Basin are not part of this volume. Chapters are organized by region, starting in Central Mexico and moving south to Guatemala. The introductory chapter attends to Preclassic sites and monuments not covered in other chapters.

Julia Guernsey, John E. Clark,
and Barbara Arroyo
20 February 2009

Stone Monuments and Preclassic Civilization

JOHN E. CLARK, JULIA GUERNSEY, AND BARBARA ARROYO

OUR PURPOSE IN THIS INTRODUCTORY chapter is to set the stage for those that follow by providing information that will make them more intelligible for non-Mesoamericanists. Contrary to standard practice, we do not summarize the individual chapters or hype their obvious significance. Rather, our objectives are to provide a time-space-culture frame for Preclassic Mesoamerican civilizations and to explain the basic terms and foundational concepts used in their study. We also propose a sculpture chronology for Preclassic Mesoamerica and introduce its most common forms. In the final section we consider the historical spread of sculpture across Mesoamerica and some of the functions and meanings these monuments may have held for their creators.

Terms, Assumptions, and Premises

The title of this book is a mouthful, but it well delimits the primary goals of the volume and the premises underlying them. It specifies time, space, cultural content, cause, and method, but does so in academic jargon that deserves some decoding. The key terms of the title also implicate important assumptions, so we begin with definitions and assumptions.

The following chapters consider a block of time in the Preclassic period. "Preclassic" is a relational and developmental term that no longer means what was originally intended—a non-complex prelude to climax forms—but scholars continue to use it, because no better label has yet been accepted. Early archaeology in Middle America assumed that the high point of cultural attainment occurred during a past "golden age" designated as the Classic period. Elaborate sculpture, stone architecture, and cities were thought to be part of this Classic cultural florescence, with the Preclassic conceived as a prelude era lacking such things. However, research over the past forty years has demonstrated that all features that originally defined and delimited Classic civilization actually occurred first in Preclassic times.

The term "Formative" is often used in place of "Preclassic" to signal the same cultural crescendo. These terms no longer retain developmental value and are used here only as markers of sequential periods.

The temporal range of the Preclassic period —and its subdivisions (Early, Middle, and Late) —varies from region to region. The range shown in Figure 1.1 aligns with historical developments in eastern Mesoamerica. Also depicted are finer sequential divisions among different regions. Each column lists phases defined by significant changes in material culture—sculpture, architecture, and ceramic forms—within a region or site. Both the

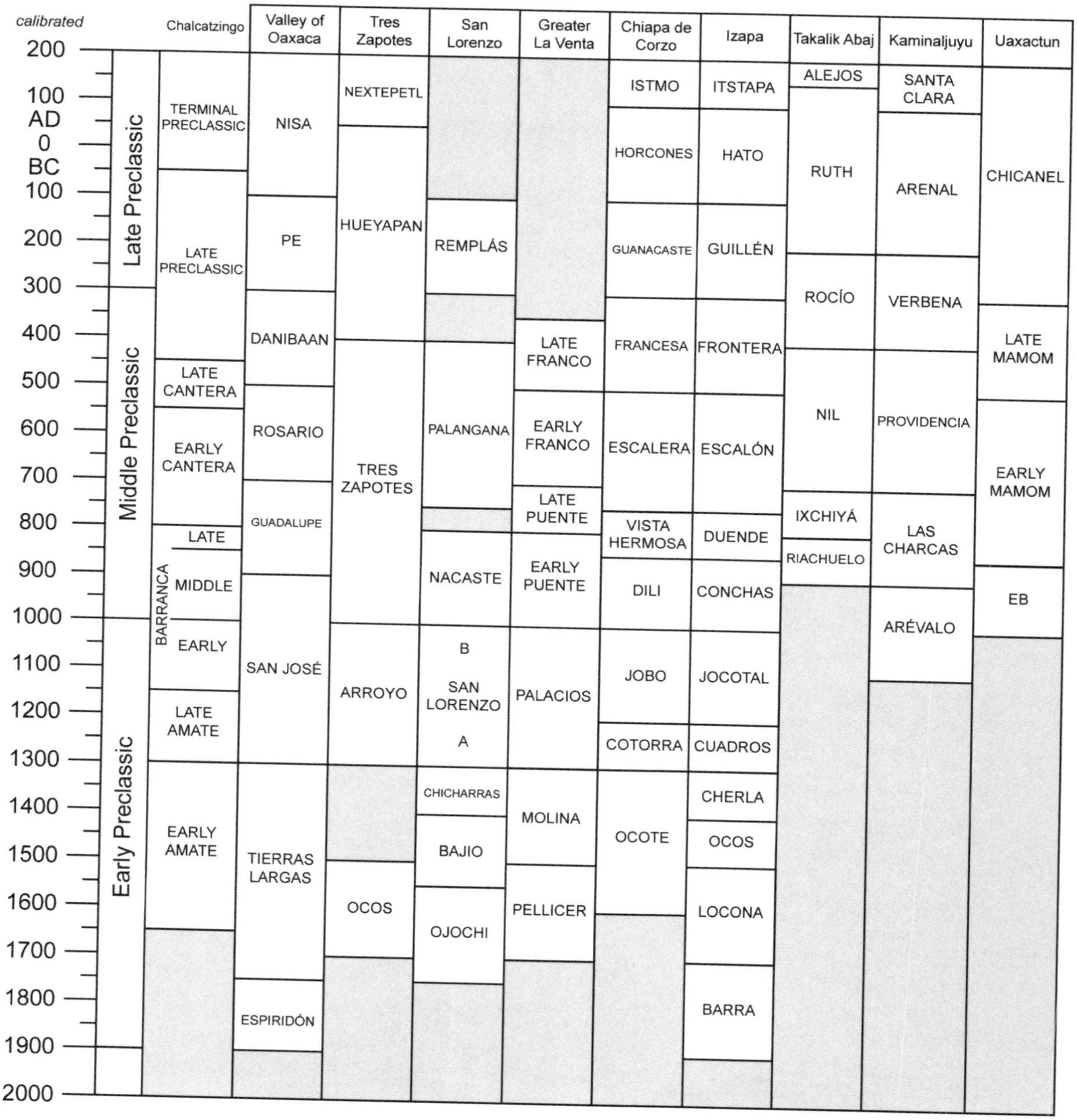

Comparative chronology of Preclassic Mesoamerica. Phases by region (approximate, from ~2000 BC to AD 200):

Period divisions (left margin): Late Preclassic, Middle Preclassic, Early Preclassic.

calibrated	Chalcatzingo	Valley of Oaxaca	Tres Zapotes	San Lorenzo	Greater La Venta	Chiapa de Corzo	Izapa	Takalik Abaj	Kaminaljuyu	Uaxactun
200 / 100 AD	TERMINAL PRECLASSIC	NISA	NEXTEPETL			ISTMO	ITSTAPA	ALEJOS	SANTA CLARA	
0 BC / 100			HUEYAPAN			HORCONES	HATO	RUTH	ARENAL	CHICANEL
200	LATE PRECLASSIC	PE		REMPLÁS		GUANACASTE	GUILLÉN			
300								ROCÍO	VERBENA	
400	LATE CANTERA	DANIBAAN			LATE FRANCO	FRANCESA	FRONTERA			LATE MAMOM
500								NIL	PROVIDENCIA	
600	EARLY CANTERA	ROSARIO		PALANGANA	EARLY FRANCO	ESCALERA	ESCALÓN			
700			TRES ZAPOTES		LATE PUENTE					EARLY MAMOM
800	LATE (BARRANCA)	GUADALUPE				VISTA HERMOSA	DUENDE	IXCHIYÁ	LAS CHARCAS	
900	MIDDLE (BARRANCA)			NACASTE	EARLY PUENTE			RIACHUELO		
1000						DILI	CONCHAS			EB
1100	EARLY (BARRANCA)	SAN JOSÉ		B / SAN LORENZO	PALACIOS	JOBO	JOCOTAL		ARÉVALO	
1200	LATE AMATE		ARROYO							
1300				A		COTORRA	CUADROS			
1400	EARLY AMATE	TIERRAS LARGAS		CHICHARRAS	MOLINA		CHERLA			
1500				BAJIO		OCOTE	OCOS			
1600			OCOS		PELLICER		LOCONA			
1700			OJOCHI							
1800		ESPIRIDÓN					BARRA			
1900 / 2000										

figure 1.1

Comparative chronology of Preclassic Mesoamerica. (Drawing from the New World Archaeological Foundation.)

period and phase divisions are keyed to absolute dates determined by radiocarbon assays.

Our delimitation of space is less obvious. Contributions are restricted to Mesoamerica, a complex term that specifies time, place, and cultural practices as an indivisible trinity. Mesoamerica represents an amalgam of cultural practices and beliefs; it is not a spatial term for a geographic region, although for any given time it specifies a region in the central sector of Middle America (Kirchhoff 1943, 1966). The boundaries of Mesoamerica fluctuated through time and territory as peoples adopted or abandoned particular cultural practices (see Litvak King 1975). It started quite small and

expanded through time. The spread of city living, frequently signaled by the presence of stone sculpture and monumental architecture, represented the growth and expansion of Mesoamerica itself. By the end of the Preclassic era (ca AD 200), Mesoamerica had nearly reached its maximum extent. The locations of the principal Preclassic cities and sites discussed in this book are shown in Figure 1.2.

The main idea held by scholars is that all Mesoamerican peoples shared a common history —as reflected in similarities of core cultural practices and beliefs. Nevertheless, significant differences persisted among them, including distinct languages. At the time of the Spanish conquest,

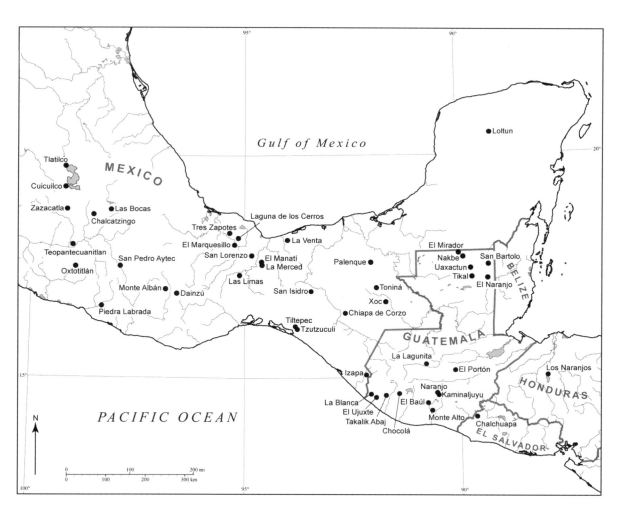

figure 1.2
Map of Preclassic Mesoamerica showing the locations of its principal sites. (Map from the New World Archaeological Foundation.)

more than three hundred languages were spoken in Middle America, representative of twenty-one major language families (Campbell 1979:904). Fewer languages were spoken in Preclassic times, but Mesoamerica was still ethnically and linguistically diverse. The sites and regions in Morelos and Guerrero of western Mexico (see Chapters 2–4) are of uncertain cultural and linguistic affiliation, but they were likely occupied by peoples who spoke ancestral forms of Otomanguean (Grove 1999:257). It is thought that the Olmecs of the Gulf Coast lowlands of Veracruz and Tabasco (or a majority of them) spoke some form of a Mixe-Zoque proto-language at the beginning of the Early Preclassic before the split into Mixe and Zoque languages (see Chapters 5 and 6; Campbell and Kaufman 1976; Justeson and Kaufman 2008; Kaufman and Justeson 2008). Mayan peoples occupied much of the region that now includes southern Mexico and the Yucatan Peninsula, Guatemala, Belize, and the western portions of Honduras and El Salvador (see Chapters 8 and 10–12). The linguistic identity of ancient peoples along the Pacific Coast and piedmont of modern Chiapas and Guatemala is a subject of ongoing debate (see Chapters 7 and 9). In summary, peoples of at least three major language families were involved in early Mesoamerica and its Preclassic Transition. From northwest to southeast, these were Otomangueans, Mixe-Zoqueans, and Mayan peoples. We can trace some of these peoples through their artistic production to modern descendants.

The book title asserts that a major developmental transformation occurred in Mesoamerica during the Preclassic period. In fact, at least two revolutionary transitions occurred. The first marked a change in lifestyle and the second in society. Precursors of the Preclassic period were "Archaic" nomadic foragers who did not live in permanent villages or depend on agriculture. The evolution of city living from this rudimentary beginning involved many significant transitions, most of them poorly known. However, it is becoming increasingly clear that a major transition to city living occurred ca 1300 BC in the Early Preclassic (instead of the Classic) period with the foundation of a city at San Lorenzo in the

Gulf Coast lowlands of Veracruz (Clark 2007; Coe and Diehl 1980; Cyphers 1996, 1999; cf. Morley 1946). A second social transition during the Middle/Late Preclassic (1000 BC–AD 200) involved the rise of cities in many different regions and the creation of distinct sculptural forms and styles by various peoples, as described in the following chapters.

This book is about the place of stone monuments and sculptures in Preclassic Mesoamerica, an allusion to their installation in cities and of the need to conceptualize them in their original settings. The term "place" serves double duty, referring to spatial coordinates and ambient associations as well as to the social and cognitive significance of sculptures and monuments for Mesoamerican peoples. In this latter sense, the term calls attention to the role of sculpture in Preclassic Mesoamerica. Use of this term in the title assumes that stone monuments and sculptures had a place in Mesoamerican societies in both senses.

Our presumption about the place of stone monuments in Preclassic Mesoamerica demands contextual analyses. We believe that the developmental significance of sculptures in different Preclassic societies depended on the uses and messages they had for the peoples for whom they were made and displayed. We are further committed to the proposition that the meanings of sculptures depended on their contexts. The central premise of this book is that the functions and meanings of stone monuments in their ancient settings must be deduced from details of their spatial, temporal, and associational contexts, as evaluated at multiple scales.

The search for meaning is a complicated topic that deserves more attention than we can accord it here. The following chapters discuss various levels of meaning, but none provides a full exegesis, because space limitations preclude detailed arguments. Some primary identifications are entailed in the classification process itself, such as identifying a monument as an altar instead of a throne, or as an image of a deer rather than a rabbit (see Chapter 8). After this first step of identification, some authors explore the metaphorical meanings of forms and entities, as documented for Late Mesoamerican peoples or their living descendants.

When it comes to exploring deep levels of meaning, we are all amateurs—archaeologists and art historians alike—doing our best with imperfect and incomplete information. Devising sound methods for ascribing meaning to stone sculptures is a critical need for future research. As a first step, it will require the kind of careful reconstructions of monuments and their contexts attempted by the authors in this book. Our purpose here is to advance the topic, with the understanding that final solutions are still far off. Interpretations in the following chapters are the responsibility of their authors; we have not attempted to forge a consensus among those with contrary views. Given the state of the art, the variety of approaches to meaning showcased here should generate positive discussion. The chapters in this book mostly concern lower levels of meaning, beginning with accurate reconstructions and clear drawings of monuments, moving to identifications of forms and representations, and then considering possible metaphorical meanings. At times this sequential process represents a naive hermeneutics that presumes transparency for primary identifications—a "what you see is what there was" perspective. At other times it involves analogies that go beyond motifs to recurring patterns of symbols. We draw attention to this caveat to stimulate future discussion and to warn readers that the clarity and certainty with which individual authors express opinions do not necessarily relate to the broad acceptance of their claims. In studying stone monuments, we have to guard equally against seeing too little and imagining too much.

The book title entails four additional foundational premises that inform the following chapters: (1) that the Middle/Late Preclassic era witnessed the elaboration and spread of city life to different peoples across Mesoamerica; (2) that stone sculpture played a dynamic role in this process; (3) that the positive effects of stone monuments in this process depended on what the monuments meant to the peoples who made and viewed them; and (4) that plain stone monuments were selected, and sculptures intentionally carved, to convey particular messages. These last two premises dictate that

our studies of stone monuments employ methods for interpreting their past uses and meanings.

Stone sculptures for the Middle and Late Preclassic periods are frequently smashed, broken, defaced, and dislocated from their original contexts. If they were as significant as we think, our first tasks are to reconstruct them and some of their original contexts, as illustrated by Travis F. Doering and Lori D. Collins (Chapter 11) in their analysis of Monument 65 from Kaminaljuyu in highland Guatemala. Another troublesome fact is that Preclassic sculptures are generally underreported, understudied, and/or poorly illustrated. These facts bring us to the paradoxical state of affairs that inspired the Dumbarton Oaks conference in Antigua: the sculptures implicated in the key social and political transformation in Mesoamerica are the most poorly known. This book hopes to reverse this state of affairs.

Preclassic Sculptures and Their Ages

The enduring qualities of stone monuments that made them useful props for gaining, retaining, and contesting power and authority in ancient times—and make them useful today for thinking about past social and political conditions—are those properties that make their historical placement and analysis difficult. Stone monuments were made to last. Thus they routinely outlived their original functions, messages, and meanings and were put to other uses by later peoples. Function and meaning were labile properties dependent on sliding historical and social circumstances. Most of the stone monuments described in this book are more than 2,000 years old, and some are more than 3,000 years old. They are being exhibited in museums, at archaeological sites, or in private collections, so they are still being put to meaningful uses after all this time. The various uses they served during their full existence are of interest, but we are especially anxious to know when they were first made and what their original uses and functions may have been. What messages and meanings did they convey, and with what results? Answers to these questions depend on correctly placing sculptures in their original temporal, spatial, and cultural frames. For the moment, no reliable methods exist for dating stone monuments directly, so archaeologists have to infer their ages from associations with other artifacts. For many Maya sculptures of the Classic period, the dates of their manufacture were carved into the stones themselves, but almost all Preclassic monuments lack this handy information.

At the present time, most Preclassic stone monuments and sculptures are dated by association with the "strong phase" of the archaeological site where they were found. Such attributions are logically weak and hinder evaluations, as a brief consideration of an infamous case illustrates. One of the difficult decisions of the Antigua conference

was to exclude Early Preclassic sculpture known principally from San Lorenzo (Figure 1.2). Sculptures at this site (see Coe and Diehl 1980; Cyphers 2004b) include colossal heads, table-top thrones, figures of seated men carved in the round, carved pillars, ornamental drain stones and spouts, and an assortment of other forms (Figure 1.3). They are all made of basalt imported from about 60 km away. Some of the monuments weigh more than twenty tons, so impressive amounts of labor were involved in bringing in finished monuments or the boulders for carving them on site. The colossal heads are thought to be portraits of kings, and the massive table-top altars are considered their thrones. Other kinds of sculptures also emphasize the kingship theme, whereas a few portray biologically impossible entities that may represent gods

figure 1.3
Early Preclassic sculptures from the Gulf Coast lowlands. (a) San Lorenzo Monument 61 (Cyphers 2004b:125–127, fig. 73); (b) San Lorenzo Monument 14 (Coe and Diehl 1980:321, fig. 439); (c) San Lorenzo Monument 10 (Coe and Diehl 1980:316, fig. 434); (d) San Lorenzo Monument 41 (Coe and Diehl 1980:350, fig. 478); (e) San Lorenzo Monument 58 (Cyphers 2004b:123, fig. 71). (Drawings from the New World Archaeological Foundation based on the images listed.)

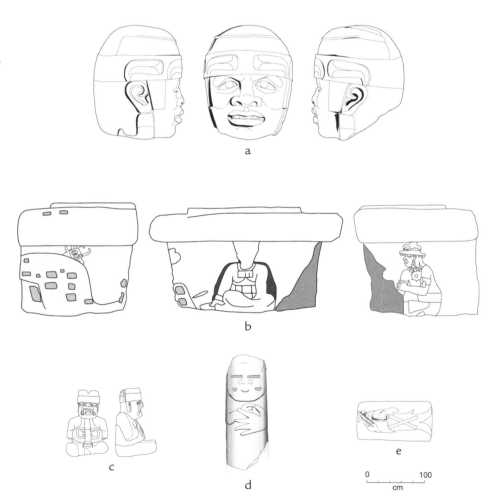

or supernaturals (Clark 2004, 2008). The labor involved in hauling basalt and transforming it into awe-inspiring images of leaders is clear evidence of a stratified society and civilization. A point of controversy is the age of these sculptures and of the developments in social and political complexity they implicate.

Coe and Diehl (1980) argue that most of the sculptures date to the apogee of the site, 1300–1000 BC. Older and younger occupation layers are known for San Lorenzo, however, so this chronometric assignment is open to debate. Some authors propose that the monuments date to the Middle Preclassic period and postdate San Lorenzo's climax (Graham 1989; Hammond 1988). If so, the San Lorenzo monuments would be coeval with the earliest sculptures known for other regions of Mesoamerica. Some of this debate arises from confusion between marginal possibilities and likely realities. Another problem is categorical thinking. It is likely that some sculptures at San Lorenzo date to the Middle Preclassic, but we believe most are older.[1] One should not assume they all date to the same phase. Several centuries of sculpture production are represented in San Lorenzo's sculptural corpus, and the same is true for sculptures described in the following chapters for other Preclassic sites. The main point for consideration here is that most of the sculptures at San Lorenzo have been recovered from secondary depositional contexts, and many of them in archaeological levels with Middle Preclassic artifacts, so many of the archaeological contexts for monuments recovered there do not unambiguously support the antiquity attributed to them.

In terms of stylistic or technological sequences, the San Lorenzo sculptures are again problematic, because they lack antecedents. The massive, realistic style of early Olmec sculptures appears to have come out of nowhere sui generis. If these sculptures are as old as claimed, their creation represents the conjunction of genius on many levels. They are some of the most sophisticated monuments, technically and aesthetically, known for Mesoamerica for all time periods, and they are also the oldest. Coe and Diehl (1980:246) and Coe (1981:128, 139)

argue that a small fragment of sculpture at San Lorenzo came from an archaeological deposit that can date to no later than 1300 BC, thus establishing a base date for the beginning of the sculptural tradition (see Clark 2007; for contra, see Graham 1989). Excavations at San Lorenzo have also recovered a colossal head and throne (Figure 1.3a,b) that date to no later than 1200 BC (Cyphers et al. 2006).

An implication of these and other corroborative data is that the tradition of carving stone sculptures began with the early Olmecs at San Lorenzo and spread from there to other parts of Mesoamerica during the period we call the "Preclassic Transition." Middle Preclassic sculptures all across Mesoamerica derived from early Olmec forms, as described by authors in this book (see Chapters 2–8). The oldest monuments are some of the most accomplished. Stone sculpture first appeared in a region bereft of the necessary raw material to create it. Antecedents of this sculpture, in terms of techniques and representations, have not been identified. We suspect the tradition of carving stone involved a transfer of techniques and forms from one medium to another, such as from wood to stone. The discovery at El Manatí, a site near San Lorenzo, of wooden sculptures that date to 1200–1000 BC (Ortíz and Rodríguez 1994, 1999, 2000) shows that they are about as old as the early stone sculptures. Some of the earliest sculptures mimic wooden forms (Clark 2004).

The difficulties of dating stone sculptures are such that most of us feel good if we can approximate the age of a Preclassic monument to within a century of its original carving date. In this situation site associations prove useful. The earliest sculptures occur in the Gulf Coast lowlands and at sites that seem to have been sequential Olmec capitals. These capitals also appear to have been abandoned before their successor came into full power, so the rise and fall of lowland Olmec centers has allowed scholars to map out a rough sequence of sculpture forms and styles associated with the sequential capitals, starting with San Lorenzo, followed by La Venta (see Chapter 6) in the Middle Preclassic, and succeeded by Tres Zapotes (see Chapter 5) during the Late Preclassic period. Coe (1966, 2005) has long proposed that other Late Preclassic sites, such as Izapa on the Pacific Coast of Chiapas, Mexico (see Chapter 9), fit in this sequence alongside Tres Zapotes. Coe argued for a unilinear sequence of major styles: Olmec, Izapan, Mayan. This popular and widely accepted view no longer is plausible because sculptures that are stylistically Maya date to the late Middle Preclassic (see Chapters 8 and 10) and thus are coeval with the latest Olmec monuments at La Venta and are earlier than Izapan-style sculptures at Izapa.

As evident in Figure 1.3, most of the earliest stone sculptures of Mesoamerica were carved in the round. Some low-relief images were also carved on the flat sides of thrones and other monuments (Figure 1.3e; see also Figures 6.5–6.8), but low-relief carvings appear most often as secondary elements on three-dimensional sculptures in the Early Preclassic. Most of the sculptural forms seen at San Lorenzo have also been found at La Venta. The continuity of forms and themes between San Lorenzo and La Venta sculptures is remarkable and has generated some confusion about the relative ages of these cities and the duration of the early sculptural style. A sculptural form seen more frequently at La Venta was the stela: a freestanding stone monument that could include low-relief

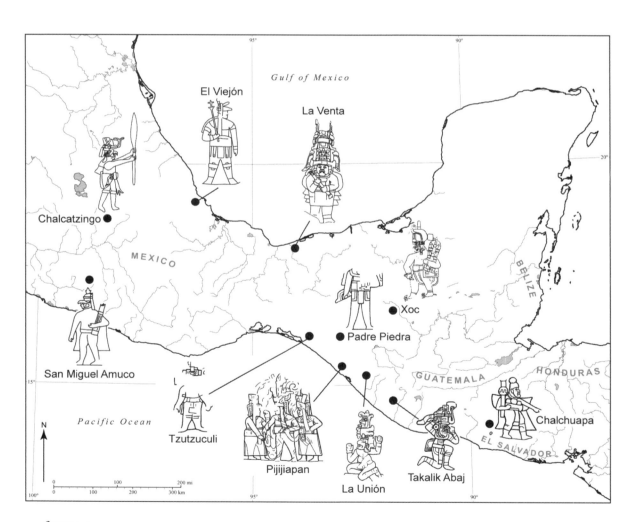

figure 1.4
Distribution of low-relief sculptures and carvings in the early Middle Preclassic period. (Map from the New World Archaeological Foundation.)

a

b

figure 1.5
Middle Preclassic low-relief carvings. (a) Chalcatzingo "Procession" (compare to Angulo 1987:143, fig. 10.13; Grove 1984:plate 9); (b) carvings on the four faces of a large boulder in Chalchuapa (compare to Boggs 1950:92, fig. 1). (Drawings from the New World Archaeological Foundation based on an examination of the carvings.)

carving on its surfaces. The carving techniques and images clearly derived from those practiced at San Lorenzo, but the underlying form was different (Clancy 1990). Low-relief images have been found across Mesoamerica, as illustrated in Figure 1.4. Outside of La Venta, many of these images were carved on exposed rock faces or giant boulders (Figure 1.5). These date to the first part of the Middle Preclassic period, or ca 950–750 BC (see Clark and Pye 2000:228, fig. 15); they depict standing men and women in elaborate garb.[2]

Full-round sculptures appear to have been less frequent in Middle Preclassic times. Sculptures in the round, probably dating to the first half of the Middle Preclassic period, have been found at La Venta, Tres Zapotes, Chalcatzingo, Takalik Abaj, and in Honduras at the site of Los Naranjos (see Chapters 5, 6, and 8; Grove and Angulo 1987; Joyce and Henderson 2002). All of these full-round figures are associated with Preclassic regional centers. In contrast, the aforementioned low-relief carvings are found near mountain passes, perhaps marking critical junctures along trade routes (Clark and Pye 2000) or territorial boundaries (see Chapter 5). Both the round and flat monuments are in the Olmec style known from La Venta. Overall, the few early Middle Preclassic monuments scattered across Mesoamerica evince a homogeneity of style and a consistent representation of limited themes.

Sculptures in the round appear to have been designed to be movable, whereas many of the low-relief carvings outside the Gulf Coast lowlands were carved on rock surfaces that could not be moved. The low-relief Olmec carvings became permanent features of the landscape. Most stelae at city centers were also designed to be planted in relatively fixed locations by burying their prepared tenons in the ground, so the monuments could be stood on end. However, small stelae are known for Preclassic sites (the stela at Ojo de Agua is 1 m tall) and from Middle Preclassic imagery (e.g., the Xoc monument from central Chiapas; Figures 1.4 and 12.2a). These examples indicate that small stelae may have been used and transported for ritual performances (Guernsey 2006a).[3] Many of the larger low-relief carvings portrayed multiple individuals in the same scene, as especially evident with monuments from Chalcatzingo and Chalchuapa (Figure 1.5). Thus one trend in Middle Preclassic sculptures was toward flat narrative scenes showing multiple individuals, most of whom appear to have been high-status persons in elaborate clothing.

An unusual and little investigated or understood development during the early Middle Preclassic period was the erection of "plain" monuments, meaning uncarved monoliths. These monuments were popular in the Guatemalan Highlands during the Middle Preclassic and on the coast of Guatemala during the Late Preclassic (see Bove n.d.a). At the early center of Naranjo in the Valley of Guatemala, more than twenty-two plain monuments have been identified in the central part of the site, and all date to Middle Preclassic times. These plain monuments are of two kinds: large basalt boulders with one smoothed surface and natural, columnar basalt pillars with six flat facets (see Figure 12.1b). Placement of these plain monuments in the main plaza at Naranjo shows they were meant to be seen by everyone. These monuments were set up in three parallel, north-south rows. The first row, facing the main mound, has a combination of columnar and boulder monuments; the second row is composed of five large basalt boulders, each with one smoothed surface; the third row consists of four natural pillars of columnar basalt. The placement of these monoliths appears to have commemorated some type of astronomical or cyclical event rather than portray individuals, as was the case for coeval monuments at La Venta, La Blanca, and Takalik Abaj (see Chapters 6–8). The presence of the two forms of plain monuments at Naranjo and their placements near major geographic features (such as springs and hills) suggest they could have also functioned as boundary stones and may have marked significant units of social and sacred space, as argued by Christie (2005) for later Maya monuments. Because of the wide distribution of plain monuments in Mesoamerica, use of such stones should be considered an important Middle Preclassic practice.

Development of the sculptural arts during the Late Preclassic period makes Middle Preclassic efforts look like exercises in modesty (Figures 1.6 and 1.7). For the Late Preclassic there is an explosion of new forms, themes, and styles (see Chapters 7–11; Parsons 1986). Sculptures show up at many more sites, in greater frequencies, and in different styles. The same trend is apparent in architecture, with the Late Preclassic period seeing a proliferation of cities, pyramids, stone architecture in regional styles, and significant differences in the basic layouts of cities (Clark n.d.). This period also witnessed the establishment of state societies all across Mesoamerica, each with its own regional style. These distinct styles probably marked culture and language differences. Regional differences started to manifest themselves before the end of the Middle Preclassic period, or ca 500–400 BC, the time that La Venta was abandoned (see Chapter 6). The overall pattern of temporal change was the

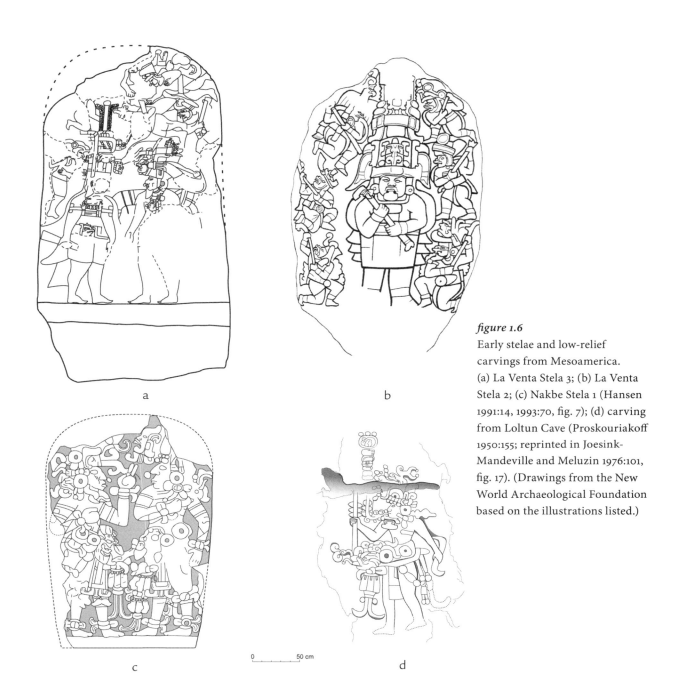

a

b

c

d

figure 1.6
Early stelae and low-relief
carvings from Mesoamerica.
(a) La Venta Stela 3; (b) La Venta
Stela 2; (c) Nakbe Stela 1 (Hansen
1991:14, 1993:70, fig. 7); (d) carving
from Loltun Cave (Proskouriakoff
1950:155; reprinted in Joesink-
Mandeville and Meluzin 1976:101,
fig. 17). (Drawings from the New
World Archaeological Foundation
based on the illustrations listed.)

0   50 cm

emergence of regional variety from preceding homogeneity.

The Late Preclassic saw the elaboration of stelae and low-relief carvings of elite individuals shown in profile (Figures 1.6 and 1.7). Some of the earliest stelae were carved on stones having a natural, elongated form, with the carving typically confined to one face. By the Late Preclassic, some stelae in eastern Mesoamerica were carved into

shaped slabs by dressing the two faces, squaring the edges, and then carving images on the front (and in rare cases, also on the back; see Chapter 11). Other forms that were popular in eastern Mesoamerica were pedestal (see Figure 10.5b) and potbelly sculptures (see Figures 7.21, 8.6, 9.14, and 9.15). Good evidence for pedestal sculptures shows they date to the latter part of the Middle Preclassic and into the Late Preclassic (see Chapters 7 and

figure 1.7
Late Preclassic sculptures. (a) Alvarado Stela showing a foldout of two sides (Covarrubias 1957:69, fig. 29; Pérez de Lara and Justeson 2006); (b) Cuicuilco (Pérez Campa 1998:37, drawing by Graciela Rodríguez León); (c) La Venta Monument 63 (compare to Joralemon 1971:44, fig. 132; Piña Chan 1982:fig. 78); (d) Kaminaljuyu Stela 9 showing wraparound designs on adjacent sides (Scott 1978:29, fig. 13). (Drawings from the New World Archaeological Foundation based on the monuments or images listed.)

a   b   c   d

0   50 cm

10). Parsons (1986:23) mentions that pedestal monuments were carved from basalt columns. This association suggests that both plain basalt monuments and short pedestal sculptures date to the Middle Preclassic. Miles (1965:248) commented on the wide geographic distribution of pedestal sculptures in Mesoamerica and noted their association with boulder sculptures. Pedestal sculptures include representations of jaguars, monkeys, other animals, and men carved in the round on top of carefully shaped, and usually square, shafts (see Figure 10.5b; Miles 1965:248). The so-called "fat-boy" or "potbelly" sculptures probably date to the same time period (see Chapters 8 and 9).

A significant trend in the Late Preclassic was the proliferation of stela-altar pairs. Because of the history of research and the sequence of archaeological discovery, stela-altar pairs are generally considered a Maya trait, as they were first identified at Classic Maya cities. However, Naranjo in highland Guatemala has three stela-altar pairs that date to 800 BC or earlier. Early stela-altar pairs are also known for Central Mexico (Grove 1984, 1987a). One of the large, plain stelae at Teopantecuanitlan stands

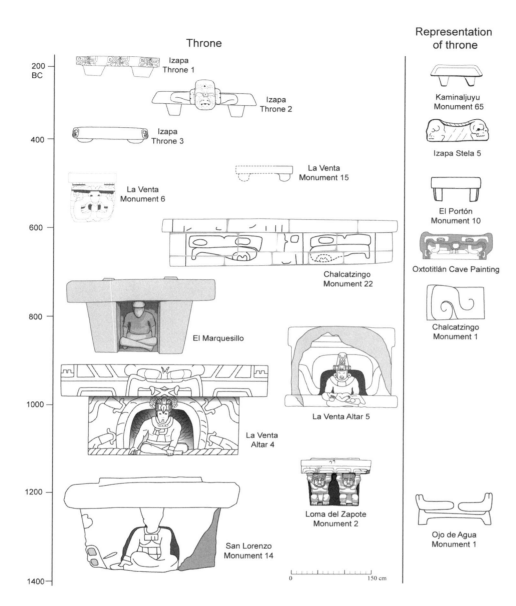

Throne

200 BC

Izapa Throne 1

Izapa Throne 2

400

Izapa Throne 3

La Venta Monument 15

La Venta Monument 6

600

Chalcatzingo Monument 22

800

El Marquesillo

La Venta Altar 5

1000

La Venta Altar 4

1200

Loma del Zapote Monument 2

San Lorenzo Monument 14

1400

Representation of throne

Kaminaljuyu Monument 65

Izapa Stela 5

El Portón Monument 10

Oxtotitlán Cave Painting

Chalcatzingo Monument 1

Ojo de Agua Monument 1

0   150 cm

figure 1.8
Evolution of thrones and their representations in Preclassic Mesoamerica. Thrones are shown at the same scale; representations of thrones are not to scale. (Drawing from the New World Archaeological Foundation.)

beside a toad altar (see Figure 3.19), and the pair dates to ca 700 BC. The Late Preclassic pairing is most evident at Izapa (see Chapter 9). At this site many of the stelae were carved with scenes that inserted images of rulers into mythic narratives (Guernsey 2006b; Lowe et al. 1982; Norman 1973, 1976). The Izapa stelae were often fronted by thick, circular altars, some of which were carved to represent three-dimensional toads similar to the Teopantecuanitlan altar from centuries earlier (see Chapters 7–9).

Another new sculptural form in the Late Preclassic was the four-legged throne (Figures 1.8

and 1.9). Many of the objects today called thrones were once thought to be altars (see Grove 1973) and are described as such in the older literature. By the Late Preclassic there were clearly formal differences between altars and thrones, although the two forms sometimes appear in similar architectural settings and may have served some of the same multiple uses (see Chapter 8). The blocky table-top thrones of the Early Preclassic became, by the Late Preclassic, thick slabs of stone supported by four short feet whose small scale made them more easily portable. Pedestal sculptures of individuals

figure 1.9
Kaminaljuyu Stela 10,
actually a throne.
(Drawing from the New
World Archaeological
Foundation based on
originals by Luis Luin and
Federico Fahsen and by
Guillermo Grajeda Mena in
Girard 1966:194; reprinted
in Parsons 1986:plate 174.)

seated on benches or seats with four legs, which date to the Middle and Late Preclassic periods, suggest a transitional form of thrones (Figures 1.8 and 10.5b; Fuente 1977:fig. 63; Navarrete 1972; Norman 1976:251; Parsons 1981:268–269, 1986:22–24, figs. 31–34; Princeton 1995:fig. 34).

No actual throne of this type has been found, and they are only known from representations on pedestal sculptures or small, serpentine "bench figures" (see Miles 1965:fig. 10e; Navarrete 1972; Parsons 1986:figs. 31, 32, and 34). The small serpentine sculptures were obviously more portable than the pedestal sculptures. A late Middle Preclassic transition from large thrones to smaller, more portable ones is also indicated by La Venta Monument 15, which, although fragmentary, appears to have had a flat, slab top and stubby feet (Drucker 1952:182, plate 64). Certainly the concept of legged seats that literally and figuratively "raised" the status of certain individuals is ancient, as evident in the Early Preclassic ceramic figurines from Mazatan, Chiapas, which represent seated village leaders (Clark and Pye 2000:fig. 25; Lesure 1999:213). Marcus (1998:56) describes a homologous case of seated figurines and stools for early societies in the Valley of Oaxaca. Figure 1.10 shows the distribution of different kinds of Preclassic thrones, and representations of them, in Mesoamerica. As a symbol of authority, the distribution of thrones is a clear indicator of the spatial and temporal distribution of powerful rulers in ancient Mesoamerica and of the importance of sculptures in marking and defining the political landscape (see Cyphers 2004a; Cyphers and Zurita-Noguera 2006). As indicated by stone thrones and representations of them, sequential centers of kingship and power in Preclassic Mesoamerica were the Gulf Coast lowlands and the Pacific slope and adjacent highlands of Guatemala.

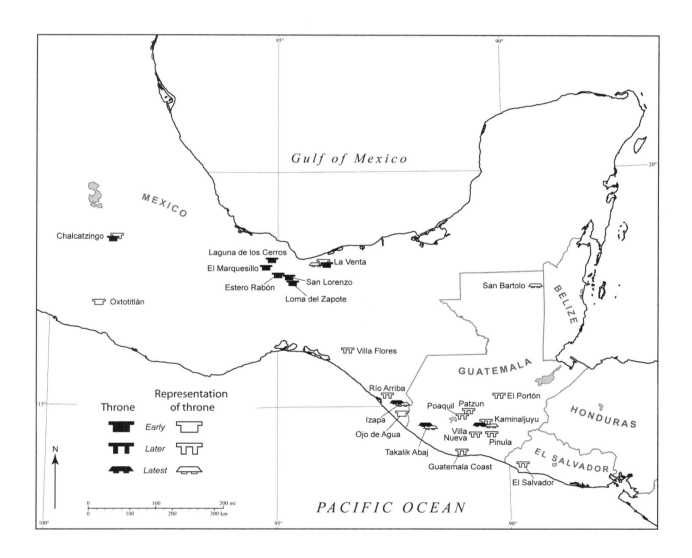

figure 1.10
Distribution of Preclassic thrones and their representations. (Drawing from the New World Archaeological Foundation.)

Distribution of Preclassic Stone Monuments

The current best evidence suggests that the tradition of carving stone sculptures started at San Lorenzo. The sculptural arts appear to have spread from there to other parts of Mesoamerica during Middle Preclassic times. The earliest sculptures were of dark volcanic stone. In the Middle and Late Preclassic a wider assortment of materials was used, including limestone, schist, gneiss, serpentine, and sandstone. The distribution of monuments varied widely in time and space, and they show clumped associations at individual sites as well. Location apparently mattered a great deal. Most regions had suitable hard stone for monuments rather close by,

so ecological explanations for the distribution of stone monuments cannot account for their limited dispersal. The basic techniques for shaping hard stone were known to all peoples who fashioned metates (grinding stones). These same peoples also had traditions of representing the human form in figurines and paintings. Therefore, arguments concerning technical knowledge and/or proscriptions against representing the human form likewise cannot account for the distribution of early sculptures. Their unequal distribution suggests that power and cultural beliefs were involved.

Early Preclassic

Considerations of the size and number of San Lorenzo's early monuments, and their obvious

figure 1.11
Distribution of Early Preclassic sculptures. (Drawing from the New World Archaeological Foundation.)

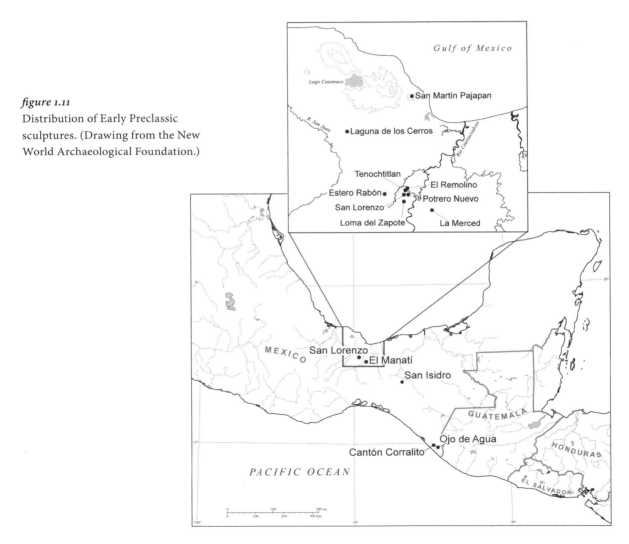

power themes, substantiate (un)popular notions that Mesoamerican civilization had a single origin among the Olmecs and later spread to all of Mesoamerica. The principal alternative view argues for multiple hearths of social and political innovation and of the pooling of cultural accomplishments from Olmecs, Mayas, Zapotecs, and others to create a blended civilization to which many different peoples contributed on essentially an equal footing. As more data have been gathered for San Lorenzo, arguments against the early age of this city and its monuments have become untenable.

The distribution of stone monuments and sculpture in Mesoamerica during the Preclassic was always decidedly lopsided. More than ninety percent of all known Preclassic sculptures come from fewer than ten sites, and this disparity becomes even more pronounced the farther back in time one goes, with most of the sculptures in the Early Preclassic period coming from San Lorenzo and its secondary centers (Coe and Diehl 1980; Cyphers 2004b; Lowe 1989). As shown in Figure 1.11, Early Preclassic sculpture is currently known from only three sites outside the Gulf Coast region.[4] The headless body of a full-round jaguar sculpture was recovered at San Isidro in northern Chiapas (Lowe 1998:46, fig. 20), and three fragments of sculptures in the round and one stela that date to 1300–1000 BC have been recovered in the Mazatan region of coastal Chiapas (see Figure 3.6; Clark 2007; Clark and Pye 2000:222, figs. 4–6; Lee 1989). All these sculptures come from sites with strong connections to the early Olmecs, so the choice to carve and erect sculptures appears to have been related to cultural practices and, quite likely, to the political prerogatives of rulers. The choice may have also depended on ideology (Grove 1993; Grove and Gillespie 1992). The absence of sculptures in other regions of Middle America at this time may indicate that the peoples of these regions were not part of the San Lorenzo polity and not closely affiliated with it (Clark 1997).

Middle Preclassic

We have already noted that the hotspots for sculpture production shifted through time, as evident in the sequence of capital centers in the Gulf Coast lowlands. The chapters in this book indicate another spatial-temporal trend. Chapters are organized geographically but also inadvertently represent a temporal succession from Middle to Late Preclassic times. This distinction is also cultural and quite likely political and social as well. The centers of sculpture production during the Middle Preclassic were La Venta, Chalcatzingo, and Takalik Abaj (Figure 1.2). Each site has more than thirty stone sculptures or monuments that date to this time. A few monuments appear at other centers, but not in these numbers.

The principal center was La Venta. This city was abandoned by 400 BC, so the seventy-three sculptures and seventeen other stone monuments found there must date to the Middle Preclassic or earlier. As described by Rebecca B. González Lauck (1988, 1989, 1994, 1996, 1997, 2000, 2004, Chapter 6), the sculptures at this site were associated with public architecture and with its northern and southern entrances (see also Grove 1999; Reilly 1999). The La Venta Olmecs imported tons of stone that they incorporated into their architecture and massive offerings, which are not generally considered stone monuments (Drucker 1952; Drucker et al. 1959). For instance, the natural basalt pillars used to enclose the northern compound at the site (see Chapter 6), and which were part of at least two tombs, should probably be considered analogous to the plain monoliths from Kaminaljuyu, Naranjo, Takalik Abaj, and elsewhere. As illustrated in Figure 1.4, low-relief monuments in the La Venta style are known from Guerrero and Morelos in the north to El Salvador in the south (Figure 1.5). These clearly were related to La Venta sculptures and likely mark the early influence of this polity on neighboring peoples. A remarkable feature of the distribution is that these Olmec-style monuments are rarely associated with pyramids or large sites, as they were at La Venta.

Chalcatzingo was the heart of Middle Preclassic sculpture production in western Mesoamerica. It is a small ceremonial center next to a split mountain, with terraces and platforms descending from the talus slope that abutted the northern face of this mountain. Many of the sculptures at Chalcatzingo correspond stylistically and thematically with those from La Venta, so a connection between the two centers is not disputed (Grove 1999, 2000), although the nature of the connection is. Other sites from regions adjacent to Chalcatzingo also had sculptures, as described by Guadalupe Martínez Donjuán (Chapter 3) for Teopantecuanitlan, Guerrero, and Giselle Canto Aguilar and Victor M. Castro Mendoza (Chapter 4) for Zazacatla, Morelos. What is remarkable about all three sites is that sculptures have been found associated with public architecture in primary settings. These rare examples allow us to view the significance of stone sculptures in their specific and wider settings within sites and landscapes. Grove (1999, 2000; see also Reilly 1991) makes a case that the thematic content of the Chalcatzingo sculptures corresponded to their place in the ceremonial precinct and landscape. "Rulership monuments and stone-faced platforms occur in the sector north of [the central] platform, and the mythico-supernatural carvings are in the sector to the south. In the far south, high on the natural sacred mountain, a 'sky cave' entrance to the otherworld is depicted (Monument 1), while its complementary opposite, a sunken patio—an entrance to the earthly otherworld—is positioned in the far north" (Grove 1999:265).

Monuments at Teopantecuanitlan and Zazacatla clearly related to the shape, size, and orientation of buildings and ultimately to the landscape and the sky above. The few monuments at La Venta in primary locations evince similar relationships (Grove 1999). The implication of the placements of stone monuments at these sites is that the meanings and functions of particular monuments depended on their place in a total scheme of cognized landscape.

The sculptures at Chalcatzingo all date to the Middle Preclassic, but it is unlikely that they date to the same centuries of that period. Much of the art at Chalcatzingo is engraved on the skin of the mountainside, but more than half of the monuments are stone stelae in the northern sector. More stelae are known from this site than from any coeval centers (David C. Grove, personal communication

2007). The stelae are probably younger than the images incised on the mountainside. One full-round sculpture is known, but this seated figure is now headless (Grove 1984:plate 19; Grove and Angulo 1987:125, fig. 9.18; Guzmán 1934:250, figs. 11–13). The small, twin sculptures from Zazacatla are also carved in the round, as are several monuments from Teopantecuanitlan. Otherwise, the sculptures from these Central Mexico sites are two dimensional.

After the Middle Preclassic, the carving of stone sculptures in the central highlands of Mexico ceased (Grove 2000). It looks like the practice of erecting stone monuments was derived from the Gulf Olmecs ca 900 BC and abandoned ca 500 BC. In contrast, in eastern Mesoamerica, especially along the Pacific slope of Guatemala, Olmec-style sculptures were succeeded by several different yet interrelated styles at Izapa, Takalik Abaj, Chocolá, Monte Alto, and Kaminaljuyu (see Chapters 7–9). This proliferation of sculpture in southern Guatemala and adjacent coastal Mexico (see Chapters 7–11) corresponded to a reduction in the number of sculptures carved in the Gulf Coast area during the Late Preclassic (see Chapter 5).

As described by Federico Fahsen (Chapter 10), the sculptural tradition was earlier and stronger in the Guatemalan Highlands than in the Maya Lowlands and clearly dates to the end of the Middle Preclassic period. The sequence of stone monuments for the Valley of Guatemala is of particular interest, given the development there by 300 BC of the Kaminaljuyu state. The earliest stone monuments in the valley have been found at Naranjo (Arroyo 2007, n.d.; Arroyo, ed. 2007). They are plain monuments set up in north-south rows. Among them are the three stela-altar pairs described above (Pereira 2008; Pereira et al. 2007). The importance of uncarved monuments in this region was noted early on by Shook (1952, 1971). Of the thirty-eight Preclassic sites he recorded for the central highlands of Guatemala, thirteen had uncarved basalt columns, often placed in plazas or in front of low platform mounds. Similar plain stelae are found throughout much of Preclassic Mesoamerica in later contexts than those of Naranjo but in similar configurations (Bove n.d.a).

The earliest known carved monument from the adjacent and succeeding center of Kaminaljuyu is a basalt pillar designated Stela 9 (Figure 1.7d). It was found in an early tomb of an elite individual and dates to ca 500 BC (Parsons 1986:16, plate 5; Shook and Popenoe de Hatch 1999:297). Stela 9 is a low-relief carving on a natural, five-faced basalt pillar and was found associated with two plain, columnar pillars and the bases of two pedestal sculptures. It is not clear how many of the more than three hundred sculptures from Kaminaljuyu date to the Middle Preclassic period, because so few have been recovered from primary archaeological contexts. Although numerous carved stelae and altars are known, many more sculptures from this site are fragments of low-relief monuments that stylistically appear to date to the Late Preclassic period (see Figure 10.14; Parsons 1986), a time when Kaminaljuyu was the most extensive state in southern Guatemala (see Chapters 7 and 10). Plain basalt pillars at Kaminaljuyu are similar to those known from La Venta and Tres Zapotes (see Chapters 5 and 6). A similar but longer natural pillar with grooved geometric designs is known for the coeval city of Cuicuilco in the Valley of Mexico (Figure 1.7b). It was associated with the early pyramid there (Pérez Campa 1998:37); no other early sculptures are known for this site or valley. Clancy (1990:22) proposes that such naturally occurring columnar basalt pillars provide a plausible antecedent for the erect stela form, and she suggests that the sculptors of Kaminaljuyu Stela 9 and the Alvarado Stela from Veracruz (Figure 1.7a) took advantage of the smooth faces of these columns whose regular, vertical contours did not require additional shaping. Both of these early monuments were innovative for their visual presentation in which the incised image wrapped around the faces of the monument (shown rolled out in Figure 1.7a,d). This feature links them developmentally to older boulder sculpture traditions (see Chapter 8; Clancy 1990:25; cf. Graham and Benson 2005). It is worth pointing out as well that they had antecedents in the carved basalt pillars at San Lorenzo (Figure 1.3d; see Reilly 2002:45, fig. 4.5).

Several of the stone monuments known from the Mirador Basin of northern Guatemala (Hansen 1991, 2001) might also date to this period (Figure 1.6c). Given the proliferation of stone sculpture among the Classic Maya, it is particularly interesting to see how rare carved stone monuments were in the Maya Lowlands before the Classic period. This region appears to have been a sculpture desert in Early and Middle Preclassic times. The absence of stone sculptures in the Maya Lowlands could be due to the limited exploration undertaken so far at early centers of this date. Usually, Middle Preclassic deposits are deeply buried, hard to reach, and sampled mostly by accident, so the sample of relevant deposits is still modest. Another possible reason for their rarity is that the uses and functions performed by stone sculptures in other regions were fulfilled in different ways at early lowland Maya sites and in different media. The stucco masks that decorated early stone pyramids come to mind (see Freidel and Schele 1988; Hansen 1990, 1998; Reese 1996).

Masked buildings represented tremendous labor investments and resulted in a monumental message, with the whole stone building being the message. Sculptures on these buildings were made by constructing a stone skeleton for each mask. These stone armatures were then covered with thick plaster and painted. Most masks are thought to be representations of various gods; representations of kings in monumental art do not appear to have come into vogue until the end of the Late Preclassic period, but this observation may stem from a recognition problem. Richard Hansen (personal communication 2000) has proposed that the Preclassic sculptural program of the Maya Lowlands varied inversely with the production of architectural masks. This proposal suggests a larger point that stone monuments, as devices for communicating information, must be seen in the broader context of all material means used for conveying such important messages. This topic is an exciting one for another day. What we do know for sure is that no obvious Middle Preclassic sculptures have been found standing around lowland Maya sites in original contexts.

The wide dispersal of Olmec low-relief monuments in Mesoamerica masks the actual spotty distribution of stone monuments in the Middle

Preclassic period.[5] Most sculptures are from three sites: La Venta, Chalcatzingo, and Takalik Abaj. Other sites in the same general regions as these three centers have a few monuments, sometimes created from alternative, non-stone materials, such as rammed earth (see Chapter 7; Love and Guernsey 2007), but most sites and regions lack monuments completely. Stone monuments were rare and spectacular, which was probably a primary part of their function and meaning in Middle Preclassic times. Why did some centers have monuments and others not?

The difference between La Venta and Chiapa de Corzo is instructive, because multiple lines of archaeological evidence reveal a strong historical and commercial relationship between the peoples of these centers. Both cities were laid out on the same ground plan (Clark and Hansen 2001). A few fragments of sculptures have been found at Chiapa de Corzo, but they are all Late Preclassic (Lee 1969). The absence of sculptures at Chiapa de Corzo during the Middle Preclassic is highly significant, especially given its geographic location between La Venta to the north and Tzutzuculi (McDonald 1983) to the south, two centers with stone sculptures (Figure 1.2). Raw materials for monuments were readily available, and the leaders of Chiapa de Corzo ruled a large polity with a huge labor pool. Why did they not put up stone monuments? They could have afforded the time and labor.

Sculpture is also absent from all other Middle Preclassic centers of central Chiapas at this time (Clark n.d.). Perhaps this distribution of sculptureless centers indicates political prerogatives for sculpting. We suggest that not every center had the right to carve and erect sculptures—notwithstanding technical and social capabilities for doing so—because of the regal themes and messages of legitimate authority involved (cf. Chapter 7; see Clark 1996, 1997, 2004). It may have been no accident that the proliferation of stone sculpting in Mesoamerica began during the final decades of La Venta, after the polity lost its clout in Mesoamerica. The increase in the number of monuments, and the places of their occurrence, also correspond to the creation of regional styles

(non-Olmec), new forms, and new themes. After the Middle Preclassic, there never again was a pan-Mesoamerican sculptural style.

Late Preclassic

The Valley of Oaxaca is the most significant case study not represented in the following chapters. It is already well published in the Dumbarton Oaks series (Scott 1978; Urcid 2001). The Middle and Late Preclassic city of Monte Albán (Figure 1.2) has a greater number of stone sculptures than is known for any other city in Mesoamerica. Some of its monuments are in their primary contexts and are associated with a single structure, Building L-sub, located on the southwestern edge of the main plaza. The production and display of carved stones there are thought to have been critical to the development of a state society in the Valley of Oaxaca ca 300 BC (Marcus and Flannery 1996; cf. Urcid 2006). Some of the monuments seemingly date to the last part of the Middle Preclassic, but most date to the Late Preclassic.

The carved stones in the Valley of Oaxaca are stylistically distinct and are clear evidence of the regionalization of styles and forms in Late Preclassic Mesoamerica (Figure 1.12). It is telling that none of the comparative treatments in the following chapters refers to the sculptures from the Valley of Oaxaca. Oaxaca sculptures differ from those in the rest of Mesoamerica in their time horizon. The most frequent forms are the famous *danzantes* or "dancers" and "conquest monuments." Most danzantes are earlier than "conquest" monuments. The latter date to the end of the Late Preclassic period (100 BC–AD 200) (Caso 1947). Danzantes consist of outlined adult males depicted in diverse poses (Figure 1.12a). Heads are shown in profile, whereas bodies are shown in three-quarter or frontal view. The portrayed individuals have been interpreted as courtly mourners, sacrificial victims, pregnant women, prisoners, court buffoons, dancers, sprawling corpses, emasculated priests, swimmers, shamans in ecstatic trance, or diseased persons (Orr 1997; Scott 1978; Urcid 2006). They are depicted naked in horizontal and vertical poses, with open mouths, closed eyes, and most often

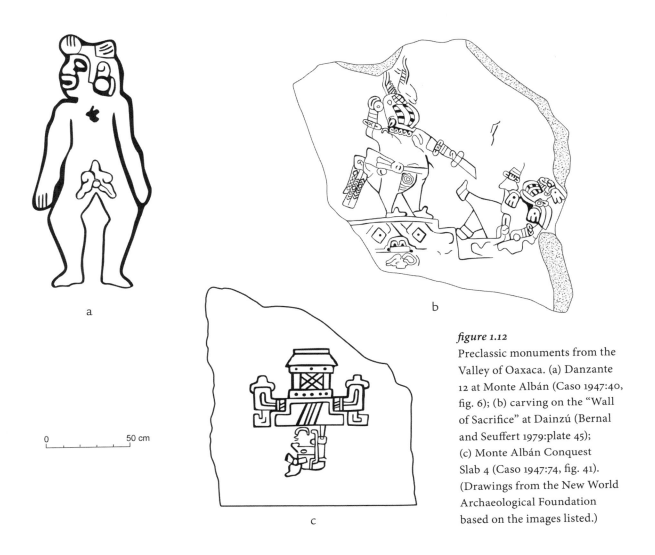

a

0   50 cm

c

figure 1.12
Preclassic monuments from the
Valley of Oaxaca. (a) Danzante
12 at Monte Albán (Caso 1947:40,
fig. 6); (b) carving on the "Wall
of Sacrifice" at Dainzú (Bernal
and Seuffert 1979:plate 45);
(c) Monte Albán Conquest
Slab 4 (Caso 1947:74, fig. 41).
(Drawings from the New World
Archaeological Foundation
based on the images listed.)

with scrolls in the groin area. These stones were
set into the facade of Building L-sub in alternat-
ing vertical and horizontal rows (Figure 1.13). The
images were carved by groove-outlining in "coun-
tersunk relief" (Kubler 1990:162) created by pecking shallow lines and grooves into stones with flat
surfaces. The ballplayer monuments from nearby
Dainzú are in a similar style (Figure 1.12b). These
danzante and ballplayer sculptures are technologi-
cally different from Olmec low-relief carvings, in
which the background of the carved images was
removed and recessed to leave the carved image as
the salient surface of the monument (Figures 1.3e,
1.5, 1.6a, and 1.7c).

"Conquest monuments" follow the same
idea of shallow designs pecked into flat surfaces
(Figure 1.12c). Yet the technique is different, and
the details are more intricate and finer than those
on danzantes. More than forty of the sixty-eight
carved images found at Building J were incorporated into the outer walls. The carved stones now
associated with this building are not in their original contexts. This building had a complex history
and went through four building stages. The carved
"conquest" slabs date to the first stage. In the second stage they were rearranged, and some danzante monuments were also incorporated into the
facade. In the final two building stages the walls

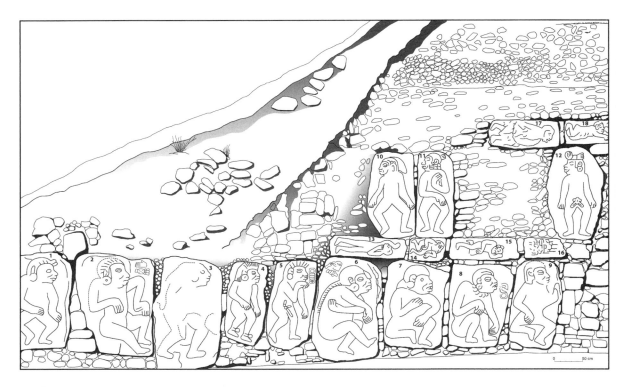

figure 1.13
Section of Building L at Monte Albán showing the arrangement of the danzante sculptures. (Drawing from the New World Archaeological Foundation based on Batres 1902:lám. V.)

of this structure were covered with thick plaster, so none of the monuments would have been visible (Carter 2008).

The large center of Kaminaljuyu in the central highlands of Guatemala also appears to have produced sculpture outside the Olmec tradition. It is not clear how developments in highland Guatemala related to those at La Venta, if at all. The earliest monuments at Naranjo and Kaminaljuyu were plain monuments (Arroyo 2007; Arroyo, ed. 2007; Parsons 1986:16). There is minor evidence of contact with the Olmecs of the Gulf Coast, but it was not nearly as strong as that evident at Takalik Abaj (see Chapter 8).[6] Early Kaminaljuyu represented a regional style (Figure 1.9). The later monuments at Teopantecuanitlan and Chalcatzingo in Central Mexico also show their own regional styles. The earliest carved stone in danzante style from Oaxaca may be as early as 600 BC (Marcus and Flannery 1996:129, fig. 137). Stylistically, the danzante forms

relate more to Stela 9 at Kaminaljuyu (Figure 1.7d) than to La Venta monuments (Figure 1.7c; Parsons 1986:16; Scott 1978:29), but we know of no corroborative evidence of contact between Kaminaljuyu and Monte Albán for this time. We imagine that similarities in their early monuments derive from an earlier, common source.[7]

Other major centers with Late Preclassic monuments were Izapa, Takalik Abaj, Chocolá, and Monte Alto (see Chapters 8 and 9) located on the Pacific slope of Guatemala and Mexico (Figure 1.2). Outside of Monte Albán, this region was a hub of sculpture production. In the adjacent highlands of Guatemala, the main centers of sculpture were Kaminaljuyu (see Chapter 11), El Portón, and La Lagunita (see Chapter 10). Fewer sculptures are known for the Maya Lowlands, but some stelae and altars clearly date to this time (Awe and Grube 2001; Estrada Belli 2006; Fahsen and Grube 2005; Hansen 1991, 1998, 2001). A particularly interesting feature is the beginning of writing and calendric notation in the Maya Lowlands and the Valley of Oaxaca. Early texts and calendar dates are known on a few monuments dating to the last century BC. The earliest writing in the Maya Lowlands is known from wall paintings at San Bartolo, a Middle and Late Preclassic site in northeastern Guatemala (Houston 2006; Saturno, Stuart, and Beltrán 2006). The earliest occurrences of calendric notation and writing on stone monuments are outside the lowland Maya region (Coe 1957; Lowe 1977; Marcus 1992), but these scribal-sculptural practices did not continue after AD 200 (see Chapters 8 and 10). Because of their great age and archaic forms, few of the early texts have been deciphered. It is clear on some, however, that special dates were involved for the accession of some persons to kingship (Figure 1.9; see Chapter 10). Writing and calendric notation are features of Classic Maya monuments but rarities on Preclassic ones. The cessation of these practices in the highlands looks like a cultural revolution, perhaps instigated by new groups of people moving into the region (see Chapter 10).

Concluding Remarks

We have provided a brief overview of stone monuments in Preclassic Mesoamerica and tracked their variation in time and space. The operational assumption of the chapters in this book is that if we can properly place sculptures in their cultural, historical, social, political, religious, and cognitive contexts, we can infer original and secondary uses and meanings for them and, subsequently, interpret the role(s) they may have played in the origins, growth, and spread of civilization in Middle America. This dictum is simple in principle and frustrating in practice, because most monuments did not stand still. As Parsons (1986:6) explains, "One of the bothersome factors in the study of Pre-Columbian stone sculpture is the mobility and mutability of objects. They usually manage to endure, but in a new location, or in a broken, mutilated, reused, or even recarved form." Preclassic monuments were part of different meaningful

ensembles during their long lives. As described in the following chapters, we can recover the final, primary contexts for some monuments but rarely the original, primary contexts. We can also postulate original meanings by reconstructing some of the life history of each stone and sequential modifications from its original condition (see Chapter 11).

Studies of Pre-Columbian art predominated during the first 150 years of casual exploration of Middle American ruins, and sculpture was the major interpretive tool for understanding the vanished civilizations in this part of the world. It was not until the first decade of the twentieth century that scientific archaeology—with its obsession with layers of dirt, potsherds, and terra cotta human figurines—began to offer a rival view of these civilizations and their achievements. For the past century there has been an uneasy accommodation in Mesoamerican research between the agendas of art and science, with radical swings of opinion over the past decades. We originally planned to review this intellectual history to show the place of this book in the larger debate, but skirmishes in this turf war have been too numerous and complex to detail here. Our main point can be made by considering a single episode of the creative tension between art and stone, an exchange between Michael Coe and William Sanders about Kaminaljuyu that occurred at MIT in 1972.

M. Coe: I may be accused here of ideationalism, or something vile like that, but that is all right with me. My current research centers on religious systems as expressed in art. In my estimation, there was strong ideological motivation in these early societies, particularly as embodied in religious systems, and this is something that materialist archaeologists tend to ignore. If some of these scholars found themselves transported to some of these societies they pretend to reconstruct, they would not recognize, I suspect, much around them. It is symptomatic that Sanders has totally neglected the evidence for mental life in ancient Kaminaljuyu, even when it is present, such as the important and large group of stelae from the Terminal Formative that have much to say on evolving Maya religion. I am sure that a great deal of the Maya pantheon was present at that time. [Coe 1974:117]

W. Sanders: Coe is absolutely right. I have no or little interest in prehistoric style and ideology since this type of study does not lead to scientific generalization. In fact, Coe is self-contradictory—if we cannot reconstruct a social system from archaeological data how can we reconstruct prehistoric mentality and ideology? [Sanders 1974:119]

This exchange about Preclassic Mesoamerican sculpture highlights two problems that we do not explicitly address in this book but that are evident in some of the following chapters: the issues of different interpretive paradigms and the research methods appropriate for them. Coe and Sanders have valid points, and both perspectives need to be included in a broader view that can accommodate their insights. The cultural ecological approach championed by Sanders (see Sanders and Price 1968), and still one of the dominant paradigms in Mesoamerica, viewed sculptures as epiphenomena of civilization and accorded them scant attention. This view reversed the prominence paid to sculptures in earlier decades and centuries, but Sanders's analytical step has not been a positive one. In this book we restore sculpture to its former preeminence—with the proviso that we view it as a means for understanding general processes. To turn Sanders on his heels, one cannot understand how sculptures functioned in the general course of events without understanding what they stood for and what they meant to ancient peoples.

This book attempts to bridge the material and the ideal with an interpretive approach grounded in fundamental facts of context, artifact forms, iconography, representations, and co-associations of sculptures with everything around them. In particular, we wish to understand the ancient functions, uses, and meanings of stone monuments in terms of social and political processes. To recover function and meaning we have to see sculptures and stone monuments in context. As Coe so aptly argued, the cultural practices and beliefs of ancient

peoples quite likely bear little resemblance to modern reconstructions of them. We have to move beyond the earthiness of the material record and attempt to understand past systems of thought. To get at these issues, the authors in this book attempt to reconstruct the temporal and spatial occurrence of sculpture forms and representations and relate these to other events. We consider monuments as cultural creations made for specific purposes, some of which can be inferred from the monuments themselves when viewed in context.

We view this book as opening research questions rather than shutting them down. Our joint efforts here are more concerned with appropriate questions and points of view than with ephemeral conclusions about what things mean to us today. If nothing else, the nearly 250-year history of art historical and archaeological explorations in Middle America shows that interpretations come and go, based on the changing shape of the facts in hand. We suspect that our efforts here will eventually be overtaken by new facts as scholars refine sculpture and site chronologies, take more care in documenting the contexts of sculptures, use modern technology to derive better images of monuments, and analyze stone monuments in full context. Many past interpretations of Preclassic sculpture never really had a chance, because so many of the objects of interpretation were floating in time and space; no one knew where they really were found or their ages. Their contexts were a matter of conjecture, and thus their interpretive significance was bound up in circular arguments based on guessing their contexts and ages in the first place. With better documentation and images, scholars can start to pin down sculptures in time, space, and culture context. These goals are well illustrated in the following chapters, as are the interpretive payoffs of the analytical approaches taken.

This said, it is too soon to come to final conclusions about the functions and meanings of Preclassic stone monuments. We have offered some interpretations here based on the facts currently available, but these are not set in stone. When better information forces different interpretations, we hope to be around to cheer them on. The limited, reliable information available indicates that the production and use of stone monuments in Preclassic Mesoamerica varied widely from group to group and within individual polities. Middle and Late Preclassic sculptures were particularly abused, shattered, and tossed about. These observations indicate that stone monuments played a meaningful role in the social and political process. The chewed-up scraps of sculptures show they were caught up in rival claims of remembering and forgetting. As Coe pointed out to Sanders in the exchange quoted above, stone sculptures were about communicated messages, such as religious concepts and ideology. Most of the monuments considered in the following chapters point to kingship as another dominant theme in Preclassic times.

Sculptures memorialized critical messages at particular times and places and for particular individuals. Agents with motives, resources, and opportunity carved some of their claims in stone. Later agents with other motives, means, and opportunities erased these earlier claims. As described in this volume, at some sites even later agents found it useful to reuse fragments of old monuments in ways that had little to do with their original meanings. In the varied histories of these early monuments we find a generative tension between symbols and power that affected the development of Preclassic civilization. Stone monuments were well suited for serving purposes of state, and they did so throughout Mesoamerica's long Preclassic Transition.

Acknowledgments

Our efforts in this chapter and in editing this book would not have been possible without the able assistance of Arlene Colman, Megan Wakefield, and Kisslan Chan of the Brigham Young University–New World Archaeological Foundation art and editorial staff. We deeply appreciate their work. We are also particularly grateful for comments on this chapter by Gerardo Gutiérrez, Michael Love, Mary E. Pye, Javier Urcid, and two anonymous reviewers. And we thank Robert Sharp of the Art Institute of Chicago for his editorial advice and Kent Reilly and Logan Wagner for assistance with images and documentation.

NOTES

1. This topic is complex, and it should remain open until sufficient concrete observations and good arguments resolve the matter.

2. A small, 1 m tall stela showing two standing Olmec figures in profile has just been discovered at Ojo de Agua, Chiapas. It dates to the Jocotal Phase, 1200–1000 BC (John Hodgson, personal communication 2009). This date makes it the oldest attested stela currently known in Mesoamerica. Monuments at San Lorenzo with low-relief carvings are probably at least this old.

3. For example, the Middle Preclassic imagery of Chalcatzingo Stela 21 (see Grove 1984:60, fig. 12; Grove and Angulo 1987:127, fig. 9.21), in which an individual grasps what appears to be a stela form, suggests that the very act of moving or erecting a stela was imbued with significance, as was certainly the case among the later Classic Maya (Stuart 1996).

4. We restrict this claim to large pieces (see Parsons 1986:11). Marcus and Flannery (1996:109, fig. 114) report two early Middle Preclassic, low-relief carvings from the site of San José Mogote in the Valley of Oaxaca that portray the face of a jaguar and a bird. The larger one is only 20 cm long, less than the diameter of a common ceramic serving bowl and shorter than most Olmec votive axes. These carved stones do not qualify as sculptures in the sense used here.

5. The stone sculptures should not be divorced from paintings in the same style. Middle Preclassic paintings evince the same distribution as the low-relief carvings. Polychrome paintings have been found in caves in Guerrero (Grove 1970) and on

cliff faces in Guerrero (Gutiérrez 2008), the Valley of Mexico (Niederberger 2000:fig. 3b), and in a valley south of Kaminaljuyu, Guatemala (see Coe 2005:53, fig. 15).

6. The most compelling evidence of contact between the peoples of Kaminaljuyu and La Venta is the mortuary offering associated with Stela 9. This stela was found in a burial in Structure C-III-6 with other stone monuments and with a necklace consisting of 290 jade beads, several spoon-shaped pendants, and a duckbill pendant. Also included was a small gray stone figurine similar to stone figurines from La Venta (see Shook and Popenoe de Hatch 1999:297, fig. 116). Ceramics found in the 2007 excavations at Naranjo include some with the Olmec dragon motif and Olmec-like profiles on some polished black bowls.

7. The earliest image we know of that portrays a human figure in a posture comparable to those of the danzantes—although the face is frontally represented rather than in profile like the danzantes—is incised on a serpentine axe found at La Merced, a small site located near San Lorenzo (Rodríguez and Ortíz 2000). The axe dates to ca 1000–900 BC (Ponciano Ortíz and Mari Carmen Rodríguez, personal communication to John E. Clark, 2002). An analogous axe in similar style comes from Arroyo Pesquero, a Middle Preclassic site near La Venta (Medellín Zenil 1971:45, plate 58). An early Middle Preclassic sculpture showing a profile head with a frontal view of the body, as with the danzantes, is known from El Viejón in central Veracruz (Figure 1.4). Monuments from Padre Piedra and Tzutzuculi in Chiapas may have been in the same format, but the faces have been erased, so we cannot tell for sure. Finally, some of the figures carved in low relief on the sides of La Venta thrones are in this same format (see Chapter 6).

Iconography of the *Nahual*

Human-Animal Transformations in Preclassic Guerrero and Morelos

GERARDO GUTIÉRREZ AND MARY E. PYE

NAHUALISM IS A CONCEPT THAT HAS LONG been identified in the Mesoamerican belief system: some individuals were believed to be endowed with certain powers, among them the control of natural elements—rain, hail, wind, thunder, and lightning—and the ability to transform into an animal. The importance of this concept in Olmec iconography was raised at early Dumbarton Oaks conferences in 1967 and 1970 (Coe 1972; Furst 1968). Although the Olmec pantheon includes other animals and zoomorphic combinations,[1] we focus here on the human-jaguar transformation, the most powerful nahual of the Mesoamerican cosmology, an attribute that was appropriated and monopolized by native rulers as early as the Preclassic period. Nahualism has been argued to have been present in Classic and Postclassic contexts, particularly in relation to political leadership (Houston and Stuart 1989; Navarrete Linares 2000; Urcid 1993). According to many colonial and ethnographic sources, the Mesoamerican jaguar-nahual ruler was believed capable of exercising control over key elements of nature. The transformation process may have been a ritual event or a metonymic process to be undergone by the ruler to channel these special powers (Navarrete Linares 2000). In the case of the Olmecs, the powers were those of avian-serpent and rain deities (Taube 1995) to prevent destructive winds and rains. We present here a transformation figurine recently identified in a collection from Huamuxtitlan, Guerrero. We believe it was locally crafted by someone who knew how to carve and was well versed in the Olmec style. Its discovery prompted our review of the role of nahualism in the Preclassic period.

One of the key characteristics of nahualism is the transformation of a human into an animal form. Furst (1968) first presented the argument that certain Olmec figurines represented a human transforming into a nahual. Drawing from his knowledge of lowland South American ethnography, he described practices in which shamans transform into jaguars, further endowing these individuals with the powers of the great predator.

a   b   c

figure 2.1
Transformation figurines from the collection of
Dumbarton Oaks, Washington, D.C. (a) PC.B.603;
(b) PC.B.008; (c) PC.B.009. (Dumbarton Oaks,
Pre-Columbian Collection, Washington, D.C.)

Although the corpus of transformation figurines is small, they share significant characteristics.[2] For example, three of them are kneeling individuals with human bodies but have faces undergoing transformation into jaguars. Two other figurines from the Dumbarton Oaks collection are figures with jaguar physiognomy, albeit they are standing —as only humans can. Using these figurines, Reilly (1989:figs. 15a–c and 16a–c) mapped out a sequence showing a human progressively transforming into a jaguar by stages. Illustrated here are three of the six figurines Reilly cited, which offer an abbreviated version of his transformation sequence. Figure 2.1a is kneeling; he has a human torso, although his hands are ambiguously shown either with fingers beneath the palms or rounding into paws, and there are both human and jaguar ears present (Taube 2004:59–60) with suggestive horizontal tears depicted across the shoulders, presumably indicating the act of transformation in process (Benson 1981:106; Reilly 1989:12). The two other figurines (Figure 2.1b,c) present later stages of

the transformation sequence—the almost-jaguar and the jaguar. The figurines were carved standing to inform the viewer, particularly in the case of Figure 2.1c, that what is being depicted is not a jaguar but a human transformed into his nahual form.

Although Furst's and Reilly's arguments focused on the literal transformation depicted in this group of figurines, there are other examples, particularly sculptures, which depict humans transforming or transformed into nahuals. Cyphers's (2004b) catalogue of sculpture from San Lorenzo and surrounding sites offers a number of Early Preclassic candidates. For example, Monument ER-5, a head with human and feline features (Cyphers 2004b: 270) or Monument SL-90, a seated feline with exaggerated fangs and mouth (the upper half of the head is missing) are likely transformation figures. The back legs of Monument SL-90 appear to be feline with paws, but the front legs seem to be hands with nails, although the left hand is missing a thumb (Cyphers 2004b:156–158). Cyphers argues that Monument SL-36, a seated feline body (broken above the neck) with two parallel elements, presumably hanging from its mouth, is also a "human (decapitated) in a feline posture using an animal skin and holding a serpent in its mouth." Its backside appears human, and it lacks a tail (Cyphers 2004b:98). The feet of the sculpture at its base have wavy lines suggesting that other paws, feet, or hands are found beneath those depicted (Cyphers 2004b:fig. 50). We also note the Zazacatla sculptures recently recovered from Morelos (see Chapter 4), and there are many others.

In the examples just cited, the transformation process is not necessarily a literal presentation. Joralemon (1976, 1996) highlighted the *pars pro toto* aspect of Olmec iconography in his explication of the Olmec jaguar-dragon, represented by the paw-wing motif, and further noted the multivalent nature of these motifs, depending on the presence of other iconographic elements. Reilly (1995:32) argues that Olmec style has a multi-perspective and multihorizon aspect, much like later Mesoamerican codices. Despite the congruence of three-dimensional Olmec figurines and sculptures with Western aesthetics, Preclassic peoples may have been "seeing" far more than we do. The depictions of persons, person-animals, and animals may represent a seamless range of the same category of person or being who inhabited the Preclassic world. We may be attempting to classify human versus feline where there was no distinction, as Lévi-Strauss (1966) argues in his apologia for indigenous epistemology. Hence, the Tuxtla Chico standing jaguar dressed like a human or the San Lorenzo Monument 10 figure holding knuckle-dusters (Benson and Fuente 1996:161, 169) could fall into the single category of a being or person with changeable human/jaguar physical aspects. Further meanings were communicated by the accompanying symbols, such as knuckle-dusters (*manoplas*), scepters, costumes, or by postures or the object's location in a particular landscape or association with other sculptures (Cyphers 1999, 2004a).

We begin with a description of the Huamuxtitlan figurine, particularly how it relates to other transformation figurines. Drawing from a variety of sources, we then review what is known about nahuals. Who were they, how did they transform, and what precisely were their powers? Also of interest here is the geography of the nahual, not just where the Huamuxtitlan figurine came from, but where the preponderance of nahual accounts has been documented. We then focus on the nahual in Preclassic iconography, in particular, for Central Mexico and Guerrero. We argue that investigation into the nahual theme provides insights into Preclassic cosmovision and the development of political authority.

Transformation Figurine from San Pedro Aytec, Guerrero

The Archaeology and Ethnohistory of La Montaña Guerrero Project began in 1997 as a program of systematic research in eastern Guerrero. Its objectives were to understand better the archaeological material culture of this region and locate and register Pre-Hispanic sites, as well as document collections of archaeological objects located in the municipalities and small towns of the region (Gutiérrez 2007, n.d.).

Among the archaeological objects recorded in the towns of the Huamuxtitlan Valley, located along the border between Guerrero and Oaxaca, we documented a beautiful piece with complex symbolism from the village of San Pedro Aytec (Figures 2.2 and 2.3). Don Pablo Domínguez Lázaro, caretaker of one of the collections, told us that this piece had been donated by a family from Tlalquetzala. We visited this town to speak with the family directly. There we interviewed don Quirino Dolores, whose deceased wife had purchased "a group of pieces" from a poor peasant family from San Pedro Aytec. Unfortunately, don Quirino, a man of advanced years, did not remember who the family was but did note that the people of San Pedro Aytec were always finding these stones in their fields on the hills. Although we could not further pursue the provenience of the piece, don Quirino confirmed for us that his wife, prior to her death, had donated the group of pieces to the collection of don Pablo.

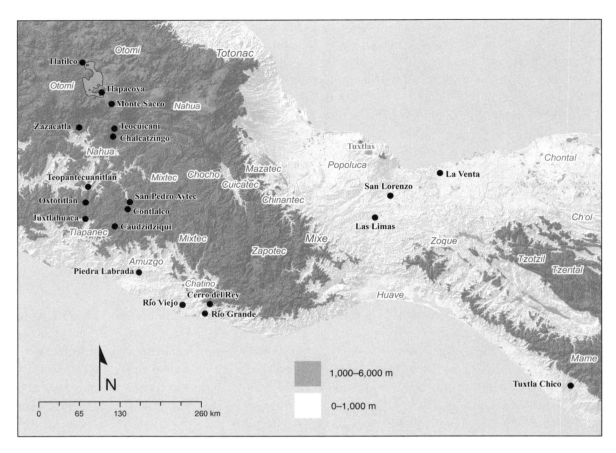

figure 2.2
Map showing locations of various Mesoamerican ethnic groups and archaeological sites mentioned in the text. (Drawing by the authors.)

Although the precise original location remains uncertain, there is a local context for it. In addition to the Cuadzidziqui Cave (Gutiérrez 2008; Gutierrez et al. 2006), our excavations in the enormous platforms at the sites of Contlalco and Cerro Quemado, a few kilometers from San Pedro Aytec, provided radiocarbon dates from the late Middle Preclassic, confirming significant construction activity in the Huamuxtitlan and Tlapa valleys beginning as early as the Middle Preclassic (Gutiérrez n.d.). We believe the San Pedro Aytec figurine is contemporaneous with the large platforms in the adjacent Tlapa Valley.

The piece in question (Figure 2.3) is 12.5 cm high, 5.5 cm wide across the shoulders, approximately 2.5 cm thick, and can stand alone. The front part depicts an individual with arms at his side, the elbows slightly bent at a sixty-degree angle, and his hands at his waist. The genitals are covered by a simple loincloth. A key iconographic element is the mask, seemingly made from the skin of an animal, which also covers his shoulders and chest. The mask displays jaguar features, especially the downturned mouth with its wide upper lip; the upper gum has no teeth, and the lower lip is slightly curved. There are two straps that run along both sides of the head and end in a large knot at the back of the head. The mask seems perfectly molded to the face, as can be appreciated in the side view of the figurine. The garment on the shoulders and chest is similarly flexible, with a clasp at the back of the figure. The head of the figure suggests tabular-erect cranial

Front   Back

figure 2.3
Several views of the San Pedro Aytec figurine.
(Photographs by the authors.)

modification, and the ears are human and realistically detailed, as is typically the case with transformation figurines.

The most important feature of this figurine is not just its front, but the combination of front and back sides (Figures 2.3 and 2.4). On the lower half of the back side the San Pedro Aytec figurine exhibits another face. When one flips the figure forward or backward, head first like an acrobat, up pops the second face in a visually surprising way, as the anatomical and decorative elements used on the backside of the front figure are reused for the abstract figure on the back (Figure 2.5). The second face on the back side bears similarities to that on the front, in particular, the feline mouth and flaring nose. But the relief carving on the back side is less detailed, and the lines thicker and more geometric. The most striking feature is the way the eyes are represented, somewhat rectangular and slightly mounded, with curved grooves in the middle. In contrast, the eyes of the front figure are almond shaped and catlike. The two faces, front and back, measure exactly 4.8 cm high.

The style, excellent carving, balance, and integration of anatomical elements between the characters on the front and back of the piece,

Front   Back

figure 2.4
Two views of the San Pedro Aytec figurine showing its two faces. (Photographs by the authors.)

figure 2.5
Three views of the San
Pedro Aytec figurine.
(Photographs by the
authors.)

and the conversion of one figure into another by means of an acrobatic flip suggest that this piece was a special achievement by a Preclassic stone carver. The elbows of the front figure convert into the shoulders of the reverse figure. In turn, the feet of the front figure, and the space between them, transform into the pronounced cleft on the head of the back figure. Finally, the leather cape of the front figure is tied with a brooch that becomes the forearms and clasped hands of the reverse figure (Figure 2.5). This back figure lacks legs and feet; instead, the back of the head of the front figure creates the appearance of a tied bundle where the legs and feet should be; this side of the figure obviously cannot stand alone.

The San Pedro Aytec figurine was carved from a local rock, a green serpentine with microfractures revealing fine hematite inclusions. This rock has a hardness of 5.5 on the Mohs' scale and is identical to samples of serpentine we have collected from the municipality of Cualac, as well as from other areas in southern Puebla around Tulcingo. These serpentine deposits have formed in contact with layers of igneous rocks and are found in association with schist and gneiss. Also abundant in these outcrops are a great variety of crystalline minerals that were used in ancient times for healing and witchcraft. These sources of greenstone were likely mined since Preclassic times, as seen by the San Pedro Aytec figurine and documented in the Postclassic in the Codex Mendoza, which shows that the towns of this region paid tribute to the Aztecs in the form of raw and carved greenstone (Codex Mendoza 1992:folio 40r).

We propose that the San Pedro Aytec figurine presents a masked and costumed human ready to begin transformation. The figurine depicts a high-status individual wearing the appropriate attire prior to performing an acrobatic flip, which will catapult him metaphorically into his jaguar nahual, presumably ready to control the meteorological forces of nature.

The Path to Nahual

In 1944, George Foster offered the first systematic overview of the concept, laying out a basic framework that separates nahual (transforming witch) from the related concept of *tonal* (animal companion). Subsequently it has become the norm to distinguish between the tonal and the nahual as manifested in specific indigenous groups (e.g., Saler 1964). In this approach, the nahual is defined strictly as a person believed capable of human-animal transformation, a process associated with a broader system of beliefs related to the control of wind, rain, and group behavior. In contrast, Foster defined a tonal as the animal spirit that accompanies an individual from birth to death. A tonal was assigned to each individual through one of many methods. In Central Mexico, as reported by Ruíz de Alarcón (1953:24 [1629]), the tonal could be dictated by the ritual calendar, with the animal corresponding to the day sign on which an individual was born. In ethnographic cases, individuals might need to visit a *brujo* (witch) to have the tonal manifest itself (Gossen 1975; Kaplan 1956). In southern Mexico, the tonal was assigned by the appearance of footprints from the first animal to visit a child after birth (Aguirre Beltrán 1978:13 [1955]).

This conceptual distinction between the tonal and nahual may be useful at an academic level; however, in ethnographic practice it has proved difficult to maintain (see Medina Hernández 2001:100–113). For example, in Weitlaner's (1977) accounts from Chinantla and the Cuicateca zone, his informants could not distinguish between the tonal and the nahual; Kaplan (1956) reported a similar inability in her Mixtec ethnography from coastal Oaxaca. Because of the frequent conflation of these concepts, some investigators have combined them as a single item of broader inquiry related to the "co-essence of the souls" or with studies of "animal companion spirits" (Gossen 1975, 1994; Houston and Stuart 1989; Urcid 1993). In the past, there may not have been such a clear distinction either. Although everyone may have had a tonal, how could one distinguish between a ruler who had a jaguar tonal or transformed into a jaguar nahual? The metaphysical distinction was a challenge undoubtedly left to the *tlacuilos* (painters and stone carvers) (Navarrete Linares 2000).

The word "nahual" originates from Postclassic Nahuatl speakers, with the word "*naualli*" used to describe the purported ability of individuals to transform into animals or natural phenomena, such as lightning or whirlwinds (Aguirre Beltrán 1978 [1955]; Foster 1944; Moscoso 1990). The etymology of the word "naualli" is obscure. Ruíz de Alarcón (1953:28 [1629]) noted in the first half of the seventeenth century three possible etymological origins: (1) *nauatia* (to command), (2) *nauatia* (to command [as a prince]), and (3) *nuaultia* (to cloak oneself or to mask one's face). Ruíz de Alarcón preferred the third interpretation; he believed that "nahual" made reference to a masked individual hidden in an animal form. López Austin (1967) elaborated on this idea and suggested that "naualli" could have derived from the roots *ehua, ahua* (clothing), *ehuatl* (skin, shell), *anahuac* (around me, around), and *naual* (cape), which together would mean "that which is my outfit," "that which I have on my skin, or around me" (López Austin 1967:95). According to Molina's (1977:63) vocabulary and Simeón's (1997:303–304 [1885]) dictionary, "naualli" makes reference to spells and sorcery in general, but also to the ability to do things with shrewdness, cunning, discretion, and deception. The verb "*naualtia*" expresses the idea of hiding oneself, hiding behind someone else, or hiding in the shadows. Similarly, the verb "*naualteca*" means to hide someone secretly in a secure place. "*Naualchiua*" means to obtain or steal something with caution and discretion, whereas "*naualla-chia*" includes the verbs to spy on or to lie in wait.

The term for a person who expresses things skillfully and cautiously and who speaks deceptively to seduce or swindle others, or to speak the language of the nahual, is "*nauallatoa*" or "*naualli tlatoa*." When one writes, or a tlacuilo paints in ciphers, one is using the writing of the nahual: *nauaulicuilo* or *naualli icuiloa*. What these dictionary entries indicate is that the nahual knew secrets and had the capacity to modify his human form and obtain his own ends through stealth and from the shadows. All three of Ruíz de Alarcón's meanings could have been correct. Some rulers were nahuals. Those who were not, perhaps because they had not been born on the correct calendrical day, could have acquired the services of a nahual as the Aztecs rulers did, thereby creating a class of political operators capable of working in the shadows. And in colonial times, nahuals had to remain in the shadows to avoid the Spanish religious authorities.

The metamorphosis of a human into an animal is intrinsic to Mesoamerican religion. Mesoamerican gods, as detailed in Postclassic myths, were transformers. For example, during the destruction of Tula, Tezcatlipoca first descended from the sky as a spider and then transformed himself into a jaguar when he played the ball game against Quetzalcoatl (Mendieta 1993:82 [1870]). It is said that the god of the underworld Mictlatecutli enjoyed taking the form of an owl to announce a death (Paso y Troncoso 1953:221 [1892]), which is why the man-owl or *tlacatecolotl* was one of the most feared ghosts or transformed witches of Pre-Hispanic populations (Garibay 1989:905; Mendieta 1993:94 [1870]).

The gods were also not limited to animal transformations, as they could convert into celestial bodies as well. Notably, however, in these situations the transformation was not reversible. An example of permanent metamorphosis is given in the story of the god Nanahuatzin, whose self-immolation in a bonfire transformed him into the sun (Sahagún 1989:432–433). Nanahuatzin, once transformed, gave courageous individuals the ability to transmute permanently into eagles, jaguars, and other animals of merit, whereas weak individuals who were unable to sustain the requisite period of fasting were condemned to turn into ever-hungry vultures (Paso y

Troncoso 1953:196–201 [1892]). For others, the most important metamorphosis occurred at the moment of death because, based on their earthly achievements in warfare, some could become beautiful birds accompanying the solar star (Aguirre Beltrán 1978:16 [1955]; Sahagún 1989:204). These examples demonstrate that the ability to transform, whether temporarily or permanently, was a concept deeply rooted in indigenous beliefs.

Early ethnohistoric accounts of Pre-Hispanic practices usually mention that nahuals had a supernatural origin at birth (Garibay 1989:904), but in modern ethnographies nahualism is an activity that has to be learned by the candidate from other nahuals (e.g., Kaplan 1956; Weitlaner 1977). Colonial sources offer the intermediate point between these two extremes, stating that the ability to be a nahual was inherited from one's ancestors; however, it was also possible for interested individuals to acquire this capacity by submitting themselves for training to a specific animal at the intercession of other nahuals (Paso y Troncoso 1953:204 [1892]). These accounts indicate that shifts were occurring in the practice of nahual belief provoked by the demographic losses and social change that had begun with the Spanish conquest. Prior to this event, transforming into a nahual was seemingly an exclusive practice reserved for a few elites, which then later adapted to include more followers through apprenticeship.

Astrology practiced at the time of the conquest dictated that nahuals were born exclusively under two signs of the *tonalamatl* or ritual calendar: *ce quiahuitl* (1 Rain) and *ce ehecatl* (1 Wind). Both days were considered disastrous, and baptisms of children were avoided on those days. The bad fortune of the day sign 1 Rain continued for a period of thirteen days when the Cihuateteo goddesses descended to earth and caused illnesses in children. Similarly, these thirteen days were not good for traveling, and merchants ceased their commercial activities during this period. The thirteen days of 1 Rain were ruled by the god Nahui Ehecatl (4 Wind), a mysterious deity who, according to the codices Telleriano-Remensis and Vaticanus A, possessed a group of attributes and powers over the rain and wind (Quiñones Keber 1995:172–173). The presence of 4 Wind and his identification as one of the Tepictoton gods of rains reveal one of the principal abilities of nahuals—control of the weather.

The thirteen days beginning on 1 Wind were governed by the goddess Chantico. Also poorly known, it was said that Chantico annoyed the creator god Tonacatecutli, who turned her into a dog (Quiñones Keber 1995:186–187). Thus Chantico suffered a permanent metamorphosis from human to animal form. The story of Chantico is relevant, as her calendar name, 9 Dog, was a special day for nahuals to perform their magical practices. The other deity associated with the thirteen days of 1 Wind was Quetzalcoatl, powerful god of the winds and whirlwinds (Sahagún 1989:248). Thanks to the association of this deity, nahuals were given the power to transform themselves into whirlwinds and call the winds to their aid. In summary, the thirteen-day periods of 1 Rain and 1 Wind were governed by deities related to rain and wind—weather phenomena that could harm crops.

Although indigenous sources extol the powers of nahuals, often describing them as prosperous and prestigious (Codex Borbonicus 1988: folios 7, 8; Garibay 1989:904; Weitlaner 1977:171, 180), the Spanish sources characterize them as poor and disgraced individuals (Paso y Troncoso 1953:166 [1892]; Sahagún 1989:248). This contradiction is not surprising, as the indigenous belief system was strongly attacked by the Spanish religious orders attempting to convert native peoples to Catholicism, forcing them to abandon their public rituals and subsequently giving rise to clandestine indigenous worship. Ironically, this stigma and secrecy provided the appropriate environment for nahualism to flourish, and the practice acquired a reactionary role against the impositions of the Spanish clergy, leading to a guerrilla war of ideology between Catholicism and the core of Pre-Hispanic religion. Some famous confrontations between nahuals and priests are described by Mendieta (1993:109 [1870]), who recounts the story of Friar Andrés de Olmos, who captured a nahual and then challenged him to escape from his jail cell.

To the great mortification of Olmos, the nahual did precisely that without being seen by any witnesses. Numerous manuals on native idolatry written by Spanish priests between the seventeenth and eighteenth centuries attest to the fact that more than a century after the conquest, Catholicism controlled the public space, but nahualism prevailed in the private sphere in everyday domestic cults, agricultural rituals, and medical practices (Paso y Troncoso 1953 [1892]).

As to the status and role of the nahual in the Pre-Hispanic era, the best source of information was provided by Friar Bernardino de Sahagún's native informants (Garibay 1989:904). In these accounts, the nahual was an astrologer who gave strength and advice to kings and commoners. The nahuals, men or women, were celibate and specialized in forecasting the weather, preventing hail, predicting the future, and curing sicknesses. The conservative nature of the nahual manifested itself through constant exhortations on the annual debt owed to the gods of rain, as the nahual reminded everyone that the only way to avoid hunger was to pay for the water needed to nourish the crops in the fields. The required payment was human sacrifice. The nahual would also rebuke any deviations from codes of conduct, as judged by the collective norms of the group. To control such powerful forces as the weather, illnesses, and behavioral deviations, the nahual needed the extraordinary powers obtained through transformation into his or her animal companion(s).

Interestingly, the nahuals mimicked Pre-Hispanic social hierarchy among themselves with a status hierarchy for their animal companions. This hierarchy of animals is detailed by Sahagún (1989:621–659), who provides a classification of animals based on their strength and other positive or negative attributes. In the indigenous view, the fauna of the world could be classified into discrete, ranked groups, within which the members were also ranked. The most important member in each group was typically a desirable companion for nahuals. The first group comprised wild beasts, among which the most powerful was the jaguar (*tigre*). In the second most important group of wild animals, the coyote, an animal admired for its intelligence, reigned supreme. Following these two groups were many others. Bird groups were distinguished according to their plumage and songs; the most important bird group had the quetzal at its head. In a separate group were the birds of prey, with eagles at the head. Fish, reptiles, insects, and aquatic animals all had their groups and individual rankings.

Such animal rankings and nahual preferences have been described for modern indigenous groups. Based on work among the Mayas of Chamula, Gossen (1975:453) describes a classification of animals into three groups, which he relates to the social status perceived by the individuals in this community. According to this ranking, Group 1 consists of carnivorous mammals (jaguar, ocelot, coyote, and fox) that, like man, have five digits on their paws. This group of potential animal companions is reserved for rich and powerful people, brujos, and healers, as well as those who seek and exercise *cargos* (duties and responsibilities) in the community. Ordinary people can only aspire to have animal companions in Group 2: rabbit, raccoon, opossum, skunk, and squirrel. Finally, the third group includes domestic animals introduced by the Spaniards, such as cows, sheep, pigs, etc., which are reserved only for brujos, who could take these forms as well as those of Group 1. This more simplified Chamula ranking does not contradict the schema given by Sahagún's informants. The significant novelty is the inclusion of European animals into the hierarchy and the fact that only witches can claim them as companions; according to the brujos, it allows them to approach the houses of their victims without being noticed. The control of domestic animals as a source of wealth and power is also undoubtedly related to these animals being attractive forms for nahual transformation.

For the Chamulans, however, the most powerful animal of all is the jaguar, and those individuals who have a jaguar as their animal companion are fortunate, rich, powerful, and live long lives. Sahagún's informants echo this sentiment, describing the jaguar as the "prince and lord of all other animals" (Sahagún 1989:621). These classifications and rankings conform to the ideological core of the indigenous social system in which inequality and the existence of hierarchy among humans is considered a normal fact of life (Gossen 1994:566).

Such a system justifies the greatness of its leaders based on the qualities of their animal companions and their perceived ability to transform themselves into different animals; therefore it is not surprising that people believed their rulers, including Moctezuma Xocoyotzin and various K'iche' lords, had the power to transform themselves into jaguars and eagles as well as lightning (Aguirre Beltrán 1978:6 [1955]; Recinos 1984:71–94). An individual born into a high-status family would receive a high-status animal companion, and if the calendrical date were appropriate, he or she could be a powerful nahual. The self-fulfilling logic of this system allowed the ruling class to monopolize the use of superior animal forms as well as other highly valued elements, both supernatural and sumptuary (e.g., lightning, clouds, fog, whirlwinds, beautiful birds and their feathers, and precious stones). For their part, commoners had to be content with lesser animal companions and therefore lesser strength and will to undertake extraordinary deeds (Mendieta 1993:97 [1870]). The exceptional aspect of this ideology is that it minimized internal social stress, because individuals were not encouraged to stand out but rather to conform, as their destiny to be commoners was fated from birth with the assignment of a weak animal companion. Since the conquest, nahualism functioned as an economic leveling process that punished those who tried to stand out from the group without having accomplished prescribed feats at prescribed moments according to social norms (Villa Rojas 1947).

In the Pre-Hispanic era, the system would have instituted a series of restrictions to prevent individuals from trying to be nahuals. These restrictions would have operated according to the ritual calendar, particularly by limiting the birth of nahuals to specific dangerous days of the calendar. Clearly, however, the danger depended on family status (Sahagún 1979:4:100). According to the glosses of the Codex Borbonicus (1988:folios 7, 18), those arriving into the world on 1 Rain would be rich. The nahual born on 1 Wind was a conjuror of hail and ice and also had power over the winds. With the help of the god Nahui Ehecatl, the nahual could force the threatening clouds to release their load of ice on places that were not under cultivation (Sahagún 1989:437). Notably, the manipulation of the weather by the nahual was not exercised directly over water, which was the domain of the Tlaloque (storm gods), but rather over the winds as a member of the Ehecatotontin (wind gods). Given that water in general was believed to flow through serpents driven by the winds (Beals 1973:94 [1945]), the nahual, through spells, could divert the serpents of water and wind or cut them into smaller pieces so that they did not fall in long destructive downpours (Codex Borgia 1980:folios 9, 19; Paso y Troncoso 1953:78 [1892]).

Sahagún's informants also demonstrated an understanding of complex meteorological phenomena. They clearly distinguished four types of winds and their effects on humans, landscape, and bodies of water (Sahagún 1977:14–15), as well as various kinds of clouds and precipitation (Figure 2.6). They specifically describe the conditions for hail as "when very white clouds settled on the mountain tops. . . . Now it will hail; now our food will be hailed out" (Sahagún 1977:7:20). The importance of understanding and controlling weather continued into the colonial period. At the end of the sixteenth century a well-organized system of storm conjurors operated in the Toluca Valley in Central Mexico. They worked in groups of up to seven conjurors, who were synchronized to launch evocations against clouds that brought hail. There were different techniques and prayers, but they all included great puffs of air directed at the clouds. The people of the region, including the Spaniards, paid one real (Spanish coinage) per field and had an administrative procedure with indigenous collectors to facilitate payment. When Bishop García Guerra attempted to curtail these activities, the residents rebelled and demanded that the rituals against storms be continued (Paso y Troncoso

1953:77–80 [1892]). Today religious specialists (*graniceros*) are still actively practicing agricultural and meteorological rituals on hilltops throughout Central Mexico as a way to control natural forces that could impact a community's agricultural livelihood (see Albores and Broda 1997).

Also of interest is an understanding of how the nahual performed the act of transformation. One might suppose that the nahual simply transformed at will, as in the case of the indigenous leader Quilaztli who appeared to the Aztec captains transformed into an eagle (Paso y Troncoso 1953:202 [1892]). However, ethnohistoric and ethnographic accounts refer to methods for conversion. During an Inquisition trial in Tula, Hidalgo, in 1536, two nahuals named Tlacatectectle and Tenixtecle reportedly transformed into jaguars by applying an ointment (Fábregas Puig 1969:98). Friar Diego Durán also mentions the use of ointments and invocations during a meeting of sixty nahuals summoned by Moctezuma Ilhuicamina in Coatepec, Hidalgo (Durán 1984:2:217). Other procedures demanded that the nahual be cloaked with animal skins, like Tecun Uman, who cloaked himself with bird wings on his arms and feathers on his legs and body before flying off ahead of his army (Recinos 1984:86–87). Part of the transformation process seemingly entailed the removal of the legs and/or feet and then jumping seven (Fábregas Puig 1969:4, 107) or three (Galinier 1987:436) times. This belief parallels Sahagún's informants characterizing the sorcerer born on the day 1 Rain: "He was a magician, one who removed his legs" (Sahagún 1979:43).

Later colonial cases indicate that the magical procedures to perform a transformation had to be taught by other nahuals. According to reports in 1687 by the Bishop of Chiapas, Friar Francisco Nuñez de la Vega, powerful nahuals trained groups of three apprentices, instructing them in the arts of nahualism. These arts included (1) reading fortunes or horoscopes, (2) controlling rain, (3) clairvoyance, (4) healing, and (5) human-animal transformation. The novices had to keep their identities secret (Brinton 1894:24–30). Among the Chinantecos of Ozumacin, transformation was done at night. The

figure 2.6
Illustration by one of Sahagún's informants defining dangerous precipitation (hail, snow, and ice) and the particular S-shaped design of the associated cloud formation. (Drawing from the New World Archaeological Foundation based on original in Sahagún 1977:illus. 13.)

novice was taken to a mountain and all clothing removed. The novice was then told to get down on all fours and wait in this position until a real jaguar appeared that would transmit the ability to take jaguar form. The jaguar would lick the novice or jump over the individual seven times, after which the power of transformation would be received (Weitlaner 1977:172).

Geography of the Nahual

We believe the nahuals moved easily through extensive Mesoamerican communication networks. These circuits were highly dynamic and continued operating after the conquest, but secretly: "they back each other up and keep their distance from us more than any nation in the world" (Durán 1984:2:217). Given this geographic mobility, it is likely that during the Pre-Hispanic era high-status nahuals had similar training in divination, ritual calendars, magic formulas, and transformation rules, as well as meteorological knowledge. Famous nahuals traveled across the provinces, provoking beneficial rains and stopping hail; the same sources describe how recognized nahuals were brought from all over Mesoamerica to serve the Aztec kings (Aguirre Beltrán 1978:3 [1955]; Durán 1984:2:217; Fábregas Puig 1969:98–102).

The way in which the reported nahual cases are distributed geographically across Mesoamerica provides some insight into clusters of activity at certain locations. By no means an exhaustive list, we have documented sixty locales from ethnohistoric or ethnographic reports where nahual activity existed (Figure 2.7; Table 2.1). The northernmost case of nahualism found so far is reported from Sombrerete, Zacatecas (Archivo General de la Nación, Mexico [AGN], 1696, ramo Inquisición, libro 497, exp. 23), which consisted of a magical healing performed by invoking nahuals from two lakes. Presented before an Inquisition tribunal, this case is interesting for the use of the word "nahual" to refer to spirits associated with permanent bodies of water. The southern cases included one in the city of Antigua, Guatemala, at the beginning of the seventeenth century, in which an indigenous woman died at the same time and with the same wounds as an alligator that had been caught at a nearby river (Ruíz de Alarcón 1953:26–28 [1629]). Another is a report by Antonio de Herrera y Tordesillas, cited by Brinton (1894:42), describing the transformation of the Honduran ruler Coamizagual into a "Thunder Bird." Overall, however, 43 percent of the cases found to date (*n* = 26) are concentrated in a corridor that connects the present-day Mexican states

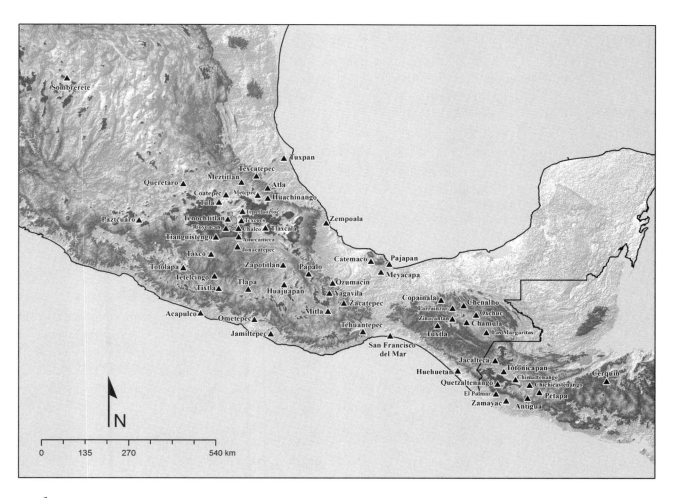

figure 2.7
Map showing the locales where nahual activity has been reported in colonial accounts and ethnographies (see Table 2.1). (Drawing by the authors.)

Table 2.1
Documented cases of nahual activity

LOCATION		NAHUAL FORM	SOURCE
ZACATECAS	Sombrerete	Water	AGN, 1696, Inquisición, l. 497, e. 23, in Aguirre Beltrán (1978:12 [1955])
MICHOACÁN	Patzcuaro	Turkey	AGN, 1696, Inquisición, l. 674, e. 14, in Aguirre Beltrán (1978:18 [1955])
QUERETARO	Queretaro	Dog	AGN, 1696, Inquisición, l. 486, e. 51, in Aguirre Beltrán (1978:6–7 [1955])
HIDALGO	Coatepec	Various	Durán (1984:2:217)
	Meztitlan	Jaguar	AGN, 1696, Inquisición, l. 303, e. 64, in Aguirre Beltrán (1978:7 [1955])
	Tula	Jaguar	Fábregas Puig (1969:98)
VERACRUZ	Catemaco	Various	Foster (1944:97)
	Huaxteca (Tuxpan)	Jaguar	Aguirre Beltrán (1978:1 [1955])
	Meyacapa	Lightning	Brinton (1894:21–22)
	Pajapan	Turtle	Fábregas Puig (1969:5)
	Texcatepec	Jaguar, eagle	Galinier (1987:432–433)
	Zempoala	Various	Foster (1944:99)
TLAXCALA	Tlaxcala	Various	Foster (1944:99)
MEXICO CITY	Coyoacan	Various	Navarrete (2000:166)
	Tenochtitlan	Serpent, jaguar, puma	Aguirre Beltrán (1978:6 [1955])
STATE OF MEXICO	Amecameca	Jaguar	Chimalpáhin (1998: 1:135–136)
	Chalco	Jaguar	Fábregas Puig (1969:97)
	Metepec	Water	AGN, Inquisición, l. 705, e. 5, in Aguirre Beltrán (1978:13 [1955])
	Tepetlaoztoc	Coyote	Fábregas Puig (1969:93)
	Texcoco	Jaguar	Fábregas Puig (1969:95)
	Tianguistengo	Dog	Paso y Troncoso (1953:81 [1892])
MORELOS	Jonacatepec	Jaguar, serpent	Durán (1984:1:166)
PUEBLA	Atla	Various	Fábregas Puig (1969:3)
	Huachinango	Serpent	Fábregas Puig (1969:98)
	Zapotitlan	Various	Brinton (1894:36)
GUERRERO	Acapulco	Lizard	Ruíz de Alarcón (1953:26 [1629])
	Taxco	Fox	Ruíz de Alarcón (1953:25 [1629])
	Tetelcingo	Various	Fábregas Puig (1969:6)
	Tixtla	Woman	AGN, Inquisición, l. 513, e. 5, in Aguirre Beltrán (1978:10 [1955])

LOCATION	NAHUAL FORM	SOURCE
GUERRERO (continued)		
Tlapa	Crocodile	Foster (1944:100)
Totolapa	Lightning	Fábregas Puig (1969:5)
Ometepec	Jaguar	Foster (1944:96)
OAXACA		
Huajupan	Bat	Ruíz de Alarcón (1953:25 [1629])
Jamiltepec	Caiman, jaguar	Kaplan (1956)
Mitla	Various	Foster (1944:99)
Ozumacin	Jaguar	Weitlaner (1977:171)
Papalo	Puma	Weitlaner (1977:188)
San Francisco del Mar	Various	Fábregas Puig (1969:7)
Tehuantepec	Feathered serpent	Brinton (1894:40)
Yagavila	Fire	Alcina Franch (1971:24–25), in Urcid (2001:247, n.18)
Zacatepec	Various	Foster (1944:96)
CHIAPAS		
Chamula	Jaguar, fox, others	Gossen (1975)
Chenalhó	Various	Medina (2001:102)
Copainala	Various	Wonderly (1946:97)
Huehuetan	Various	Brinton (1894:36)
Larráinzar	Various	Holland (1961:167)
Las Margaritas	Lightning	Fábregas Puig (1969:12)
Oxchuc	Various	Villa Rojas (1947:583)
Tuxtla Gutiérrez	Various	Fábregas Puig (1969:11)
Zinacantan	Jaguar, others	Vogt (1970:1156–1158)
GUATEMALA		
Chichicastenango	Various	Foster (1944:100); Tax (1949:131)
Chimaltenango	Various	Fábregas Puig (1969:15)
Guatemala	Lizard	Ruíz de Alarcón (1953:26 [1629])
Petapa	Puma, jaguar	Gage (1958:273–275)
Quetzaltenango	Dog, eagle	Brinton (1894:43); Recinos (1984)
Santiago El Palmar	Various	Saler (1964:309–310)
Totonicapan	Various	Brinton (1894:30–31)
Zamayac	Various	Brinton (1894:37)
HONDURAS	Cerquin	Various	Brinton (1894:12–13)

Note: AGN, Archivo General de la Nación, Mexico.

of Hidalgo, Puebla, Tlaxcala, the Federal District, the State of Mexico, Morelos, eastern Guerrero, and western Oaxaca. In general, these are cold highlands with a marked seasonality between rainy and dry seasons. In this difficult environment the nahual predominated, capable of bringing rain or altering the path of hail and ice. The two most common animal nahual forms in this area were jaguars and serpents.

Five locales (8.3 percent) are concentrated in the Gulf Coast plains of Mexico, including the Huaxteca, Totonac, and Popoluca regions. This area has abundant rainfall but is subject to strong cold winds blowing from the north, which are damaging for both agricultural and fishing activities (*Relación de la provincia de Coatzacualco* 1984:116). In this region the nahual fulfills the primary functions of healing and weather control, particularly control of the north winds. The northern mountains of Oaxaca, with an extension to the Isthmus of Tehuantepec, has six locales of nahual activity (10 percent of the sample). These include Chinantec, Mazatec, Mixe, and Zapotec communities (Figure 2.2). The nahual beliefs of this cluster are very similar to those found in the Gulf of Mexico, specifically around the Tuxtla Mountains, so these two clusters could be merged.

The second largest cluster of nahual activity (31.6 percent) has been documented in the Chiapas and Guatemala areas. The central Chiapas Highlands presents eight locales; another eleven locales are reported in the Guatemalan Highlands and the Pacific Coast, from the Huave zone in coastal Oaxaca to the Department of Suchitepequez, Guatemala. The most interesting case of this group is the Tlazoalayan shrine at Huehuetan, Soconusco, where there was a nahual altar dedicated to the "Heart of the Town" as late as 1687. This sanctuary contained greenstone (*chalchihuites*), a stone with the calendar names of the gods, and ceramic vessels with covers (Brinton 1894:47). In this vast area, the predominant nahual function is the exercise of social control in groups and the practice of healing (Gossen 1975; Moscoso 1990). The preferred animal of these nahuals is the jaguar; however, this

zone also exhibits the greatest variety of animal transformations.

Evaluation and comparison of clusters of known nahual activity from the colonial period to early ethnographies of the twentieth century may indicate a possible origin of these practices. Brinton (1894:63–64) believed that the word "nahual" had its origins in a language from which the root "*na*" was derived, which he proposed meant "to know" or "to be in the know." He proposed that the Zapotec, Mayan, and Nahuatl languages acquired this monosyllabic word elsewhere, but he did not venture a possible origin language, although he noticed that the only Mayan language that did not have this root was Huastec. Based on their Mixe-Zoque linguistic studies, Campbell and Kaufman (1976:85) proposed a Proto-Mixe origin for the word "*na?wa*" (old man) and associated the nahual complex with the Olmec culture. We do see centers of nahual activity in areas where Olmecs formerly lived, as in the Tuxtlas, or where Olmecs had strong contacts, such as the Soconusco. Subsequent linguistic work by Wichmann (1995:223, no. 23), however, notes that Proto-Mixe had a separate word for "brujo" or "nahual"—"*cok?a*"—making it "unlikely that *na?wa* would mean anything but 'old man' or 'husband,'" and therefore would not explain why other languages would borrow "*na?wa*" instead of "*cok?a*." Given the geographic distribution of nahual cases, the other possible source from which the word "nahual" might have derived could be the Otomanguean language family, although further linguistic work is required to support this idea.

Our map presents a bias toward those cases that were brought to the attention of the colonial Europeans and early ethnographers; still, the concentrations of such cases in the central-southern section of Mexico is suggestive of the strength of this belief in areas where ancient occupations of Amuzgo, Chocho, Mixtec, Otomí, and Tlapanec peoples once lived (Figure 2.2). Notably, these peoples live in the highlands and in areas of central and southern Mexico with marked seasonality of rainfall patterns. Although the rainy season brings water to the agricultural fields, this precipitation arrives in many dangerous forms, such as hail, sleet, and *agua-viento* ("water-wind," sheets or ropes of rain). Such problematic rainfall is very frequent in the highlands, in contrast to the lowlands, where excessive flooding and winds are more common threats to agriculture. So perhaps the core precept of the nahual as weatherman comes from the highland area.

The final point to consider in the geography of the nahual is that the network of nahual sanctuaries is also found along the principal trade routes that connected Mesoamerica. We believe that the majority of the shrines controlled by the nahuals were located precisely along these routes. In particular, we note the route connecting Morelos with the Pacific Coast and the Soconusco, the route connecting Puebla to Tuxtepec that runs through the Tehuacan Valley and the Mazatec and Chinantec regions (Pye and Gutiérrez 2007), and finally the route that connects Hidalgo to the Huaxteca through the Huauchinango road (Gutiérrez 1996). Perhaps for this reason Aztec merchants not only avoided travel during the thirteen-day period beginning with the day 1 Rain, but they also celebrated their feast days at this time—a period dominated by nahual rituals.

Interpretations of the San Pedro Aytec Figurine

We return to the San Pedro Aytec figurine to highlight some of its important features in light of our survey of nahual practices. The front figure wears a mask with features including the downturned mouth, almond-shaped eyes, and flattened nose with pronounced nostrils. The back figure has the downturned mouth and a cleft at the top of its head. This second complex of features is seen beginning in the Early Preclassic period on monumental sculpture and baby-faced figurines; these elements are often referred to as were-jaguar characteristics and are believed to be associated with the Rain God (Joralemon 1996:56; Taube 1995:95).[3] In the Middle Preclassic this complex is not only seen on the Gulf Coast but also in Morelos, Guerrero,

and numerous unprovenienced portable objects throughout Mesoamerica. In particular, we note the four faces (see Figures 3.11 and 3.12) seen on the architectural facades of the Teopantecuantitlan sunken plaza (see Chapter 3; Martínez Donjuán 1994:156) and a series of plaques or large pendants in the collection of the Spratling Museum in Taxco (Villela 2006:9), as well as the recently uncovered sculptures from Zazacatla (see Chapter 4).

Contortionism was an important theme in the Preclassic period and is relevant to the San Pedro Aytec figurine. Such physical feats, as indicated by the famous Tlatilco contortionist figurine (Figure 2.8), are possible for a restricted few who are double-jointed, suffer from Ehlers-Danlos syndrome, practice intensive yoga, are in the throes of an epileptic seizure, or are perhaps specifically trained for the task from a young age (Tate 1995:63–64). Shamanic contortions, as referred to by Tate (1995), may be one of the behaviors practiced by those who were about to transform themselves into their animal forms. The Tlatilco figurine, depicting an individual lying on his stomach, head and upper torso upright, his legs curved back, and his feet on his head, was found with Burial 154. The adult male in this grave exhibited cranial modification and dental mutilation and was found with a variety of other grave goods, including clay pieces shaped like mushrooms or phalli, small metates that could have been used for grinding mushrooms, quartz amulets, jadeite and bone earspools, an iron-ore mirror, flint, obsidian artifacts, and greenstone (Niederberger 1996:fig. 4; Ochoa 1996:189). The implication of these grave goods is that the interred individual was of high status and practiced shamanism. Other two-dimensional depictions of contortionists on flat, carved monuments depict what would be a frontal view of the Tlatilco figurine: the upper half of an individual with arms crossed, no torso or legs, and the soles of the feet jutting upward from the top of the head. A round altar from San Lorenzo (Monument 16) depicts the jutting feet, although the rest of the image has eroded off (Figure 2.9; see Cyphers 2004b:75; Tate 1995:figs. 24–28). The Shook Panel from coastal Guatemala (see Figure 10.7b) shows a similar scene.

It presents two abstract views of the same individual (cf. Tate 1995), one sideways with a hand reaching back to grab his feet, his entire figure encircling the panel, and a frontal view depicting a ruler's upper torso with two footprints above the headdress. The individual has a were-jaguar face. The frontal view depicts a jester god headdress and a pendant, perhaps a stone spoon or bloodletter (Tate 1995:63). This technique of two views of the same person for a two-dimensional surface may intend to depict an individual in motion, potentially in the act of tumbling past the viewer.

On the San Pedro Aytec figurine, the two faces of the figurine are not back to back, as in a Janus-faced image. Rather, one must rotate the figurine to see the other face (Figure 2.3), hence the suggestion of contortion or tumbling. Contortion is also indicated in one of two other ways. The back

image shows only the upper torso and head, and the cleft above the head could also be seen as its two feet swinging up and around, as in the low-relief images described above (see Figure 10.7b). The second possibility is that the reverse figure's shoulders are carved at an angle and could appear to be the thighs, knees, and upper calves of the front figure (Figure 2.4, back); note also the clear lines demarcating these legs from the forearms and hands of the backside individual. In fact, the carver could have intended both interpretations to convey the sense of a whirl of legs in motion as in acrobatic tumbling. This fascination with contortionism can be demonstrated from at least the Early Preclassic on, as evidenced in San Lorenzo Monument 16. Also, Christine Niederberger correlated the figurines in the Tlatilco burials, including the acrobat, with her Tlapacoya figurine sequence and dated them to the

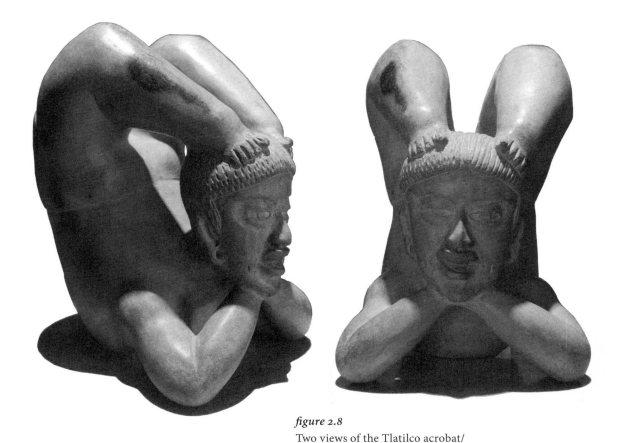

figure 2.8
Two views of the Tlatilco acrobat/
contortionist figurine. (Photographs
by the authors.)

figure 2.9
San Lorenzo Monument 16.
(Drawing from the New World
Archaeological Foundation.)

0   50 cm

Manantial phase, or the late Early Preclassic in the Basin of Mexico (Niederberger 1987:1:230, fig.107, 2:452–453, figs. 308–309, 2000). Other figurines and monuments depicting contortionists lack context, albeit the Shook Panel presents iconography attributed to the Middle Preclassic (see Chapter 10; Shook and Heizer 1976).

The lack of legs depicted on the back figure of the San Pedro Aytec figurine calls to mind the removal of the legs in the transformation process, according to ethnohistoric and ethnographic accounts. If, in fact, the legs were supposed to "disappear" or change, then the kneeling position used by felines would be a viable posture. It also represents a reversal of roles: the human kneeling like a jaguar before metamorphosis and the nahual in jaguar form standing like a human (Figure 2.1). The artistic solution for depicting disappearing legs could be a kneeling human; the other would be the solution presented by the San Pedro Aytec figurine, showing two states of transformation: with legs and without.

The figure on the back presents the roughly ovoid shape seen in some of the votive axes, such as the Kunz axe (Benson and Fuente 1996:262), the Tenochtitlan axe (Cyphers 1997:227), and a series of axes from private collections that appeared in the Princeton Olmec exhibition (Princeton 1995:201–204). These carved axes all have simply drawn anthropomorphic arms and legs; the legs, in particular, consist of a single incised line in the lower half of the torso, and not even that in some cases. These schematic anthropomorphic torsos greatly contrast with their elaborate heads with large jaguar mouths, fangs, and headdresses and/or ears, perhaps indicating that the amorphous anthropomorphic torso is in the process of changing into a feline form to match the well-defined jaguar head, or that in fact the legs have already essentially disappeared. The suggestion of the two legs would cue the viewer that he or she was looking at a transformed nahual. Although the San Pedro Aytec figurine may not present clean axe lines or shape, such as the Kunz axe (Benson and Fuente 1996:262), the figure on the back does have the wide head and cleft at what could be its "bit" end, whereas the "poll" end is considerably narrower. This pattern is typical for many of the Olmec greenstone axes, particularly the cleft imagery, which Taube (2004:270) relates to the Maize God, a common theme in Middle Preclassic iconography.

An alternative interpretation of the figurine is indicated when comparing the two faces (Figure 2.4), suggesting an interesting duality. One image presents an adult in a jaguar costume and the other could be seen as an infant with legs swaddled. One could argue that the eyes of the back face appear to be closed, perhaps indicating death. This image brings to mind the Las Limas sculpture, which depicts a human, presumably of high status, holding the drooping body of a were-jaguar baby that is perhaps dead, given that these were-jaguar babies have been shown full of life in other depictions, such as on La Venta Altar 5 (see Figure 6.7; González Lauck 1994:111, fig. 6.28). If accurate, the two sides of the San Pedro Aytec figurine would have represented alter egos of a single being or person (Javier Urcid, personal communication 2008). Others have interpreted the were-jaguar being as a young Rain God (Taube 1995); hence, the front figure could be the acting jaguar nahual calling the winds, with the Rain God on the backside calling the rains.

Nahualism in Central Mexico and Guerrero

At this point we turn our attention to a specific zone of nahual activity in Central Mexico. We define this region as the southern half of the State of Mexico, all of Morelos, central and eastern Guerrero, as well as western Puebla and Oaxaca. This region had a network of sanctuaries or shrines dedicated to the gods of rain and wind (Durán 1984:1:166). The indigenous chronicler don Domingo Chimalpáhin comments that when the Nahuatl speakers arrived in this zone they found inhabitants who spoke a different language from Nahuatl, and among them were some who were called the Quiyahuizteca (People of the Rain). Chimalpáhin identifies them as *quiyauhnahualleque* (rain nahuals) and as *tecuannnahualleque* (jaguar nahuals), or those who use the mask of the jaguar ("disfraz de tigre") (Fábregas Puig 1969:43–51). These rain nahuals and jaguar nahuals were experts in the magical arts and could transform themselves at will into beasts

and provoke rains. They could be found from the province of Chalco to the Mixtec-Tlapaneca zone of eastern Guerrero. It was said that the Nahua people learned from them the art of transformation. The Nahuas then captured their temple Chalchiumomozco and the precious items within it, apparently also robbing them of their transformation abilities as well (Chimalpáhin 1998:1:135–145). Chimalpáhin describes Chalchiumomozco as a shrine dedicated to water that was situated on a hill with a cave beneath it and a natural spring in the cave. Mendieta (1993:602 [1870]) mentions how Chalchiumomozco became a Christian shrine after the conquest, today called Monte Sacro in Amecameca, a destination for pilgrimages.

Friar Diego Durán describes in detail another water shrine in Morelos, which is called Ayauhcalli (house of repose and shade of the gods), located on the hilltop Teocuicani. Durán (1984:1:166) states that Teocuicani means "divine singer," because when the clouds passed over it, "great thunder and lightning were emitted, so loud and reverberating that it scared one to hear it." He notes that everyone from the province came to worship this hill and to sacrifice men there. There was a large greenstone idol in the sanctuary that the Indians hid when the conversion efforts began in the area. Durán informs us that, like Teocuicani, there were many hilltops with shrines and that "only to mention all of them one would have to write a thick book" (Durán 1984:1:166). According to Grove (1972:35–36), Teocuicani is known today as Cerro Jantetelco, located a few kilometers from Chalcatzingo.

This great network of rain sanctuaries controlled by the jaguar nahuals extended from Chalco-Amecameca to the Pacific Ocean. In Guerrero, rituals petitioning for rain still take place on mountain tops. During the months of April and May, the *tecuani*, men wearing jaguar masks and costumes, come out to fight one another and to draw blood in sacrifice to the Rain God. From the sanctuaries located on the hilltops, the tecuani call the good rains by striking the air with their whips, imitating the sounds of thunder, and asking the winds to guide the rain to the fields (Díaz Vázquez

2003:76–77). Although our knowledge of this ritual network of shrines is limited, Late Preclassic and Postclassic sites have been located on hilltops in the valley of Mexico (Aranda Monroy 1997) and Morelos (Broda and Maldonado 1997); this last investigation in Morelos uncovered three offerings in a cave. It is likely that this system originated at least by the Middle Preclassic period. We propose this age because of the presence of three caves with Middle Preclassic rock paintings in central and eastern Guerrero: Oxtotitlán, Juxtlahuaca, and Cauadzidziqui (Grove 1970; Gutiérrez et al. 2006). Paintings in two of these caves depict individuals dressed in jaguar costumes and dominating other individuals in nonjaguar dress. The other cave, Oxtotitlán, apart from depicting a human-bird seated on an altar, also has a painting of a human whose body is shown with black paint and who wears a headdress; a jaguar stands in front of him, and his tail reaches back and is attached to the genital area of the individual (Grove 1970:17, fig. 13), perhaps an example of a jaguar nahual. All three caves are located on mountains where rain-petition rituals occur today.

Other Examples of Transformation Iconography in Guerrero and Morelos

In addition to the colonial and ethnographic reports of nahualism, we describe a Postclassic case dating to AD 1475. In the Azoyú codices 1 (folio 26) and 2 (folio 7), one of the most powerful rulers of the Tlachinollan Kingdom in eastern Guerrero[4] is depicted, a person called Quiyahuitl Tecuhtli, or Lord Rain (Gutiérrez 2002, 2008; Vega Sosa 1991). Although we are not completely sure of the numerical day of his birth, we can infer that Lord Rain was born on a "Rain" day of the calendar. This birthday partially satisfies the conditions for a powerful nahual in Pre-Hispanic times: (1) one had to be a noble, and (2) one had to be born on the days 1 Rain or 1 Wind.

The folios in question paint Lord Rain at the moment of his death in his mortuary bundle. In Codex Azoyú 2, the bundle is associated with a jaguar sacrificing a man. In Codex Azoyú 1, his bundle is tied to a jaguar devouring a man (Figure 2.10). This action is significant, as we know that powerful nahual rulers could transform themselves into their animal companion at the moment of death (Brinton 1894:42). We suggest that these scenes from the Azoyú books depict the final transformation of Lord Rain into his primary nahual, a jaguar-sacrificer and devourer of men, a role he performed during his life. We also believe that it is not a coincidence that Lord Rain purportedly died in the year 11 Ehecatl (11 Wind) of the Tlapanec calendar. The symbolic link of these elements—Rain (day of the ruler's birth), Wind (his year of death), and the image of the jaguar sacrificer—reflects the use of a form of *naualli tlatolli* (language of hidden meaning) to underscore these related cosmic elements and to support Lord Rain's designation as a great jaguar nahual.

Given these scenes from the Azoyú codices, we note that San Lorenzo Monument 107 (Figure 2.11; Cyphers 2004b:183–186) may parallel this theme—a dead lord with his nahual. This sculpture depicts a seated, snarling feline with disk-shaped eyes, fangs, and a single front tooth. The jaguar appears to be holding a human with eyes closed and wearing an avian helmet. Cyphers (2004b:186) draws attention to a volute or S-shaped relief between the legs of the human, and possibly more around the depressions noted on the backside of the sculpture. The snarling pose of the feline is directed outward; it is not directly menacing the human, as in other scenes of snarling jaguars dominating humans (e.g., Chalcatzingo Monument 4) (Angulo 1987:145–146, figs. 10.16 and 10.17; Grove and Angulo 1987:121, fig. 9.11). Nonetheless, on the San Lorenzo monument, the feline is touching the human—the feline is connected to him. The human individual, perhaps dead, also appears to be in flight, although downward into the underworld.

Chalcatzingo Monument 31 (Grove 1996:113, fig. 8) may also depict a transformed ruler acting in his capacity as nahual (Figure 2.12). A jaguar with an avian crest and slightly beaky nose is attacking a human. Above the jaguar are three raindrop motifs and the inverted S-shaped volute.

We believe this scene depicts the transformed man-nahual, who also has avian characteristics emphasizing the sky element of wind. The nahual performs his role as sacrificer to provide the offering required to the rain and sky gods and to use his powers over wind and rains. Notably, the three-raindrop motif and inverted S-volute also appear together on Chalcatzingo Monument 1 of El Rey (Figure 2.13), leading Grove (1996:113) to suggest that these two monuments are contemporaneous. On Monument 1, El Rey holds an inverted S-volute in his arms, sits on an inverted S-volute throne, and his headdress has two sets of the three-raindrop motif. From his seat in the serpent cave/niche (Grove 2000), scrolls emerge, perhaps indicating the wind, while rain falls from clouds overhead. The inverted S-glyph and raindrops may represent a particular type of wind and rain: agua viento, rain that falls in sheets or ropes, as it is referred to in Morelos today, over which the nahual has control (Reilly 1996). Additionally, the inverted S-volute is also seen in the bundles held by the four personages arranged around the Teopantecuanitlan sunken patio (see Figures 3.11, 3.12, and 3.15). Some of the bundles depict one volute, in the middle, whereas others show two (Figure 2.14), one in the middle and one below, a repetition that recalls El Rey, Chalcatzingo Monument 1 (Figure 2.13). The volutes seem to function as clasps for the bundles of what Taube (1995:89–91) believes were quetzal plumes,

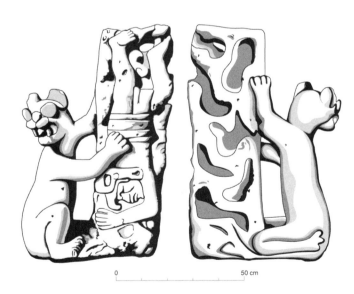

figure 2.11
San Lorenzo Monument 107. (Drawing from the New World Archaeological Foundation.)

which can also refer to green vegetation, thereby connecting rain and wind to agriculture.

We now turn to our final examples of nahualism from the archaeological site of Piedra Labrada, Guerrero, which dates to the Late Classic period (Gutiérrez 2008). Two of the monuments from that site are of interest here: one a stela, the other a sculpture in the round. Both depict a high-status person, likely a ruler of the site. The two sculptures demonstrate two stages in the nahual transformation. The stela, Monument 3 of Piedra Labrada (Figure 2.15), portrays an individual with the name Lord 10 Knot[5] on his chest. He is depicted as a jaguar-man standing upright, holding tri-glyphs in both claws (hands), while tri-glyph speech scrolls emit from his mouth. These tri-glyphs have been interpreted as bleeding hearts (Fuente 1995b:292). We believe the image of ruler 10 Knot is fulfilling his function as jaguar nahual, specifically, reminding people that the moment had arrived for paying the blood sacrifice owed to the rain gods. In the second sculpture, Monument 13 at Piedra Labrada (Figure 2.16), the same ruler, Lord 10 Knot, is shown completely transformed and now appears to be a seated jaguar. Unfortunately, the sculpture is decapitated, but the posture of the figure and its claws are feline. Another interesting element is that the typical jaguar spots on the body have been replaced by raindrop motifs, like those seen on the Preclassic Chalcatzingo monuments, reinforcing the idea that the ruler 10 Knot is a jaguar nahual with the ability to control rain. Urcid (1993:156, fig. 18) has also highlighted the Piedra Labrada stela, along with three other stelae from the coastal Oaxaca sites of Río Viejo, Río Grande, and Cerro del Rey, as representations of rulers with jaguar features, alluding "to the powers of the elite in transforming themselves into jaguars" (Urcid 1993:152). Stela 3 from Cerro del Rey is particularly unusual in presenting a standing figure, split in half—half human, half jaguar—providing a literal depiction of a "co-essence form" (Urcid 1993:149, 152) as discussed by Gossen (1975, 1994) and Houston and Stuart (1989).

These public monuments not only refer to the jaguar-transformation capacity but also to human sacrifice, jaguar-avian elements, and motifs for rain

figure 2.12 Chalcatzingo Monument 31. (Drawing from the New World Archaeological Foundation based on the authors' photograph.)

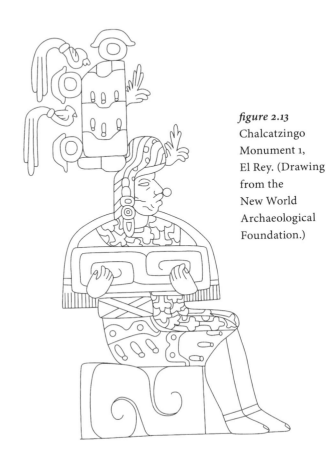

figure 2.13 Chalcatzingo Monument 1, El Rey. (Drawing from the New World Archaeological Foundation.)

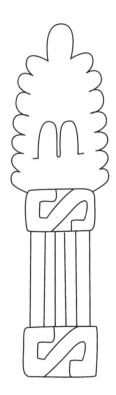

figure 2.14
One of the bundles carried by a figure in the Sunken Patio at Teopantecuanitlan. (Drawing from the New World Archaeological Foundation.)

and wind—all presumably related themes intrinsic to the ruler's role. Taube (1995) describes two gods in early Olmec iconography: one an avian-serpent and the other a rain deity. Although the rain deity is primarily a jaguar in form, along with its snarling mouth it also displays other elements, such as a single front tooth (perhaps from a shark), a furrowed brow, and in some cases, slitted eyes. Elements of this Olmec Rain God can be discerned in the later depictions of the rain gods Chahk, Cocijo, and Tlaloc (see Chapter 9; Covarrubias 1957:62), and like the later rain gods, the Olmec version is probably also quadripartite in nature. Taube (1995:97) describes four Olmec Rain God heads on the inner thighs of the Young Lord figurine, which probably count among their many aspects specific types of rain (e.g., hail, rain with winds). The avian-serpent specifically represents the sky realm, ancestral to later Mesoamerican sky serpents (Taube 1995:92–99). As these two are often depicted separately (e.g., Taube 1995:fig. 19a), it would seem that the avian-serpent god and the Rain God together were responsible for weather phenomena, with the avian-serpent providing transportation for rain, and the Rain God providing the precipitation itself. Such

0   50 cm

figure 2.15
Piedra Labrada Monument 3, Lord 10 Knot. (Drawing from the New World Archaeological Foundation based on the authors' photograph.)

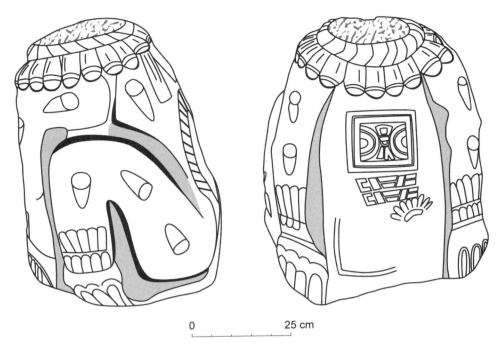

figure 2.16
Piedra Labrada Monument
13, Lord 10 Knot in nahual
form. (Drawing from the
New World Archaeological
Foundation based on the
authors' photograph.)

0   25 cm

a combination is indicated in ethnographic, colonial, and codex accounts that describe serpents of water and wind. It is also suggested by the seated jaguar monuments with cords or serpents hanging from their mouths, such as San Lorenzo Monument 37 (Cyphers 2004b:97) and La Venta Monument 80 (Figure 2.17; see also Taube 1995:93, fig. 13f). It has previously been posited that San Lorenzo Monument 37 depicts a transformed nahual (Cyphers 2004b:98–99).

Other components of nahual activity by rulers depicted in the Morelos and Guerrero examples include human sacrifice, as the blood was to be offered to the gods to propitiate the rains. Rituals to propitiate rain occur today on mountain tops in Guerrero and still include blood sacrifice, although it is chickens, dogs, and cats that are sacrificed, the last for its role as predator (Dehouve 2007:109). Chalcatzingo Monument 31 depicts the disemboweled human victim beneath the jaguar nahual (Figure 2.12). As part of the rain god complex, Taube argues that the Olmecs, like later Mesoamerican groups, practiced human sacrifice in conjunction with the ballgame, noting that Tenochtitlan Monument 1 (Cyphers 2004b:219) is a ballplayer sitting on top of a bound victim;

ballplayer figurines also often wear the mask of the Olmec Rain God (Taube 1995:100). A ballplayer may imply the traditional Mesoamerican ballgame, but Orr (2003) and Taube and Zender (2009) highlight another possible event that was conceptually linked to the ballgame: boxing. Boxing combatants have slightly different attire, including helmets and padding, and they perhaps used knuckle-dusters in contests to draw the human blood required to bring the appropriate rain. In small towns of La Montaña, Guerrero, men and boys gather to engage in the ritual *pelea de tigre* (jaguar fights) to attract winds that will bring the clouds that carry the good rains (Díaz Vázquez 2003:8). Wearing full costumes of black-spotted yellow-and-orange cloth and elaborate leather masks, the participants engage in fisticuffs, in pairs, with other jaguars typically their own age, with the intent to draw blood from their opponents (Díaz Vázquez 2003:116–123; Saunders 1983). A boxing ritual for drawing the sacrificial blood could explain the posture of the standing nahual figurines: the body tense, upright, knees bent, legs separated, arms doubled, and fists clenched. In the case of two of the transformation figurines (Figure 2.1b,c), the clenched

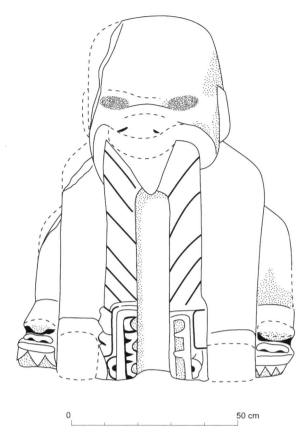

figure 2.17
La Venta Monument 80. (Drawing from the
New World Archaeological Foundation.)

0   50 cm

fists have holes in the palms, perhaps to hold
removable knuckle-dusters (Taube 2004:63).

Concluding Remarks

We propose that the San Pedro Aytec figurine is
one of a group of portable sculptures that represents human-to-animal transformation or nahualism, an important component in the Mesoamerican
belief system from Pre-Hispanic to modern times.
Cyphers (1997) has documented the predominance
of felines and human-feline composites in the
sculpture of San Lorenzo and argues that they also
represent a jaguar-to-human transformation. We
concur and believe that the corpus of jaguar nahual
depictions is much greater than the few figurines
with literal depictions of half-jaguar, half-human

beings. The San Pedro Aytec figurine is remarkable
for sharing iconography with the corpus of other
literal depictions of transforming nahual figurines,
as defined by Reilly (1989), albeit more evocative
and less literal than they are. For example, the San
Pedro Aytec figurine does not show the tearing of
the skin at the shoulders like the Dumbarton Oaks
example (Figure 2.1a). The important question is
not whether the human-to-jaguar transformation
is occurring, but rather, what is the nahual doing?
Is the nahual in the posture of the boxer about to
engage in a fight for ritual blood? Is the nahual half-
jaguar/half-human or a full jaguar (Figure 2.1a,b),
and why does the distinction matter? What is the
nahual holding or wearing? What is the difference
between the small portable objects, such as the San
Pedro Aytec figurine, and the public monuments of
San Lorenzo? Perhaps the small figurines were used
in private elite rituals, or perhaps, as was suggested
by our informant, don Quirino, they were buried
in agricultural fields. They could have been planted
during rituals and, in effect, believed able to call the
winds to attract the good rains to their specific buried locations. Or, as some greenstone is referred to as
"*quiauhteocuitlatl*," which literally reads "precious
rain," the planted greenstone could have represented
rain that was "planted" to nourish the crops.

In addition to the jaguar nahual, the San Pedro
Aytec figurine highlights another Preclassic theme,
that of the acrobat or contortionist. The San Pedro
figurine cleverly connotes the idea of tumbling by
the position of the two faces—not back to back but
requiring one to flip the figure over—and by the suggestion of the legs flipping over and feet appearing
above the head of the second figure. These visual
cues, together with the ethnographic accounts referring to jumping as part of nahual transformation,
indicate that contortionism and tumbling were part
of the transformation process, as well as confirming two-dimensional depictions of these physical actions on stone sculptures, namely, the Shook
Panel (Shook and Heizer 1976) and San Lorenzo
Monument 16 (Figure 2.9). Tumbling and contortion
were also seemingly practiced by elites, as evidenced
by the Shook Panel and by the presence of the acrobat figurine in Burial 154 of Tlatilco.

We suggest that the nahual belief became entwined with ruling elites sometime in the Preclassic, at least as early as the San Lorenzo Olmecs, who were depicting nahuals in their stone monuments. Why would early leaders appropriate nahual powers for themselves? It would confer on them the ability to mediate natural forces, as we have explored here for wind and rain. Implicit in the role of mediator is the ability to communicate and travel to the various realms of the Mesoamerican cosmos in the guise of the nahual. This concept of travel and communication with sky and underworld gods and, later, with ancestors, is more explicitly indicated in Late Preclassic iconography, when all of Mesoamerica seems to have been filled with rulers advertising this ability on stone monuments (Guernsey 2006b).

Weather control became an important tool for ruling nahuals by the Middle Preclassic. We lack Early Preclassic sculptural depictions emphasizing the importance of rain and wind, such as on Chalcatzingo Monuments 1 and 31 (Figures 2.12 and 2.13); however, the inverted-S volute is present on the jaguar of San Lorenzo Monument 8 (Cyphers 2004b:fig. 17). (Ceramic examples from the Early Preclassic that may fit into this conceptual scheme are not included in this discussion; see note 3.) Perhaps here this element, expressing the concept of sky, and particularly strong winds, could also have referred to the periodic *nortes* (northern winds) and hurricanes, weather phenomena of the Gulf Coast that would have required mediation. Colonial and ethnographic accounts explicitly state that nahuals can control the winds that bring rain or hail, and Sahagún's informants drew a depiction of S-shaped clouds associated with hail and snow. Granicero activities in Central Mexico attest to the continuance of this belief in the control of weather phenomena.

We also propose that the concept of nahualism and its relationship to weather control, including the word itself, may have origins with Otomanguean peoples, who are believed to have occupied the central areas of Mexico at this time, particularly the highlands. This is not to say that

coastal lowland peoples, primarily Mixe-Zoques in the Preclassic period, did not have a concept of shamanic transformation. The idea of transformation probably originated with the peoples who crossed the Bering Strait. Gulf Coast peoples seem to have been the first to put this imagery on stone sculpture. Still, highland Otomanguean peoples may have had an earlier dependence on domesticated cultigens. We know from research in the Soconusco that Early Preclassic subsistence consisted of a broad range of exploited plants and animals, and there does not seem to have been reliance on maize until the Middle Preclassic period (Blake, Chisholm, Clark, and Mudar 1992; Blake, Chisholm, Clark, Voorhies, and Love 1992). Coastal areas, such as the Soconusco and the Gulf Coast, offered a plurality of subsistence options, as well as more time in which to grow crops, particularly compared to the highlands. Hence the seasonally destructive forces of the rainy season could have had a greater impact on subsistence in the highlands than in the lowlands. The concepts of nahual and weather control would have provided highland leaders with the means to present themselves as being able to mediate natural phenomena, which could simultaneously impact their Preclassic livelihood and enhance their prestige. We believe these concepts are exemplified in the Middle Preclassic monuments of Chalcatzingo and, later, in the Late Classic monuments of eastern Guerrero and coastal Oaxaca as well as the depictions in the Azoyú codices 1 and 2.

In this chapter we have called attention to a variety of research on nahualism, its graphic representation, and its time depth. Using ethnographic and ethnohistoric information, codices, and Classic and Postclassic iconography to help interpret Preclassic iconography can be problematic, because shifts in meaning can occur over long time periods (Kubler 1961). Nevertheless, when multiple lines of evidence overlap and coincide, then the belief in question likely represents a core concept that has not greatly changed in substance. The nahual concept is active today in communities throughout Mexico; Báez-Jorge (2008:175) argues that many patron saints have been "nahualized"—identified with animal form alter-egos and believed capable of controlling weather phenomena.

Although the Mesoamerican cosmovision has roots in the beliefs of Late Archaic hunter-gatherers, the impact of a sedentary lifestyle in the Early Preclassic period and its profound changes on engagement with objects and people in economic production and sociopolitical organization was fundamental in creating the Mesoamerican cosmovision we know today (Clark 2004; López Austin 2001:49). Derived from the hunter-gatherer tradition were beliefs about inanimate objects, sky and earth, as well as individuals and shamans who could mediate these natural forces. Whether Pre-Hispanic rulers (and their subjects) truly believed themselves capable of transforming into jaguars and controlling the weather, or by donning masks and costumes were simply personifying the gods who could do these things, is a metaphysical distinction we cannot resolve from our vantage point. Nevertheless, this distinction does not negate the nahual concept as a core precept in the Mesoamerican cosmovision that had profound implications for the organization of societies and their political leadership, beginning with the Preclassic period. The centrality of these concepts is evident in their early occurrence on stone sculptures, such as the San Pedro Aytec figure; the widespread distribution of transformation figures during the Preclassic period; and the persistence of this theme throughout the rest of Mesoamerican history even up to the present day.

Acknowledgments

We thank John E. Clark, Julia Guernsey, and Barbara Arroyo for the opportunity to present our work at the symposium, as well as for their suggestions for improving this chapter. Additionally, we thank Javier Urcid for his detailed and insightful comments on our first draft and two anonymous reviewers for their useful comments. All errors, however, are our responsibility.

NOTES

1. Our discussion focuses on the jaguar nahual as mediator of the natural forces of weather, hence our emphasis on rain and sky beliefs and iconography. However, we also believe that the nahual's mediation abilities extended to the forces of the earth and underworld, but we do not address this aspect of jaguar symbolism here (see Chapter 4).

2. Other transformation figurines are: (1–3) Dumbarton Oaks, Washington, D.C., figurines PC.B.603, PC.B.008, and PC.B.009 (Taube 2004:59–67), (4) "Shaman in Transformation Pose" (Princeton 1995:169–170; Reilly 1989), (5) half-kneeling figurine from the Constance McCormick Fearing collection of the Los Angeles County Art Museum (Princeton 1995:174–175), and (6, 7) two figurine heads with half-human/half-jaguar features in the collection of the Museo Nacional de Antropología in Mexico (Furst 1968:fig.2) and a private collection (Princeton 1995:no. 47). Other possibilities are illustrated in the catalogue from the Princeton, New Jersey, Olmec exhibition (Princeton 1995:172–176).

3. Space limitations preclude discussion of ceramic vessels, which also include depictions of these motifs. Dating the primacy of the iconographic complex of Preclassic ceramics has been the subject of protracted debate, most recently since the publication by Blomster and colleagues (2005). We direct the reader to recently published data and analysis from San Lorenzo addressing this issue (Di Castro and Cyphers 2006).

4. The capital of this kingdom lies beneath the modern city of Tlapa.

5. See Urcid's (2001:156, 159) identification of Glyph A as "knot" and also the discussion of Late Classic sculpture of eastern Guerrero in Gutiérrez (2008).

3

Sculpture from Teopantecuanitlan, Guerrero

GUADALUPE MARTÍNEZ DONJUÁN

IN LATE FEBRUARY 1983, A REPORT OF looters' activities brought me and other archaeologists to the site of Teopantecuanitlan, located in a small intermontane valley of eastern Guerrero. There, reburied by looters at the bottom of their deep trench, we found two blocky monoliths that were so heavy that the tow truck commandeered by the looters had been unable to remove them— so they had covered the monuments pending a later attempt at removal with better equipment (Figure 3.1). The monoliths were lying face down, so we could only see part of the carved design on their obverse sides. The find was astonishing. Our surprise was complete when we stood the sculptures upright and saw for the first time the jaguar visage of each (Figure 3.2). The monuments lay among a jumble of large rectangular blocks of limestone. The wall from which all these had fallen was also exposed. Government backing allowed us to start salvage operations several weeks later to investigate the original settings of these monuments. We found another pair of jaguar sculptures

in the same Olmec style associated with the opposite wall and eventually discovered other monuments with other buildings. Several seasons of excavations at Teopantecuanitlan revealed that ca 1000–900 BC four large stone carvings of were-jaguar gods had been placed on top of the walls of a sunken court in a very deliberate manner. We call this complex the "Sunken Patio." The name of the site references these jaguar gods in this setting. "Teopantecuanitlan" means "place of the jaguar temple" in Nahuatl. In this chapter, I describe these monuments and their architectural setting and detail what has been learned so far of their functions and meanings (see Jiménez García et al. 1998; Martínez Donjuán 1984, 1986, 1994, 1995; Niederberger 1986, 1996, 2002a, 2002b; Reilly 1994a). Different sculptures were associated with different construction stages at the site.

Teopantecuanitlan lies in a small, semi-arid valley of the highlands of central Guerrero. The valley is part of the Balsas River drainage, with the site located 8 km from the confluence of the Mezcala

figure 3.1
View of the looters' trench at Teopantecuanitlan. (Photograph by the author.)

figure 3.2
First view of the monuments, wall stones, and a portion of the eastern wall at Teopantecuanitlan in 1983. View from the north, looking south. Monument 2 is visible in the foreground. (Photograph by the author.)

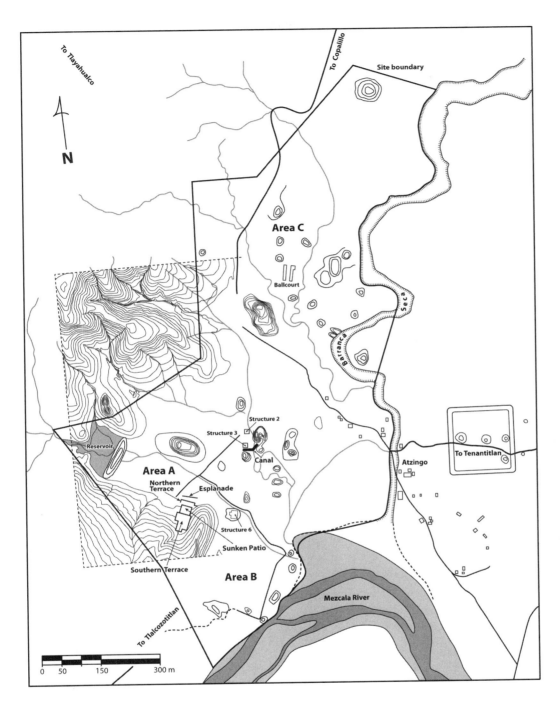

Area C

Ballcourt

Structure 2
Structure 3
Canal

Reservoir

Area A

Northern
Terrace
Esplanade

Structure 6

Sunken Patio

Southern Terrace

Area B

Mezcala River

To Tlayahualco

To Copalillo

Site boundary

Barranca Seca

Atzingo

To Tenantitlan

To Tlalcozotitlan

N

0   50   150   300 m

figure 3.3
Map of
Teopantecuanitlan
and the surrounding
area. (Drawing from
the New World
Archaeological
Foundation.)

and Amacuzac rivers (see Figure 4.1). This region of Guerrero is geologically complex, with limestone, volcanic rock, and metamorphic stone all nearby (Niederberger 1986). The site covers at least 280 ha and consists of three mound groups (Areas A, B, and C) as well as residential areas (Figure 3.3).

The principal occupation of the site was during the Middle Preclassic. There is evidence of some local development going back to the Early Preclassic ca 1250 BC and a final episode during the Postclassic ca AD 1200. The apogee of Teopantecuanitlan was from 1000 to 700 BC, when it functioned as a regional center. The people of this site participated in the Middle Preclassic interaction and trade sphere that included Chalcatzingo, Zazacatla, and La Venta, among others (see Chapter 4; Grove 1987a:429, 1989:142–145; Niederberger 1996, 2002b). The best evidence of their participation is the foreign goods brought into the site, monumental stone monuments in their architectural settings in Area A, and Olmec designs carved on sculptures and ceramic vessels.

The complex of Area A is located on the northeast flank of Cerro Leon, 400 m west of the Mezcala River. Area A is 45 ha in extent and has several mounds and terraces, a reservoir, and a special Sunken Patio. This area of the site went through five construction stages, and monuments and architectural associations changed with each stage. The earliest buildings were of yellow clay over a core of river cobbles; later buildings were faced with cut limestone blocks. I focus here on the last part of the architectural and sculptural sequence of the Sunken Patio.

The Sunken Patio

The Sunken Patio lies about 2 m below the current ground surface and is located between the northern and southern terraces or platforms. Architecturally, it is composed of a central patio surrounded by a raised walkway (Figure 3.4). Excavations revealed four construction stages, described in detail below, and a fifth and final stage that resulted in the decommissioning of the Sunken Patio. For the first stage, only a floor has been identified. A second floor has been identified above the first, and this second stage is also evident in two fragments of stairs near the northwest corner of the structure. These were covered over in the third construction stage wherein the raised walkway and central patio were built. The third stage was finished with a yellow clay surface. In the fourth construction stage, a stone veneer was added to the interior of the patio.

In several publications I have referred to the Sunken Patio as the most important ceremonial construction at Teopantecuanitlan (Martínez Donjuán 1984, 1986, 1994, 1995). Given the theme of this book, it is worth repeating its importance. In this structure are clay and stone monuments in their original architectural contexts, and some of their past functions and meanings can be reconstructed. Associations with different buildings confirm that stone monuments followed clay ones.

Features pertaining to the third construction phase of the Sunken Patio, built ca 1000 BC, are made of the same yellow clay and are associated with the southern stairs. At this time, the Sunken Patio measured about 32 m east-west and 26 m north-south, with an enclosing walkway roughly 1.2 m high. Small platforms lay on the east and west sides, each with its own stairway. On the north of the walkway was a stairway, and on the south was a space in the walkway that allowed access from the ground level into the patio itself. The two platforms and the northern stairway were adjoined to the interior wall of the patio. Closing the south side, two double stairways allowed access to the walkway, and these had decorated balustrades, as described below. Small alleys led past these stairways from the south into the patio. The precise interior dimensions of the patio are not known because of subsequent rebuilding. In its final stage, with its cut-stone facade of dry-laid blocks in place, the inner patio measured 18.6 m by 14.2 m. The elevated walkway around the patio was 2–4 m wide and had four stairways symmetrically placed on each of the sides, as well as small platforms or viewing areas on the east and west sides (Figure 3.4). There is no evidence of perishable buildings on these platforms or that the patio itself was covered.

In the fourth and last building stage of this structure, the interior walls of the patio were covered with a layer of thick, well-shaped limestone blocks, and the four stone monoliths were incorporated into the upper course of stones of these walls. The stone for the blocks and monuments was transported from a location 3 km from the site. Two small, low platforms were constructed inside the patio. There is evidence that they were built during the second construction stage. Each platform measures 7 m from east to west, 3.5 m from north to south, and is 35–60 cm high. They were constructed of river

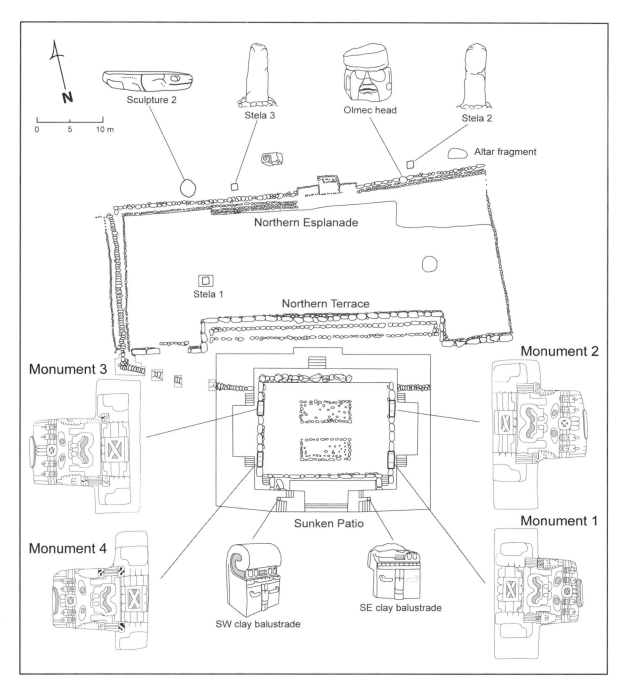

Labels within the figure:

N

0 5 10 m

Sculpture 2

Stela 3

Olmec head

Stela 2

Altar fragment

Northern Esplanade

Stela 1

Northern Terrace

Monument 2

Monument 3

Monument 1

Monument 4

Sunken Patio

SW clay balustrade

SE clay balustrade

figure 3.4

Map of Area A of Teopantecuanitlan showing the location of the various monuments, including Monuments 1–4 of the Sunken Patio. (Drawing from the New World Archaeological Foundation adapted from the author's originals [Martínez Donjuán 1994:152, fig. 9.10; 1995:59].)

cobbles of various sizes, set in a clay mortar, and together they formed a small, symbolic ballcourt.

The Clay Sculptures

At the lower terminus of the balustrades between each of the southern double stairways, my colleagues and I found decorated, short, squared pillars of clay, or clay monuments, one facing east and the other facing west (Figure 3.4). They are the earliest sculptures at the site. They were modeled around stone nuclei and decorated with Olmec symbols and stylistic elements that suggest representations of jaguars (Figure 3.5). These clay sculptures were formed with a voluminous mass of rounded clay at the top, shown as volutes on the sides. On the better-preserved monument, just

under the projecting upper fold on the front of the monument, is a recessed flat plane with molded representations of four rectangles with cleft "V" marks flanking a small central niche. Below this niche is another horizontal band with eight contiguous small semicircles that mark the top of the face, and immediately below these are eyebrows represented by a long horizontal border with two small upward projections at their ends. I interpret the vertical band down the middle of the sculpture as a bifid tongue because of the vertical division of the top portion. Flanking this tongue or vertical bar are two more elements that serve as a second pair of upturned split eyebrows or eyes. Stylistically, some elements on this clay sculpture are similar to those of a stone sculpture of similar size and form

figure 3.5
West-facing clay sculpture at the south staircase. (Photograph by the author.)

Eyebrows

Tongue

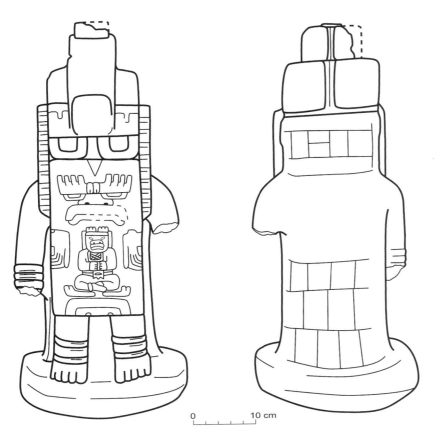

figure 3.6
Two views of the Ojo de
Agua monument, which has
eye and eyebrow elements
similar to those on the clay
sculptures at Teopantecuanitlan.
(Drawings from the New World
Archaeological Foundation.)

0   10 cm

from Ojo de Agua, Chiapas, dating to ca 1200–1100
BC (Clark and Pye 2000; Navarrete 1974), a date
that corresponds well with the clay sculptures at
Teopantecuanitlan. The lower set of eyebrows on
the clay sculptures is in a position similar to those
on the front of the Ojo de Agua sculpture. As seen
in Figure 3.6, on the Ojo de Agua sculpture these
eye elements form a jaguar throne beneath the
small seated figure.

In the schematic representations of the clay
balustrade monuments at Teopantecuanitlan, the
jaguar is symbolically represented. It was an animal associated with darkness and night (Seler
2004:33). The stairways conjoined with these sculptures may have been understood as portals of communication between the earthly world governed by
humans and the threshold to the underworld, as
represented by the interior of the Sunken Patio. The
exterior cruciform plan of the Sunken Patio resembles the open mouth of the earth monster and was

probably meant to convey the threshold between
worlds, as is evident when comparing the overall
shape of the patio plan to Chalcatzingo Monument 9 (Figure 3.7; Grove and Angulo 1987:125–126).
It is unfortunate that other sculptures have not
been preserved from the clay building stage. They
would provide a more ample vision of what appears
to have been an early representation of the cosmos.
The small platforms attached to the elevated walkway on its east and west sides may once have had
clay sculptures that were the antecedents to the
four stone monoliths placed in the patio during
the final construction phase.

In support of the notion of ideological and cosmological continuity between the clay and stone
sculptures, a fragment of stone sculpture with the
same curled topknot seen on the clay sculptures
has been found at the site (Figure 3.8) and may
have represented another stylized jaguar head. If
so, it would demonstrate that the ideas molded in

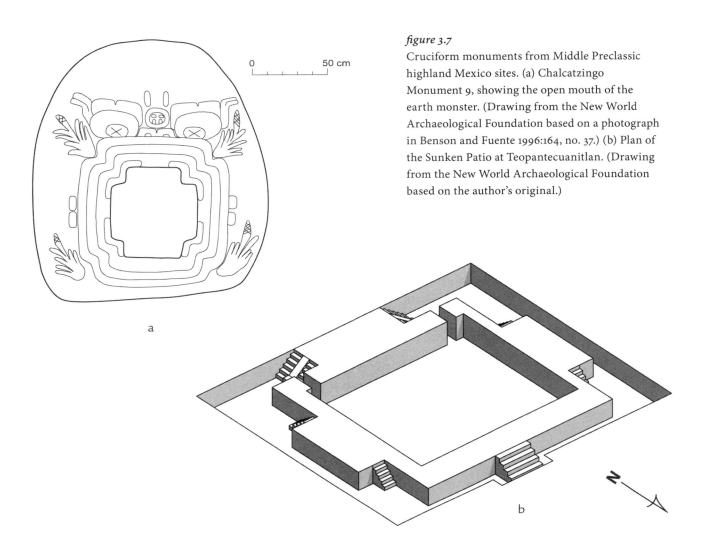

figure 3.7
Cruciform monuments from Middle Preclassic
highland Mexico sites. (a) Chalcatzingo
Monument 9, showing the open mouth of the
earth monster. (Drawing from the New World
Archaeological Foundation based on a photograph
in Benson and Fuente 1996:164, no. 37.) (b) Plan of
the Sunken Patio at Teopantecuanitlan. (Drawing
from the New World Archaeological Foundation
based on the author's original.)

clay in the third construction phase persisted into
the fourth phase when these same symbols were
carved into the stone itself, rather than modeled
in clay around a stone core. The stone sculpture
fragment was found lying discarded in front of the
Northern Esplanade (see below) and out of its original context (Figure 3.4). In searching the corpus of
Olmec artifacts for other possible examples of this
form of headdress, the closest image I could find is
a fragment of a serpentine figurine from Tuzapan,
Veracruz, in the collection of Dana B. Martín (Figure 3.9; Benson 1996:290; Pohorilenko 1990:1675,
fig. 167.7). The headdress or topknot on this piece
is clearly associated with a were-jaguar, as sus-
pected for the clay sculptures at Teopantecuanitlan.
In the latter case, the head curl is the reverse of

those on the Teopantecuanitlan sculptures, with
the curl starting at the back of the head rather than
in front. This piece also has an eyebrow-like element on its cheek in the same position as on the clay
sculptures.

This type of sculpture integrated into architecture, with an associated sunken patio, is not
currently known outside of Teopantecuanitlan.
The incorporation of sculptures with architecture during the Middle Preclassic appears to have
varied from site to site, all of which suggests ideological diversity in the religious sphere among peoples of the same economic network, a point made
by Giselle Canto Aguilar and Victor M. Castro
Mendoza for Zazacatla (see Chapter 4) in nearby
Morelos. The Sunken Patio at Teopantecuanitlan

may have been a temple, meaning a space reserved for the gods. Alternatively, this recessed place may not have been appropriate for the gods, who required more exalted vantage points to oversee the works of humans.

Centuries later, decorated balustrades on pyramids show up again in Mesoamerican architecture. Decorations are serpent heads carved in stone. It is possible that decorated balustrades were associated with other types of building platforms, but being the most vulnerable part of the architecture, they have not been preserved. One example is Structure 40A of the West Plaza at Teotihuacan (Cabrera et al. 1984). In the earliest stage, the end of the balustrade was a serpent head with a bifid tongue that extended to the floor (Figure 3.10). In the second construction stage of this building, the head was of a jaguar with a four-petaled flower at the back of its head. The first head also has jaguar elements (the head and face) combined with serpent elements (the split tongue and the volute at the back of the head)—both features seen on the clay sculptures of the Sunken Patio at Teopantecuanitlan. The split tongue of the Teotihuacan serpent is like the split vertical band on the Teopantecuanitlan clay sculpture, and both sculptures have the same volute at the top or back of the head, almost in the form of a headdress.

Another, later, example of a serpent balustrade is from Chichén Itzá. Serpent heads decorate the balustrades of the pyramids of the Great Priest's Tomb and the Castillo. In the latter case, the sculpture had a cosmological function that involved the building platform and its orientation to the sun. During the spring equinox, "the great heads cease to be mere adornments and come to life with the light of the sun for about 10 minutes, in which we can see the spectacular [undulating] body of the serpent about 43.18 m long" (Arochi 1976:74, photo 154, translation by J. Clark). Toward the afternoon, the head on the west is connected to an undulating body that simulates the movement of the serpent, as suggested by the changing shadows of the corners of the steps of the pyramid along the length of the balustrade. The special orientations of building stairways, the decorated sculptures at

figure 3.8
Fragment of a stone sculpture of a schematic jaguar head from in front of the Northern Esplanade. (Photograph by the author.)

figure 3.9
Serpentine figurine from Tuzapan, Veracruz, showing a similar top-knot to the one on the clay sculptures and the sculpture fragment from the Northern Esplanade. (Drawing from the New World Archaeological Foundation based on photographs in Benson 1996:290, no. 200; Coe 1965b:fig. 14; Covarrubias 1957:plate XI; Piña Chan and Covarrubias 1964:94.)

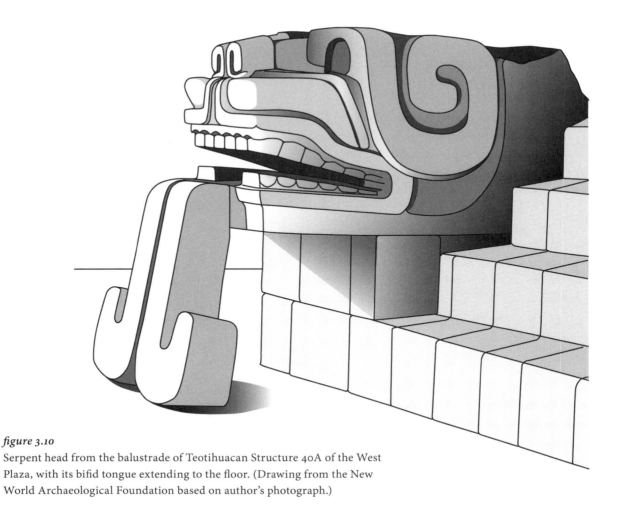

figure 3.10
Serpent head from the balustrade of Teotihuacan Structure 40A of the West Plaza, with its bifid tongue extending to the floor. (Drawing from the New World Archaeological Foundation based on author's photograph.)

the end of the balustrades, and the play of light and shadow at the equinox are all features evident at the Sunken Patio at Teopantecuanitlan by ca 900 BC. Evidence for the dance of shadows comes from the final building stage and the erection of stone monuments on opposite walls of the Sunken Patio.

The Stone Sculptures

In the fourth construction stage, from ca 1000 to 700 BC, the walkway around the Sunken Patio was carefully refinished, and the clay surface of the patio walls was covered over with dry-laid stone blocks. Two monolithic sculptures were placed in the upper row of stones on both the east and west walls. In contrast, the floor and the two small, parallel platforms in the center of the patio were

maintained with minor modifications, presumably serving their original purpose dating back to the second construction stage.

The four limestone monoliths crowning the walls (Monuments 1–4) are similar in theme and show only modest differences in detail and execution on their faces (Figures 3.11 and 3.12). The faces of all four gazed over the patio and at one another, so they could only have been seen at close range by people on this patio. The heads of standing celebrants would have been about half a meter below the penetrating gaze of the four gods who held constant vigil on the patio. Because of its small size and restricted access, it is probable that the patio was reserved for small ceremonies rather than large ones. The four monoliths all portray were-jaguars,

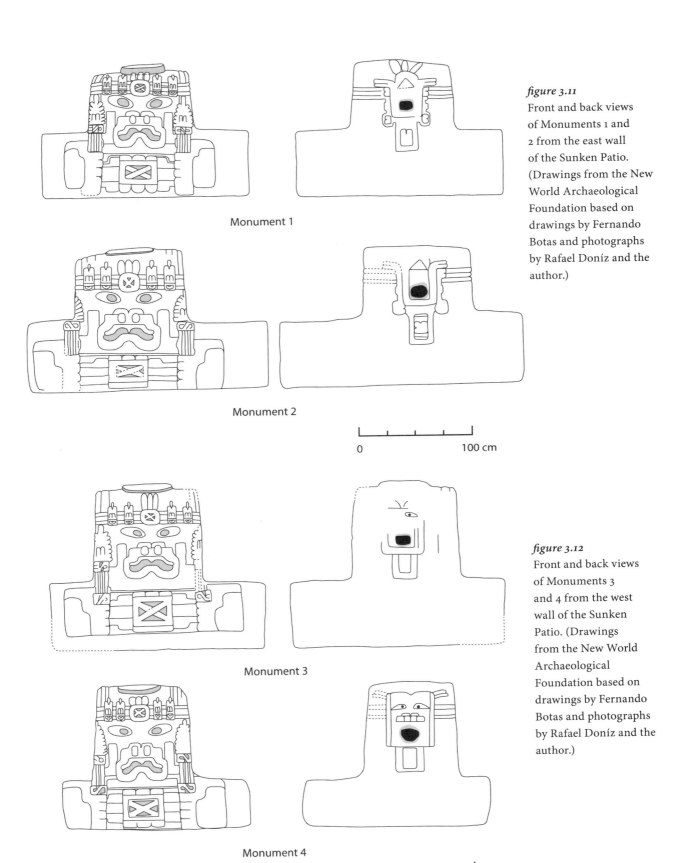

Monument 1

Monument 2

figure 3.11
Front and back views
of Monuments 1 and
2 from the east wall
of the Sunken Patio.
(Drawings from the New
World Archaeological
Foundation based on
drawings by Fernando
Botas and photographs
by Rafael Doníz and the
author.)

0   100 cm

Monument 3

Monument 4

figure 3.12
Front and back views
of Monuments 3
and 4 from the west
wall of the Sunken
Patio. (Drawings
from the New World
Archaeological
Foundation based on
drawings by Fernando
Botas and photographs
by Rafael Doníz and the
author.)

0   100 cm

Sculpture from Teopantecuanitlan, Guerrero   65

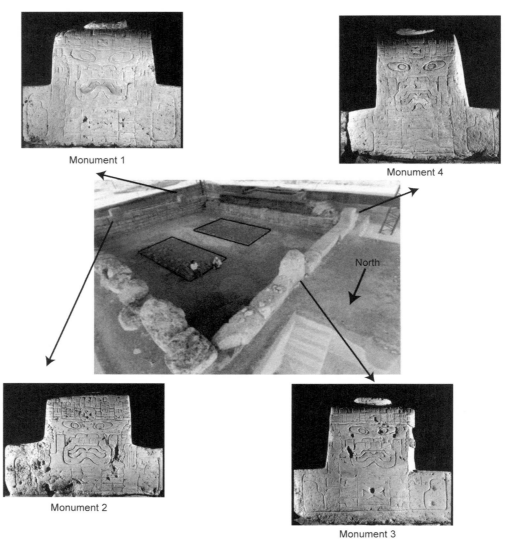

Monument 1

Monument 4

North

Monument 2

Monument 3

figure 3.13
The Sunken Patio and the four monuments on the walls. (Central photograph by the author and photographs of the monuments by Rafael Doníz.)

presumably gods. These images were carved on massive stones with an unusual inverted "T" shape. They range from 1.4 to 2.2 m long, 1.15 to 1.5 m high, and 0.70 to 0.90 m thick. They weigh from 2.5 to 4.0 tons each. These massive, fine-grained, beige sculptures were built into the final line of blocks on top of the wall of the patio and placed in a symmetrical manner that appears to have been related to a practical function.

Our excavations confirmed that these sculptures and the upper two courses of wall stones

had been pushed over into the patio ca 700 BC, two centuries before the abandonment of the site (500 BC). My colleagues and I were able to reconstruct these walls and restore the monuments to their original positions. Our reconstruction was informed by photographs of the original wall fall (Figure 3.2) and experiments in pushing large blocks off a wall of this height to monitor the displacement of stones. The largest building blocks were in the upper course, with the monolithic sculptures near the ends of each wall. For each wall, four long stones separated the paired monuments, and two flanked them on the outside ends, these end stones being flush with the outside corners of the original wall (Figure 3.13). Thus the relative position of the monuments, the size of the building stones, and the known corners of the walls virtually locked these sculptures into place, their current restored position, a point worth emphasizing given the reconstruction of their ancient function. These paired monuments faced one another exactly across the small patio. The lower portion of the T-shaped monuments was the equivalent of one of the long building stones and, once set into place, would have been very stable. The upper portions of the monuments projected above the wall line like double merlons (see Reilly 1994a), as on a medieval castle turret.

The four monuments represent gods. The facial attributes and iconography of these entities with human-feline faces reference their various responsibilities related to water, vegetation, earth, sky, and as ballplayers. Among the many duties accorded these gods and their respective monuments, astronomy and cosmology were, I believe, the most important. Ideological functions were linked to their unusual inverted T-shape, complex iconography, and exact positions on the walls of the Sunken Patio. These stone monoliths were carefully aligned and set up above the patio to record the passage of the equinoxes and solstices. This was done by observing the play of their shadows throughout the year as they swept across the small ballcourt on the patio floor. The stone monuments functioned as gnomons for telling time and making calendrical observations, likely related to the agricultural cycle. Their role as gnomons for monitoring the seasons for planting was reinforced by their detailed representations as jaguar gods associated with agricultural fertility.

The chronometric function of these monuments was accomplished by the projecting heads of the T-shaped monuments above the upper line of the inner patio wall. For example, the head of Monument 2, with the rising sun about 7 a.m. on the spring equinox, casts a shadow on the floor that reaches the foot of Monument 4 across the patio,

and as the sun arcs across the sky it casts a reverse shadow that retraces the diagonal line through the center of the ballcourt and ends at the southeast corner of the northern platform in the patio. In this case, the evening shadow of Monument 4 projects toward Monument 2 but only reaches part way across the patio, unlike the longer length of the morning shadow (Figure 3.14). During the autumn equinox, only the evening shadow is visible between Monuments 3 and 1. The morning shadow is blocked by Cerro Filo. The conjunction of these two equinox diagonal shadows duplicates the Olmec "X" symbol known as the Saint Andrew's cross that intersects in the middle of the symbolic ballcourt on the floor of the patio. Such precision astronomy and engineering would have required years of observation to create this equinox shadow effect before the patio was built and the monument sizes calculated for the patio width and wall height. These astronomical monuments were built into place with the fourth construction stage. I would not be surprised if the final shaping of the width of the heads of these monuments was done once they were in place, as a final refinement of the shadows. The three previous floors and patios appear to have been about the same size and alignment as the last one, which suggests the intention of building a solar observation platform from the very first construction stage.

The same "X" symbol traced on the patio floor over the course of the solar year appears as the central element of the headbands, on both sides of each headband, and on the chests of each of the four monuments (Figures 3.11, 3.12, and 3.15). These sun lines, in addition to linking the monuments to cosmological concepts, allowed the inhabitants at Teopantecuanitlan to record and calculate time, as suggested by glyphs carved on the back of Monument 2, which show a four-petaled flower above two bars, interpreted as the calendar day 10 Flower (Figure 3.11). I also suggest that the decorative facade of Teopantecuanitlan Structure 3, which shows three round stones on two flat slabs, represents three dots over two bars, or the number thirteen in bar-and-dot notation (see Figure 4.13), thus making it another indicator of time-keeping.

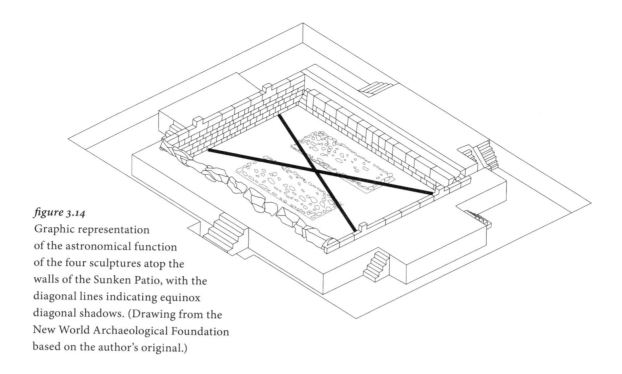

figure 3.14
Graphic representation
of the astronomical function
of the four sculptures atop the
walls of the Sunken Patio, with the
diagonal lines indicating equinox
diagonal shadows. (Drawing from the
New World Archaeological Foundation
based on the author's original.)

figure 3.15
The iconographic elements
of the four sculptures of the
Sunken Patio. (Drawing
from the New World
Archaeological Foundation
based on the author's
original.)

In their cosmological function, I would argue that the identity of the monuments as representations of ballplayer gods is evident (see Angulo 1994), as indicated by the knuckle-dusters, elbow protectors, and the objects in their hands (Figure 3.15), interpreted as torches. Regarding the objects clasped in their hands, the upper element may have symbolized clouds, the recumbent "S" design of the middle part may have indicated hurricanes or wind (Oliveros 1994), and the vertical lines the final rain (Piña Chan 1993). The complete image of the handheld objects represent "torches" associated with handstones (knuckle-dusters) and elbow guards, which identify these gods as ballplayers

(Angulo 1994). In contrast, Taube (1996:75) interpreted the objects clasped in their hands as feathered maize fetishes and argued that they embodied aspects of the Olmec Maize God. The faces and jaguarian features of these four monuments represent the same deity; the distinguishing differences among them appear on their backs in the clasps for the headdresses.

The Sunken Patio and its crowning sculptures embodied the movement of the universe and the earth and the struggle between life and death (Figure 3.16). In this function, the conjunction of sculpture, architecture, and the orientation of the Sunken Patio and its walkway had no precedent in

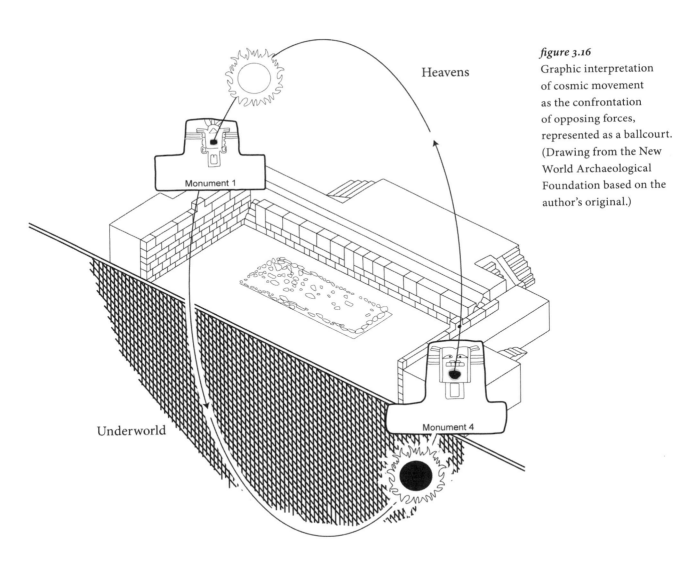

Heavens

Monument 1

Underworld

Monument 4

figure 3.16
Graphic interpretation of cosmic movement as the confrontation of opposing forces, represented as a ballcourt. (Drawing from the New World Archaeological Foundation based on the author's original.)

its day. The entities with jaguarian countenances, in their role as gods, discharged sundry duties according to the attributes signaled in their symbols.

The iconography on the fronts of the four sculptures appears to be the same, but one element is different—the double, recumbent "S" held by the personages on the west wall (Monuments 3 and 4), the direction of the strongest winds at the site. Another difference is found on the backs of these monuments, even though all have a deep hole carved into the back of their heads. The eastern sculptures bear a representation of a bird with an open beak, which includes the hole, and their spread wings; the western monuments show jaguar faces with their open jaws, also represented by holes (Figures 3.11 and 3.12). The position of these animals in the cardinal directions is not random. I suspect their significance was similar to the interpretation of the same animals found in much later Mesoamerican cultures.

In later Mesoamerican traditions, the bird, although not identifiable as to species, symbolically represented light, day, and heat—and by extension, life; in contrast, the jaguar was associated with night, darkness, cold, and the underworld (Caso 1978:53; López Austin 1984:87; Seler 2004:127–133). These sculptures in their aspects as ballplayer gods represented antagonistic forces by taking on the attributes and perhaps the flesh of these animals. They confronted one another in an eternal contest or ballgame, with the sun as the ball and the two parallel platforms in the patio the ballcourt. The squarish plan of the ballcourt represented the surface of the earth, and its subterranean position in the Sunken Patio stood for the threshold of the underworld. In this endless struggle, triumph and defeat alternated, because the bird won victory for the eastern gods when it arose with the sun in its beak, but the jaguar eventually defeated them when the last rays of the sun were swallowed in its open jaws, thereby wresting victory for the gods of the west (Figure 3.16). Lighting the way to the underworld with the torches they hold in their hands, these gods pursued this contest through the underworld until the sun rose again the next day in the bird's beak. This representation of universal

movement, of life and death, was shown as an alternation between antagonistic forces and the diurnal equilibrium between them. This dynamic harmony, in my opinion, is the core cosmology that distinguished Teopantecuanitlan.

These sculptures also represented the four cardinal points at the edges of the earth, understood as the four quarters of the world. The intersection of the diagonals that connected these points marked the fifth point, the *axis mundi*, thereby constituting a quincunx with five world directions. The cosmology implicit in the layout of the ballcourt and the concept of the four world quarters, I believe, is part of the Olmec legacy to the worldview of later Mesoamerican peoples, one enriched with later additions. From these concepts, many of the interpretations of symbolism implicit in the sculptures and their iconography can be found in the beliefs and practices recorded for later peoples.

Before describing the last episode of sculpture and building at Teopantecuanitlan, I consider two isolated sculptures that correspond to the last construction stage of the Sunken Patio. They are two fragments that were found in the fill that covered the Northern Terrace. The first is a human torso 32.4 cm tall, 23.3 cm wide, and 14.2 cm thick carved in limestone with no body decoration indicated (Figure 3.17a). The second is a limestone head with the face mutilated and with Olmec characteristics. It is 31.0 cm tall, 25.0 cm wide, and 17.0 cm thick. It also lacks any indication of personal adornment or iconographic elements (Figure 3.17b). The importance of these monuments, even in the absence of a primary context, is that they are the only naturalistic sculptures of humans chronologically associated with the Sunken Patio. The breakage and mutilation of these monuments indicate some conflict and violence at the site that is also suggested by numerous fragments of burned floor material found in the fill. These finds confirm that Teopantecuanitlan was no stranger to economic, social, political, and religious conflict. Incorporation of the monument fragments in the fill of the Northern Terrace was part of the episode during which the four jaguar monoliths on the eastern and western walls of the

figure 3.17
Fragments of broken and mutilated limestone sculptures found in the fill that covered the Sunken Patio. (a) Torso; (b) bust. (Photographs by the author.)

Sunken Patio were pulled down and the patio filled in. It is interesting that none of these monuments was mutilated at this time, and that the only mutilation was to sculpture representing humans, a pattern Clark (1997) describes for Olmec sculpture in the Gulf Coast lowlands. I suspect the four monuments of this patio were not mutilated because they represented gods rather than humans. Filling in the Sunken Patio may have been a reverential act to protect this space from invaders or new peoples coming into the site who did not share the ideology of the original inhabitants. This activity of decommissioning the Sunken Patio was the beginning of the fifth and final building stage at the site.

The Northern Esplanade

After the Sunken Patio had been filled in and the place leveled, an enormous wall was built just to the north of it on the Northern Terrace, which encompassed the Northern Esplanade (Figures 3.3, 3.4, and 3.18). This massive north wall was comprised of large stones, but no stone sculptures in the round. Some stones, however, have small faces carved on them in cartouche form, with one low-relief

carving of a human figure. An unusual element in this wall is perforated boulders (Figure 3.18). The holes through these stones are similar to the deep holes in the backs of Monuments 1–4, and both sets represent the opposite of gnomon—the play of shadows in a hole rather than projected on the ground. Just north of this wall, another low stone wall was built at the same time for the Northern Esplanade. It has a small stairway in the center that is flanked on both sides by stone sculptures. These structures date from 700 to 500 BC. Structures 2 and 3 (for locations, see Figure 3.3), with their decorated stone facades, date to this period (see Chapter 4). It is worth noting that the massive north wall also may have served as a solar observatory and for tracking time, as had the monuments in the Sunken Patio. In the case of the north wall, time was monitored with megaliths and holes carved through them to follow sun shadows at a much smaller scale than before (Figure 3.18). The stonework of this wall and of the facades of Structures 2 and 3 shows much coarser construction than for the earlier building, and less care was taken in the shaping and placement of wall stones.

The Northern Esplanade is part of the Northern Terrace and lies north of the Sunken Patio. In

figure 3.18
Wall of the Northern Terrace and some of its carved stones. (Photograph by the author.)

this last phase of occupation there is a radical shift in the sculpture and architecture at the site—from Olmec norms to new ideas and influences brought in by different peoples. The architecture was more rustic, although still monumental. The representations of human and animal attributes in sculpture mark the arrival of other ideas and groups from the south. This influence is evident in a limestone head and two stela-altar groupings that were associated with the Northern Esplanade (Figures 3.4, 3.19, and 3.20). The limestone head is carved in the round and is about a meter tall and a meter wide and was set into the wall to the east of the access stairway that led up to the esplanade (Figure 3.20). The head is reminiscent of Gulf Coast colossal head sculptures and conveys a sense of monumentality, but not at the same scale or with the same aesthetic (Martínez Donjuán 1986:70). The differences between this sculpture and the colossal heads

from the Gulf Coast lowlands caused me to look to other regions for sculptural similarities. The stela-altar pairs are more similar to monuments from the Guatemalan coast (Tránsito, Bilbao, and Monte Alto, among others) than to those from La Venta, which suggests a connection between Teopantecuanitlan and the coastal cultures of Guatemala and Chiapas (Martínez Donjuán 2008; Pye and Gutiérrez 2007).

Two stela-altar groupings flank the stairs to the east and west. These monuments are placed side-by-side rather than front-to-back, as known for later stela-altar pairs in the Maya area. In the first set, the two sculptures remain in their original positions (Figure 3.19). The 2.5 m long altar known as Sculpture 2 represents a toad. This monument is 2.0 m wide and 0.55 m thick. Near its right eye is a low-relief carving that cannot be made out and farther back is a Saint Andrew's cross. Stela 3 is plain;

it is 2.7 m tall, 1.0 m wide, and 0.55 m thick. It is located 5.6 m east of Sculpture 2. The altar is on the outside, and the stela on the inside, closer to the central stairway.

The other pair of sculptures is located near the stone head east of the stairs. The altar was destroyed in antiquity, and only a fragment now remains, but enough of it has been preserved to show that it was a large monument (Figure 3.20). The associated Stela 2 was broken in half by looters. Some elements of low-relief carving are still visible on the defaced altar, such as the right eye, part of the mouth, and possibly digits. These suggest that the monument was another depiction of a toad. Stela 2 was also plain; it is 2.4 m tall, 1.0 m wide, and 0.60 m thick. It has been provisionally restored; it is located 3.5 m inside and to the west of the broken altar. The altar probably represents a bufo toad, an animal that may have symbolized an earth monster. Altars with this representation are known from Izapa, Kaminaljuyu (see Chapters 5, 7, and 9), and Takalik Abaj (see Chapter 8). These stylistic and iconographic similarities corroborate the idea that people and ideas came from the south along the Pacific Coast.

The last two sculptures I consider also lack secure context but are of interest for the overall history of the site. They are carved in limestone and were found together about a kilometer north of the Sunken Patio and within 1.5 m of each other. They appear isolated and out of context, but because of the position in which they were found, it is possible that they may have been rolled down from a nearby terrace located to the west. The first represents a low-relief carving of a toad with fangs, with the feet together and lacking any features that would identify it as an Olmec carving (Figure 3.21). This late Preclassic sculpture is 1.47 m long, 0.50 m wide, and 0.48 m thick.

The other sculpture is also carved from limestone. It is 1.40 m tall, 0.90 m wide, and 0.66–0.40 m thick. It portrays a fat personage with a long, false beard or a duckbill mask (Figure 3.22). The face has been destroyed by plowing. He is seated, with the knees flexed to the side of the body and the bottoms of the feet turned to the outside, so the toes are

figure 3.19
The Northern Esplanade showing Stela 3 (left) and Sculpture 2 (right foreground). (Photograph by the author.)

figure 3.20
The Northern Esplanade showing Stela 2 (to the left of the tree) and the Olmec head (under the awning). (Photograph by the author.)

figure 3.21
Sculpture in the round of a toothy toad, found in the northern part of the site. (Photograph by the author.)

figure 3.22
Different views of a boulder sculpture of an obese seated person (a "potbelly" sculpture), found in the northern part of the site. (Photographs by the author.)

visible. The left foot is better defined than the right. The back of his head is round and lacks any indication of hair or ornaments; the neck is thick, and the arms are folded over the abdomen. The left arm appears to be holding an object that is barely visible, but from the rounded upper part looks somewhat like the object carried by the entity depicted on the Xoc monument from northern Chiapas to the southeast (Ekholm-Miller 1973). However, these similarities may be due to the erosion of both sculptures. The waist is encircled with a band visible on the back and the sides, with a flap that stretches between the buttocks, like a *maxtlatl*. By its form and finish this sculpture represents a complete break with the earlier sculptural tradition at Teopantecuanitlan and appears similar to, but not as obese as, some potbelly sculptures from Bilbao and Monte Alto from coastal Guatemala (see Chapters 7, 8, and 9; Parsons and Jenson 1965) and two from Tlaxcala (Delgadillo Torres and Santana Sandoval 1989). The difference is that the Teopantecuanitlan monument is not a typical potbelly sculpture with legs in front, as they are generally portrayed in Guatemala. The eroded "beard" feature could be a buccal mask

or even a duckbill mask, such as those depicted on the Tuxtla Statuette and on La Venta Altar 7. Overall resemblances among the latest sculptures at Teopantecuanitlan suggest a connection to cultures of coastal Guatemala rather than to the Olmec heartland of the Gulf Coast (see Chapters 7–9).

Concluding Remarks

The excellent context of the clay and stone monuments at Teopantecuanitlan, and their changes through time, provide insights into the ancient use and meaning of these monuments and of architecture-sculpture complexes. Had only one or two of these monuments been recovered, or all of them recovered out of context, most of the observations presented here would not have been possible. The meaning is not in the faces described, but in the faces combined with what they faced.

The iconography of the monuments shows some foreign influence as well as local traits from the very beginning. What is particularly interesting at Teopantecuanitlan is that the first sculptures were of thick clay modeled over stone cores. Such ephemeral sculpture is rarely recovered at Mesoamerican sites. At Teopantecuanitlan there is some continuity between clay and stone sculptures, and both of these relate to stone sculptures and small serpentine figurines from the Gulf Coast area. Had conditions of preservation been less ideal and the clay melted away, we would only have recovered the standing stones in front of stairways. They would have looked like small, plain stelae. Plain stela are known for the last period of the site, but only because of the context. Teopantecuanitlan has thousands of stone orthostats at the site that are the same size and shape as plain stelae, but most of these were used to line and cover canals (see Martínez Donjuán 1994, 1995) or in the wall of the Northern Terrace. What the plain stelae signified remains to be determined. They may have been covered with clay or stucco and not been plain at all. They appear to have been associated with toad altars by ca 700 BC and are some of the earliest stela-altar groupings known in Mesoamerica.

The excellent state of preservation of the Sunken Patio and the likelihood of its accurate reconstruction demonstrate the benefits of having precise context. Beyond the usual messages evoked by large and expensive stone sculptures integrated into public architecture—and the lessons of their complex iconography—it is evident that the real context of the monuments is related to the passage of the sun overhead through its annual cycle and the play of shadows on the floor of the patio and its symbolic ballcourt. This display also involved local geography and natural features, because the hills block some shadows and winds and permit others. As gnomons on opposed walls, the heads of the four jaguar gods constituted a precise chronometric device for keeping track of the seasons. This use required that the patio be left uncovered.

I have not explored here the phenomenological aspects of what would have been required for specialists to track the sun through its annual travels through the heavens. Who were the watchers, and what other rituals might have been involved with the shadow play on the patio floor or in the recesses carved into monuments and boulders? The Sunken Patio could not have accommodated many people, and fewer still on the occasions for which the shadows from the wall monuments had to be left unimpeded on the floor. Bystanders on the walkway and its adjoining platforms likewise may not have been possible on some days when monitoring the shadows was important.

As mentioned, the faces of the monuments could only have been seen and appreciated close up by those in the patio. I believe the representation of the jaguar gods as ballplayers captures some of the ancient meaning of the arrangement of these monuments on this ceremonial court and their continual play in the ballcourt at their feet. This association evokes the story of the *Popol Vuh* and the contest among the gods in the underworld (the sunken ballcourt) at the dawn of creation. It also evokes the eternal contest between day and night, life and death. These concepts represent only a small portion of their original meanings, especially if the Sunken Patio had been the site of rituals, as it probably was. Additional insights must await further clues to the specific and regional contexts of these monuments, as revealed by excavations of other structures at this site and related sites. This possibility is dramatically shown in the finds at Zazacatla in Morelos, which evince a complementary pattern to the one described for Teopantecuanitlan (see Chapter 4).

The importance of the sculpture at Teopantecuanitlan also relates to its interregional connections and changes through time. At Teopantecuanitlan there is evidence of some internal and local development as well as signs of influence during the last phase from the Pacific Coast of Guatemala and Chiapas. The presence of post-Olmec sculpture at Teopantecuanitlan indicates that further investigation of other areas of the site needs to be undertaken, followed by a revision of site history. Finally, the cosmological program built into the Sunken Patio and its sculptures, with all the interpretations that can be made of them, represent one of the important legacies of the Olmecs to later Mesoamerican peoples.

Acknowledgments

I am grateful to Dumbarton Oaks for the invitation to participate in the symposium on Preclassic sculpture held in Antigua, Guatemala. There I had the opportunity to learn of field investigations that helped me understand better the connections in sculptural styles among Preclassic peoples of Guerrero and Guatemala through time. I was also able to evaluate my own forays into the subjective field of iconographic interpretation and Olmec cosmology. I especially appreciate the kindness and support of the symposium organizers, who were always ready to help with the smallest details. I thank John Clark for translating my chapter into English and for his help with some references and illustrations.

Zazacatla in the Framework of Olmec Mesoamerica

GISELLE CANTO AGUILAR AND VICTOR M. CASTRO MENDOZA

RECENT DISCOVERIES IN MORELOS, Mexico, have revealed the presence of a Middle Preclassic ceremonial center affiliated with Olmec culture at the site of Zazacatla. It is in the archaeological zone previously known as Los Capulines de Atlacholoaya (Sapio 1982). Like its coeval sister centers at Chalcatzingo, Morelos, and Teopantecuanitlan, Guerrero, by 800–600 BC Zazacatla had formal public architecture with elaborate stone facades, pottery, and stone sculptures in Olmec style. Two small Olmec sculptures were found in the wall niches of a broad platform called the "Lajas Structure" and are among a handful of early monuments found in their primary settings. In this chapter we describe the Lajas Structure at Zazacatla and its associated sculptures and explore their ancient meanings.

Zazacatla was planned and built by, and for, a stratified society. Public construction projects there required political and social control of a large workforce. Zazacatla also participated in the Middle Preclassic Olmec interaction sphere,

which stretched from Guerrero on the northwest to Honduras on the southeast and was a participant in what Kent Reilly calls the "Middle Formative Ceremonial Complex" (MFCC). This complex "consists of the physical evidence—artifacts, symbols, motifs, and architectural groupings—for the rituals practiced by, and the ideology and political structures of, the numerous ethnic groups forming the demographic and cultural landscape of Middle Formative period Mesoamerica" (Reilly 1995:29).

We pay particular attention here to the connections between stone sculptures and architecture and consider their association as messages and visual metaphors for the ancient inhabitants at Zazacatla. We attempt to recover some of the ancient meanings of these messages as they concerned Pre-Columbian ideology and integrative principles for the body politic, as related to the MFCC. We begin our discussion with an overview of the site and its buildings and sculptures. We then consider the signs and symbols at the site, their combinations as texts, and some possible meanings of their joint arrangement vis-à-vis the site and its natural setting. For this, we offer a hypothetical reconstruction of the Lajas Structure at Zazacatla, based on excavation data, and its iconographic elements. In the final section, we explore similarities and differences among different participant centers of the MFCC and weigh the effects of possible ethnic differences on its different manifestations. We present different levels of interpretation of these signs and texts. Of special interest are the perceived variations in the symbols used by each group. We understand an ethnic group to be a group formed apart from others, with whom they coexist, based on perceptions of cultural differences (Jones 1997:xiii).

Zazacatla

Zazacatla is located in the Mexican Highlands in the state of Morelos, 16 km south of the modern city of Cuernavaca and 50 km west of the ancient

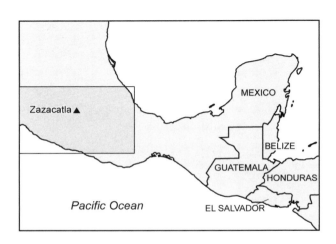

figure 4.1
Map of the Mexican Highlands showing the location of Zazacatla and other Middle Preclassic sites. (Drawing from the New World Archaeological Foundation.)

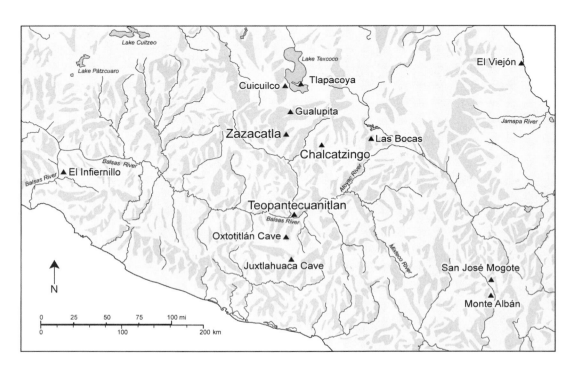

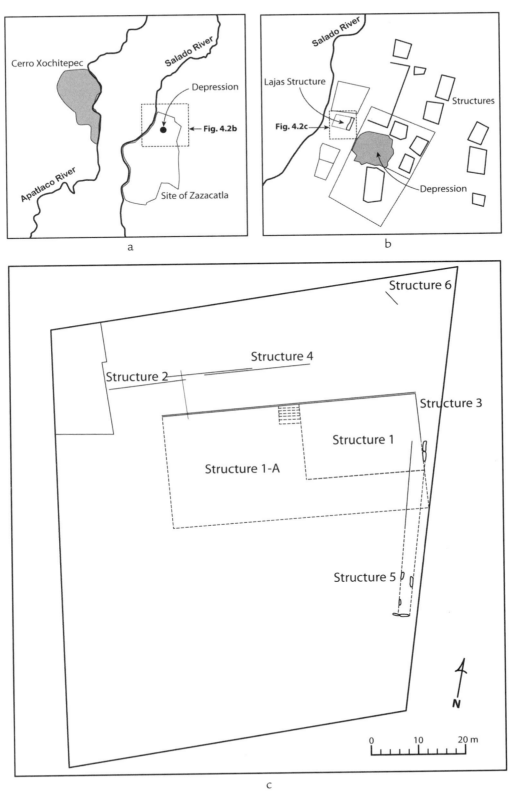

figure 4.2
Map of Zazacatla showing the locations of the principal platforms. (Drawing from the New World Archaeological Foundation based on maps by the authors.)

center of Chalcatzingo (Figure 4.1). The modern toll road from Cuernavaca to Acapulco passes through the site, and its construction was one of the reasons salvage excavations were undertaken there. Zazacatla was built on a flat rocky outcrop or very low rise with thin soil, and it extended over an area of approximately 2 km². The site was advantageously placed with respect to the abundant natural resources of the region. To the north, east, and south are deep soils and numerous springs that today make this place one of the most fertile agricultural zones of western Morelos. To the west, the Salado River forms the limit of the Zazacatla site (Figure 4.2). Farther west but in view from the site lies Cerro Xochitepec, located near the Apatlaco River. This river runs through Morelos, from the Chichinautzin Mountains to the north until it joins the Amacuzac River at the beginning of the Huautla Mountains to the south. It is possible that by means of the Apatlaco River route the inhabitants of Zazacatla had access to forest resources, such as firewood and game. Alternatively, site location could have been dictated more by the control of, or access to, communication routes.

Zazacatla differed from its sister centers at Chalcatzingo and Teopantecuanitlan. Both of the latter sites were constructed on the slopes of prominent hills, and this close association with hills and mountains appears to have been meaningful (see Chapter 3; Grove 2000, 2007). In contrast, Zazacatla is located on the valley floor next to a river. The site surrounds a circular depression 100 m in diameter in the otherwise level limestone bedrock. The buildings of the civic-ceremonial center explored archaeologically were built to the east and west of this depression; the habitation area of Zazacatla was located to the south (Figure 4.2). In Pre-Hispanic times, this central depression may have been a lagoon, or at least might have held water during the rainy season. It has largely been filled in with various kinds of garbage during the past twenty years of intensive construction activity at the site, so precise observations of its ancient character are not currently possible.

All three Middle Preclassic highland Olmec centers mentioned so far were constructed near signal geographic features of likely cosmological significance. In the Mesoamerican worldview, mountains were considered aquatic worlds from which came gifts (see Chapter 2; López Austin 1994). They were also the cosmic tree or axis mundi that connected the human world with the supernatural one (Reilly 1995:31). López Austin (1994:19, translation J. Clark) describes the cosmic trees as "the four posts—trees or gods or men—that became the roads of the gods . . . via their hollow trunks they traveled and accessed the divine." Entrance to this other world was by means of caves, mountains, and cosmic trees (Reilly 1994a:255). In the case of Zazacatla, the pool at the bottom of the central depression, a mirror of water, took the place of the cave and represented the entrance to this supernatural, aquatic world. Features of the terrestrial world were built at the site on the rim of this hole. Of particular interest are two construction phases of the Lajas Structure.

The Lajas Structure

Excavations at Zazacatla have identified six construction stages, two of which concern the Lajas Structure. The earliest stage at the site is represented by cutting and leveling activities and the creation of tamped floors of pulverized travertine and marble. Floors of domestic houses of this age are dispersed across the site. The same leveling activities continued into the second stage, with the addition of platform construction in the ceremonial center. This process required the leveling of some houses, the removal of some travertine bedrock, and the filling in of low spots to create a large, level area for public platforms. On this broad, level surface were built Structures 1 and 1-A (the Lajas Structure) and Structure 2 (Figure 4.2), which is north of Structure 1. The third construction stage began with the partial dismantling of the Lajas Structure and the filling in of the area, which covered what remained of the structure, thus preserving part of the building. The construction of Structure 3 covered Structures 1 and 1-A and recycled some of the stone slabs from these previous structures, but most of its building stones were of

figure 4.3
Lajas Structure: Structure 1, north facade.
(Photograph by the authors.)

figure 4.4
Lajas Structure:
Structure 1, north
and east facades.
(Photograph by
Jorge Pérez de
Lara.)

Monument 1   Monument 2

Structure 1   0 _____ 5 m

figure 4.5

Drawing of the north facade of Structure 1. (Drawing from the New World Archaeological Foundation based on original by Bernardo A. Flores Bonilla.)

larger size and did not come from these earlier platforms. In the fourth construction stage the builders partially demolished Structure 3 and the west facade of Structure 2 and created Structure 4, a large plaza or low platform. In the fifth construction stage large slabs of limestone, up to 3 m long, were placed between slabs of smaller size, creating the Megalajas Structure, Structure 5. This structure has been mostly destroyed, but it is evident that the facades were put together with less care than those for earlier platforms. For the last construction stage, Structure 6, the context is incomplete, and evidence of only one wall has been recovered. This wall has a different orientation than those of earlier platforms, and it may date to the Late Preclassic. It is not possible to determine whether more construction levels existed at this part of the site, because the area has been largely destroyed in recent years by urban sprawl and the construction of housing projects, gas stations, factories, and the like. This chapter focuses on the Lajas Structure, which was constructed during the second construction stage at the site.

The Lajas Structure is located to the west of the central depression and near the Salado River (Figure 4.2). In the construction of its vertical walls, long slabs of bluish-gray limestone, or *lajas,* were used (hence the name of this building). This type of stone is rare in the locale, so these building stones were likely brought in from elsewhere. These flat slabs were dry laid like bricks against the face of an earthen-core platform. This was decorative work, with most stone slabs stacked horizontally, but offset with groups of stones placed vertically

and diagonally in the facade. Several squarish niches were also built into the lower register of the facades (Figures 4.3–4.5). The Lajas Structure had two construction phases: Structure 1, on bedrock, was built first; Structure 1-A was added later over floors associated with Structure 1.

Structure 1 and Its Monuments

The north and east faces of Structure 1 have been excavated, but the south face has not. The west face no longer exists. It was dismantled by the ancient builders of Zazacatla in the second building phase, and its bluish-gray slabs were reused in Structure 1-A. The maximum height of Structure 1 preserved in the walls is 1.5 m and corresponds to the height of the central, vertical stone on the north facade. We estimate the original height of the wall at 2.2 m.

The north facade is the best preserved and measures 22.93 m in length. The northeast corner of this building was found partially collapsed, and no evidence was found for the northwest corner. From the observed pattern of the placement of inclined slabs we suppose that only three diagonal slabs are missing from the northwest corner, perhaps removed when the recessed stairs were added to the west with the construction of Structure 1-A. Based on these data, we estimate that the original length of the north facade was 24 m. The orientation of this wall is 285° 47′.

On the north facade, groups of three diagonal stones, inclined toward the right and toward the left—thus forming a broad, truncated "V"—delimit two panels, each with a central niche (see Figures 4.3 and 4.5). These niches contained Monuments 1 and 2 (monuments at Zazacatla are numbered in their order of discovery) (Figures 4.6 and 4.7). As mentioned, diagonal slabs also marked the corners of the building. The minimal differences in the dimensions of the two niches of the north facade indicate that the placement of the sculptures and the construction of the building were done simultaneously. At the center of the facade, flanked by the two panels, was placed a large, vertical stone, which may have once been painted with designs. It is the size and shape of plain stelae known from other sites, but it was not freestanding; rather, it was incorporated into the decorated facade. The possibility of painted stones is supported by fallen fragments of what appears to have been a painted mural on a wall in Structure 2.

The east facade of Structure 1 shows a greater degree of destruction than does the north facade (see Figure 4.4); only the lowest course of wall stones of the north half of this facade was recovered. A niche was also found, much better made than those of the north facade, located in the upper part of the wall in a small panel outlined by two groups of three slabs inclined to the right and to the left. Because the stone that once capped this niche was not found, we think the sculpture that rested there was removed during the construction of Structure 3, as much of the Lajas Structure was dismantled to build the later structure. The length of the east facade of Structure 1 is 10.52 m. The niche, located 9.10 m from the northeast corner, probably marked the center of the east facade in the same structural position as the plain orthostat in the north facade. If so, the original length of the east facade would have been about 18 m, giving an estimated volume of fill for Structure 1 of 950 m³.

As mentioned earlier, two stone monuments were found associated with Structure 1. The stone used for Monument 1 was gray andesite, originating from the volcano of the Chichinautzin Mountains (Figure 4.6). The sculpture is 57 cm tall, 31 cm wide, and 27 cm thick; it weighs about 50 kg. The head-to-body ratio for this seated monument is 1:1.25. The sculpture is partly polished

but still has a slightly rough finish. The sculpture portrays a human figure with body bent forward. The figure's headdress consists of a wide rectangular band around the head. At its ends, in front, the headdress has two circular bosses flanking the face. From the forehead band hang two flaps, which cover the ears and frame the face. Above the band the cap sweeps upward toward the back in the hammer-claw pattern of a cleft head. The large head with its headdress makes up nearly half the composition. The eyebrows are thick frames separated by a double wrinkle gathered above the bridge of the nose. The eyes are rectangular in form, sunken, and have downturned outside corners. The nose is wide and flat, and the mouth is wide and slightly open, with downturned corners. The figure wears a buccal mask that projects outward just below the nose. The shoulders of this figure are clearly defined. The arms are straight and cylindrical in form, coming out to the front of the body and ending in well-defined hands, where it is possible to see the fingers resting on the calves. The torso appears to be nude and without decoration. The legs are crossed, left over right; the left foot is indicated but not the right.

Monument 2 appears to have been carved of gray tuff or consolidated ash, a type of stone found near the site (Figure 4.7). This light gray statuette is similar in size and form to Monument 1. Monument 2 is 46 cm tall, 32 cm wide, and 28 cm thick, and it weighs about 30 kg. The head-to-body ratio of this monument is 1:1. The texture of the piece is rough because of the softer and more granular type of rock from which it is carved. It depicts a human figure in a seated position, with the body leaning forward. This figure wears the same headdress as described for Monument 1, although it is not as well preserved. A piece of this headdress broke off when the stone slab that capped its niche broke and fell on it. The shoulders of Monument 2 are clearly defined. The arms are straight and cylindrical in form and come straight out in front of the body, ending with well-defined hands draped over and obscuring the feet. One can count five fingers on the right hand and four on the left. The torso appears without decoration. The legs are bent

figure 4.6
Three views of Zazacatla Monument 1. (Photographs by Jorge Pérez de Lara.)

figure 4.7
Three views of Zazacatla Monument 2. (Photographs by Jorge Pérez de Lara.)

in the lotus position, and the bottoms of the feet are concealed.

Both sculptures retain traces of red pigment around their eyes and in small recesses on their bodies. They were probably completely covered with red paint in ancient times. This preservation of pigment is remarkable and warrants more attention, as it could shed insight into how ancient sculptures were painted in the ancient past.

Structure 1-A and Its Monuments

The builders of Zazacatla enlarged Structure 1, giving the final form to the Lajas Structure by extending the platform to the west and south. They created and joined this new addition by means of a stairway on the west corner of the north wall. To make this enlargement, builders first disassembled the west facade of Structure 1 and, presumably, reused the stone slabs to build the north facade add-on for Structure 1-A. For this later addition, only the north facade and two slabs from the northwest corner were recovered in our excavations. The west facade has disappeared completely stemming from modern destruction. The northeast corner was not excavated, because it is located below various later floors and levels of stairways of the corner that also partially covered Structure 1-A. We estimate that this extension of the north facade

figure 4.8
Lajas Structure: Structure 1-A, north facade. (Photograph by the authors.)

figure 4.9
Drawing of the north facade of Structure 1-A. (Drawing from the New World Archaeological Foundation based on original by Bernardo A. Flores Bonilla.)

Monument 4   Monument 3

Structure 1-A   0   5 m

was approximately 24.5 m long and, with the added stairs, represented more than a doubling of the length of this facade from Structure 1 to Structure 1-A. The final building was 58 m by 36 m and about 2.2 m high, representing a volume of about 4,600 m³ for this platform. Thus 3,650 m³ of volume was added to the original Structure 1. There were probably summit buildings on this platform as well, but we currently have no evidence for them. In terms of platform fill, the addition of Structure 1-A required nearly four times the original volume of construction materials as was amassed for Structure 1.

Although the method of construction for both structures was the same—limestone slabs arranged horizontally and diagonally to create a wall pattern—the limited available evidence suggests that the triads of diagonal stones were arranged less carefully in Structure 1-A. The slabs do not bracket central niches; rather, they appear above and to the side of them (Figures 4.8 and 4.9). Like Structure 1, the later building has two niches, and Monuments 3 and 4 were found in them. These niches differ in size. The central position of the facade of Structure 1-A has a vacant place for a large, vertical stone slab, but none was found. Perhaps it was removed in a later construction stage. The recessed stairway that joined the two construction stages of the Lajas Structure was 5.13 m wide. The six steps of this stairway were made of rammed earth rather than stone.

The smaller niche of Structure 1-A contained a small sculpture, Monument 3, carved from iron-rich basalt and very heavy for its size (Figure 4.10). The figure is abstract and represents a zoomorphic being, with minimal carving that took advantage of the natural irregularities of the stone to outline its features. The sculpture is 31 cm long, 15 cm wide, and 21 cm thick, and it weighs approximately 15 kg. It is a sculpture of a supernatural being represented by the neck and head. The head is rounded with a blunt rectangular snout; it is possible to distinguish the rounded ears at the back of the head. Eyes are indicated with small depressions. The piece is covered with red pigment.

Zazacatla Monument 4 is made from a natural form of cave flowstone, probably a stalagmite (Figure 4.11). The stone conveys the sense of a seated anthropomorphic being, and this resemblance is probably why it was selected. Its similarity to Monuments 1 and 2 is striking, given its natural form. It is 64 cm long, 62 cm wide, and from 42 to 21 cm thick, which gives it a general trapezoidal shape. It weighs approximately 100 kg. The back part of this stone shows no evidence of having been worked—the only marks on it are those made to break it off a cave floor. The rock appears to show flexed arms and legs of a seated entity holding a small object. Had this stone not been found in a niche in Structure 1-A, we would not have identified it as a monument, nor would we have accorded it so much attention. But the care taken to display it at the site testifies to its significance. Of the four sculptures found in niches it is the most unusual, and it has the most obvious ties to caves and the

figure 4.10
Zazacatla Monument 3. (Photograph by Jorge Pérez de Lara.)

figure 4.11
Zazacatla Monument 4.
(Photograph by Jorge Pérez
de Lara.)

underworld. At the time that Structure 1-A was in use, all four monuments would have been visible in their niches on the north face of the building. It is significant that all four sculptures were made from different kinds of stone, brought from different corners of the surrounding region. The origins of these stones were clearly part of the message communicated by their linear display along the northern side of the Lajas Structure, as most clearly signaled by the unmodified Monument 4 brought up from the bowels of the earth and placed in its niche. This display appears to emphasize the notion of "stone" and its connection to the earth as part of the structure's message (see Chapter 12). As detailed in the following sections, the message of the building was conveyed through the positioning of the sculptures in the Lajas Structure and their changing arrangements through time.

The Mountain and the Cave

Based on information from the excavation, we present a hypothetical reconstruction of Structure 1 as its builders might have conceived it (Figure 4.12). It consisted of a rectangular platform, approximately 24 m by 18 m in basal dimensions, and had straight, vertical walls about 2.20 m high, with the stairs likely located on the western side. The east facade had one central niche, whereas the north facade had two. The facades on the four walls were not the same. The west facade probably lacked a niche and instead had a recessed stairway. The south facade was probably the mirror image of the north facade, having two niches and sculptures. In this regard, Zazacatla Structure 1 may have been analogous to La Venta Structure D-8, a building with a rectangular foundation that had east and

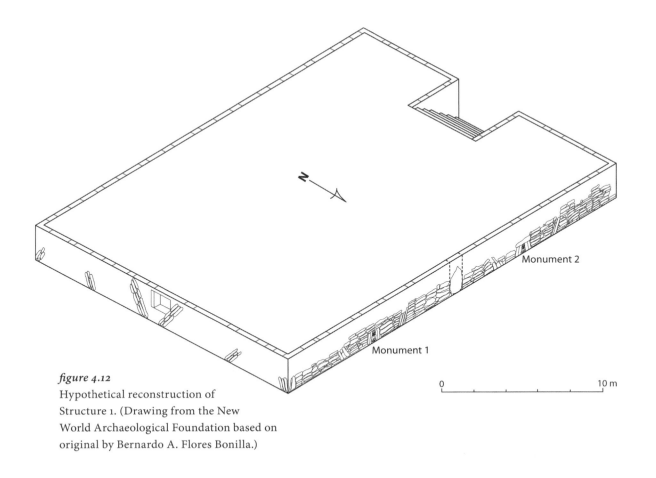

figure 4.12
Hypothetical reconstruction of
Structure 1. (Drawing from the New
World Archaeological Foundation based on
original by Bernardo A. Flores Bonilla.)

Monument 2

Monument 1

0   10 m

figure 4.13
Teopantecuanitlan Structure 3.
(Photograph by Giselle Canto Aguilar.)

west facades marked, respectively, with Altars 4 and 5 (see Chapter 6; González Lauck 2004:98). It is possible that in Zazacatla Structure 1 the stairway was located in the west facade, as it was in Teopantecuanitlan Structures 2 and 3 (Figure 4.13; see Chapter 3; Martínez Donjuán 1994, 1995).

It seems likely that the central concept that the masons built into Structure 1, undoubtedly at the behest of the elites who commissioned the structure, was that of a sacred mountain, with the flanking niches representing caves and entrances into the mountain. This concept is emphasized by the presence of V-shaped architectural elements in the facades. As Reilly (1995:37) argues, these elements have two different connotations. When this cleft symbol appears in representations of the Olmec dragon, such as that on the Tlapacoya vase or on the table top of La Venta Altar 4, it is associated with the sky and other common Middle Preclassic celestial motifs, such as the Saint Andrew's cross. When the "V" appears in a headdress containing a maize plant, the sign represents the cosmic tree, the earth, and ancestors (the maize plant being a metaphor for lineage). Thus the connotation of the "V" symbol or sign depends on its context. In the case of Structure 1, the presence of "V" signs formed by diagonally-placed building slabs to frame the niches probably marked the entrance to the interior of the mountain, to the supernatural world, and possibly to the celestial realm.

Monuments 1 and 2 represent human beings, as indicated by the use of buccal masks and bodies inclined in reverent postures. Their faces exhibit attributes of the Olmec dragon: the eyes in the form of reclining "L"s; the wide, flat nose of a jaguar; and the mouth with downturned corners. The eyebrows were not carved in the form of flames, but the wide frame above the eyes could have been painted with flaming eyebrows, an attribute of birds of prey. These compound faces could indicate that the individuals represented were in a trance state. Such a state comes by means of autosacrifice and/or ingesting hallucinogenic drugs and would have shown a leader's ability to communicate with supernaturals (see Chapter 2). Such transformed

persons are not found on the earth but reside in the supernatural realm, to which they arrive by means of the cave portal, in this case indicated by the niche framing the sculpture. The buccal mask carved in the form of a jaguar mouth would have been the artifact that permitted persons transported to the supernatural world to communicate with the ancestors. These small statues in their niches are reminiscent of the figures in niched thrones or altars from the Olmec region of the Gulf Coast (see Figures 6.7 and 6.8 in Chapter 6).

Beyond this narrative of mountains, caves, and trance states, Structure 1 and its monuments also could have represented cosmic order and the three levels of existence: the earth, the underworld, and the sky, with the earth's surface divided into four quarters. The connection between the earth and the other two cosmic planes was by means of four world trees (one in each quadrant) plus a fifth tree (the largest one in the center position), the five forming a quincunx pattern. If this hypothetical reconstruction of Structure 1 is correct, it is possible that the position of the four sculptures along the north and south facades represented the four world trees. Two sculptures for the south facade are inferred from extrapolating building symmetry. The two sculptures from the north facade wear split headdresses with a V-shaped cleft. On other monuments and representations, a young corn sprout or plant emerges from this cleft, as incised on a jade axe from Arroyo Pesquero, Veracruz (Figure 4.14; Reilly 1995:38–39).

Other representations of the same theme show a central personage flanked in four directions by cleft axes, from which grow young corn plants (see Taube 2000a:301). If the cleft sculptures associated with Structure 1 had the same meaning, the postulated quartet of seated sculptures at Zazacatla represented corn plants/cosmic trees that surrounded a pivotal person/tree, or ruler, at the center of the platform. At the contemporaneous site of Teopantecuanitlan there are four sculptures mounted on two opposite walls of its sunken court that convey the same message (see Chapter 3). These four sculptures at Teopantecuanitlan (see Figures 3.11 and 3.12 in Chapter 3) depict entities with cleft

figure 4.14
Jade axe from Arroyo Pesquero, Veracruz.
(Drawing from the New World Archaeological
Foundation.)

headdresses and are thought to be representations of the Maize God (Taube 2000a, 2004). Martínez Donjuán (Chapter 3) offers an alternative explanation and interprets them as gods and ballplayers. In Taube's interpretation, these supernaturals hold in their hands gifts for humans: bound maize plants. At nearby Chalcatzingo, the person shown on Monument 32 wears a cleft headdress, from which emerges a maize plant (see Aviles 2000:fig. 14). On Chalcatzingo Monument 36, cleft celts appear in the headdress of the supernatural being (see Córdova Tello and Meza Rodríguez 2007:65), as also shown on the Teopantecuanitlan monuments. The "V" designs in the facades of Structure 1 could have conveyed a similar meaning of an opening in the earth from which maize emerges.

The architectural layout, facade designs, and niched were-jaguar figures at Zazacatla all point to the central area of the platform as the designated place for the fifth element of the cosmic order. The fifth tree, the center one and axis mundi (Reilly 1995), was possibly found in a temple at the high part of the platform, but it need not have been another sculpture. Instead, the fifth tree and monument could have been the living flesh of the ruler himself adorned as the axis mundi. Access to this central area was by a western stairway, so devotees climbing the stairs in the early morning would have faced the rising sun.

A principal message broadcast by Structure 1 and its sculptures was the legitimate right of the local ruler to exercise power because of his capacity to mediate among the three levels of the cosmos and to communicate with gods and ancestors. A variation of this theme can be seen on La Venta Altar 4, where a ruler-priest is shown seated in the entrance of a cave and holding a rope that binds him to his ancestors, depicted on the side of this throne (see Figure 6.8 in Chapter 6). His bird headdress indicates he has passed to a different cosmic plane (Reilly 1995:41). Part of the same theme is depicted on Chalcatzingo Monument 1 (Angulo 1994:224, fig. 14.1; Grove and Angulo 1987:117, fig. 9.3). This narrative, carved on a cliff face, shows a ruler-priest inside a cave from which billow rain clouds (Figure 4.15). In these two cases, the ruler

figure 4.15
Chalcatzingo Monument 1. (Photograph
by Víctor M. Castro Mendoza.)

is represented as having the ability to communicate with the gods and to transmit divine messages or blessings back to the local population. At Zazacatla, the ruler as the axis mundi would have been found in the temple, in the bowels of the mountain. Zazacatla Monuments 1 and 2 were representations of mythical ancestors who justified the ruler's right to rule.

The Underworld

The major modification of Structure 1—which included the dismantling of the west facade and the addition of Structure 1-A, which was joined to the earlier building by means of a recessed stairway—implies a designed expansion of the Lajas Structure (Figure 4.16). The platform continued to represent a sacred mountain, but its recessed stairway and entrance was now to the north. Priests and other celebrants who carried out rituals on this structure faced south as they climbed the stairs. The stairway that joined the two structures essentially segregated the platform into halves (represented by the two different construction episodes). This axial division suggests a new narrative based on dualities or complementarities. On the eastern side, Structure 1 continued to be the mountain abode

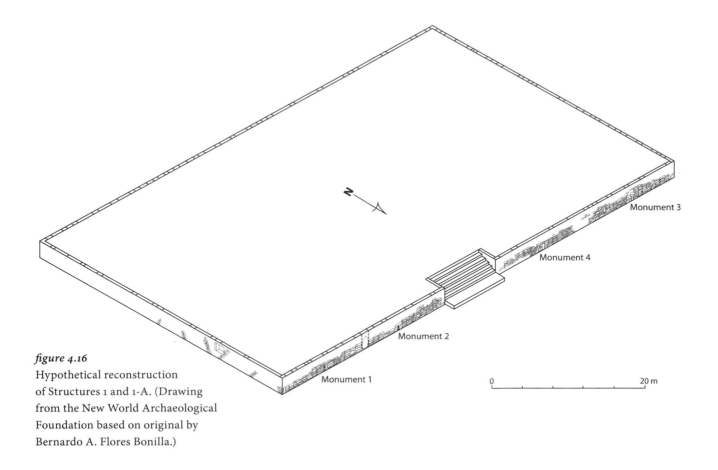

figure 4.16
Hypothetical reconstruction
of Structures 1 and 1-A. (Drawing
from the New World Archaeological
Foundation based on original by
Bernardo A. Flores Bonilla.)

of the mythical ancestors and cosmic trees that legitimized the right to rule. The new, western, half represented cosmic events that occurred inside the mountain.

We believe the concept represented in Structure 1-A and part of the MFCC was the birth of the mythical ancestor, progenitor, and protector of the ruling class by means of the alliance of the ruler with the supernatural (Bernal-García 1989:117). This genealogical concept is generally represented by three elements. The first is the figure of an adult, the ruler. Next is an infant with supernatural facial features held in the arms of the ruler. Third is a supernatural being in all its splendor (see Gonzáles Lauck 2004:96–98). The explicit expression of this theme is found on La Venta Altar 5 (see Figure 6.7 in Chapter 6), where the ruler projects outside a cave and holds a were-jaguar baby in his arms. The top of the altar portrays the Olmec dragon.

Another example is the Las Limas sculpture. This well-known figure holds a cleft-headed were-jaguar infant in his arms, and five supernatural faces are incised on his face, shoulders, and knees (see Fuente 1995a:fig. 10, 1996). At Chalcatzingo this theme is not so explicitly portrayed. However, parts of it are depicted on different relief carvings. The connection between humankind and the Olmec dragon is represented on Chalcatzingo Monument 4, which portrays relations between jaguars and humans (Angulo 1987:figs. 10.16 and 10.17, 1994:234, fig. 14.17; Grove and Angulo 1987:121, fig. 9.11) and on Monument 5, which depicts a man being swallowed by a saurian monster (Angulo 1987:147, fig. 10.18; Grove and Angulo 1987:122, fig. 9.12). No clear representations are known in the relief carvings of were-jaguar infants, but perhaps Monument 13 could qualify; it shows a personage inside a cave who has an elongated, swept-back, cleft head

(Angulo 1987:141, fig. 10.12), similar to the person who appears on the side of La Venta Altar 5. Chalcatzingo Monument 1, "The King," would have completed this narrative at that site (Figure 4.15).

At Zazacatla Structure 1-A, Monuments 3 and 4 may have represented the concept of a ruler removing a mythical ancestor from a cave. Monument 4 could represent a ruler holding an infant. In contrast to the sculptures from the Olmec Gulf Coast region mentioned above in which the persons are leaning partially out of a cave, the personage at Zazacatla is in the interior of the mountain at the moment of creation, a supernatural world represented as cloudy—hence the nebulous features and the selection of a stalagmite for this monument. The Olmec dragon was present at this cosmic event in the roughed-out figure on Monument 3.

As with Structure 1, the meaning of Structure 1-A in the MFCC narrative was that of the mountain. But in contrast to the former, in Structure 1-A there was no cosmic passage formed by the "V" sign on the facade. The placement of groups of three diagonal slabs was without order; this disorder could indicate that the cosmic event just described was portrayed as having taken place in the interior of this structure. As discussed, the "V" sign has two connotations, depending on context: as part of the Olmec dragon, which wears a Saint Andrew's cross, and as associated with the sky. When it appears on headdresses the "V" is associated with the earth and the cleft in the earth from which maize grows. The images on the sculptures associated with Structure 1-A indicate that the intended narrative concerned a supernatural realm, possibly the underworld, as the latter is often represented as being in the interior of a mountain. If the addition to the Lajas Structure represented the underworld as a deliberate contrast to the original Structure 1, then this earlier structure probably represented the sky. If so, the connotation of the "V" sign would have been sky rather than earth. It would not have represented the cleft in the earth but instead that associated with the Olmec celestial dragon. Thus the eastern side of Structure 1, where the sun rises, would have been associated with the celestial realm, whereas the

western side, where the sun sets, would have been linked to the underworld. If this interpretation is correct, the Lajas Structure would then have been the representation of the three planes: underworld, earth, and celestial world. During the rituals that took place on the platform, the ruler-priest moved from one plane to the other as the embodiment of the axis mundi.

The construction of Zazacatla Structure 2 closed the plaza space in front and north of Structure 1-A, leaving an aisle 7 m wide between the two buildings. This aisle is oriented toward the west and would have ended at the Salado River, with Cerro Xochitepec visible in the distance. Even more important, the floor associated with the first building stage of Structure 2 completely covered the niche containing Monument 3 and the lower half of the niche with Monument 4. A subsequent reflooring episode completely covered the latter niche. At the same time, Structure 1 was maintained at the same level, which meant that Monuments 1 and 2 were still exposed to view. It is possible that the partial burial of Structure 1-A and its sculptures was a way of emphasizing its significance as the underworld. This burial does not mean that the Lajas Structure fell into disuse or lost its significance. There are many examples in Mesoamerican sculpture of hidden details that continued to be significant, as best exemplified with the Coatlicue monument found in the Templo Mayor of Tenochtitlan. Its base is carved with an image of the earth god Tlaltecuhtli. This carving could not have been seen with the monument in upright position, so only the faithful would have known it was there.

Ethnic Differences

We have discussed two of the concepts embodied in the MFCC: (1) the cosmos and its order and (2) rulership tied to and bolstered by ancestors and gods. We have considered stone sculptures and buildings from La Venta, Chalcatzingo, and Teopantecuanitlan to demonstrate that these concepts were widespread in Middle Preclassic

Mesoamerica. The main message in these concepts is that of the position of the ruler in the cosmos as the axis mundi, capable of mediating earth and sky, of carrying offerings to supernatural beings, and of obtaining otherworldly gifts for humans by communicating with deceased ancestors and lineage founders.

This MFCC narrative is well represented at La Venta and Chalcatzingo as well as at Zazacatla, albeit in different ways. We interpret the variance in presentation of core themes as having arisen from different practices or preferences that reveal ethnic identity. Each difference in the use of common symbols manifested the existence of distinct groups who shared the same view of the cosmos. An example of different ways of symbolizing common themes with the same symbol set is the representations of caves on La Venta Altars 4 and 5, on Chalcatzingo Monuments 1 and 9, and the stone niches in the Lajas Structure at Zazacatla. Another example of transformed symbols is the "V" sign created by diagonal stone slabs in building facades. At Zazacatla, the "V" appears in two places on the north facade of Structure 1. A variant of this same sign is found on Teopantecuanitlan Structures 2 and 3 (Martínez Donjuán 1994:fig. 9.19). The "V" sign there is the lower part of a diamond shape that is only apparent if the upper wall stones are in place

figure 4.17
Wall associated with the altar of Chalcatzingo Monument 22, showing detail of the slabs forming an inverted "V." (Photograph by Víctor M. Castro Mendoza.)

(Martínez Donjuán 1994:162–163, fig. 9.19). In contrast to Zazacatla, at Teopantecuanitlan the number of "V" signs varies from two to four, and the same for the number of niches, depending on the structure (Figure 4.13). This mutability was probably due to variations in the message, because the sign appears to have carried the same meaning. At Chalcatzingo, the "V" sign appears on the walls of the patio that flank Monument 22, the Olmec composite throne (see Figure 1.8 in Chapter 1), but in this case the sign is inverted and is essentially the upper half of a diamond design. Although Chalcatzingo Monument 22 is similar to altars or thrones in the Gulf Coast region, it lacks a representation of a cave, and instead of portraying an Olmec dragon, it only depicts the eyes of a supernatural (Grove 2000, 2007). By this means, the concept of "cave" is represented by an inverted "V" sign on the walls next to this altar (Figure 4.17).

If Zazacatla Monuments 1 and 2 can be read individually as signs, and together as a conjunction of signs, they can also be read as part of a single text or narrative, one repeated in the MFCC at numerous sites. The use of these signs permits a variety of messages to be generated. For example, the observed postures of Monuments 1 and 2 are similar to that of the Cruz de Milagro sculpture known as "The Prince" (see Clark and Pérez Suárez 1994:267, fig. 16.6; Fuente 1995a:fig. 4, 1996). In contrast, the facial attributes on the Zazacatla monuments are significantly different. The buccal masks, cleft heads, and zoomorphic faces of the Zazacatla monuments suggest a state of transformation, such as on San Lorenzo Monument 10 (see Figure 1.3c in Chapter 1; see Angulo 1994:226, fig. 14.5; Coe and Diehl 1980:316, fig. 434; Cyphers 2004b:62–64, fig. 22). Thus the new combination of posture and head attributes created a novel message and narrative claim. This capacity to create new messages by recombining symbols is characteristic of a sign system, and this pan-Mesoamerican system could have been used by different groups to mark their distinctions. As Reilly (2005:31) argues, it is necessary to know the relative position of a sculpture within its ensemble to understand its meaning. We

have such information for the Zazacatla sculptures but not for the Cruz del Milagro or San Lorenzo Monument 10 sculptures, so comparisons of meaning among them cannot be taken very far until we have more information on other monuments in their original contexts.

Concluding Remarks

In the three-dimensional model of the cosmos, the Lajas Structure represented the earth and also symbolized the worlds above and below. Structure 1 corresponded to the terrestrial plane; its seated sculptures referenced the four world trees located at the four corners of the earth, with the niches indicating cave entrances to the underworld. In turn, Structure 1-A represented the supernatural— the creation of the ancestors under the tutelage of the supernatural jaguar. These two worlds were joined by a stairway at the north end of the platform that marked the division between the two.

The conjunction of architecture with sculptures at Zazacatla created a stage for ritual performances related to the renewal of political power based on the connections of rulers with deified ancestors and gods. The ruler in the role of the axis mundi mediated between the celestial and mundane and brought the local population in line with divine will. This narrative of rulership forms part of the MFCC, and it was represented in different ways in ancient centers, such as La Venta, Chalcatzingo, and Teopantecuanitlan. The observed differences in the signs used to communicate this narrative may indicate ethnic differences among peoples.

Acknowledgments

We thank the organizers of the Dumbarton Oaks conference for inviting us to participate. We especially thank Fred W. Nelson and John Clark for translating our chapter and the graphic artists of the New World Archaeological Foundation for helping with the illustrations.

Stone Monuments and Earthen Mounds

Polity and Placemaking at Tres Zapotes, Veracruz

CHRISTOPHER A. POOL

THE FORMATION OF A POLITY IS FUNDA-mentally an act of placemaking. It is not simply an abstract act of social reorganization through the development of governing institutions, but necessarily the practical creation of a territory—a political landscape that encompasses the spaces perceived, experienced, and inhabited by the subjects of the regime (Smith 2003:154–160). In ancient Mesoamerica, as in most other regions of the world, regimes created such spaces by erecting buildings and sculptures, which formed the settings for ceremony and administrative practice. To a substantial degree we should expect that the political spaces so created will reflect the governmental precepts of the regime. At the same time, the modification of existing spaces (and in a different way, the construction of new ones) also involves a dialogue with the past, not only stemming from the inertia of old forms but also because of the necessity of resolving the current regime with history.

Tres Zapotes, Veracruz, is a good place to study political placemaking because of its prominence as the center of a regional polity and its long history of stone monument carving and architectural construction. Recent research has documented the growth and decline of the site from ca 1250 BC to AD 1000 (all dates are calibrated), achieving its maximum size between 400 BC and AD 300 (Pool and Ohnersorgen 2003; Pool et al. n.d.). The sculptural corpus includes stylistically Middle, Late, and Protoclassic examples (Pool 2000, 2006; Porter 1989). Mound construction appears to have begun by the late Middle Preclassic period and to have continued into the Early Classic period (Pool 2000, 2008). Changes in modes of sculptural representation and architectural plans suggest realignments of political strategies in the Late Preclassic period and again in the Protoclassic (Pool 2008). Furthermore, recent archaeological surveys have begun to provide badly needed context with data on regional settlement history, and new Olmec sculptures with clear ties to La Venta, Tabasco, have been recovered (Loughlin and Pool 2006).

Nevertheless, it is important to recognize the limitations in the data I draw on in this chapter. Stratigraphic context is available for only three stone monuments from Tres Zapotes, among which is Stela C, with its 32 BC Long Count date (Millet Cámara 1979; Pool 1997; Stirling 1939). Consequently, the temporality of the remaining forty-seven monuments must be inferred on the basis of style and spatial association, and the original find locations of about half of these are uncertain. Similarly, most data on construction stages of mounded architecture are limited to brief summaries by Drucker (1943), Stirling (1943b), and Weiant (1943), written before radiocarbon dating existed and when ceramic sequences were only starting to be understood. A notable exception is Millet Cámara's (1979) excavation of an earthen "altar" or adoratory with associated offerings and a nearby platform standing 2 m high and partly stone faced. These earlier excavations within structures are complemented in the present study by recent stratigraphic excavations that were designed to test middens adjacent to formal architecture, plazas, and household contexts but also encountered some structural remains (Pool 2005). Additional data on the current conformation of architecture and associated materials come from intensive surface collection and mapping (Pool 1997).

The Setting

The archaeological site of Tres Zapotes occupies about 500 ha on the floodplain and adjacent terraces of the Arroyo Hueyapan where it emerges from the piedmont of the Tuxtla Mountains onto the coastal plain. The distribution of deeply buried materials found in excavations and auger tests suggest that Tres Zapotes began its history as a modest village of between 7 and 17 ha (Pool et al. n.d.). Over the course of the Middle Preclassic period (1000–400 BC) Tres Zapotes grew into a regional center with some 80 ha of continuous settlement, surrounded by another 70 ha of settlement dispersed among thirty localities within 1.5 km of the center (Pool 2006; Pool and Ohnersorgen 2003).

Regardless of whether these satellite settlements are included in the total, only La Venta clearly surpassed Tres Zapotes among Gulf Coast centers at this time (González Lauck 1996; Pool 2006). A total of eight to nine Olmec monuments, including two colossal heads and two stelae, underscore the emergence of Tres Zapotes as a Middle Preclassic political center (Pool 1997, 2006).

The end of the Middle Preclassic saw major disruptions in Olmec political economies. Greenstone ceased to be imported on anything approaching the scale at La Venta during its heyday. At Tres Zapotes, greenstone imports, which were always modest by comparison to those arriving at La Venta, virtually ceased. In the Tuxtla Mountains and at Tres Zapotes the dominant obsidian source shifted from the area around the Pico de Orizaba volcano to more distant deposits at Zaragoza and Oyameles, Puebla (Knight and Pool 2008; Santley et al. 2001).

In contrast to other Gulf Coast Olmec centers, however, Tres Zapotes not only survived the end of the Middle Preclassic period but flourished, growing to its full 500 ha extent in the Late Preclassic period (400–1 BC) (Figure 5.1). Cultural continuity across this transition is evident in ceramic technology (Ortíz 1975; Pool 2006; Pool and Ortiz 2008) and in the persistence of Olmec sculptural themes, despite changing technique and form (e.g., Pool 2000), as discussed below. The urban landscape of Tres Zapotes also experienced profound change, with an explosion in the construction of formal architecture (Pool 2008). Excavations have shown that Olmecs at Tres Zapotes had begun to erect platforms in the Middle Preclassic period (Millet Cámara 1979; Pool et al. n.d.; Weiant 1943). Nevertheless, none of the documented examples exceeded 2 m in height.[1] During the Late Preclassic and Protoclassic periods, the rulers of Tres Zapotes began to erect earthen pyramids and platforms in formal arrangements, some of which continued to be enlarged in the Early Classic period (Pool 2008).

My interpretation of architectural layouts at Tres Zapotes (Pool 2008) emphasizes the practices of individuals and groups within societies, particularly as regards competition and alliance building among factions, defined as "structurally

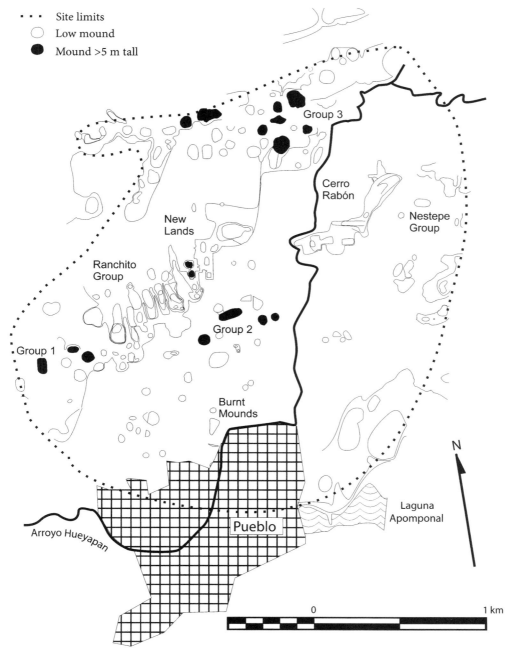

figure 5.1
Planimetric map of Tres Zapotes, Veracruz. (Drawing by the author.)

and functionally similar groups which . . . compete for resources and positions of power or prestige" (Brumfiel 1994:4). It also incorporates the distinction between exclusionary and corporate (i.e., "collective" [Kolb 1996:59]) politicoeconomic strategies elaborated by Blanton and his colleagues

(1996). Exclusionary strategies refer to those by which political leaders seek to monopolize material and symbolic sources of power and authority. Such efforts often focus on establishing individual control over prestige-good networks or exclusive patron-client relationships with craft specialists

(Blanton et al. 1996:5). Conditions of factional competition provide fertile breeding grounds for exclusionary strategies, but the successful monopolization of power sources by leaders of a single faction will result in a highly centralized political economy. Collective strategies, in contrast, restrict the ability of individuals and factions to monopolize power; they promote the sharing of power among multiple segments of society. As a result, one hallmark of collective strategies at the level of polity governance is an assembly that permits the representation of society's constituent groups (Blanton 1998:154).

In applying this framework, I take seriously the idea that both kinds of strategies coexist to some degree in all societies. Blanton and his colleagues (1996:2) concede this point, but in the same sentence they insist that one "will be dominant in any particular time and place." This, they assert, is because these strategies "result in dissimilar and antagonistic political economies" (Blanton et al. 1996:7), although they acknowledge that "elements of both approaches may, however, be employed in certain complex cases" (Blanton et al. 1996:7). The Mesoamerican examples they offer of these complex states include the Aztec Triple Alliance and Chichén Itzá, which suggest that the dominance of one politicoeconomic strategy over another at the scale of polity-wide administration may be accompanied by other strategies at smaller scales within polities and at larger scale in interactions among polities (Pool 2008:123). Therefore my interest in applying this framework at Tres Zapotes lies not in characterizing polities as either exclusionary or corporate but in ascertaining how and at what social scales exclusionary and collective strategies were employed by political leaders at different times.

The material expressions in art and architecture of the ideologies that underpin exclusionary and collective strategies provide an important entrée into their implementation in ancient societies, especially the "patrimonial rhetoric" that supports exclusionary claims to authority by virtue of descent from the ancestors of ruling lineages (Blanton et al. 1996:5, 8). In contrast, collective strategies promote a corporate "cognitive code"

that emphasizes collective solidarity and interdependence among constituent groups of the society, expressed as "collective representations and the accompanying ritual based on broad themes such as fertility and renewal in society and the cosmos" (Blanton et al. 1996:6). These observations inform my analysis of sculpture. With regard to architecture, I argue that, compared to exclusionary strategies, collective strategies implemented at the level of the polity should emphasize architectural layouts designed to provide more open public access to communal ritual. Where collective strategies mediate among political factions, there should be greater replication in the layouts of contemporaneous civic-ceremonial complexes, thereby reinforcing a common vision of the proper relationship not only among architectural elements but also among the institutions they represent (see Pool 2008). Differences in the scale of civic-ceremonial complexes should be reduced compared to those built in more hierarchically ordered polities, and such size differences should correspond to the duration of their use more than to differences in wealth and political power, as expressed in access to exotic resources, finely crafted goods, or sculptural programs.

At Tres Zapotes, Late Preclassic and Protoclassic civic-ceremonial architecture is concentrated in four plaza groups—Groups 1, 2, 3, and the Nestepe Group (Figure 5.1). Each conforms to a basic Tres Zapotes Plaza Group plan consisting of a plaza with a temple pyramid to the west, a long platform to the north, and a low platform or adoratorio on the central east-west axis. Three of these four complexes contain additional platforms, including one or two temple pyramids at the eastern end of the plaza (Pool 2008:table 2). Radiocarbon dates from middens behind the long platforms and plaza resurfacings confirm that the use of these plaza groups overlapped in the Late Preclassic and Protoclassic periods (Pool 2008). Although these groups vary in area and construction volume, no one was clearly dominant in these respects (Sullivan 2002), and there is little indication of differential access to exotic goods (Pool 2008). Thus I have argued that the Late Preclassic Tres Zapotes polity was governed by an alliance or confederation of factional leaders instead of a single ruler. During the Protoclassic period, however, construction and sculptural programs began to diverge, suggesting the assertion of individual power by factional leaders and a weakening of the ruling confederation (Pool 2008).

Stone Monuments of Tres Zapotes

The approach I take in analyzing the monuments of Tres Zapotes is fundamentally a behavioral one. I see the transport, carving, and placement of monuments as meaningful acts intended to convey power through references to political and religious authority. In this perspective the shaping of monuments into conventional forms, the rendering of standard thematic content, and the arranging of monuments in relation to one another and to features of the built and natural landscape all were done with the intent of conveying messages understandable to particular audiences and consistent with the political ideology and practices of the day. By the same token, as political practices change, we should expect shifts toward new conventions of expression, including new formal classes of monuments. Furthermore, as the many cases of recarving and resetting ancient monuments attest (e.g., Graham 1989; Porter 1989; Stirling 1940a), the acts of transport, carving, and placement need not all have taken place at the same time or necessarily in a short time frame, and old forms could have been reused in new settings to invoke history or convey new meanings.

With regard to form, the stone monuments of Tres Zapotes and its environs can be divided into a dozen or so categories (see Porter 1989): colossal heads (three examples); full-round figures (twelve); tenoned busts (eleven); composite figures (three or four); stelae (eight), including plain, celtiform, and proscenium or "niche" examples (to use Porter's [1989] term); a round altar (one); cylindrical basins and perforated cylinders (four); boxes (two); possible box tops (two); throne fragments (two); bedrock carvings (one); and basalt-column enclosures (one). (The one example of a basalt

enclosure contained basalt slabs, one perforated, and a carved serpentine column.) Additionally, pieces of columnar basalt with uncertain uses are found widely scattered over the site. Such diversity is hardly surprising at a site that was regionally prominent for something on the order of a millennium (Pool 2008). However, neither form nor iconography alone provides a secure footing for reconstructing a sculptural chronology, as several art historians dealing with Preclassic art have argued (e.g., Graham 1989; Kubler 1962; Milbrath 1979; Porter 1989; cf. Clewlow 1974; Clewlow et al. 1967). Instead, such authors as John Graham, Susan Milbrath, and James Porter argue for close attention to stylistic traits that include techniques of carving and execution of detail, as well as overall modeling, general proportions, and posture for anthropomorphic and zoomorphic figures. Variation in sculptural techniques suggests that particular classes of monuments at Tres Zapotes, particularly full-round figures, tenoned busts, and stelae, were created over a significant time span. That said, the number of different solutions proposed to the puzzle of Olmec sculptural chronology in general, and that of Tres Zapotes in particular, does little to instill confidence in stylistic seriations (compare the authors above as well as Coe [1965b], Fuente [1977, 1981], and Wicke [1971]).

For certain questions, the chronological sequence in which monuments were carved at Tres Zapotes is unimportant. Using the behavioral perspective, it is possible to analyze the meaning of monuments strictly with respect to the contexts in which they were placed during the site's Late Preclassic and Protoclassic apogee when, I argue, the majority would have been observable. Such a narrowly synchronic view, however, ignores the historical significance and associations of certain Olmec monuments that were already ancient by the time they were incorporated into epi-Olmec construction plans. Therefore some consideration of the sculptural chronology is in order. I view such chronologies, which focus on when the monuments were carved, as part of a broader problem of the temporality of sculptures, which includes their continued reuses and recarvings.

Several authors have included a handful of Tres Zapotes monuments in their analyses of Preclassic Gulf Coast sculptural chronology (e.g., Bernal 1969; Lowe 1989), often focusing on the site's colossal heads (Clewlow et al. 1967; Fuente 1977, 1981; Kubler 1962; Wicke 1971) and/or its stelae (Coe 1965a, 1965b; Pool 2000; Stirling 1965). Milbrath (1979) includes five monuments from Tres Zapotes in her chronology of Olmec figural sculptures and reliefs. She defined three broad stylistic/chronological groups for seated figures and reliefs, the first two subdivided on the basis of sculptural detail and posture, and a fourth group restricted to reliefs. Rather than focusing on iconography, as Clewlow (1974) had, Milbrath considered the manner of representation (degree of overall modeling, treatment of detail, and body postures and proportions) as paramount in defining styles that cross-cut regional variation.

Two of the Tres Zapotes seated figures (I and M, Figures 5.2 and 5.3) fall into Milbrath's Group IIa, which "are carved in an angular manner, and most frequently are posed seated cross-legged, leaning forward with the arms extended.... Costuming... is rendered by incision and low relief, without any great emphasis on three-dimensionality," and musculature and extremities are less detailed than her more sensitively modeled Group I figures (Milbrath 1979:9–10). A third seated figure, Monument J, she classifies with the "extremely angular and crude" Group III in which "hands and feet are rendered as rough blocks" and "costume detail is virtually absent" (Milbrath 1979:18). Basing her chronological ordering on comparison with sculptures from sites with dated archaeological sequences, Milbrath inferred a progression from the naturalistic and sensitively modeled forms of her Group I through Group II to the geometric, angular, and "cruder" forms of Group III. Milbrath also included Tres Zapotes Stela A (Figure 5.4) and Stela D (Figure 5.5) in her Group IV reliefs, which, she admits, do not represent a highly unified style, but rather the incorporation of elements characteristic of later Mesoamerican styles. Interestingly, the elements she describes are mainly iconographic rather than stylistic in the narrow sense she invokes for her other groups.

Porter (1989) has made the most complete attempt to order the Tres Zapotes monuments chronologically by style. His six groups are defined by the manner of carving (e.g., incised, grooved, incised relief, flat relief with incised detail, modeled half-round or full-round), the extent to which natural surfaces are modified, and the degree and manner of representation of such details as body ornament and clothing. As does Milbrath (1979),

figure 5.2
Tres Zapotes Monument I. (Stirling 1943b:plate 9a). (Photograph by Matthew Stirling/National Geographic Image Collection.)

figure 5.3
Tres Zapotes Monument M. (Stirling 1943b:plate 11b). (Photograph by Richard H. Stewart/National Geographic Image Collection.)

figure 5.4
Tres Zapotes Stela A. (Photograph by the author, adjusted for perspective.)

figure 5.5
Tres Zapotes Stela D. (Photograph courtesy of John Justeson.)

Porter (1989:6) emphasizes the distinction between simple-closed forms and complex-open forms but assumes a progression from the former to the latter (see also Graham 1981). Therefore his Group 1, consisting entirely of petroglyphic boulder sculptures "in which the natural surface of the stone is minimally modified by cupping, grooving, and incision" (Porter 1989:16), precedes his Group 2, "in which major features are represented in incised relief or flat relief with incised detail" and "the natural surface of the stone is retained wherever its removal is not essential to the depiction and the surface of the sculpture adheres closely to the natural surface of the stone" (Porter 1989:17). Porter hints that these two groups include pre-Olmec and very early Olmec sculptures, including the colossal head of Cobata (Figure 5.6). Porter's next two groups, 3 and 4, both consist "of sculptures in which major features are represented in the round or in the half round with relief detailing" (Porter 1989:19–20) but differ in that Group 4 exhibits more extensive modification and modeling of surfaces; deeper declivities and perforations separating limbs from the torso; and more abundant, complex clothing and body ornament. Group 5 "consists of sculptures in which flat surface patterns with combinations of swirling and angular forms are executed in a linear style" (Porter 1989:23). Some stylistic latitude seems to be granted in the inclusion of sculptures in this group, which includes the heavily carved Monument C stone box (Figure 5.7) as well as the plain stone box, Monument B. Also included are Stela C (Figure 5.8) and Stela D. Group 6 is a late, catchall category of "sculptures in which

figure 5.6
The colossal head of Cobata. (Photograph by the author.)

figure 5.7
Tres Zapotes
Monument C.
(Photograph by
the author.)

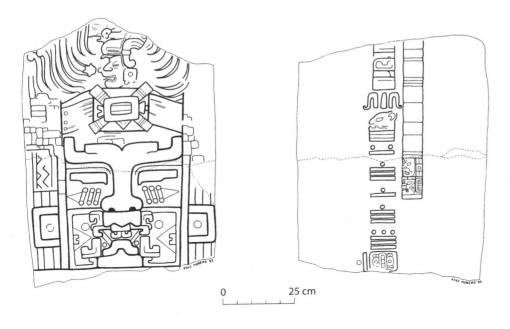

0   25 cm

figure 5.8
Tres Zapotes Stela C,
obverse (left) and reverse
(right). (Drawing from the
New World Archaeological
Foundation by Ajax Moreno.)

forms, themes, compositions, features, and motifs unique to Olmec art do not appear at all." In fact, six of the eight pieces in Group 6 are unadorned basins and altars; the exceptions are a numeral or date inscribed in bedrock (Monument E [Stirling 1943b:fig. 5]) and a fragment of a possible Izapan-style throne (Stela E [Stirling 1943b:plate 7c]).

It is notable as well that ten of the fourteen monuments in Porter's more rustic Groups 1 and 2 were found in small sites in the countryside around Tres Zapotes. The techniques of cupping, grooving, incision, and incised relief, as well as the minimal modification of the natural surface of the stone, are characteristic of rock carvings widely distributed in time and space in Mesoamerica (e.g., Early Preclassic Chalchuapa, El Salvador, and the Late Postclassic shrine of Cerro Tlaloc, Mexico). I suspect what Porter has identified here is an

Table 5.1

Approximate sequence of monuments from Tres Zapotes and nearby sites

DATE	COLOSSAL HEADS	FULL-ROUND SCULPTURES	TENONED BUSTS	CARVED STELAE AND COLUMNS	PLAIN STELAE	BOXES AND BASINS
AD 300						
Protoclassic				La Mojarra Stela 1, Stela C (reset)	Monument 44, Stela B?	
				Stela C (Long Count date)		
AD 1				El Meson Stela 2		Monument D, Monument N?
						Monument B
Late Preclassic				Stela E?		Monument C
		Monument J	Hueyapan de Mimendez Monument 1	El Meson Stela 1		Monument 39
			Monuments F, 19, 29	Alvarado Stela 1		
400 BC			Pajonal Monument 1	Stela D, Stela C (obverse)		
		Monument 37	Monuments G, R	Monument 33 (serpentine)		
Late Middle Preclassic				Stelae A, F		
		Monument M				
700 BC		Monument I				
		Monument H				
Early Middle Preclassic	Monument Q	Lerdo Monument				
	Monument A	Cabada Monument				
1000 BC						

figure 5.9
Tres Zapotes Monument
A, the colossal head of
Hueyapan. (Photograph
by the author.)

figure 5.10
Tres Zapotes Monument
Q, the colossal head of
Nestepe. (Photograph
by the author.)

urban-rural distinction rather than a chronological one. Further, although I recognize that styles and techniques of carving change through time, I am not convinced that the direction of change can be assumed to always follow the simple-closed to complex-open sequence characteristic of some historical spans of Western art; rather, I consider that a hypothesis to be tested in other settings.

My own assessment of the sequence of monument carving at Tres Zapotes is more archaeological and so better aligned with that of Milbrath in tying forms and modes of representation to dated archaeological sequences. As do Clark and Pye (2000), I view monuments as artifacts that were employed to particular ends in their initial carving and setting, as well as (and often for different reasons) in subsequent reuses and resettings. It is likely that as political practices and the ideologies that underpinned them changed, themes and representational conventions also changed. However, I also expect, as with other artifact styles, that the replacement of one set of techniques or conventions will often be gradual, unless social and cultural upheaval dictates a rejection of the old ways (events that are more likely to affect iconography and representational content than technique). Furthermore, although the final setting of a monument does not date its carving, it does provide a useful *terminus ante quem* for the carving. Moreover, if a large number of monuments of a particular style can be shown to have been set in their final positions within a particular time frame, that time frame should provide a reasonable estimate of when they were carved as well, in the absence of contradictory evidence. In the following paragraphs I outline the sculptural sequence I employ in my analysis of placemaking at the end of this chapter.

Three sets of carvings provide anchors of varying certainty to the Tres Zapotes sculptural sequence (Table 5.1). The mid-second-century radiocarbon-dated setting of Monument 44 (a plain stela), and the 32 BC Long Count date of Stela C (Figure 5.8) lie toward the upper end, and the typically Olmec colossal heads (Monuments A and Q) (Figures 5.9 and 5.10) mark the lower end of the sequence. Between are two high-relief stelae

A and D (Figures 5.4 and 5.5), which fairly clearly correspond to the late Middle Preclassic period. Though the later monuments are the most securely dated, I will proceed in approximately chronological order and organize my discussion by monument classes to underscore changes in political practice.

Figural Sculptures in the Round

The temporal placement of Tres Zapotes's colossal heads is a matter of considerable disagreement. Most authors have identified them as more similar in their overall proportions to the heads of La Venta than to most of those from San Lorenzo (Clewlow et al. 1967; Fuente 1977; Kubler 1962; Wicke 1971). Authors writing after radiocarbon dating proved the greater antiquity of San Lorenzo (Coe et al. 1967) have usually argued that the Tres Zapotes heads are later than those of the other two sites (Fuente 1977). Clewlow and others (1967), however, saw little evidence for a long span for carving the colossal heads, speculating that perhaps all were carved within two hundred years of one another, and they attributed differences in costuming and proportion to regional variation. Lowe (1989) and Grove (1997) concurred with Clewlow that all heads were produced in a short span during the Early Preclassic period. When I began working at Tres Zapotes, I favored this argument. However, our archaeological investigations, which indicated only a modest Early Preclassic component at Tres Zapotes, convinced me that the leaders of Tres Zapotes would not have had the political prominence or the labor force required to commission and transport these monuments before the expansion of the site in the Middle Preclassic period (Pool 2000, 2006). Nevertheless, I find it difficult to believe that this distinctive Olmec tradition extended much beyond its Early Preclassic apogee at San Lorenzo. Therefore I favor an early Middle Preclassic date for the colossal heads of Tres Zapotes (and possibly those of La Venta). Quite likely Monuments A and Q were carved in succession (Figures 5.9 and 5.10); Monument Q is certainly more deeply modeled and finely detailed than Monument A. However, I do not think we can assume an evolution toward finer carving, as Porter (1989) argues; certainly that would seem to run against the documented priority of some of the finest San Lorenzo heads. The unique location, size, and style of the Cobata head on nearby Cerro el Vigía (Figure 5.6) raise several issues of function and temporality (Pool 2006). Here I note only that the rustic, unfinished appearance of the Cobata head (see Hammond 2001) seems more a consequence of its rural setting than the antiquity favored by Porter (1989) or the late decadence favored by Fuente (1977). It may also be the case that the carving of the Cobata head was left unfinished, as Hammond (2001) has argued. It does not necessarily follow, however, that this most colossal of Olmec heads was destined for Tres Zapotes or another center; certainly 50-ton basalt boulders of comparable shape could have been obtained from the flanks of Cerro el Vigía with considerably less effort. Rather, I argue that the Cobata head, located in an important pass at the divide between the lower Papaloapan and the Tepango valleys, was intended to serve as a territorial marker for the Tres Zapotes polity (Pool 2006).

Twelve full-round figures have been recovered to date from Tres Zapotes and the nearby site of Hueyapan de Mimendez. Tres Zapotes Monument H (an elongated were-jaguar head; Figure 5.11), seated figures (Monuments I, M, and 37, the last discovered in 1995; Figures 5.2, 5.3, and 5.12), and Hueyapan de Mimendez Monument 2 (Figure 5.13) all fit comfortably within classical Olmec canons, with rounded contours and details of facial features and costume represented by a combination of modeling and incision (Milbrath 1979; Porter 1989). Recently, two additional Olmec figures have come to light in the vicinities of Lerdo de Tejada and Angel R. Cabada. The Lerdo monument (Figure 5.14) is nearly identical to the San Martín Pajapan monument (Benson and Fuente 1996:162–163, no. 5), which in turn bears a headdress and ear ornaments similar to La Venta Monument 44 (González Lauck 1994:fig. 6.23). The seated Cabada monument (Figure 5.15) is very similar to La Venta Monument 77 (Benson and Fuente 1996:172–173, no. 10) in the incised rope-like elements on its stiff cape. Interestingly, the element worn on the belt of the Lerdo monument also links it to La Venta

Monument 77, which displays an identical belt. In general, these well-modeled figures seem to represent a sculptural style present in Early Preclassic contexts at San Lorenzo that persisted with some tendency toward greater abstraction at La Venta and elsewhere into the Middle Preclassic (Fuente 1977; Milbrath 1979).

Another seated figure, Tres Zapotes Monument J (Stirling 1943b:plate 9c), is executed in a blocky, geometrical style, which seems absent at San Lorenzo (Cyphers 2004b) but which Milbrath relates to La Venta Monuments 21 (Drucker et al. 1959:plate 51b), 40 (Clewlow and Corson 1968:plate 11a), 74, and 75 (Fuente 1973:118–119) as well as to La Venta Altar 6, which most authors regard as late Middle Preclassic (e.g., Parsons 1986). Similar in its severe geometry is Tres Zapotes Monument 35, a torso with hands held to its chest, which my colleagues and I encountered on an archaeological survey in 1995 (Pool 1997). Another Tres Zapotes figure, Monument L, is heavily battered, but its contours identify it as a potbelly figure with an unusually large head (Stirling 1943b:plate 10c, misidentified in the caption as "Monument H"). Porter (1989:107–108) describes Tres Zapotes Monument L as "primitive" and considers it early Olmec or pre-Olmec. In favor of Porter's position, the style and quality of its carving share a general resemblance to small anthropomorphic statues from San Lorenzo (Monuments 130–133 [Cyphers 2004b:208–215, figs. 144–147]). The dating of potbelly sculptures has long been a matter of debate. Miles (1965) placed the potbelly sculptures in her stylistic Division I, which she assigned to the Early Preclassic, and Graham (1981, 1989) argued for a pre-Olmec component of the potbelly corpus at Takalik Abaj. Most other scholars have since favored a Late Preclassic placement, consistent with the earliest documented final settings at San Leticia, El Salvador; Monte Alto, Guatemala; and elsewhere (e.g., see Chapter 9; Demarest et al. 1982; Parsons 1986). The remaining full-round figures from Tres Zapotes (Monuments 20, 26, and 30) are simply too battered or fragmentary to attempt to place them in time.

Tenoned busts seem clearly to be an adaptation of carving in the round to specific,

figure 5.11
Tres Zapotes Monument H.
(Photograph by the author.)

figure 5.12
Tres Zapotes Monument 37. (Photograph by the author.)

figure 5.13
Hueyapan de Mimendez Monument 2. (Photograph
by the author.)

figure 5.14
Olmec monument, Lerdo de Tejada, Veracruz.
(Photograph by the author.)

figure 5.15
Olmec monument, Angel R. Cabada, Veracruz.
(Photograph by the author.)

probably architectural, functions (cf. Stirling 1965:731–733). In contrast to the full-figure sculptures with attached pedestal bases that are common in Late Preclassic Guatemala (see Chapters 7 and 10; Parsons 1986:figs. 15–20) and occasionally encountered in the southern Gulf Coast lowlands (Gillespie 2000:fig. 14), tenoned busts have a long, shaped but uncurved element extending either vertically or horizontally from the upper torso. With seven examples and another four from nearby sites, Tres Zapotes was arguably the preeminent Preclassic center for the carving of tenoned busts (Porter 1989:9). Stirling (1965:733) suggested that San Lorenzo Monument 6 (also known as Loma del Zapote Monument 12), a large anthropomorphic head, was originally attached to a tenon, but this is doubtful (Cyphers 2004b:260, fig. 174). The

only other Preclassic Gulf Coast example is La Venta Monument 56 (Westheim 1950; Williams and Heizer 1965:plate 1c), a monkey with hands clasped behind its neck (cf. Fuente 1973:104) carved from a hornblende andesite that is probably from La Unión (Chichonal) volcano (Williams and Heizer 1965:20). Perhaps because they are so rare elsewhere, this class of monuments has received little systematic attention, with most authors commenting only on the largest and most complete examples, Tres Zapotes Monuments F and G, and assigning them a Late Preclassic date (e.g., see Bernal 1969; Coe 1965b; Parsons 1986; Stirling 1943b, 1965; cf. Porter 1989).

Although Fuente (1973:297–299) doubted its Olmec attribution, Monument G (Figure 5.16) is most reasonably interpreted as an Olmec sculpture of a person wearing a were-jaguar mask (Porter 1989:94–95). The head, which projects from the upper surface of the tenon, is thrown back like that of La Venta Monument 11 (Drucker et al. 1952:plate 61g; see also Benson and Fuente 1996:164–165, no. 6) and wears a buccal mask having a downturned mouth with angular upper-lip bracket and out-curving fangs. The mid-face is heavily battered and exfoliated, but human eyes are clearly visible on either side of the broad nose region. Heavy ear ornaments terminating in large, beehive-shaped elements frame the face. The upper arms and wrists are adorned with bands. Like the other tenoned monuments, the arms are bent at the sides below the head, but in Monument G they clasp a pectoral with flanges to either side of a raised central element. The musculature of the arms is modeled in the typical swelling volumes of Olmec sculpture, and incision is employed to indicate hair on the back of the head falling to the neck. The carving of the fragmentary Monument R is similar, and it possesses arm bands and the traces of a down-turned mouth, but its clenched fists grasp nothing (Porter 1989:plate 26, figs. 26–28).[2] Were it not for their horizontal tenons, these two carvings would fit comfortably in a Middle Preclassic assemblage. The fully human tenoned bust of Panatlan Monument 1 (Fuente's [1973:308–309] catalogue no. 247, "unknown provenience") is similar to Monument R in the way its back expands toward the shoulders, neck, and upward-projecting head (Fuente 1973:plate 245; Porter 1989:187, plate 56). The feline La Providencia Monument 1 (Figure 5.17) seems related in theme to Monuments G and R, although the overall style of carving appears more blocky, possibly an effect of the many angular fractures that mar its features.

The bulbous features of the face of Monument F (Figure 5.18) diverge more from typical Olmec canons, but nevertheless seem related in their smooth, rounded contours. The top of the head projects less from the horizontal plane of the tenon, and less attention is paid to the modeling of the arms. The modeling of the arms of Monument 19 is similar, although the musculature of the back is also indicated, and the face and

most of the head are missing (Figure 5.19). Also in this group of tenoned busts is Monument 43, with similarly positioned arms (Pool 1997). Porter (1989:19) comments that La Venta Monument 56 is an example of his stylistic Group 3, to which he also assigns Monument F, although he places Tres Zapotes Monuments G, R, 19, and 27 in his more extensively modified Group 4.

Quite different from these is the severely angular Hueyapan de Mimendez Monument 1, which resembles an anthropomorphic metate (Figure 5.20). Also unusual is Tres Zapotes Monument 29, rendered in an angular fashion but apparently meant to be set vertically; it has an abstract, curving design in place of a face (Porter 1989:fig. 36). Tlapacoya Monument 1 is likewise a vertical tenoned monument with zoomorphic form, but the crude carving is less angular (Stirling 1943b:plate 15b). Vertical tenoned monuments are particularly rare. La Venta Monument 56, for example, is currently set vertically, but its original intended position is unknown (Fuente 1973:104).

Still in the tradition of sculpture in the round, but apparently restricted to Tres Zapotes and its environs, are flexed arms, possibly components of composite sculptures. Tres Zapotes Monument O and Monument P (Figure 5.21) were found together in the Arroyo Hueyapan, where they had evidently fallen from a low mound on the east bank and have become heavily worn by the flowing water. Stirling (1943b:24–25) cautiously described these two monuments as U-shaped pieces of basalt with a stone "web" in the inner curve and a short cylindrical piece attached to the longer segment. Comparison with the monument found in a mound group at La Puente leaves little doubt that they were carved to represent human arms (Porter 1989:22; Stirling 1943b:26, plate 13a). Monument 25, found near O and P several years later, is likewise heavily smoothed by water. Porter (1989:135, plate 33) regards it as a large, unfinished head with a short tenon. Porter included all these monuments in his Group 4, suggesting a late Middle Preclassic date. Their ornamentation and flexed position are also reminiscent of the arms on the tenoned busts Monuments G and R. The lack of context for these

figure 5.16
Tres Zapotes Monument G: (a) three-quarter view; (b) frontal view. (Photographs by the author.)

figure 5.17
La Providencia Monument 1. (Photograph by the author.)

figure 5.18
Tres Zapotes Monument F. (Photograph by the author.)

figure 5.19
Tres Zapotes Monument 19. (Photograph by the author.)

figure 5.20
Hueyapan de Mimendez
Monument 1. (Photograph
by the author.)

figure 5.21
Tres Zapotes Monuments O and P. (Photograph by the author.)

pieces and the absence of comparable sculptures from other sites make their dating particularly uncertain.

Reliefs and Plain Monuments: Stelae, Boxes, and Basins

The carved stelae of Tres Zapotes present a reasonably clear sequence from Stela A and the recently discovered fragment Stela F, through Stela D to Stela C. Coe's (1965b:773) oft-repeated contention that Stela A (Figure 5.4) is an Izapan monument is based on a highly inaccurate drawing published by Stirling (1943b:fig. 3), as Graham (1989:239) and Porter (1989:37–38) both noted. Although the proscenium monument is very heavily weathered and has continued to degrade since it was discovered, it is clearly Olmec in theme and presentation. The central figure, carved in very high relief, sports a tall headdress, much like the principal figure on La Venta Stela 2 (Stirling 1943b:plate 34). Figures carved in low incised relief flank the central figure, a technique that calls to mind not only the carving on La Venta Stela 2 but also the earlier relief carving of figures on the sides of altar-thrones with half-round figures at San Lorenzo and La Venta (see Chapter 6). Stirling's (1943b:11–14) description and the accompanying drawing indicated that the figure on the observer's right held a severed human head, and this trait formed the basis for Coe's identification of the stela as Izapan. As Porter (1989:38) correctly observed, however, the postulated "eye" of the severed head is formed by a pebble in the volcanic breccia from which the stela is carved, and the rest of the carving is too indistinct to identify it securely as a head. Other elements are very much Olmec, including the sky-monster mask at the top of the stela and the shark-like, triangular-toothed mask of the underworld monster below. Also distinctly Olmec are the incised-relief carvings of diminutive figures on the right side of the stela, one facing upward and the other downward, which recall similar diminutive beings floating around the human figures on La Venta Stelae 2 and 3. Incised reliefs on the left side of the monument depict a feline and a serpent, which, although not exclusively Olmec, are certainly consistent with Olmec themes. Thus

what is represented here is the ruler as axis mundi or world tree, situated between the underworld and sky, attended by human servants, and watched over by supernatural beings and forces (see Chapter 4). Chronologically, Stela A was most likely carved in the late Middle Preclassic period, as were La Venta Stelae 2 and 3 (Lowe 1989:61), whose iconographic and technical parallels have been noted. In terms of composition, however, the closest parallel to Tres Zapotes Stela A comes from the Pacific piedmont site of Tiltepec, Chiapas, the ceramic assemblage of which corresponds to the 500–200 BC time span (John E. Clark, personal communication 2008; cf. Clark and Pye 2000:230; Milbrath 1979:28, 41, fig. 51; Parsons 1986:18). A date of 500–400 BC for Stela A would accommodate its technical, compositional, and thematic similarities to the La Venta and Tiltepec stelae.

In 2003 my colleagues and I recovered the monument fragment we have named Stela F (Figure 5.22) in a field located east of Group 1 near Mound 111, where we excavated three Middle Preclassic burials. Stela F was carved in high relief, which consisted of removing material around the figure and leaving a raised border around the edge of the monument. Even though the face of the figure has been effaced, the carving is very clearly Olmec, with subtly modeled musculature of the shoulder and arm bordered by the raised outline of a cape.

Also belonging to the late Middle Preclassic period is Monument 33 (Figure 5.23), a carved serpentine column that Millet Cámara (1979) recovered in a basalt-column enclosure. The short serpentine column is carved with the crisscrossing lines of a mat design and has a cleft in its upper extremity, thereby combining symbols of political and ideological authority. Interred upright in a perforated slab set on a low platform at the heart of the Middle Preclassic center, the column is another clear representation of the axis mundi. Several lines of evidence point to a late Middle Preclassic date for Monument 33. Most strikingly, the form of the basalt enclosure and the carving of the serpentine columns recall monuments and practices from Phase IV at La Venta. In addition, the platform lies stratigraphically below levels containing ceramic

figure 5.22
Tres Zapotes Stela F.
(Photograph by the author.)

types consistent with the Late Preclassic Hueyapan phase, including fine paste, black and white, and "imitation black and white with orange rims" (Millet Cámara 1979:65–69; cf. Ortíz 1975). Below the platform Millet Cámara (1979:45–53) encountered an offering containing the disarticulated bones of a spider monkey, howler monkey, and several other species of mammals and birds wrapped in bark as well as a jadeite celt, a serpentine petalloid celt, and a pseudo-celt of petrified wood (my personal observation; cf. Millet Cámara 1979:49).

Other items associated with the offering included a perforated shark's tooth and two pieces of cinnabar. The two brushed (*rastreado*) jars associated with the offering are not particularly diagnostic (Ortíz 1975:gráfica 1), but the squat shape, collared rim, medium paste, and tan surface color of a third jar are consistent with the Middle Preclassic Palangana phase pottery from San Lorenzo (Coe and Diehl 1980:203–208, figs. 180y–d′, especially 180b′). Furthermore, the depth of the platform, 175–225 cm below the surface, corresponds to Middle Preclassic deposits we excavated about 25 m to the south.

Stela D (Figure 5.5) has been identified as Izapan (Coe 1965b:773), with somewhat more justification than Stela A. Like Stela A, Stela D is a proscenium monument with three figures arranged in a niche surmounted by a monster mask. The softly rounded contours of the relief carving are very different from the plano-relief style of most Izapa stelae. Nevertheless, the use of the monster's maw to frame the figures recalls Izapa Miscellaneous Monument 2 (Norman 1976:figs. 5.25 and 5.26) and a niche figure from Tiltepec (Norman 1976:fig. 5.27). The depiction of a two-headed serpent hanging from the monster's mouth likewise resembles both Izapan and earlier Olmec monuments. Also reflecting participation in a Late Preclassic transisthmian communication network are the inclusion of a downward-facing figure at the top of the scene and long-lipped serpent profiles on the sides of the monument (Taube 1995:fig. 13), as well as the overall narrative composition. What looks like a double column of glyphs appears between the headdresses of the central and left figures (cf. Porter 1989:59), but the details are too effaced to determine the affiliation of the writing system.

Stela C (Figures 5.8 and 5.24) is the most precisely dated of Tres Zapotes's monuments with a Long Count date of 7.16.6.16.18 6 Etznab securely placed in 32 BC (Coe 1957; Stirling 1940a), although there is some discussion at to whether the precise date would be September 3 or twenty days earlier on August 17 (John Justeson, personal communication 2006). Stela C, however, dramatically illustrates how the longevity of a monument extends beyond its initial carving. As is well known, Stela C was broken in antiquity, and the lower of the two parts so far recovered was reset on its side behind a circular altar (Altar 1) at the north end of Plaza B in Group 3 (Stirling 1940a:1, figs. 1 and 2). Stirling (1940a) does not provide detailed information about ceramics associated with Stela C that would help date its resetting. In 1997, however, my colleagues and I excavated Monument 44, a plain stela set approximately 20 m south of Stela C on the plaza centerline. An associated offering of a

figure 5.23
Tres Zapotes Monument 33, a carved serpentine column. (Photograph by the author.)

differentially fired bowl covered by a plate of the same ware yielded a radiocarbon date of 1870 ± 50 BP (2σ cal AD 55–250). This date is also compatible with the changing patterns of diagnostic pottery distributions in and around Group 3, which indicate that Plaza B was maintained free of refuse during the Protoclassic Nextepetl phase (Pool 2008). It therefore provides a reasonable estimate for the establishment of Plaza B and, by extension, the setting of Stela C. Another plain monument, Stela B, was found in Group 3, "about 25 yards southeast of Mound C" (Stirling 1943b:14). Depending upon one's interpretation of Weiant's (1943) Map 3, this could place it on the south end of Plaza B.

Early discussions of Stela C focused on the reconstruction of its Cycle 7 date and whether the date was contemporaneous with its carving or referred to an earlier event (Coe 1957; Morley 1946; Stirling 1940a; Thompson 1941). The argument over the Cycle 7 date was effectively settled when radiocarbon dates showed Olmec culture to be older than Stela C. This relatively late age for Stela C was corroborated much later when its missing top piece was found, also in Group 3, in 1970 (Beverido Pereau 1987; Porter 1989; Pugh 1981). One of the early arguments in favor of the contemporaneity of the date with its carving was the presence of the monster-mask panel on the opposite (obverse) face of the monument. Interestingly, Stirling (1940a:4) noted that the mask panel was more severely weathered than the reverse, but he explained the differential weathering by suggesting that the monument had lain on its back for a long time before it was reset. That is, he used the heavy erosion of the obverse face to argue for the antiquity of the monument in general. In fact, one might just as well argue that the date was inscribed substantially after the derived Olmec-style earth monster-mask panel, from which a profile head emerges amidst the curving branches on the upper fragment—a powerful image of a ruler as axis mundi (Figures 5.8 and 5.24).[3] I do not mean to argue that Stela C began its life as a Middle Preclassic Olmec monument, but that its obverse might well have been carved much earlier in the Late Preclassic than the Long Count date. Graham (2005) has also called attention to differences in the relief carving of the Long Count date and the scratchy incision of the accompanying

figure 5.24
Tres Zapotes Stela C, obverse, upper section. (Photograph by the author.)

text, questioning whether they might also have been carved at different times. Graham's question is well put, but I would point out that the Etznab day sign at the base of the Long Count is carved in a similar manner to the rest of the text, which is also incised into raised columns. Thus the history of Stela C may have begun with the carving of the obverse axis mundi scene sometime in the Preclassic after 400 BC, then the inscription of the Long Count and accompanying isthmian text in 32 BC, after which it was broken and its pieces separated, with one piece eventually reset perhaps two centuries later.

Stela E may also have been recarved. When it was found, this smooth slab retained a fragment of incised-relief carving on one side, possibly in an Izapan-related style. Stirling (1943b:16) surmised that the stela had been broken off just above the portion that was intended to be set in the ground, but his photograph (Stirling 1943b:plate 7c) seems to show a fragment that had been reworked along its edge, destroying most of an earlier carving, and thereby creating a plain stela from a previously carved one. Stirling's description suggests that Stela E was found on Cerro Rabón (Porter 1989). In 1995, my colleagues and I recorded on Cerro Rabón another well-worked stone slab, Monument 42, which might well have functioned as a plain stela (Pool 1997:fig. 13). Other possible plain stelae are Monuments 38 and 39, found with other stones used to reinforce a modern well southwest of the Ranchito Group. Plain stelae, of course, are difficult to date without contextual information, but it is worth noting that they are common

figure 5.25
Tres Zapotes
Monument 39.
(Photograph by
the author.)

in Late Preclassic sites in southern Chiapas and Guatemala (see Chapter 7).

Several stone monuments from Tres Zapotes apparently functioned as containers. Most obvious are two large stone boxes, Monuments B and C. Monument C (Figure 5.7) is the better known because of its elaborately carved scenes of figures struggling among scrolls, representing either water (Smith 1984) or clouds (Coe 1965b). Not only the dramatic scene, which incorporates long-lipped gods among the scrolls, but also the plano-relief carving make this the most Izapan-like monument at Tres Zapotes. Monument B is fragmentary but was apparently uncarved (Stirling 1943b:plate 7a). A possibly related form is represented by Monument 39 (Figure 5.25), a semirectangular slab with a thinned border, which could have served as a cover for a stone box, similar to the function suggested for San Lorenzo Monuments 21 and 58 (Coe and Diehl 1980:figs. 452 and 433; Cyphers 2004b:123, figs. 41 and 72; Fuente 1973:110; Graham 1989:245). Stone boxes or sarcophagi are known from La Venta (Monument 6, late Middle Preclassic [Stirling 1943b:plate 47a,b]), San Lorenzo (Monument 8, Early Preclassic [see Cyphers 2004b:37–38; see also Coe and Diehl 1980:fig. 432]), and Laguna de los Cerros (Monuments B and F [Gillespie 2000:101–102, fig. 5]). Monument C, however, is clearly of Late Preclassic vintage, and the similar form and proportions of Monument B suggest a similar age. Later stone boxes have been found in highland Guatemala (see Chapter 10).

Monument B was found on a low platform east of the Burnt Mounds group about 3 m from Monument D, a barrel-shaped stone with a basin-like depression at the top (Stirling 1943b:17, 21, plate 10b). Another cylindrical stone basin, Monument N (Stirling 1943b:24, plate 10a), was recovered outside Tres Zapotes proper, near the seated were-jaguar figure, Monument M. Monument 40, a biconically perforated cylinder (Figure 5.26), was found with Monuments 38 and 39 among the stones supporting the side of a modern well. A stone cylinder was also recovered from San Lorenzo (Monument 39 [Coe and

figure 5.26
Tres Zapotes Monument 40. (Photograph by the author.)

Diehl 1980:348, figs. 474 and 475]), but the form of the perforation is cylindrical rather than biconical, and its walls are much thinner than those of Tres Zapotes Monument 40. More similar is Monument 14 of La Venta, which was recovered in the excavation of Mound A-3 (Drucker 1943:71, fig. 21, plate 12b). Although the perforation of Monument 14 is also cylindrical, the walls are thicker, and the end was fitted with a stone plug to allow the cylinder to function as a basin. It was set upright on the surface of the red clay mound and covered with drift sands, indicating a very late Middle Preclassic setting. Although we cannot be sure of the date of the original shaping of the cylinders at Tres Zapotes, their contexts and associations suggest that most were set in place during the Late Preclassic period or later.

Summary

All in all, stylistic comparisons suggest that the Tres Zapotes monuments were carved over a long period, beginning early in the Middle Preclassic and continuing at least through the Late Preclassic (Table 5.1). The Middle Preclassic monuments, particularly the colossal heads and stelae, evince a focus on the ruler as an individual as well as a concern with mythicoreligious themes. In the Late Preclassic, however, such representations appear to have been much scarcer at Tres Zapotes. The obverse of Stela C (Figures 5.8 and 5.24), for example, appears to illustrate the role of the ruler as the conduit between underworld and sky, but not the individual person of the ruler. Unfortunately, we do not know what the inscription on the reverse states, although John S. Justeson (personal communication 2003) and Malmström (1997:141–144) tie the date to astronomical events. An exception to the rule of Late Preclassic monuments not depicting individuals is Stela D (Figure 5.5), with its apparent representation of a person in obeisance to a ruler. It was found in an outlying mound group, away from Tres Zapotes proper. Other Late Preclassic and Protoclassic monuments in the lower Papaloapan Valley, such as La Mojarra Stela 1, El Mesón Stelae 1 and 2, and the Alvarado stela, likewise appear to emphasize the personal authority of rulers. In Tres Zapotes, however, the absence of personal representations in the Late Preclassic sculptural corpus is consistent with a confederation in which individual authority was subsumed to a more communal governmental practice at the polity level.

The carving of Tres Zapotes monuments was not the last meaningful event in these sculptures' history. Rather, as the biography of Stela C illustrates, monuments were reused, reset, and sometimes reshaped in ways that conferred new meanings upon them and the spaces they occupied. As I discuss in the remainder of this chapter, the creation of a polity was not just an abstract act of social reorganization but also a concrete exercise in placemaking.

Polity and Placemaking at Tres Zapotes

My analysis of political placemaking at Tres Zapotes draws on Smith's (2003:154) characterization of a polity as "a horizon of action, a field of political practices that produce boundaries, frontiers and places steeped in memories within a landscape that aspires to cohere as a locale of sovereign authority" and as "a political landscape defined through the practical relationship of regime and subjects" (Smith 2003:160). Particularly relevant to the following analysis is Smith's (2003:181–182) argument that "what establishes the polity are certain configurations of political practice established through the experience, perception, and imagination of landscapes that (1) regularize demands of regimes on subjects and (2) legitimate these demands in reference to both senses of place and the proper world order."

Smith's observations resonate strongly with the importance of place and history shared by the inhabitants of Mesoamerica in indigenous concepts of polity. For example, Berdan (2008:108–109) argues that place and common history were fundamental factors in the formation of group identity in Late Postclassic Central Mexico, particularly with regard to forging the basic unit of political organization, the *altepetl* (often glossed as "city-state"). Also resonant is the emphasis Smith gives to architectural spaces and sculptural monuments as practices to imprint "experience, perception, and imagination" on the landscape, although his examples come from Anatolia and Mesopotamia rather than Mesoamerica. The identification of sacred landscapes defined by monuments, places of offerings, and temples is now well advanced in Mesoamerican studies (e.g., Ortíz and Rodríguez 2000; Reilly 1994b; Tate 1999; Townsend 1992), and many of these authors comment on the relationship between the sacred and the political in their reconstructions. That relationship is especially notable in the Preclassic literature (e.g., Cyphers 1999; Grove 1999).

Placemaking in the Olmec Center of Tres Zapotes

Undoubtedly, the Early Preclassic inhabitants of Tres Zapotes defined it as a place, distinct from others, through the normal practices of living there, including the construction of houses and the burial of their dead. However, the creation of Tres Zapotes as a place of political authority—an administrative center—apparently occurred over the course of the Middle Preclassic, and it was materialized from an early time with carvings of rulers' portraits represented by Monuments A

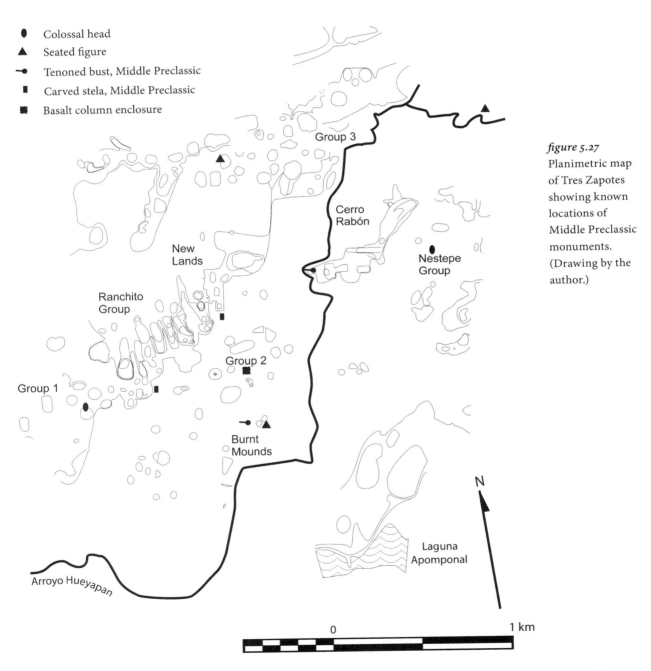

figure 5.27 Planimetric map of Tres Zapotes showing known locations of Middle Preclassic monuments. (Drawing by the author.)

and Q.[4] It is likely that these monuments were reset during the Late Preclassic period (Pool 2008), as discussed below. Nevertheless, if these colossal heads did remain near their original locations, it is interesting that they are located on the edges of the Middle Preclassic site (Figure 5.27). That is, they seem to mark the perimeter of the center, perhaps announcing the entrance to the heart of the Olmec polity. Similarly, three of the colossal heads at La Venta were placed at the northern edge of the ceremonial zone (see Chapter 6; Grove 1999:267, 275). Consequently, it seems possible that before the end of the Middle Preclassic the colossal heads had acquired a meaning different from that assigned to those at San Lorenzo, not just as rulers and their ancestors, but as icons and guardians of the polity.

In contrast, five of the monuments that can be attributed to the late Middle Preclassic are concentrated at the center of Tres Zapotes as it then existed. It was at about that time that the local zapoteños began to construct clay platforms like the one encountered in Unit 12, dating between 780 and 400 BC. In the heart of their capital, rulers erected the basalt-column sanctuary with its serpentine column representing the world tree at its center. Middle Preclassic rulers also represented themselves in less abstract form as individuals by means of relief-carved stelae, and they apparently placed these monuments outside the core of their capital but not as distant as the colossal heads. The number of Middle Preclassic monuments at Tres Zapotes is small, and future discoveries may well change the current perspective. Nevertheless, it is not difficult to see a spatial pattern related to the themes of these monuments, with the portraits of ancient rulers guarding the periphery of the capital, the stelae of late Middle Preclassic rulers arrayed around the ceremonial center, and the sanctuary of the serpentine column at the center of everything. The distributions of other Olmec figures, both human and supernatural, do not present a clear pattern, but the spatial arrangement of the serpentine column, the stelae, and the colossal heads emerges as a powerful act in the creation of Tres Zapotes as the capital of an Olmec polity.

Placemaking in the Epi-Olmec Center of Tres Zapotes

Of course, the creation of places of power continued as Tres Zapotes grew during the Late Preclassic period. The epi-Olmec inhabitants of Tres Zapotes incorporated some of the old monuments into their new spaces, which they also defined through the setting of new monuments and, especially, through configurations of formal architecture. Elsewhere I have reported in detail on the configurations of plaza groups at Tres Zapotes (Pool 2008). Here I simply underscore contrasts with the Middle Preclassic architectural arrangements.

The four plaza groups at Tres Zapotes shared a basic and distinctive plan, which consisted of a pyramidal or conical temple platform on the east, a long administrative-residential platform on the north, and an adoratorio on the central axis of the large, open plaza. To this basic plan additional temples and other platforms were often added; for example, the plaza of Group 3 was reoriented in the Protoclassic period. Furthermore, the long platforms and some of the old Olmec monuments were arranged in a consistent manner. The long mound of Group 2 was erected opposite the sanctuary of the serpentine column, and the colossal heads gazed toward the long mounds of Group 1 and the Nestepe Group. It is likely that the colossal heads were repositioned to correspond better to the new platforms, but that was not possible with the sanctuary in Group 2, whose tall basalt column perimeter would still have been visible in the Late Preclassic. In each case, the relationship between the long platform and the Olmec monument defined an administrative axis that contrasted with the ceremonial axis defined by temples and adoratories. The portraits of more recent Olmec rulers on stelae and such possible Olmec monuments as the tenoned Monument G, however, received less reverential treatment: their faces were deliberately destroyed.

Other monuments attributable to the Late Preclassic and Protoclassic periods tend to be associated with the platforms and open spaces of the plaza groups as well as other groups dispersed around the site (Figure 5.28). For example, the stone box, Monument C, was set at the central point at the base of the Long Mound in Group 2 (Stirling 1943b:18), opposite the sanctuary. Whether Monument C once contained a dedicatory offering, the blood of sacrifices, or the remains of a ruler is unknown. Tenoned monuments do appear to be associated with mounds, consistent with their hypothetical use as architectural embellishments, but only Monument 19 was recovered from within a formal plaza group (Group 1; Porter 1989:125).

The Protoclassic use of monuments to define political and ceremonial space at Tres Zapotes is

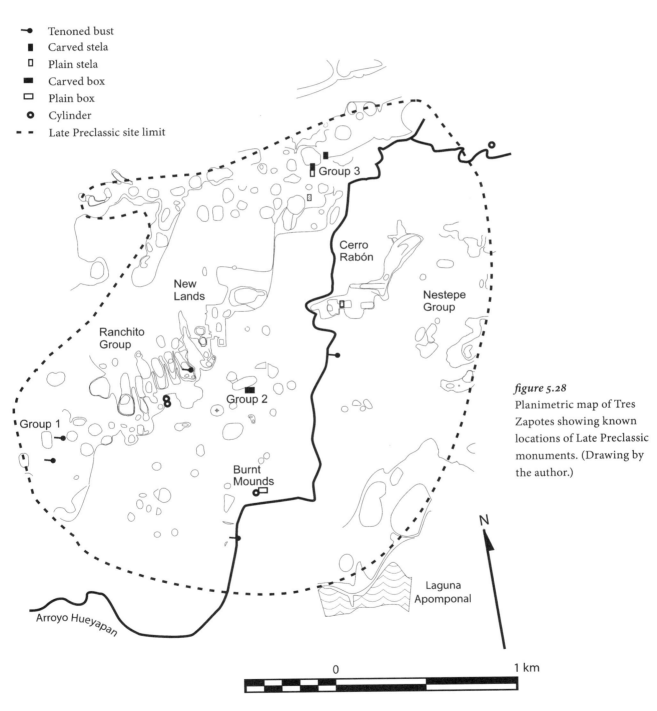

figure 5.28
Planimetric map of Tres Zapotes showing known locations of Late Preclassic monuments. (Drawing by the author.)

particularly evident in Plaza B of Group 3, where the leaders embarked on a construction plan that violated the old spatial order of the Tres Zapotes Plaza Group (Pool 2008; Sullivan 2002). Long after it was originally carved, a fragment of Stela C was set on its side behind a circular altar, and a rough slab (Monument 44) was set a few meters to the south. By this time, the carving and text on Stela C had apparently lost its original significance, although the isthmian script continued in use elsewhere in the southern and south-central Gulf Coast lowlands, as at La Mojarra and the San Andres Tuxtla vicinity. Instead, at Tres Zapotes in Group 3, it was the setting of the stones themselves and the accompanying offerings that defined the long axis of a new plaza with a new orientation.

Concluding Remarks

Throughout its Preclassic history, the inhabitants of Tres Zapotes employed stone monuments to represent the relationship among rulers, their subjects, and the cosmos. During the Middle Preclassic period, Olmec rulers commissioned carvings that emphasized their exclusionary strategies aimed at monopolizing sources of material and ideological power. By the close of the Middle Preclassic, with Tres Zapotes flourishing as a regional center, they reinforced that message with colossal heads, stelae, and a carved column of exotic greenstone in a sanctuary ringed with basalt columns that was positioned to emphasize the concentration of authority at the very heart of the polity. In the Late Preclassic period, however, growing factional competition, likely exacerbated by the breakdown of prestige-good networks, forced changes in politicoeconomic strategies at Tres Zapotes. The apparent solution to the threat of political fragmentation was to share power among factions

ruling from the plaza groups of Tres Zapotes (Pool 2008). New monuments were created that emphasized the office of rulership rather than the person of the ruler. Some old monuments that smacked too much of personal political power were defaced, and others were incorporated into the plans of newly built plaza groups in a manner that acknowledged the ancient political authority of Tres Zapotes but balanced power among its leaders. Ultimately, as the governing coalition began to weaken in the Protoclassic and factional leaders began to reassert their individuality, new building and plaza constructions redefined and challenged old spatial orders, and the old stones of Tres Zapotes were broken and reset to give meaning to the newly created spaces.

Acknowledgments

Fieldwork at Tres Zapotes was supported by grants from the National Science Foundation (SBR-9405063, SBR-9615031, and BCS-0242555), which were administered by the University of Kentucky and Ithaca College. The Instituto Nacional de Antropología e Historia (INAH) of Mexico issued field permits. Since its inception, the Tres Zapotes Project has benefited from the kind assistance of the staff at the Centro INAH, Veracruz, and the Tres Zapotes Museum. I particularly thank the directors, past and present, of Centro INAH, Veracruz, Arqueólogo Fernando Pérez Vignola and Antropólogo Jacinto Daniel Goeritz. I am also most thankful to John E. Clark, Julia Guernsey, and Barbara Arroyo for inviting me to participate in the Dumbarton Oaks Pre-Columbian symposium and for providing thoughtful suggestions for improving this chapter. The responsibility for all errors of fact or interpretation, however, lie squarely with me.

1. The documented examples are Cabeza Group Mound E (Group 1, Mound 5) red clay platform, about 1 m (Weiant 1943:6); Arroyo Group (Group 2) altar and platform, about 180 cm (Millet Cámara 1979); Group 2, Unit 12 gray clay cap, about 80 cm (Pool et al. 2010).

2. Porter (1989:123–124) identified this monument as Tres Zapotes Monument 18, which, in his numeration, should correspond to Tres Zapotes Monument R in Fuente's (1973:306) catalogue. Fuente's description of the dimensions and appearance of Monument R is sufficiently similar to Porter's description and illustrations of Monument 18 to leave little doubt they are the same monument (cf. Porter 1989:179–181).

3. This interpretation is not inconsistent with an identification of Stela C as a personification of maize or as a maize god (e.g., Taube 1996:57). As Reilly (1995:39) argues, "the world tree has reptilian as well as maize associations," particularly as represented on Olmec celts from Río Pesquero and other sites. Taube (2000a:303) builds on Reilly's observation, arguing that La Venta Monuments 25/26, 27, 58, and 66 portrayed "images of the Olmec Maize God" and represented "embodiments of the central world tree."

4. Stirling (1955:20) first argued that Olmec colossal heads were portraits of prominent individuals. Citing the overall realism of the heads and the individuality of their facial features, expressions, headdresses, and ear ornaments, most scholars agree with Stirling and regard these massive monuments as portraits of Olmec rulers (see Grove 1981:61).

6

The Architectural Setting of Olmec Sculpture Clusters at La Venta, Tabasco

REBECCA B. GONZÁLEZ LAUCK

THE OLMEC CITY OF LA VENTA, TABASCO, holds a unique place in the ancient history of Middle America. Its great antiquity (1200–400 BC), monumental earthen architecture, and impressive stone sculptures are a few of La Venta's outstanding features. The sculptures are most extraordinary because of their quantity, great thematic variety, and impressive scale. Considering that the stone source for these massive sculptures was more than 80 km distant (Heizer 1966; Williams and Heizer 1965:18–20, maps 1 and 2), the significance of importing these stone monuments to La Venta becomes all the more awesome.

Because La Venta's corpus of stone sculpture is one of its exceptional features, it has been subjected to myriad studies and interpretations by different specialists in the course of the past eight decades (Bernal 1969; Clewlow 1974; Coe 1965a; Drucker 1952; Drucker et al. 1959; Fuente 1973, 1977; Gillespie 2008; González Lauck 1994, 2004; Heizer 1967; Milbrath 1979; Ochoa and Jaime 2000; Piña

Chan 1982, 1989; Porter 1992; Reilly 1990, 1994b, 1995, 1999, 2002; Stirling 1943b, 1968; Tate and Bendersky 1999). These studies have contributed to understanding Olmec art and, for the most part, they share the common denominator of treating each sculpture individually, that is, segregated from its sculptural and architectural context. In contrast to most previous studies, I propose to look at La Venta sculptures as clusters of monuments, as they were found in situ.[1] Special attention is paid to four considerations: (1) the placement of stone monuments in the architectural layout of this ancient city, (2) the repetition of themes in each group or cluster of sculptures, (3) the relationship in terms of size and proportion of each sculpture in its display group, and (4) the different raw materials involved. Interesting patterns emerge when this information is combined, indicating that sculpture was used as a sophisticated visual language whose messages are still, for the most part, undeciphered.

A Brief History of the Architecture and Sculpture at La Venta

The current data on La Venta's stone sculptures and the site's earthen architecture are inconsistent and incomplete. During the first three decades (1925–1955) of scientific research at the site, most of the architectural information was presented as a series of partial sketch maps (Blom and La Farge 1926:84, fig. 68; Drucker 1952:7, fig. 1). The exception was La Venta's ceremonial precinct (Complex A), which was partially excavated (Drucker 1952; Drucker et al. 1959; Stirling 1943a, 1955; Stirling and Stirling 1942) and provided rich architectural data as well as material for a detailed map (Drucker et al. 1959:fig. 4; González Lauck 2007:49). It is fortunate that the University of California at Berkeley project at La Venta, directed by Robert Heizer, carefully mapped this part of the site, because it was subsequently nearly completely destroyed (Heizer et al. 1968:139). During the Berkeley project, the unearthing of stone sculptures was a significant component of the work undertaken. Forty-two monuments, whole and fragmented, were reported, including colossal heads, altars, and some of the stelae discussed below (Blom and La Farge 1926:79–90; Drucker 1952:173–184; Drucker et al. 1959; Heizer et al. 1968; Stirling 1943b:48–60; for a summary, see González Lauck 2004:tables 1 and 2). The map that best exemplifies this period of emphasis on sculpture was published in the report detailing the 1955 field excavations (Drucker et al. 1959:fig. 2). On this map, the symbols representing the sculptures are about the same size as those for the architectural elements, perhaps an unconscious acknowledgment of the importance of sculpture in the research programs of that time vis-à-vis the monumental earthen architecture.

Beginning in the 1950s and continuing for the following three decades, the archaeological site of La Venta underwent radical alterations. The scattered dwellings of twelve families said to have been living at La Venta prior to the 1940s—amidst a lush tropical forest environment—were transformed into a densely packed settlement of 17,000 inhabitants by 1985 (Correa Villanueva et al. 1986:49). The principal causes of this population growth were the establishment of a petroleum processing facility at the southern edge of La Venta, the exploration and exploitation of the oil resources in the region, and the construction of the infrastructure (such as an airstrip, roads, streets, private and public buildings) that accompanied these activities. The extent of the damage to the archaeological remains is unknown, because the most complete map of the site was rendered in 1985 (González Lauck 1988). A conservative estimate is that fifty percent of the architectural remains were modified or destroyed in this period of rapid growth.

In terms of sculpture, today there are seventy-three carved stone sculptures identified as being from La Venta. In addition, there are seventeen stone artifacts that are not sculptures per se but that were classified as "monuments" in the various La Venta sculpture catalogues, as well as hundreds of basalt columns and blocks and a few green-colored columns, all with architectural functions. Most of these monuments and other stone artifacts were removed from the site in 1957–1958 to "protect" them from the above-described modern construction projects. These "protected" monuments are displayed in two state museums in Villahermosa. Unfortunately, close to fifty of these sculptures are exhibited in an open-air park exposed to the elements (González Lauck and Solís Olguín 1996:152; Ochoa and Jaime 2000). The original locations of a third of these La Venta sculptures are unknown, because they were unearthed and removed from the site without proper archaeological supervision or recording (González Lauck 2004:81, tables 1–3). This situation might help explain why years later it was claimed that "Olmec sculpture can be dealt with separately, since it has little connection to architecture" (Bernal 1969:55).

Despite this distressing attitude, the architecture and sculpture that survived the modern devastation provide some information about how monuments were displayed in relationship to earthen platforms and plazas. The vestiges of earthen mounds in this ancient Olmec city form north-south rows of rectangular buildings (Figure 6.1). Between these rows, avenue-like spaces and plazas were created; on the east-west axis there

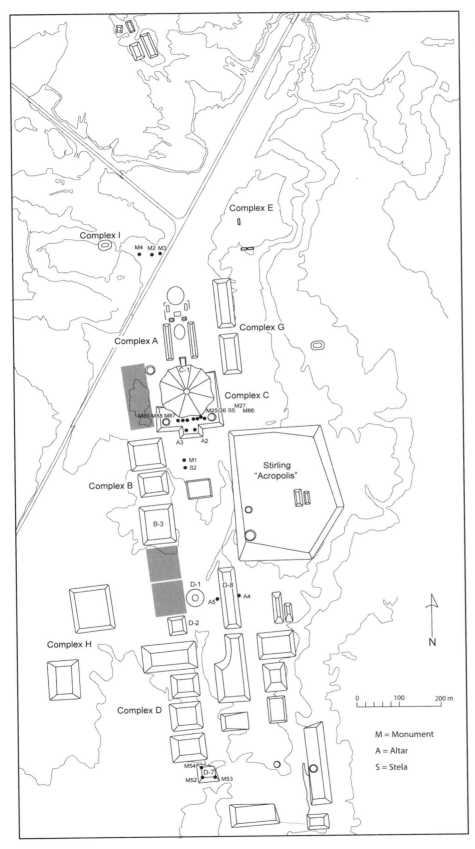

figure 6.1
Architectural layout of
La Venta, showing the
locations of sculptures
discussed in the text.
(Drawing from the New
World Archaeological
Foundation based on a map
by Proyecto Arqueológico
La Venta, Instituto Nacional
de Antropología e Historia.)

Complex E

Complex I

M4 M2 M3

Complex G

Complex A

C-1

Complex C

M25/26 S5 M27 M86

M89 M88 M87

A3 A2

Stirling "Acropolis"

M1
S2

Complex B

B-3

D-1 D-8
A5 A4

D-2

Complex H

Complex D

M54
D-7
M52 M53

0 100 200 m

N

M = Monument
A = Altar
S = Stela

The Architectural Setting of Olmec Sculpture Clusters at La Venta, Tabasco   131 are street-like spaces, a few of which cut across the width of the site. The traffic flow among the public buildings seems to have been extremely well planned and regulated. The architectural bilateral symmetry, for which Complex A is famous (see Drucker et al. 1959), does not extend across the rest of the site. Nevertheless, there is a certain harmonious equilibrium in the way the buildings were laid out, creating open public spaces—such as the 4 ha plaza south of Complex C—in addition to secluded and private areas, of which the north "courtyard" of Complex A is the best example.

For my purposes in this chapter, a partial reconstruction of what may be referred to as the western row of buildings is necessary (Figure 6.1). These buildings might not have composed the westernmost row in the original site plan, because there is evidence of possible additional rows farther west, as indicated by the presence of the structures in Complex H. My reconstruction of the western row of platforms is based on the following observations: (1) architectural vestiges can still be appreciated on the surface, (2) information provided by the pioneering archaeologists who sometimes misidentified mounds as "small hills," "knolls," and "low ridges" (see Drucker et al. 1959:1), and (3) oral reports describing the destruction of mounds in the period between 1950 and 1980. To the south, this row begins with Structure D-7, a platform a bit off-center from the rest of the mounds in this row. To the north of it are five platforms of different sizes and shapes that form part of Complex D. To the west of Structure D-1, north of Structure D-2, and south of Structure B-3 is an area that today is occupied by modern houses and an elementary school, which was built between 1960 and 1970. Oral reports indicate that two mounds, indicated by shaded squares in Figure 6.1, were leveled to build the school.

The row of buildings continues to the north with the three platforms of Complex B. To the north of the northernmost platform in Complex B and directly west of Complex C the topography indicates another large mound, again indicated by a shaded rectangle. This area was one of the most densely inhabited sectors of the site in the mid-1980s, occupied by locals during the three decades of destruction. Because of this residential activity, it is presumed that the platform was basically leveled, even though one can still appreciate what might be its contours on the surface and in a 1985 aerial photographic restitution map (González Lauck 1987).

Continuing to the north, the 1968 map of La Venta (Heizer et al. 1968:end map) indicates a circular structure slightly off the northwest corner of Complex C. This mound was not found when the site was surveyed and remapped in 1984. The 1968 map also indicated a similar structure off the northeast corner of Complex C but, instead of locating it, the two rectangular mounds of Complex G that lie directly to the east of Complex A were identified in 1984. Based on the harmonious placement of the earthen mounds in the architectural layout of this ancient Olmec city, I presume that structures similar to those of Complex G were found to the west of Complex A—in alignment with the row of buildings that form the southern tip of Complex D. These presumed mounds would have been destroyed when the airstrip, road, and streets were laid out with bulldozers in the late 1950s. Because Monuments 19, 20, and 21 appeared when this part of La Venta was leveled (Drucker et al. 1959:197), it seems that mounds were most certainly destroyed during the leveling process. This conclusion is reinforced by the present-day recognition of the frequently symbiotic relationship between sculpture and architecture in ancient La Venta and other contemporaneous Olmec sites (see Chapters 3–5).

If my reconstruction is correct, the row of buildings initiated by Structure D-7 in the southern sector of the site would have continued for a distance of about 1,400 m. This proposed reconstruction is not far-fetched, considering that the easternmost row of buildings of the site plan—which includes part of Complex D, the Stirling "Acropolis," and Complex G—measures close to 1,200 m in length.

Clusters of Sculptures

In this chapter I discuss five clusters or groups of sculptures that include sixteen monuments for which there is adequate information about their ancient placement in La Venta's architectural layout. These groups include two pairs of altars, three colossal heads, three monumental human figures, and six stela-like monuments, all of which were associated with specific buildings or architectural spaces. I assume these sculptures were found in their final positions or, in other words, the last positions where the Olmecs placed them. There exists the possibility that these stone monuments were moved by Late Classic squatters at La Venta, but it is improbable, given the size of these sculptures, the patterns of their placement in the site, and their arrangement in each group.

North and South Sculpture Triads: Entryways to the Ancient City?

Two triads of colossal sculptures, one at the north end and the other at the south end, marked the boundaries of the monumental architectural sector of La Venta. The northern group consists of a row of three colossal heads carved in basalt. The southern group consists of representations of human figures carved in sandstone in a crouched or squatting posture and with disproportionately large heads.

Matthew Stirling unearthed the three northern colossal heads, known as Monuments 2, 3, and 4, in 1939 (Figure 6.2). These basalt sculptures were found to the north of the city's ceremonial precinct (Complex A) in an east-west row and facing north (Drucker 1952:9; Stirling 1940b:328–332, 1943b:57–58). The information on possible buildings associated with this group of sculptures is unclear. In the literature, there is an early perplexing reference to "stone foundations" for the sculptures (González Lauck 2004:86). However, in the 1940s sketch maps of the site, there are two "low ridges" to the east of the colossal heads that might have been unrecognized earthen platforms (Drucker 1952:fig. 5). Thus it is possible that there may have been low platforms in association with the three colossal heads. Unfortunately, this area is too disturbed today to be able to confirm this possibility.

If one were to reconstruct the northern entrance to La Venta as it existed 2,500 years ago—at the point where these three colossal heads were placed—the largest head (Monument 4) would

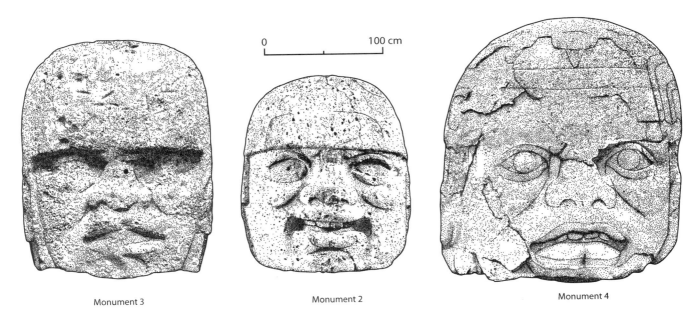

0   100 cm

Monument 3   Monument 2   Monument 4

figure 6.2
La Venta Monuments 3, 2, and 4. (Drawing from the New World Archaeological Foundation based on originals by Hermelando Ramírez Osio.)

have been to the right of a viewer approaching from the north. The smallest head (Monument 2) would have been in the center and the mid-sized one (Monument 3) to the left. These monuments were displayed in an east-west row about 100 m long. These sculptures repeat a variation of the same theme: exaggerated representations of a human head with a tight-fitting helmet. This trio shares the unusual feature on colossal heads of parted lips, as if the individuals are speaking (Monuments 3 and 4) or smiling (Monument 2) (Figure 6.2).

Despite the general thematic similarity, each sculpture differs in size, volume, weight, facial features, helmet insignia, and ear ornaments, indicating a differential reading of each. Monument 4 is by far the largest of the triad, weighing 17.9 tons[2] and measuring 2.20 m high. Its facial features indicate a middle-aged male with thick lips and a broad, flat nose, pronounced cheekbones, and almond-shaped eyes. The insignia on his helmet depict three elements that have been described as feline claws and a series of horizontal and curved bands

running along the sides and back of the head. The one surviving ear ornament is circular with a cross in its interior. Stirling (1943b:58) reported finding a fragment of this head with "a smooth-surfaced dark purplish paint." Monument 2 is the smallest of the triad: it weighs only 10.7 tons and stands 1.71 m in height. Its facial features, similar to those of Monument 4, are those of a young adult male, the difference being that he is smiling. The distinguishing insignia on the helmet is a bifurcated, curved, and elongated element (leaves? feathers?) whose juncture is over the right eye of the figure. The ear ornament is circular, and from it descends a curved pendant. The last sculpture of this group, Monument 3, weighs a little more than 11 tons and measures 2 m in height. Its facial features are eroded and difficult to discern. It does wear a helmet, but no insignia are identifiable. Its ear ornament seems to be a circular disk from which hangs a band.

At the southern end of the site, three monumental human figures carved in reddish sandstone were located (Figure 6.3). One of these monuments

figure 6.3
La Venta Monuments 54, 52, and 53. (Drawing from the New World Archaeological Foundation based on originals by Hermelando Ramírez Osio.)

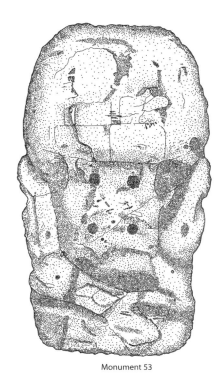

0   100 cm

Monument 54   Monument 52   Monument 53

was initially reported by Blom and La Farge (1926:89, fig. 68) and, later the trio was excavated by Stirling (1968; cf. Drucker 1952:175). Monuments 52, 53, and 54 were again excavated in the 1987 season of the Proyecto Arqueológico La Venta (Gallegos Gómora 1990; González Lauck 1988:150–152). Because these sculptures were left in situ (whereas most were removed from the site in 1957) and this part of the site was not disturbed in the three subsequent decades of residential havoc, it was possible to ascertain that they were found on the surface of Structure D-7.

This earthen platform can be described as U-shaped and is almost 50 m square. Its south slope measures 3.5 m in height, whereas its east and west sides diminish in height, as with a terrace, until they reach the surrounding ground surface at the northern edge. The top of the platform slopes downward toward the north and seems to have been slightly lower in elevation at the middle of the structure, as if there were a sunken patio-like area. This structure seems to be unique at La Venta; likewise, it is not fully aligned with the westernmost row of buildings described previously (González Lauck 1990:59–60).

All the monuments were found lying on their sides: Monument 53 was found at the southeast corner of D-7, Monument 52 at the southwest corner, and Monument 54 at the northeast edge of the same platform (Gallegos Gómora 1990). If their horizontal positions were any indication as to how they were oriented when upright, then Monuments 53 and 52 would have faced south and Monument 54 north. That is, two of the monuments faced outward, similar to the colossal heads at the north, and the other would have faced inward toward the pyramid at the center of the site.

As with the basalt colossal heads, these sandstone sculptures share a single theme. They are massive representations of crouched or squatting human figures with arms raised to touch the bottom edges of their helmets and elbows resting on bent knees. These sculptures are quite eroded: they were carved in sandstone (which erodes more easily than basalt) and were exposed to the elements for more than two millennia. Nonetheless,

it is possible to determine that between sixty and seventy-five percent of each figure consists of the representation of the face and helmet. It is not possible to distinguish distinct facial features or helmet insignia, but one can appreciate the hollows of the eyes, the volume of the noses, and the mouths with the downturned lips. The bodies of the figures are relatively small, yet it is possible to distinguish the frontal and lateral volumes of the bent legs and raised arms. Stirling (1968:35) described Monument 52 as a bust. Tate and Bendersky (1999) argue that these sculptures represent human fetuses.

Because of the eroded condition of this triad, the main discernible difference among the group members is relative size. Monument 53 is one of the largest sculptures at La Venta; it is 3.80 m tall and weighs almost 36 tons.[3] As with the triad of colossal heads to the north, the middle sculpture in the southern triad, Monument 52, is the smallest: it stands 2.60 m high and weighs 14 tons. The midsized sculpture, Monument 54, measures 3.10 m tall and weighs 17 tons.

Similar to the colossal heads to the north, if these massive monuments marked the southern entryway of the site, it would have been awe inspiring to approach by canoe or enter on foot into this ancient Olmec city. Particularly impressive would have been the almost 4 m high Monument 53, perched atop the 3.5 m high Structure D-7, while approximately 40 m to the west on the same platform stood Monument 52 and, at about the same distance to the north, Monument 54 (Figure 6.1).

The Main Pyramidal Edifice and Its Ensemble of Sculptures

The main pyramidal edifice at La Venta, known today as Structure C-1, is the most prominent architectural feature at the site. This landmark of the local landscape can be seen for many kilometers, because not only is it the tallest mound at La Venta, but it was also constructed on the 20 m high natural elevation of the site itself. This earthen structure, 30 m in height, measures 114 m on the east-west axis and 128 m on the north-south axis (González Lauck 1990:51). The surface of its last construction phase dates to ca 400 BC, though the construction history of the building itself has yet to be defined. A basal platform surrounds it on all sides except the north. Excavations on Structure C-1's southern flank revealed a possible central staircase as well as six sculptures, most of them with their tenons embedded in the basal platform. Three of the sculptures, carved of greenish-colored stone, were placed to the east of the stairway, and the remaining three monuments of gray volcanic stone were placed on the western side. All except one were carved in low relief (Figure 6.4; González Lauck 1997).

Four of the sculptures (Monuments 25/26, 27, 88, and 89) repeat a similar theme, and two were placed on each side of the central stairway. Porter (1992) refers to Monuments 25/26 and 27 as "celtiform stelae," implying that they were monumental representations of Olmec carved celts. It might be more accurate to view carved celts as miniature versions of the pyramid bas-relief stelae. Perhaps incised celts were mementos for outside visitors to this impressive and sacred site, which might explain their presence in the far reaches of ancient Mesoamerica. It is important to note, however, that none of the known incised Olmec celts follows precisely the image format of the stone monuments in front of Structure C-1. The image represented on these celtiform stelae consists of three sections: the top is a headdress, the middle portion a squarish face, and the bottom a series of horizontal and vertical bands probably representing a woven textile and/or binding cords. Fuente (1977:92) refers to these monuments as composite figures, or depictions that mix naturalistic elements with fantastic features to create images that have no representation in the real world. In this chapter the term "supernatural" is also employed to describe composite images. Although none are identical, the four examples are either incomplete or partially defaced, but all seem to represent a similar image. Taube (2000a:310) refers to this image as the "Maize God." Grove (2000:291) refers to these monuments as "mountain faces." It is interesting that the special precinct at Teopantecuanitlan, Guerrero (see Chapter 3), also has four images of a singular theme associated with a single structure, and these images

possibly represent the same Olmec supernatural entity carved on the stelae in front of La Venta's main pyramid.

The headdress is preserved only on Monuments 25/26 and 27; in both cases it is a half-circle, and its perimeter is indicated by a series of semicircles resting on a basal band (Figure 6.4). The interior of the headdress seems to have an abstract design, whereas the basal band consists of upright bifurcated rectangles, and in Monument 27 there is a central "X." The Monument 25/26 headdress is crowned with a trilobed element (leaves?). The headdresses sit directly on top of the serrated eyebrows of the figures, as can be seen in Monuments 25/26, 27, and 88. The eyes in Monuments 88 and 27 are oval in shape, and only in the first are the irises visible. The noses of the figures are flat and wide, and the nostrils are evident in all except Monument 89. Directly below the nose is a buccal mask that hides the upper lips of the figures and exposes the gums. This mask is basically rectangular in shape, though its lower edge is curved, and it has two protrusions on its lower corners. The gums of all figures show a central tooth and two fangs. The fangs on Monuments 88 and 89 represent snakes in profile. The corners of the lower lips are downturned, and Monument 89 shows a lip plug. On the surface of the face of Monument 88 are fine incisions that might represent tattoos.

Framing the faces are vertical bands, which in Monuments 88 and 89 show faint traces of profiles of inward-facing, human-like faces. Adjacent to the exterior and lower part of the band, one can discern different ear ornaments that, for the most part, are simple rectangular earplugs with rounded corners. However, in the case of Monument 88, half of a human face (one eye and half of the nose and mouth) is represented. Above the ear ornaments on Monuments 27, 88, and 89 there are three somewhat squared, cartouche-like elements placed in a column, and within them are three vertical rectangles with a circle on top of each.

Directly below each face, three horizontal and two vertical bands are depicted in a woven fashion; they contain horizontal and diagonal incisions. They seem to represent a mat, textile, or knotted

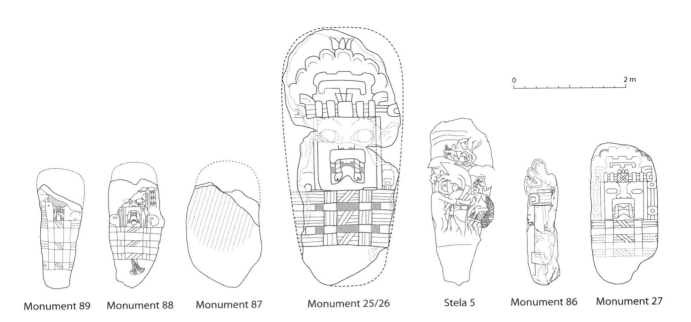

figure 6.4
La Venta Monuments 89, 88, 87, 25/26, Stela 5, Monument 86, and Monument 27. (Drawing from the New World Archaeological Foundation adapted from originals by Hermelando Ramírez Osio and Alfredo Arcos Rivas.)

cords. Monument 88 has a fishtail-shaped pendant that hangs from this woven design. Because of the eroded condition of the lower part of Monument 27, only the edges of this textile/mat are visible.

Stela 5 was found between Monuments 25/26 and 27. In contrast to its counterparts, this sculpture portrays a narrative scene rather than a supernatural entity. There are three standing figures, all with their faces in profile; a fourth figure is represented above them. The lower figures stand on what seems to be a simple horizontal line, while the upper one seems to be floating and emerging from a band that frames the scene at the top. The principal human figure is at the center of the composition, and the other figures face him. His head and legs are shown in profile, while his torso is represented frontally. His left arm is bent at a right angle, and he clasps in his hand a ceremonial bar, weapon, or scepter that extends diagonally over his left shoulder. This arm is also intertwined with that of the figure to his left, while his right arm reaches out toward the midriff of the figure to his right. He wears a short skirt above the knees, held in place by a sash around his waist that includes a feline head

in profile. The individual to the left of the principal figure is also human and is depicted completely in profile. This figure's right arm extends toward the principal figure's hand that holds the bar, and the figure's knees appear to be slightly bent. The figure wears a less elaborate and smaller headdress held in place by a chin strap; not much else can be said of other accoutrements because of their state of conservation. The individual to the left of the principal figure does not seem to be human and could be considered a supernatural. The figure's face (eyes, nose, and mouth areas) has feline-like features; the arms are unusually long and thin, and one entwines with the central figure. The other arm hangs alongside the body. The figure's legs are also thin and bent. The supernatural wears a large and intricate headdress as well as a short skirt; a cape decorated with finely incised lines hangs from the shoulders to the knees. Only the upper section of the body of the fourth figure can be seen above the three just described. The facial features of this figure are more easily distinguishable than those of the other two human figures. The figure's arms are outstretched and slightly bent around a small bar.

An elaborate headdress, crowned by a pointed bar and leaf-like elements and held in place by a chin strap, is also visible.

The sixth sculpture of this set is Monument 87, which was erected between Monuments 88 and 25/26. It is a slab finely pecked to create smooth surfaces. No image can be discerned on its sculpted surface, nor are there traces of pigment. It is therefore classified as a plain stela. We do not know whether it was once painted or draped with textiles with painted images on them.

A seventh sculpture, Monument 86, was found with this set of stela-like sculptures. Two fragments of it were found associated with Stela 5 (González Lauck 1997:fig. 4). Unlike the other sculptures in this group—except Monument 27—it did not have its tenon embedded in the earthen platform at the southern foot of Structure C-1. It is thus difficult to ascertain with precision its final position, or whether it was part of this composition. It may be part of the mound fill. Unlike the other monuments in this group, it is more column-like and narrower. It was carved in low relief on green-colored stone; its broken fragments are quite eroded, and most of its carved design has been obliterated. A wide central band extends vertically over most of the length of the sculpture and is interrupted near the top and bottom by narrower horizontal bands. On one of its extremities the top band is carved and incised in what scholars call a "knuckle-duster" design. Above that a series of diagonal lines indicate a feathered element similar to those on the celtiform stelae. Monument 86 appears to be a gigantic version of a scepter, as depicted on the four monuments from Teopantecuanitlan (see Figures 2.14, 3.11, 3.12, and 3.15) and as known from a carved jadeite "maize fetish" in the Peabody Museum at Harvard (see Taube 2000a:308, fig. 11g).

As with the previous groups of sculptures described, even though four of the sculptures in this ensemble repeat the same theme, they are not identical. The differences are in size, raw materials employed, and the accoutrements of the entities depicted. Though it is not possible to determine the original height of some of the sculptures because of their current broken states, it is clear

that Monument 25/26 was the largest, measuring almost 5 m tall (González Lauck 2004:table 6).

Based on the quadruple repetition of the composite-figure theme, it is absolutely clear that this theme was the main topic in this ensemble at the southern flank of the main pyramid of La Venta. Stela 5, with its worldly and stately scene, played a subordinate role. Yet it was sufficiently relevant to have been carved from a green-colored stone, been accompanied by four supernatural figures, and been placed at the foot of Structure C-1. The use of green-colored stones for the sculptures on the southeastern edge of the pyramid was not accidental. Monuments 25/26 and 86 were carved of schist; Monument 27 of gneiss, and Stela 5 of serpentine (Drucker et al. 1959:204–208; Jaime 2004:97–99). If one were to reconstruct the architectural landscape in this part of the sacred city, a commanding view must have been visible from the great plaza or from the western flank of the Stirling "Acropolis" to the south of Complex C where, with or without ritual activity, these monumental stelae were set upon the basal platform, with the pyramid as a backdrop. This ensemble, like those previously described, displays repetition, symmetry, and nuanced differences.

Pairs of Altars

Olmec "altars," like the colossal heads, are a type of sculpture known since the pioneering explorations of Mexico's southern Gulf Coast (see Chapter 1 for a discussion of these Olmec altars that Grove [1973] first identified as thrones). Olmec altars display a variety of forms, themes, and stylistic differences. Generally an Olmec altar refers to a typically rectangular block of stone that has a central niche in its front, in which a human figure is depicted in the round. The altar may have a ledge at its top or bottom margins, and it may have additional low-relief figures or designs on the front and wrapped around the lateral surfaces. At La Venta eight sculptures have been classified as altars, but this count depends on definitions. If altars are defined as sculptures that include a niche figure, as most do, then La Venta Altar 1 is not an altar, but La Venta Stela 1 would be included in this category (Fuente 1977:238).

figure 6.5
Two views of La Venta
Altar 3. (Photographs
courtesy of the New
World Archaeological
Foundation.)

figure 6.6
La Venta Altar 2.
(Photograph courtesy
of the New World
Archaeological
Foundation.)

Only two pairs of altars are discussed here: Altars 2 and 3 and Altars 4 and 5 (Figures 6.5–6.8). These four altars were found as pairs associated with specific buildings. The first pair was found on Complex C's southern basal platform; the second pair was associated with Structure D-8 (Figure 6.1). Altars 2 and 3 were found lying on their backs, with their niched figures facing the sky (Blom and La Farge 1926:84). When placed upright, the niche figures face the pyramid to the north. As with stelae at the foot of Structure C-1, these two altars were also placed on an east-west axis, with Altar 2 to the east of Altar 3 (Stirling 1943b:53). More than 400 m to the south, Altars 4 and 5 were found associated with Structure D-8, a long mound 150 m in length and 40 m wide. Altar 4 was found on the east side of the mound with its carved face facing east (its back to the building), whereas its partner, Altar 5, was located on the west side of the same structure

facing west toward Structure D-1, a 7 m high pyramid (Figure 6.1; Blom and La Farge 1926:87; Lowe 1989; Ochoa and Jaime 2000:32, fig. 18; Stirling 1943b:55–56).

All four altars were carved from basalt, although Altar 4 is the only one whose stone type has been verified through petrography (Williams and Heizer 1965:32). These pairs of altars share two themes. Altars 2 and 5 depict a human figure seated in the central niche and cradling an infant, whereas Altars 3 and 4 exhibit a single seated human figure in the central niche without an infant. Despite the partially fragmentary state of each of these sculptures, it is important to point out that this second theme of a seated human without an infant is represented in a larger size than its counterpart in each pair. Altar 3 weighs more than 12 tons in contrast to the almost 5 tons of its complementary Altar 2; Altar 4 weighs more

figure 6.7
Three views of La Venta Altar 5. (Photographs courtesy of the New World Archaeological Foundation.)

than 30 tons as opposed to the 17 tons of Altar 5 (González Lauck 2004:table 7).

As with the previous groups of sculptures described, although the altars present similar themes, they are not identical. Altar 3 is severely damaged, but one can distinguish a seated human figure in high relief (Figure 6.5). The figure leans slightly forward and, in the mid-chest area, wears a large square pendant with a fringe composed of small triangles. His facial features have been

battered, but large circular earspools are depicted, and his headdress is tall and conical. Viewed from the front, on the right surface adjacent to the niche stands a human figure carved in low relief and about one-third the size of the niche figure it faces. The head of this figure is basically obliterated, but one can discern its silhouette. Its torso is depicted almost completely frontally and the right arm is bent at a right angle and extended toward the niche, although the hand cannot be seen; the

figure 6.8
Two views of La Venta
Altar 4. (Photographs
courtesy of the New World
Archaeological Foundation.)

left arm hangs down, also handless. The figure wears a wide belt and a skirt that extends over the knees, and his legs and feet are depicted in profile and point toward the niche.

The left side of the altar was destroyed in ancient times and presents a pecked surface, whereas the back presents a slightly recessed, smooth surface. The right side of the altar is also a smooth surface on which two low-relief human figures are depicted on the same scale as the one just described.

These figures are seated, cross-legged, facing each other. The figure at the center of this panel is placed on a raised dais or bench, and the figure in front of him is depicted on the floor. Beneath these figures is a horizontal line under which two medallion-like elements are incised (originally there were probably three of these elements). The central figure's head and lower limbs are shown in profile, and his torso is depicted frontally. His left hand rests at his waist, and his right arm is raised in the direction of the second seated figure. The central figure wears a small headdress, which might have a bird profile, and a long, pointed beard. The other figure is also shown in profile. His right arm rests on his lap, and his hand almost touches the raised hand of the central figure. He sports a small beard and wears a small headdress held in place by a chinstrap. The top part of this side of the altar is delimited by a horizontal band under which a series of scallops is depicted above a series of circles.[4]

Altar 2, the partner to Altar 3, is more damaged and mutilated (Figure 6.6). This altar shows an oval-shaped central niche in which sits a cross-legged figure. The niche hugs the upper torso of the figure, and only the head and part of the legs project from it. One cannot discern the facial features of this figure, though he seems to wear a turban-like headdress with a tight headband, and faint outlines of a possible ear ornament are also visible. A smaller body lies horizontally across the lap of the central figure, and the head of this small figure rests on the left knee of the seated individual. The panels to the right and left of the niche show no evidence of low-relief images. The top of the altar reveals a partially destroyed projecting ledge, still conserved in the central area. The two sides and back of the altar are smooth surfaces. On the back and on a very small part of the left side one can see part of the top projecting ledge of this table-top altar. There is no evidence of low-relief carving on these surfaces.

In contrast to the above pair, Altars 4 and 5 are the best preserved examples of Olmec altars at La Venta and are certainly the most "classic" of all known. They flank opposite sides of the long D-8 mound. Three plain columnar basalt pillars were set up on top of this mound and were associated with these altars. Altar 5, unlike the others described here, has projecting upper and lower ledges, remnants of which can be seen on all four sides (Figure 6.7). The central niche is small and holds only the torso of the figure, in contrast to the full seated body of the other altars. The central figure is carved in high relief and sits cross-legged. He holds in his arms and lap a small infant. The central figure leans forward, and around his neck he wears

a two-banded flat collar with a large square pendant. The facial features of this figure are generic and no longer represent an identifiable individual, such as those depicted on the colossal heads. The figure's eyes are narrow slits, his nose and upper lips have been damaged, and his lower lip is downturned. He wears circular earspools and a conical headdress. The headdress has a wide band at the base, decorated symmetrically, with a square on each side containing an "X." At the center of the band is a medallion with a carved face crowned with three dots and triangles. There seems to be another medallion at the top front of the conical headdress.

This seated figure cradles an infant. The infant lies horizontally with its legs draped over the left leg of the adult figure. A remnant of its right arms indicates it was held against the adult's body with the latter's hand resting on its belly. The facial features of the baby have been obliterated, but the contours of the eyes and nose can still be discerned. Its lips are downturned. The infant wears no clothing, and its head is elongated, indicating a possible headdress. The infant's relaxed pose suggests it is either asleep or dead. An unusual feature of these two figures is the use of volume to indicate musculature, particularly in the upper arms of the adult and the chest and belly of the infant.

The two short sides of Altar 5 are finely carved in low relief. Four figures are depicted on each side: two adults and two composite figures. The latter have infant bodies with heads that seem to depict supernatural qualities. The adults and composite figures are shown in pairs, with the adults holding the infants. In most cases, the infant has an arm around the shoulder of its adult companion. All the adults are seated. The adult figures on the right side of the altar are seated cross-legged, and it seems that those on the left are kneeling. Their faces are shown in profile and face toward the front of the altar, whereas their bodies are depicted almost fully frontally. All of them are richly garbed: distinctive headgear with or without chinstraps, elbow-length capes, large circular pendants hanging on the chest, earspools, bracelets, and tasseled waistbands. The composite infant figures are naked but can be distinguished by the shapes of their heads: bulbous, bifurcated, or elongated. In contrast to the infant held by the adult in the central niche, the low-relief infants on the sides of the altar are in dynamic poses and depict movement. On each side of the altar, one infant faces the niche figure whereas the other faces its adult holder; one is held in the arms of its adult companion whereas the other is standing.

Altar 4 is the largest altar at La Venta and is probably the best known. It is rectangular in shape when viewed from the front and presents a wide overhanging ledge (Figure 6.8). The front surface of this ledge is carved in low relief, unlike the "table-tops" of the other altars described above. In the central section of Altar 4 is depicted a face with oval-shaped eyes and an open mouth with no lower lip. The upper gum and two fangs are identifiable. Between the fangs two crossed bands form an "X." Between the eyes a bifurcated or "cleft-head" design is incised. At the height of the eyes, a horizontal band extends on both sides of the face to the edges of the ledge. Above it, one vertical and two diagonal bands are depicted; at the extreme left side of the ledge there is a rectangle with two square protrusions. Toward the bottom edge of the ledge, inverted "U" elements are depicted on each side of the animal's face. In my opinion, this composite figure gives the impression of an avian head with extended wings. Most authors, however, interpret this image as the face of a jaguar (e.g., Stirling 1943b:54). Unlike the other altars described here, the top of Altar 4 is also carved. It consists of a raised central area, which could be interpreted as a representation of the body of the composite figure depicted on the front of the ledge.

Below this projecting ledge, the front of Altar 4 is composed of a central, oval-shaped niche in which a male sits cross-legged. He is carved almost fully in the round and, unusual for Olmec sculpture, evinces musculature in the upper arms and chest. His torso leans forward but remains in the niche; his head and headdress extend out of the niche. Both of his arms are outstretched; his left hand grasps his right ankle and an oval-shaped

object, while his right hand holds the carved rope depicted along the bottom edge of the altar. The man wears a wide, flat, double-banded collar. The upper band seems to be of cloth and has a knot in the center. From the lower band hangs a D-shaped pendant that seems to have a clasp; a wide band descends from the pendant to the waistband of the figure's knee-length skirt. The facial features of the human figure are either very eroded or have been purposefully defaced. In any case, they now seem quite generic in nature, with small slits for the eyes, cavities for the nostrils, and a volumetric rendering for the mouth. This figure does not seem to be wearing ear ornaments. The headdress represents an avian head. This bird's head has two symmetrical cavities for the eyes, from which two diagonal incised lines extend to the top of the headdress; the buccal area is broken off. At the center of the top of the headdress is a protuberance. There are two rectangular cartouches with intertwined bands on the bottom on each side of it.

The inside of the niche presents a series of curvilinear incisions extending to the front surface of the altar around the headdress of the figure. These could represent a matted backdrop or feathers. The front panel of the altar presents a series of low-relief decorations, the principal one being a band with curvilinear incisions that follows the contours of the niche. On each side of it are two U-shaped designs that enclose an inclined vessel-like object from which two curvilinear bands (smoke? water? leaves?) emerge and terminate at the edge of the front surface of the altar.

The short sides of the altar were also carved. The projecting ledge on the left side was broken off in ancient times. On the flat surface below this broken edge is a seated figure in low relief that is not as well preserved as the imagery currently indicates.[5] The figure is shown in profile, facing toward the front of the altar, and basically only the eye cavity can be seen. The figure wears a headdress and is seated so that the torso is presented almost fully frontal. The figure's right arm is bent over the chest and the thumb and index finger are clearly depicted; the index finger points toward the front of the altar. The figure's left arm rests on one knee. Wrapped around the wrist of the figure's rather listless hand is a rope, which runs from the bottom of the front of the altar to the side of the monument. The figure has a band around the waist area and seems to be sitting on bent legs.

The projecting ledge on the right side of the altar is complete and shows no evidence of carved designs. The original flat surface beneath this ledge was modified in ancient times over more than fifty percent of its area, especially affecting the lowermost part and thus obliterating the rope that ran along the bottom of the altar, if it indeed continued to this side. Two small rectangular niches are carved in the stone on this side. On what remains of the original surface, toward the upper part, the silhouette of a head in profile of a human figure with an incised eye can be discerned, and it faces toward the front of the altar. Behind it is a raised rectangular surface unidentifiable in design. The back of the altar is irregular and not smooth like the other altars, and the wide, projecting ledge seen on all the other faces of this altar is not present. The back of this altar does not ever appear to have been dressed for viewing.

These detailed descriptions of Altars 2, 3, 4, and 5 aim to present the type of discourse conveyed by this sculptural form. As westerners, we are accustomed to reading words in texts, but few of us have been trained to read images or groups of images. In any case, despite the thematic differences in the altar pairs, their dual display was not random. Their placement in close association with the only two pyramidal structures at the site indicates that these mounds were also a fundamental element of the full message. It is also evident that the main theme in these sculptural pairs was the figure of a male adult human, and that the composite or supernatural figures played only a secondary role in this visual discourse. This message is the reverse of that reconstructed for the line of stelae at the base of Structure C-1. The relative sizes of the altars seem to indicate that the theme of a single individual emerging from the niche carried more significance than the theme of an individual holding an infant.

Concluding Remarks

Over the past 112 years, controlled and uncontrolled excavations at La Venta have revealed one of the largest and most diverse collections of stone sculpture in the Olmec style. As with all other vestiges of the material culture of past peoples, the context of sculptures is essential for gaining an understanding of them; the less we know of context, the greater the chance for misinterpretation and limited understanding. Unlike many other material culture remains, stone sculptures may have had long individual histories, and their use and meaning may have changed from the time of their creation to their final moment of Pre-Columbian use. This is a cautionary note that must always be borne in mind when ancient stone sculptures are the subject of inquiry.

In this chapter, sixteen La Venta sculptures, found in pairs, triads, ensembles, and groups, were examined in light of their architectural contexts. It is assumed that these sculptures were recovered as the Olmecs last exhibited them between 600 and 400 BC—even if they were carved in earlier times and had been exhibited elsewhere on the site and/or with different monuments. The emphasis in this analysis is on their placement in the architectural layout of La Venta as last displayed, as well as the internal organization of each group in terms of size, raw materials employed, and distinguishing elements.

Analysis of this small sample of sculptures shows that particular themes were exhibited in association with specific buildings or areas of La Venta. Two trios of sculpture, each repeating a single theme, were found at the southern and northern limits of the site. I argue that they marked the main entrances to this ancient city. Two pairs of altars sharing similar themes (seated human figures emerging from a niche) were associated with the only two pyramids at the site, whereas six slabs of stones carved in low relief were placed at the foot of the main pyramid where the repeated theme was that of a composite or supernatural being. The lines of important adult males, perhaps kings, defined the northern and southern edges of this ancient city, whereas the principal line of monuments at the city's center honored a supernatural entity depicted on four different but similar monuments that framed the southern ascent to the pyramid.

Despite the repetition of a theme within each group, ensemble, and cluster, each sculpture was distinct in size and identifying elements (such as headdresses, ear ornaments, and facial features). These differences were surely significant components in the reading and meaning of each image and its role in the group. It might be simplistic to propose that the largest sculptures—such as Monument 25/26 at the foot of Structure C-1 or Altar 4 in the pair associated with Structure D-8—were the most important in their groups. Differences in the sizes of the sculptures in each ensemble were intentional and easily recognizable. In the absence of written inscriptions on the monuments, the imagery of the monuments had to be understood by artistic representations, perhaps by peoples of different languages. Size may have reflected some type of scale hierarchy, a technique commonly employed in visual depictions to make an image or an element more conspicuous.

This simple visual device contrasted with the use of others much more sophisticated and nuanced, such as the detailed minutiae included in the images themselves. Distinct details were clearly significant for reading imagery and should not be dismissed or glossed over. The use of different kinds of stone (basalt; sandstone; possibly andesite; and green-colored stones, such as schist, gneiss, and serpentine), for example, might have been another kind of visual cue in which stone color was relevant to a monument's meaning. This is particularly manifest in the group of six sculptures at the southern foot of the main pyramid (green:gray::east:west) or in the rust-colored sandstone triad at the southern entrance to the site and the gray colossal heads at the north of the site (red/brown:gray/black::south:north). Color differences evident in these sculptures might have referenced the cardinal directions but could also have referred to the domain of distant rock outcrops accessed by the La Venta Olmec (see Chapter 4 for a possible related example). An equally plausible possibility is that technological considerations dictated the choice of stone, as sculpture in the round may have been more readily accomplished with stones of volcanic origin, whereas metamorphic rock may have been better suited to low-relief sculpture.

It could be proposed that the sixteen sculptures reviewed here played a fundamental role in the official discourse of ancient La Venta, but such a claim would be dismissive of the other fifty-plus sculptures, whole and fragmentary, found at this ancient city. The carved stone monuments of known context were a small fraction of the whole. I have not yet explored why other sculptures with similar themes at La Venta were exhibited in different manners. Examples abound, but to mention just one, consider the case of Monument 1 found near Stela 2 in the plaza south of Complex C (Figure 6.1). This colossal head has no accompanying thematic counterpart in this setting, and it was placed in the middle of the largest plaza at the site, in contrast to the setting of the triad of colossal heads at the northern limit of the site. It would seem that these variations were purposeful, but just what was meant by the overall pattern remains to be determined.

Almost four decades ago, Proskouriakoff (1971:147) provided one of the most succinct explanations for the development of early monumental sculpture in ancient Middle America, and her explanation may help explain the use of sculptures at La Venta. She argued that in the absence of a writing system, it was through visual imagery, hand-in-hand with ritual activities, that hierarchical Mesoamerican societies validated themselves. At the same time, this visual imagery served as a permanent form of communication between the "administration and the populace." In the same vein, Fuente (1977:193) stated that Olmec art was an official art: the repetition of themes was undoubtedly imposed on the sculptors—but this reiteration of themes facilitated their mental retention by viewers. As I have discussed, some of these themes concerned kings and their thrones ("altars"; see Chapter 1), supernatural beings, and the relationships among them.

Few traces of a written language have been directly associated with the Middle Preclassic

Olmec stone sculptures, a situation similar to later impressive cultural manifestations in Pre-Columbian America, such as that of the Incas or at Teotihuacan.[6] Great strides have been made in Maya studies since decipherment of their hieroglyphic script, and this knowledge has significantly affected our understanding of sculptural images accompanied by texts. The paucity of written texts for Olmec sculpture greatly limits our interpretations of the meaning or significance of the themes depicted in Olmec sculptures.

In their classic study of the changes in content and representation of the myth of Pandora's box, Panofsky and Panofsky (1956) demonstrated that a theme may be represented in different and various forms through time. They established that the best way to address diachronic changes in form and meaning in images is through a careful and detailed correlation with written texts. With relevant exceptions, this basic tenet in the field of art history has not been applied to the study of Pre-Columbian images by art historians or archaeologists focusing on Olmec art. It has been most unfortunate that Olmec-style images have been interpreted using frameworks derived from Aztec, Maya, and other cultures. This practice is not only

nescient of the vast temporal and cultural differences that existed among different Mesoamerican groups, but it also obscures the uniqueness of the Olmecs. We should attempt to deal with these early monuments on their own terms by putting them in context.

Thus what can be said about the meaning of the sculptures discussed in this chapter must be limited to formal analysis. The detailed descriptions of the sculptures presented here emphasize the differences of each image, which I believe are essential clues that signal their individual distinctiveness, even though the overall structure of the image might follow a thematic pattern. The meaning of each sculpture—and pair, group, cluster, or assemblage of monuments—is contained in these details, in its combination with its counterpart(s), and is intimately connected to the highly structured manner of display at strategic locations in the site. The basic message conveyed by La Venta's monumental sculptures and architecture is that of manifest power. It is an unequivocal demonstration of control over people, ideas, landscape, and distant resources. Its predominantly homocentric images provide a glimpse of the primary preoccupations of the Olmecs, both historical and mythical.

NOTES

1. I use "in situ" to signify the locations of monuments found in excavation. In Pre-Columbian archaeology there is always the problem of determining whether the find locations of sculptures were original placements. Changes in settings imply different meanings and functions for relocated sculptures during their individual life histories.

2. Unless otherwise noted, weights for sculptures were taken from Williams and Heizer (1965:24), which were calculated in short tons (907.18 kg). To provide readily comparable data, all weights provided here have been converted to metric tons (1,000 kg).

3. The scale on the PEMEX crane that was used when the monuments were moved from Structure D-7 to

the La Venta site museum provided the weight of these monuments.

4. This part of the altar seems to have been modified when moved from Villahermosa to La Venta Park. One can discern what seems to be the steel rope burns or marks on the top band, which almost totally destroyed the circles below the scallops. In addition, Carlos Pellicer Cámara filled the natural vesicles in the stones with cement. This modification can easily be seen by comparing the early Smithsonian Institution or National Geographic Society photographs to recent ones or to the sculpture itself. Pellicer also liked to highlight or accentuate the low relief, which seems particularly intrusive in the hand area of the secondary seated

figure. There are no written records or reports of these "restorations" in the archives of the Instituto Nacional de Antropología e Historia. These modifications seem to have been done on Pellicer's own initiative. Similar modifications can be seen on other La Venta sculptures in La Venta Park. In careful iconographic analyses of La Venta sculptures, it is necessary to work with earlier images that have not been modified through modern "restorations."

5. This figure is one that Carlos Pellicer Cámara heavy-handedly "restored." His modifications can be seen by comparing the sculpture as it is today with the photograph of it when it was unearthed (Stirling 1943b:plate 37b). Pellicer reconstructed the mouth, chin, nose, part of the headdress, the necklace, the left forearm, the right shoulder area, and the right leg and foot—in short, most of the figure.

6. Early scripts have recently been claimed for the La Venta area. Pohl and her colleagues (2002) argue for the presence of simple writing for San Andrés, a small subsidiary of La Venta, by ca 700 BC. Rodríguez and others (2006; see also Ortíz et al. 2007) argue for an even earlier and more complex script already having rules of syntax for the Cascajal serpentine block, found about 40 km west of La Venta and thought to date to at least 900–700 BC. These claims remain controversial. Early scripts and writing may have existed by La Venta times, as Coe (1965b:755) argued for La Venta Monument 13, although this monument may be late in date (Houston 2004). The absence of writing or glyphs on most La Venta monuments is all the more remarkable if the option to do so had been available, which was likely the case. In other words, then, the lack of text would indicate a deliberate choice to employ a form of expression that was based on image rather than text.

Thinking Outside the Plaza

Varieties of Preclassic Sculpture in Pacific Guatemala and Their Political Significance

MICHAEL W. LOVE

SCULPTURE HAS ALWAYS BEEN AN IMPORtant source of information for the study of ancient social and political organization, insofar as monumental sculpture and architecture are often taken to be prima facie evidence for the power of ancient rulers as well as serving as media for the presentation of ideologies of power. In ancient Mesoamerica the Preclassic period was a time of radical social transformation, manifested in the development of tremendous social inequality and centralized institutions of government. All of the many dimensions of social complexity increased during that period, including population size and nucleation, social inequality, craft specialization, and political centralization. Large centralized polities that could be classed as paramount or complex chiefdoms appeared in the Pacific Coast region by the Middle Preclassic (900–400 BC; all dates are uncalibrated), and by the Late Preclassic period (400 BC–AD 250) state-level forms of government were widespread in the region, as elsewhere in Mesoamerica (Traxler and Sharer n.d.). The

widening social gulf between elites and commoners was accompanied by an ideology in which rulers claimed divine powers and likened their own actions to those of the gods at the time of creation to justify their political and economic dominance of the masses (Guernsey and Love 2005).

In this chapter, I examine Preclassic sculptures from the Pacific Coast and highlands of Guatemala with an eye to analyzing the nature of political power during the early stages of state formation at the transition from the Middle to Late Preclassic. The main argument of this chapter is that there is much to learn from sculpture if we can appreciate its diversity and give greater attention to the sculpture found outside the main plazas of the largest cities. That examination, I believe, supports Yoffee's (2005) proposition that archaeologists often overstate the power of rulers in early states. Yoffee presents the image of powerful rulers exerting near total control over an awed populace as one of the central "Myths of the Archaic State" and believes that we have grossly overestimated the amount of control by early rulers, failing to see the evidence that their success at integrating disparate social factions under their rule was only partial. Mesoamerican scholars are as guilty as anyone else of such exaggeration. Seduced by the beauty of Preclassic art, they often have taken at face value the claims of elites, both in image and in text, as evidence of a shared cultural construct rather than as a political ideology asserted by a specific social group, the elite. We have too willingly assumed that the nonelite sectors of ancient Mesoamerican society believed the claims of rulers, and we have failed to see evidence to the contrary.

The data presented below show that, although Preclassic sculpture does indeed portray themes of elite power and the glorification of rulers, representations of other kinds are more frequent and more widespread. The iconography of these latter monuments is poorly understood, but I suggest that they are linked to elements of religious practices shared by all social sectors and used in both domestic and public rituals. Moreover, the distribution of sculpture outside of the central zones of major capitals in the Late Preclassic period displays little overt interest in rulers or rulership, suggesting that the bulk of the populace may not have perceived the rulers to be as important as the rulers portrayed themselves.

I begin with a consideration of the diversity of sculpture in materials, formal attributes, and themes. I argue for a broad definition of sculpture and for a multifaceted analysis of its meaning, because I see no justification for defining sculpture solely as monumental stone art. A broad definition helps identify the conceptual overlap among representations in various media and contexts. Many problems in sculptural analysis stem from an artificial division among sculptural forms. Old divisions between high "art" and lowly "craft," while seldom used explicitly nowadays, have not been completely abandoned, nor have distinctions such as "Great Tradition" and "Little Tradition." The sculptural corpus of Preclassic Mesoamerica was not a unified class of material culture but was formed by a multiplicity of material products that were made and used by diverse social groups in different types of settings. By examining the distribution of the many forms of sculpture, I hope to show that the creation and use of sculpture formed a broad but overlapping set of social practices performed by different kinds of social actors across a varied cultural landscape.

The meaning and social import of the many dimensions of sculpture demand both new empirical analyses and new theoretical contemplation if we are to fully mine their potential. Empirically there is a need to document sculpture in all of its formal diversity as well as its iconographic themes and distributional contexts. Theoretically there is a further need to consider the way sculpture was made and used in those multiple contexts, and by whom. I hope to contribute on both fronts in this chapter by presenting evidence of new sculptures while also considering who made and used these sculptures.

Sculpture of Preclassic Pacific Guatemala

The highlands and Pacific Coast of Guatemala (Figure 7.1) are home to one of the most significant bodies of Preclassic sculpture in Mesoamerica. The corpus includes stelae with early hieroglyphic texts, plain stelae, potbellied sculptures, toad altars, petroglyphs, pedestal sculptures, silhouette sculptures, colossal heads, animal representations, human representations, boxes, thrones, mushroom stones, and more. Pre-Columbian sculptors in the region worked in multiple media and also dealt with many different themes. It is not my intention to provide an exhaustive overview of the corpus, as many excellent syntheses already exist (Miles 1965; Parsons 1986). Rather than provide encyclopedic coverage, my goal is to situate the study of Preclassic sculpture in the region by examining its variety, distribution, and relationship to other forms of material culture. Although the tremendous diversity of sculptural forms in the highlands and coastal region has been widely recognized, many aspects of that diversity remain unanalyzed, not merely in the formal characteristics of

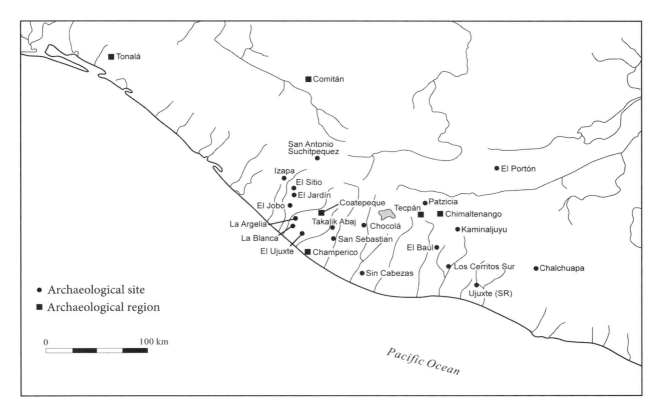

figure 7.1

Map of coastal Guatemala showing the sites and regions mentioned in the text. (Drawing by the author.)

sculpture or its iconography but also in the variety of its social settings and social uses. Much has been made of the representational stelae, including portraits of rulers and supernatural beings, found in the midst of formal architectural settings in the largest sites, such as Kaminaljuyu, Takalik Abaj, and Izapa. These representations and their settings have been reasonably linked to elite power and an ideology of rulership that crossed cultural and ethnolinguistic boundaries (Guernsey 2006b). Nonetheless, Preclassic sculpture is also found in secondary and tertiary centers, in domestic contexts, and outside of site centers altogether. The wide distribution of highly diverse forms suggests that sculpture was made and used by groups other than the elite and that practices linked to sculpture transcended what was once called "the cult of the ruler."

My focus in this chapter is the transition from the Middle Preclassic period (900–400 BC) to the

Late Preclassic period (400 BC–AD 250). It was during this time that many regional polities grew from complex chiefdoms to early states (Love n.d.). I focus on the southern highlands and Pacific Coast of Guatemala, the area of previous sculptural surveys by Miles (1965) and Parsons (1986). This is a highly diverse region geographically, linguistically, and culturally; the Preclassic sculptural corpus in its boundaries includes Olmec, Maya, and Izapan styles, along with other works not easily classified (see Chapter 8; Schieber de Lavarreda and Orrego Corzo 2002).

Despite some claims (Graham 1981, 1989; Miles 1965), there is no sculpture in the Guatemalan Highlands and coast that can be dated to the Early Preclassic, pre-Olmec period. The earliest stone carvings on the Guatemalan coast date to the Middle Preclassic Olmec manifestation, beginning at ca 900 BC (Love 1999b). Earlier monuments are known from coastal Chiapas, Mexico (Clark and

Pye 2000; Navarrete 1974), but these are also works by sculptors trained in the early Olmec tradition(s).

For both the Middle and Late Preclassic periods, there are significant difficulties in our ability to accurately date sculptural materials. First, there are general problems of chronology, as the ceramic periods used by most archaeologists for the temporal placement of sculpture and architecture are still in need of refinement. Second, there are problems specific to sculpture, such as the reuse and re-placement of works in periods after their initial manufacture and dedication (Graham 1989). We rarely find pristine sculptures in their initial placements. For example, Graham et al. (1978) and Parsons (1986) describe the reuse and placement of Preclassic sculpture in Classic contexts at Takalik Abaj and Kaminaljuyu, respectively. Sculpture was also frequently mutilated, recycled, or entirely destroyed after its initial carving. These ancient activities not only curtail our ability to interpret the formal properties and iconography of sculpture but rob us of its context and the supporting evidence of rituals and acts of veneration that may aid in interpreting its cultural meaning. It is somewhat amazing that despite all these problems we can still say something meaningful about Preclassic sculpture. Although we are often limited to formal study and analysis of iconography, an analysis of context, though difficult, is still possible on a broad scale, that is to say, at the regional level.

In what follows, I begin at the formal level with a consideration of sculptural media and forms. Following that, I attempt a contextual analysis by looking at a limited number of examples from the area of my work on the western Pacific Coast of Guatemala. To enliven the discussion, I present a number of works previously unpublished and others not widely known.

Describing Sculptural Diversity: The Media

A description of the diversity of sculpture can begin with a consideration of the materials used by ancient sculptors. Normally when one discusses sculpture in Mesoamerica, it is understood that the medium is stone. Other sculptural media generally require a clarifying adjective—wooden statue, stucco head, or ceramic figurine. Small ceramic figurines, a sculptural form in any objective definition, are generally excluded from an analysis of sculpture, although, as detailed by Guernsey (Chapter 9), they show important thematic correspondences with stone sculpture. Although I follow convention here and exclude ceramic figurines, it is nonetheless clear that even if we limit consideration to larger works, Preclassic artists used a variety of media other than stone. I illustrate the point by reference to a few examples.

I begin in the Middle Preclassic period at La Blanca, located in the western extreme of modern Guatemala. La Blanca was occupied principally during the Conchas phase, dated 900–600 BC (Love 2002). La Blanca has two known stone monuments (Figure 7. 2). Monument 1 is a small head recovered by Edwin M. Shook in 1972, and Monument 2 is a fragment of the knee and thigh from a sculpture in the round, found on the surface of the site in 1985 during a visit by Shook. There are other sculptural works, presumably looted, which are attributed to the site, such as the Young Lord statuette and a large greenstone saurian creature illustrated in the *Lords of Creation* catalogue (Fields and Reents-Budet 2005:103, 126). Other looted pieces are somewhat more vaguely attributed to the site and held in private collections in Guatemala.

Three additional works, discovered during recent excavations, are of material other than stone. La Blanca Monument 3 is an altar formed of unfired, rammed earth and fine clay (Figure 7.3). The altar is in the form of a quatrefoil, symbolic of a portal to the supernatural, which has consistent associations with fertility and elite power throughout Mesoamerican history (Guernsey n.d.; Love and Guernsey 2007). The bulk of the monument is formed of clay loam compacted to a hard consistency and then shaped. After forming, a finish coat of fine dark clay was applied, and the inner rim was painted red with hematite. The monument was probably used for rituals of divination and ancestor communication, possibly using water (Love and

a   b

figure 7.2
La Blanca Monuments (a) 1; (b) 2. (Photographs by the author.)

figure 7.3
La Blanca Monument 3. (Photograph by the author.)

Guernsey 2007). It is dated to the early part of the Conchas C subphase, ca 800 BC.

La Blanca Monument 4 (Figure 7.4), found in a domestic trash pit, demonstrates the use of fired clay at a large scale. This sculptural fragment is the nose and eye of a piece that probably represented a supernatural creature or possibly a human with supernatural attributes. The nose is very similar, both in size and shape, to that of La Blanca Monument 1, but the mouth is represented by a glyph-like element. The features of the figure (eye, nose, and mouth) are defined by skillful differential firing of the ceramic, and the eye is highlighted further by a circle of red paint. If Monument 1 can serve as a guide, the head of Monument 4 would have originally been approximately 40 cm high. Although it is possible that Monument 4 is a piece of a mask or other ornament rather than a free-standing sculpture, the wall thickness of more than 4 cm gives the piece tremendous weight, and the complete piece would have been far too heavy to wear as a mask. The thickness of the piece was created in two steps, as revealed in the two distinct layers of clay evident in the broken profile. Its bulk and extreme weight were intentional, designed to make it durable rather than wearable. Thus the interpretation of the piece as a fragment of a free-standing sculpture is most likely.

The creativity of Middle Preclassic sculptors extended to the use of pumice. A small fragment from the fill of La Blanca Mound 1 is a pumice cobble carved in low relief (Figure 7.5). Clearly a fragment of a larger piece, the surviving representation depicts two hands and forearms, although from the

figure 7.4
La Blanca Monument 4.
(Photograph by the author.)

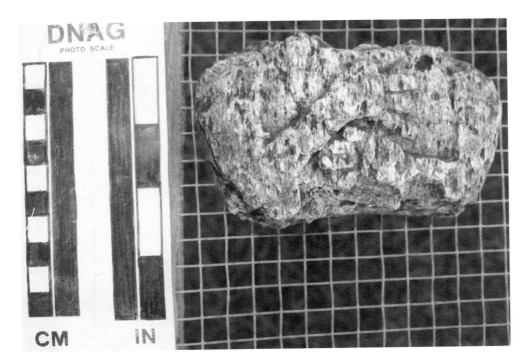

figure 7.5
La Blanca sculpted
pumice. (Photograph
by the author.)

limited portion that was recovered it is impossible to discern whether the limbs belong to a single individual or a pair. If it is one individual, the overall representation may be a three-dimensional work, such as a potbelly, with the hands resting on the stomach. Although pumice was used extensively as a utilitarian material, normally in the form of small pebbles for scraping or cleaning, the example from La Blanca is, to my knowledge, the only case of sculpted pumice. The piece comes from within the first episode of construction of Mound 1, which occurred ca 900 BC.

A Late Preclassic piece from the site of El Ujuxte, located 13 km east of La Blanca in the department of Retalhuleu, demonstrates further the use of ceramic as a sculptural medium (Figure 7.6). The large ceramic disk formed the base of a scene with four figures: two standing and two kneeling. More than just figurines placed on a pot, the traces suggest a dynamic composition similar to the representations of vassals and/or captives kneeling before lords, known from stone stelae, such as Kaminaljuyu Stelae 2, 6, 10, and 66; Kaminaljuyu Monument 165 (Fahsen 2002; Parsons 1986); El Jobo Stela 1 (Shook 1965); Chocolá Stela 1

(Jones 1986); and Takalik Abaj Monument 42. The El Ujuxte sculpture is thus another example of the thematic overlap of works in ceramic and stone.

Given the documented use of such a wide variety of materials, the use of wood as a sculptural medium seems quite likely, and perhaps we should avoid the hubris of thinking that all sculpture is preserved in the archaeological record. After all, the use of wood as a sculptural medium is well documented in Mesoamerica from Preclassic to Postclassic times (Coggins 1992; Ekholm 1964; Ortíz and Rodríguez 1999; Reents-Budet 1998), and wooden images were an important part of highland Maya religious practices in the ethnographic record (Orellana 1981).

Although not documented directly on the Pacific Coast or in the highlands for the Preclassic period, the use of wood may be suggested by other representations. A pottery sherd from El Ujuxte appears to represent a stela placed between two mounds (Figure 7.7). Such a stela has eluded discovery to date, and at present the only sculptural works in stone known from El Ujuxte are three uncarved altars and two miniature potbellies (described below). A small and badly battered sculptural

figure 7.6
Base of ceramic sculpture from El Ujuxte. (Photograph by the author.)

fragment found at Chiquirines Viejo and sculptures from La Argelia, both secondary centers of El Ujuxte, hint that there may be stone sculpture yet to be found in the area, but such a suggestion is purely conjectural. Although some studies have hypothesized the lack of a well-developed sculptural tradition along the western portion of the coastal plain (Bove 1981; Guernsey and Love 2005), it simply may be the case that materials other than stone were used.

As discussed by Stuart (Chapter 12), stone had special meaning in ancient Mesoamerica, and its use in sculpture held tremendous symbolic importance. Nonetheless, for the Preclassic period, especially on the coastal plain where all monumental architecture was earthen and built without use of stone, other media may also have held symbolic importance. For example, the techniques of

construction evident in La Blanca Monument 3 are the same as those used to construct the monumental pyramid at the site. The rammed-earth technique made the body of both the monument and the pyramid rock hard, and the use of a coat of fine dark clay was also the same in both cases. The techniques of making earth as hard as stone, whether by ramming it or firing it, may have had just as much symbolic importance as using stone itself.

We do not yet have enough examples of nonstone sculpture to fully evaluate their forms, distribution, and meaning. However, many of the extant examples, such as La Blanca Monuments 3 and 4, have analogues in stone and other materials. La Blanca Monument 3 is directly comparable to several stone monuments from Chalcatzingo, Morelos, as well as a stucco sculpture from Aguacatal, Campeche, Mexico (Houston et al. 2005;

figure 7.7
Pottery sherd
from El Ujuxte.
(Photograph by
the author.)

CM   IN

Love and Guernsey 2007). As mentioned above, Monument 4 greatly resembles Monument 1 from La Blanca as well as Takalik Abaj Monument 55 (Love 1999b). These similarities may indicate that the artists who manufactured the sculptures of clay and ceramic were schooled in the same aesthetics as sculptors who worked in stone. If we conjecture that sculptors who produced stone representations displayed in the ceremonial centers of major sites were working under the patronage of elites, then we might reasonably conclude that the sculptors of nonstone monuments with similar themes displayed in similar settings were also acting under such patronage.

It would be erroneous, however, to conclude that all sculptures, whether in stone or other materials, were produced under the same social and economic relationships. It is commonly assumed that sculptures in major centers were created under the patronage of elites or possibly by members of the elite. In the following section, I describe the distribution of some different formal categories of stone sculpture across the landscape of highland and Pacific coastal Guatemala. The nature and distribution of these forms suggest that nonelites were making and using sculpture and that although there was much overlap in themes, we cannot assume a purely top-down model for the production of sculpture and the choice of themes represented in the art.

Diversity of Sculptural Forms

A full inventory of sculptural forms for the Middle and Late Preclassic periods would require more space than available here. My focus in what follows is on the distribution of those forms, both geographically and socially. That is, I am equally concerned with what types of sites have sculpture as with where those sites are located with respect to hypothesized culture areas or where they fall in a seriated temporal ordering. It will be necessary, however, to briefly discuss some of the more prominent classes of sculpture for both the Middle and Late Preclassic before examining their distributions.

Middle Preclassic Period

Sculpture dating to the early part of the Middle Preclassic period is known from sites all along the coastal plain and the piedmont, from Mexico to El Salvador (Figure 7.8). The sites include Pijijiapan, Chiapas (see Figure 1.4; Navarrete 1974),

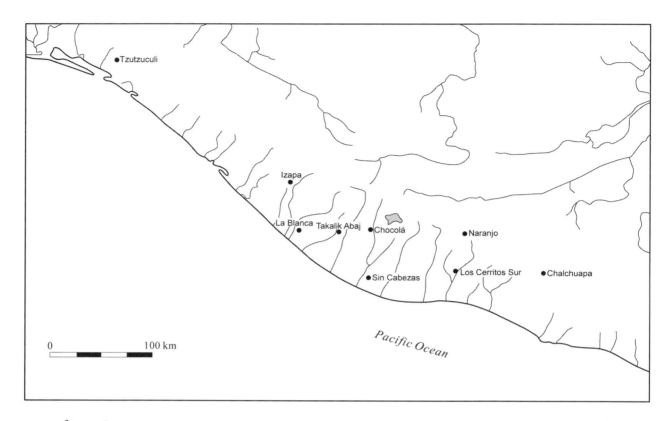

figure 7.8
Sites with Middle Preclassic sculptures. (Drawing by the author.)

Tzutzuculi, Chiapas (McDonald 1983), La Blanca (Love 2002), Takalik Abaj (Graham et al. 1978), Los Cerritos Sur (Parsons 1986), and Chalchuapa (Sharer et al. 1978). The formal categories of art include petroglyphs, freestanding human figures, supernatural figures in the round, niche figures, and altars. Smaller portable sculpture is also known, such as the head from El Baul (Shook 1956) and the Young Lord sculpture. The stone disk, often called the "Shook Altar" (see Figure 10.7b; Shook and Heizer 1976), was recovered near San Antonio Suchitepequez and may be attributable to Chocolá. The Sin Cabezas pedestal sculptures (Parsons 1986:plates 15–18), so distinctive from the other potbellies, are placed in the Middle Preclassic by some authors (Graham 1989; Love 1999b). The largest corpus of Middle Preclassic sculpture from the coastal zone comes from Takalik Abaj, which is discussed by Schieber de Lavarreda and Orrego Corzo in Chapter 8.

In the Guatemalan Highlands, the use of plain stelae is documented at a number of sites during the Las Charcas phase, or the early Middle Preclassic (800–600 BC), in the Department of Guatemala (see Chapter 1; Arroyo, ed. 2007; Shook 1952). Sculptural forms began to diversify in the latter portion of the Middle Preclassic, or the Providencia phase (600–400 BC) (Miles 1965; Shook 1952; Shook and Kidder 1952). Kaminaljuyu Stela 9 (see Figure 1.7d) and several fragments of pedestal sculptures were found in a large pit in Mound C-III-6, a secure Providencia phase context (Shook and Kidder 1952).

Despite the far-flung geographic distribution of Middle Preclassic sculpture and its variety of forms, its distribution in political terms is quite narrow. On the coastal plain and piedmont the known Middle Preclassic sculptures come from the largest regional centers, those that were likely the primary settlements of their regional polities. The veracity of this statement is most evident in the western portion of the Guatemalan coast, where Takalik Abaj and La Blanca were the largest centers of their respective regions. Farther east, Middle Preclassic sculpture is more rare, but Los Cerritos Sur, with its Olmec-style profiles, was also a large primary center (Bove 1981). In the highlands, the largest corpus of Middle Preclassic stelae comes from Naranjo, arguably the political center of much of the Valley of Guatemala during the Las Charcas phase (Chapter 1), but it is unclear whether other Las Charcas phase sites with plain stelae, such as Piedra Parada, Virginia, and Santa Isabel, were politically independent (Love n.d.). By Providencia times, Kaminaljuyu was the valley's major political center, and little sculpture in the Valley of Guatemala is found outside of that center.

Late Preclassic Period

Despite the wide geographic distribution of Middle Preclassic sculpture in the highlands and Pacific Coast region of Guatemala, its overall frequency is low compared to other regions of Mesoamerica, especially the Gulf Coast of Mexico (see Chapters 5 and 6). It was in the Late Preclassic that sculpture reached its peak in both frequency and diversity in the southern highlands and Pacific Coast, achieving dazzling heights on both counts. In spite of the aforementioned problems of chronology and context (pieces moved, reutilized, mutilated, or excavated without controls), the sheer size of the corpus means that for the Late Preclassic period as a whole we have better data for the social context and cultural significance of sculpture than for any other period. Regrettably, for some sites with large numbers of sculpture, notably Kaminaljuyu, such contextual data are largely lacking, because so few pieces from that site have been excavated under controlled conditions.

In contrast to the Middle Preclassic period, sculpture in the Late Preclassic is much more

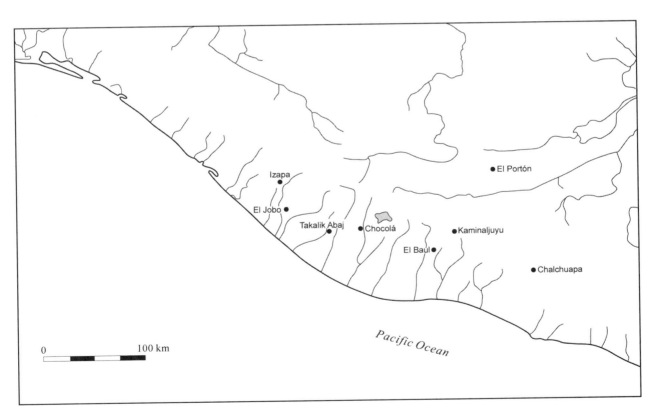

figure 7.9
Sites with representational stelae. (Drawing by the author.)

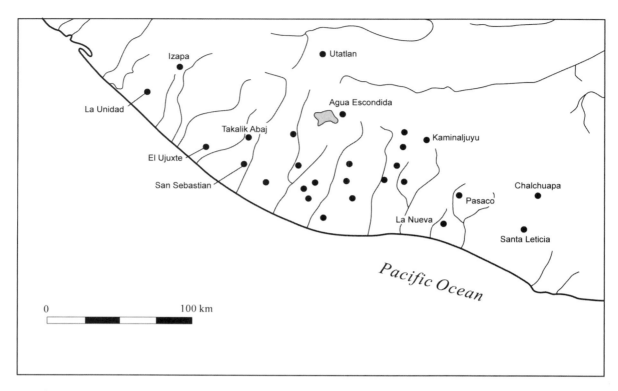

figure 7.10
General distribution of potbellied sculptures along the Pacific coastal plain of Guatemala, Chiapas, and El Salvador. Dots indicate locations of potbellies. (Drawing by the author, based on Rodas 1993.)

widespread across different types of settlements. That is, although Middle Preclassic sculpture is overwhelmingly concentrated in just a few of the largest settlements, Late Preclassic sculpture is found in a much wider variety of sites and contexts. Most of the sculpture known for the Late Preclassic period comes from the very largest sites; Kaminaljuyu has more than 300 pieces, Takalik Abaj more than 320, and Izapa more than 200. Nonetheless, a quick survey of Parsons's (1986:fig. 2) catalogue shows sculpture found or attributed to more than thirty sites in the Late Preclassic period. Parsons's number can be increased, based on recent discoveries. The total number of sites with sculpture now exceeds fifty. Rodas's (1993) catalogue of potbelly monuments found them distributed at more than thirty sites, ranging from the largest centers to small sites with only a single public mound. Bove's (n.d.b) study of plain stelae also finds them at more than twenty-seven sites. Beyond the studies of Bove

and Rodas, I know of no detailed considerations of the distribution of monument types across space on the Guatemalan coast and Highlands, but these studies make clear that much sculpture in the Late Preclassic period comes from outside the largest political and religious centers.

Nonetheless, not all forms of sculpture are widespread or evenly distributed. Representations of rulers on low-relief stelae appear only at the largest of sites in the highlands and in the piedmont stretching from El Salvador to Mexico: Chalchuapa, Kaminaljuyu, Takalik Abaj, El Baúl, Izapa, and El Jobo (Figure 7.9; see also Figure 1.4). These sites, most of which may be labeled as supraregional centers, probably represent the capitals of state-level polities and/or entrepots for long-distance trade networks (Love n.d.). So, although being relatively rare (compared to other themes), ruler portraits also have an extremely limited distribution in political terms.

The most frequent formal category in the highlands and on the coast during the Late Preclassic period may well be the potbellies, which have also received much scholarly attention (Guernsey and Love 2008; Miles 1965; Navarrete and Hernández 2000; Rodas 1993). Potbelly sculptures are widespread, stretching from western El Salvador to Veracruz, but their concentration is greatest on the Guatemalan coastal plain, with the largest number in the Department of Escuintla (Figure 7.10). As Guernsey discusses in Chapter 9, potbellies may emerge out of a Middle Preclassic figurine tradition, so that the elite and public nature of representational stelae contrasts with a domestically derived and perhaps nonelite potbelly form. Following Graham's (1979) analysis of the formal qualities of Preclassic sculpture, I suggested that the potbellies and representational stelae may represent different cultural traditions (Love 2004). The two interpretations are not mutually exclusive, but much work is needed on these topics.

Whereas representational stelae are found only at the largest sites, potbelly sculptures are much more widely distributed, occurring at primary, secondary, and tertiary settlements (see Bove [1981] for a discussion of settlement hierarchies in the Escuintla region). In his catalogue of potbelly sculptures, Rodas (1993) documents them occurring principally at primary and secondary centers. The quantity of potbellied works, however, at a site may correlate with its regional importance. Thus the three sites with the greatest number of potbellies are Kaminaljuyu, Monte Alto, and Takalik Abaj.

Plain stelae, or large worked freestanding stones without graven representations, have a wide distribution in the Late Preclassic period, rivaling that of the potbellies. Bove (n.d.b) has analyzed the distribution of these works and found them associated with sites with monumental architecture but, like the potbellies, they are also present in secondary and tertiary centers. There are chronological problems in analyzing the distribution of plain stelae, as they appear first in the Middle Preclassic (at least in the Valley of Guatemala) but continue well into the Late Preclassic in this region (although the use of plain stelae is known until the Late Classic in other regions). As discussed below, plain stelae may also be found at even more diverse locations beyond secondary or tertiary centers.

At many major sites, alignments of plain stelae may mark important astronomical events (Estrada Belli 2002; Shook 1952). Shook noted that in many cases plain stelae were placed on platforms east of the largest mound, suggesting that the stelae were used for observing solar passages. Such usage has been documented for Late Preclassic sites on the coastal plain, such as Ujuxte (in the department of Santa Rosa; Estrada Belli 2002) and Monte Alto (Shook and Hatch 1981). At other sites, however, there is no apparent astronomical rationale for the alignments. At Naranjo, alignments were created to structure space in a large plaza but without any known astronomical function (Arroyo, ed. 2007; Pereira et al. 2007). Isolated plain stelae were also found at Naranjo, such as one placed at the mouth of a spring, suggesting that they served to mark sacred locations as well (see Chapter 1).

Minor Forms

Other classes of sculpture, including toad altars, pedestal sculptures, and zoomorphs, are found in smaller numbers (see Figure 7.11 for the distribution of pedestal sculptures). These forms are frequently found at locations outside the major centers, but their distribution has not been fully analyzed, nor have their meanings or functions been studied in detail. In many cases, the works can only be attributed to a region rather than to a specific site. The pedestals and altars hint at religious beliefs and rituals partially or perhaps completely unassociated with elite power. Examining these works helps us to better understand the special nature of elite works and the contexts in which they were placed, but they also make it clear that we have yet to fully comprehend the great variety of Preclassic sculpture. These minor works, and the locations in which they occur, have not been systematically investigated by archaeologists, but they merit attention. In what follows I illustrate by case studies the potential importance of such works.

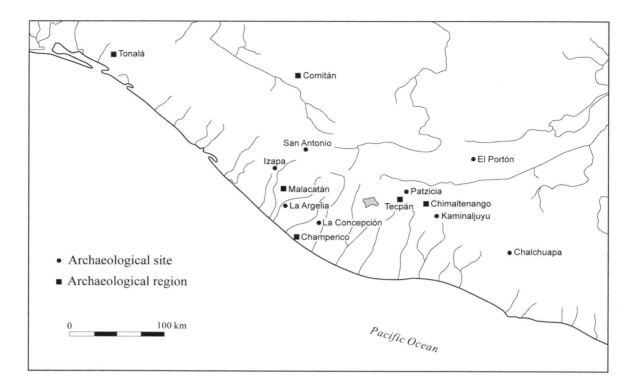

figure 7.11
Distribution of pedestal sculptures in Guatemala and Chiapas. (Drawing by the author.)

Distribution of Sculpture in Pacific Guatemala: Sculpture in Minor Sites

My case studies for the distribution of sculpture come from a small selection of sites on the western coast of Guatemala (Figure 7.12). These sites represent different types of settlements and have distinctive forms of sculpture. I do not presume that these sites represent a typical or full pattern, but I do think that analysis of the sculpture found there contributes toward understanding the overall role of sculpture by highlighting its use outside of primary centers.

Smaller Sites in the Takalik Abaj Hinterland

San Sebastian is a small center on the Samalá River, approximately 20 km southeast of Takalik Abaj. Shook (n.d.) recorded two large mounds at the site, but I found only one, approximately 10 m in height. When I first visited the site in 1981, all monuments had been removed from the site's plaza and taken to

various parts of the eponymous modern town. They have since been consolidated at the Museo Horacio Alejos in the departmental capital of Retalhuleu.

No formal survey of Takalik Abaj's hinterland has been conducted, but if San Sebastian were part of the political sphere of that large city, an ad hoc analysis would place it as a tertiary center. San Sebastian has fewer and smaller mounds than do other sites close to Takalik Abaj, such as Flamenco, Sitaná, and La Sultana. San Sebastian Monument 1 appears to be a head, approximately 1 m in height (Figure 7.13a); portions of it appear to have been reworked. San Sebastian Monument 2 (Figure 7.13b) is a toad altar. This altar form has a wide distribution in the coast and highlands, being documented at Kaminaljuyu, Takalik Abaj, and Izapa (Guernsey Kappelman 2000; Norman 1973, 1976; Parsons 1986), and the distribution extends even to Veracruz and Guerrero (see Chapter 3). However, to my knowledge there are no detailed studies of the formal variation in toad altars nor of their

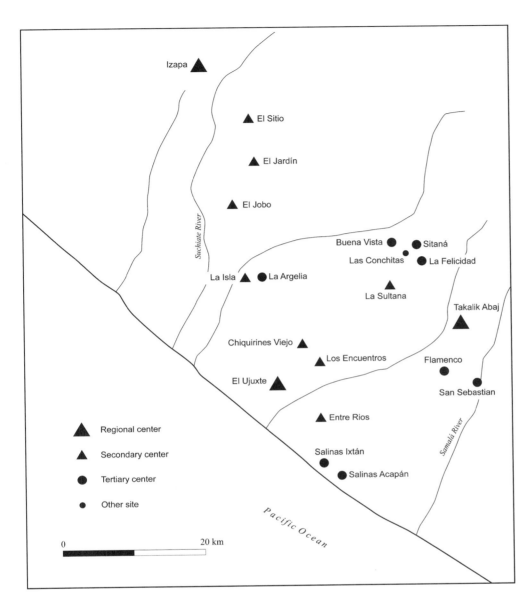

figure 7.12
Sites of southwestern Guatemala and Chiapas. (Drawing by the author.)

distribution. The example from San Sebastian is notable for the skill of its carving, which contrasts with the more rustic examples discussed below.

San Sebastian Monuments 3–6 are potbellied sculptures of various forms (Figure 7.14a–d). Monument 3 is carved in high relief, but it is not fully in the round, a style noted also for Takalik Abaj Monument 58 (see Figure 8.12b). Monument 4 is carved in the round, with a very distended belly. Monument 5, badly battered, is carved fully in the

round and most nearly approaches the full-round potbellies of Monte Alto. Monument 6 is carved in relief similar to Monument 2.

The subjective evaluation of the quality of a piece and the skill of the carver is always a dangerous proposition. Nonetheless, the varying degrees of sophistication shown in the San Sebastian works demands explanation. Monuments 1 and 2 are undeniably expert carvings. The forms are perfectly symmetrical, the features are sharply carved, and

figure 7.13
San Sebastian Monuments (a) 1; (b) 2.
(Photographs by the author.)

a

b

a   b   c   d

figure 7.14
San Sebastian Monuments (a) 3; (b) 4; (c) 5; (d) 6. (Photographs by the author.)

the depth of relief is even. In contrast, Monuments 4 and 6 are somewhat awkward in that the forms are less clearly rendered and the relief barely passes the depth of engraving. Thus Monuments 1 and 2 suggest the work of expert carvers, Monuments 4 and 6 look to be the work of less-skilled crafts-people, and Monument 5 is too badly battered to make a determination. The pattern of more sophisticated works appearing alongside relatively crude works is repeated at other sites detailed below.

All Roads Lead to Coatepeque

Like San Sebastian, a cluster of sites in and around the modern city of Coatepeque, Department of Quetzaltenango, may also be among the secondary and tertiary centers to Takalik Abaj. Located in the piedmont at an elevation of around 300 m, modern Coatepeque lies approximately 20 km west of the great city of Takalik Abaj (Figure 7.1). Each of the Coatepeque sites with moderate public architecture and two or more plain stelae appears

figure 7.15
Monuments from La Felicidad. (Photographs by the author.)

figure 7.16
Monuments from
La Sultana and a map
showing where they
were found. (Photographs
and map by the author.)

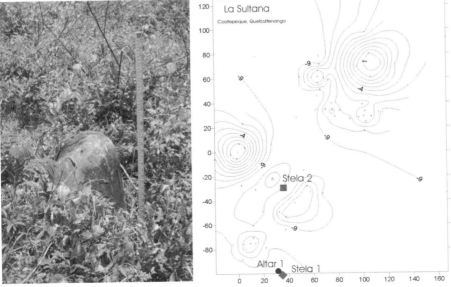

to represent a small ritual and/or administrative center. Much smaller than Takalik Abaj or Izapa, they lack stelae with portraits of rulers. The distributional pattern of sculpture at these sites fits well within that noted by Bove (n.d.b) in that plain stelae and altars are frequently found at secondary centers where they apparently served to create structured space.

There are at least four sites with small architectural groups in the immediate vicinity of Coatepeque: La Sultana, La Felicidad, Buena Vista, and Sitaná. Sitaná was described by Shook (n.d.) as having a 5 m tall mound and two plain stelae. Buena Vista also has two mounds between 5 and 6 m in height, along with two plain stelae. La Felicidad has two large mounds, one approximately 6 m tall, the other 10 m. Three plain monuments were found at the site. Two are stelae, the third may be a plain altar (Figure 7.15).

La Sultana is a larger site than the other three, with several large mounds and a triadic group located atop a massive acropolis. Donaldo Castillo, Julia Guernsey, Scott Johnson, and I visited La Sultana in 2006 and found a large architectural group with two plain stelae (Figure 7.16). A plain altar was associated with one of the stelae.

Secondary Sites of the El Ujuxte Polity

La Argelia is an extensive site, located approximately 10 km north of La Blanca and 10 km east of the border of Mexico and Guatemala. Shook (n.d.) recorded La Argelia as a large Late Preclassic site whose major architecture was destroyed by road construction in 1972. I have found materials from the Early Preclassic onward at the site, but the pottery was predominantly Late Classic. The Late Preclassic component of La Argelia may be a residential area associated with the larger site of La Isla, which has extensive formal architecture and may have been a secondary center of the El Ujuxte polity (Love n.d.).

Guernsey and I (Guernsey and Love n.d.) recorded three sculptures from La Argelia. The sculptures were removed from the site many years ago by Juan López, the now-deceased owner of the Finca Argelia, and moved to his house at

Hacienda Las Conchas. My attempts to record the sculptures in 1985 were frustrated by the untimely death of Señor López, but Guernsey and I traced them to the estate of Fernando López, the son of Juan. There the sculptures were stored in the large barn qua chicken coop, amidst used tractor parts, rotting tires, and a plethora of Late Preclassic artifacts.

All three monuments from La Argelia (Figure 7.17) are pedestal sculptures, a form well known from Kaminaljuyu, the Guatemalan Highlands, and the western Pacific Coast of Guatemala. Monuments 1 and 2 are representations of monkeys. A broken tail section seems to best match Monument 1, with which it is displayed in Figure 7.17. Monument 3 presents a seated jaguar (or possibly another species of large cat) with a curved and elongated appendage, superficially resembling a maize cob, arching forward from the head. The ears of the cat spiral backward in a manner similar to the sculptures of supernaturals found at Monte Alto and in western El Salvador (Miles 1965; Richardson 1940). Miles (1965) noted the similarity between the spiral ears of the feline pedestal sculptures from the Malacatán district (which includes El Jardín and El Sitio) and those sculptures from Monte Alto and El Salvador, which she considered to be jaguars. Both Guernsey (Chapter 9) and Taube (1995) now associate these latter images with the rain deity Chahk, and the feline pedestal sculptures sharing the spiral ears may also be associated with that same supernatural.

All three monuments from La Argelia greatly resemble, indeed nearly replicate, other documented pedestal sculptures from the region of the modern border between Guatemala and Mexico. Feline pedestal sculptures closely resembling La Argelia Monument 3 come from El Sitio and El Jardín in the Malacatán district (Miles 1965; Shook 1965) of southwest Guatemala, and others are documented from Izapa (Norman 1973), Tonalá (cited in Miles [1965] but not illustrated) in Chiapas, coastal Retalhuleu (Pye 1995), and Takalik Abaj. An unpublished example, attributed to the Champerico region along the Pacific Coast of the Department of Retalhuleu is on display at the Museo Horacio

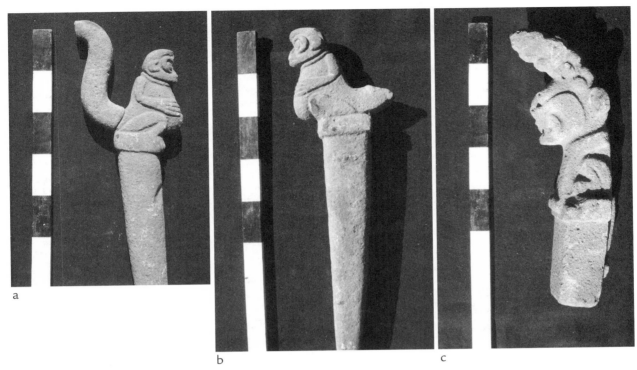

figure 7.17
Pedestal sculptures from La Argelia. (a) Monument 1; (b) Monument 2; (c) Monument 3. (Photographs by the author.)

Alejos. Monkeys on pedestals, complete with tails similar to that of Monument 1 from La Argelia, are also known from the Champerico region. It is interesting to note that in western Pacific Guatemala there is a great concentration of pedestal sculptures at what appear to be secondary political centers. It is likely that El Sitio and El Jardín, which are most likely the sources of the monuments attributed to the Malacatán region, were secondary centers to Izapa, whereas the sites of the Champerico region were secondary to El Ujuxte. More interesting, however, may be the marked similarity between the numerous feline pedestal pieces.

The remarkable similarity of both the monkey pedestals from southwestern Guatemala and the group of feline sculptures from same region raises the possibility, certainly far from demonstrated, that they were produced by the same individual artist or a group of artists trained in similar concepts. I comment on some implications for such a model of sculpture production below.

Thinking Outside the Plaza: Sculpture Beyond the Political Centers

Possibly more interesting than the secondary and tertiary centers discussed above is a fifth site in the Coatepeque region. A number of sculpted monuments were recently discovered at Finca Las Conchitas, which lies approximately halfway between La Felicidad and Sitaná, separated from each by about 1 km. During the excavation of a drainage canal for a housing development, four carved monuments were found. Subsequent to these discoveries a salvage archaeological project was undertaken by Juan Luis Velásquez, who published four of the sculpted monuments (Velásquez 1999). Later at least three other large stones, worked but without representational imagery, were found.

The Las Conchitas site is an area without obvious mounds. There is a Late Preclassic residential area near where the sculptures were found, perhaps 150 m distant, but the primary association of

figure 7.18
Las Conchitas Altars (a) 1; (b) 2; (c) 3; (d) 4. (Photographs by the author.)

the monuments is with a spring that gives birth to the San Francisco River, a small stream tributary to the Naranjo River. The published carved monuments are all altars. Although showing thematic and some formal similarities to altars known from larger sites, none could be considered an exemplar of the high tradition of Mesoamerican sculpture.

Altar 1 is well formed, with a flat rectangular surface bound by a band of triangles (Figure 7.18a), recalling the treatment of Kaminaljuyu Altar 1 (Parsons 1986:fig. 161) and Izapa Altar 16 (Norman 1976:245). This shared detail indicates the widespread use of many sculptural conventions, even in the smallest of sites. All sides of the Las Conchitas monument are well formed and carefully shaped. One side of the altar bears the partially eroded image of a dancing human in high relief. The figure holds an object in the right hand, possibly a percussion instrument. The image thus suggests performance, evoking the theme of many ruler representations (Guernsey

2006b), but with perhaps a nonelite person represented here.

Altar 2 (Figure 7.18b) is expertly worked and shaped but unadorned, except for an animal image carved in high relief on one side. The type of animal represented is ambiguous, but the long snout suggests that it is most likely either a dog or a *pisote* (also known as a coati; it is a member of the raccoon family).

Altars 3 and 4 are both toad altars (Figure 7.18c,d). As already discussed, toad altars are a widespread sculptural form in the Late Preclassic period, known from the Guatemalan Highlands, the Pacific Coast, and coastal Veracruz and Guerrero (see Chapter 3). The two examples from Las Conchitas are from any point of view rather crude examples of the form. The boulders are not dressed, and they appear to have been selected because of their natural resemblance to the shape of a somewhat flattened amphibian. The mouth, legs, and eyes of the toad are indicated by shallow

figure 7.19
Las Conchitas Altars (a) 5;
(b) 6. (Photographs by the
author.)

a

b

grooving rather than the skillful pecking and relief carving shown in the altar from San Sebastian.

In addition to the four altars recorded by Velásquez (1999), there are at least three other monuments at the Las Conchitas locality. The first of these, Stela 1, is a plain stela more than 3 m in length that was discovered during the excavation of the drain trench for a real estate development within Finca Las Conchitas. According to Luís Solórzano, administrator of Las Conchitas, the stela was too large to be lifted by the available machinery, so it was simply pushed to one side and reburied. For that reason, no photographs are available. Licenciado Solórzano reported to me that the stela was very finely worked and well proportioned, but I have not observed the monument personally.

Thinking Outside the Plaza   169

A second monument lies just east of the place where the stela and altars were found, immediately below the fountainhead of the San Francisco River. This monument, Altar 5, is a large slab of andesite with minimal working around the edges (Figure 7.19a). Five grooves have been ground into the surface, evidence of some form of extensive use. The third uncarved piece, Altar 6 (Figure 7.19b), lies in the streambed of the San Francisco River. Monument 6 has been smoothed by water action, but the perfectly square corners indicate shaping by human hands. Still more stones in the streambed may have been shaped by human actions, but the evidence of working is not definitive.

Sculpture from Domestic Contexts

Although we generally think of sculpture as being of stone, it can also be considered as something found in public contexts, either in large architectural complexes or in communal ritual spaces, such as caves or springs. Nonetheless, Pacific Guatemala yields some examples of sculptures found in domestic contexts.

Returning to the Middle Preclassic period, the La Blanca Monument 3 quatrefoil (Figure 7.3) was associated with an elite residence fronting the sunken plaza east of Mound 1, a monumental temple pyramid originally 25 m in height (Love

and Guernsey 2007). The artifact assemblage from the elite residence exhibits high indices of utilitarian pottery, faunal remains, and other domestic indicators (Love and Guernsey 2007). Despite its association with a domestic context, the quatrefoil monument stood adjacent to what might be interpreted as a public space, the sunken plaza. Thus its context is somewhat ambiguous, and perhaps that ambiguity was intentional, meant to blur the lines between the public and private functions of a ruler.

More clearly associated with domestic contexts are three small sculptures from El Ujuxte, Retalhuleu. Miniature Sculpture 1 is a small work, barely 20 cm long, found on the surface of a small residential mound. The piece is a representation of a turtle, carved from andesite (Figure 7.20). Several turtle shells were recovered from El Ujuxte, and they may have been a staple of domestic ritual, perhaps as drums, although their exact function is as yet unclear.

Two miniature potbelly sculptures were also found in surface collections. Miniature Sculpture 2 (Figure 7.21a) has been decapitated, and it is possible that it was the base of a mushroom stone sculpture (see Ohi and Torres [1994] for an excellent compilation of mushroom stones). Miniature Sculpture 3 is nearly complete, though badly damaged by plow scars (Figure 7.21b). These two miniature potbellies from El Ujuxte share a prominent feature of the full-scale Late Preclassic sculptures: the placement

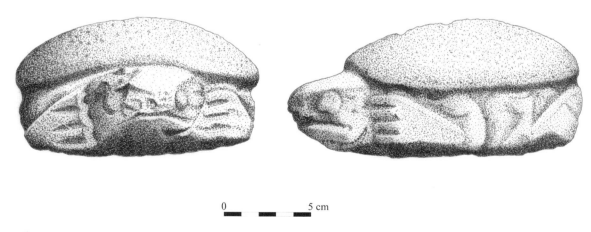

0   5 cm

figure 7.20
Two views of El Ujuxte Miniature Sculpture 1, a small turtle sculpture. (Drawing by Araceli Alzamora.)

figure 7.21
El Ujuxte Miniature
Sculptures (a) 2;
(b) 3, small potbelly
sculptures.
(Photographs
by the author.)

of hands on a prominent belly. They were located on a low domestic mound in the eastern portion of the site, separated by a distance of about 1.5 m, and both facing east. My supposition is that they were placed on each side of a doorway, perhaps as talismans. It is interesting to note that several potbellied sculptures at Takalik Abaj also occur at passageways or points of transition, such as the potbellies found associated with the stairway that leads from Terrace 2 to Terrace 3 (see Chapter 8).

Camahuiles

Two small greenstone sculptures from El Ujuxte fall within the class known as *camahuiles* in K'iche' (Figure 7.22). Camahuiles (a name that Orellana [1981] derives from *c'abawil* or "deity") are generally defined as small figures with angular features and lacking sexual characteristics. Typically they are carved only on the front, with the back being flat (Orellana 1981). Ichon (1977) dates similar examples from La Lagunita to the Protoclassic period, and Orellana (1981) documents their continued use during the Postclassic period and into ethnographic times in the highlands of Guatemala. Although the El Ujuxte examples strongly resemble the camahuiles from La Lagunita (Ichon 1977:fig. 5) as well as those recorded by Schultze Jena (1933; see Orellana 1981:fig. 1), more distant relationships can be seen with Mezcala-style stone

figurines from Guerrero (Lister 1971) and stone figurines from Veracruz (Drucker 1955).

Ciudad Ruíz (1984) considers the camahuiles to be generally associated with the K'iche' Maya, though he notes that Carmack and Lamer (1971) see similarities with Mixteca-Puebla–style figurines from Oaxaca. Ciudad Ruíz views the camahuiles of the highlands during the Classic period as predominantly associated with a conservative folk tradition and used largely in domestic rituals. Ichon (1977), however, recovered caches of camahuiles in La Lagunita in the central zone of the site, notably in Sarcophagus 4, so they are not necessarily strictly domestic items (see Chapter 10).

The El Ujuxte examples both come from domestic trash deposits of the Pitahaya phase, ca 100 BC–AD 100. One (Figure 7.22a,b) was associated with a residence in the middle of El Ujuxte's socioeconomic scale (Operation 7). The other (Figure 7.22b) comes from a deposit (Operation 17) associated with the highest ranked residence at the site, Mound 36. Made of greenstone, the camahuiles superficially resemble potbelly sculptures in that the figures have their hands placed on their stomachs. In one figurine, the belly is enlarged, as in the potbelly mode. The two examples from El Ujuxte were not associated with burials but, judging by the context, may have been used in some form of domestic ritual.

figure 7.22
Camahuiles from
El Ujuxte. (a) Profile
view of Camahuile 1;
(b) frontal view
of Camahuile 1;
(c) profile view of
Camahuile 2;
(d) frontal view
of Camahuile 2.
(Photographs by
the author.)

If the correspondences between Preclassic camahuiles and potbelly sculptures can be sustained, they would be further examples of the links between potbellies and domestic rituals. Guernsey (see Chapter 9; Guernsey and Love 2008) proposes that large stone potbelly sculptures of the Late Preclassic may have derived from Middle Preclassic figurines used in domestic rituals. The camahuiles, in conjunction with the miniature potbellies from El Ujuxte, may show continuity in the use of such images in the domestic context throughout the Preclassic period. Thus although ceramic figurines underwent a very dramatic decline during the Late Preclassic period, possibly reflecting the movement of ritual from domestic to public contexts (Guernsey and Love 2005; Love 1999b), some aspects of domestic ritual may have continued.

Limited as these examples may be, they serve to illustrate the presence of Preclassic sculpture in domestic contexts. With the exception of La Blanca Monuments 3 and 4, however, there are few data with which to discuss their contexts or uses. The mounds at El Ujuxte where the small sculptures were located were not excavated, so measures of socioeconomic status are limited. All miniature sculptures from El Ujuxte came from very low mounds, an indication that they are not from elite residences (Love n.d.).

Discussion

What do these disparate examples tell us about the role of sculpture in Preclassic Mesoamerica? First and foremost, they indicate that the role of sculpture was much broader and more varied than is often appreciated. In form, subject matter, and location, sculpture was highly diverse. Although is it undeniably true that most monumental sculpture was located in major centers, sculpture was extremely widespread in the southern highlands and Pacific coastal plain.

Second, although it would be facile to say that everyone sculpted in Preclassic Mesoamerica, it does appear that sculpture was made and used by diverse sectors of society. There is every reason to believe that sculptures, such as the portraits of royalty and deities in the largest cities, were undertaken by specialized artists commissioned by the elite. The sculptors may well have been members of the elite themselves. The combination of skill, along with demonstrated knowledge of sacred precepts, iconography, calendrics, and (in some instances) writing, make that proposition almost certain. The sculptors working on these elite-sanctioned works probably trained as apprentices, studied the works of master sculptors, and participated in a tradition of sculpting that spanned many hundreds of years.

Other sculptors may have been vernacular, having little formal training and drawing upon folk interpretations of religion and ritual. The sculptures from small sites sometimes show familiarity with many techniques and formal elements of sculpture from larger sites, but often they do not show expert execution. That is to say, the sculptors at smaller sites were not the best and may not have been formally trained, as were the sculptors of larger sites. The less sophisticated potbellies of San Sebastian and the simple toad altars of Las Conchitas may represent the works of nonspecialists, the residents of the locales. Although it is problematic to equate simplicity with unspecialized artisans, quality does count for something, and attributing unskilled carving to untrained carvers seems the most parsimonious way to explain the juxtaposition of simple works with sophisticated works at Las Conchitas and San Sebastian.

Third, we can see from these examples that there was great variation in subject matter in sculpture. For instance, the monuments from Las Conchitas illustrate that sculptural forms outside the largest sites do not focus on rulers and rulership. Instead, Late Preclassic monuments from these sites show a great deal of thematic overlap with ritual objects used in the domestic sphere during both the Middle and Late Preclassic. Guernsey (Chapter 9) makes the point that Late Preclassic potbellied sculptures may be derived from Middle Preclassic figurines that were used principally in domestic rituals, and that the presence of potbelly sculptures in ritual centers may represent a concession to populist concerns. Similarly, dogs, pisotes, and other animals (possibly talismanic) are represented in the Middle Preclassic corpus of figurines and could be viewed as images used in religious or healing rituals by all members of society. Las Conchitas Altar 2 may thus be another example of thematic overlap and the incorporation of nonelite concerns into the sculptural programs of the Late Preclassic. We should not assume that the works by nonelites were simply imitations of the works carved by elite specialists, but we should entertain the idea that some sculptures in site centers may have necessarily conformed to shared practices of elites and nonelites, or they may have reflected the conservative traditions of nonelites (Guernsey and Love 2008).

Fourth, these materials say something about the social conditions under which sculpture was produced. As just noted, many sculptures were probably produced as commissioned works by specialists patronized by elites, a relationship also known as "attached specialization" (Clark and Parry 1990). In these cases, the product would have been inalienable and controlled by the patron, who determined its initial placement. Other sculptures, however, may have been produced for exchange as commodities by independent specialists. These works were alienable, and may have been exchanged over varying distances. Still other works, as suggested above, may have been produced by nonspecialists for either individual or communal use.

The remarkable similarity of both the monkey pedestal sculptures from southwestern Guatemala—and the group of feline sculptures from same region—raises the possibility that these small monuments were produced by the same individual artist or a group of artists trained in similar concepts. The pedestal sculptures are highly portable and, if made by independent specialists, could have been objects of exchange. The idea of sculpture as a trade item may seem radical, but the idea seems more plausible than to assume that the small sites of the Champerico region, a locale that lacks local stone and has few works of sculpture, would have had skilled resident sculptors who precisely copied works from sites in the piedmont zone. We often think that sculptures were produced at the place where they were displayed, even if both the rock and the sculptor were brought from a distance, but we should entertain the idea that some small forms

of sculpture may have been produced at centralized workshops and traded. A similar conclusion may be drawn from the camahuile figures from El Ujuxte. The stone from which they were made is clearly not local, and the strong resemblance to examples from highland Guatemala and Guerrero suggests that they were trade goods. The source of the stone has not been determined, so the point of origin as well as the conditions of their manufacture are both unresolved.

Concluding Remarks

This chapter began with the proposition that the power of Preclassic rulers in Mesoamerica may be overestimated. My presentation has focused chiefly on sculpture that does not depict rulers, is located outside of site centers, and whose subject matter, I propose, is unrelated to rulers or rulership. My interpretation is based on the assertion that such sculptural representations as pisotes, dogs, toads, and potbellies represent widespread (common to all sectors of society) religious precepts that focused on natural (possibly sacred) forces and perhaps ancestor veneration. Other interpretations are certainly possible, and it must be admitted that the iconography of these various representations is still poorly developed. Nonetheless, the overlap between these sculptures and the ceramic figurines used so commonly in domestic ritual may provide some clues. That is, themes represented in stone sculptures outside the public areas of major sites overlap considerably with the paraphernalia of domestic ritual, but most especially with ceramic figurines.

The lack of ruler representations outside major centers is also subject to multiple interpretations. It may be that those residing in secondary and tertiary centers were forbidden by rulers in regional capitals to erect monuments depicting local elites, or it may be that the local populace forbade rulers to erect portraits in the center of their towns (see Chapter 1). Which interpretation we choose may ultimately depend on archaeological evidence for political and economic organization at the regional level.

Acknowledgments

Investigations at La Blanca and El Ujuxte were carried out under the auspices of the Instituto de Antropología e Historia de Guatemala; I thank the personnel of the Departamento de Prehispánicos y Coloniales for their help and support. Research at El Ujuxte was supported by National Science Foundation Grants (SBR-9807304, SBR-96171123, and SBR-9510991), with additional support from the Heinz Foundation, the Wenner-Gren Foundation for Anthropological Research, Sonoma State University, and the Universidad del Valle de Guatemala. Financial support for the excavations at La Blanca came from the New World Archaeological Foundation, the Wenner-Gren Foundation for Anthropological Research, the National Geographic Society, the Mesoamerica Center in the Department of Art and Art History at the University of Texas at Austin, and National Science Foundation Grant BCS-0451024. A grant from the Foundation for the Advancement of Mesoamerican Studies helped support the analysis of materials associated with La Blanca Monument 3. The late Henry Sierra first introduced me to the sculptures of Las Conchitas, and Luís Solórzano, the administrator of Las Conchitas, S.A., graciously guided me around the location where the monuments were found. Byron Lemus first informed me of the monuments of La Felicidad and Buena Vista. Valerio Sowa served as guide to the monuments at La Felicidad during a visit in 2007. Donaldo Castillo helped to locate La Sultana and coordinated a visit to the site, where Scott Johnson assisted in mapping the mounds. I thank the staff of the Museo Horacio Alejos in Retalhuleu for kindly allowing me to photograph the monuments housed at the museum. The late Juan López first informed me of the sculptures from Argelia housed at Hacienda las Conchas, and his son Fernando López kindly gave permission to take photographs. I thank Julia Guernsey for helping to develop many of the ideas presented here and for her close editing of earlier versions of the chapter.

8

Preclassic Olmec and Maya Monuments and Architecture at Takalik Abaj

CHRISTA SCHIEBER DE LAVARREDA AND MIGUEL ORREGO CORZO

Takalik Abaj lies on the Pacific slope of Guatemala at the nexus of several major trails, most significantly one connecting the coast to the central highlands (Popenoe de Hatch et al. 2000:160, 164, 170, fig. 3). Myriad peoples and goods passed through this center during the seventeen centuries of its existence (800 BC–AD 900). The cosmopolitan nature of Takalik Abaj is readily apparent in the wide variety of sculptural styles and themes present there. In contrast, ceramic wares at this site from 800 BC onward appear strictly local and give little indication of foreign influence (Poponoe de Hatch 2004:437–447, fig. 3.7). Instead the ceramic tradition suggests indigenous peoples occupied the site continuously, so the dramatic changes in sculptural fashions implemented during the Preclassic likely indicate adoption of different styles rather than population replacement.

Takalik Abaj is a modern Mayan name meaning "Place of the Standing Stones" (Graham et al. 1978:85; Orrego Corzo 1990:7; Tarpy 2004:72).[1]

Takalik Abaj has been the object of systematic archaeological investigations since 1976, resulting in the discovery of 326 stone monuments and more than 80 mounds. Most of the monuments date to the Middle and Late Preclassic periods. Except for two examples (Stela 18 and Monument 27), all recovered monuments are from locally available volcanic rock. John Graham and Robert Heizer of the University of California at Berkeley excavated this site, because it was, and continues to be, the only one known to have both Olmec and early Maya styles of stone sculpture (Graham 1977, 1979, 1980, 1981, 1982, 1989, 1992; Graham et al. 1978; Graham and Benson 2005).[2] They wished to discover the relationship between these two cultures. There are also other monument styles at the site, as described here. The only other Preclassic site with similar diversity and number of stone sculptures is Kaminaljuyu, but so far Olmec style sculptures have not been found at this contemporaneous highland center (see Chapter 1; Miles 1965; Parsons 1983, 1986).

The functions and meanings of these stone monuments have changed through time and will continue to do so as long as they remain exposed to view. These monuments are still objects of veneration by modern indigenous peoples (Bruehl 1888; Schieber de Lavarreda and Orrego Corzo 2002:75; Tarpy 2004). In this chapter, we consider past meanings and functions and how both may have varied during different eras. After a brief introduction to the site we consider the meaning(s) of its monuments. Constituents of meaning include (1) the characteristic of each monument in its original form (e.g., its carved representations, size, carving technique, raw material); (2) modifications to monuments after their original carving; (3) the temporal position of monuments; (4) their spatial locations; and (5) their associations with other monuments, buildings, and offerings. We are principally interested in the reasons for the plurality of styles at Takalik Abaj as they relate to site history. Why were Olmec and Maya monuments positioned side by side? Valuable information also comes from a study of the destruction of monuments and the recycling of sculptures.

Overview of Takalik Abaj

Takalik Abaj is located in the transitional piedmont zone (600–900 m altitude) between the coastal plain and the central highlands (see Figure 10.1). The deep volcanic piedmont soils at the

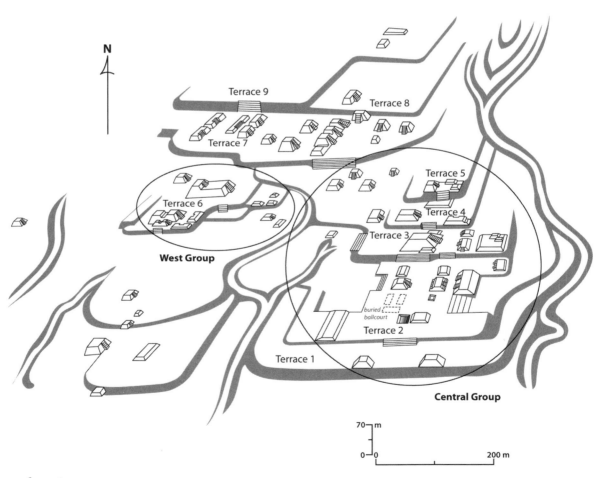

figure 8.1
Map of Takalik Abaj showing the terraces and major sectors of the site. (Drawing from the New World Archaeological Foundation based on original from the Proyecto Nacional Takalik Abaj.)

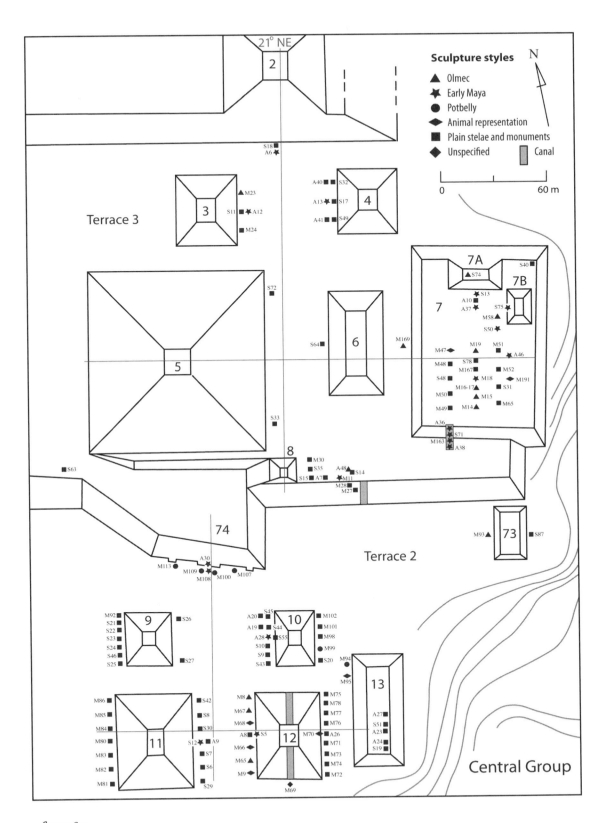

figure 8.2
Distribution of stone monuments on Terraces 2 and 3 at Takalik Abaj. (Drawing after the Berkeley Abaj
Takalik map [Map A] by Mark Johnson and Kevin Pope.)

site are extremely fertile, and this spot receives ample rainfall for growing a range of crops, especially the highly valued cacao. The site extends over 6.5 km² and ascends upslope from south to north over a series of ten largely natural terraces, each with groups of platforms. The terraces have been enhanced with retaining walls to create steep fronts 4–10 m high and 140–220 m wide (Graham et al. 1978:88). Modification to the natural terraces was accomplished by adding fill to the downslope end rather than cutting away the slope on the uphill side. A deep ravine borders the site to the east, and several small streams run through the site. The four principal architectural groups are, according to their location in the urban zone, the North, South, West, and Central groups. Stone sculptures have been found in the West Group on Terrace 6 and in the Central Group on Terraces 1–5 (Figure 8.1), with the greatest number on Terrace 2 (Figure 8.2).

Traces of Early Preclassic occupation have been reported for Takalik Abaj but no significant occupation (Popenoe de Hatch 1991:68, 2004:437–447). The city grew rapidly during the Middle and Late Preclassic until the Early Classic, when there was a collapse of traditional trade routes and interaction spheres in southern Guatemala (see Chapter 10; Popenoe de Hatch 1997; Popenoe de Hatch et al. 2000). The Early Maya sculptural tradition ceased at Kaminaljuyu and Takalik Abaj at the time of this collapse. In the Late Classic, Takalik Abaj experienced a renaissance, evident in the remodeling of its ancient platforms and the renewed display of its early stone monuments. This resurgence lasted until the beginning of the Postclassic period. The city appears to have been abandoned at this time.

Construction of terraces and low rectangular platforms, as well as the design and alignment of the plazas, began in the Middle Preclassic. The principal, north-south, axis of the plazas was 21° northeast of true north, and this alignment was maintained throughout the history of Takalik Abaj. The earliest platforms were constructed of tamped clay and rammed earth. Some of the earliest clay structures uncovered are buried beneath the current plaza surface of Terrace 2. Structures Sub-1, Sub-2, and Sub-4 constituted three sides of an open-ended ballcourt

with a playing surface about 34 m long (Schieber de Lavarreda 1994:78). Structure Sub-1 was built before Structures Sub-2 and Sub-4, which defined the north-south–trending playing alley; the whole ballcourt came together on the third plaza floor laid down in the Nil phase (700–400 BC). Recent analyses of associated ceramics suggest the ballcourt dates to the early part of that phase (Marion Popenoe de Hatch, personal communication 2008). The long axis of this court was 23° northeast of magnetic north. This ballcourt appears to have been carefully buried when the terrace was raised (Schieber de Lavarreda 1994, 1997).

During the Late Preclassic (400 BC–AD 150), the clay buildings were enlarged and given stone cobble facings set in a mortar of clay mixed with sand and *taxcal*.[3] These platforms were taller and broader than their predecessors. They also slanted outward and provided greater stability to the buildings and better resistance to erosion from heavy rainfall. The river cobbles used in platform facades increased in size through time. Many of the Late Preclassic buildings at Takalik Abaj were built over and incorporated Middle Preclassic platforms. One interesting architectural feature of Late Preclassic platforms was inset corners on rectangular buildings, a common trait in the lowland Maya region (Orrego Corzo 1998:55; Schieber de Lavarreda 1994:78).

The Middle/Late Preclassic occupation at Takalik Abaj was strong, but the site's construction apogee and building boom occurred in the Terminal Preclassic (Ruth phase, 200 BC–AD 150) and lasted until ca AD 200, the beginning of the Early Classic. Most of the visible platforms and pyramids at Takalik Abaj date to the Terminal Preclassic, and the placement of monuments at their bases corresponds to this time. As mentioned, the majority of the Terminal Preclassic buildings have Middle Preclassic cores that were maintained and added to during the Late Preclassic. The clay ballcourt under the southwest corner of Terrace 2 is an outstanding exception. It was deliberately buried ca 400 BC, and no platforms or buildings were built above it. No other ballcourt is known to have replaced it during the Preclassic period. It is likely that closure of this ballcourt corresponded to the shift in sculptural styles at Takalik Abaj from Olmec to early Maya (see below).

No new buildings or sculptures were added to the site in the Early Classic, and many extant monuments were purposely broken and defaced. Long-distance trade also appears to have ceased at this time. As noted, Takalik Abaj experienced a political and economic rebirth during the Late Classic (until AD 900). Many buildings were refurbished, and new stairways added to the then-ancient platforms. There is evidence of long-distance exchange and commercial ties with neighboring polities (Popenoe de Hatch and Schieber de Lavarreda 2001; Popenoe de Hatch et al. 2000; Schieber de Lavarreda and Orrego Corzo 2001b:25, 2002). Stone monuments placed along the bases of the main mounds during the Late Preclassic to Early Classic era retained their positions. New drainage canals were built for some of the mounds. Construction activity has not been identified for the Late Postclassic (Popenoe de Hatch 2005:1037–1043).

To summarize, all contexts for stone monuments at Takalik Abaj are final ones but rarely first ones. Most placements apparent today represented a change in original settings, functions, and meanings. In some Late Preclassic alignments, Olmec, early Maya, and other style monuments commingle with no apparent regard for age or culture. We have speculated that some Olmec sculptures relocated to Structure 12 of Terrace 2 may originally have been associated with the clay ballcourt (Schieber de Lavarreda and Orrego Corzo 2002:34). Olmec sculptures were certainly contemporaneous with this ballcourt, and there are some intrusive holes at the edges of the ballcourt platforms, pointing to the possibility that sculptures may have been placed there originally. The Olmec sculptures found on Terrace 2 are all unique, so even if some had been associated with the ballcourt, there is no evidence for a quadripartite arrangement of nearly identical ballcourt sculptures, such as described by Martínez Donjuán for Teopantecuanitlan, Guerrero (see Chapter 3).

The stone monuments at Takalik Abaj have a long history of use, reuse, and abuse. The initial placements of all Middle Preclassic and a few Late Preclassic monuments cannot be recovered, but some original meanings may possibly be inferred from individual carvings.

Types and Styles of Sculpture at Takalik Abaj

Most of the basic formal types of Preclassic sculptures described in Chapter 1 are present at Takalik Abaj—large stone heads, thrones, boulder sculptures, petroglyphs, niche figures, stelae, altars, and unspecified monuments (see Graham 1979, 1981, 1982, 1989, 1992; Graham and Benson 2005; Graham et al. 1978; Orrego Corzo 1990, 1995, 1997, 1998; Orrego Corzo and Schieber de Lavarreda 2001). Middle/Late Preclassic sculptures were reset to highlight new Terminal Preclassic/Early Classic constructions and perhaps to tie them to the power and spirituality of ancestors. Graham (1981:168, 1982:14) characterizes the rows of monuments in front of some of the cobble-faced platforms as one of Mesoamerica's first museums.

A preoccupation since the beginning of research at Takalik Abaj has been to separate Olmec from Maya monuments. This stylistic division is also temporal. Olmec monuments date to the Middle Preclassic, and Maya monuments came in at the beginning of the Late Preclassic period, ca 400 BC. As mentioned, Middle Preclassic monuments were reset, so sculptures cannot be dated solely from their architectural associations. Our assessment of the relative ages of stone sculptures relies on styles, forms, themes, and iconography. We classify stone monuments at Takalik Abaj as Olmec, early Maya, potbelly, animal representations, smooth or plain, and unspecified (Figure 8.2). Some monuments cannot confidently be identified as either Olmec or Maya. Within these general categories, sculptures are subdivided by form, such as stelae, altars, boulder sculptures, and petroglyphs.

Distinctions among Olmec, Maya, and Izapa styles in the Pacific slope region are based on carving techniques, forms, themes, iconography, and modes of representation. Graham and Benson (2005)

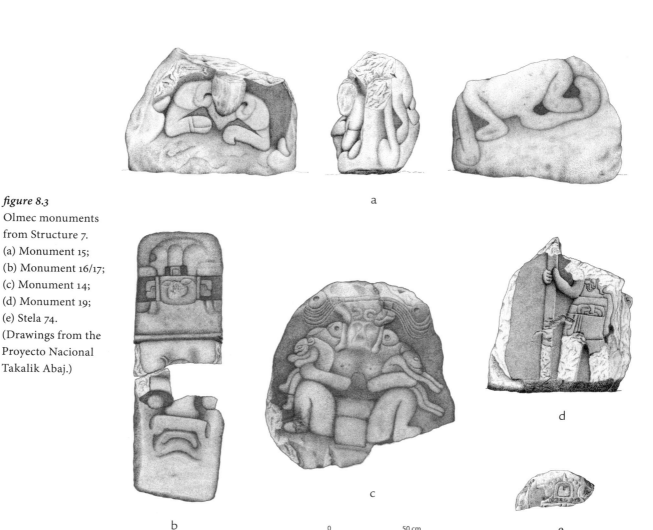

figure 8.3
Olmec monuments from Structure 7.
(a) Monument 15;
(b) Monument 16/17;
(c) Monument 14;
(d) Monument 19;
(e) Stela 74.
(Drawings from the Proyecto Nacional Takalik Abaj.)

distinguish between Olmec and Maya styles in their description of boulder sculptures from Takalik Abaj. Boulder sculptures refer "to the use of large stones in which the natural contours remain substantially recognizable or distinguishable" (Graham 1982:16); they can be relief sculptures or in the round. The "Olmec style is above all characterized by a pre-occupation with volume, that is, a feeling for full, swelling masses, which together with consistent application of a highly refined system of proportion accounts for the overall impression of grand, inherent monumentality which distinguished even the smallest of fine Olmec objects" (Graham 1982:9; see also Graham and Benson 2005:357; see Figure 8.3). "These works contrast strikingly with the early

Maya vision which required flat slab-like surfaces for the expression of their more pictorially oriented, two-dimensional, decoratively patterned relief surfaces" (Graham and Benson 2005:362; see Figures 8.4 and 8.5).

In Graham's (1982:9) opinion, the Izapan style shares more features with Maya art than with Olmec art: "Izapan art...displays almost no feeling for volume, systematic proportion, or monumentality, but concerns itself instead almost entirely with the sometimes amazingly sophisticated creation of notional or depicted space, a natural predisposition for artists whose chief purpose seems to have been the depiction of narrative scenes." As he elaborated, "Izapa sculptures characteristically

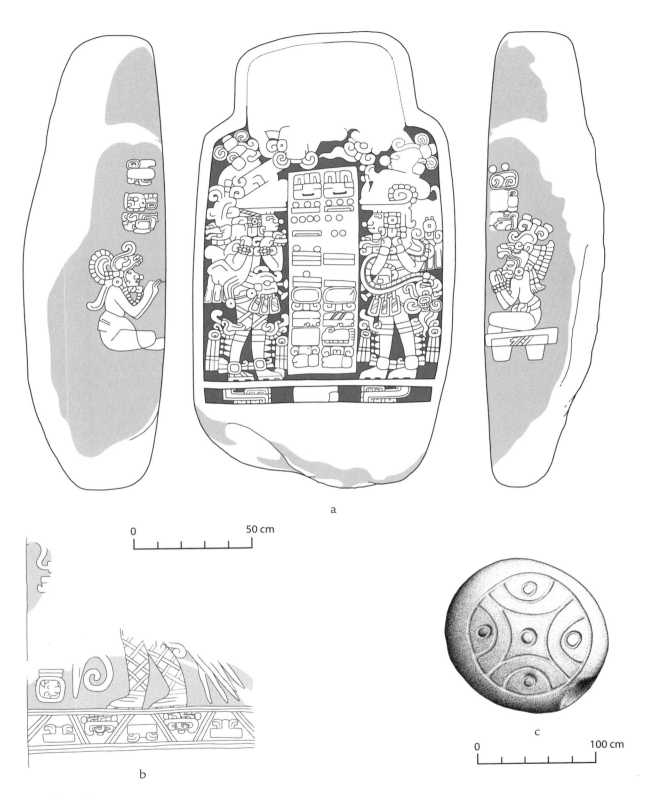

a

0   50 cm

b

c

0   100 cm

figure 8.4
Early Maya sculptures from Terrace 2. (a) Front and side views of Stela 5; (b) Stela 12 (drawings a and b from
the New World Archaeological Foundation based on originals from the Berkeley Abaj Takalik Project);
(c) Monument 188 (drawing from the Proyecto Nacional Takalik Abaj). Parts a and b are to the same scale.

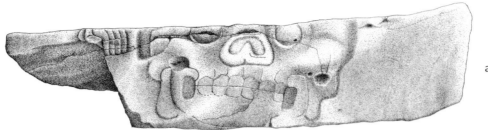

figure 8.5
Early Maya sculptures
from Terrace 2. (a) Altar 28;
(b) Altar 30. (Drawings
from the Proyecto
Nacional Takalik Abaj.)

figure 8.6
Potbelly sculptures
from Structure
74, Terrace 2.
(a) Monument 100;
(b) Monument 107;
(c) Monument 108;
(d) Monument 109.
(Drawings from the
Proyecto Nacional
Takalik Abaj.)

a

b

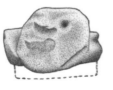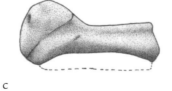

c

d

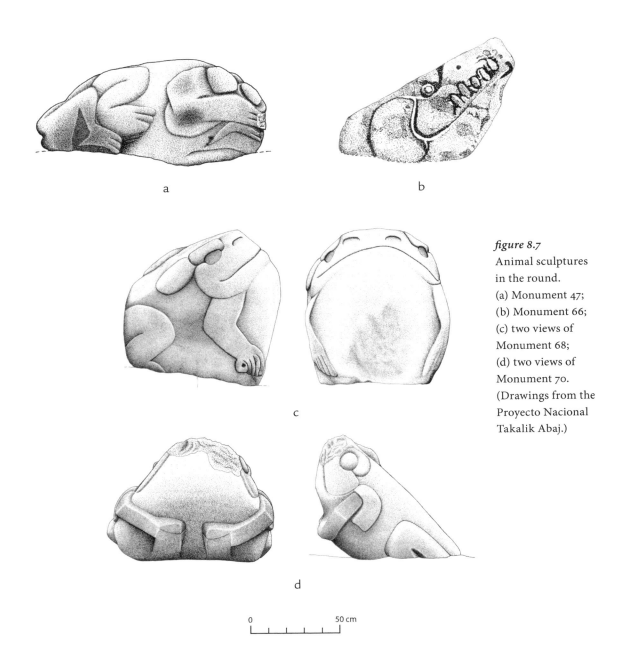

a

b

c

figure 8.7
Animal sculptures
in the round.
(a) Monument 47;
(b) Monument 66;
(c) two views of
Monument 68;
(d) two views of
Monument 70.
(Drawings from the
Proyecto Nacional
Takalik Abaj.)

d

0   50 cm

create an environment within which a figure or figures are placed and with which there is a clearly articulated interaction. Trees, water, and other phenomena constitute elements of the setting. . . . Izapa art is basically pictorial, and it is likely that it is narrative in nature, possibly mythic" (Graham 1979:186). In contrast, "early Maya stela art generally focuses upon the human figure, or figures, in an historical portrait. . . . There is seldom interest in relating figures to an environment or to depict interaction; each figure is independent of the other although placed in the same composition which is essentially a two dimensional arrangement of elements with no interest in represented space" (Graham 1979:186). Graham finds the Izapan and Maya styles "mutually contrastive" and both of them distinct from Olmec style.

Major monument forms that we cannot characterize definitively as either Olmec or Maya include potbelly sculptures and representations of animals. Both sculptural forms were likely coeval with early Maya sculptures during the Late Preclassic (see Chapter 9; Clancy 1985, 1990:27; Demarest 1986:138–139; Popenoe de Hatch 1989:25). These two general types of sculpture were fundamentally different. The first represented obese seated human beings (Figure 8.6), and the second depicted animals, predominantly those associated with water (Figure 8.7).

Terminal Preclassic Monument Ensembles in the City Center

Several general observations are apropos before diving into the placement details of Preclassic stone monuments in the ancient city center. Takalik Abaj is unusual in all of Mesoamerica because of the number of recovered Middle and Late Preclassic monuments. Izapa, Monte Albán, and Kaminaljuyu are its only rivals in quantity. The Takalik Abaj monument corpus differs from these other sites in the variety of forms and styles present, although Kaminaljuyu comes close. Takalik Abaj is the only one with abundant Olmec and Maya sculptures. Equally remarkable is the virtual absence of Izapan-style monuments at Takalik Abaj, because Izapa was its nearest neighbor with comparable sculptural output (see Graham 1979). The sculptures at Izapa display minimal variety of style; the variety is in the narrative themes (see Chapter 9; see Clark and Moreno 2007; Guernsey 2006b; Lowe et al. 1982; Miles 1965; Norman 1973, 1976; Quirarte 1973, 2007; Smith 1984). There are thematic and iconographic similarities among some Late Preclassic sculptures at Izapa, Kaminaljuyu, and Takalik Abaj, but stylistically Takalik Abaj shows the strongest connections to the Miraflores style of Late Preclassic monuments at Kaminaljuyu (see Chapter 11; Miles 1965; Parsons 1983, 1986). Fewer than a dozen Preclassic centers and cities in Mesoamerica had prolific sculptural programs. Most cities with more than one hundred Preclassic sculptures were on, or adjacent to, the Pacific slope (see Chapter 7).

In the city itself, the distribution of sculpture was not haphazard. Most monuments were placed in the Central Group on Terraces 2 and 3 (Figures 8.1 and 8.2). This distribution is not a consequence of research strategies or excavation efforts. We have excavated in the other groups at the site dating from Middle Preclassic to Late Classic, but these terraces, plazas, and platforms lack monuments. The clustered distribution of monuments in the Central Group draws attention to this sector as the ceremonial heart of Takalik Abaj—and also to the likelihood that the display of stone monuments there related to critical functions.

We focus here on the buildings and sculptures of Terraces 2 and 3 for the Terminal Preclassic. In the next section we take a historical view of how these monuments and buildings came together over a period of nine centuries. As evident in Figures 8.1 and 8.2, the platforms and pyramids on Terraces 2 and 3 share a similar arrangement, which differs from those of buildings on other terraces (Orrego Corzo 1998:55; Schieber de Lavarreda and Orrego Corzo 2001b:2). Terrace 2 steps up and north to Terrace 3. The five platforms and pyramids on Terrace 3 are larger versions of those on the terrace below. More stone monuments are known for Terrace 2 than for Terrace 3. On both terraces, the analogous eastern buildings, Structures 13 and 7, are the only ones that have lines of stone monuments on top of platforms rather than along their bases. At the foot of Terrace 3 (also known as Structure 74), six stone monuments are associated with the three broad stairways that connect the terraces (compare Figures 8.1 and 8.2). Four of these monuments are potbelly sculptures and represent one-third of the twelve potbelly sculptures known for the whole city. Clearly the distribution of sculptural forms and themes in the Central Group was deliberate (Figure 8.2).

Space limitations preclude description or illustration of all 326 monuments and their shifting contexts over the 1,700-year span of city occupation. Additional monuments are still coming to light, and we are learning more about the architectural and occupation history of the site every year. We restrict attention to the best evidence for the function and use of monuments in the heart of Takalik Abaj and propose interpretations of monument-architecture arrangements, beginning with plain monuments.

The inventory of sculptures at Takalik Abaj includes those discovered during the excavations by John Graham, Robert Heizer, and Edwin Shook with the University of California at Berkeley Abaj Takalik Project, as well as those uncovered in our own work, beginning in 1988, with the Proyecto Nacional Takalik Abaj. Currently, 326 stone monuments have been registered (Graham 1979, 1981, 1982; Graham and Benson 2005; Graham et al. 1978; Orrego Corzo 1990, 1995, 1997; Orrego Corzo and Schieber de Lavarreda 2001; Parsons 1983; Rizzo de Robles 1991; Rodas 1993; Thompson 1943). Of these, 140 have carved designs, 123 are plain stelae and other monuments, 37 are cupped-and-grooved monuments (see Chapter 10), and 26 monuments are sculptures reported by the Berkeley Abaj Takalik Project (1976–1981), which were reburied to protect them. Our classification of monument types follows those proposed by Miles (1965), Parsons (1983), and, especially Graham (1979, 1981, 1982; Graham and Benson 2005; Graham et al. 1978).

Monument 27 is a plain gneiss slab with carved grooves; it was found just south of Altar 48 (see below), with its carved face down. Stela 18, another monument of this imported material, weighs 5–6 tons, is 4 m long, and was erected as a plain or uncarved stela (Graham 1977). Given the regional geology, this stone must have been brought in from a great distance at considerable labor costs. It is worth observing that if all plain stelae at the site had been plastered over with stucco and/or painted, as some scholars have suggested, the uniqueness of Stela 18 would have been obscured. The incredible effort expended to bring it to Takalik Abaj would have been best shown by displaying it unpainted. This shiny, greenish stone was worked to a smooth polish but was not carved. Perhaps much of the message of other plain monuments was also that of the stone itself (see Chapter 12). Stela 18 was erected in one of the most prominent positions at the site as part of a stela-altar pair at the northern end of the Terrace 3 plaza (Figure 8.2).

Perhaps the best way to understand the context of Takalik Abaj monuments is to walk virtually through the site, starting with Terrace 1 and moving northward to Terrace 3. As evident in Figure 8.1, the buildings of the Central Group defined a series of long, north-south plazas. Ancient traffic flow is also evident in the locations of wide stairways. Two parallel platforms located just before ascending to Terrace 1 in the extreme south of the Central Group appear to have been the gateway that channeled movement to the central stairway leading up to the main plaza on Terrace 2. At the top of Terrace 1, there is a sunken rectangular plaza just west of Structure 14, which has a sweat bath. Monument 188, a small Maya sculpture (Figure 8.4c), was incorporated into the floor of the paved patio in the northeast sector of the sunken plaza, constructed during the end of the Late Preclassic or beginning of the Early Classic. This sculpture is carved in a rounded cartouche and represents a "Lamat" or Venus symbol (Glyph T 510a; Thompson 1962:108, 452). The monument was located with the axis of the design oriented at 0° from magnetic north.

The main plaza of Terrace 2 is about 200 m long and passes between Structures 11 and 12 and then between Structures 9 and 10. The plaza is bounded on the east and west but is open on the north and south. In the southern sector of this plaza numerous monuments line the bases of Structures 11 and 12. Each platform has a central stairway facing the plaza, and two prominent stone monuments are located at the center of these stairways. Both are early Maya stelae with texts. Stela 5 (Figure 8.4a) of Structure 12 has a plain altar in front of it, and the broken Stela 12 (Figure 8.4b) of Structure 11 has a four-legged throne in front. More monuments are displayed in the northern part of the plaza, defined by Structures 9 and 10. The center of Structure 10 has another stela-altar pair (Figure 8.5a). Each of these platforms had a row of monuments on the opposite side.

Of the five major buildings on Terrace 2, Structure 13 has the fewest monuments (there may be more; the west face has only been excavated partially), and most of them are on top of the platform rather than along its base. The small plaza defined between Structures 10, 12, and 13 is more of a narrow corridor. There are no special

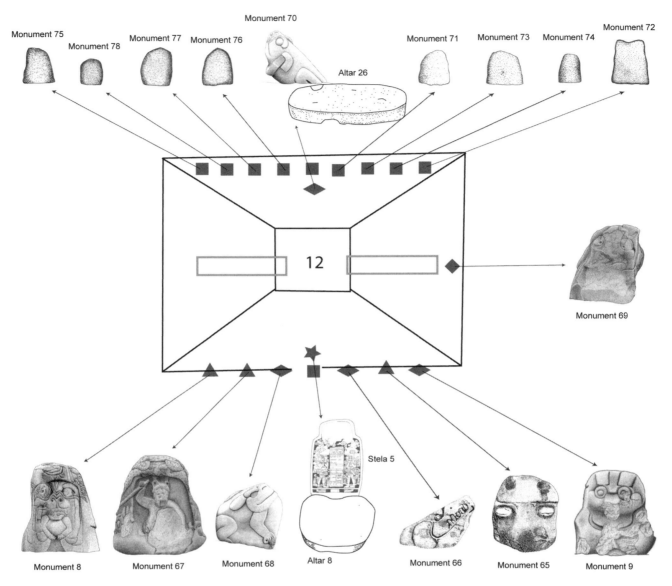

figure 8.8
Structure 12, Terrace 2, showing the distribution of monuments. The symbols
are defined in Figure 8.2. (Drawing from the Proyecto Nacional Takalik Abaj.)

Labels in figure:
Monument 75, Monument 78, Monument 77, Monument 76, Monument 70, Altar 26, Monument 71, Monument 73, Monument 74, Monument 72, Monument 69, Monument 8, Monument 67, Monument 68, Stela 5, Altar 8, Monument 66, Monument 65, Monument 9

12

paired monuments on the backsides of Structures
9, 10, 11, or 13.

Judging from the number of monuments and
their variety of forms and themes, Structure 12
appears to have been the most important one of
Terrace 2. This 3 m high platform measures 38.5 m
by 54.0 m. As evident in Figure 8.8, it had sculptures on three sides, arranged by axial symmetry.

One anthropomorphic monument (69) was found
on the south side in line with a drainage canal
beneath the mound (Figure 8.9e); no corresponding monument was found in the mirror position on
the north (Balcárcel 1995). The drainage canal was
part of a previous version of Structure 12 and was
sealed in place by the last version built in the Early
Classic period. Had a monument once been there

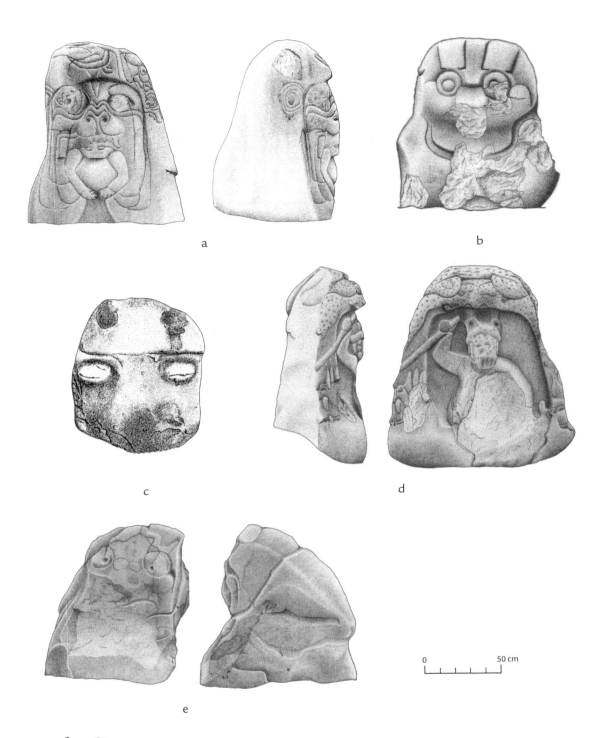

figure 8.9
Carved stone monuments from Structure 12. (a) Monument 8; (b) Monument 9; (c) Monument 65; (d) Monument 67; (e) Monument 69. (Drawings from the Proyecto Nacional Takalik Abaj.)

(to complete the symmetry), this platform would have been surrounded by twenty monuments dispersed in four directions. Eight of the nine monuments arrayed along the east face of Structure 12 are short, plain stelae. The lone exception is Monument 70, a sculpture in the round of an erect and/or croaking frog (Figure 8.7d). It is similar in theme to toad altars but unusual in its elevated posture. This sculpture faced east and fronted one of the twin stairways of Structure 13.

The west facade of Structure 12 boasts one of the most unusual monument lines at Takalik Abaj. Centrally placed Stela 5 was anchored to the base of the central stairway and faces west toward Structure 11. A large circular altar lies to the west of this stela. Stela 5 depicts two standing individuals facing each other but separated by a panel of hieroglyphs and calendric notations, the dates being AD 126 and AD 103 or AD 83 (Graham et al. 1978:92). Each side of Stela 5 depicts seated individuals; the one on the south side is shown seated on a four-legged throne (Figure 8.4a). Three monuments flank Stela 5 on each side (Figure 8.8). Moving from south to north, these are Monuments 9, 65, 66, [Stela 5], 68, 67, and 8. These represent, respectively, an owl, a large human head, a crocodile, [Stela 5], an erect toad, and two human figures emerging from niches (Figures 8.7 and 8.9). These two niched monuments located at the northern end of the facade and the owl and the large human (colossal) head, positioned at the southern end, are considered Olmec and are probably older than the rest of the sculptures in this line. In summary, there is a central early Maya Stela 5 flanked by two animal sculptures, with two Olmec monuments on each side of the paired animal sculptures. Across the plaza, Stela 5 faces Stela 12 with its associated throne in front. As noted, one lateral figure on Stela 5 is shown seated on a throne similar to the one in front of Stela 12, so the image may reference this monument in the same plaza, as described by Guernsey (Chapter 9) for some monuments at Izapa.

Stela 12 faces east across the plaza and is flanked on each side by three short, plain stelae—an exact complement to the monuments across the plaza in stela-monument pairs. Seven plain stelae grace the west face of Structure 11 (Figure 8.2); they

were all in place by the Late Preclassic period. The symmetrical spacing of monuments, their themes, and their quantities were obviously important. The altars and thrones in front of some central monuments may not have been part of the original numerology. The plain altar in front of Stela 5, for example, was added long after this monument was first put into position (see below). Structure 11 has two rows of seven stelae each. Structure 12 has rows of seven and nine; and Structure 9 has a row of seven monuments on the west side but only two on the east side. Structure 10 has six stelae along its west face but appears to be missing one monument. Five monuments line its east face. One of these is a potbelly sculpture. The central altar (28) of Structure 10 is particularly interesting, because it has a relief carving of a human skull (Figure 8.5a). It is the only carved altar in the plaza group. The few monuments associated with Structure 13 do not display any clear patterns, and certainly there was no display of monuments along its east face. Along its northwest face are a monument of a giant toad and a potbelly sculpture.

Having walked through the plaza of stelae on Terrace 2, we are now ready to ascend 5.5 m up the central stairway to Terrace 3. As mentioned, four potbelly sculptures are found at the base of this terrace (also known as Structure 74) in front of its three staircases (Figure 8.2). The east and west staircases each have one potbelly sculpture at its base. The central staircase has two potbellies. In between there is a small boulder sculpture of a head (Monument 108), which has a flat portion behind the head that suggests a function as an altar (Figure 8.6c). These monuments were in place by the Late Preclassic period, a date that accords with the age of potbelly sculptures in other regions (see Clancy 1990:27; Demarest 1986:138–139; Popenoe de Hatch 1989:25). The only other potbelly sculptures on Terrace 2 face each other across the narrow corridor between Structures 10 and 13 (Figure 8.2). All these monuments appear situated at passage points, as noted by Love (Chapter 7).

Altar 30 (Figure 8.5b) is a reused stela transformed into a throne, which, in its last use, was integrated into the fourth ascending step in the central

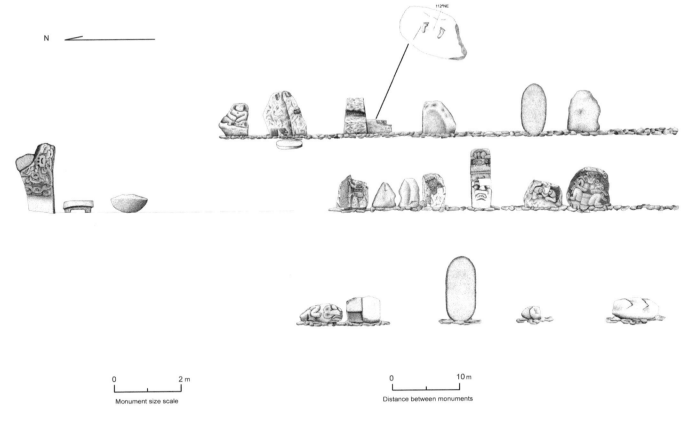

figure 8.10
Groupings of monuments on Structure 7, Terrace 3.
(Drawing from the Proyecto Nacional Takalik Abaj.)

0   2 m
Monument size scale

0   10 m
Distance between monuments

axis of the staircase of Structure 74. The position in the central axis chosen for this sculpture as part of the staircase suggests that it functioned as a sacred and special construction element. It was placed in this final position during the first part of the Early Classic period and postdates the placement of the potbelly sculptures in front of the staircase. On the upper surface of the throne, the figure of a winged human with a bird mask is depicted in low relief. The central part of this relief was intentionally erased. The edges of the throne show evidence of having been resculpted from another monument, probably a stela. For that reason, the tips of the extended wings are truncated at the edges of the monument. This Maya sculpture is the only case of reutilization of an intact monument in a building at Takalik Abaj.

More carved monuments are known for Terrace 3. Twenty-three of the thirty-three monuments are on top of Structure 7; these cluster in three long north-south rows or lines (Figure 8.10). Several large sculptures are found at the bases of platforms, and, although fewer in number, they are symmetrically distributed along the building facades, as on Terrace 2 (and as for Structures 3 and 4, with three monuments facing each other across the plaza). We focus on the monuments on top of Structure 7. At first, archaeologists considered the summit of this structure a "garden" of monuments, but more detailed study revealed three separate lines of sculptures (Graham et al. 1978; Popenoe de Hatch 2002a:437–458; Schieber de Lavarreda and Orrego Corzo 2001b:18, 2002:70). The central row of nine monuments is represented, south to north,

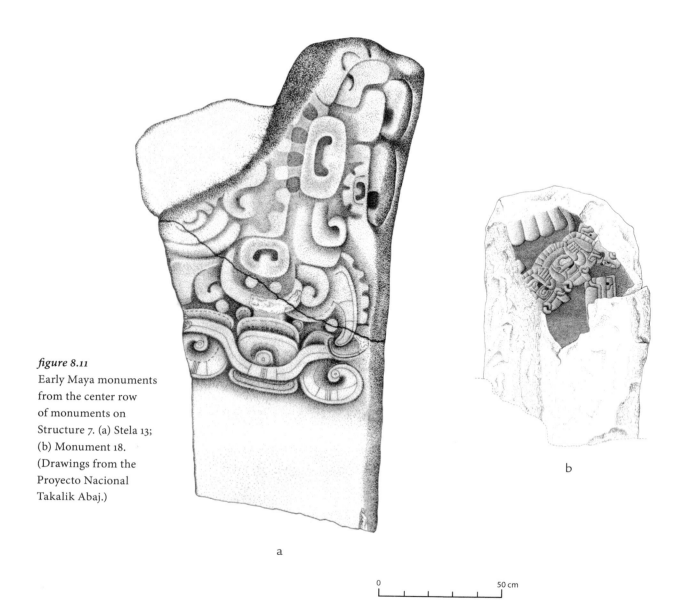

figure 8.11
Early Maya monuments
from the center row
of monuments on
Structure 7. (a) Stela 13;
(b) Monument 18.
(Drawings from the
Proyecto Nacional
Takalik Abaj.)

a

b

0   50 cm

by carved monuments 14, 15, 16/17, 18, and 19, and on the same line farther to the north is Stela 13 at the base of Structure 7A (Figure 8.2). The first three monuments of this row are Olmec (Figure 8.3a–c), and the last one is Maya (Figure 8.11a). Another Olmec monument fragment, Stela 74 (Figure 8.3e), was found underneath Structure 7A, deep in the interior of Structure 7.

The east row has seven monuments, beginning in the south with three plain stones, followed by Altar 46 in early Maya style, an unidentified monument (Monument 51), and finishing with another Maya monument (Stela 50) and an Olmec

monument (Monument 58) (Figure 8.12b). This last monument depicts a seated obese person on a throne, similar to potbelly sculptures yet distinct from them in posture, form of the face, and headdress. The west row of monuments begins in the south with three plain monuments followed by Monument 47, which depicts copulating toads (Figure 8.7a), and unspecified Monument 48.

Returning to the south end of the central row of nine monuments, Monument 14 is a boulder sculpture carved on both sides. The image on the front is locally and erroneously known as the "rabbit woman." It depicts a seated woman with an animal

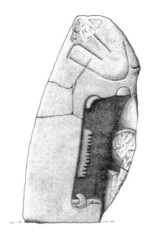

a

figure 8.12
Monuments from
the east row of
sculptures on
Structure 7.
(a) Monument 50;
(b) Monument 58;
(c) Altar 46. (Drawings
from the Proyecto
Nacional Takalik Abaj.)

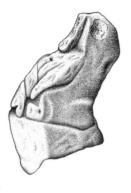

b

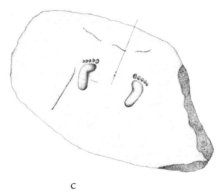

c

0   50 cm

under each arm—a jaguar under her right arm and a deer under her left (Figure 8.3c). The back of this monument shows traces of a low-relief carving. Monument 15 is particularly interesting. The front of this boulder sculpture shows a man emerging from a large jaguar mouth, with the man's head, arms, and shoulders coming out of this cave-like niche. The back shows the legs and tail of a jaguar. The top part of the monument is missing, so it is not clear whether the back shows a jaguar entering a cave or merely the back part of the jaguar (Figure 8.3a). This sculpture (as well as Monument 93) represents a transformation narrative, but in the reverse order (from jaguar to man) to that described by Gutiérrez and Pye (Chapter 2) for such figures. Monuments 16 and 17 are halves of the same long Olmec face with a tall headdress (Figure 8.3b). There follows Monument 18, a severely damaged carving that shows traces of Maya imagery (Figure 8.11b), two plain monuments, and an Olmec style stela fragment, Monument 19 (Figure 8.3d). Monument 19 shows the profile of a person standing and holding a staff. Continuing to the north, this line of monuments ends with a censer altar (Altar 37) and Stela 13 (Figure 8.11a). The stela has been broken into two pieces. The carving is

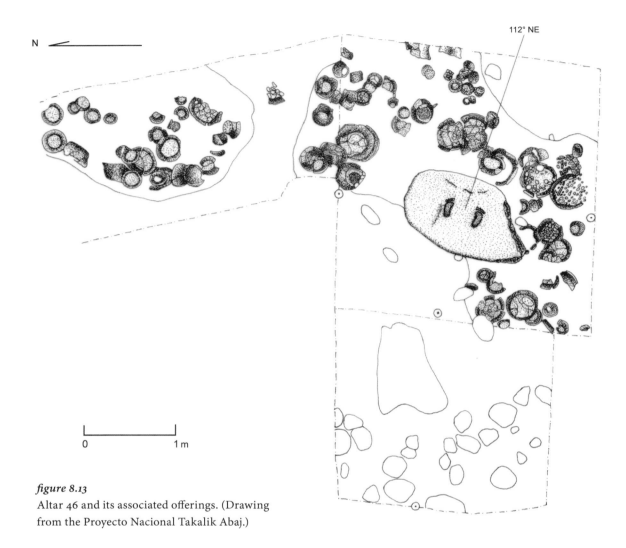

N

112° NE

0   1 m

figure 8.13
Altar 46 and its associated offerings. (Drawing
from the Proyecto Nacional Takalik Abaj.)

particularly well made and shows the stylized head
of a serpent, probably the earliest Maya sculpture at
Takalik Abaj (Fahsen 2001).

The monuments on Structure 7 form three
rows, more or less parallel, whose original orientation, we believe, was 21° northeast of true north
(see Figure 8.2). This orientation was "corrected" at
the beginning of the Late Preclassic to 23° northeast, the position of the constellation Draco in that
period (Popenoe de Hatch 2002a:442). This reorien-
tation would have coincided with the end of carving
Olmec monuments and a shift in cultural traditions. We are less sure of original alignments than
of final ones, of course. The final alignment to the
heavens suggests that at least one function of these

monuments was for astronomical observation, particularly of the night sky (cf. Chapter 3). We suspect
Terrace 3 had a more private use than did the buildings on Terrace 2, which was related to its sacred
and astronomical functions.

In the east row of monuments on Structure 7,
Altar 46 was discovered in March 2007; it consists of
a plain rock with a slightly polished surface. In the
center of this monument are two carved footprints,
24 cm long or average human size, in a natural position of a standing person (Figure 8.12c). Standing
in these footprints, an observer would be looking
about 112° northeast of magnetic north, a position
that corresponds to the sunrise on the autumn equinox (September 21). The placement and orientation

of this monument implies that, in addition to the observations of the night sky, astronomers at Takalik Abaj also observed the sun's daily passage during the year (Popenoe de Hatch 2002a; Marion Popenoe de Hatch, personal communication 2007). Altar 46 is of particular interest, because it is one of the few associated with offerings (Figure 8.13). Associated with this altar were 171 artifacts that date to the final part of the Late Preclassic period (200 BC–AD 150) and Late Classic (AD 500–700) (Popenoe de Hatch, personal communication 2007). Beneath the altar were found thirty-seven whole ceramic objects and one obsidian blade. The uppermost, principal vessel was precisely below the center of the altar. Among the lowest ceramic objects (nearly a meter below the altar) was a capped vessel containing an offering of jadeite beads and tiny pyrite mosaic pieces. Accompanying this offering vessel was an impressive upright three-pronged incense burner. The altar was carefully placed above the ceramic vessels in such a way as to not crush them. Among the 134 offerings surrounding the altar were five cylindrical censers, two of them with appliqué decorations of figures of emaciated adult males.

The arrangement of these offerings and the forms of the artifacts provide clues to the rituals involved in placing the altar. The frequency of each artifact type and its placement shows a preoccupation with numbers, particularly 3, 5, and 10. Some ceramic plates had simple offerings of stone pebbles, and these occurred in frequencies of 3, 6, 72, and up to 123. Rituals associated with this monument took place over a prolonged period and involved placing artifacts in the ground before the altar itself. The presence of numerous broken and incomplete artifacts around the altar indicates that offerings were regularly interred.

Preclassic Monuments through the Ages

Despite the history of monument movement, replacement, and breakage at Takalik Abaj, it is still possible to reconstruct or trace a history of monument production and use at this center, beginning with Middle Preclassic Olmec monuments and finishing with Maya monuments of the Late Classic. Of the thirty-eight Olmec monuments found at the site, the most frequent themes were niche figures (nine), full-figured human beings or heads (eight), animals (seven), and human prisoners (six). For the forty-seven early Maya sculptures, the predominant themes were early texts and calendrical dates (twelve), standing or seated well-dressed persons in profile (eleven), early Maya iconography (ten), and representations of animals (four). Most of the sculptures in the round are Olmec, and the stela-altar pairs are early Maya. Most of the monuments were placed in the Central Group, with the greatest number on Terraces 2 and 3. Based on the number and variety of its monuments, Graham (1979, 1981, 1982, 1989) argued that Mesoamerica's sculptural tradition began and evolved at this site. His argument was largely theoretical and founded on his notion of evolving styles and carving techniques, as well as the postulate that stone monument carving most likely evolved in a region with ready access to compliant raw materials.

Graham's thesis for the origins of Olmec and pre-Olmec stone sculpture at Takalik Abaj has not been supported by archaeological evidence at this site or from earlier sites in the Gulf Coast region. For some scholars, the more crudely made sculptures at Takalik Abaj that inspired Graham's hypothesis are not evidence of the evolution of sculpting in Mesoamerica, only of the presence of some less-skilled sculptors. The lack of extensive Early Preclassic deposits at the site support their claims that these sculptures are not early (see Chapter 1). They postulate that the rustic sculptures at Takalik Abaj postdate Monument 1 (Figure 8.14a), the well-executed low-relief sculpture just off the eastern limit of the site. From this point of view, Graham's hypothetical evolutionary and technological sequence is chronologically upside-down. Some of the earliest Olmec sculptures appear rather sophisticated in terms of technique and representation (Monuments 16/17, 19, 55 [human head in the round], 5, 4, 44 [prisoners], 42, 172 [human figure with a staff], and Stela 74). We believe these sculptures date to the Middle Preclassic period.

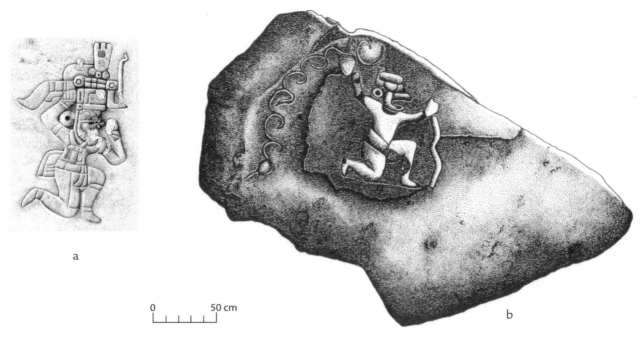

a

b

0   50 cm

figure 8.14
Early Olmec monuments at Takalik Abaj. (a) Monument 1; (b) Monument 64.
(Drawings from the Proyecto Nacional Takalik Abaj.)

Regarding Graham's thesis and arguments against it, it is important to observe that the sculptural themes and forms at Takalik Abaj are remarkably similar to those from contemporaneous La Venta (see Chapter 6). The evolution of the sculptural program at La Venta very likely was reflected at Takalik Abaj. Apparently La Venta sculptures had temporal, formal, technical, and stylistic antecedents at the earlier city of San Lorenzo (see Chapter 1). The archaeological record shows that Takalik Abaj postdates San Lorenzo but was coeval with La Venta. As for the conjectured more rustic appearance of some Takalik Abaj sculptures vis-à-vis monuments from La Venta and Graham's postulated origin of the sculptural arts at Takalik Abaj, archaeological data for these sites (and numerous contemporaries) indicate a significant role for long-distance trade. Trade was an important social mechanism for the transmittal of ideas and practices in Middle Preclassic Mesoamerica, probably including the purpose and meaning of stone sculpture, sculpting techniques, visual themes and symbols, and codified representations. Changes

occurred in themes as a consequence of transmission. In some cases, specialized artisans and sculptors may have traveled to different regions to create certain works. More frequent would have been local artisans creating sculptures according to forms and themes known from San Lorenzo and La Venta. Circumstances of social interaction and the increasing popularity of stone monuments would have given rise to regional differences in stone sculpture (see Chapter 1). We think that these circumstances are reflected in the corpus of sculptures at Takalik Abaj. There are obvious formal and iconic connections to other times and places, but much of the sculpture at the site was a local tradition.

The best-known Olmec monument at Takalik Abaj is Monument 1, a low-relief carving of a kneeling man facing east, with an elaborate headdress and special dress and ornaments. It is a petroglyph carved on a huge boulder in the ravine just east of the site (Figure 8.14a). It is similar to other low-relief Olmec carvings along the Pacific Coast from Chiapas to El Salvador (see Clark and Pye

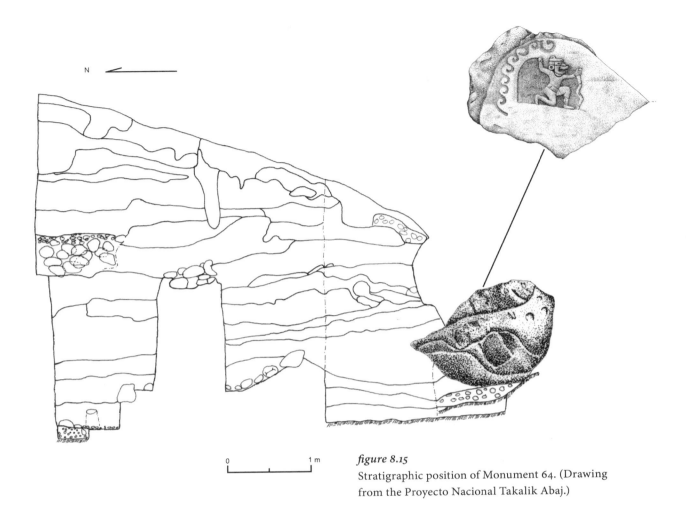

figure 8.15
Stratigraphic position of Monument 64. (Drawing
from the Proyecto Nacional Takalik Abaj.)

2000:figs. 1, 7, and 15) that appear to mark trade
routes. Monument 1 could have served a similar
marking function. We cannot date Monument 1
based on its archaeological context, but we have
solid information for a similar monument.

Monument 64 is another petroglyph carved
in low relief on a boulder. Found to the west of the
Central Group in a natural depression intersected
by the El Chorro rivulet, this kneeling figure is more
simply carved than the figure depicted on Monument 1. We believe Monument 64 depicts a ballplayer (Figure 8.14b; cf. Chapter 9). The petroglyph
represents a slightly outlined human figure, facing
east and shown in profile in a niche. He wears a
possible mask with jaguar features and assumes
a ballplaying posture. His right arm is raised, and
in his left hand he holds a kind of undulating bar in

front of him. Behind the figure and outside the niche
space there are partially marked volutes forming an
ascending arc. The figure's posture and feline mask
resemble those of the "ballplayer" on Monument 1
(Graham and Benson 2005:fig. 2 lower left).

Excavation of Monument 64 revealed a clear
stratigraphic sequence (Figure 8.15) that places
it in the first part of the Middle Preclassic period
(Ixchiyá phase, 800–700 BC) (Popenoe de Hatch
2004:437–447; Schieber de Lavarreda and Claudio
2004:429–436; Schieber de Lavarreda and Popenoe
de Hatch 2006). This monument was subsequently
buried during the latter half of the Middle Preclassic (Nil phase, 700–400 BC) and the Late
Preclassic (Rocío phase, 400–200 BC). Its burial
may indicate that the ballgame theme was no longer viable. As mentioned, the clay ballcourt on

Terrace 2 was covered over about this time, and there was none to replace it until the Late Classic period. The practice of playing ball appears to have been discouraged beginning ca 400 BC, the time of transition from Olmec to Maya monuments. This change in sculptural themes and cultural practices may have been caused by the arrival at the site of new ideas and/or new overseers.

Evidence of a transition to the Late Preclassic period comes from excavations in Structure 7, the large platform on Terrace 3. In the heart of Structure 7, located close to the east edge of Terrace 3 and on the same east-west axis as Monument 64, a small platform of clay was found that dates to the first part of the Middle Preclassic (800–700 BC). This platform was covered with a rose-colored floor of finely ground taxcal, thus the name Rosada Structure I. It was followed by Rosada Structure II and a construction that covered both called the Núcleo or "Core" (Schieber de Lavarreda 2005). During the latter part of the Middle Preclassic (Nil phase) and at the beginning of the Late Preclassic, these early structures were covered over by fill that corresponds to the first construction stage of Structure 7. We believe this building sequence indicates that by 400 BC, Olmec sculptures and small clay platforms were obsolete and superseded. During this time there is a change in architecture to large platforms and pyramids.

The discovery of a fragment of Stela 74 reinforces this interpretation. This stela fragment depicts a foliated maize and "U" symbol from the upper portion of a stela with a rounded outline (Figure 8.3e). The low-relief design represents a trefoil symbol with a cartouche in the form of an arc. A "U" is evident inside the cartouche. Below this basal line are found three other small "U" shapes. The entire symbol is similar to one represented in the upper part of Monument 25/26 at La Venta (see Chapter 6; Figure 6.4; Diehl 2004:65, fig. 30d). We propose that this symbol was part of a headdress or crown of a person represented on the stela. Stela 74 was found in the fill that covered the Rosada structures. Destruction of this stela and placement of its fragments in the Structure 7 fill confirm two things. First, Stela 74 corresponds to the Olmec sculptural

tradition at Takalik Abaj. Second, breakage of this sculpture coincided with the shift in its architectural program ca 400 BC.

The transition from Olmec to Maya sculpture at the site was confirmed by the discovery of Altar 48 in March 2008 (Schieber de Lavarreda and Orrego Corzo 2009). The stratigraphic information for this altar indicates a placement at the very beginning of the Maya era (Rocío phase, 400–200 BC). With a sculpted face and four sides, this altar portrays a beautifully rendered mythological theme and a hieroglyphic text in an early writing style, likely related to the person depicted in the center of the monument (Figure 8.16). This individual is shown as emerging from the body of a crocodile represented in the form of a quatrefoil, a visual rendering of the Mesoamerican belief that the earth represents the back of a crocodile floating on a primeval sea. Altar 48 indicates the use of powerful mythological concepts for political purposes and might represent the founding monument for the first Maya dynasty at Takalik Abaj.[4]

The second level of construction for the great platform of Structure 7 was completed during the final part of the Rocío phase, and construction of Structure 7A followed. In front of this small structure a massive ritual was performed for the placement of Stela 13 (Schieber de Lavarreda 2002:459–473). This monument depicts a serpentine creature looking east and was placed as the terminal monument of the center row of monuments on Structure 7 (Figures 8.10 and 8.11a). This ritual, similar to that performed with the dedication of Altar 46, began before the stela was put in place, and it continued afterward as well. Stela 13 appears to be the earliest occurrence of Maya monuments at Takalik Abaj (Fahsen 2001). It was probably carved near the beginning of the Late Preclassic (Rocío phase). Its placement in front of Structure 7A occurred later (Ruth phase, 200 BC–AD 150) and is another example of the reuse of monuments. This Maya monument and Altar 48 indicate that the early Maya cultural tradition was established at Takalik Abaj by the early Late Preclassic. At the end of the Late Preclassic, one of the last of the early Maya kings at Takalik Abaj was buried

figure 8.16
Takalik Abaj Altar 48.
(Drawing from the Proyecto
Nacional Takalik Abaj.)

0   50 cm

in Structure 7A, just north of Stela 13 (Schieber de Lavarreda 2003:797–805; Tarpy 2004). He could be the leader depicted on Stela 5 holding the serpent scepter (Graham and Benson 2005:fig. 6). The stone monuments, offerings, and burial of a king indicate that Structure 7 was an extremely important place at Takalik Abaj that was revered and periodically commemorated.

Sculptural programs during the Late Preclassic period are also well attested for Structure 12 on Terrace 2. This structure was built after the clay ballcourt, and some of the monuments along the west facade of Structure 12 may have been taken from this old ballcourt. Structure 12 experienced eight building episodes, the last three of which have cobblestone revetments and are associated with sculpture placements. Stela 5 was erected on the central axis of Structure 12 during the sixth

construction phase and was positioned on its west face in front of the central stairway, commemorating it with Long Count dates of AD 83 and AD 126. Monuments 66 and 68, which flank Stela 5, were put in place during the seventh construction episode. Monuments 9 and 65, situated at the south end of the west facade, and Monuments 67 and 8, on the north end, were put in place during the eighth and final construction episode corresponding to the beginning of the Early Classic period. Altar 8 in front of Stela 5 appears to have been positioned during Late Classic times.

On the opposite side of Structure 12, Monument 70 was put in place during the seventh construction episode, and its facing altar was placed during the eighth episode. The associated plain monuments date to the last construction phase. Thus Stela 5, one of the youngest monuments (at

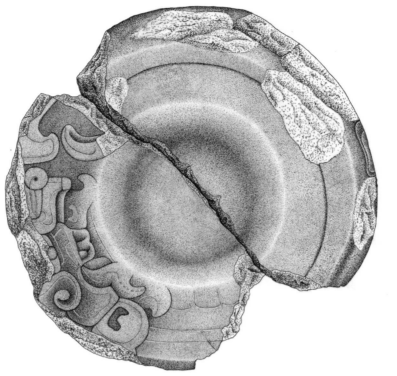

figure 8.17
Takalik Abaj Altar 36/38 from a
Late Classic canal on the south edge
of Structure 7. (Drawing from the
Proyecto Nacional Takalik Abaj.)

0   50 cm

least stylistically) associated with Structure 12, was the first one set in final position, and older monuments were added through time until the final configuration seen today had been assembled. Of course these other monuments could have been part of the original line and might have been merely bumped out of their original positions with each subsequent refurbishing episode of Structure 12.

If the final placement outlined above accurately reflects the sequence, then the Late Preclassic was a time of significant movement of monuments. The meaning of individual monuments would have shifted with every move and with each new association of each ensemble. Throughout these reassignments, the images of the two kings and their historic texts on Stela 5 were central. Stela 5 was the central monument of the Terrace 2 plaza. Stela 12 faced it across the way, but at some point

in prehistory it was broken off below the knees, and most of it was carried off (Figure 8.4b). Stela 5 shows no signs of defacement or intentional damage, only the effects of erosion (Figure 8.4a).

Movement and breakage of monuments at Takalik Abaj continued into the Late Classic, as apparent with "rattlesnake" Altar 36/38 (Figure 8.17). This circular monument has four cylindrical supports. The circular cavity in its center indicates a function as an incense altar, a usage confirmed by remains of carbonized material impregnated in the bottom of the cavity. A low-relief carving of a serpent encircles this altar in such a manner that its tail rattles conjoin the serpent's head. The altar was broken into two parts; one part included the head and tail and the other the serpent's body. The fragments of this monument were placed in separate locations, hence its two monument numbers. Both fragments were incorporated into a stone-lined drain associated with the south end of Structure 7 (Figure 8.2). This drainage channel was built with cobblestones in Late Classic times (Marroquín Alvarez 2005:999–1000, 1007–1008, figs. 7–9). The portion with the sculpted body of the serpent was found at the head of the drain in the area where water accumulated on the surface of Platform 7. The head-and-tail fragment was at the lower end. As evident in Figure 8.2, two more fragments of sculpture were integrated into the construction of this drain: a fragment of Stela 71 (Marroquín Alvarez 2005:1008, fig. 9) with early Maya iconographic elements served as a capstone, and a fragment of a seated human pedestal sculpture (Monument 163) (Marroquín Alvarez 2005:1008, fig. 9) was a lateral stone of this drain. The special locations where sculpture fragments were placed indicate they were not casual building material but were sacred stones incorporated into the new construction.

Concluding Remarks

Perhaps the most lasting impression of the stone sculptures at Takalik Abaj is of their diversity. The final disposition of monuments along the facades of Terminal Preclassic buildings makes it difficult to tease out the sculptural stratigraphy and history of this site, but such is our purpose in this final comment. The preceding discussion focused on providing contexts for monuments on Terraces 2 and 3. Here we speculate on the possible functions and meanings of monuments based on likely changes in monument programs through time. Most monuments at the site are plain. Of the carved ones, most have been broken, defaced, mutilated, or mistreated in various ways, all of which makes the task of understanding their original functions and meanings difficult. We have argued for the pervasive movement, resetting, and recycling of monuments through the end of the Preclassic period. A remarkable feature of stone sculptures at Takalik Abaj is that they appear to have maintained their stations after ca AD 150. There is little evidence that monuments were created, destroyed, or moved

after this time. In short, stone monuments were virtually frozen in place by the beginning of the Early Classic period, and this probably indicates the waning fortunes of local elites and also a pervasive change in the meaning and function of the monuments themselves.

The general sculptural sequence at the site is from Olmec to Maya monuments, with potbelly sculptures wedged in between, probably near the transition point between the two traditions and styles. Sculptures of animals correspond to both traditions and are ambiguous in our analyses. Monument 1 is likely the earliest Olmec monument at the site, and it is the most expertly carved and the one that best conforms to the La Venta style (Figure 8.14a). It was carved on the face of a huge boulder in a ravine, along the Ixchiyá River in the barranca just to the east of the site. It is likely that a specialist sculptor from the Gulf Olmec region carved this monument. Some scholars consider other Olmec sculptures at Takalik Abaj as less well done and outside the canons of Gulf Coast art. At the moment, there are no table-top altars known for Takalik Abaj, and the two colossal heads from the site (Monuments 23 and 65) are not accepted as such by some scholars, although at least one follows this theme (see Chapter 3 for another example). The niche-boulder sculptures at Takalik Abaj were probably conceptually equivalent to the table-top altars from the Gulf Coast region. The correspondences between them become evident in their comparison (Monuments 8, 14 [backside], 15, 23, 67, 104, and Stela 50 [backside] compare favorably with thrones; see Gillespie [2000:106, fig. 8]). Evident at Takalik Abaj is a proliferation of Olmec themes and iconography, but not strictly in the same forms as known from La Venta. There are more boulder sculptures at Takalik Abaj, and these include various niche figures. All these characteristics suggest that Olmec sculptures at Takalik Abaj might be rather late in the Middle Preclassic period; they show as many affinities to the sculptures at Tres Zapotes (see Chapter 5) as to those from La Venta.

If these speculations are correct, the first shift in the sculptural program at Takalik Abaj was from commemorations of natural features to setting up monuments at the site itself, and a change from immobile art to the creation of smaller, movable monuments. In general, these trends also involved a shift from rounded sculptures to flat ones. Olmec monuments, and the animal sculptures made at the same time, were carved in the round and were meant to be viewed from all sides. They were designed as freestanding monuments that could have been placed in the middle of plazas. Whether they were so displayed is another issue. For the moment, we have not recovered any stone monuments associated with Middle Preclassic clay platforms. We lack concrete evidence of where these movable monuments were originally placed; we suspect they were out in the open in the early plazas of the Central Group.

Potbelly sculptures, as previously described, are stylistically and temporally between Olmec and Maya monuments. They were carved in the round and meant to be freestanding and viewed from all sides. Thematically, potbelly sculptures clearly derived from earlier boulder sculptures of seated individuals, such as Monument 58 (Figure 8.12b).

Early Maya sculptures represented another significant change to flat art meant to be viewed from the front and, less often, from the sides. Most of these monuments were designed to be positioned in front of buildings or as parts of buildings rather than as freestanding sculptures. The fusion of building and sculpture appears to have been part of a larger program for directing traffic through the major plazas and placing monuments along the sides of the plaza for maximum exposure, as at La Venta and Izapa (see Chapters 6 and 9). Another feature was the deliberate coupling of standing and recumbent stones as stela-altar pairs. At least three of these pairs at Takalik Abaj are plain. Absent is the Izapa pattern of carved stelae associated with carved altars. Instead, we see the lowland Maya pattern of plain altars fronting carved stelae. Also represented are carved altars with plain stelae. At Takalik Abaj, some altars were carved more elaborately than the stelae, and some altars and stelae are exceptionally large compared to those from other sites.

The limited reliable contextual evidence for early Maya monuments shows that elaborate stelae with images of kings, and with carved texts and calendar dates, were set up on the central axes of platforms and pyramids (see Figure 8.2). These honored spots were maintained through time. As best evident with the sequence of monument placements around Structure 12, older monuments and plain ones flanked and drew attention to the principal stela-altar pair of these buildings. We suspect the main meaning of flanking sculptures was that of "old" or "venerable" monuments rather than assigning significance to the particular toad or niche figure portrayed. The number and placement of monuments as constituents of overall patterns appear to have been significant, with the whole giving a sense of age, variety, history, and probably of sacred connections to ancestors—a message that became fixed by Early Classic times. Stone monuments conveyed a sense of ancient power and spirituality. They continue to convey that same message today for modern Mayas who perform ceremonies in front of them. Given this intrinsic meaning of ancient and sacred stones carved by the ancestors, it perhaps mattered little that many were battered or broken.

There was a time, of course, when these modifications mattered, principally at the moment the sculptures were desecrated. Great effort was required to break and damage the sculptures, and it must have been done with the express purpose of destroying their previous meaning and significance. Because so many broken monuments were subsequently reset and placed in honored positions during the Terminal Preclassic, we lack the information needed to reconstruct the details of monument breakage. As discussed, Takalik Abaj underwent a major transition ca 400 BC. Some Olmec sculptures had already been broken and interred by this time. It was also the time of architectural change, including the burial of the ballcourt on Terrace 2. Our best guess is that most Olmec monuments had been broken and/or decommissioned by this time. This period was one of transition across Mesoamerica (Lowe 1977:222), as is particularly evident in the abandonment of La Venta (Chapter 6). At Takalik Abaj, Olmec-related things gave way to Maya-related objects, but without a displacement of the city's residents. We believe the replacement of Olmec monuments with Maya ones was likely a shift in political affiliation and ideology rather than a change in population (see Lowe 1977:214–215). The original research focus at Takalik Abaj was to discover a transition from Olmec to Maya, largely conceived as a replacement of ethnic groups. Art styles changed, but the population did not. Local residents stayed put and appear only to have redirected their loyalties. They continued to engage in international trade but changed its focus from the La Venta network (which apparently collapsed) to a Maya network associated with Kaminaljuyu and cities in the Maya Lowlands.

This explanation is only partial, of course, because many of the Maya sculptures created after this Late Preclassic transition were also subsequently broken and defaced. Potbelly sculptures were not destroyed, for the most part, nor were the sculptures of animals. By far the most common incidents of destruction and defacement involved images of humans, thus suggesting that iconoclasm was linked at some basic level with claims and counterclaims to political authority and power, with rivals destroying one another's monuments. Martínez Donjuán describes a similar pattern of monument defacement for Teopantecuanitlan (Chapter 3), and Clark (1997) claims this pattern as general for Olmec sculpture. If so, it suggests that potbelly sculptures were not implicated in such rival claims and conveyed a different message (see Chapter 9).

Most of the early Maya monuments at Takalik Abaj were also broken and defaced. Breakage appears to correspond to the presence of carved texts and calendar dates, as described by Fahsen for highland Guatemala (Chapter 10). Some of the earliest Long Count dates and perhaps the earliest texts (Monument 11, Altars 12 and 48, and Stela 2) have been found at Takalik Abaj (Graham 1980, 1981, 1989; Graham and Benson 2005; Graham and Porter 1989; Graham et al. 1978; Schieber de Lavarreda and Orrego Corzo 2009). These precocious developments came to an abrupt end ca AD 200. Whether the monuments were broken at

this time remains to be determined. As described by Fahsen (Chapter 10), the second century AD was a period of rapid change in the Guatemalan Highlands. The carving and erection of stone monuments ceased at Takalik Abaj about this time, and the monuments in front of its buildings were left in place—a testament to an earlier age.

It is not clear what the function and meaning of Olmec monuments were at Takalik Abaj or why some were destroyed and others not. Many fragments appear to have been of leaders and prisoners. The images of conquerors and conquered were both broken (as at Kaminaljuyu; see Chapter 11). More fragments of torsos and legs have been found than of heads, so maybe the heads were carried away or otherwise disposed of. We suspect that many of these monuments represented leaders and their claims to governing authority and tribute. Whatever the case in the fifth century BC, by 100 BC these old fragments of sculpture were not censored or dangerous, and their residual and imputed meaning was appropriated by placing them in the monument rows seen on top of Structure 7. Access to the top of this platform was likely restricted, so unlike the monuments at the foot of the platforms, these sculptures were not for everyone to see. They do not appear to have been associated with buildings (although links to perishable buildings are a possibility). The rows of monuments are not random, and they are aligned with the constellation Draco. We suspect that monument rows were used to make astronomical observations. This rather utilitarian function would be similar to that described for Teopantecuanitlan (see Chapter 3).

Some monuments on Structure 7 were the focus of repeated ritual offerings, so they marked special spots in the landscape. The images on these monuments may have been related to the meaning of their locations. Stela 13 with its snake image, for example, may have portrayed the constellation Draco, and its position on the centerline of monuments on Structure 7 would have reinforced this function. If true, it would be the same pattern seen for the main buildings of Terrace 2, in which pride of place was given to one monument, and the others played supporting roles of drawing attention to the principal monument, its location, and it representation. If such proves to be the case, we should probably classify monuments as primary or secondary and attempt to infer the function of their combinations in the various roles they played.

The preceding discussion has touched on monument associations and ensembles. Before the Terminal Preclassic, these appear to have varied, so meaning by association was labile until the final ensembles came together. When they did join forces, we see almost no distinction in the styles and forms of monuments and the final use of sculptures as secondary monuments. We suggest the meaning of representations for these monuments was generic, apropos of their supporting roles to primary monuments, which appear to have portrayed the deeds of the last Preclassic kings at Takalik Abaj. For the supporting monuments, the specific image of each stone does not appear to have been as important as the fact that it was an "old stone." The Terminal Preclassic guardians of Takalik Abaj appear to have kept the past alive in some capacity by incorporating relics into a living site.

More needs to be done to work out the temporal sequence at Takalik Abaj and to reconstruct the themes of shattered and defaced monuments. A necessary task is to compare the history of sculptural change at this site with those of contemporaneous centers. In comparative perspective, the sculptural corpus at Takalik Abaj seems to be rather thin on representations of gods and supernaturals and rather generous in representations of creatures. Perhaps these naturalistic animals actually represented supernatural forces and could be one reason for the infrequent representations of supernatural beings, especially in the corpus of the site's Olmec monuments. Also missing at Takalik Abaj are monuments in narrative format, as abundantly known for the nearby center of Izapa. The paucity of sculptural ties to Izapa is puzzling. The people at Takalik Abaj appear to be some of the first to put up Maya monuments with the full package: written texts, Long Count dates, and profile images of standing kings. Why this tradition did not persist is another question for future study. The early history of Takalik Abaj shows selective influence by distant neighbors and open experimentation with a range of sculptural forms and themes. The final history shows an avoidance of sculpture altogether.

Acknowledgments

The data reported here come from many years of archaeological research, for which we have had wonderful help from able colleagues and support from generous institutions. We are grateful to Oswaldo López, Armin Torres, and Fredy Guillén of our sculpture research team and to Jeremías Claudio, David Claudio, and Robin de León of our archaeological research team. These individuals helped us excavate, record, draw, analyze, and keep track of the numerous sculptures at Takalik Abaj. We express our special thanks to our friend and mentor Marion Popenoe de Hatch for her painstaking work in analyzing the eroded potsherds found at the site and devising the ceramic chronology; this chronology has been fundamental to our research and understanding of Takalik Abaj. We are also grateful to John E. Clark for his interest in our investigations and for his editorial help and questions, which made this work more complete. We thank him and the New World Archaeological Foundation for funding our radiocarbon dates. We especially acknowledge the Guatemala Ministerio de Cultura y Deportes y Dirección General del Patrimonio Cultural y Natural for its continuous institutional support of the Proyecto Nacional Takalik Abaj, which has made our long-term investigations at the site possible. Our final appreciation is for the conference organizers and volume editors, Julia Guernsey, John E. Clark, and Barbara Arroyo, for inviting us to participate in the Dumbarton Oaks conference on early sculpture and for allowing us to be part of the discussion on the place of stone monuments in Preclassic Mesoamerica.

NOTES

1. Stone monuments at this site were originally attributed to one of two coffee plantations that own part of the site (Santa Margarita and San Isidro Piedra Parada) or to nearby places (Colomba) (Coe 1957; Graham et al. 1978:85). To provide more order to the archaeological descriptions, Miles (1965:246) proposed "Abaj Takalik" for the site name, and this was the name adopted by the University of California at Berkeley Abaj Takalik Project. "Abaj Takalik" is a translation into K'iche' Maya of the Spanish term *piedra parada,* meaning "standing stone." As it turns out, Miles's literal translation violated the rules of Mayan grammar, so the terms were recently reversed to conform to proper speech. The site is now known as Tak'alik Ab'aj, and this revised name was adopted by the current Proyecto Nacional Takalik Abaj. We anglicize and simplify the name here as Takalik Abaj.

2. The terms "Olmec sculpture" and "Maya sculpture" are used throughout this chapter to indicate styles of carving but not necessarily the ethnicity of their carvers.

3. Taxcal is a local material at the site that was widely used in construction to make plaza floors of variegated colors and add strength to clay constructions. It is a clay- and mineral-rich material formed from decomposing volcanic tuffs (Franklin Matzdorf, personal communication 2006).

4. This altar, because of its discovery after this chapter was originally drafted, is not included in the numbers and percentages mentioned for monumental themes, destruction, and reuse.

9

Rulers, Gods, and Potbellies

A Consideration of Sculptural Forms and Themes
from the Preclassic Pacific Coast and Piedmont of Mesoamerica

JULIA GUERNSEY

THIS CHAPTER EXPLORES THE POTENTIAL motivations of Late Preclassic rulers for their choices of specific sculptural forms and themes in the built environment. Two seemingly disparate lines of inquiry are employed. The first considers the depiction of water deities at sites in the Pacific piedmont during the Preclassic, where their representation seems closely tied to natural features, hydraulic systems, or other sculptural objects from the public sector that directly reference the practical control and ritual manipulation of water. The second line of inquiry considers the enigmatic potbellies, or *barrigones,* a very different yet prominent sculptural type along the coast and piedmont. Comparison of the potbellies to ceramic figurines from La Blanca, Guatemala, indicates that the potbellies may trace their antecedents to Middle Preclassic household ritual and suggests that this sculptural type stems from traditions conceptually grounded in the domestic sector.

My premise is that rulers invoked particular themes and sculptural types for specific purposes

that engaged different sectors and concerns of society. In so doing, rulers orchestrated a multi-faceted sculptural program that negotiated a variety of social constituencies and ideological realms. Sculpture was adeptly integrated into its environment, making reference to other monuments, architecture, the rituals and trappings of material culture, and modifications to the natural environment. Through this brief, and admittedly tentative, exploration of the conceptual motivations for dissimilar sculptural forms, I hope to underscore the complex nature of sculpture and its role in the political and social matrix of Late Preclassic Mesoamerica.

The focus of this chapter is on the Pacific coastal plains and piedmont of Mesoamerica, which were home to a number of ethnic groups, including peoples who spoke Mayan and Mixe-Zoquean. During the Late Preclassic period (300 BC–AD 250) such sites as Izapa, Takalik Abaj, El Ujuxte, and Monte Alto occupied advantageous locations on trade routes between the coast and interior, functioning

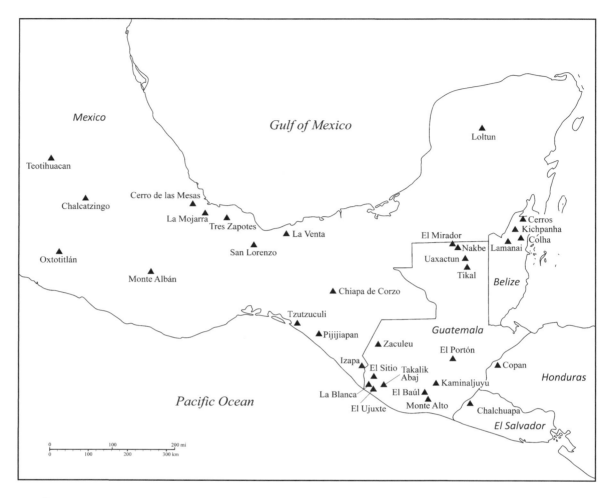

figure 9.1
Map of Mesoamerica showing sites mentioned in the text. (Drawing by the author.)

as important crossroads of communication and exchange (Figure 9.1). Despite their contemporaneity and proximity to one another, each site exhibited a sculptural corpus that—although functioning within broadly shared elite political and religious agendas and sharing certain characteristics—possessed unique components or emphasized certain themes over those of its neighbors. Certainly the diverse arrays of sculptural types in this region were one of the most prominent aspects of site centers, working in tandem with the architecture to define each center's space and the performances staged within it. The monuments were the result of the vision of the ruling elite at specific sites, whose beliefs and political ideologies were manifested in

sculptural form. Sculpture was a powerful vehicle through which a ruler could forge and display messages of supernatural well-being, economic prosperity, and political expansion, making them tangible in the built environment. In other words, sculpture was not merely reactive: it was a key player that actively asserted specific concepts, characters, and agendas, and it did so through a diversity of forms.

Gods, Rain, and Water

The site of Izapa, in Chiapas, Mexico, reached its apogee during the Guillen phase (300–50 BC), during which all of its central plaza groups reached their maximum proportions and most of its monuments were carved (Lowe et al. 1982:133). The primary sculptural vehicle at Izapa was the stela, carved or plain, which was typically paired with an altar. These stela-altar pairs were arranged at the bases of architectural mounds, defining a series of quadrilateral plazas that were the loci of performances (Guernsey 2006b; Lowe et al. 1982).

Izapa Stela 1 (Figure 9.2), located at the southern end of Group A, depicts a Late Preclassic version of Chahk, the god of rain and lightning (Coe 1962:99, 1978; Girard 1966:40; Hellmuth 1987; Miles 1965:252; Norman 1976:87–92; Taube 1992:22). Comparison to a Classic Chahk from Tikal reveals many similarities (Figure 9.3). On Izapa Stela 1, Chahk is fishing, replete with creel and woven basket; the Tikal Chahk also wears a creel on his back and clasps a fish in his hands. Likewise, both versions possess nearly identical topknots of hair, a diagnostic feature of Chahk during the Classic and Postclassic periods; the Izapa Chahk also has a curled brow or forehead, a diagnostic device in Late Preclassic representations of this god (Taube 1995:95). Celts mark the shins of the Izapa Chahk and indicate his divine nature (Taube 1996:50). He also possesses a blunt snout, prominent tooth, and curling whisker or fish barbel at the corner of his mouth.

On Stela 1, Chahk stands on a watery band flanked by two zoomorphic heads that Taube (1995:95) identified as Chahk heads based on their curling brows, which Norman (1976:91) originally associated with cloud volutes. The watery band may allude to actual water that flowed from Group A into a reservoir at the base of Mound 60, the highest mound at the site that formed the focal point of plaza construction (Figure 9.4). Water collected in the Group A plaza was channeled to a reservoir on the west side of Mound 60 by an inlet drain at the southeastern corner of Mound 58 (Gómez Rueda 1995; Lowe et al. 1982:171). Although this drain served the functional purpose of removing standing water from the plaza, it was probably part of a more symbolic scheme as well. With the series of reservoirs, dams, and aqueducts at its base that channeled water from the central plazas to the Izapa River to the east, Mound 60 would have

figure 9.2
Izapa Stela 1. (Drawing from the New World Archaeological Foundation.)

figure 9.3
Detail of carved bone from Temple I at Tikal. (Drawing by John Montgomery.)

stood at the center of a watery realm that marked the heart of the site.

Stela 1 stood adjacent to the drain at the corner of Mound 58, as if referencing the inlet drain that carried water from the plaza to the Mound 60 reservoir. Its location adjacent to this drain must have been the deliberate decision of an Izapa ruler, who in so placing Stela 1 incorporated the very hand and actions of the deity into the Izapa environment. I suggest that, through his carved representation on the stela, Chahk's presence and role as rain-bringer and fisherman were materialized, while the practical and symbolic manipulation of rainwater was also placed under his symbolic oversight. Certainly the control of water was critical in the environment of Izapa, which receives high annual precipitation.

The erection of an image of Chahk in the Group A plaza must also have testified to the successful relationship between the Izapa ruler and this deity, whose presence was evinced through this carved stone. In fact, the relationship between the carving of an image and the actual manifestation of an entity is important, as it appears to be at the very heart of Mesoamerican sculpture. For the Classic Maya, stelae were more than static monuments and more than mere surrogates for the imagery carved on them: they literally embodied the entity depicted on their surfaces, whether god or human (Stuart 1996). As Houston and Stuart (1996:304, 1998:87–88) elaborated, Stela 1 from El Zapote depicts Chahk, and the accompanying text identifies him as the god of a local lord and also records the erection of the stela itself. Moreover, the final passage of the inscription "hints at an equivalence between god and depiction of god" (1998:87), suggesting that the identities of the stela and the god

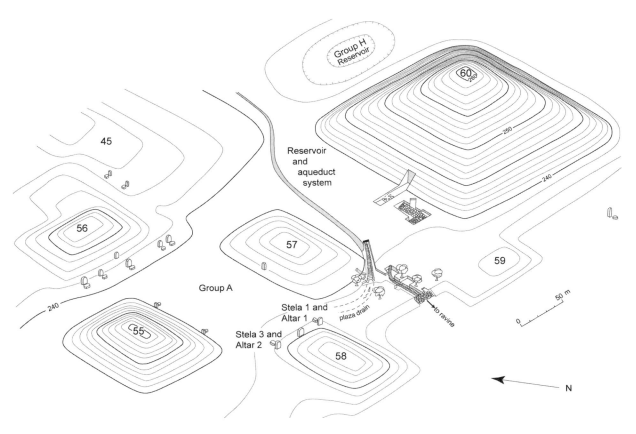

figure 9.4
Izapa Group A, Mound 60, and the associated hydraulic systems. (After the drawing from the New World Archaeological Foundation in Lowe et al. 1982:fig. 8.8.)

were fused. Recent hieroglyphic advances, such as this one, are critical to understanding how sculpture functioned in ancient times and point to its nature as a vehicle through which gods, messages, and human actors were perpetually manifested.

Although the depiction of Chahk on Stela 1 is very active, emphasizing his rain-making and fishing activities, the imagery also alludes to other sculptures at the site. Such references among sculptures not only provide information regarding the types of performances associated with these objects but also hint at the narrative programs that operated among monuments and through space. For instance, the basket held by Chahk resembles Miscellaneous Monument 24 from Izapa, a large stone basin carved in the likeness of a woven basket (Figure 9.5). There is no bottom to the basin, and its upper lips are worn, which led Norman

(1976:270–271) to suggest that it functioned ceremonially in some sort of water channel or spring. The original context of the monument is unknown, as it was relocated in ancient times to Group F at Izapa, where construction was refocused during the Early Classic period. Despite its lack of original context, however, I suggest that the basket may have originally been located in Group A, where it might have formed a tableau with Stela 1 and the stone-lined drain leading to the Mound 60 reservoir. Similar "fountain stones" were found on the bank of the Izapa River, which supports the suggestion that the original context for these monuments was in association with moving water (Lowe et al. 1982:103; Norman 1976:281). Regardless, it appears that the sculpture was a three-dimensional version of a basket, similar to the one carried by Chahk on Stela 1 and, presumably, by ordinary individuals

figure 9.5
Izapa Miscellaneous Monument 24. (Photograph by the author.)

as well. As such, its very presence in monumental sculptural form is significant on several levels. The actions of the god Chahk, phrased as an act of fishing with a basket, would have registered with viewers both as a familiar act of subsistence and also as a metaphor for the arrival of rain. The symbolism of both monuments was part of a deliberate design that addressed both the ritual and practical manipulation of water. These messages further resonated within the broader Group A plaza, whose primary theme was the supernatural performances of rulers in the guise of the Principal Bird Deity (Guernsey 2006b). Thus even the acts of the gods and the arrival of rain were phrased only in the context of the acts and authority of Izapa rulers.

A similar narrative relationship among monuments also appears in association with Stela 3 (Figure 9.6), the counterpart to Stela 1 at the northwest

corner of Mound 58. The figure depicted on Stela 3 has been compared to the Classic God K, whose leg terminates in a serpent (Lowe et al. 1982:24; Miller 1986:61), as well as to Maya rain gods who wield similar axes (Norman 1976:97). The divine nature of the figure is confirmed by the celt strapped to his shin. A new drawing of the monument, however, makes clear that the foot of the figure passes behind the serpent and is not part of the character's leg, as is diagnostic for God K. The axe-wielding figure on Stela 3 is nonetheless difficult to analyze, although it anticipates to some degree the Classic version of Chahk known as Chahk Xib Chahk, who brandishes an axe that causes thunder. Yet as Taube (1992:76) discussed, the Classic God K is also sometimes associated with rain and lightning, and composite Chahk-God K figures are known from the Early Classic. Although the Stela 3 figure does not possess the curled hair of Chahk on Stela 1, the forehead and cranium are distinctively domed, and the projecting frontal "horn" appears on other Late Preclassic versions of Chahk (see Taube 1996:fig. 17). The position of Stela 3 at the southwest corner of Mound 58 and of Stela 1 with its image of Chahk at the southeast corner of the same mound might also anticipate the directional associations of some Classic Chahks (Taube 1992:17–27, 1995:97). Likewise supporting the identification of the deity on Stela 3 as a version of Chahk is the toad altar, Altar 2, which was placed in front of the stela and mirrored by the placement of a similar toad altar in front of Stela 1 (Figure 9.7). During the Classic period, Chahk was closely associated with toads, an association that perseveres in modern Cha Chahk rituals (Freidel et al. 1993:32; Redfield 1941:95, 117).

The serpent at the center of the composition on Stela 3 might further confirm the identification of the protagonist as an aspect of Chahk. During the Classic and Postclassic periods, serpents often symbolized the lightning wielded by Chahk. On Stela 3, the enormous serpent has oval eyes, a prominently upturned snout, a squared jaw from which project curling volutes, and an open mouth. A nearly identical version of this serpent, Miscellaneous Monument 3, exists in three-dimensional form (Norman 1976:259) (Figure 9.8a). Miscellaneous Monument 3 is a drain spout that was found in a secondary context in Group F. I suggest that the serpent on Stela 3 is an animated version of the stone drain spout and that the two sculptures, like Stela 1 and Miscellaneous Monument 24, together form a narrative relationship concerning the ritual actions of water gods. Again, although the original context of Miscellaneous Monument 3 will never be known, it seems likely that it, too, was once a part of a sculptural tableau at the base of Mound 58 in which the actions of rain and water gods were visualized through the interplay between these sculptures. Such associations between rain deities and water systems were not new in Mesoamerica, as the sculptural inventory of Early Preclassic San Lorenzo suggests a similar relationship (see Coe and Diehl 1980:361–362). Interestingly,

another zoomorphic drain spout exists at Izapa (Figure 9.8b), and other plain trough fragments were recovered from secondary contexts in Group F (Norman 1976:268–269, 273).

Even though the figure on Stela 3 clearly bears an iconographic relationship to contemporary and later versions of Chahk, it may be prudent to identify it more generally as a water god. Indeed, the

0   50 cm

figure 9.6
Izapa Stela 3. (Drawing from the New World Archaeological Foundation.)

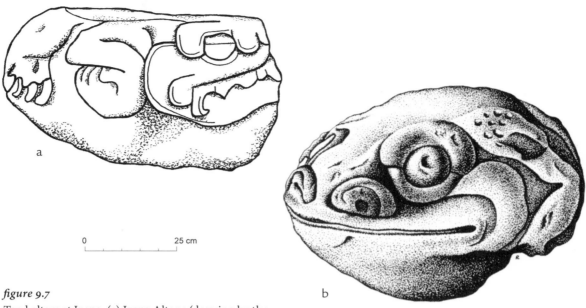

0   25 cm

figure 9.7
Toad altars at Izapa. (a) Izapa Altar 1 (drawing by the author); (b) Izapa Altar 2 (drawing from the New World Archaeological Foundation by Ramiro Jimenez).

b

differences between Stelae 1 and 3 at Izapa may indicate that, in this region during the Late Preclassic, there were flexible categories of water gods whose traits and associations could overlap in the broader conceptual category of rain and water. The ways in which water is visualized on Stelae 1 and 3 also warrants further comment. On Stela 1, the water is moving—active and teeming with aquatic life. In contrast, on Stela 3, water is referenced only through the portrayal of the animated stone trough: it is a more terrestrial vision of water, manipulated and controlled at the site center. Perhaps different types of water were the domain of specific water deities or were associated with one particular aspect of a more generic water god.

Although one can only hypothesize that the original locations of Miscellaneous Monuments 24 and 3 were in Group A, the narrative relationship between the imagery of Stelae 1 and 3 and the form of these two miscellaneous sculptures cannot be denied. Moreover, the thematic link between these diverse monuments is one of water manipulation, which was given supernatural sanction through the actions of these Late Preclassic water gods. Yet

this supernatural narrative was more than clever myth: it was anchored to an actual physical space at Izapa and a system of hydraulics that carried water from the plaza to the reservoir at the base of Mound 60 and ultimately to the Izapa River, which emptied into the Suchiate River on its way to the Pacific Ocean. The monuments manifested a vision of water as a source of dynamic sustenance and fertility while also presenting it as controlled and manipulated in the terrestrial realm.

This narrative created at the base of Mound 58 was echoed throughout the assemblage of monuments in Group A. The watery band of Stela 1 appears on Stela 5, and liquid of some sort descends from the sky band on Stela 26.[1] Altars 1 and 2, which probably represented *Bufo marinus* toads (based on the pitted parotid glands of the Altar 2 toad), also bear a relationship to Stela 6, directly opposite them at the base of Mound 56 to the north. Stela 6 depicts another *Bufo marinus* toad, which burps forth a canoe-shaped object from its mouth that recalls those on Stelae 3 and 26, also in Group A. I have argued elsewhere (Guernsey 2006b:126) that Stela 6 was an animated, or personified, version of

figure 9.8
Zoomorphic drain
spouts at Izapa. (a) Izapa
Miscellaneous Monument 3;
(b) unidentified monument
in pile of sculpture
fragments at the site.
(Photographs by the author.)

a

b

the Altar 1 and 2 toads, envisioned as an active participant in the materialization of the canoe-shaped object or vision. As such, it is further linked to the imagery of Stela 11 in Group B, in which an individual emerges from the mouth of a similar *Bufo marinus* toad in an act of birth or as the manifestation of a vision. Such imagery, in which stone monuments are not only personified but are also literally participating in ritual acts, underscores the need to understand Preclassic stone sculpture as more than just immobile lumps of stone, but as vibrant actors in the ritual narratives that were constructed

by Late Preclassic rulers. The narrative in Group A may also have been linked to other sculptures at the site, particularly Stela 23 to the north in Group D. Stela 23 (Figure 9.9) depicts an actor with a curled brow who descends from a skyband toward a watery basal band. The figure wields in one hand a curling staff and in the other a plaited object. The curled brow and associations with water suggest that the figure represents yet another aspect of a Late Preclassic water god (Norman 1976:130–131).

So why did an Izapa ruler (or rulers) choose to construct this particular narrative, which featured

figure 9.9
Izapa Stela 23. (Drawing from the New World
Archaeological Foundation.)

the actions of Chahk and other water gods, in a broader sculptural program celebrating the ruler's own political and cosmological authority? The exact motivations for this choice can never be known, but some possible rationales can be asserted. The control, manipulation, and removal of water must have been of serious importance at Late Preclassic Izapa, as it is in the region today. Implicating the hand of the gods in the hydraulic

scheme at Izapa, in effect, gave supernatural sanction for such major public works at the site. The sculpture, through its reference to objects involved in the actual movement of water (such as drains), also created a link between the supernatural realm and that of practical public works, uniting both domains under the supervision of the ruler. Through the use of sculpture—both stelae and more three-dimensionally rendered forms—a narrative program was carefully structured in the plaza that forged continuity between the diverse aspects of the daily workings of the site. One must also bear in mind the very human scale of the sculptures involved. One cannot stand at one end of the Group A plaza and discern the imagery on monuments at the opposite side: the plaza is enormous, and to view the imagery, one must approach each stela individually, moving from monument to monument in a deliberate fashion that necessitates the involvement of the viewer. Thus the references among monuments would have become clear only as one moved through the plaza, creating a narrative that unfolded as the viewer interacted with the built environment as a whole.

These narrative choices at Izapa were not unique. Rulers at other Late Preclassic sites, such as Takalik Abaj in Retalhuleu, Guatemala, also invoked water and rain deities. Takalik Abaj Stela 1, whose original context is unknown (Orrego Corzo 1990:90), depicts another version of a Late Preclassic water or Chahk-related deity (Figure 9.10a). Like the Chahks on Izapa Stela 1 and the Tikal bone, this one has a towering hank of swirled hair (or a voluted brow), a zoomorphic snout, and curling whiskers or fish barbels at the corner of his mouth. In his left hand he clasps a ceremonial bar from which emerges a serpent, perhaps an antecedent to the lightning-serpent axes wielded by Chahk during later periods. Behind his left leg and dangling from his belt is, as Taube (1992:76) observed, a small figure, partially effaced, that blends attributes of both Chahk and God K, as evidenced by what may be a leg that terminates in a serpent foot.

Likewise, Takalik Abaj Monument 64 may depict another water deity (Figure 9.10b). The figure wields a serpent staff, and flanking him is a

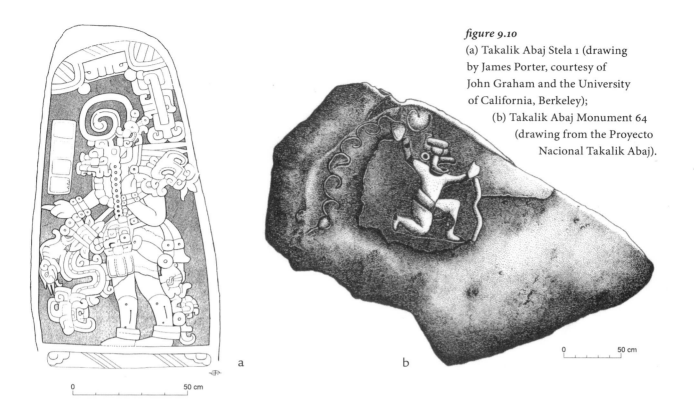

figure 9.10
(a) Takalik Abaj Stela 1 (drawing
by James Porter, courtesy of
John Graham and the University
of California, Berkeley);
(b) Takalik Abaj Monument 64
(drawing from the Proyecto
Nacional Takalik Abaj).

series of S-scrolls, closely associated with rain-bearing clouds (Reilly 1996; Stone 1996:403; Stuart and Houston 1994). Interestingly, Monument 64 was recovered in the portion of the site known as El Escondite, located directly to the west of Terrace 3 in the Central Group (see Figure 8.1). El Escondite is in a natural depression that, although probably prone to seasonal inundations, was also the locus of the earliest residential compounds that date to the early Middle Preclassic (Popenoe de Hatch 2004; Schieber de Lavarreda and Pérez 2004). Monument 64 was found on the east bank of the El Chorro rivulet, and its imagery clearly reflects its context in this watery zone. The El Chorro rivulet in El Escondite was also linked to a series of aqueducts that carried water to the south (Schieber de Lavarreda and Orrego Corzo 2001a:31; Schieber de Lavarreda and Pérez 2004). The association of Monument 64 with a hydraulic system recalls the context of Izapa Stelae 1 and 3 and again suggests a compelling relationship between images of water gods and public works designed to transport water throughout the sites.

Similar themes characterize the artistic programs of contemporaneous sites in the Maya Lowlands. As described above, the narrative of water gods at Izapa was embedded in a larger sculptural program that invoked the ruler's ability to communicate with the supernatural realm in the persona of the Principal Bird Deity. A very similar conceptualization of the water god theme characterizes a stucco facade at Calakmul in the Maya Lowlands. The facade, which dates to the Preclassic, displays a stucco frieze that frames a passage to the interior of the Substructure II-c complex (Carrasco Vargas 2005:62–66).[2] At the center of the frieze appears Chahk (Figure 9.11a), flanked by figures wearing costumes related to the Principal Bird Deity. The Calakmul Chahk's curling topknot of hair compares closely to those of the Chahks at Izapa and Tikal, and his gestures and posture—although oriented differently—are much like those of the water god on Izapa Stela 23, who also descends from a skyband.

Another Late Preclassic version of Chahk appears on the west wall of the San Bartolo murals.

a

b

c

figure 9.11

Representations of Chahk in the Maya Lowlands. (a) Detail, rotated 90° for comparative purposes, from the frieze of Calakmul Structure II-c (after Carrasco 2005:fig. 4); (b) Chahk on the west wall of Las Pinturas Sub-1 chamber, San Bartolo; (c) another water god from the west wall of Las Pinturas Sub-1 chamber, San Bartolo (details from San Bartolo after drawings by Heather Hurst, courtesy of William Saturno and the Proyecto San Bartolo).

At the center of a quatrefoil dances the Maize God, and to the left sits an enthroned Chahk (Figure 9.11b). To the right is a supernatural identified as the god of standing or terrestrial water, who may also be linked to Classic Maya personified forms of the 360-day period (or *tuun*) and to the Water Lily Serpent (Figure 9.11c; Saturno et al. 2005:650; Taube 1992:59). I would point out, however, that the curled topknot or upper brow of the supernatural closely resembles that of the figures on Takalik Abaj Stela 1 and Izapa Stela 23. Likewise the gesture made by the supernatural at San Bartolo is strikingly similar (in reverse) to that made by the figure on Takalik Abaj Stela 1. The positions of these two water deities at San Bartolo on opposite sides of the Maize God, who often marks the center, anticipates the directional associations of Classic water gods (see Quenon and Le Fort 1997:fig. 25). It is worth

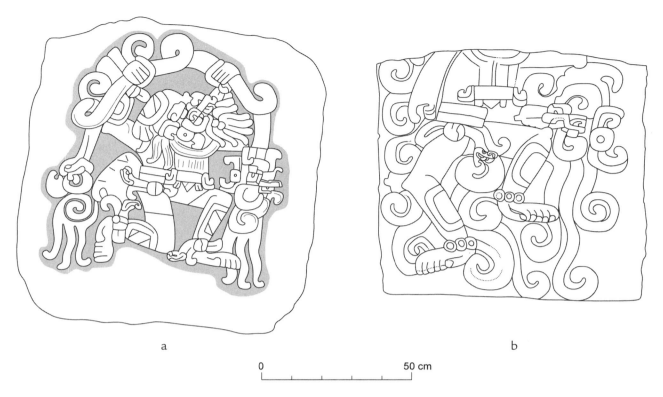

figure 9.12
(a) Kaminaljuyu Stela 19 (drawing from the New World Archaeological Foundation); (b) Kaminaljuyu Stela 4 (drawing by Luis Fernando Luin, courtesy of Federico Fahsen).

considering that this supernatural figure identified as the god of terrestrial water at San Bartolo may be linked to other water gods that appear at Izapa and Takalik Abaj during the Preclassic. Perhaps at San Bartolo, as at Izapa, the many aspects of water—as rain, storm, source of aquatic life, standing or flowing, from the sky or the earth, in streams, lakes, and oceans, or transported through hydraulic works—were envisioned through the presence of various water gods or their shifting associations. Interesting, too, is the inclusion of this vignette in the greater narrative of the San Bartolo murals, which highlights the role of the Principal Bird Deity in the creation story. This iconographic program is consistent with those at Izapa, Calakmul, and the Early Classic site of Aguacatal (Houston et al. 2005) that likewise featured water deities in broader creation stories referencing the Principal Bird Deity.

Monuments from Kaminaljuyu also relate to the water god narrative in general. Taube (1995:95)

noted the voluted "Chahk" heads that appear on the serpent clasped by the figure on Kaminaljuyu Stela 19 and amidst the scrolls on Stela 4 (Figure 9.12). Both stelae portray anthropomorphic figures with jaguarian paws. On Stela 4 the creature performs a dance in association with a series of curling scrolls and the Chahk head, which is nearly identical to the one at the base of Izapa Stela 1. Izapa Stela 90 (Gómez Rueda and Grazioso Sierra 1997) may also be related to these Kaminaljuyu monuments. A zoomorph with a voluted forehead decorates the belt of the standing figure, and a serpent, also bearing a zoomorphic face, emerges from the front of the belt. Interestingly, a Zoque ritual called the "Dance of the Jaguar" was recorded by Báez-Jorge (1983:397), in which participants donned jaguar masks and performed dances associated with agricultural fertility and the arrival of rain.[3] Such images, which evoke the rain-making capabilities of Chahk, allude to the types of performances and

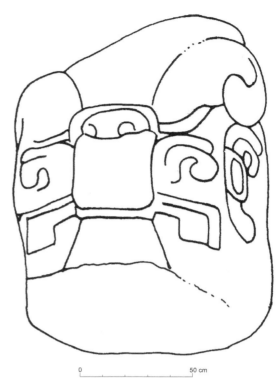

figure 9.13
Monte Alto Monument 3. (Photograph by the author; drawing by Karl Taube.)

dances that were probably staged in the plazas that held these water god monuments.

Taube (1995:96–97) also noted a series of Late Preclassic full-figure representations of Chahk. Most interesting is a large boulder sculpture from the site of Monte Alto in Escuintla, Guatemala. This sculpture, Monument 3, possesses the curling brow and whiskers that mark other versions of Chahk and was located in a monument grouping on the eastern boundary of the site center (Figure 9.13; Parsons 1986:35, fig. 6). Parsons (1986:30) noted that the double-voluted earplugs and cheek markings on Monte Alto Monument 3 are identical to those of the Chahk heads on Kaminaljuyu Stelae 4 and 19. Interestingly, this three-dimensional rendering of Chahk is unusual at Monte Alto, which is much better known for its potbelly sculptures and plain stelae. Evidence suggests that Monument 3 as well as the other monuments found grouped with it were moved in ancient times

(Popenoe de Hatch 1989:25; Shook 1971:74–75). This move makes dating the monument difficult, but its iconographic and formal attributes strongly argue for a Late Preclassic date (however, see Miles [1965:247], Parsons [1986:3], and Richardson [1940] for alternative classifications and dating).

Evidence like that discussed above indicates that the sculptural programs of Late Preclassic sites along the Pacific piedmont were not operating in a vacuum—instead they were related to those found at contemporaneous sites in other regions of Mesoamerica. The theme of Chahk, or water gods in general, obviously reflects concerns and motivations shared by many rulers. The choice of this theme for public programming enabled rulers to relate their actions and authority to practical and natural concerns, such as the arrival of rain and its control and manipulation in the form of hydraulic systems, as well as more conceptual concerns, such as the involvement and sanction of the gods in the affairs of their communities. Through such narratives, rulers could articulate their continued successes in maintaining the delicate balance of well-being, both practical and spiritual, in their communities.

Potbellies, Puffy Faces, and Domestic Ritual

The theme of monumental water gods and hydraulic works, although critical to a consideration of how authority was visualized during the Late Preclassic, limits discussion to the public sector and site centers, whose very organization and conceptualization was the domain of the rulers and elites. Yet the broader sculptural context of the Chahk monument from Monte Alto alludes to other sources of inspiration for the sculptural themes of the Late Preclassic that have less to do with the public domain than with the residential sector. As a counterpoint to the discussion above, I consider a very different potential origin for a recurring form of sculpture along the Pacific piedmont during the Preclassic—that of the potbellies. This brief and exploratory essay is part of an ongoing exploration into the relationship between public and private ritual during the Middle to Late Preclassic transition along the Pacific Coast (Guernsey and Love 2005, 2008; Love and Guernsey 2007).

Potbellies are a sculptural form found frequently throughout the Pacific slope and highlands during the Preclassic period (Amaroli 1997; Bove 1989:5; Chinchilla Mazariegos 2001–2002; Miles 1965:242; Navarrete and Hernández 2000; Parsons 1986:38–44; Popenoe de Hatch 1989; Richardson 1940; Rodas 1993; Shook 1971), although they are also known from elsewhere in Mesoamerica (e.g., see Chapter 5; W. Coe 1965:fig. 18; Craig 2005:fig. 3; Delgadillo Torres and Santana Sandoval 1989; Fialko 2005; Lothrop 1926; Richardson 1940:fig. 37; Scott 1980, 1988; Stirling 1943b:24). A few scholars have argued for a Middle Preclassic date for the potbellies (Girard 1969; Graham 1980, 1989:236–238; Miles 1965:242), but most agree that the earliest occurrence of this sculptural form coincides with the Middle to Late Preclassic transition and that

their major florescence unfolded during the Late Preclassic (Bove 1989:5; Demarest 1986:42, 138–139; Parsons 1986:39–44; Popenoe de Hatch 1989; Shook 1971:75). The potbellies are often rotund human figures, carved in the round from boulders, with distinctive facial features that typically include puffy faces with closed eyes and puffy eyelids. Monte Alto Monument 4 typifies these features (Figure 9.14). However there is variation among them, including some who are more stout than obese but still grasp their stomachs in a consistent manner and wrap their legs around their bellies, such as Finca Sololá Monument 3 (Figure 9.15; Rodas 1993:fig. 7). Other sculptures from Monte Alto, such as Monuments 8 and 10 (Figure 9.16), consist of the head alone with its puffy features and closed eyes, as if the essence of these "potbelly" sculptures was conveyed by the closed, puffy-lidded eyes and bloated facial features alone, without need for the obese body. In fact, based on these examples from Monte Alto and others noted below, I suggest that the closed eyes and puffy facial features are more diagnostic than the obese bodies of Late Preclassic stone potbelly sculptures.[4] At Monte Alto the Monument 3 Chahk head was grouped along the eastern edge of the site with four massive boulder sculptures (Parsons 1986:44–45; Popenoe de Hatch 1989; Shook 1971:75; Shook and Popenoe de Hatch 1981). Monuments 4–6 are potbellies, whereas Monument 2 is one of the massive heads that bears the typical bloated facial features and puffy-lidded, closed eyes associated with potbellies. Along the western margin of the site stood another grouping of three heads (Monuments 7, 8, and 10) and one potbelly, Monument 9. Monument 11, another potbelly, stood alone at the northern end of the site; fifteen plain stelae, three altars, and sixty-eight plain boulders were also recorded at the site (Shook 1971:75).

As scholars have commented (Popenoe de Hatch 1989:25; Shook 1971:75), the location of the Monte Alto sculptures does not reflect their original context, as they were apparently moved in ancient times and more recently. This situation obviously hinders any discussion of their contextual significance. As a result, most scholars have considered the Monte Alto potbellies and heads

figure 9.14
Monte Alto Monument 4.
(Photograph by the author.)

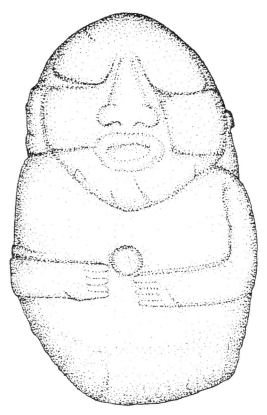

figure 9.15
Finca Sololá
Monument 3.
(Drawing from
Rodas 1993:fig. 7,
with permission of
Fred Bove.)

within broader discussions of the potbelly phenomenon and its distribution, or their relationship to Middle Preclassic Olmec sculpture and the Gulf Coast tradition of monumental heads (Girard 1969; Graham 1980, 1982; Miles 1965:242; Parsons and Jenson 1965). In an attempt to sidestep these debates, which cannot be resolved because of consistently poor contextual data, I briefly present an alternative avenue of investigation. Although not by any stretch an encompassing discussion of the potbelly phenomenon or its symbolic significance, this approach instead presents new data that address the distinctive puffy features of the potbellies and monumental heads and their relationship to domestic figurine traditions. By moving discussion beyond the domain of public sculpture alone and considering potential alternative sources for this genre of sculpture, I hope to offer insight into the choices for sculptural programming that were made by Late Preclassic rulers.

Based on comparisons to domestic figurines from the Middle Preclassic site of La Blanca,

a   b

figure 9.16
Monte Alto sculptures. (a) Monte Alto Monument 8; (b) Monte Alto Monument 10. (Photographs by the author.)

Guatemala, it can be tentatively suggested that the origins of certain attributes of the potbellies can be traced to Middle Preclassic domestic ritual (Guernsey and Love 2008). La Blanca, located on the Pacific Coast of Guatemala, was the major center in this region during the Middle Preclassic period and one of the largest sites of its time in ancient Mesoamerica (Love 2002). Large earthen mounds were constructed during the Conchas phase (900–600 BC, uncalibrated), and it retained its prominence for more than three hundred years until it declined ca 600 BC. The site center was characterized by monumental architecture, including Mound 1, which stood more than 25 m tall, and a sunken plaza to the west and adjacent to a ridge that supported an elite residential precinct (Love et al. 2006).

One of the most noteworthy characteristics of domestic assemblages—from both elite and non-elite households—at La Blanca is the abundance of hand-modeled ceramic figurines. They are virtually omnipresent at La Blanca, as in many other Preclassic households throughout Mesoamerica (Cyphers 1993; Joyce 2003; Marcus 1998). The figurines have been interpreted as objects invoked in rites associated with important life-history events, stages in the life cycle, the creation of social identity (Cyphers 1993; Joyce 2003), and ancestor veneration (Grove and Gillespie 2002; Marcus 1998, 1999). What unites these interpretations is the consensus that figurines were used in rituals, particularly within the household, a pattern that is confirmed at La Blanca.

Importantly for this discussion, a series of figurines from La Blanca bear the puffy facial features associated with Late Preclassic potbellies and the massive heads from Monte Alto (Arroyo 2002; also see Ivic de Monterroso 2004:420). The most complete example represents an adult female (Figure 9.17).[5] Most significantly, she exhibits facial features that anticipate those of the Monte Alto heads and potbellies, including the closed eyes with puffy lids and swollen cheeks. In contrast to the Monte Alto examples, her arms and legs extend outward, and her belly is not obese but rather that of a mature woman. The La Blanca figurine dates to the Conchas phase, which indicates that this figurine type predates the stone potbellies, whose earliest appearance appears to coincide with the transition to the Late Preclassic period, perhaps 400–300 BC. Although the modeling of the figure's body does not anticipate later potbelly sculptures, the striking similarities between the facial features of this figurine and those of the later Monte Alto sculptures are noteworthy.

Monte Alto–like facial features also characterize a number of incomplete figurines found throughout La Blanca, all in Conchas phase contexts (Figure 9.18), as well as in adjacent regions, such as La Victoria, Guatemala (Coe 1961:fig. 55p), and Cuauhtemoc, Chiapas (Rob Rosenswig, personal communication 2008), during the Conchas phase. The facial features are fairly consistent, emphasizing closed eyes, puffy lids, and often a bulbous nose. At least one La Blanca example purses its lips in a manner identical to figurines from other regions, to potbellies from Finca Sololá (Parsons 1986:fig. 92) and San Juan Sacatepequez (Figure 9.19a; Parsons 1986:fig. 103), and to the puffy-faced figures on the boulder sculptures from Tiltepec, Chiapas (Figure 9.19b,c; Navarrete and Hernández 2000), among

figure 9.17
La Blanca Middle Preclassic female figurine. (Photograph by Michael Love.)

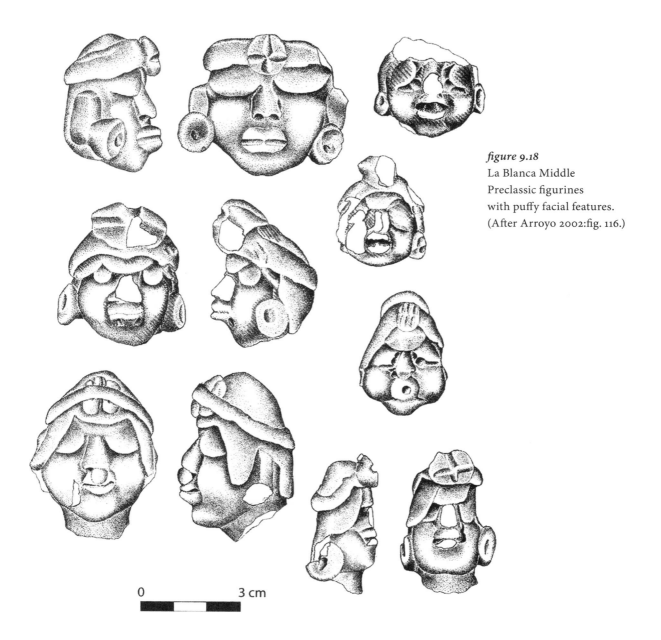

figure 9.18
La Blanca Middle
Preclassic figurines
with puffy facial features.
(After Arroyo 2002:fig. 116.)

0   3 cm

other examples. Others exhibit variation in the hairstyles and headdresses yet retain relative consistency in the puffy facial features and closed eyes. Examples of strikingly similar puffy-faced, closed-eye figurines exist from Preclassic sites elsewhere in Mesoamerica, indicating that this figurine type was not limited to the Pacific Coast (see, for instance, Dahlin 1978:fig. 3, d3; Drucker 1943:plate 28w, 1952:plate 40A,l).

Given these examples, it appears that the Late Preclassic stone potbellies and Monte Alto heads

trace their antecedents—or at least the puffy facial features and closed eyes—to early Middle Preclassic ceramic figurine traditions. These Late Preclassic monuments, ubiquitous in the Pacific piedmont and highlands by the Late Preclassic, are grounded in a tradition of representation well documented in Middle Preclassic domestic assemblages.

The implications of this origin are provocative, as it suggests that the use of Late Preclassic puffy-faced stone potbellies in public contexts reflected the adoption or appropriation, by rulers, of motifs

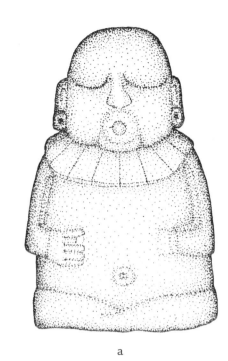

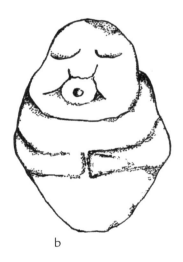

figure 9.19
Potbellies with pursed lips. (a) San Juan
Sacatepequez Monument 1 (drawing
from Rodas 1993:fig. 7, with permission
of Fred Bove); (b) Tiltepec Monument 23;
(c) Tiltepec Monument 25 (drawings of
Tiltepec monuments by the author, after
Navarrete and Hernández 2000:fig. 8).

from earlier domestic ritual traditions. This suggestion correlates well with evidence discussed elsewhere (Guernsey and Love 2005; Love 1999a, 2002) that points to a dramatic decline in figurine use at the household level between the Middle and Late Preclassic periods along the Pacific Coast. For example, the abundance of domestic figurines and feasting vessels at Middle Preclassic La Blanca indicates that household ritual, outside the supervision of the ruler, was of major importance during this period. However, by the beginning of the Late Preclassic period at the nearby site of El Ujuxte, which rose to power following the decline of La Blanca, domestic figurine use ceased almost completely, and there was also a concomitant decline in household feasting (Guernsey and Love 2005; Love et al. 1996:8). By contrast, there is dramatic evidence for increased public ritual at El Ujuxte, materialized in the form of rigidly programmed public space and ritual caches. Likewise at other regional sites, such as Izapa, Takalik Abaj, and Monte Alto, new emphasis was placed on public sculpture that defined each ritual center.

Such evidence suggests that Late Preclassic elites along the Pacific piedmont of Guatemala succeeded in deemphasizing ritual at the household level and moved it—literally and symbolically —into sacred centers. The transformation from puffy-faced figurines to the stone sculptural forms of potbellies or massive heads was one of the ways in which this transition in ritual was made visible. The trappings and symbols of Middle Preclassic domestic ritual, in the form of the puffy-faced figurines, became reconfigured in the form of larger, public stone sculpture whose presence in the sacred environment was controlled by rulers. The exact nature of this reconfiguration is less clear from the available evidence: did it involve an overt appropriation of certain domestic rituals by Late Preclassic rulers? Or, perhaps less dramatically, did it represent a concession or nod to more traditional domestic rituals and belief systems, tolerated when under a ruler's direct supervision and control?

The transition from small ceramic figurines to large boulder sculptures is interesting to ponder. Although the dating for most of the stone potbelly sculptures is admittedly problematic, Parsons (1986:39) asserted that "smaller potbelly sculptures are generally earlier and the larger Monte Alto boulder effigies and heads . . . are generally somewhat later." If true, the transition from smaller to larger versions of the stone potbellies could be a reflection of their origin in smaller ceramic forms. Interestingly, two small stone potbellies were discovered at the site of El Ujuxte (Chapter 7), which, as described above, exhibited a drastic decline in figurine usage and increased evidence of centralized authority at the beginning of the Late Preclassic period (Figure 9.20a). Miniature potbellies from elsewhere, for example Monuments 57 and 58, are also known (Figure 9.20b).[6] Although one of the small potbellies from El Ujuxte is missing its head, the other, like Monuments 57 and 58, bears the puffy-faced attributes of the La Blanca figurines; Monuments 57 and 58 also purse their lips in a manner nearly identical to at least one of the La Blanca figurines. Parsons (1986:42) observed that the arms of the figures on Monuments 57 and 58, which are cut free from their bodies, suggest an early date; it also links them to earlier figurine forms, which often had an open space between the arms and torso. Also noteworthy is the more "slender" form of these miniature potbellies; none is particularly obese. Nor do the figures of Monuments 57 and 58 cohere to the typical potbelly posture of wraparound legs and bodies. I suggest that these variations in the miniature potbellies point to their origins in figurine traditions, like those represented at La Blanca, and also indicate that the puffy facial features are the more critical diagnostic trait.

Importantly, rotund bellies were a frequent and long-standing attribute of Preclassic figurines, sometimes alluding to pregnancy and in other cases appearing to reference obesity. At La Blanca and elsewhere, however, the attributes of a fat belly and wraparound arms and legs are also associated with hybrid human-animal characters. In other words, the attribute of a rotund belly (or potbelly) is not unique to human figurines (Guernsey and Love 2008). Although perhaps a seemingly minor point, it indicates that "potbelly-ness"—defined only by the obese torso and wraparound arms and legs—was

fluid and could be shared by animals, humans, and composite characters during the Preclassic period. This inclusiveness is particularly significant given that numerous individuals have postulated a link between Preclassic potbellies and the so-called "Fat God" complex identified early on by such scholars as Beyer (1930) at Teotihuacan (see, for instance, Feuchtwanger 1989:32; Scott 1988:34–35; Taube 2004:156–161). There is indeed a geographically and temporally widespread phenomenon of fat or jowly individuals in the corpus of art throughout Mesoamerica, but the distinctions and unique features discernible among these obese characters are important. Various attributes of the Preclassic potbellies, such as the distended stomach or jowly cheeks, are associated with a range of characters—human, animal, and composite—suggesting that during the Preclassic this "fat" attribute was not associated with a specific deity (such as a singular "Fat God"), character, or type.

Rather than trying to interpret the meaning or symbolic significance of the stone potbellies and Monte Alto heads, this brief analysis seeks only to suggest that certain key aspects of their iconography can be traced to Middle Preclassic domestic figurine traditions. Yet it is also important to acknowledge that these monuments undoubtedly reflect a diverse mix of influences and long-standing conventions regarding the representation of obese characters that appear in the iconographic record, beginning in the Early Preclassic. Nonetheless, despite any formal resemblance to other, ubiquitous Preclassic "fat" characters found in a variety of media, the most consistent and conspicuous characteristics of the potbellies and Monte Alto heads are the closed, puffy-lidded eyes and puffy facial features that are well attested in the Middle Preclassic figurine assemblages found in the same Pacific coastal region where the stone sculptures are concentrated.

Perhaps most significantly, the puffy-faced figurines at La Blanca factor into broader discussions of the relationship between Middle Preclassic domestic ritual and its trappings, and the symbols and themes employed—or appropriated—by Late Preclassic rulers in the form of public sculpture.

a

figure 9.20
Potbelly carvings. (a) Miniature potbellies from El
Ujuxte, each between 14 and 20 cm in height (photograph
by Michael Love); (b) Monument 57, possibly from
Kaminaljuyu (photograph courtesy of the Museo Popol
Vuh, Universidad Francisco Marroquín, Guatemala).

b

At such sites as Monte Alto, the massive potbellies visually dominated the site center, monumen-
talizing in sculptural form imagery conceptually
grounded in household rituals. The rationale for
this choice is less clear. Was it an active appropriation of specific themes from the domestic sector by
rulers, in which they controlled and limited the use
and ritual associations of this imagery? Or was it a
form of concession, in which Late Preclassic rulers sought to assert their power while also choosing representations that resonated with the general
populace? Such questions cannot be adequately
addressed by the archaeological data at Monte Alto,
which does not include evidence from the domestic
sector on the nature of ritual at that time. However,
the data from La Blanca and El Ujuxte are provocative, as they point to a very definite cessation
of household rituals, or at least the use of ceramic

figurines, at the transition from the Middle to Late Preclassic. At this juncture in time, specific aspects of domestic ritual appear to have been moved to the public domain under the control of rulers; concurrently, the first stone potbellies debuted on the scene. At El Ujuxte, where figurines are virtually absent in the archaeological record, the small potbellies make their appearance in conjunction with a more rigidly defined public sector, careful astronomical alliances of architecture, and elaborate caches in the site center (see Chapter 7).

Despite this consideration of a developmental trajectory, the meaning of the stone potbellies remains enigmatic. Nor do their ties to earlier domestic traditions explain the permutations in form that the potbellies and puffy-faced sculptures exhibit, including the massive heads at Monte Alto; the potbellied figures along the Pacific Coast and highlands; the unusual puffy-faced characters on monuments at Tiltepec, Chiapas; and the puffy-faced motifs decorating a monument at the site of San Miguel, Tabasco (Navarrete and Hernández 2000:591–595). What also needs to be borne in mind is that sculpture had been employed by ruling elites on the Pacific slope of Guatemala long before the appearance of the stone potbelly tradition (see Chapter 1). Yet by considering Middle Preclassic domestic ritual as a source of inspiration for this unique type of sculpture, I hope to initiate discussion about how innovative sculptural forms may reflect and quite literally embody the dynamics and changing social circumstances that characterized the transition from the Middle to the Late Preclassic period in this region of ancient Mesoamerica.

Concluding Remarks

So how, and why, were these two very different conceptual schemes—water gods on one hand and stone potbellies on the other—integrated in sculptural form during the Late Preclassic period? The presence of the massive Chahk head, Monument 3, in a sculptural grouping of potbellies at Monte Alto illustrates the potential for incorporating multiple narratives. Rulers there commissioned a sculptural corpus that referenced both the acts and the presence of the gods as well as ritual traditions rooted in the domestic sector. In fact, this combination suggests that rulers created sculptural programs that addressed differing concerns and diverse social sectors or constituencies. The combination also reflects the deliberate choices by rulers to create a complex sculptural interchange among the supernatural world, the public sector, and the domestic sphere, all articulated in the domain controlled by the ruler. Even at Izapa, where supernatural entities, such as Chahk, played leading roles in the construction of sacred space, potbellies also make an appearance. A 80 cm tall crudely carved potbelly, Miscellaneous Monument 70, was found at Izapa on Mound 30b, where it was associated with a small irregularly shaped stone altar in a context that Lowe et al. (1982:107, fig. 6.15) assigned to the Late or Terminal Preclassic. This configuration of potbelly and altar mirrored the arrangement of stela-altar pairs throughout the site. Likewise such sites as Takalik Abaj and Kaminaljuyu, where carved stelae were abundant and narratives involving water gods and water control were also featured, included potbellies as part of their sculptural programming (see Chapter 8; see García 1997; Parsons 1986). The potbellies, having their origins in domestic ritual, may have carried powerful associations with ancestor worship. As such, they perhaps bridged—or at least mitigated—some of the differences among various sectors and socioeconomic levels of society, forging a link between household ritual and ancestor veneration on one hand and the esoteric realm of the ruler and his responsibilities to communicate with the gods of the supernatural realm on the other. Numerous scholars (see Lucero 2006) have discussed the dynamic relationship between domestic and public rituals, describing how the material aspects of ritual were manipulated, replicated, expanded, and contracted within and between these two domains. The relationship between the stone potbellies, massive Monte Alto heads, and Middle Preclassic figurines clearly points to a similar dynamic that was explored through the vehicle of sculpture by elites during the transition to the Late Preclassic period.

Although worth pondering, the questions raised in this chapter concerning the choices and motivations of Late Preclassic rulers will most likely elude definitive answers. Yet one thing remains abundantly clear: the sculptural assemblages at various Late Preclassic sites along the Pacific slope reflect the diverse choices made by rulers. Some emphasized carved stelae and altars, others erected plain stelae, and yet others focused on the potbelly form and associated puffy-faced boulder sculptures. Interestingly, sites with strikingly diverse sculptural inventories were located within a few kilometers of sites where rulers chose to eschew sculpture almost completely, focusing on architecturally defined spaces and a rigidly axial site layout, as at El Ujuxte. These variations in assemblages warrant further analysis, because the choices by rulers may be a reflection of a variety of factors, including ethnicity or cultural affiliations, political alliances, ideological platforms, ecological considerations, availability and quality of stone, and complex factors governing the relationship between the types of sculpture a ruler was expected to erect and the relative size or regional authority of the site. In the end, such diverse monumental themes along the Pacific slope clearly attest that Late Preclassic rulers negotiated their power—political, social, and supernatural—in part through sculptural programs whose narratives were multifaceted and rooted in long-established ritual and belief systems.

Acknowledgments

I thank all of the individuals who provided images, insights, and editorial assistance for this chapter, which is part of an ongoing study of the relationship between public and domestic art traditions in the Preclassic: Mary Jane Acuña, Barbara Arroyo, Fred Bove, Kat Brown, Karen Olsen Bruhns, Oswaldo Chinchilla, John Clark, Federico Fahsen, John Graham, Gerardo Gutiérrez, Norman Hammond, Lucia Henderson, Michael Love, Heather Orr, Christopher Pool, Mary Pye, Kathryn Reese-Taylor, Sergio Rodas, Rob Rosenswig, Bill Saturno, Erin Sears, David Stuart, and Karl Taube.

NOTES

1. For drawings of these related monuments (Izapa Stelae 5, 6, 11, and 26), see Clark and Moreno (2007:figs. 13.7, 13.8, 13.13, and 13.25), Guernsey (2006b:figs. 6.9 and 6.11), and Norman (1976:figs. 4.1, 3.6, 3.11, and 3.30).

2. Carrasco Vargas (2005:64) dates Substructure II-c to 390–250 BC. However, stylistically the facade of Substructure II-c1 compares favorably to designs on Late Preclassic stelae from Izapa and Takalik Abaj.

3. These rain- and jaguar-associated images trace their origins to the Middle Preclassic (Angulo 1987:133; Covarrubias 1957; Reilly 1996; Taube 1995:100); see Chapter 2 for further discussion of these associations.

4. Only a small percentage of the stone potbelly sculptures and Monte Alto heads has open eyes that diverge from the typical closed, puffy-lidded features. For example, of the more than fifty potbellies illustrated by Rodas, only four or five have open eyes (see Rodas 1993:figs. 3, 17, 23, 24, and possibly 11). Likewise Popenoe de Hatch (1989:30, plate 2.6) observed that Monte Alto Monument 6's open (yet puffy-lidded) eyes are unusual.

5. This nearly complete figurine comes from Mound 9, a household located on the elite residential precinct west of Mound 1 that was also associated with a quatrefoil-shaped clay sculpture (Love and Guernsey 2007).

6. Parsons (1986:42, fig. 102) attributed Monuments 57 and 58 (37 and 38 cm tall, respectively) to Kaminaljuyu; however, Rodas (1993:23) questioned this attribution. For other small potbellies from various regions, see Guernsey and Love (2008), Scott (1980:fig. 3), and Stirling (1957:plate 62c).

Preclassic Stone Sculpture in the Guatemalan Highlands

Broken Monuments and Forgotten Scripts

FEDERICO FAHSEN

FOR THE PAST TWENTY CENTURIES IN THE territory that became Guatemala, the history and archaeology of the highland Maya have been overshadowed by the vainglorious detritus left behind by their lowland cousins: pyramids, palaces, sculptures, tombs, and texts. Pyramids, tombs, and stone monuments with artistic portraiture and inscribed texts have also been found at highland sites, as I describe here, but not in the same frequencies or rendered in the same graceful aesthetic. Hence the highlands have consistently attracted less scholarly attention and public acclaim than the lowlands. Ironically, some of the earliest Maya ceremonial centers, stone sculpture, and writing—and the cultural practices they implicate—appeared in the highlands and may have spread some 2,600 years ago from this temperate clime to the lowland jungles of Belize and northernmost Guatemala. If we are eventually to understand Maya cultural practices, the early contributions of highland Maya peoples need to be taken into account. In this chapter I advance

this objective by analyzing one important cultural practice: the creation and use of stone monuments. What do early sculptures in this region tell us of early Maya history?

In accord with the parameters of this volume, I restrict my coverage of sculpture largely to monuments from the Preclassic period, which ended in the highlands ca AD 200 (Sharer and Sedat 1999:213; Shook and Popenoe de Hatch 1999:291). Few Preclassic sites have been identified in the Guatemalan Highlands, and fewer still are known to have had stone monuments (see Figure 10.1). Most sculptures in the highlands have been found at the site of Kaminaljuyu, located in the central highlands (see Chapter 1; Fahsen 1999, 2000a, 2000b, 2002; Kaplan 1995, 1996, 1999, 2002; Kidder 1961; Kidder et al. 1946; Parsons 1983, 1986; Miles 1965; Valdés 2003) and in two valleys of the northern highlands (*sensu* Ivic de Monterroso 1999) in the modern departments of Quiché (Bailey 1980; Ichon 1977, 1992; Ichon and Viel 1984) and Baja Verapaz (Sedat and Sharer 1972; Sharer and

figure 10.1

Map of Guatemala showing its principal regions and the locations of Preclassic sites with stone sculpture. (Drawing from the New World Archaeological Foundation adapted from Sharer and Sedat 1987:3, fig. 1.1, with the archaeological regions based on Ivic de Monterroso 1999:168, fig. 62.)

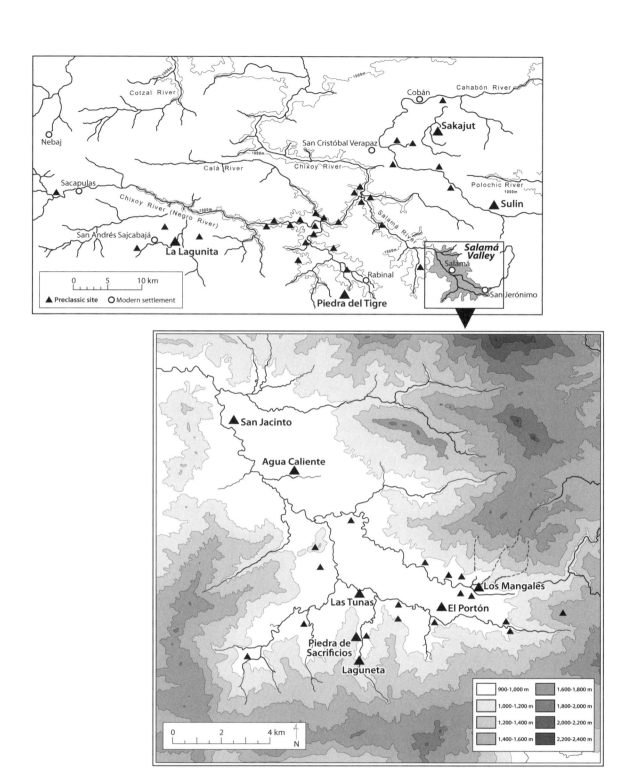

figure 10.2
Map of the northern highlands of Guatemala showing the Preclassic sites of the Salamá and San Andrés Sajcabajá valleys. (Drawing from the New World Archaeological Foundation adapted from Sharer and Sedat 1987:448, fig. 21.1.)

Sedat 1973, 1987, 1999). I describe and analyze stone sculptures found in the Salamá Valley (Baja Verapaz), mostly from the sites of El Portón and Los Mangales, and in the San Andrés Sajcabajá Valley (Quiché) located 60 km to the west, with La Lagunita being its principal center (Figure 10.2, inset map). Separated by rugged terrain and ranging in altitude from 900 to 1,200 m above sea level, these highland valleys were occupied by 1200 BC and had ceremonial centers by 500 BC; they continued to be occupied into the Postclassic and contact periods (Arnauld 1986; Ciudad Ruíz 1984; Iglesias Ponce de León and Ciudad Ruíz 1999; Smith 1955).

Preclassic stone sculptures from these highland valleys evince stylistic similarities with one another and also with sculptures from Kaminaljuyu, located about a three days' walk south of the Salamá Valley (Sedat and Sharer 1972). I explore the similarities and differences among these early monuments and explain what their correspondences might mean in terms of their ancient uses and meanings. The earliest sculptures are from the Salamá Valley, so I begin there and then consider the sculpture from the San Andrés Sajcabajá Valley. I next review the pattern of monument creation and destruction in both regions in light of coeval developments from other areas of Guatemala, especially those at Kaminaljuyu. Attention is paid in each region to script traditions, which appear to have flourished in the highlands until just before the beginning of the Classic period. I conclude with a consideration of how the sculptural corpus from the highlands—its creation, display, as well as its destruction—provides insight into the social and political dynamics of this region. Before delving into the sculptural inventory of the highlands and an explanation of individual monuments and their significance, however, it is useful to provide some historical background of the peoples who made and revered these monuments.

Overview of the Highland Preclassic Era

As pictured in Figure 10.1, the highlands of Guatemala constitute just over fifty percent of this country's land mass and comprise its most broken and difficult terrain. On their southern margin, the highlands are delimited by the chain of majestic volcanoes that parallels the Pacific Ocean and separates the highlands from the coastal lowlands, or Pacific slope region. To the north, volcanic peaks and metamorphic mountains give way to the karstic topography of the lower limestone hills and canyons that divide the northern highlands from the flat lowlands of northern Guatemala. Trending east to west, the Guatemalan Highlands abut Chiapas, Mexico, on the west, and Honduras and El Salvador on the east. Most of the important Pre-Hispanic trails and commercial routes in the highlands cut across this east-west mountain belt and connected the Pacific slope region to the Maya Lowlands. Most early sites known for the highlands were located on overland trails connecting these three regions (see Chapter 8; Sharer and Sedat 1987, 1999).

In many archaeological studies, the Guatemalan Highlands are treated as unwelcome middle ground—an inconvenient obstruction that hindered free communication between coastal peoples and the lowland Mayas. This bias may be a simple consequence of the number of studies published for each area. Other than the research and salvage projects undertaken at Kaminaljuyu in present-day Guatemala City (see Kaplan 2002; Kidder 1961; Kidder et al. 1946; Michels and Sanders 1973; Popenoe de Hatch 2002c), the northern, western, and eastern highlands have received minimum attention. Smith (1955) surveyed the highlands and reported seven possible Preclassic sites out of sixty-seven; most sites dated to the Postclassic period (Smith 1955:table 1). Extensive excavations were also carried out at Zacualpa (Wauchope 1975), Zaculeu (Woodbury and Trik 1953), and Nebaj (Becquelin 1969; Becquelin et al. 2001; Smith and Kidder 1951), but none of these sites has a significant Preclassic occupation. Zacualpa has a Protoclassic occupation. The monuments I analyze here were recovered in conjunction with two different projects along the Chixoy River and its tributaries: the University of Pennsylvania's Verapaz Archaeological Project in Alta and Baja

Verapaz (Sedat and Sharer 1972; Sharer and Sedat 1973, 1987) and various projects of the French Archaeological Mission in Quiché (Arnauld 1986; Arnauld et al. 1993; Bailey 1980; Ichon 1977, 1979, 1992; Ichon and Arnauld 1985; Ichon and Cheesman 1983; Ichon and Viel 1984). Even this modicum of research, however, demonstrates that the Preclassic history of the highlands was complex and developmentally important, as clearly implied by the current distribution of Mayan speakers, the descendants of these early villagers.

Of the twenty-eight Mayan languages still spoken today, speakers of seven languages live in Mexico and speakers of the other twenty-one live in Guatemala, with eighteen of these languages confined to the highlands and three to the lowlands (see Sharer and Traxler 2006:figs. 1.2 and 1.3). This linguistic diversity and uneven language distribution goes back before the Spanish conquest (see Kaufman 1974, 1976; Kaufman and Justeson 2008) and by all logic reflects a complex history and long residency for highland Maya peoples, one only now beginning to be appreciated. At the time of the conquest, most of Guatemala was occupied by many different Maya peoples, and it is likely that Mayas have tended most of this ground for more than 4,000 years. For the moment, however, any claim for their deep antiquity remains a supposition, because Maya residency in Guatemalan territory cannot be traced archaeologically beyond 1200 BC (Popenoe de Hatch 2002c:279; Robinson et al. 2005). The earliest sedentary villages in Guatemala, found in the Pacific coastal lowlands, date to ca 1850 BC (Arroyo 1995; Valdés and Rodríguez Girón 1999), but it is not certain that these coastal farmers were Maya (see Love 1999b). To the north, occupants of the territory now known as Belize were probably speaking a form of proto-Maya by 2400 BC, more than a millennium before they settled down there in permanent agricultural villages (Clark and Cheetham 2002). As they did in Belize, it is likely that early Mayas hunted and gathered in the Guatemalan Highlands during the Archaic period, perhaps as early as 2400 BC (Sharer and Sedat 1987:427, 1999:215). But for the moment, no artifact traces of late Preceramic peoples have

been found in the highlands—or anywhere else in Guatemala, for that matter (Neff et al. 2006).

The Preclassic period considered here covers 1,400 years, beginning with the earliest villages in the highlands and ending with the advent of the Classic period at AD 200. The best evidence for the early colonization of the Guatemalan Highlands comes from Sharer and Sedat's (1987) research in Baja Verapaz and Alta Verapaz of the northern highlands. Small villages began there by 1200 BC and were located in fertile valleys near reliable water sources. These villages were undifferentiated, an indication that early villagers probably followed a simple, egalitarian way of life (Sharer and Sedat 1987, 1999:215). In addition to farming, they participated in networks of long-distance exchange involving obsidian, jade, and other products. During the Early Preclassic period, seven small sites were established in the Salamá Valley (Sharer and Sedat 1999:215). To the south, the earliest known occupation of the Valley of Guatemala dates to ca 1100–1000 BC at Kaminaljuyu (Popenoe de Hatch 2002c:279; Valdés and Rodríguez Girón 1999). These early village experiments look like attempts by outlanders to colonize the highlands. It is not clear where these first villagers came from, but the oldest pottery in the Valley of Guatemala and the Salamá Valley shares many characteristics with pottery from the Pacific slope, so this region is a likely homeland of early highland immigrants (Barbara Arroyo, personal communication 2008; Love 2007; Sharer and Sedat 1987, 1999; Shook and Popenoe de Hatch 1999). Other peoples may have come from the north (Sharer and Sedat 1999:215). To keep these pioneering efforts of early Mayas in historical perspective, at the time the first villages were growing up in the Guatemalan Highlands and northern lowlands, coastal peoples were already supporting hereditary leaders, constructing ceremonial centers graced with monumental architecture and stone monuments, and pursuing trade in a variety of products, including obsidian and jade from the highlands (see Chapters 7–9). Perhaps the desire for highland resources stimulated the immigration of peoples to the highlands in the first place.

The comparative histories of the major regions of Guatemala indicate that sedentary agricultural communities began in the highlands later than they did on the coast. The same is true of the establishment of stratified society. By 900 BC, coastal La Blanca was probably a complex chiefdom (see Chapter 7); villages were barely getting started in the central and northern highlands at this time. Naranjo, located 5 km northeast of Kaminaljuyu, may have been the earliest ceremonial center in the central highlands, beginning ca 850 BC. But it did not last long and appears to have been eclipsed by the growth and development at Kaminaljuyu by 500–400 BC (see Chapter 1; Arroyo, ed. 2007).

In the northern highlands, population increased throughout the Middle and Late Preclassic periods, with the greatest concentration of people in the Salamá Valley (Sharer and Sedat 1999:213). El Portón became the largest ceremonial center of its region. Evidence found in the Salamá Valley shows that chiefdom societies were in place there by 600–500 BC, as most apparent from the burials of leaders. Sharer and Sedat (1987:136–138, 147, 1999:216) argue that an adult male buried at Los Mangales may have been a headman or chief. Among the special goods interred with this individual were three human skulls, probably trophies, and twelve bodies placed outside his stone-lined crypt, apparently sacrificed retainers. A slightly later burial in the San Andrés Sajcabajá Valley to the west, at the site of La Lagunita, is also thought to have been a village leader and shaman (Ichon 1984:19, fig. 15; Valdés and Rodríguez Girón 1999:146).

The first evidence of stone sculpture in the northern highlands postdates the development there of chiefdoms and hierarchical society, so sculpture was probably adopted as one means of reinforcing extant status distinctions. Of particular interest are two different sculptural traditions that were present in the Salamá Valley by the end of the Middle Preclassic period (Sharer and Sedat 1987, 1999:219). Population in the Salamá Valley continued to increase at this time and spill over into adjacent areas. Some of the earthen platforms constructed at El Portón hint at ceremonial functions combined with residential use. Stone

monuments with carved figures and early hieroglyphic inscriptions were associated with Structure J7-4B at El Portón (Sharer and Sedat 1987:74), and other stylistically distinct monuments have been found at Los Mangales and Laguneta (a site in the Salamá Valley that is distinct from the similarly named La Lagunita, located farther to the west in the Quiché region). Both the latter sites were positioned close to passes leading south to the Motagua Valley and also to the routes north to the lowlands of the Peten (Arnauld 1986; Sharer and Sedat 1987). People at these sites probably benefited from their involvement in interregional trade and may have served as intermediaries for other people in the valley.

In the Quiché region to the west, the dominant center—beginning in the Late Preclassic and lasting through the Early Classic—was La Lagunita. El Portón, La Lagunita, and other Late Preclassic centers in the highlands appear to have been the products of local sociopolitical evolution, with the centers of different valleys being independent of one another. In the Terminal Preclassic, El Portón appears to have fallen under the dominion of rulers at Kaminaljuyu (Sharer and Sedat 1999:222, 224). During this time the highlands also appear to have experienced an era of conflict. Population declined in the Salamá Valley, as evident from the diminishing number and size of sites (Sharer and Sedat 1999:214, 221). Stone sculptures at Kaminaljuyu dating to this era depict bound prisoners, probably K'ichean Maya speakers from the western highlands, a region that included the area around La Lagunita (Fahsen 2002). The people living at Kaminaljuyu and in the Salamá Valley were probably speakers of Cholan Maya.

Rivalries among highland Maya groups probably explain the complex history of this region as well as the eventual destruction of most Preclassic stone monuments in the highlands. Other interactions among peoples included active trade. Clear evidence of past interactions and connections among peoples is found in the similarities seen in stone monuments, pots, and potsherds. Based on such observations for the Terminal Preclassic and Early Classic periods, Popenoe de Hatch (1997,

1999, 2002b, 2002c) argues for massive movements and replacements of populations ca AD 200, as indicated by demographic declines and abrupt changes in utilitarian ceramic vessel inventories at various sites. Her hypothesis implicates a linguistic and ethnic division in the highlands during the Late Preclassic that divided the northern highlands between the Salamá and San Andrés Sajcabajá valleys. The Salamá Valley was part of what Demarest and Sharer (1986) call the "Miraflores ceramic sphere"; the San Andrés Sajcabajá Valley was just outside of this interaction sphere. Popenoe de Hatch (1999, 2002c) postulates the replacement of Cholan speakers at Kaminaljuyu (the inferred people of the Miraflores ceramic sphere) by K'ichean peoples who came into the Valley of Guatemala from the northwest, perhaps ultimately from Chiapas. This replacement of the population at Kaminaljuyu, and in the central highlands more generally, was part of the same string of historical events that witnessed the wreckage of most stone monuments at Kaminaljuyu and the subsequent absence there of stone texts. To understand this story, we must start at the beginning, and that takes us to El Portón and the earliest known Maya hieroglyphic text carved on a stone monument.

Preclassic Sculpture in the Salamá Valley

The explorations by the University of Pennsylvania in the Salamá Valley recovered twenty-nine Preclassic stone monuments or monument fragments, fourteen of which were from primary contexts. Most of the monuments come from three sites, and most are plain stelae or altars. There are also carved pedestal sculptures and several stelae carved in low relief (Sharer and Sedat 1987:359–377). Carved monuments from primary contexts were found at El Portón and Los Mangales, and four carved stelae were recovered from the site of Laguneta (see Figure 10.2 for site locations). These last monuments are from a secondary context and are thought to once have been at El Portón (Sharer and Sedat 1987:368). In the following discussion I

consider first the sculptures from El Portón and Laguneta, and then two monuments recovered from Los Mangales in a burial context.

The site of El Portón is located in the center of the upper Salamá Valley near the La Estancia River (Fig. 10.2). Its fifteen mounds are distributed over four broad, artificially constructed terraces (Figure 10.3). The tallest mound (J7-10; Structure 10 on the map) is 12 m high and located on the northernmost terrace. The earliest occupation at the site goes back to 1200 BC, and it was occupied continuously until AD 200. Circa 500 BC El Portón became the dominant center in the Salamá Valley (Sharer and Sedat 1987:431; Sharer and Traxler 2006:197). Two other sites in the valley, Las Tunas and Los Mangales, are known to have had earlier public platforms. Both these sites continued on into the Late Preclassic as secondary places to El Portón. Las Tunas appears to have been a special elite residential site, and Los Mangales appears to have been a special burial site (Sharer and Sedat 1987:428). The first major construction at El Portón dates to the Middle to Late Preclassic transition, or 500–200 BC (Sharer and Sedat 1987:431). The four terraces constructed at the site appear to have had different functions. Terraces 1, 3, and 4 served residential and ritual functions, and Terrace 2 had a more ritual function (Sharer and Sedat 1987:431). Structure J7-4B (Structure 4 in Figure 10.3) on Terrace 2, a 3 m high mound, is of special interest because most of the stone monuments and caches recovered from El Portón were found along the central axis of this building (see Figure 10.4). The earliest phase of the 1 m high Terrace 2 was constructed at the same time as the first phase of Structure J7-4B (Sharer and Sedat 1987:48).[1]

Monuments 1 and 2 were associated with one of the earliest building phases of Structure J7-4B. They are said to constitute one of the oldest stela-altar pairs (Sharer and Sedat 1999:219; Sharer and Traxler 2006:197), but there is a significant spatial gap between them (Figure 10.4); the juxtaposition is not as close as for the stela-altar pairs known for Naranjo in the central highlands or for the later Classic lowland Mayas. Monuments 1 and 2 have been dated to ca 400 BC (Sharer and Sedat 1987:59;

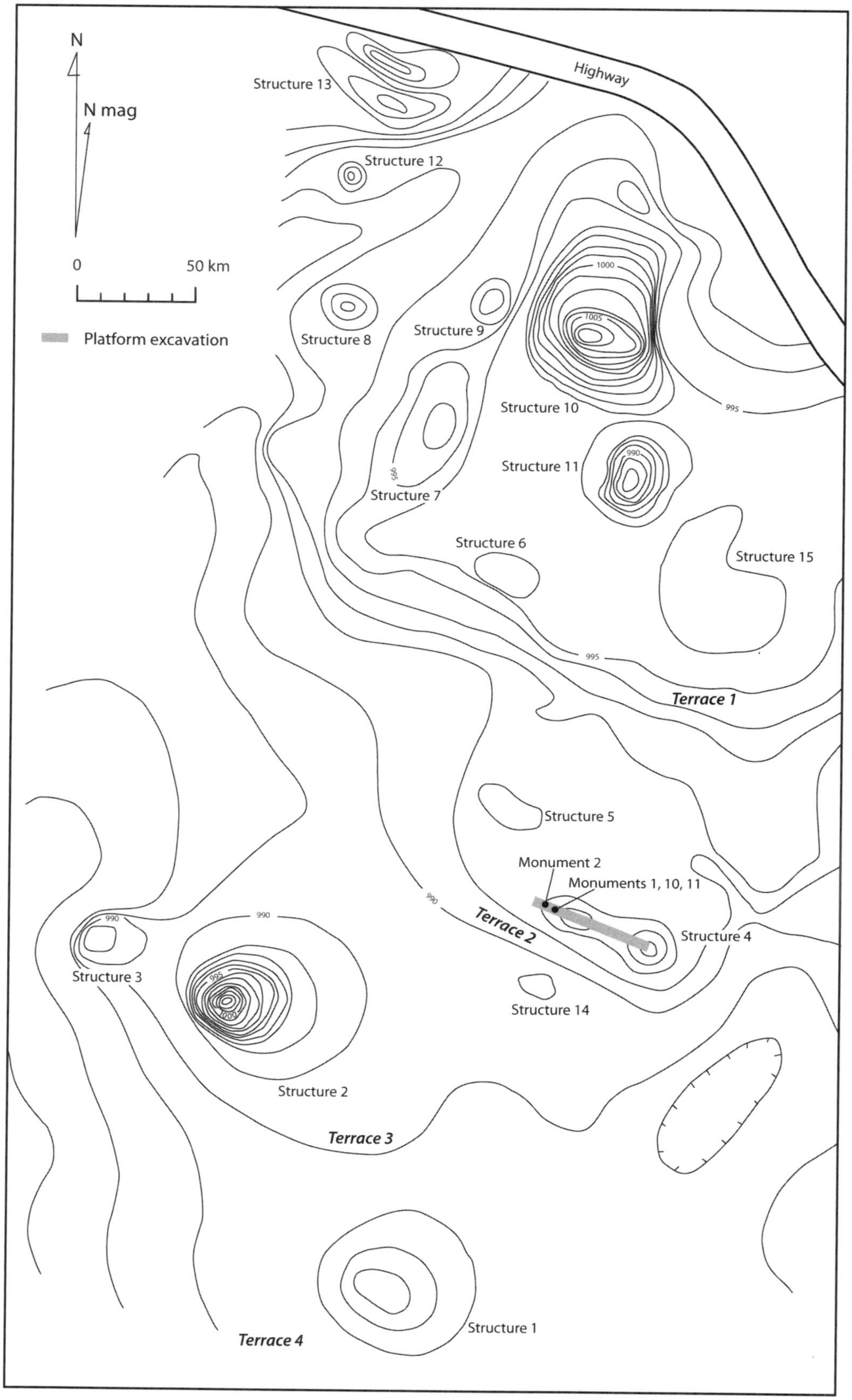
N
N mag
0
50 km
Platform excavation
Highway
Structure 13
Structure 12
Structure 8
Structure 9
1000
1005
Structure 10
995
Structure 11
990
995
Structure 7
Structure 6
Structure 15
995
Terrace 1
Structure 5
Monument 2
Monuments 1, 10, 11
990
Terrace 2
Structure 4
Structure 14
990
990
Structure 3
995
1000
Structure 2
Terrace 3
Terrace 4
Structure 1

figure 10.3
Map of El Portón, Baja Verapaz, Guatemala, showing the archaeological context of Monument 1. (Drawing from the New World Archaeological Foundation adapted from Sharer and Sedat 1987:35, fig. 3.1.)

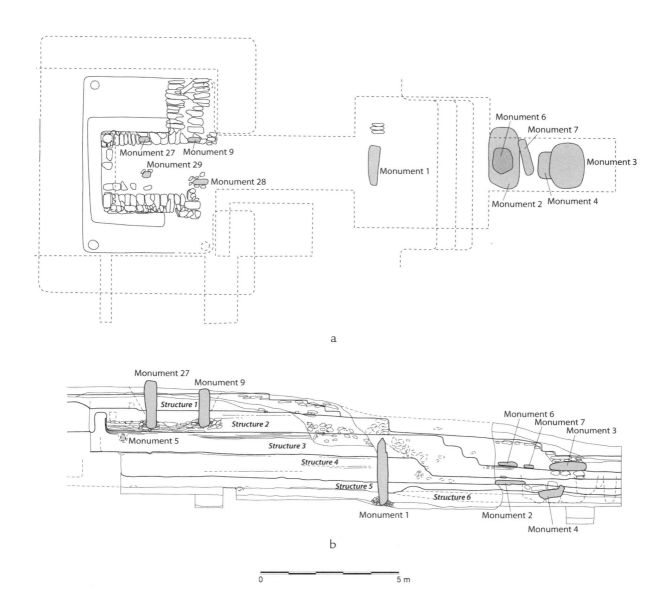

figure 10.4
Schematic plan and profile drawings of excavations in Structure J7-4. (a) Plan view of excavations showing the locations of Monuments 1–4, 6, and 7 in Structures J7-4B-5 and J7-4B-3 (adapted from Sharer and Sedat 1987:fig. 3.10); (b) profile of the excavations at Structure J7-4B, showing the building and monument sequence (adapted from Sharer and Sedat 1987:fig. 3.8). (Drawings from the New World Archaeological Foundation.)

Sharer and Traxler 2006:fig. 5.9) but are probably much younger. Monument 1 is a large stela carved on one face (Figure 10.5a), and Monument 2 is a horizontal, flat rectangular slab with slightly rounded corners, thought to have been an altar; it was placed 4 m to the west of the west-facing Monument 1. Both monuments were placed to the west of Structure 5, a small westward-facing clay-walled building (Figure 10.4). These stone monuments were meant to be seen by the people participating in the rituals carried out on Terrace 2. Both monuments were on the projected central east-west axis of Structure 5, as marked by other caches. Caches were associated with most stone monuments of this building, and some fragments of broken monuments were clearly placed in caches along the same line (Sharer and Sedat 1987:63).

Two pedestal monuments (Monuments 10 and 11) are reported to have been found in association with Monument 1 (Sharer and Sedat 1987:49, 364). These smaller monuments carved in the round were removed before archaeologists could see them in context, but they must have been located west of Monument 1 and east of Monument 2. (Monument 1 abuts undisturbed strata on its eastern face or back side, so Monuments 10 and 11 could not have come from this side; see Figure 10.4b.) A black pot and various jade artifacts were found with these monuments (Sharer and Sedat 1987:49). The presence of these pedestal monuments complicates the postulated coupling of Monuments 1 and 2 as a stela-altar pair. Monument 1 would have been closer to Monuments 10 and 11, the two pedestal sculptures, with the three of them constituting a triad facing Monument 2.

figure 10.5
Monuments from El Portón, Structure J7-4B-5. (a) Monument 1 (adapted from Sharer and Sedat 1973:figs. 2 and 3, 1987:plates 18.1 and 18.2; some added details taken from photographs by Luis Luin); (b) front and side views of Monument 10 (adapted from Sharer and Sedat 1973:194, fig. 6, 1987:plate 18.8). (Drawings from the New World Archaeological Foundation.)

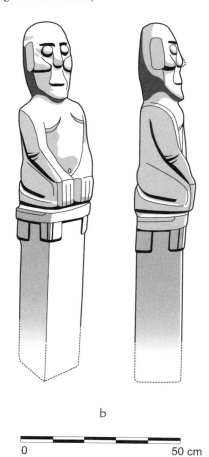

a

0   100 cm

b

0   50 cm

Monument 10 was the better preserved of the pedestal sculptures (Figure 10.5b). Monument 11 was apparently broken; Sharer and Sedat (1987:364) were not able to recover an image of this monument.

Monument 10 (Figure 10.5b), like other known pedestal monuments from El Portón, shows a male on a four-legged stool or throne (see Sharer and Sedat 1987:plates 18.9 and 18.30). Six semicomplete pedestal monuments and another possible destroyed monument have been found at El Portón. The discovery of the Monument 10 pedestal sculpture and its counterpart, Monument 11, in association with the last building phase of Structure J7-4B, which corresponds to the end of the Terminal Preclassic, warrants retelling. As Sharer and Sedat (1987:66) described, a farmer found the pedestal sculptures and associated large stone slab while plowing. Reports from the subsequent amateur excavation describe the removal of the large stone slab, reportedly some 2.5 m long and 1.5 m wide (without any carving); beneath this they found Monument 1 as well as two additional (later located) pedestal sculptures (one intact, one fragmentary). The location of this large slab directly above Monument 1 demonstrates a memory of place and a consistent placement of these monuments through time (Sharer and Sedat 1987:66). Another fragment of a pedestal sculpture (Monument 5) was found in the same general location for the middle building phase (Structure 3), but as an offering rather than as a standing monument (Sharer and Sedat 1987:63). In sum, the association of pedestal sculptures with stelae in Structure J7-4B appears to have been a long-lived pattern that began with the association of Monuments 1, 10, and 11. Pedestal sculptures are characteristic of the Preclassic period and have been found at Kaminaljuyu, on the Pacific Coast, and in Honduras, El Salvador, and coastal Chiapas (see Chapter 7; Miles 1965; Parsons 1986).

The primary locations of Monuments 1 and 2 were verified by excavation. Monument 1 was broken in antiquity, and most of its carved surface was abraded away. Sharer and Sedat (1987:60) speculate that this stela may have been broken with the construction of Structure 4 ca 30 BC. There are insufficient clues as to its original height, but it is still 2.3 m tall. The extrapolated total length of this monument shown in Figure 10.5a is based on the supposition that the uncarved lower portion of the monument (which would have been buried in the ground) would have been about one-third of the monument's length. The lower 50 cm portion of this broken stela was actually found in its original emplacement. "Numerous angular white quartzite stones and round cobbles were found around the base of the monument . . . apparently to provide a stable footing" (Sharer and Sedat 1987:51). These white stones were probably also an offering (their total number was not recorded). Twenty-two white pebbles were found with three offering pots in a cache just 4 m east of Monument 1 (Sharer and Sedat 1987:59). For its part, Monument 2 was placed over a small offering of two obsidian blades (Sharer and Sedat 1987:59), so these complementary monuments in perpendicular positions were planted in contrasting matrices of round white and sharp black stones—with the sculptures in between (Monuments 10 and 11) associated with jade artifacts and pebbles. The relative positions of monuments and associated caches of pots and rocks along the east-west center line of Structure J7-4B indicates that their placements were meaningful and that part of the meaning of vertically or horizontally oriented stones derived from their associations with caches placed beneath them or on each side of them.

As evident in Figure 10.4b, the broken base of Monument 1 was eventually covered over during the end of the Late Preclassic phase (Structure 3). The profile drawing of the building phases of Structure J7-4B is particularly informative, because it shows a consistent history of stone monument use at this building. Portions of Monument 1 were visible for about two or three centuries, and although completely stationary, it was associated with different monuments and buildings through time. The complete monument in its pristine condition was associated with Monument 2 and Structure 5. Perhaps only the upper meter or so of Monument 1 was visible (depending on its breakage history) with the completion of Structure 4 (Sharer and Sedat 1987:60), at which time it may have been associated with a new altar (Monument 4). This altar was later broken into pieces and interred as an offering alongside a new basin altar, Monument 3, which was put in place with the construction of Structure 3 (Sharer and Sedat 1987:64). Monument 1 was probably associated with the pedestal sculptures (Monuments 10 and 11) by this time if not earlier. The important point is that associations of monuments and buildings changed with each new construction episode or movement of some of the monuments, so their contexts were not constant through time; thus their uses, functions, and meanings would also have evolved (see Sharer and Sedat 1987:64).

Monument 2 was buried under Structure 4 (Sharer and Sedat 1987:60), and Monument 3 was placed above it with the construction of Structure 3. Both Monuments 1 and 2 (and presumably Monuments 10 and 11) were eventually completely buried in place. Subsequent stelae and altars were positioned above them on the same center line and in the same relative locations with three other structural elements: the one-room building to the east, the vertical stones in the medial position in front of the entrance to this structure, and altars to the west of the building and the stelae. A minor exception is the last plain stelae associated with Structure 2, which were placed inside the one-room building instead of in front of its entrance (Sharer and Sedat 1987:66), so these last stelae were not immediately visible to people who may have congregated on Terrace 2 (Figures 10.3 and 10.4a). These later monuments were all uncarved, and several of the plain stelae (Monuments 9, 27, 28, and 29) may, in fact, have been the reworked butts of pedestal sculptures (Sharer and Sedat 1987:374). These observations suggest some continuity in the general function and meaning of this architectural-sculptural complex from the beginning of the Late Preclassic to the end of the Terminal Preclassic. Just what that function and meaning were remain to be determined, but in the case of Monument 1, some of the original meaning can still be read from the stone itself.

El Portón Monument 1 (Figure 10.5a) bears one of the oldest known Mayan texts that can be analyzed (Sharer and Traxler 2006:197). An associated radiocarbon date places the monument at ca 400 BC, but analysis of the writing would date it to ca 200 BC.[2] Even though the hieroglyphs carved down the right edge of this monument are not completely decipherable, the glyph in the lowest and last position relates to a title (Figure 10.6a,d). It consists of the head of a bird, similar to those depicted on Nakbe Stela 1 (see Figure 1.6c; Hansen and Guenter 2005:fig. 2), Kaminaljuyu Stela 11 (Fahsen n.d.), Takalik Abaj Stela 3 (Figure 10.7a), and the Shook Altar from San Antonio Suchitepéquez (Figure 10.7b; Shook and Heizer 1976). All these examples except for the earlier San Antonio Suchitepéquez Monument 1 date to the Late Preclassic period. The bird head also occurs on a text found on a block of stone from San Bartolo in the Peten region of Guatemala (Figure 10.6c). This sign has been interpreted as an earlier form of the AJAW title, which was later used during the Classic period in reference to rulers or "lords." The superfix is an early form of the title also. The other four glyphs on El Portón Monument 1 are difficult to interpret. A mistake made by Sharer and Sedat (1973, 1987) in reporting this monument was to assign a glyphic value in the text and drawing to separations "b," "e," and "j" (see Figure 10.5a), which are simply horizontal divisions between the vertical glyphs of the column rather than glyphs or numbers. Glyph "c" may be the expression CHUM, which is later understood as the verb "to sit," with a phonetic complement in the "d" position. In other words, the text could refer to "seating," the action of assuming the throne as AJAW or "Lord." Presumably, the other glyphs and images on this stone as originally carved referred to a specific lord.

The text merits more extensive epigraphic study than I can provide here. Since the publication of El Portón Monument 1 (Sharer and Sedat 1973), other Preclassic texts have appeared elsewhere, which can be used for comparison. A published photograph of Monument 1 at the time of its accidental discovery (Sharer and Sedat 1987:plate 18.2, b) shows an extended hand in vertical position (probably the back of the right hand) for the first glyph in the column. The hand does not appear in later photographs; it was apparently broken off after the monument was discovered. This

a

b

c

d

figure 10.6
Panel of hieroglyphs from
El Portón Monument 1 and
related hieroglyphs from other
monuments. (a) Panel from El
Portón Monument 1 (adapted
from Sharer and Sedat 1973:figs.
2 and 3, 1987:plates 18.2 and 18.3
and photographs by Luis Luin);
(b) head from Kaminaljuyu
Stela 11 (see Figure 10.14b);
(c) head from mural at San
Bartolo, Guatemala (adapted
from Saturno, Taube, Stuart,
Beltrán, and Román 2006:574,
fig. 4); (d) final glyph of the
El Portón text. (Drawings from
the New World Archaeological
Foundation.)

hand glyph has been restored in Figures 10.5a and 10.6a. In Mayan texts, an open hand often supports another glyph above it. In the famous early script on Kaminaljuyu Stela 10, for example, there are two hand glyphs (Houston 2004:281, fig. 10.3), and in the Mayan syllabary used by epigraphers, another eight hands in different positions are listed (Montgomery 2002; Stuart et al. 2005). If the hand on El Portón Monument 1 was part of a compound verbal expression, it would have been read along with the next-lower glyph to strengthen the verb CHUM, with an expression such as "K'AL JUN," also an ascension-to-the-throne verb. In Mayan syntax, a verb followed by its subject is used for intransitive expressions, as in this case (Lacadena 2008).

The meaning and function of Monument 1 may not have been in the details of its carved image and text of an ascending lord, but in the meta-message of its essence and placement as perceived by the public (see Chapter 12):

Monument 1 and the altar that accompanied it [Monument 2] required considerable collective effort to transport. They also represent great skill in carving and writing. These sculptures were placed in a sacred place in a large, elevated area, thereby becoming the focal point of public ceremonial activity in the principal ceremonial center in the valley. This context indicates that this carved monument and its hieroglyphic text were artistically sculpted to record an event.

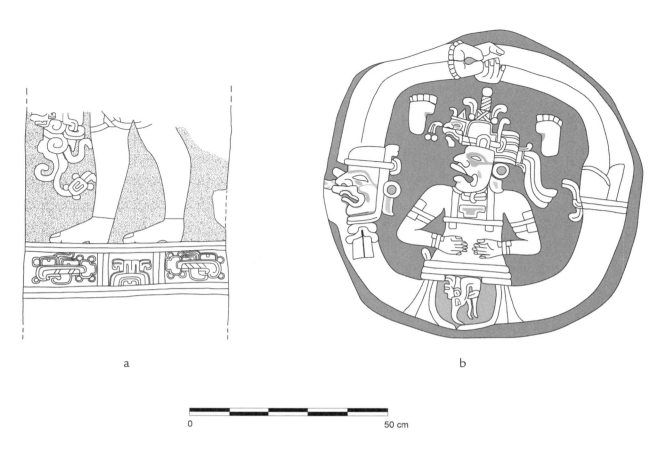

a   b

0   50 cm

figure 10.7
Stone sculptures with bird representations from the Pacific slope of Guatemala. (a) Takalik Abaj Stela 3 (adapted from field illustration by John Graham); (b) the Shook Altar from San Antonio Suchitepéquez (adapted from photograph taken by Edwin Shook). (Drawings from the New World Archaeological Foundation.)

It was part of the privileges enjoyed by governing authorities, and one evidently evoked, to have their images carved to commemorate their accomplishments, to justify their membership in certain lineages, and by so doing affirm their right to rule. One may well suppose, in the social context of the Preclassic, that carved hieroglyphs on public monuments would have been interpreted by the general public as ideological signs whose purpose was to reinforce effectively the extant social and political structure. [Sharer and Sedat 1999:219; translation by John Clark]

The sculptural history evident at Structure J7-4B indicates that, with the exception of pedestal monuments, carved monuments were the earliest form of monument and were replaced in time by plain monuments. Such an interpretation, however, represents a biased picture of the monument history of this region, as indicated by monuments found at the site of Laguneta, also in the Salamá Valley (Figure 10.2). Several Preclassic stelae were recovered in a Late Classic or Postclassic context at this site and were obviously reused. Sharer and Sedat (1987:368) speculate that the Laguneta stelae (Figure 10.8) were originally from El Portón, located 4 km to the northeast. If so, these unbroken monuments must have been left at El Portón when it was abandoned ca AD 200 in places where later peoples could access and appropriate them for new purposes. These virtually whole stelae further indicate that not all Preclassic monuments in the Salamá Valley were broken up or mutilated at some point in their histories—in contrast to the monuments from La Lagunita, in the San Andrés Sajcabajá Valley in Quiché, described in the next section.

The Laguneta monuments clearly belong to the later part of the Late Preclassic period (Figure 10.8). Their fine carved scenes and motifs show a close relationship to Kaminaljuyu Terminal Preclassic monuments, such as Stelae 21 and 15. According to Shook and Hatch (1999:291), this similarity would mean that they were carved in the Arenal phase (300 BC–AD 100). They are more similar to monuments from Kaminaljuyu than to El Portón Monument 1, and they have their own style, which Sharer and Sedat (1987:384) christened the "Verapaz Sculptural Style." The monuments are carved in hard, local gray-to-brown schist. They display a dynamic style similar to that of contemporaneous stelae from La Lagunita in the San Andrés Sajcabajá Valley (see below). Monuments 16 and 17 (and Monument 19) incorporated geometrical designs, and they also depict individuals in active postures. According to Sharer and Sedat (1987:367), the spirals in front of the face of the individual on Monument 16 may represent his name or his voice.

The other sculptural tradition in the Salamá Valley is the "Pecked and Grooved Sculptural Tradition" (Sharer and Sedat 1987:376), best represented at the small site of Los Mangales, located about 2 km east-northeast of El Portón. This tradition is represented by stone shafts, columns, and boulders on which are pecked grooves and small circular depressions or "cupules," thought by some to represent dots in a numeric or calendrical notation system. The cupules or dots might represent an alternate form of message transmission to that of hieroglyphic texts:

> The cupulate tradition, as expressed on the stone monuments of the Salama Valley, was an early notational system. Its function, at least in part, seems to have been to record and preserve cyclical events such as the passage of days or seasons. As such, it would have conveniently served to preserve calendrical computations and to stimulate the development of more functional writing systems. [Sharer and Sedat 1987:381]

a　　　　　　　　b

0　　　　　　　50 cm

figure 10.8
Low-relief stelae from Laguneta from the Salamá Valley of Baja Verapaz. (a) Monument 16 (adapted from Sharer and Sedat 1987:plates 18.16–18.18); (b) Monument 17 (adapted from Sharer and Sedat 1987:plates 18.19 and 18.20). (Drawings from the New World Archaeological Foundation.)

Four cupulate monuments have been found at Los Mangales; other monuments with pecked circles have been found at Piedra de Sacrificios, Salto West (located about 6 km northeast of Los Mangales [Sharer and Sedat 1987:378]), and El Portón (Figure 10.2). Two monuments with cupules come from the tomb of Burial 5 at Los Mangales. Monuments 13 and

14 (Figure 10.9a,b) were reused as covering stones in this Preclassic stone crypt of a village leader (see Sharer and Sedat 1987:plate 4.3; Sharer and Traxler 2006:fig. 5.10). The monuments show evidence of significant use before having served their final function as stone lintels in a grave. Figure 10.9 illustrates Los Mangales Monuments 13, 14, and 15 as well as La Lagunita Sculpture 16. All these monuments were found with burials. Given their final context of secondary use, some cupule monuments must date at least to the last part of the Middle Preclassic and be older than El Portón Monument 1. If so, it would follow that the cupulate system of notation is older and possibly ancestral to the glyphic system. "The occurrence of the cupulate tradition in an elaborate transitional Middle-Late Preclassic burial also indicates that this system was probably the prerogative of, and developed by, elite specialists versed in its concepts and usage" (Sharer and Sedat 1987:381).

Cupule marks or notations have been discovered on monuments at Naranjo (Barbara Arroyo, personal communication 2007) as well as on monuments in other regions of Mesoamerica (Piedra Santa and Morales 2007). According to Sharer and Sedat (1987:378), these inscriptions are not pictograms and are not solely decorative; rather, they are symbolic motifs or signs for communicating information. These scholars suggest that the three-dot cluster or triad form of cupules appearing on Monuments 13, 14, 15, and 21 could be forms that precede the Mayan day signs for Ix (T524) and Ajaw (T533) (Sharer and Sedat 1987:379). I believe it more plausible that these circular marks relate to calendrical notation rather than to early day signs. The

figure 10.9
Preclassic cupule monuments. (a) Los Mangales Monument 13 (adapted from Sharer and Sedat 1987:plates 18.10 and 18.11); (b) Los Mangales Monument 14 (adapted from Sharer and Sedat 1987:plates 18.12 and 18.13); (c) Los Mangales Monument 15 (adapted from Sharer and Sedat 1987:plates 18.14 and 18.15); (d) La Lagunita Sculpture 16 (adapted from Ichon 1977:39, fig. 29). (Drawings from the New World Archaeological Foundation.)

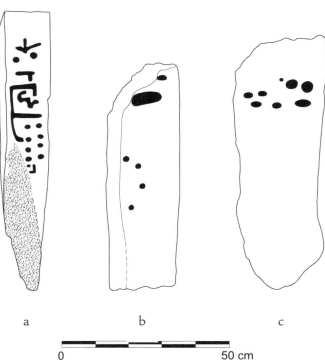
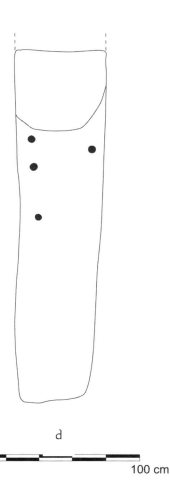

a   b   c   d

0   50 cm   0   100 cm

way the signs are ordered does not hint at syntax, so the signs probably are not true writing. As mentioned, one cupulate monument, Sculpture 16, has been found at La Lagunita, Quiché (Figure 10.9d). It also came from a tomb and is much older than its final context suggests (Ichon 1977:38–39, fig. 29).

Preclassic Sculpture in the San Andrés Sajcabajá Valley

La Lagunita is located at an altitude of 1,200 m in the San Andrés Sajcabajá Valley in Quiché (Figures 10.1 and 10.2). It was the principal Preclassic center

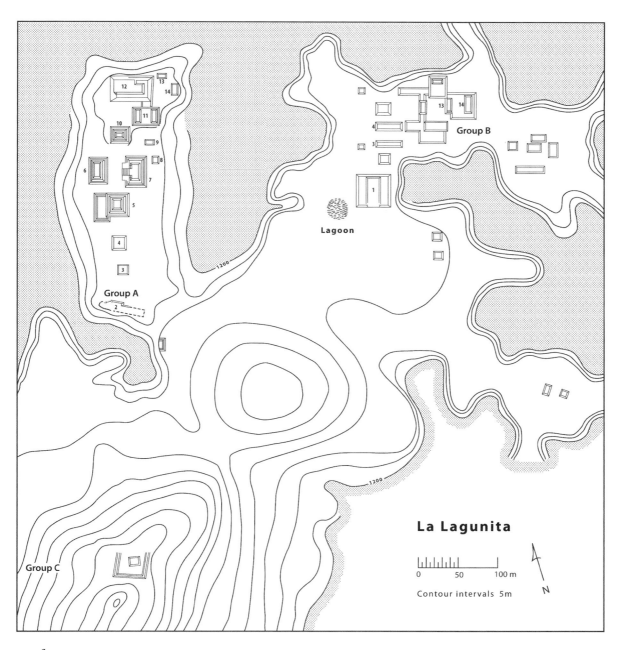

figure 10.10
Map of La Lagunita, El Quiché, Guatemala, showing the different architectural groups. (Drawing from the New World Archaeological Foundation adapted from Ichon 1977:fig. 57.)

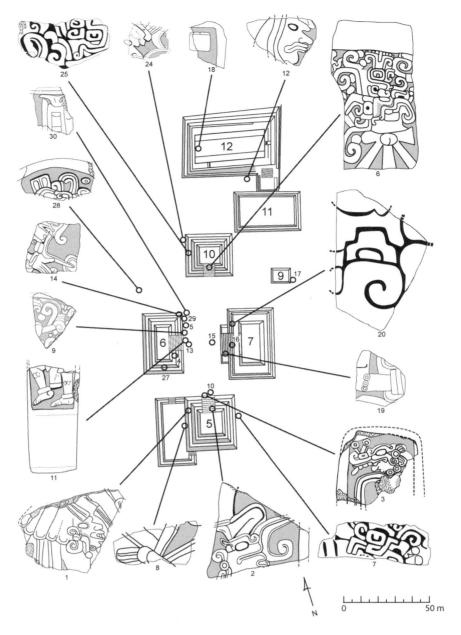

figure 10.11
Map of Group A from La Lagunita showing the locations of low-relief sculpture fragments. (Drawing from the New World Archaeological Foundation; most monument locations from Ichon 1977:fig. 3.)

in a cluster of sites (Ichon and Viel 1984). As illustrated in Figure 10.10, the site is comprised of three groups of structures, and remains of houses have been found in the neighboring peripheral zones. La Lagunita was occupied from the beginning of the Middle Preclassic through the Late Classic period. Thirty stone sculpture fragments and four

sarcophagi have been reported from Group A at the site (Ichon 1977; Ichon and Viel 1984); most date to the Late Preclassic and Protoclassic periods (also known as the Terminal Preclassic) and show affinities to sculptures from Kaminaljuyu.

Group A has four large mounds arranged in a cruciform pattern around a plaza. An artificial cave was found in the middle of this plaza underneath Structure 7 in Group A (henceforth referred to as "Structure 7A"), thus completing the quincunx pattern (Ichon 1977). Four stone sarcophagi with Early Classic burials were found in two of the mounds. The rest of the sculpture fragments come from secondary contexts on the mounds. Thus the contextual information for the Preclassic sculptures from La Lagunita is less specific than that just presented for the Salamá Valley. We can be reasonably sure that the sculpture fragments recovered from La Lagunita come from sculptures once displayed there. It is also clear that these were all broken after their first use and prior to their incorporation into Early Classic mounds. Thus the Protoclassic period (AD 0–200) appears to be the likely period of monument destruction at this site. Fragments of these sculptures appear to have been displayed in the plaza in Early Classic times or may have been intruded into the base of the principal mounds as offerings, as described for El Portón. In any event, the distribution of pieces in Group A does not appear to have been random. Sculpture fragments with the most complete images appear to have been set up in prominent positions on these mounds (Figure 10.11). This nonrandom ordering suggests that remnants of broken sculptures were sought out and placed in Group A in places of reverence. These carved stones appear to have had some sacred associations, power, or historical memory left in them that was tapped by later peoples.

The La Lagunita sculptures have at least two stories to tell: that of their final placement in the Early Classic plaza of Group A, and the more fragmentary story that must be pieced together based on reconstructing their original forms, themes, chronology, and local and regional associations. Most of the fragments come from low-relief stelae that stylistically date to the Terminal Preclassic period. Some of the thicker pieces may be fragments of altars. Most monuments are carved from a rather soft volcanic tuff, available locally. Fragments of low-relief sculpture with recognizable motifs are illustrated in Figures 10.12 and 10.13. A few sculptures in the round are also known from La Lagunita. Monument numbers do not

correspond to their co-associations. In the following discussion, I consider monuments by type and theme and then turn to the question of their final distribution in Group A.

The low-relief carvings depict animals, humans, articles of dress, and unidentified designs. Monuments 2, 3, and 6 represent zoomorphs carved in low relief (Figure 10.12b–d), and Monuments 4 and 13 are animals carved in the round. Human individuals are shown on Monuments 1, 11, 12, 14, 23, and 24 (Figures 10.12a,e,i and 10.13a,f,g). Fragments 14 and 24 are of the same thickness and look like they could be conjoining fragments from the same broken monument. Some sculpture fragments depict scrolls or other decorative elements and cannot be specified as to whether they are human or beast. Monument 11 is a four-sided column with images carved on each face (Figure 10.12e). Ichon (1977) states that it could have been as tall as 1.5 m, with about two-thirds of it carved on all four sides. The monument shows traces of red paint and portrays an individual on the front side who appears to be dancing, whereas on the back side this person is shown in a pose. The other two sides have a reclining "S" design that could be a symbol for clouds, as known for Preclassic and Classic sculptures (see Chapter 2). Two zoomorphic monuments are similar to several sculptures from Kaminaljuyu. Sculpture fragments 27, 28 (Figure 10.13i), 29, and 30 (Figure 10.13j) show several forms in outline. Another five sculpture fragments in a Kaminaljuyu style were found at the sides of Pyramid 5. Sculpture fragments 1, 2, 3, and 6 depict heads of persons or animals (Figure 10.12a–d). The other two sculpture fragments, which are mostly destroyed, show parts of decorations or headdresses. The bottom portion of Sculpture 6 compares very closely with the tripod incense burners depicted in the San Bartolo murals (Karl Taube, personal communication 2008), indicating that they belong to the same time frame and perhaps the same cultural tradition. The tripod base with the central knot on top supports the same kind of creature as seen in the San Bartolo murals (see López Bruni 2006:54).

Structure A7 had three sarcophagi and four sculpture fragments. The monument catalogued as

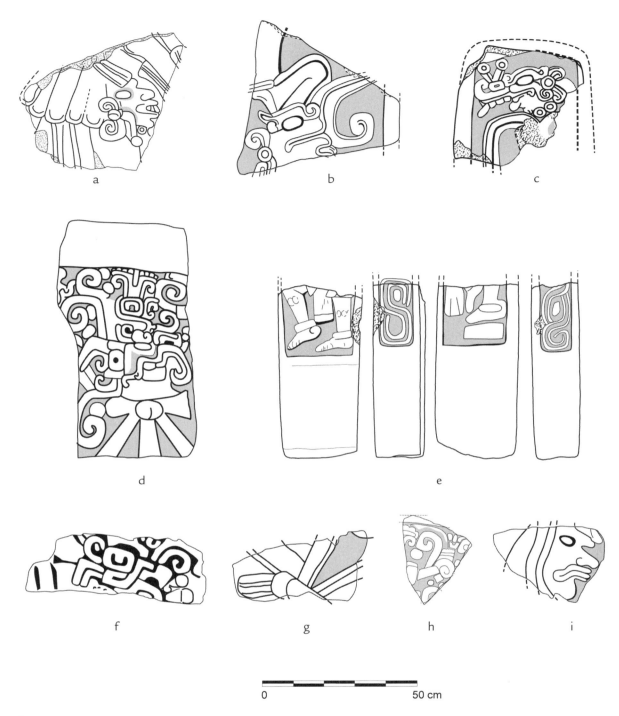

figure 10.12

Fragments of low-relief sculptures from La Lagunita. (a) Sculpture 1; (b) Sculpture 2; (c) Sculpture 3; (d) Sculpture 6; (e) four faces of Sculpture 11; (f) Sculpture 7; (g) Sculpture 8; (h) Sculpture 9; (i) Sculpture 12. (Drawings from the New World Archaeological Foundation based on photographs from Ichon 1977 and on photographs and drawings made by Luis Luin.)

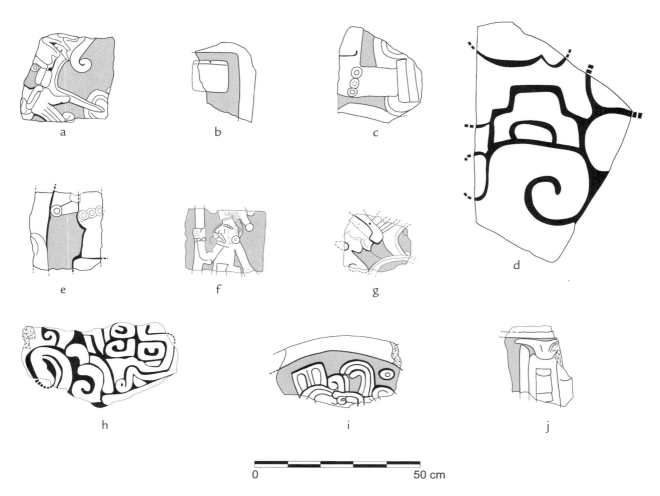

figure 10.13

Fragments of low-relief sculptures from La Lagunita. (a) Sculpture 14; (b) Sculpture 18; (c) Sculpture 19;
(d) Sculpture 20; (e) Sculpture 22; (f) Sculpture 23; (g) Sculpture 24; (h) Stela 25; (i) Sculpture 28; (j) Sculpture 30.
(Drawings from the New World Archaeological Foundation based on photographs from Ichon 1977 and
on photographs and drawings made by Luis Luin.)

Sculpture 15 is a round sculpture from a column, described by Ichon (1977) as a section of a column, but it may have been an altar. Sculpture 16, made of schist and in the form of a stela, is the only one at the site with cupule marks (Figure 10.9d). The stone material and its style would fit better in the Salamá Valley, and it is possible that this monument is from there. It was found closing the entrance to Tomb C-44. Sculpture 20 (Figure 10.13d) has details similar to those of Sculpture 9 of Structure 6 (Figure 10.12h), but it was found buried in Structure 7.

Sculpture 22 (Figure 10.13e), similar to Sculpture 19 of Structure 7 (Figure 10.13c), shows

a person's leg and was part of a stela. There are three sculptures with profiles of human heads (Sculptures 11, 19, and 22). The heads and other decorations depicted on Sculpture fragments 1, 6, 12, 14, and 22 (Figures 10.12 and 10.13), show an emphasis on commemorating real persons and so of establishing lineages and royal dynasties (Valdés and Fahsen 2007). The sarcophagi described below were found buried inside Mound A7. Fragments 22, 24, 25, and Sarcophagus 3 were also found in a group. The individual shown on Sculpture 12 displays Olmec traits (Figure 10.12i). Sculpture fragments 17 and 18 could be from a slightly later period but are still Preclassic. Sculpture 18 (Figure 10.13b), found in the patio of the ballcourt, has a glyph that also appears on Sarcophagus 3, being one of the few signs that could represent a name (Ichon 1977).

The sculptures of La Lagunita display a dynamism and iconography very similar to sculptures found at Kaminaljuyu (see Figure 10.14). Although close-knit relationships could have existed, these centers were probably politically independent from each other, especially during the Middle Preclassic period. La Lagunita remained the most significant ceremonial center of the fifteen Preclassic sites located in its region. During the Protoclassic or Terminal Preclassic period, construction of public buildings was suspended at El Portón, and new ceramic wares showed up in La Lagunita. The Protoclassic was key for K'iche control, as can be seen in the buildings at La Lagunita and in affinities with the Mexican Highlands.

La Lagunita Sculpture fragments 2 and 14 are stylized versions of Kaminaljuyu monuments (Figure 10.14). Such examples have fine incised work and show human faces, and so they could have been derived from monuments like Stelae 21 and 15 at Kaminaljuyu. Others (Sculptures 2, 3, 7, and 9) are also done with great care, thus producing excellent quality work that is similar to Kaminaljuyu Stelae 10, 12, 28, and some silhouetted reliefs (see Parsons 1986).

Almost no sculptures were found in the other architectural groups at the site. In Group B there was a ballcourt marker carved in schist (Sculpture 21) or a portable sculpture in the form of a jaguar, with the body of a serpent and the head portrayed

figure 10.14
Kaminaljuyu Monuments.
(a) Stela 6 (adapted from
Parsons 1986:fig. 159 and
line drawing in Fahsen n.d.);
(b) Stela 11. (Drawings from
the New World Archaeological
Foundation.)

0   25 cm

a

0   50 cm

b

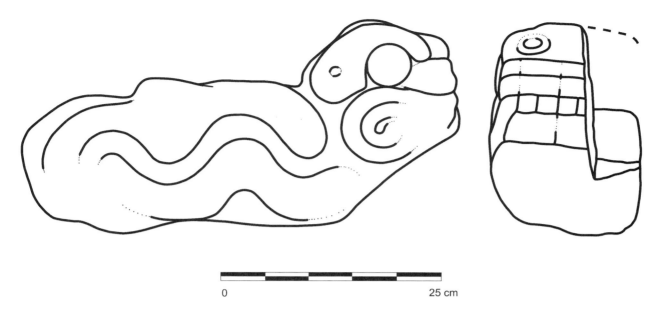

figure 10.15
La Lagunita Sculpture 21 from Group B. (Drawing by Luis Luin.)

in a rather realistic manner, with lips, two rows of teeth, and canines that convey ferocity (Figure 10.15). Half of the head has broken away along a natural fault plane. Group B, with several structures, appears to have been an elite residential area. Two similar animal sculptures were reported by Smith (1955:figs. 7 and 9) in the middle of the ballcourt in Chalchitán, Huehuetenango. These sculptures and the one from La Lagunita are likely Late Classic.

The most impressive sculptures from La Lagunita are four stone boxes called "sarcophagi" by the French Mission and "*pilas*" ("water basins") by the local population. Three were found in Structure 7 (Sarcophagi 1, 2, and 4), and one was recovered in Structure 10 (Sarcophagus 3). Sarcophagus 4 was found in the lowest part of the structure, near Burial C-44, and as such, it is probably the oldest of the four. It was carved from a rectangular block of tuff and measures 1.80 m long by 1.08 m wide. Sarcophagus 4 was painted bright red (Ichon 1977) and contained two skeletons, and several offerings were placed in the chamber. According to Ichon (1977:53), the sarcophagus weighs more than a ton.

The east face of this sarcophagus has a low-relief panel with a step-fret design that resembles three uneven pyramids with three steps each (see Ichon 1977:55, fig. 46). The west side has the most elaborate carving (Figure 10.16). It depicts two individuals facing each other; between them are plant-like volutes with flowers at their ends, similar to that on Sculpture 14, a stela fragment (Figure 10.13a). The individuals have similar headdresses and earflares. The volutes and flowers could represent water plants and refer to the primordial sea before the creation of the cosmos. The person on the right side has the back part of a bead collar that descends downward, and under it a small head with an oval eye and a circular earflare. A speech scroll comes out of the figure's mouth.

The individual on the right has a flexed left leg as if dancing or walking. The faces of both figures have distinct oval eyes: the elongated central portion of the eye is surrounded by another outer oval ring. These eyes are different from those on the other monuments at La Lagunita, and Ichon (1977:54) compared them to the protective goggles worn by Mexican deities, especially Tlaloc. The hands of the two figures show nails on the side nearest the observer. An element that seems to be flexible hangs from their noses—this element is lacking

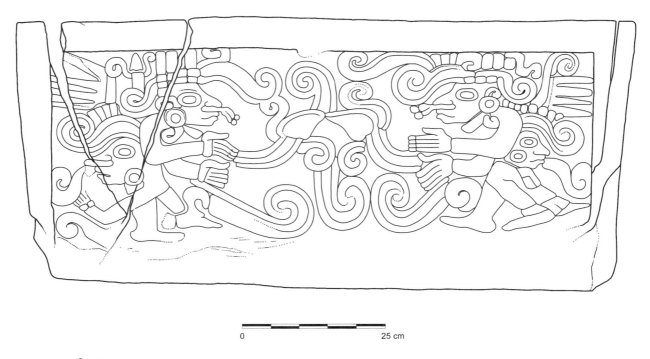

figure 10.16
La Lagunita Sarcophagus 4, west side. (Drawing by Luis Luin, redrawn from Ichon 1977:fig. 49.)

on the heads of the small faces worn on the backs of the standing individuals. Instead, these small faces emit speech scrolls, and the face looking to the left also wears a tubular element beneath the nose.

The overall composition of Sarcophagus 4 depicts five individuals on three sides of the box in opposed pairs and involved in conversation. The south side (Ichon 1977:fig. 51) shows a single individual in a dynamic pose dressed in a loincloth and possibly pants. The individual's arms are extremely long. In all cases, the individuals are shown out of true proportions (small torsos, long arms and legs, and big heads).

The north side of Sarcophagus 4 (Ichon 1977:fig. 50), like the west side, depicts two individuals. One has another flexible element hanging from the nose, and the other has only a tubular element. Even though the earspool on the figure to the left is more impressive than that of the opposing individual, the opposing headdress is more elaborate. The individual on the right seems to be moving. Ichon (1977:59) believes the figure is sitting and balanced on a stool: "assis sur un sorte tabourette." The individual on the left has both arms in motion and is standing on a somewhat lower surface. There is a large circular motif in front of both individuals that could be a ball, and the portrayed individuals could be ball players.

Sarcophagi 1 and 2 of the same Pyramid 7 are large square boxes of tuff buried near the surface. Sarcophagus 1 lacks carved decoration but was found painted red, both inside and out. It has an opening on one of its sides, as if to drain some liquid, and a hole coming out from the lower side. Sarcophagus 2 was found buried somewhat deeper than Sarcophagus 1. It also has a frame surrounding it and a drain. According to Ichon (1977), these coffins or sarcophagi were used to store water, hence the name "pilas" used by the present-day inhabitants of the region. However, in the case of Sarcophagus 4, it was used as a burial casket for two people whose skeletons rested one atop the other. The other two stone boxes contained human remains, but the skeletons were incomplete.

Sarcophagus 3 was found on the south side of Structure 10, north of the main plaza.

According to investigations from the French Mission, these stone boxes, although called sarcophagi (refer to Smith 1955 for Nebaj), were not necessarily designed for that purpose and could have been most often used for baths in ceremonies and rituals for sacred cleansing. Other large stone boxes are known from the sites of La Iglesia, Chalchitán (Smith 1955), Pacagüix, and Nebaj. The one in Chalchitán in the plaza of the town of Aguacatán was undecorated, except for an upper carved strip and another below, forming a frame. The one in Nebaj contained human remains. These stone boxes appear to have served different functions at different times. What is evident is that the sarcophagi with reliefs on the sides, and with human remains inside, were used to bury important individuals, perhaps rulers or other elites.

There are no name glyphs with clear titles on the Preclassic sculptures in the northern or western highlands, therefore it is only by inference that stelae in these regions, as well as other sculptures, can be related to individuals. In the Late Preclassic murals of San Bartolo, Peten, there is an accession scene (see Kaufman 2003; López Bruni 2006; Saturno, Taube, Stuart, Beltrán, and Román 2006). If such a ceremony occurred at San Bartolo, it is plausible that similar ceremonies could also have taken place in the highlands during the same time frame, particularly given the images on the stelae, such as those at Laguneta.

The site of La Lagunita probably suffered incursions by populations from the north and west. Circa AD 100–250 was a period of general social stress and change that included the northern and central highlands. The change was brought about by the group responsible for the destruction of monuments at La Lagunita and Kaminaljuyu, especially monuments depicting human figures and glyphic texts (Fahsen 2000a). These new K'ichean inhabitants did not use any type of writing and do not appear to have had much respect for the monuments with written texts. The texts they destroyed were probably of the Choltian language branch (Fahsen 2000a; Fahsen and Grube 2005).

Some Trends in Making and Breaking Highland Sculptures

Comparisons of the styles of monuments, their contexts, and breakage provide fundamental historical clues to the social and political dynamics in part of the Guatemalan Highlands during the Middle and Late Preclassic. Unlike the Baja Verapaz region and the Salamá Valley, the sites of Quiché, principally La Lagunita, show a greater affinity with Kaminaljuyu in terms of shared sculptural programs, monument style, carving techniques, and age of the sculptures. Kaminaljuyu is the older site of the two, and the first stone sculptures at this site had different themes than those at La Lagunita. The sculptures at La Lagunita date from the Late Preclassic to the Early Classic. The low-relief stelae date to the Late Preclassic, which, according to Shook and Popenoe de Hatch (1999:291), corresponded to the Arenal phase at Kaminaljuyu (300 BC–AD 100). These sculptures and their themes are similar to coeval sculptures at Kaminaljuyu (see Parsons 1986). For example, La Lagunita Sculpture 6 (Figure 10.12d) depicts the same Principal Bird Deity appearing on Stela 11 of Kaminaljuyu (Figure 10.14b). La Lagunita Sculptures 1, 2, 3, and 7 (Figure 10.12a–c,f), even though damaged, appear to be of the same sculptural school as those from Kaminaljuyu.

The La Lagunita stelae with human figures correspond more closely to Aurora phase or Early Classic (AD 200–400) monuments at Kaminaljuyu. This period was a time of great disturbance in the Guatemalan Highlands that witnessed the appearance of western peoples. These groups, I believe, were responsible for the destruction of the stone monuments at La Lagunita, Kaminaljuyu, and surrounding areas (Fahsen 2000a). However, in Baja Verapaz at the sites of El Portón, Los Mangales, and Laguneta, the stone monuments are better preserved. Nonetheless the breakage of the Los Mangales pedestal monuments and their missing heads attract attention as probable evidence of their ritual termination. As noted, even at this early time the stela-altar complex was present at El Portón (Structure J7-4B) and at La Lagunita

(Structure 7), although the stelae from Salamá Valley differ stylistically from those at La Lagunita. For example, Monument 1 of El Portón displays more similarities to lowland Maya stelae, as is evident from its column of glyphs and probable standing individual portrayed at the center of the monument (Figure 10.5a).

The almost complete absence in the northern highlands of potbelly sculptures, monuments common along the Pacific Coast (see Chapters 7–9) and in the central highlands, merits comment. For some reason, potbelly sculptures were not part of the sculptural tradition of the northern highlands, perhaps for ideological reasons or perhaps because comparable messages were articulated in a different sculptural form. In contrast, sculptures with cupules are reported from both highland valleys. In the Salamá Valley they probably represent the oldest sculptures with encoded messages, though of esoteric or maybe divinatory character, available for reading only to a privileged group of readers.

Four Kaminaljuyu monuments could have had strong influence on the La Lagunita sculptures: Stelae 4 and 19 and Altars 9 and 10. These four sculptures show dramatic movement in their carved figures as well as some iconographic signs, which eventually become words in later inscriptions (see Parsons 1986). On Stelae 4 and 19 the legs of the figures display the mirror glyph that emphasizes their supernatural condition (Taube 1996:50), and on Altars 9 and 10 the Principal Bird Deities have K'IN and A'KBAL signs in their wings (representing "day" and "night," respectively) and "mirror" signs on their bellies. These birds have the same beaks as has the figure on La Lagunita Sculpture 6, but this monument is closer in style to Kaminaljuyu Stela 11, which is perhaps 100 years later (Figure 10.14b). The adobe relief mask from Kaminaljuyu Mound D-III-1 is also a long-snouted being, although this mask is Early Classic (Ohi et al. 1994; Parsons 1986:fig. 187).

Kaminaljuyu Stela 10 (Figure 1.9; Parsons 1986:fig. 175) shows a male person and a possible human female figure as well as a long text, as do other Arenal phase monuments from Kaminaljuyu

whose texts were readable before their destruction. For example, Kaminaljuyu Stela 21 (Parsons 1986:fig. 157) has a possible emblem glyph at the end of a text preceded by a face that could have been a nominal or the equivalent of the AHAW glyph. The above mentioned similarities in themes and styles between Kaminaljuyu and La Lagunita can serve to place monuments in relative chronological order, and in this sense it seems that monuments from Kaminaljuyu can be used as benchmarks because of the duration of their use before they were destroyed. I suggest that the monuments of La Lagunita be placed somewhere in the middle time span of the Kaminaljuyu sequence of monuments. The monuments from El Portón are in a similar position.

Some of the earliest monuments from Kaminaljuyu and El Portón have similar characteristics. For example, pedestal Monuments 10 and 22 from the Salamá Valley (Sharer and Sedat 1987:plates 18.9 and 18.30) and one monument from El Portón photographed by Shook (see Parsons 1986:fig. 40) are similar to two fragments from Kaminaljuyu (Monuments 3 and 7). Sculpture 6 from Kaminaljuyu is virtually identical to El Portón Monuments 12 and 22. According to Parsons (1986:23–24), these sculptures date to the "Transition Phase," or ca 700–500 BC. He argued for a regional phase of sculptures that imitated nature and local animals. When figurative monuments later appeared at these three sites, the human figures took on an important role, and glyphs carrying messages complemented the narrative images (e.g., Kaminaljuyu Altars 1, 2, 9, and 10, Monument 65, and Stelae 15 and 21). Similarly, El Portón Monument 1 (Figure 10.5a) and Laguneta Monument 16 (Figure 10.8a) are in the same category. These figurative monuments with texts began to be carved with the initiation of writing after 400 BC and show individuals, verbal communications, and personal titles. However, they do not have Long Count dates. Sharer and Loa Traxler (2006:197) believe that these monuments represented individuals who were assuming power, but with no specific dates related to the history of the later Maya tradition of time cycles. Two monuments from La Lagunita, Sarcophagus 3 and Sculpture 18 (Figure 10.13b), also have what could be interpreted as glyphs but not texts. Monuments from Kaminaljuyu, besides showing figures of supernaturals (e.g., Stelae 4 and 19, Altars 9 and 10, and Monument 63), depict individuals performing ceremonies (e.g., Stelae 10, 11, 15, 16, and 21), with texts and dates indicated, and some had what must have been complete texts.

The breakage and destruction of monuments appear to have occurred initially with pedestal sculptures. Some breakage could have resulted from the mishandling of fragile monuments (e.g., El Portón Monuments 12 and 22; Kaminaljuyu Monument 23, Sculpture 6, and many silhouette monuments from this site). Most pedestal monuments have lost their heads. The neck was the weakest part of these sculptures and thus the most susceptible to breakage. However, the breakage of most monuments from La Lagunita and Kaminaljuyu appears to have been deliberate rather than accidental. Kaminaljuyu monuments show deliberate breakage, most clearly evident on Monument 65 and the socketed holes carved on its face for breakage and the erasure of the images (see Chapter 11). Kaminaljuyu Stela 21 (Parsons 1986:fig. 157) shows the last two glyphs of a double column of text with two individuals, one kneeling in a submissive position beneath the text, the other standing adjacent to the inscription.

Although there are few texts at El Portón and fewer at La Lagunita, the deliberate destruction of monuments in these places, especially La Lagunita, relates to a similar situation as described for Kaminaljuyu. Popenoe de Hatch (1997, 1999, 2002b, 2002c) believes that by AD 200 massive numbers of people moved to the central highlands from the northwest. These were probably K'ichean peoples. Archaeologically they are manifested by what Popenoe de Hatch calls the "Solano" ceramic tradition. These peoples appear to have moved south and eventually invaded such places as La Lagunita and Kaminaljuyu. They displaced much of the local population and replaced the elites, which, in the case of Kaminaljuyu, were likely Cholan speakers. The displaced inhabitants of Kaminaljuyu fled the area with the arrival of the people of the Solano tradition (Popenoe de Hatch 1997, 2002b).

Several monuments from Kaminaljuyu (see Fahsen 2002:figs. 16.1, 16.4, and 16.6) show captives or other submissive individuals, sometimes naked, bound, or with their genitals exposed, cowering before standing persons (compare to Chapter 11). Such imagery perhaps points to a revisionist strategy of invaders to destroy images that depicted their own previous humiliation at the hands of Kaminaljuyu elites or warlords. I think the prisoners depicted at Kaminaljuyu were likely of K'ichean affiliation, and the invaders destroyed these denigrating depictions of themselves once they took over Kaminaljuyu (Fahsen 2002).

El Portón fared better than either La Lagunita or Kaminaljuyu in terms of its stone sculptures. Recall that El Portón Monument 1 maintained its position of honor in its architectural complex throughout the history of this regional center. It was defaced and broken sometime early in its history, probably long before the monument destruction that took place at either La Lagunita or Kaminaljuyu at the end of the Late Preclassic period. Based on the later pattern seen at Kaminaljuyu, it is particularly interesting that the text on El Portón Monument 1 was preserved and that the image—presumably that of a standing king—was almost completely erased. The text continued to have a place of honor. At Kaminaljuyu, the monuments with writing were destroyed, and the written texts themselves effaced. These differences in the patterns of monument breakage suggest that different social forces and/or rationales were involved. I believe that the K'icheans who destroyed monuments at La Lagunita and Kaminaljuyu were less concerned with the inhabitants of the Salamá Valley. It was a key spot on the trade route for resources coming out of the central highlands, but their focus appears to have been to take control of the primary resources themselves rather than trade routes.

The persisting, unanswered question meriting much more research is why different Preclassic Maya groups were at odds with one another. I believe one of the most plausible reasons was the desire to profit from the control of valuable resources—especially jade and obsidian located in the central highlands. This concern persisted until Postclassic times. Study of the different styles of stone monuments and their breakage provides evidence of a shift in power and control in the central highlands at the end of the Late Preclassic period (by AD 200). Future studies of more sculptures in context, and in light of other indicators of group affiliation, will help establish the complex history of highland Maya peoples in Guatemala.

Acknowledgments

It was a privilege to participate in the Dumbarton Oaks symposium that inspired this book. I thank John Clark, Julia Guernsey, and Barbara Arroyo for organizing this event and encouraging my participation. I am particularly grateful to those who helped with the artwork for my presentation and for this chapter. Several monuments found at La Lagunita and in Baja Verapaz have disappeared or have been reburied for their protection and could not be rephotographed. Most monuments were photographed and drawn by Mr. Luis Fernando Luin, a specialized draftsman. The National Museum of Archaeology and Ethnology of Guatemala authorized the sketching of the sculpture fragments from La Lagunita, Quiché, which are currently in their collection. Mr. Luin visited and photographed some of the monuments in San Jeronimo, Baja Verapaz, especially El Portón Monument 1. His drawings and photographs were compared to published versions of these monuments by John Clark, who combined these data with the help of artists of the New World Archaeological Foundation in the final illustrations presented here. I thank all involved for their contributions in bringing to light the early sculpture of the Guatemalan Highlands. A CD with the photographs taken by Luis Luin can be obtained from the author.

NOTES

1. To simplify the discussion, I refer to specific building stages of Structure J7-4B by their sequential numbers; hence "Structure J7-4B-5" is simplified to "Structure 5." Archaeological convention usually numbers buildings in the sequence of their discovery, from youngest to oldest, meaning that the higher the number, the older the building.

2. Sharer and Sedat (1987:59) assign a date of 400 BC to Monument 1, but based on comparisons to the San Bartolo murals, which Saturno, Stuart, and Beltrán (2006) place at ca 150 BC, a date of 200 BC seems more likely. One of the San Bartolo texts shows a vulture glyph or serpent-form bird head at the end of the inscription, similar to the one on Monument 1. Thus I believe these inscriptions were nearly contemporaneous, with the San Bartolo date being more accurate. Both would coincide with Kaminaljuyu Stela 11, which shows a serpent-form ornament in the belt. Edwin Shook (personal communication 1999) dated this monument to 200 BC.

11

Revisiting Kaminaljuyu Monument 65 in Three-Dimensional High Definition

TRAVIS F. DOERING AND LORI D. COLLINS

THREE-DIMENSIONAL LASER SCANNING IS A state-of-the-art spatial data acquisition technology that significantly improves, enhances, and increases the extraction of detail and information carved on Preclassic sculptures. The extremely high resolution, accuracy, and density of the data acquired by three-dimensional scanning can be used for a number of purposes. Minimally, this technique provides the finest archival documentation possible through the implementation of "best-available technologies" for museum or collection registration, heritage preservation planning and management, and educational applications (United Nations 2005). Perhaps the most exciting capability of three-dimensional scanning, however, is its ability to capture data that can be used to rescue or resurrect details of damaged monuments that have not been previously recognized. Our purpose in this chapter is to demonstrate the utility of three-dimensional laser scanning for capturing such detail. In particular, we showcase Monument 65 from Kaminaljuyu in highland Guatemala to demonstrate the power and potential of this technique.

Kaminaljuyu is considered one of the most significant and politically influential Preclassic settlements in southern Mesoamerica (Coe 1999; Evans 2003; Kaplan 1995; Michels 1979; Parsons 1988). Stone sculpture created during the Miraflores phase of the site's occupation (400 BC–AD 200) is regarded as a "forerunner of the Classic Maya" (Coe 1999:71). In the site's sculptural corpus Monument 65 is deemed "a most important stone, the largest sculpture at Kaminaljuyu" (Parsons 1986:57–58). Furthermore, the two discrete low-relief images carved on opposite faces of this monument are interpreted as early depictions of Mesoamerican "rulership ideology" (Kaplan 2000:185). We believe the scenes on the two faces differ substantially in content, style, and presentation, but both were precursors of Classic Maya symbolic representations of rulership and political acquiescence.

The iconographic significance of the carving on Monument 65 is noteworthy and merits close scrutiny. The information presented in this chapter was generated by an innovative application of ultrahigh-definition three-dimensional laser scanning that was used to record and analyze the stone and its carvings. The scan data produced substantial new imagery and clarified earlier representations. Examination of these new images suggests alternative possibilities for, and interpretations of, its carved scenes. The data resulting from the laser scans also permit a partial reconstruction of the monument's history of use and reuse. Before detailing new observations, we provide some technical background on three-dimensional laser scanning and its use on Preclassic sculptures. Subsequent discussion focuses on Monument 65 and its context, use, and meaning.

Three-Dimensional Laser Scanning

As the name implies, three-dimensional laser scanning allows researchers to visualize sculpted objects as three-dimensional images. Such images also raise new questions and open fresh avenues of inquiry. We selected Kaminaljuyu Monument 65 to test this new technology, because this sculpture embodies many of the diverse factors and problematic conditions that are regularly encountered with early monuments. Monument 65 presents two carved faces, abraded and eroded surfaces, illegible details, and evidence of reuse and recycling, all obstacles to archaeological interpretation that laser scanning data can help overcome.

Laser scanning is a noncontact, noninvasive, and nondestructive technique for accurately and, in most cases, more completely recording sculpted artifacts than can be done using conventional methods of documentation.[1] Typically, high-definition scanning is considered to be the systematic and automated collection of three-dimensional data of a particular surface or object at a relatively high rate and in near real time (Boehler et al. 2001, 2004; Frei et al. 2004). Because of the extreme accuracy and exceptional density of the three-dimensional data acquired, objects can be analyzed, visualized, measured, and evaluated

more effectively and precisely than if the researcher were in the field or had the physical object in her presence. Once an object has been scanned in the field, detailed and comprehensive examinations of the stone and its sculpture can be conducted for the captured data in a virtual environment. The objects can be virtually rotated 360° and viewed in true three dimensions. The virtual light sources of the laser images can be manipulated to observe and accentuate the object from any angle, submillimeter measurements can be made of any portion of the piece on the computer screen, and numerous visualization techniques can be used to enhance and clarify details.

Over the past six years, we have developed three-dimensional data acquisition and postprocessing techniques that significantly improve and facilitate the ability to visualize and analyze Mesoamerican sculptures (Collins and Doering 2006; Doering and Collins 2007, 2008; Doering et al. 2006). The continued development of these techniques is an ongoing effort that will provide archaeologists, epigraphers, iconographers, and other researchers increased capacity to recognize and interpret information that ancient peoples left on their stone monuments. These techniques well complement conventional methods (e.g., photography and drawings) for the study of stone sculpture. Additionally, the life history of a stone can be traced through the identification of tool and other marks on it that can assist in determining the manufacturing process, detect transport methods, and distinguish reuse and recycling of the stone.

Three-dimensional laser scanning is also critical for the documentation of monuments. As Price (1996:30) stated, "If we cannot preserve stone forever, it is imperative that we make the best possible record of it. Indeed, one could argue that recording should have a higher priority than preserving the stone itself." Photographic techniques have, until now, been the most common methods used to record stone sculptures and, while exceptional results have been achieved, there are considerable limitations on its use as a stand-alone method. Stereophotography offers only an illusion of depth and is limited to a single viewpoint, and similar drawbacks are present in photogrammetry (Price 1996). Raking-light photography is a method in which the light source is placed at an acute angle to the stone to cast shadows across the surface in an effort to enhance faint details and reveal contours carved in a stone (see Kaplan 2000:187, 188, 190). This technique is helpful in many cases but is laborious and presents fundamental problems of spatial control and the introduction of parallax, the visual displacement of an object caused by the position or angle from which the image was acquired. This type of spatial distortion causes a progressively increasing dimensional error when used for analysis or the production of drawings from photographs. Furthermore, the intentionally created shadows can hide significant details and exaggerate others, a point addressed by Graham (1989:242–243), who noted that such inconsistencies can result in misconceptions or hinder interpretation. Another consideration is that these types of produced images, although visually striking, do not provide a measurable or quantifiable record.

Inherent in traditional techniques of recording are also problems and limitations imposed by the subjective nature of the procedures. Decisions as to what is important, what is recorded, and what is not exposed are some of the biases that are introduced into conventional documentation methods. Outstanding or obvious elements may be recorded at the expense of others deemed unimportant by an individual recorder that in reality may be vital to the interpretation of the artifact. The singular or limited viewpoint can prevent the visualization of details and thus skew the interpretation of elements critical to understanding the object and its meaning. Drawings made from photographs or rubbings introduce a second level of subjectivity. Well aware of these interpretive dangers, Graham (1989:243) stated that "our apprehension of [Preclassic] art has also suffered greatly" through "distortions in repeatedly republished drawings" that result in erroneous observations. Most Preclassic sculpture has not been sufficiently documented to permit critical comparative morphologic, iconographic, or epigraphic analyses.

Although three-dimensional scanning can substantially lessen many of the difficulties and limitations of photography and other more subjective methods of documentation, it has its own limitations. Nevertheless, in the majority of cases, three-dimensional scanning is considerably more rapid and acquires more robust and accurate data than any other method of documentation presently available. Because the scan data can include the entire piece and supply a precise, quantifiable digitization of the actual surface of the object (accurate to 50 microns or 0.002 inch), the initial level of recorder subjectivity is basically eliminated.

Our analysis of Monument 65 began with close-range three-dimensional laser scanning that was combined with software visualization, which transformed the data into line drawings and generated images of the surfaces of the sculpture. It should be noted that the images provided in this chapter are two-dimensional representations of three-dimensional images and do not illustrate the full capabilities and the exceptional clarity and detail in the actual data sets. These features can best be appreciated by viewing the three-dimensional data.[2]

Preclassic Kaminaljuyu and Its Sculpted Stone Corpus

The ancient settlement of Kaminaljuyu is located in the northwest part of modern Guatemala City (see Figure 10.1), but most of this exceptionally large site has been lost to modern urban sprawl (Coe 1999:70–71; Michels 1979). The site was first occupied in the Early Preclassic period or Arévalo phase (1100–900 BC) when, according to Arroyo (2003:1), "an intensive interaction of Early Formative societies" was occurring along the Pacific Coast of Guatemala. By the early Middle Preclassic period (Las Charcas phase, 900–700 BC), evidence suggests that Kaminaljuyu was densely populated and that complex sociopolitical, economic, and religious institutions had been established (Shook 1951:98). The florescence of Kaminaljuyu took place in the Late Preclassic Miraflores period, spanning the Verbena (400–200 BC) and the Arenal phases (200 BC–AD 200), and varying levels of occupation extended into the Late Classic period (Cole 2006).

During the Late Preclassic, Kaminaljuyu was one of the largest settlements in the Guatemalan Highlands and the location of one of the region's most powerful chiefdoms or states (see Chapter 7; Demarest 2004; Michels 1979; Popenoe de Hatch 2001:387). Its advantageous position on a natural pass connecting the Pacific Coast and the interior of Guatemala allowed its occupants to act as conduits of communication and exchange in an interaction sphere that extended through the Motagua Valley and into El Salvador, throughout Chiapas and the Maya Lowlands, and as far northwest as Teotihuacan and the Gulf Coast region. In addition to this geographic advantage, Kaminaljuyu controlled two major obsidian sources, El Chayal and San Martín Jilotepeque, and an expansive acquisition and redistribution system that included jade, salt, cacao, fruits, and ceramics.

Kaminaljuyu has been described as cosmopolitan or international in character, with multiple ethnic affiliations that suggest it may have served as a port-of-trade or gateway community (Brown 1977; Popenoe de Hatch 1993). Some scholars have also suggested that it was a key point of interaction between Mixe-Zoquean and Mayan peoples (Mora-Marín 2001). A major factor contributing to these interpretations of the site is the eclectic nature of the monumental sculptures erected in plazas and in front of platforms and temples around the sprawling city (Parsons 1986; Popenoe de Hatch 1997).

Much of the increasingly complex iconography manifest in stone sculptures at Kaminaljuyu and elsewhere in Mesoamerica at this time dealt with depictions of rulership and ideology (see Chapter 1; Figures 1.9 and 10.14). A comparative study of the iconographic content on monumental stone sculpture at coeval sites, such as El Portón, Takalik Abaj, El Baúl, Chocolá, and Izapa, suggests that similar themes were being depicted, often with analogous imagery and symbols (see

Chapters 8–10; Arroyo 2007; Guernsey 2006b; Sharer and Sedat 1987). In particular, we believe that the imagery on Kaminaljuyu Monument 65, recovered in great part through the three-dimensional scanning process, sheds insight on the themes of hereditary inequality, the divine right to rule, and political domination (see Clark and Blake 1994; Earle 1997; Guernsey 2006b; Hayden 1995). Before we begin a more focused discussion of the monument's interpretive potential, however, we discuss the process involved in the scanning of this important monument.

Scanning Kaminaljuyu Monument 65

The laser scanning of Monument 65 was conducted as part of the Kaminaljuyu Sculpture Project,[3] an endeavor that involved the high-definition three-dimensional recording of the available corpus of 119 stone carvings and selected decorated ceramics from the site of Kaminaljuyu (Doering and Collins 2008). We have also documented numerous Preclassic stone monuments from Takalik Abaj in Retalhuleu, Guatemala, and La Venta in Tabasco, Mexico (Doering et al. 2006; Pohl 2008). These opportunities have helped us better appreciate the context, media, artistry, and effort involved in the production of monumental sculptures and to recognize both the stylistic variation and the representational correspondences present among the widespread contemporaneous monuments.

The content and condition of Monument 65 and its carvings presented numerous challenges. This sculpture contains palimpsest-like carvings; some are readily observable, whereas others are practically imperceptible, and the laser scanning permitted us to distinguish previously indiscernible features as well as analyze multiple modification events in the stone's history.

In the first line-drawing attempt from scan data, Geomagic v. 9 software was used to view the three-dimensional model, from which we created a hand tracing and line drawing of Monument 65. This procedure was conducted in an effort to see whether conventional line drawings could be made by working directly from the scan data. The benefit of drawing directly from three-dimensional images is that spatial control is maintained even though lighting and orientation can be varied. Two other hand drawings were made using the same three-dimensional model by separate artists who had never seen a representation of Monument 65 and were unfamiliar with Mesoamerican sculptural styles. This procedure was done to evaluate the visual content and clarity of the scan data from an unbiased perspective. The similarities of the three independent drawings were exceptional. This correspondence supports the strength and validity of the scan data for interpretive purposes. It is important to stress that each of these illustrations contained significantly more detail across Side B of Monument 65 than has previously been published. This method of drawing, however, still included a degree of artist subjectivity when moving from the digital environment to a line drawing. In an attempt to further reduce this subjectivity, a method of surface detail depiction that was fully maintained in the computerized digital platform was instituted using new advances in graphic input hardware and software. Using an Intous3 professional pen tablet, static screen images of three-dimensional data from various lighting perspectives were used as base layers to create digital line drawings of Monument 65 using Corel Painter software. The finalized drawing, with the base layer removed, exhibited a high degree of conformity with the hand-drawn line art, but this method of depiction was completed much more rapidly, possibly because of the maintenance of the digital environment. Interpretive error was also minimized by drawing directly over first-generation data. This method, conducted in the digital realm, is not unlike previous methods using Mylar and pen to trace over sculpted stone or photographs (see Norman 1973, 1976).

Using Adobe Photoshop Element 5.0 software, static screen images of the original three-dimensional data sets were brought in and computer enhanced to examine areas of the carving.

Although in some cases it can be difficult to differentiate between naturally occurring and human-produced elements, it is possible to obtain an image that depicts the carving in a more contrastive way by using the filter threshold tool. Similar photographic filtering and enhancements have proven useful for pigment analysis and carved-stone documentation in petroglyph studies (see Brady 2006).[4]

Another approach using the three-dimensional scan data to determine surface elevational differences is possible using the Geomagic software, which essentially allows a topographic contouring of the area. When applied to Monument 65, this method highlights elevational differences in the carved surface. Our images derived from laser scanning relate well to those drawn from photographs, the major difference being the greater number of verified details from the laser images. These additional details are significant and call for a reevaluation of previous interpretations of this monument, a task we begin here.

In his study of Monument 65, Kaplan (2000:185) described Monument 65 as a "single oversized pale volcanic stone" that was modified "from the original boulder slab." He gives the height of the sculpture in its existing state as 290 cm but estimates the overall height may originally have been 330 cm; he adds that Side A shows evidence of deterioration (Kaplan 2000:190). He used raking-light photography, line drawings, and close visual inspection to examine and decipher the carvings on both sides of this relatively flat monolith.

We continue the use of his arbitrary assignment of Side A (recto) and Side B (verso) to identify and differentiate between the opposite carved faces (Figure 11.1; Kaplan 2000:186). We also use Kaplan's report as a point of departure in our examination of the monument but stop short of a final interpretation of the carved images, for reasons detailed below. The evidence, even with the addition of the new data, remains ambiguous and supports divergent interpretations. However, we believe a reassessment of the previously recognized iconographic elements in light of the new details from the laser scans is warranted.

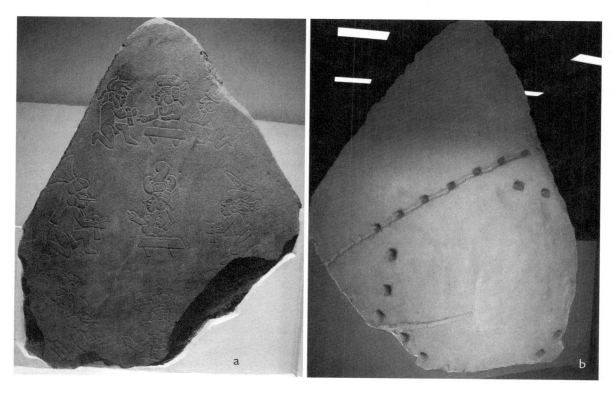

figure 11.1
Kaminaljuyu Monument 65. (a) Side A (recto); (b) Side B (verso). (Photographs by the authors.)

Side A

Monument 65, Side A, contains a series of relatively well-defined figures and objects whose positions and actions have been commented on previously (Brady 2003; Houston and Taube 2000; Kaplan 2000:185; Parsons 1986). The scene shows three vertical series of figures arranged in three horizontal registers (Figure 11.2). Each register or series of figures increases in size, from top to bottom. The upper two series include a central personage seated on a throne (personages 1b and 2b in Figure 11.2; see Grove 1973; Kaplan 1995). The monument is made from a stone that is broken at the bottom and sides, but based on the symmetry of the scene, it is likely that the original lower series would have included a throne and a third figure to the viewer's right. This hypothetical depiction is illustrated in Figure 11.2 by dashed lines. The details of our drawing of Side A are derived from the three-dimensional scan data as base referent combined with photographic data. The illustration

represents a collaborative effort between us and John Clark and Kisslan Chan.

A common presumption is that this scene depicts rulers seated on thrones with captives arrayed to either side (Fahsen 2002; Kaplan 2000:186–191; Parsons 1986:57–58). We do not rule out this interpretation, but an alternative explanation suggested to us by Julia Guernsey (personal communication 2008) is that the flanking individuals are not necessarily either prisoners or hostages. The primary basis for the "captive" interpretation came from the observation that the outer figures had been stripped naked (Houston and Taube 2000:265; Parsons 1986:58), had their wrists bound, and were in a kneeling position. Kaplan (2000:190–192) argued that the imagery referenced warfare, humiliation, and human sacrifice, and that "every detail of the carving was included for a conscious purpose."

We agree with this statement about the sculpted details but not their interpretation. We consider the posture, attitude, and physical disposition of the personages on Side A to be significant clues to understanding the scene's meaning. New image details derived from the three-dimensional scan data suggest that all five figures to the left and the right of the scene (1a, 1c, 2a, 2c, and 3a) are wearing loincloths and are not naked (Figure 11.2). This is a difference that makes a difference. These individuals are also wearing distinctive headdresses,

various types of ear ornaments, and are in a position of genuflection on one knee.

An important principle in Mesoamerican art is "verticality . . . the higher a seated figure in a scene, the higher the rank" (Houston 1998:343). The individual figures in each of the three horizontal scenes on Side A are of equal size and vertical position in their respective registers. They look each other directly in the eye, and none has an elevational

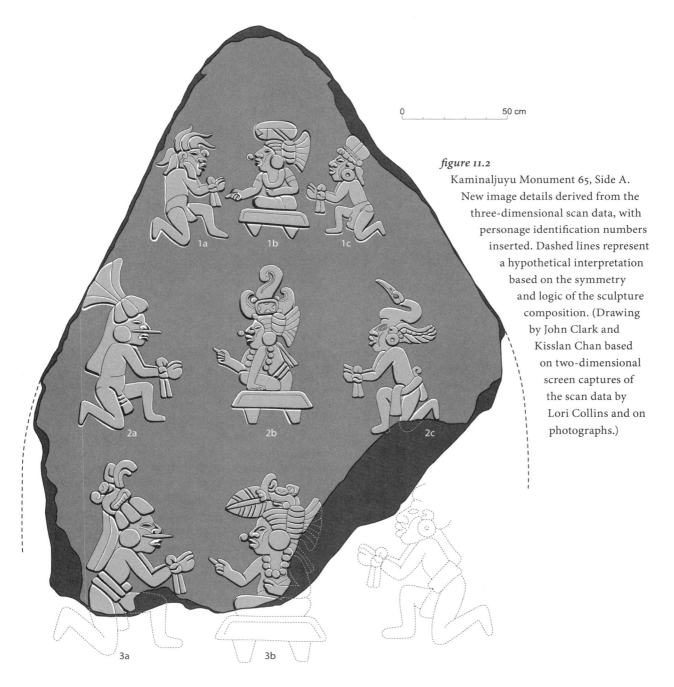

figure 11.2
Kaminaljuyu Monument 65, Side A.
New image details derived from the
three-dimensional scan data, with
personage identification numbers
inserted. Dashed lines represent
a hypothetical interpretation
based on the symmetry
and logic of the sculpture
composition. (Drawing
by John Clark and
Kisslan Chan based
on two-dimensional
screen captures of
the scan data by
Lori Collins and on
photographs.)

advantage. The three figures to the viewer's left (1a, 2a, and 3a) wear nose ornaments. All eight figures in the scene wear the same clothing as well as variations of headdresses and ear ornaments. Other than being seated on a throne, the central figures differ because they wear necklaces and different types of nose ornaments (see Houston and Taube 2000:265–273).

The positions of the face, arms, and hands on both the seated and kneeling figures may illustrate a sociopolitical relationship among the actors. Personages 1a, 1c, 2a, 2c, and 3a appear to be in submissive or reverential postures. When considering other contemporaneous sculpted images, the combination of a forward-facing or uplifted head, genuflection or kneeling, arms extended in front of the torso, and wrists placed together may not be evidence that the depicted individuals represent captives, warfare, or sacrificial victims. Rather, this particular placement of the head, arms, and wrists may signify subservience or deference to another actor in the scene. Julia Guernsey (personal communication 2008) pointed out to us that the same posture appears in imagery at such contemporaneous sites as San Bartolo and Takalik Abaj (see Chapter 8; Figure 8.4a), and these other occurrences suggest submission, respect, or secondary status. On the San Bartolo west-wall mural, the two kneeling figures located directly behind the Maize God are shown with their arms and wrists in the same pose as the five kneeling figures on Monument 65, and they have similar knotted strips on their wrists (see Kaufmann 2003; López Bruni 2006; Saturno, Taube, Stuart, Beltrán, and Román 2006). We would further note that the arms and wrists of the San Bartolo Maize God himself are depicted in the same manner. Accordingly, the rear figures are showing deference to the Maize God who may, in turn, be showing deference to an ancestor or deity. Guernsey (personal communication 2008) further noted that the figure on the right side of Takalik Abaj Stela 5 (see Figure 8.4a) makes the same gesture with arms lifted and wrists extended and has band-like elements on his wrists. In this case, the Stela 5 figure is seated on a throne, and his status as captive, ancestor, or individual of some secondary

status or political rank relative to the figures on the front of the monument is ambiguous.

In contrast, on Izapa Stela 89, another contemporaneous Preclassic monument, a kneeling individual has his arms bound behind his back and is propped up in an obviously unnatural and uncomfortable pose (Norman 1976:162–164). In numerous Classic Maya depictions, prisoners of war and sacrificial victims are shown in similar positions and usually portray a sense of despondency or hopelessness. Examples of these scenes are present on monumental sculpture, ceramic vases, and figurines from Jaina, Piedras Negras, Tikal, Toniná, Yaxchilan, and other sites (Coe 2005; Martin and Grube 2000; Miller 1999).

The depictions of the band-like objects on the wrists of the kneeling figures on Side A of Kaminaljuyu Monument 65 seen in the laser scan data illustrate a specific and consistent type of knotting. The items on the wrists of the outer five characters cannot be definitively interpreted as a binding tying the wrists together. They may be a type of bracelet-like ornament on each wrist that, because of the profile view of the arms, cannot be seen individually. The personage on Kaminaljuyu Stela 11 (see Figure 10.14b) also wears analogous bands and knotting on each wrist but, in this case, they are clearly not tied together. The same is true of the figures on Izapa Stelae 4 and 11 (Clark and Moreno 2007:285, 294; Guernsey 2006b:56, 126; Norman 1973:plates 7, 8, 21, and 22, 1976:98, 112) and Kaminaljuyu Stela 10 (see Figure 1.9).

Even if the bands on the Monument 65 individuals do represent a tying of the wrists, their presence may be indicative of something other than captivity. On La Venta Altar 4 (see Figure 6.8), for example, the primary niche figure, who is believed to be the ruler, grasps a central portion of a rope that extends around the left side of the altar and is wrapped around the wrist of a second personage. This individual on the side of the altar has been variously interpreted as a captive or ancestor (Drucker 1981:45; Grove 1970; Guernsey and Reilly 2001)—the scene may depict a demonstration of real or fictive kinship or a subordinate sociopolitical position (see Kaplan 2000:192).

The individuals seated on the thrones on Side A of Kaminaljuyu Monument 65 are thought to be rulers and are depicted with their right arms bent at the elbow and right hands closed, with the index fingers extended in what we would call a pointing gesture. This arm, hand, and finger configuration is seen on the prominent figure on the right-hand portion of Side B (see below), and it is a common pose on numerous geographically dispersed Preclassic monuments. Individuals on Tres Zapotes Stela D (see Figure 5.5); La Venta Altars 3, 4, 7, and Monument 13 (see Chapter 6); Izapa Stela 5 (Clark and Moreno 2007:286–288; Guernsey 2006b:3; Norman 1973:plates 9 and 10, 1976:165); and many other monumental sculptures display the same gesture. In these scenes, the context suggests that the actor with the bent arm, closed hand, and extended finger is acknowledging or accepting the action(s) of other persons or elements in the scene. We are not aware of sculpted depictions of rulers posed in this position who are lording over captives or sacrificial victims.

The meaning of the kneeling actors before the acknowledged sovereigns on Kaminaljuyu Monument 65, Side A, may be mirrored by events that occurred at Piedras Negras centuries later. Stuart (2007) analyzed the sculpture on Panel 12 from this Classic Maya site, the context and presentation of which appear to have a notable correspondence to Monument 65. In the Piedras Negras case, texts explain the actors and their actions. Three rulers from neighboring territories are shown with their arms extended in front of them and wrists together. They are kneeling in front of the standing king of Piedras Negras and are clothed with the regalia and accoutrements associated with their high office. To the rear of the standing ruler is what appears to be a captive in a distinctively different posture. His arms are tied behind his back, he is bare headed, with hair disheveled, and his physical demeanor suggests discomfort.

Stuart (2007) considers the scene "performative," a symbolic message of political dominance. He argues that the three kneeling figures are rulers of subsidiary realms. That they are not sacrificial victims or prisoners of war is confirmed by the

knowledge that these individuals returned to their home territories and continued to rule for several more years after this event was memorialized on the stone panel at Piedras Negras (Stuart 2007). Stuart (2007) also maintains that "later Maya kings represented subject rulers as bound prisoners, even though the subservient lords continued to rule for many years."

In summary, new data provided by high-resolution scanning of Side A of Monument 65 has allowed a clearer representation of what was actually carved on the surface of this stone and permits a more thorough analysis than was previously possible. All actors on Kaminaljuyu Monument 65 Side A, in each of the three scenes, are shown as equals in physical stature and are at a level to look each other in the eye. The presence of thrones does not place the kneeling figures in a diminished position, and minor differences in dress do not appear to suggest indignity. Nevertheless, the supreme ruler is clearly identifiable in each scene, but not to the social detriment of his allies. There is no indication of weapons or overt signs of warfare, belligerence, or threatening or aggressive postures. Therefore we believe that the new data support the possibility that the kneeling individuals are not captives but might instead be signaling their allegiance or deference to more powerful rulers (cf. Kaplan 2000:190–191). We would also suggest that, in return, the sovereign may be acknowledging the fealty of his vassals.

Side B

The verso side of Kaminaljuyu Monument 65, Side B, has received a more cursory examination and significantly less description than Side A (Pool 2007:274). The primary reason for this relative inattention is due to the faintness and indistinctive nature of the carving that makes comprehension of the scene exceedingly difficult. Kaplan (2000:193) claims that the "thematic depiction" present on Side B was effaced and is, therefore, more difficult to see and interpret. We agree that portions of Side B containing low-relief carving appear to have been intentionally smoothed or abraded. Our review of Side B first focuses on the elements of the

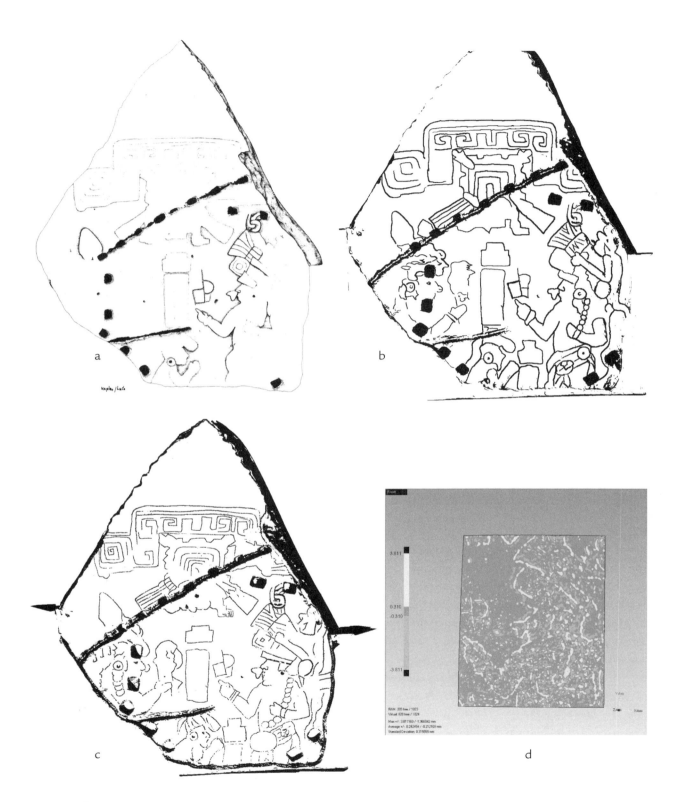

figure 11.3

Kaminaljuyu Monument 65, Side B. (a) after Kaplan 2000:190; (b) from tracing of scan data; (c) digital drawing in scan software environment; (d) detail of area of line contour confirmation using scan software analysis tools.

figure 11.4
Kaminaljuyu Monument 65, Side B. The four actors
are identified by letter in the line drawing that was
made by tracing over the scan data. (Drawing by
Lori Collins and Rebecca O'Sullivan.)

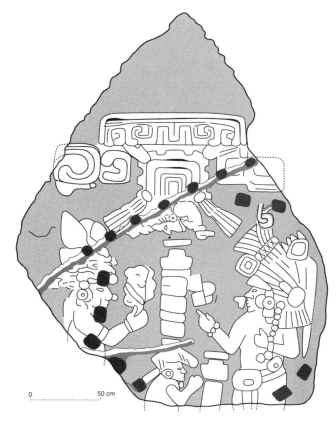

figure 11.5
Kaminaljuyu Monument 65, Side B.
(Interpretation by John Clark and Kisslan
Chan using two-dimensional screen captures
of scanned data and Kaplan 2000:fig. 2).

carved scene, then in the following section we discuss other intrusive elements present on this side
of Monument 65.

Raking-light photography has previously been
used to extract details not otherwise visible on Side
B (Figure 11.3a; Kaplan 2000). The resulting published photograph and line drawing displayed a
spatially restricted view that focused on the right
portion of the monument. The left portion, which
contains the faintest carving on Side B, was not
fully recorded. Close-range three-dimensional
laser scanning captured the extant carved scene in
its entirety and without the spatial limitations and
parallax distortion of raking-light photography
(Collins and Doering 2006). This technique also

revealed additional information, which enables us
to make fresh interpretations of carved details in
the scene on Side B (Fig. 11.3b–d).

Side B depicts four actors who are in a zone
of contact (the area between the personages). They
are shown in profile and identified in Figure 11.4.
The overall format or spatial organization of the
scene is similar to that in sculptures from other
Late Preclassic sites along the Pacific piedmont of
Guatemala, including an altar fragment from Polol
(Patton 1987). In the upper center portion of the
scene, a downward-facing individual (A) emerges
from the bottom of a lozenge-shaped medallion
(David Freidel, personal communication 2008). A
second figure (B) is on the left in the carved scene, a

third (C) is on the right, and the fourth (D) is near the lower center of the stone and faces character C. Personage C is often considered the peak or highest status figure based on his placement in the scene (Houston 1998:341). This individual has been considered the largest and most discernible on Side B and is facing figure B on the carved scene. Figure C is more complete but is really no larger than the facing figure B. The faces of both are the same size, and both have tall elaborate headdresses. Another rendition of what the monument may have originally looked like is shown in Figure 11.5. This illustration is an interpretation by John Clark and Kisslan Chan using two-dimensional screen captures of our scan data and photographs published by Kaplan (2000). It is a work in progress.[5] Individuals B and C flank the central glyph block, and both are likely royal personages of similar rank (Stephen Houston, personal communication 2008).

The text of the glyph block may begin with an introductory glyph, given its size, position, and separation from the rest of the text (Federico Fahsen, personal communication 2008). Figure D is kneeling in front of a second, smaller vertical glyph block. The emergent figure A is revealed by the scan data to consist of a profile face and hand. The facial features of this individual remain relatively indistinct.

The organization of the scene, including body placement, directionality, and items of personal adornment, are important indicators in the depiction of social power, identity, interaction, and meaning. Spatial orientation and handedness, left or right, appear to be linked to demonstrations of power and authority (Palka 2002:419) and can be examined in the scan data. For example, the data show that figure C uses his right hand to gesture toward the central glyph block, and contrary to previous suggestions, he is not seated (see Kaplan 2000:193). Given the position of his thighs, figure C must be standing. He is presenting with the right side of his body and right hand (see Figure 11.4), and he wears an elaborate headdress. Other personal adornments include earspools, bracelets, chains or ringlet-like objects, a nose ornament, and an elaborate belt.

The lower personage D appears to be kneeling and lifting his bound or braceleted wrists up toward personage C. This supplicant gesture, as discussed above for Side A, appears to be aimed at both the primary figure (C) and a second vertical glyph panel, which could contain the name of this individual (Figure 11.6; Federico Fahsen, personal communication 2008). The monument has been broken across the bottom of the scene, a circumstance that precludes much further observation other than to note that figure D is wearing an earspool and headdress. Figure B faces toward the center of the scene and holds a scepter or staff-like object in his right hand. This personage also wears a nose ornament, earspool, bracelet, and elaborate headdress that possibly contains a zoomorphic figure (Figure 11.7). The breakage and modification of Monument 65 prevents examination of the actor below the waist, but the figure appears to have been standing as the mirror image of figure C.

The symmetry of the left and right figures (B and C) is balanced by the central glyph panel and the celestial or sky band above. These sky bands are frequently marked with diagonal and vertical elements, and they first appear on stone sculptures of the Gulf Olmecs (e.g., Portrero Nuevo Monument 2, La Venta Altar 4 and Stela 1) (Norman 1976:23; Quirarte 1973:17; Stirling 1943b:62). Their use continued into the Late Preclassic and Protoclassic (e.g., Alvarado Stela and Izapa Stela 12), and Guernsey (2006b:78–79) illustrates several types of these bands. Preclassic depictions of sky bands are thought to represent the celestial sphere, as in the Classic period, when this type of element was prevalent in Maya art (Clancy 1990; Miller and Taube 1993:154–155).

A prototypical Preclassic sky or celestial framing band is scrolled along the top of the scene on Side B. It also may be that the rectangular spiral-like elements to the left and right of the Side B band are serpents. Reilly (1995:37) refers to the serpent as a bicephalic ecliptic monster. An alternative interpretation of these elements is that they could represent clouds (Federico Fahsen, personal communication 2008). A comparable framing band is present on Izapa Stela 3, which contains dual serpent

figure 11.6
Detail of Kaminaljuyu Monument 65, Side B. Three-dimensional scan (left) and sketch (right) show the profile and upper torso of Personage D and a proposed introductory glyph and glyphic text box.

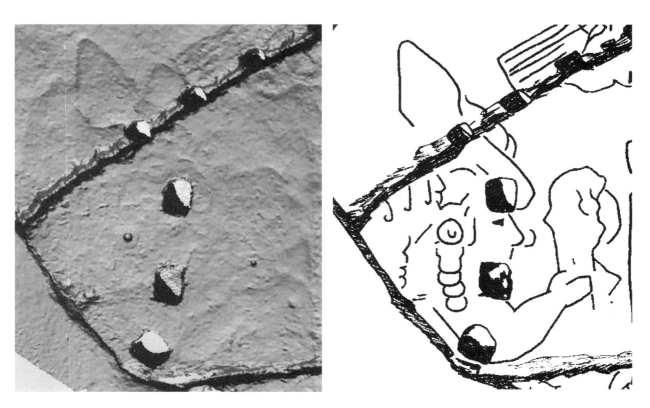

figure 11.7
Detail of Kaminaljuyu Monument 65, Side B. Three-dimensional scan (left) and sketch (right) shows Personage B.

heads at either end (Clark and Moreno 2007:284; Guernsey 2006b:3, 125; Norman 1973:plates 5 and 6). Clark and Chan (Figure 11.5) interpret this element as scrolls rather than as serpent elements.

Other similar sky bands appear on Izapa Stelae 1, 4, and 11 and Takalik Abaj Stela 1, among others. The left and right extremities of the Side B band fold downward, forming a niche containing what appears to be a lozenge-shaped medallion from the bottom of which emerges a personage with an outstretched hand (Figure 11.8; David Freidel,

personal communication 2008). A profile of a downward-gazing personage is a feature present on Izapa monuments (see Guernsey 2006b:56, fig. 3.11), and a tradition of portraying persons in profile emerging from serpents continued among the Classic Maya.

In both the Preclassic and Classic periods, the personages emerging from serpents are thought to be ancestors. Comparisons can be made with Yaxchilan Lintels 14 and 15 (I. Graham 1979, 1982; Graham and Euw 1977), which illustrate not only the emergent profile of ancestors but also their

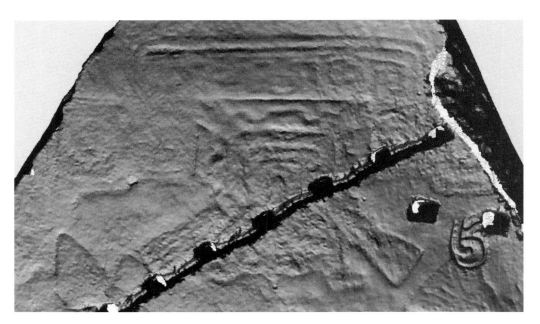

figure 11.8
Detail of Kaminaljuyu Monument 65, Side B. Three-dimensional scan (top) and sketch (bottom) show a celestial band and downward-facing Personage A emerging from the bottom of a medallion.

outstretched hands. El Baúl Stela 1, also known as the Herrera Stela (see Schele and Miller 1986:27, fig. 8), has a niche-like element in what Coe (1999:64–65) describes as a "cloud-scroll." Tucked into the niche is a lozenge-shaped medallion from which emerges a downward-facing profile. Similar to the Side B scene, the actor in the El Baúl sculpture is standing to the viewer's right and faces a vertical glyph block that contains a series of illegible glyphs. The individual holds a scepter-like object in his right hand, and his arm is bent. Takalik Abaj Stela 1 offers another close comparison (Guernsey 2006b:fig. 3.3b). The standing actor faces a carved block containing four glyph-like but illegible components, and the index finger on his right hand is extended in what can be described as a pointing gesture.

As this discussion illustrates, scan data sets, such as those for Kaminaljuyu Monument 65, significantly increase the level of observable detail compared to other types of available documentation. Given the new details visible on Monument 65 and their similarities with other carved pieces from southern Mesoamerica, we believe there is a more plausible interpretation of the scene on Side B than has been offered before. We contend that the scene may depict individual C's hereditary right to rule. Figure A may be an ancestor of the peak character (C). As such, figure A provides the connection, real or fictive, that was required for actor C, the assumed ruler, to exert or claim the right to rule. The bent arm and extended finger may be actor C's acknowledgment of that relationship. This power and authority may be further documented in the dominant central glyphic text. The meaning of the presence of figure B is not clear at this time. The personage could represent a political or military alliance or may have been the immediate predecessor of the new ruler, as in the relationship depicted on the Palenque Oval Palace Tablet, the House A-D Palace Tablet, the Tablet of the Cross, and numerous other depictions from this Classic site (Robertson 1985, 1991). Figure D is also ambiguous but could represent subordinate allegiance, and the associated text may hold documentation of this loyalty.

We realize that others will have differing interpretations of the scene described and portrayed here. As more information and details are extracted from the scan data, interpretations will be refined and modified. It should be clear, however, that the insights provided by the three-dimensional scan data significantly expand our view and understanding of this important monument and will be integral in moving us to a fuller explanation of the monument's meaning.

Comparison of Sides A and B of Kaminaljuyu Monument 65

The additional iconographic information that has become available from the three-dimensional scan of Monument 65 has also raised additional questions regarding the meaning and chronology of the sculpture. The sequence of the carving of the scenes on Sides A and B has been a point of contention that cannot be definitively resolved. Parsons (1986:58) raised questions about the chronology of the carvings and speculated that they were made at different times. Kaplan (2000:193) declared unequivocally that they are contemporaneous, based on his interpretation of styles and artistic elements, and that "Side A reflects an exoteric, Side B an esoteric, view of the same themes." Other conclusions based on style suggest that the carving of Side B was later than the creation of Side A (Stephen Houston and Julia Guernsey, personal communications 2008). Pool (2007:274) believes there are two different styles present, and he comments that Side A was carved in a local style, whereas Side B presents a form and arrangement that suggests an Izapan style or one following early Maya conventions. Federico Fahsen (personal communication 2008) believes that there are similarities between the individuals portrayed on Sides A and B.

We think the artistic styles, composition, and content of the scenes are noticeably different. Both scenes relate to rulership, but specific aspects of that office are depicted from distinct perspectives. Side A is an uncluttered, rudimentary display of power and authority, whether it was communicated through representing captives or subservient nobles. It demonstrates the dominance and control of the Kaminaljuyu ruler or rulers. Side B appears to be a much more complex demonstration of the right to rule, possibly authorized by divine or ancestral relationships. Compared to the austere presentation on Side A, Side B contains a panoply of ceremonial regalia and paraphernalia, glyphic texts, and celestial bands. These dramatic differences argue for separate carving events and substantially different presentations. In addition to the formal differences, the presence of a glyphic text on Side B has also been seen as a factor that indicates a later date than the more symbolic Side A (Stephen Houston, personal communication 2008).

Evidence of Ancient Reuse and Recycling

The three-dimensional laser scanning data have allowed us to look at Monument 65 in ways that were not previously feasible. This stone monolith has undergone repeated and distinct modification events since its initial production. Observation of the surfaces, marks, and condition of the extant stone demonstrates an active history. With the scan data profiles and cross sections, measurements accurate to 0.01 mm can be made directly on the computer screen. These perspectives open new avenues of inquiry regarding the monument's use and reuse.

At some point or points in the stone's history, all outer edges were broken, possibly more than once (Figure 11.1). Figure 11.9 illustrates the vertical and horizontal medial cross sections of the stone; Figure 11.10 provides a key for the various regions of the carving discussed. The cross-section views show a significant difference between the planes of Side A, which is relatively flat, and Side B, which has a notable convex curvature horizontally. Defacement or a wearing away of the surface has occurred on both sides of the monument. On Side A, the deterioration appears limited to isolated portions of the carving and seems to be a result of natural wear on the surface. This condition is possibly

due to extended time on or under the ground or was caused by dragging the monolith along the ground with Side A down. Side B presents a very different appearance that may have been produced by the smoothing of the original carved surface in preparation for another, future carving or recycling event.

We argue that the surface of Side B was intentionally modified by a process of abrading and pecking to remove or diminish the earlier sculpted scene. The remnants of the erased, original carved surfaces across the entire face are relatively consistent, a condition that suggests the carving was intentionally smoothed. The substantial curvature of Side B (Figure 11.9b) makes it unlikely that natural weathering of the carving occurred at such a uniform rate and level across the bowed surface. Supporting the hypothesis of intentional abrasion is the fact that at the lower left corner of cut hole B9 is a carving of what may be a portion of an earflare or ornament that is clearly intrusive over the original scene (Stephen Houston, personal communication 2008). The sculpted lines of this invasive element are substantially deeper and wider and are cut in a different style and manner than those of the underlying sculpture. The more recent lines are literally carved down into the underlying sculpted scene and have no artistic or iconographic relationship to any portion of the scene on Side B. Why this earflare-like sculpture was initiated, and why it was not continued, is not known. The edges of this element, however, as well as other intrusive perforations and incisions to the surface of Side B, do not show a corresponding type or degree of wear present on the earlier underlying scene.

Directly above the right hand of figure C is an unusual design element that has been incised into Side B. The shape and depth of this element appears to be different from other portions of the sculpture. At this time, we cannot determine whether this feature was part of the original scene—or when it may have been carved.

The other invasive elements on Side B include two channels on the surface and two separate series of rectangular tapering holes in the stone. The grooving of the surface and the alignment

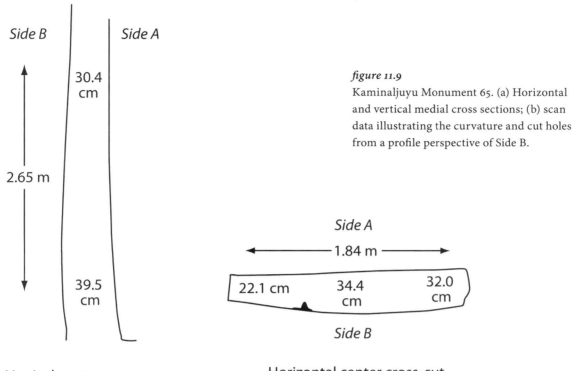

Side B   Side A

30.4 cm

2.65 m

39.5 cm

Vertical center cross-cut

figure 11.9
Kaminaljuyu Monument 65. (a) Horizontal and vertical medial cross sections; (b) scan data illustrating the curvature and cut holes from a profile perspective of Side B.

Side A

← 1.84 m →

22.1 cm   34.4 cm   32.0 cm

Side B

Horizontal center cross-cut

a

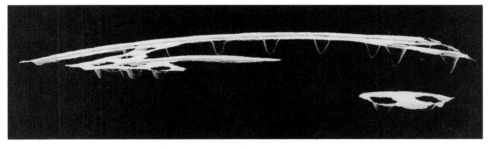

b

of the cut holes suggest that the stone was being readied for further modification but was abandoned before the process was completed. A series of cut sockets (B1–B7 in Figure 11.10) was placed along a diagonal groove incised across the surface of Side B. This layout suggests that a controlled break of the stone was going to be attempted along the perforated line. Evidence of this type of method for sectioning large stones is present on Takalik Abaj Monument 23, which was actually broken along a series of similar cut holes (Miguel Orrego Corzo and Christa Schieber de Lavarreda,

personal communication 2008). From the outline produced by the holes and incised grooves on Monument 65, it appears the ancient stonemasons were attempting to produce three slabs of stone of specific sizes and shapes. Cut hole B9 is intrusive over a portion of the earflare-like carving, indicating it and probably the other cut holes and scribed lines were made during a subsequent modification event.

The data listed in Tables 11.1–11.3 suggest that there were two distinct series of holes cut into the stone on Side B and that these penetrations

figure 11.10
Kaminaljuyu Monument 65, Side B, showing cut holes B1–B16.

were calculated and executed with exceptional care and precision. The widths of cut holes B1–B7, which comprise the upper line of perforations, vary by only 1.5 mm, the height varies by 3.5 mm, and the depth varies by 2.3 mm. These minimal dimensional differences demonstrate exceptional planning, consistency, and skill. Because of the precision and uniformity of these features, as well as a number of other observations, we do not believe the holes were made with a modern jackhammer, as conjectured by Kaplan (2000:193). The two upper wedges outlined by the pecked and drilled holes appear to represent axe-shaped blanks that could have been used as stelae

(Figure 11.11; John E. Clark, personal communication 2008). All the cutting work on Monument 65 is very regular and carefully done.

The existing outline or morphology created by the edges of Monument 65 suggests that the stone was recut after the two opposing scenes had been carved. The inwardly tapering upper edges of the monument intrude into the scenes carved on both Sides A and B. An assessment of the overall spatial position of the scenes indicates that neither one is complete, nor are they symmetrically placed on the stone as it exists today. These skewed spatial arrangements run counter to most other monumental sculptures from Kaminaljuyu, which are

Table 11.1
Dimensions of cut holes B1–B7, Kaminaljuyu Monument 65, Side B

CUT HOLE NUMBER	WIDTH (MM)	HEIGHT (MM)	DEPTH (MM)
B1	70.6	64.4	71.3
B2	70.1	61.3	71.8
B3	70.9	63.1	73.3
B4	70.7	61.7	73.2
B5	69.8	61.5	73.6
B6	70.0	61.5	73.5
B7	69.4	60.9	73.6

Table 11.2
Distance between cut holes B1–B7, Kaminaljuyu Monument 65, Side B

HOLE PAIR	DISTANCE (MM)
B1 and B2	117.7
B2 and B3	118.6
B3 and B4	149.2
B4 and B5	128.7
B5 and B6	130.4
B6 and B7	121.9

Table 11.3
Dimensions of cut holes B8–B16, Kaminaljuyu Monument 65, Side B

CUT HOLE NUMBER	WIDTH (MM)	HEIGHT (MM)	DEPTH (MM)
B8	107.1	90.1	91.9
B9	101.6	87.4	91.2
B10	102.3	86.5	na
B11	107.1	93.2	na
B12	106.5	93.9	na
B13	106.6	94.7	na
B14	104.5	94.7	na
B15	106.1	91.0	91.4
B16	107.8	90.3	91.7

Note: na, not available.

figure 11.11
Kaminaljuyu Monument 65, Side B. Three-dimensional scan data clipped to reveal the two upper wedges outlined by pecked and drilled holes that could be recycled as stelae.

centered on the stone and symmetrical in layout and design (e.g., Altar 2 and Stelae 3, 4, 5, and 23; see Parsons 1986).

A glance at Side A shows that the three rows of figures are not in a vertically central position relative to the edges of the stone. The horizontal spacing between each of the figures in the upper and middle tiers is exceptionally consistent, yet personages 1a, 2a, and 3a are at or near the left edge of the stone, whereas personages 1c and 2c

have at least twice the space between them and the right edge (Figures 11.1 and 11.2). Furthermore, the top of the headdress on personage 2a has been cut into by a later modification of the stone's edge; the same thing has happened to personage 1c. Although the top lines of their headdresses are still discernable, they have been affected by edge modifications, and these changes appear to have been made without regard for the carved scene. The lower left and right portions of the stone were both broken and, along with the bottom, are now covered by the concrete mounting that supports this massive monument.

Similar observations of Side B also suggest the shape of the stone was modified after the scene was carved. The upper inward-tapering edges of Side B have cuts into both the left and right extremes of the celestial band, but if the scene were originally symmetrical, the right side has been invaded to a greater degree (Figure 11.5). This modification of the stone shifted the scene to the viewer's right; the shift on Side A was in the opposite direction. These conditions suggest the opposing carvings were originally centered with each other and probably on the stone itself. Thus it appears that the tapered upper edges were the result of intentional breakage of the stone, a conclusion based on the faint remnants of cut holes visible from Side B that are present along the two edges.

Based on observations that are supported by the scan data, we can deduce or identify the following events in the life of Monument 65:

1. The stone was quarried and hauled to Kaminaljuyu.
2. Both faces of the monument were carved.
3. The outer edges of the monument were intentionally modified to create a new form after the scenes on Sides A and B were carved.
4. Side B was partially abraded.
5. An earspool-like element was carved into the surface of Side B.
6. Two diagonal grooves were pecked into the surface of Side B.[6]
7. A series of seven consistently sized holes were cut along the upper of the two inscribed grooves on Side B.
8. A second series of consistently sized holes, which differ significantly from the dimensions of the previous series, were also cut into Side B.
9. The monument was abandoned and experienced deterioration and erosion from exposure to the natural elements.
10. The bottom of the stone was broken in 1983 during its rediscovery and excavation.

11. The monument was moved from its location near the intersection of Avenida 30 and Calle 6, Zone 7, in present-day Guatemala City to the National Museum of Archaeology and Ethnology, and its base was imbedded in cement so it could be exhibited in an upright position.

Currently the temporal order of these events cannot be established unequivocally, but the general history of the stone's use and reuse is reasonably clear. It is also evident that the precision and care taken to produce the actions described in steps 6–8 do not constitute monument destruction but instead demonstrate intentional recycling of the monument. It was very likely going to be the source of two or three new monuments. Had the ancients wanted to break this stone as an act of iconoclasm, they could have done so easily with a few well-directed blows with another heavy stone (John Clark, personal communication 2008).

The reasons for the abrading of the surface of Side B, as opposed to Side A, are also uncertain. It is possible that Side B was effaced to change the political message on the stone. Alternatively, Side B may have served a more technical function, or it could simply have been a matter of convenience (i.e., Side B was easier to access). In any case, it does not appear that the completed or anticipated modifications to Kaminaljuyu Monument 65 were made with a concern for preserving the scenes carved on Sides A or B. Figure 11.12 illustrates that the breakage of the stone along the perforated cut holes would have destroyed the scene on Side A just as effectively as they would have eliminated the scene on Side B. Therefore it is possible that the modifications were not intended to maintain or preserve either of the earlier low-relief scenes. We do not know the timing or circumstances surrounding the attempted partition of Monument 65 into derivative monuments, but the meaning of the original carvings does not appear to have been something that the later artisans tried to save. It may be that the principal attribute of concern was the essence of this ancient, sacred stone as a connection to ancestors and other cosmic forces, as described by David Stuart in Chapter 12.

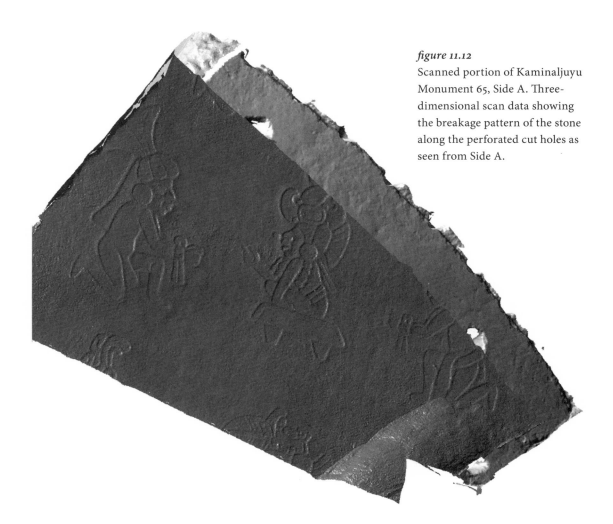

figure 11.12
Scanned portion of Kaminaljuyu
Monument 65, Side A. Three-
dimensional scan data showing
the breakage pattern of the stone
along the perforated cut holes as
seen from Side A.

Concluding Remarks

Parsons's (1986:58) statement that Kaminaljuyu Monument 65 has "not yet been fully interpreted" remains true, but three-dimensional laser scanning has advanced us toward this goal. The successful retrieval of new information and iconographic details from the close-range scanning of Monument 65 demonstrates that laser scanning technology can significantly enhance the analysis of Mesoamerican sculptures (Figure 11.13). The multiple challenges to perception and interpretation presented by Monument 65 are representative of those encountered for monuments across Mesoamerica.

We have demonstrated that substantial new information can be extracted from defaced and eroded monuments through the capture and processing of scan data. Previously indistinguishable features can be recovered. As demonstrated with Monument 65, sculptures can be viewed in three dimensions, as their original creators intended them to be seen. Furthermore, the life history of a monument can be traced through identification of tool marks and other traces of production, modification, use, and recycling. With laser scanning, the formal and metric documentation of a sculpture is complete and serves as the best-available recording technique for multiple types of analyses, as well as for use in preservation and conservation.

Three-dimensional laser scanning and the associated software needed for its presentation are advancing at a rapid rate. Our own efforts demonstrate that the capabilities of the data will continue to expand, and refinements will offer even greater detail and insight. This technology is a powerful evolving tool for the documentation

figure 11.13
Kaminaljuyu Monument 65,
Side B. Three-dimensional
scan data visualized.

and interpretation of Preclassic Mesoamerican sculpture. High-resolution three-dimensional laser scanning can be routinely incorporated into research designs. These data and images, if used by archaeologists, epigraphers, and iconographers, would allow the analysis and interpretation of Preclassic sculptures to move to a new, more inclusive, and definitive level. Our initial efforts with Monument 65 show the promise of this technique—and the need for it.

Acknowledgments

We thank Jan M. Ziolkowski, director of Dumbarton Oaks, and Joanne Pillsbury, director of Pre-Columbian Studies at Dumbarton Oaks, for the opportunity to participate in the symposium on Preclassic sculpture, where the original version of this chapter was presented. We are especially grateful for the assistance, comments, and editorial suggestions of John Clark, Julia Guernsey, and Barbara Arroyo, the organizers of this conference. The open communication and sharing of ideas with Stephen Houston, Federico Fahsen, David Freidel, Mary Pohl, Miguel Orrego Corzo, and Christa Schieber de Lavarreda has significantly improved our work. The exceptional cooperation and assistance provided by Claudia Monzón Sosa de Jiménez, director of the Museo Nacional de Arqueología y Etnología, Guatemala City, and her staff made the documentation of Kaminaljuyu Monument 65 possible. We are also grateful for the cooperation of the Ministerio de Cultura y Deportes and the Dirección General del Patrimonio Cultural y Natural de Guatemala. Thanks to Dan Perreault of NeoMetrics Technologies for lending his technical expertise and to James McLeod, Rebecca O'Sullivan, and Edward Krause, students from the University of South Florida, for their assistance. Funding for portions of this documentation project was provided by the New World Archaeological Foundation of Brigham Young University and a major research grant from the Foundation for the Advancement of Mesoamerican Studies. We thank these institutions for their support.

NOTES

1. To document Mesoamerican monumental sculptures, we used a Konica-Minolta VIVID 9i Laser Digitizer, a close-range scanner that excels at high-precision three-dimensional measurement and is capable of a fast processing speed for rapid and straightforward merging and editing of large amounts of measurement data. The choice of the VIVID 9i was also due to its proven ability to produce exceptional results in a variety of locales (e.g., labs, bodegas, museums, and archaeological sites) and under a range of physical and climatic conditions (Doering et al. 2006). The remarkable accuracy, detail, and clarity of the images are due to the ability to record surfaces at an accuracy approaching 0.05 mm (Konica-Minolta 2007), less than the diameter of a human hair.

2. To view the fully three-dimensional data sets available, the Geomagic Review free inspection software is one example of an available product that allows viewing of files created by Geomagic software. This software is available for free downloading and use at http://www.geomagic.com/en/products qualify/review/index.php.

3. The Kaminaljuyu Sculpture Project, funded by the Foundation for the Advancement of Mesoamerican Studies, provides the basis for an expandable three-dimensional database of sculpted stone monuments for all periods, and the results (Doering and Collins 2008) are available at http://www.research.famsi.org/3D_imaging/index.php. Further technical information can be found at http://www.AIST.cas.usf.edu.

4. Enhancements in software image editing are not without subjective decisions, but the level of subjectivity is reduced over artistic renderings (Read and Chippindale 2000:75).

5. This collaborative effort is designed to devise the best ways to translate the data into clean line drawings that are faithful to the quality of the original lines on the stone or to its calligraphic quality. A critical issue is to sort out verified details versus possible details. Figure 11.5 is more generous than Figure 11.4 in its assessment of confirmed and tenuous details of the carved image.

6. The scenes on Sides A and B may have been sculpted simultaneously or during discrete events. The final carving of Mesoamerican stone monuments was usually completed close to the location where the monument was placed. This procedure eliminated damage to the piece or its carved details during transport (Stephen Houston, personal communication 2008).

12

Shining Stones

Observations on the Ritual Meaning of Early Maya Stelae

DAVID STUART

ARCHAEOLOGICAL INVESTIGATIONS IN THE past two or three decades show that free-standing stone monuments have a considerable time depth in the Maya area, with its beginnings traceable as far back as the Middle Preclassic. Such time depth of stelae and altars would no doubt surprise Mayanists of earlier generations, when the so-called "stela cult" was seen as a hallmark of lowland Classic Maya civilization, a relatively late adoption of a monumental tradition originating far afield among cultures to the south or west. But just as other key aspects of what has traditionally been considered "Classic"—urbanism, monumental architecture, and the institution of kingship—have been pushed back centuries in time, so too has the dating of monumental sculptures and the meanings we associate with them.

The present chapter considers the difficult issue of how we interpret early stelae and related stone monuments, in the very broadest sense, as material representations in and of themselves, putting aside their role as media for sculptural decoration.

In doing so, I assume that some of these meanings can be extrapolated from textual and iconographic evidence from Classic Maya sources. The rich language the ancient Maya used to describe and label monuments surely had considerable time depth, and their words therefore presumably illuminate a number of far older meanings and metaphors associated with monuments and the idea of monumentality. Stelae were very complex symbols in their own right, far richer in their ritual cosmological significance than is implied by the deceptively simple term Maya scribes used to refer to them—"*lakam tuunoob*," or "large stones."[1]

The Question of Sculpture

A short distance to the west of the main plaza at the Classic Maya site of Palenque, Chiapas, beside the trail that winds its way among the unexcavated ruins in the dense forest, stands a tall, thin erect stone known as La Picota (Figure 12.1a). It is uncarved and bears little evidence of being shaped by human hands, making for a strange sight among Palenque's other better-known buildings and artworks (all the more so because Palenque has only two stelae in its corpus of monuments). The significance of La Picota remains a mystery, but it may be significantly earlier in date than most other Palenque monuments, given the early remains so far identified in the surrounding area (Rands 1974).

The very presence of such a monument in the great Classic city raises one simple question at the heart of this study: what does an undecorated upright monument "do"?

Palenque's La Picota is one example of a widespread phenomenon—plain monuments in fact abound at many Classic Maya sites. At Tikal, in fact, uncarved stelae outnumber carved ones and dominate at the ritually important Twin Pyramid

a

b

figure 12.1
Plain monuments from the Classic and Preclassic Maya area. (a) La Picota monument, Palenque, Chiapas; (b) basalt column stela from Naranjo, Guatemala. (Photographs by the author.)

complexes. Some have wondered whether "plain" is a proper description. Could they have once been elaborately painted, sometimes with a plaster veneer? Certainly this is a possibility, and such early writers as Maler (1911:62) and Morley (1938:235) suggested as much, apparently unable to believe that stelae could serve any purpose without any decorative imagery. The same argument has been made more recently in connection with plain monuments on the Pacific slope region of southern Mesoamerica (e.g., Norman 1973). However, I am struck by the lack of physical evidence of stucco relief or of painted line work on any so-called "plain" monuments. Given the large number of such stones in the archaeological record, I would expect to see at least some evidence of preserved plaster on exposed stone. The evidence suggests that uncarved stelae alone were somehow significant, or that, as Clancy (1985:60) notes, "the plaza monument, whether or not carved imagery was added, must have had a special meaning in itself."

The discovery of several basalt stelae and altars at the early highland site of Naranjo, Guatemala, shows that the public display of upright stones has far greater time depth in the Maya area than previously supposed (see Chapter 1; Arroyo et al. 2007; Pereira et al. 2007). The stones, some shaped and some in their natural form as basaltic columns (Figure 12.1b), seem to date to ca 750 BC, making them among the earliest known stelae in Mesoamerica (Barbara Arroyo, personal communication 2007). Their familiar shapes and linear arrangements in front of architecture manifests a pattern that would last for two millennia, culminating in the vast number of Classic stelae, with their images of kingly ritual. The Naranjo monuments are for the most part uncarved, existing on their own as imposing erect shapes on a landscape. Their natural form and lack of decoration suggest a very ancient concern with the intrinsic idea of stone monumentality—as form and as material—without so much emphasis on their potential role as a medium for carved images and portraits. It is a pattern that lasted well into the Classic period, when even complex carvings seem to complement the more elemental idea behind the stone

into which they were hewn. As Clancy (1985:60) has noted:

> The earliest Maya stelae tended to be used in a freshly quarried, rough state. There was little concern for smoothing the stone into flat surfaces; it was left in a more natural state with the protrusions, cavities, and pits typical of limestone. The relief-carved images were forced to follow the irregularities of the stone, and the images often seem of secondary concern.

Such ancient regard for a sculpted stone's natural shape and form, even including the rock's imperfections, does indeed seem to have been important in the design and production of monuments. We see this vividly in a number of early stelae from the region of Peten, Guatemala, such as Stela 31 from Tikal, with its tapered and somewhat irregular top—its carved surface follows the stone's natural contours, accommodating several dips and irregularities. I disagree slightly with Clancy, however, in her characterization of such early stelae being in a "rough state." Maya artists and sculptors took great pains to smooth and burnish these intricate monuments, to the point where the finished surfaces almost shine and reflect light. When such monuments as Stela 31 are found extremely well preserved—not a commonplace happening, unfortunately—their sculpted and finished surfaces can still be spectacular, even as they adhere to the natural shape and contours of the stone.

The ancient Maya terminology for stone monuments reflects a similar emphasis on material substance. Classic inscriptions make constant use of the Mayan word for "stone" in various terms that refer to stelae and altars of various types. Most common is simply *tuun* or *lakam tuun*, both generic terms used for stelae (Justeson and Mathews 1983; Stuart 1996). The word "lakam tuun" survived in colonial Yucatec Mayan as "*piedra enorme*" and also served as a place name, Lacantun, or Lacandon. Other smaller types of stones mentioned in the inscriptions took a variety of names that are more descriptive of the sorts of ritual actions associated with them, including *sibik tuun* ("soot stone"), *kuch tuun* ("carrying stone"), or *taj tuun* ("torch stone"). These terms probably describe certain forms that we would class as altars. Other hieroglyphic terms also exist that still elude decipherment, but the common thread among all of them is "tuun," the very basic idea of "stoniness." The consistency of such language suggests that wood and other potential materials were far less important in monument production and had their own specific roles as artistic media.

The self-referential phrases inscribed on Classic stelae typically describe the rituals surrounding the stone's dedication and placement. On key calendrical dates many stelae were "erected" (*tz'ap*) like a post, and others were "stood up" (*wa'*) on the ground. The later word wa' in Mayan languages refers mainly to an erect bodily position, and it is probably no coincidence that this term occurs most commonly on statue-like stone sculptures from Toniná, Chiapas, where the bodily metaphor is most obvious. The short inscription on the back of the three-dimensional Monument 30, for example, revealingly says: *"wa'laj u lakam tuunil ? Chapaht"* (the big stone of ? Chapaht stands up.)

The use of a standard dedication phrase, such as "his big stone stands up," emphasizes the corporeal quality for the vertically placed monuments and the figural images they bear. As the discussions below attempt to demonstrate, the meanings of stelae were more multilayered, based on the material substance of stone and metaphors of the human body, but at times also referencing animate qualities, other types of precious stones, and ideas of temporal permanence.

The Materiality of Animate Stone

We have seen that the substance of stone was somehow an elemental and meaningful attribute of monuments of many varied designs and settings. Basic to this concept, presumably, was the notion that stone is an inherently powerful and timeless substance, a permanent material both of the earth and transcendent, evoking other spatial realms and categories. Stone lines the walls of caves, and it also juts out into the air in mountainous terrain, often as pinnacles or large exposed cliffs. This approach to thinking about stone and stones might seem obvious at first—permanence seems a de facto requirement of any true monument, after all—but I believe that the Maya and other Mesoamericans saw upright stones and associated altars, both carved and uncarved, as evoking the very natural substance of the earth and its interior. This emphasis on the intrinsic meanings of stone—on its materiality—offers rough but interesting parallels with recent interpretations of megalithic stone monuments elsewhere in the ancient world, most particularly in Neolithic Europe (Tilley and Bennett 2004).

The placement of stone monuments in ritual architectural settings dates to the Early Preclassic, but it becomes much more formalized and widespread by the Middle Preclassic (Clancy 1990), when we also find the curious appearance of large and carefully composed figures hewn into exposed surfaces of bedrock and cliffs, very far removed from built-up ceremonial centers (see Chapter 1). One outstanding example from the Maya region is the figural sculpture from Xoc, Chiapas (Ekholm-Miller 1973), with its Olmec-style representation of a standing deity or deity impersonator (Figure 12.2a). The immense relief of a ruler carved above the entrance to Loltun Cave, Yucatan, is a Late Preclassic example of a similar phenomenon (Grube and Schele 1996; Thompson 1897). These cases represent two of the earliest reliefs found anywhere in the Maya region, predating or at least contemporary with (in Loltun's case) the earliest known carved stelae in the lowlands. I suggest that these two settings for sculptural presentations—rock faces and monuments—might therefore be intimately related conceptually. The more natural settings of sculptures at Xoc or Loltun operate as part of a landscape, as monuments carved into the hard material substance of the earth. Even well into the Classic period we see the same idea at work in the immense cliff carving at San Diego, Peten, with an overall design indistinguishable from the

a

b

figure 12.2
Early cliff sculptures from the Maya area. (a) Middle Preclassic
Olmec relief carving at Xoc, Chiapas (after Ekholm-Miller
1973:9, fig. 8); (b) Early Classic relief at San Diego, Peten (after
VanKirk and Bassett-VanKirk 1996:131–132).

image and text presentation of a freestanding stela
(Figure 12.2b). The isolated images of kingly ritual
on caves and cliffs at Loltun and San Diego might
at first seem odd and out of place, but I believe that
they reveal a telling natural aspect of stelae and
their significance as extensions of the earth's core
substance, a sort of portable bedrock.[2] The simplicity of the very name "lakam tuun" ("large stone")
thus takes on a more complex significance, as the
material of tuun is one of the underlying points of
any stela's existence in the first place. One might
also easily imagine how the placement of monuments in and around ceremonial plazas, platforms,
and pyramids added a key naturalistic element of
exposed rock to the design of artificial landscapes,
with their human-made mountain-pyramids,
cave-shrines, and pool-like courtyards.

The importance of naturally exposed rocks,
boulders, and cliffs in ceremonial landscapes is
well known both archaeologically and ethno-
graphically in Mesoamerica and beyond (Brown
2005; Bullard 1963; Dean 2007; Kintz 1990; McGee
1990:57; Wisdom 1940:428). The basic connection
I draw between such natural features and monumental stones is reflected in Mayan languages.
Among the Ch'orti' Maya, for example, the word
"*ch'en*" means not only "cave" (its old and widespread significance) but also any kind of craggy
boulder or large expanse of a cliff or of bedrock.
The exposed faces of prominent rocks, fissures,
and waterholes are known among the Tzotzil of
Zinacantan as *ch'enetik*: "'openings' in the earth's
crust, hence means of communication with the
Earth Lord" (Vogt 1969:387). In some highland

a   b

figure 12.3

The animate spirit of tuun ("stone") in Maya art and writing. (a) Support for Piedras Negras Altar 4;
(b) stone molar from mouth-doorway of Copan Temple 22. (Photograph and drawing by the author.)

Mayan languages the meanings of ch'en, or its cognate form *k'en,* came to be extended simply to "stone" and/or "metal" (e.g., Poqomchi'[Popti'] ch'en, "piedra, metal, *hierro*" ["stone, metal, iron"] < proto-Mayan *k'eʔn, "cueva"* ["cave"] [Kaufman 2003])—an important association of two materials that is important in the following discussion.

The ancient Maya also saw an essential animate essence in precious rocks and prominent stones. Evidence of this concept comes from numerous ethnographic and iconographic sources. In highland Chiapas, numerous ritual objects are thought to possess a *ch'ulel* ("soul"), including stone crosses and sacred images (Vogt 1969). Kintz (1990:15, 38) observes that the present-day Yucatec Maya of Coba acknowledge the existence of spirits called *"tun"* that inhabit large stones found in the forest. Although Kintz does not say so, one wonders

whether this spirit or essence of tun holds a special significance at Coba, amidst the vast ruins and stone monuments still standing in the dense forest surrounding the present-day village. As a youngster living in Coba in the mid-1970s (when Kintz was also living and working there), I well remember how the ancient stela reset before the La Iglesia pyramid was considered a *rey* ("king"). The pyramid was regularly the site of family rituals and an object of veneration and prayer among the members of the community (also a common occurrence at Takalik Abaj; see Chapter 8).

This animate spirit of stone appears with great frequency in Maya iconography, where it assumes the form of a so-called "cauac monster" (Spero 1991; Tate 1980; Taylor 1978).[3] Some of the best examples of the stone entity appear on the pedestal stones of Piedras Negras Altar 4, as supports for a larger table top representing a jaguar's paw. Together the components of the altar "spell" the hieroglyphic elements of Piedras Negras's place name, "Paw Stone," otherwise shown using a standard tuun glyph. These pedestals are literally the faces of animate stone, seen throughout much of Maya art and hieroglyphic writing (Figure 12.3a). In other examples, we see how more subtle stone elements take on a living form, as in the large molar teeth that flank the cave-doorway on Temple 22 at Copan, Honduras (Figure 12.3b). Even the teeth of a mountain are considered alive.

Curiously, this animate tuun entity in Classic Maya art bears a very strong resemblance to Chahk, the animate force of rain and storms. Both share a basic reptilian countenance not found on other supernatural beings, characterized by large curled eyes, a long muzzle, a large fanged mouth, and a frontal hair knot. Some tuun heads also display the distinctive shell ear (or ear ornament) that is a key diagnostic of many Chahk portraits (Taube 1992). What accounts for this association? It derives, I think, from two related concepts. One is that Chahk is himself considered an inhabitant of stony environments, such as mountain tops and mountain caves, where the clouds and mists of rain emerge from the earth. As I explore in more depth below, the other conceptual link between the rain god and stone concerns the more specific idea of lightning. The "strike of Chahk," as it is called in some Mayan languages, was seen as the creative force behind special stones holding sacred qualities. Even to this day, Maya and other Mesoamerican peoples commonly believe that obsidian, jade, and other special rocks that shine and reflect light appear as a result of lightning striking the earth (Taube 2000b:290–291). The brilliant surfaces of these stones no doubt account for this idea, and it is surprisingly widespread. Such notions of shining, sacred "lightning stones" probably had considerable time depth among the ancient Maya, and as a category they may well have encompassed large worked monuments and sculptures.

Also related to this array of meanings is the important concept of monumental stones as embodiments of abstract time. Among the Classic Maya, a 360-day period of the Long Count was sometimes called a "tuun." These periods were individually tallied into groups of twenty, corresponding to the K'atun period (Stuart 1996). For the Maya of Yucatan, at least up to the sixteenth century, large stones also served as direct markers for K'atun periods and their subdivisions. As Friar Diego de Landa described in the sixteenth century:

> There are in the plaza of that city (Mayapan) seven or eight stones, each about ten feet long and rounded on one side, well worked and containing several lines of characters which they use, and which cannot be read . . . the native, when asked about this, reply that they were accustomed to erect one of these stones every twenty years, which was the number they use in counting their cycles. [Tozzer 1941:38–39]

The historian, Friar Diego López de Cogolludo (cited in Tozzer 1941:38) wrote more specifically: "Their lustres coming in periods of five years, which made twenty years, which they call K'atun, they placed an engraved stone upon another which was also engraved, and set it with lime and sand in the walls of their temples."

Landa's and López de Cogolludo's statements help explain why tuun came to be mistakenly translated as "year," when its true literal sense was always "stone." "Year" came about as an imprecise translation in late nineteenth- and early twentieth-century scholarship, from settings where Yucatec tun clearly stood for the 360-day unit of the calendar. Properly speaking, "year" in Mayan languages is "haab" or some cognate thereof.

The role of stones as embodiments of temporal units also can be traced among the Classic and even Preclassic Maya. Inscriptions from the Classic period regularly show that numbered "stones" refer to markers for the individual 360-day units in a K'atun. The word "K'atun," in turn, surely originated as "k'altuun" ("twenty stones") or, more literally, a term for the fastening or binding (k'al) of the accumulated set of stones. This basic term was widely used in reference to the most important type of period-ending rituals. But what were these stones? No obvious archaeological remains from the Maya area show discrete sets of twenty monumental altars or stelae dedicated in a K'atun period, or otherwise seem reflective of the pattern. Landa's statement indicates, however, that tallies of actual year-stones did in fact occur among the contact-period Maya. These were not necessarily monuments, but rather, it seems, more nondescript and even unsculpted markers, and one can easily imagine that simple, shaped but uncarved stones and altars at Maya sites held similar meanings.

It was at major Period Endings—stations of the K'atun or its four subdivisions—that the Classic Maya did occasionally provide labels, often simply carving Ajaw day signs on them. The numerous altars of Caracol, Belize, provide excellent examples, and various similar giant Ajaw altars can be found at numerous sites, from Toniná to Copan and northern Yucatan. The same idea could also be applied to those stelae on which similar large Ajaw dates dominate textual presentations, as on El Palma Stela 5 (Figure 12.4) or Machaquilá Stela 12. The time-marking function of Classic stelae also comes across simply and directly in the designations used for many monuments, such as "The One Ajaw Stone," "The Six Ajaw Stone," where the Ajaw date stands as a short-hand reference to the period commemorated.

figure 12.4
El Palma Stela 5,
Chiapas. (Drawing
by the author.)

Monuments and Lightning Stones

In a variety of ways, then, stelae and other monumental sacred stones were used for the marking and perhaps even the embodiment of sacred time periods. And with their important functions as stones bearing portraits and images of kingly ritual, there is little doubt that stelae also held complex layered meanings revolving around embodiments of royal persons and ceremonial actions. I think we can bring some of these conceptions into sharper focus by looking at the ways that monuments themselves were described in ancient Maya inscriptions, pressing beyond the basic categories of tuun and the metaphorical beings involving time and the king.

An important step forward in the understanding of one of these metaphors was James Porter's suggestion that Middle Preclassic Olmec monuments at La Venta and elsewhere were celtiform stelae, that is, intentionally shaped and carved to echo the appearance of the ceremonial jade celts so important in Olmec ceremonialism (Porter 1992; Taube 2000a). Independently, work at about the same time in the decipherment of inscriptions on Maya stelae showed a very similar idea at work, pointing to an explicit understanding of stelae not just as vaguely precious stones, but as large, monumental celts and axes.

A key to this realization is the so-called "mirror" sign in Maya script (Figure 12.5a,b). The first detailed study of the sign was by Jeffrey Miller, who in the early 1970s began to analyze the sign as a representation of a mirror—an idea that Linda Schele greatly expanded upon in a joint work published after Miller's untimely death (Schele and Miller 1983). Miller's identification stemmed from the appearance of the same design in the smoking forehead of K'awiil (God K), a deity that Miller's mentor, Michael Coe, had suggested was the Maya precursor to the Mexica deity Tezcatlipoca, "Smoking Mirror." Although this specific identification may still be debated, Miller's idea that the simple curved parallel lines represent a reflective mirror still has much support and wide acceptance. Today we prefer to see the motif not so specifically as a mirror representation but rather as a more

general marker of shining and resplendent surfaces (Leonard and Taube 2007; Schele and Miller 1986:43). As a hieroglyphic sign, this "shiner" element is clearly a visual equal to the celts shown hanging from the ritual belts of Maya kings, nearly always in two or three sets of three. Such thin and beautifully worked and polished objects are known archaeologically, the most famous being the Leiden Plaque. Many other examples of such objects are known from Maya art, but very few have adequate archaeological context.

As a glyph, iconographic motif, or costume element, the mirror or shiner is nearly ubiquitous. It also has an animate form as a deity face with a large eye, "mirror" lines on the forehead, and a large open mouth with prominent teeth. In some cases this form seems to overlap with the animate forms of stone already mentioned, but they are largely separate forms.[4] The animate mirror or shiner face is perhaps best known as the head on the large loincloths worn on the belts of royal costumes and often misinterpreted to be representations of the trunk of a sacred tree (e.g., Schele and Miller 1986:77). The very same head, in profile, appears also as an animated axe blade or celt, often in the forehead of K'awiil, the deity that embodied Classic Maya notions of agricultural abundance and dynastic procreation (Figure 12.5c).

Establishing the precise word value for the mirror or shine glyph has proved difficult over the years. Here I tentatively suggest that it may be a logogram read **LEM**, a widespread Mayan root meaning "to shine," often derived as a noun for "flash" or for any object that possesses such a quality, such as a mirror, glass, or things made of metal or of polished stone. There is as yet no firm phonetic confirmation for the **LEM** reading, but whatever the value, there is wide agreement that the mirror sign must be semantically close to these meanings.

Lem exists too as a word for "lightning bolt," as in Ch'olti' "*u lem Chahak (vlem chahac)*," "*resplandor del rayo, relámpago*" ("light of lightning, lightning bolt"), or literally "Chahk's flash" (Morán 1689–1695 [1929]). The sacred axe wielded by Chahk in his numerous ancient portraits is

figure 12.5
The so-called "mirror" sign in Maya
art and writing. (a, b) Standard and
animate forms of the glyph **LEM?**
("shine, flash"); (c) axe in the forehead of K'awiil (drawings a, b, and c
by Ian Graham); (d) axe of the storm
god Chahk (drawing from Miller and
Martin 2004:fig. 14b).

a

b

c

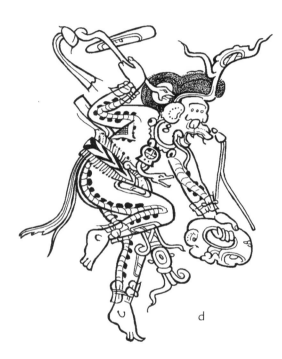

d

thought to be the very instrument of lightning
(Figure 12.5d), thereby pointing to a close connection or even equation between lightning bolts and
the polished axe of the deity, both being manifestations of lem. Ethnographic sources from across
Mesoamerica—and even well beyond—point to
the same association, with shiny ancient stones,
such as shiny greenstone axes or obsidian, considered creations of the storm god and strikes of
lightning. (More practical axes used in everyday
work are primarily made of chert, a more mundane and somewhat more readily available stone
material, at least in the Maya Lowlands.) Among
the Ch'orti' Maya, Wisdom (1940:382) noted that

ancient stone axes found in milpas and on the landscape were considered to be used by the storm gods
to make rain and lightning. Similarly, among the
Ch'ol, obsidian axes and blades found in arroyos
and forests are known as "*jacha lac mam*" ("axes
of our grandfathers") and are said to be produced
by lightning striking the ground (Aulie and Aulie
1978). We have already seen a special visual connection between the animate face of stone (tuun)
and Chahk, and I believe these same associations
among rain, lightning flashes, and precious shining stones lie at the heart of the curious overlap.

Because lightning was widely seen as caused by
the striking or throwing of Chahk's stone or metal

axe—and thus causing the appearance of shining stones—it seems appropriate that a glyph for lem would mark Chahk's axe and large hammer-like hand stone. "Lem" therefore seems to me to be a strong contender for the reading of the sign, although the evidence still remains circumstantial. In Mayan languages, "lem" can stand as a modifier on nouns ("shiny") or as a noun itself ("a shiny thing," or "a flash"). As shown below, this reading fits remarkably well with the many contexts for the shiner glyph in Maya texts. More work will be needed, of course, to confirm this proposal.

A simple use of the shiner glyph appears on an actual inscribed celt of Late Classic date, where it clearly stands as a term for the celt itself, perhaps reading **U-LEM?**, "his shiner" or "his flash." The full text reads "and then his 'shiner' gets fashioned." Another Maya celt of Early Classic date bears a more complex inscription that is also clear in equating the shining celt hieroglyph to the celt object (Figure 12.6). Much of the inscription is missing, but the text opens with the statement

?-CHAN-LEM?   U-K'ABA'   U-ka-ya-wa-ka?
Chan Lem(?) u k'aba' u kaywak ["The ?-Sky-Shiner is the name of his 'celt.'"]

Here the word "kaywak"—also found on several other inscribed celts—no doubt serves as the actual ancient term for this type of celt object (Stephen Houston, personal communication 1992). Its proper name is ?-Sky-Shiner or ?-Sky-Flash, a possible allusion to lightning. In this regard, it is perhaps relevant that many ceremonial belts worn by rulers take the form of celestial bands, from which such "flashing" celt objects were suspended. They may have been likened in some way to lightning flashes descending from the heavens.

The possible **LEM** glyph also appears in very similar types of inscriptions on stelae, drawing a clear association between celts and upright stone monuments. Numerous Classic Maya stelae had proper names, not unlike architectural spaces, deities, and people. Their identification was first made in 1986 during work on the inscriptions of Copan

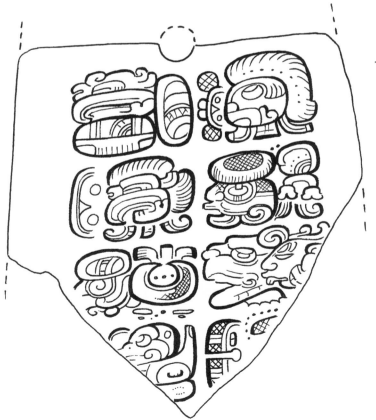

figure 12.6
Inscribed Early Classic celt (kaywak), named in the initial glyph as ?-Sky-Shiner(?). (Drawing by the author.)

and Quirigua (Stuart 1986), and the names have been studied by several writers (Looper 2003; Newsome 2001). We see the parallel use of the shiner or flash glyph most clearly in these inscriptions, where, just as on the Early Classic celt just described, the sign always appears as the final element after a string of modifiers ("the such-and-such 'Shiner'"). Copan Stela 9 bears the name Yaxk'in Tuun Lem(?), "New-Sun-Stone-Shiner(?)" (Figure 12.7a). Copan's Stela C, a Late Classic monument, bears a dedicatory

text that also includes a proper name, damaged but fairly legible as ?-Chaaj-Stone-Shiner(?).

It is interesting to note that Stela C and a few other Copan monuments preserve much of their original red paint, and where it is visible we see that the original surface of the monument was highly burnished, to the point of being almost reflective of light. The surface treatment of Maya stelae is hardly ever well preserved, but I suspect that burnishing and polishing was common on many of the fine

figure 12.7
Proper names of
(a) Copan Stela 9;
(b) Copan Stela 63.
(Drawings by the author.)

a

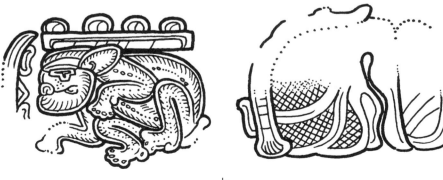

b

sculptures decorating Maya pyramids and plazas. Recent chemical analyses of preserved paint on the Rosalila Temple at Copan has shown that mica was included, clearly indicating a desire to create a reflective and sparkling appearance to the building's exterior (Goodall et al. 2006). Kaminaljuyu Stela 10 (see Figure 1.9) offers a well-preserved example of a Late Preclassic sculpture with a heavily polished surface, and the resemblance of such examples to the treatment of portable jade and greenstone objects is probably not coincidental. I suspect that sacred stones of various sizes, shapes, and materials were intended to shine, sparkle, or reflect light.

Turning to another Copan monument from the Early Classic, Stela 63, we find another revealing hieroglyphic self-description (Figure 12.7b). This monument was dedicated by Ruler 4 of Copan to commemorate his ancestor's oversight of the great Bak'tun ending on 9.0.0.0.0 8 Ajaw 13 Keh, and it was placed inside an enclosed shrine (named Papagayo) that evidently served as a focus of ceremonial activity for nearly two centuries. The inscription refers to the stela as the lakam lem(?) ("large shiner(?)") instead of the far more customary and generic phrase lakam tuun ("large stone").

The equivalence of Maya stelae with celts and axes was also conveyed through very direct symbolic representation on monuments, with Copan Stela J being a key example (Figure 12.8). Here on its west or front side we see a large deified face, with rectangular eyes and an inverted T-shaped mouth. It is marked also by kaywak motifs near its top. Baudez (1994) has interpreted the visage of Stela J as a portrait of the Sun God, specifically a representation of the setting sun, facing westward. Yet there are no specific solar characteristics to this face. Instead, all of the basic features of the shiner are present. Indeed, the design can be equated to a glyphic conflation of both tuun and possibly lem elements, the very terms used together in the proper names of many stelae at Copan and elsewhere. This interpretation is, I believe, the true face of the animate stela, suggesting not only that Stela J was conceived as a shining lem stone, but possibly also as a massive axe or celt piercing the ground.

figure 12.8
The "shine" and "stone" faces combined on Copan Stela J. (Photograph by the author.)

In this sense, it evokes much the same pattern that James Porter described for the Middle Preclassic Olmec stelae at La Venta (see Chapter 6).

Another key Copan monument, Stela 9, makes the connection between monuments and rain and lightning even more directly. As mentioned earlier, this stone was named the Yaxk'in Tuun Lem(?) ("Dry Season-Stone-Shiner(?)"), but in a remarkable use of terminology, its dedicatory text goes on to say that this was "the name of his Chahk" (Figure 12.7a). That is, the stone monument is not simply a lakam tuun, but a direct manifestation of Chahk the rain deity. Stela 9's direct association of its "shining stone" descriptive name with the god of storms and lightning seems difficult to ignore and strongly points to it being a precious stone of Chahk, most likely a figurative axe and literal lightning stone. I suspect that the same general sense was applied to many of the carefully painted and burnished stelae that were perhaps called "stone shiners" or "stone flashes."

This line of interpretation leads me to consider its connection with other more traditional symbolic meanings and significances we typically associate with stelae and stone monuments. As discussed above and as elaborated in an earlier article touching on similar subjects (Stuart 1996), stelae and other monumental stones were sacred tuuns that embodied the Ajaw days naming the 360-day year and its larger groupings in the Maya calendar. Many such monuments were commemorations of individual rulers and their ceremonies associated with such dates, but they were more than convenient media for displaying portraits; rather, the stones were imbued with a sense of making permanent an elapsed moment in time, of freezing ritual performance and the fleeting nature of its sacred day or time period (Stuart 1996). The ajawoob ("living kings") depicted on stelae also embodied these time periods, indicating a three-part arrangement of overlapping ideas involving time, the material of sacred stone, and the royal person.

All these connections still remain true, but the discussion so far also leads me to consider another important dimension to these complementary meanings and ideas. Although it is hard to discern on eroded sculptures today, many Maya stelae were material manifestations of another key and powerful force in the Mesoamerican universe: flashing light and its reflectivity. Sacred celts were laboriously crafted and polished to highlight the quality of shininess (Taube 2000a), and a similar effect on some well-preserved monuments seems to evoke the form and surface of celts. In this sense, stelae at Copan and elsewhere were also truly shining objects—polished celts writ large—perhaps equated with the flashes of Chahk and related to celestial deities that bridged the realms of sky and earth. Lightning and its replication through material stone, often the media for royal portraits and ceremonial scenes, therefore may occupy an even more central role in the ideology of Maya rulership than has been previously supposed.

As I have argued here and elsewhere (Stuart 1996), many Maya stelae were manufactured to embody particular time periods, not just to commemorate them, and I am tempted to think that the significance of such flashing stones was related to this temporal aspect of their function. Just as a day or moment of time passes in human experience, so too does the flash of a god who brings rain and sustenance to the earth. The axes of Chahk in this way came to be thrust into the earth as sacred monuments, carrying multifaceted meanings of time, world renewal, and of rulers' active roles in those processes.

Concluding Remarks

This chapter has largely focused on Classic Maya clues for understanding the nature and significance of stone monuments, and admittedly it contains a number of general claims that may be difficult to extend to all areas and time periods. Nevertheless, it assumes that at least some of the most fundamental meanings and symbolic messages about the substance of monumental stones can be extended from Classic times into earlier centuries and might even shed some light on the motivations behind the early use of stelae and other classes of stone monuments in Preclassic Mesoamerica.

It is important to stress that such monuments were not always used as media for the presentation of royal images and iconographies of power and cosmology. Many examples from the Preclassic and Classic periods were intentional "plain" tuuns, either natural in form or somehow finished, that embodied a number of multifaceted ideas about time, permanence, and the transcendent space bridging the sky with the substance of the earth. By the Middle Preclassic, the appearance of images on stelae brought new layers of meaning to what was an already complex array of ideas, anchoring episodic representations of history, myth, and ceremony to the substance of stone itself. Throughout much of Mesoamerican history, I would argue, the medium of stone was always an elemental message communicated by monuments.

Stone monuments were conceptually related to other more intimate types of precious stone, having close symbolic connections to polished jade, greenstone, pyrite, and other prized materials. Symbolic meanings and messages must have varied considerably among these types, ranging from crystals used in divination, to jade and greenstone axes and celts, to mirrors, as well as altars and stelae. All these shared an underlying significance that was based on their materiality as substances of the earth and on their visual characteristics as shiny and light-making substances. Some impressive Mesoamerican and Maya sculptures make this connection explicit by occasionally being located on outcrops of stone, away from archaeological sites, where physical setting and connection to *roca madre* (bedrock) was evidently significant.

Although I argue that stelae can be thought of as extensions of the core stony substance of the earth and its landscape, and also of the related sacred powers of the sky and rain, they also represented the cultured realm of human agency and artistic expression. The careful and time-consuming work involved in the shaping of large and small stones (not necessarily the sculpting of them) was at the center of craft production from the Early Preclassic onward, when highly skilled craftsmen transformed the rough material of raw stone into divine objects. Like polished and shaped axes, celts, and mirrors, finished stone monuments encompassed a number of important religious ideas, but they uniquely were able to carry these and other meanings into the public arena as integral parts of artificial and architectural landscapes. As important as large monuments were as media for political and ritual messages, they never lost their basic and essential meaning as stones.

Acknowledgments

The ideas discussed in this chapter, still only partially developed in some ways, benefited greatly from comments by Karl Taube and Stephen Houston. Norman Hammond, Virginia Miller, and Joanne Pillsbury pointed me toward publications that discuss parallel ideas on the meaning of stone in Europe and the Andes. Finally, my good friend and colleague Barbara Arroyo deserves great thanks—several tours of her excavations at Naranjo stimulated a number of the thoughts presented here, especially on the time depth of symbolism surrounding Maya stone monuments.

1. Throughout this chapter I spell the Mayan word for "stone" as "tuun," to represent the long vowel present in the ancient Classic Mayan word and as reflected in the standard hieroglyph **TUUN-ni.** The more familiar "tun" spelling comes from colonial Yucatec orthography, in which vowel length and tone were unrepresented.

2. Proskouriakoff (1968:121) made a similar observation in noting that "the stela originated in the Olmec habit of recording their presence wherever they went, and that the lack of native rock at La Venta led to the substitution of artificial slabs."

3. The term "cauac monster" is now somewhat out of fashion, perhaps because it is widely acknowledged that the label has been used to encompass several similar beings that are best considered separate. For example, many such "cauac monsters" may simply be animate stone, but a great many others are mountains (*witz*) (Stuart 1987, 1997).

4. The animate shiner symbol has often been called the "*tzuk* head" (Freidel et al. 1993:418–419; Grube and Schele 1991), but this term is mistaken, being based on a false visual analysis of a different glyph spelled "**tzu-ku**" for *tzuk* ("geographic partition"). The mirror or shiner element here is not a glyph but an integral part of the **tzu** syllable sign representing a bottle-gourd. Its presence was likely meant to mark the surface of the gourd image as shiny in some sense, and elaborate forms of **tzu** go so far as to animate the shininess itself, to the point that its face visually dominates the gourd form. Linda Schele mistakenly generalized the animated head inside of **tzu** as all shiner heads and took the animated **tzu** conflated with **ku** as a single sign, **TSUK.**

CONTRIBUTORS

Barbara Arroyo, Research Associate, Popol Vuh Museum, Francisco Marroquín University, Guatemala City

Barbara Arroyo obtained her Licenciatura from the Universidad de San Carlos de Guatemala and her Ph.D. in anthropology from Vanderbilt University, Nashville, Tennessee. She has carried out research on the Pacific Coast of Mexico, Guatemala, and El Salvador, focusing on early sedentary villages. She has been directing the Naranjo Archaeological Project in Guatemala City for the past four years, uncovering a significant Middle Preclassic occupation in the region. She is one of the organizers of the annual Simposio de Investigaciones Arqueológicas in Guatemala and is also a coeditor for the published proceedings of these meetings. Her book, *Enterramientos en Balberta, un sitio de la Costa Sur de Guatemala,* was published in 1990 (BAR International Series). Arroyo has taught classes on Mesoamerican archaeology at Universidad del Valle and Universidad de San Carlos de Guatemala. She is currently a board member of the Society for American Archaeology.

Giselle Canto Aguilar, Instituto Nacional de Antropología e Historia, Mexico, Morelos Regional Center, Cuernavaca

Giselle Canto Aguilar graduated from the Escuela Nacional de Antropología e Historia, Mexico City, and is currently an archaeologist at the Instituto Nacional de Antropología e Historia. There she directs the Ceramoteca, or Ceramics Research Center, which concentrates on the archaeological materials from diverse regions and sites in the state of Morelos. Since 2003 she has been responsible for the project "Registro, conservación y rescate del patrimonio arqueológico del estado de Morelos," whose objective is the preservation, cataloging, and conservation of the archaeological patrimony of Morelos. Canto Aguilar has participated in numerous archaeological investigations, including those at the sites of Xochicalco, Hacienda Calderón, Olintepec, and Tepoztlán. She has also collaborated on didactic guides and educational materials for site museums at Xochicalco and Coatetelco, and for the Museo Regional Cuauhnáhuac, Morelos, among others. Recently she has focused her attention on the site of Zazacatla, Morelos, and its archaeology, development, and settlement during the Middle Preclassic period.

Víctor M. Castro Mendoza, Instituto Nacional de Antropología e Historia, Mexico, Morelos Regional Center, Cuernavaca

Víctor M. Castro Mendoza, an archaeologist with the Escuela Nacional de Antropología e Historia, Mexico, has participated in the surveying and mapping of the site of El Vergel, Oaxaca, with Berenice Y. Heredia Espinoza, and in excavations at the site of Nicayuhu, Oaxaca, with archaeologist Verónica Pérez Rodríguez. He has also collaborated with Ronald Spores at the site of Pueblo Viejo de Teposcolula, Oaxaca. His research appears in the journal *Arqueología mexicana* and in the cultural supplement "El Tlacuache" of *La jornada Morelos.* At present his work continues to focus on the flotation of soil and sediment samples taken during excavations at the site of Zazacatla, in Xochitepec, Morelos.

John E. Clark, New World Archaeological Foundation, Brigham Young University, Provo, Utah

John E. Clark has been doing research in southern Mexico for the past thirty-two years, with particular attention to Preclassic societies in Chiapas and their development. He received B.S. and M.A. degrees from Brigham Young University, Provo, Utah, and a Ph.D. in anthropology from the University of Michigan, Ann Arbor. For the past two decades he has directed the New World Archaeological Foundation, with headquarters in Chiapas, Mexico. His dissertation research concerned the origins of hereditary social inequality among the earliest villagers of proto-Mesoamerica. Since that time he has focused on later developments of Preclassic peoples, in particular, the creation of Olmec cities, complex government, and related rituals and beliefs—as most clearly evident in Olmec art and ritual practices. He has edited two books on Olmec archaeology.

Lori D. Collins, Alliance for Integrated Spatial Technologies, College of Arts and Sciences, University of South Florida, Tampa

Lori Collins is a cofounder of the Alliance for Integrated Spatial Technologies in the College of Arts and Sciences' Office of Research and Scholarship at the University of South Florida (http://aist.cas.usf.edu). She received her Ph.D. in applied anthropology from the University of South Florida (USF). Collins is an instructor in the Department of Anthropology at USF, teaching undergraduate and graduate courses in archaeology, heritage preservation, cultural resource management, and spatial documentation methods. Her research focus is on three-dimensional laser scanning and documentation survey strategies for cultural heritage preservation and conservation. Her interests center on integrating spatial technologies of three-dimensional laser scanning, Global Positioning System, conventional survey

tools, and Geographic Information System and software applications to assist with cultural heritage preservation and rapid inventory and analysis of archaeological sites, features, and objects. She has worked internationally with a number of projects focusing on Mesoamerican sculpture documentation.

Travis F. Doering, Alliance for Integrated Spatial Technologies, College of Arts and Sciences, University of South Florida, Tampa

Travis Doering is cofounder and director of the Alliance for Integrated Spatial Technologies (AIST) in the College of Arts and Sciences' Office of Research and Scholarship at the University of South Florida (http://aist.cas.usf.edu). He has studied ancient Mesoamerican cultures for 30 years, with a primary focus on the events and people of the Preclassic period. Doering has conducted numerous international archaeological and cultural heritage preservation projects using a suite of state-of-the-art three-dimensional spatial data collection and processing techniques along with conventional survey methods. His research objectives include the continuing development of improved methods to extract imperceptible and previously unrecognized detail from sculpted artifacts, and to make these data readily available to students and researchers worldwide through the use of web-based databases.

Federico Fahsen, School of Architecture, Francisco Marroquín University, Guatemala City

Federico Fahsen was born in Guatemala City and educated in both the United States and Guatemala. He received his B.A. in architecture from the University of Southern California, Los Angeles and his M.A. in urban and regional planning from the University of California at Berkeley. He has worked at many institutions in Guatemala, as well as for the Organization of American States in Washington, D.C., as director of the Guatemalan Institute of Tourism, and as Guatemalan Ambassador to the United States. He has served as project epigrapher for numerous archaeological projects and has published extensively on this subject. He has also collaborated with colleagues on various books concerning Maya codices and the monuments of the important Maya archaeological sites of Uaxactun and Tikal.

Rebecca B. González Lauck, Instituto Nacional de Antropología e Historia, Mexico, Tabasco Regional Center, Villahermosa

Rebecca B. González Lauck received her B.A. in anthropology from Newcomb College of Tulane University, New Orleans, Louisiana, and her M.A. and Ph.D. in anthropology from the University of California at Berkeley. Currently an archaeologist and professor of scientific investigation at the Instituto Nacional de Antropología e Historia, Tabasco, she has directed excavations at the Olmec site of La Venta, Tabasco, since 1984, in addition to coordinating the protection and restoration programs at the site. She has also worked on archaeological projects in Guatemala, Costa Rica, Yucatan, and Chiapas and has served on the editorial board for the journal *Arqueología mexicana* since 1996. Her many publications include *Olmeca, balance y perspectivas: Memoria de la Primera Mesa Redonda* (Universidad Nacional Autónoma de México, 2008), coedited with María Teresa Uriarte; essays in *Olmec Art of Ancient Mexico* (National Gallery of Art, 1996), edited by Elizabeth P. Benson and Beatriz de la Fuente; *Acercarse y mirar: Homenaje a Beatriz de la Fuente* (Universidad Nacional Autónoma de México, 2004), edited by María Teresa Uriarte; and Leticia Staines Cicero; and *Los olmecas en Mesoamérica* (El Equilibrista and Turner Books, 1994), edited by John E. Clark. She has also published articles in a variety of journals, including *Arqueología, Arqueología mexicana,* and the *Journal of Field Archaeology.*

Julia Guernsey, Department of Art and Art History, University of Texas at Austin

Julia Guernsey is an associate professor in the Department of Art and Art History at the University of Texas at Austin. Her research and publications focus on the Middle and Late Preclassic periods in ancient Mesoamerica, in particular on sculptural expressions of rulership during this time. She is also project iconographer for the La Blanca Archaeological Project, where she continues to participate in ongoing excavations and analysis of materials from this Middle Preclassic site on the Pacific Coast of Guatemala. Her most recent research appears in her book *Ritual and Power in Stone: The Performance of Rulership in Mesoamerican Izapan Style Art* (University of Texas Press, 2006). She also has essays in *Antiquity; Ancient America; Res: Anthropology and Aesthetics; Mexicon; Journal of Latin American Lore; Memorias de la Segunda Mesa Redonda Olmeca;* proceedings of the annual *Simposio de Investigaciones Arqueológicas en Guatemala;* and the exhibition catalogue *Lords of Creation: The Origins of Sacred Maya Kingship* (Los Angeles County Museum of Art, 2005), edited by Virginia M. Fields and Dorie Reents-Budet.

Gerardo Gutiérrez, Department of Anthropology, University of Colorado, Boulder

Gerardo Gutiérrez is assistant professor of anthropology at the University of Colorado at Boulder. He has a Ph.D. in anthropological archaeology from Pennsylvania State University, University Park, a M.A. in urban studies from El Colegio de México, Mexico City, and a Licenciatura in archaeology from the Escuela Nacional de Antropología e Historia, Mexico City. He has done archaeological and ethnohistorical investigations in many areas of Mexico, including the southern Huaxtec region, the Zapotec, Mixe, and Chinantec regions of northern Oaxaca, the Mixtec-Tlapanec-Nahua-Amuzgo region of eastern Guerrero, and the Soconusco region. Gutiérrez has written articles on a variety of topics, including Huaxtec religion and settlement patterns, the evolution of Mesoamerican graphic communication systems in eastern Guerrero, and the creation of Geographic Information System models to address questions about ancient communication routes of Mesoamerica. Most recently he has developed an ethnoarchaeological project to understand the process of adaptation after major disasters.

Michael W. Love, Department of Anthropology, California State University, Northridge

Michael W. Love is professor of anthropology at California State University, Northridge. His research interests focus on Mesoamerica, early social complexity, ceramic analysis, and household archaeology. Most recently, he has conducted research on political cycling and state formation on the Pacific Coast of Guatemala, working at the sites of La Blanca and El Ujuxte and concentrating on the examination of changes in household economy and ritual. He has received grants from the National Science Foundation, the National Endowment for the Humanities, the Wenner-Gren Foundation for Anthropological Research, the National Geographic Society, and the Foundation for the Advancement of Mesoamerican Studies, among others. His major publications include *Early Complex Society in Pacific Guatemala: Settlements and Chronology of the Río Naranjo, Guatemala* (New World Archaeological Foundation, 2002) and *Incidents of Archaeology in Central America and Yucatán,* coedited with Marion Popenoe de Hatch and Héctor Escobedo (University Press of America, 2002).

Guadalupe Martínez Donjuán, Instituto Nacional de Antropología e Historia, Mexico, Morelos Regional Center, Cuernavaca

Born in Zumpango, Guerrero, Guadalupe Martínez Donjuán studied education in Morelos and Mexico City, received a Licenciatura in sociology from the Universidad Autónoma de Guerrero, Chilpancingo, and a Licenciatura and M.A. in archaeology from the Escuela Nacional de Antropología e Historia, Mexico City. She has worked as an archaeologist in the states of Morelos and Guerrero, most recently as director of the Teopantecuanitlan archaeological project. She has spoken at numerous international congresses and symposia, and the discoveries at Teopantecuanitlan have been featured in several exhibitions in Mexico (Museo Regional Cuauhnáhuac, Morelos; Museo Regional de Guerrero; Museo de Antropología de Xalapa;

and Casa de la Cultura en Veracruz). Her work appears in numerous publications and journals, including *Revista mexicana de estudios antropológicos, Anales de antropología, Arqueología y etnohistoria del estado de Guerrero, Arqueología, Boletín del Consejo de Arqueología, Arqueología mexicana, Los olmecas en Mesoamérica, Historia general de Guerrero,* and *National Geographic.*

Miguel Orrego Corzo, Ministerio de Cultura y Deportes, Dirección General del Patrimonio Cultural y Natural, Proyecto Nacional Tak'alik Ab'aj, Guatemala City, Guatemala

Archaeologist Miguel Orrego Corzo was born in Guatemala City in 1945. While finishing his secondary education, he worked at the site of Kaminaljuyu (1960–1964). From 1964 to 1969 he participated in the Tikal Project of the University of Pennsylvania, and from 1969 to 1987 he collaborated on the Tikal National Archaeological Park–Instituto de Arqueología e Historia (IDAEH) project. From 1979 to 1980 he studied archaeology at the University of Pennsylvania, Philadelphia, and in 1991 he was awarded an honorary degree, Profesional honoris causa y Arqueólogo Emeritisimum, by the Humanities Faculty of the University of San Carlos, Guatemala. In 1987 he founded the Tak'alik Ab'aj National Archaeological Project in the Guatemala Ministry of Culture and Sports, and he continues to direct this archaeological project today. He has worked at many archaeological sites, including Iximché, Río Azul, Yaxhá, Seibal, Dos Pilas, Tamarindito, Aguateca, and Naj Tunich. He specializes in the architecture of the Maya Lowlands and Pacific Coast and its restoration, as well as the design and development of archaeological parks.

Christopher A. Pool, Department of Anthropology, University of Kentucky

Christopher A. Pool received his Ph.D. from Tulane University, New Orleans, Louisiana, and is an associate professor of anthropology at the University of Kentucky, Lexington. He has done archaeological fieldwork in and around the Tuxtla Mountains of southern Veracruz, Mexico, since

1983 and has directed archaeological investigations of long-term change in political economy at Tres Zapotes, Veracruz, since 1995. Pool is editor of *Settlement Archaeology and Political Economy at Tres Zapotes, Veracruz, Mexico* (Cotsen Institute of Archaeology, University of California at Los Angeles, 2003), author of *Olmec Archaeology and Early Mesoamerica* (Cambridge University Press, 2007), and coeditor (with Philip J. Arnold III) of *Classic Period Cultural Currents in Southern and Central Veracruz* (Dumbarton Oaks, 2008).

Mary E. Pye, New World Archaeological Foundation, Brigham Young University, Provo, Utah

Mary E. Pye received her Ph.D. from Vanderbilt University, Nashville, Tennessee, and is a research associate of Brigham Young University and series editor for *Papers of the New World Archaeological Foundation (NWAF)*. She has done fieldwork in Belize, Guatemala, and Guerrero and Chiapas, Mexico. Her research and writing have focused on Preclassic societies, in particular on specialized production, iconography, and communication routes; she is coeditor with John E. Clark of *Olmec Art and Archaeology in Mesoamerica* (National Gallery of Art, 2000). She is a member of the editorial group for the published proceedings of the *Simposio Anual de Investigaciones Arqueológicas en Guatemala* and was a member of the editorial board for the *Guide to Documentary Sources for Andean Studies* (University of Oklahoma Press, 2008), edited by Joanne Pillsbury. As NWAF series editor, she has overseen publication of a number of volumes, most recently *Excavations at Ojo de Agua, an Early Classic Maya Site in the Upper Grijalva Basin, Chiapas, Mexico* (NWAF, 2008) by Douglas D. Bryant.

Christa Schieber de Lavarreda, Ministerio de Cultura y Deportes, Dirección General del Patrimonio Cultural y Natural, Proyecto Nacional Tak'alik Ab'aj, Guatemala City, Guatemala

Christa Ilse Schieber Goehring de Lavarreda was born in Parramos, Chimaltenango, Guatemala, but she spent much of her youth in southern Germany. In 1991 she obtained her degree in archaeology from the University of San Carlos, Guatemala. Since the founding of the Tak'alik Ab'aj National Archaeological Project in the Guatemala Ministry of Culture and Sports in 1987, she has concentrated her attentions at this site, where she is responsible for archaeological investigations, the training of students, and the publication of project results. Her area of expertise is Preclassic archaeology, particularly the earthen architecture and associated sculpture of Tak'alik Ab'aj, as well as the conservation of this material. In 1998, she organized the Taller de Arqueología de la Costa Sur de Guatemala. She is a member of the Society for American Archaeology. She has also participated in numerous international archaeological meetings and symposia.

David Stuart, Department of Art and Art History, University of Texas at Austin

David Stuart is the Linda and David Schele Professor of Mesoamerican Art and Writing at the University of Texas (UT) at Austin. His research concentrates on the civilizations of Mesoamerica, with a focus on Maya hieroglyphic writing. His early work on Maya hieroglyphs led to a MacArthur Fellowship in 1984. He received his Ph.D in anthropology from Vanderbilt University, Nashville, Tennessee, in 1995, and he taught at Harvard University for eleven years before arriving at UT Austin. Stuart has conducted research at archaeological sites in Mexico, Guatemala, and Honduras and is currently project epigrapher for the Proyecto San Bartolo. His publications include *Ten Phonetic Syllables* (Center for Maya Research, 1987), which laid much of the groundwork for the now-accepted methodology of decipherment. His most recent publication is a collaboration with George Stuart titled *Palenque: Eternal City of the Maya* (Thames and Hudson, 2008). Stuart also directs The Mesoamerica Center at UT Austin, which fosters multidisciplinary studies and produces publications on ancient American art and culture.

REFERENCES CITED

Aguirre Beltrán, Gonzalo
1978 [1955] *Nagualismo y complejos afines en el México colonial.* Reimpresos 10 (enero). Instituto de Investigaciones Antropológicas, Universidad Nacional Autónoma de México, Mexico City.

Albores, Beatriz, and Johanna Broda (editors)
1997 *Graniceros: Cosmovisión y meteorología indígenas de Mesoamérica.* El Colegio Mexiquense, Zinacantepec, Mexico, and Universidad Nacional Autónoma de México, Mexico City.

Alcina Franch, José
1971 Nahuales y nahualismo en Oaxaca: Siglo XVIII. *Anales del Instituto de Antropología e Historia* 3:23–30. Caracas, Venezuela.

Amaroli, Paul
1997 A Newly Discovered Potbelly Sculpture from El Salvador and a Reinterpretation of the Genre. *Mexicon* 19(3):51–53.

Angulo, Jorge V.
1987 The Chalcatzingo Reliefs: An Iconographic Analysis. In *Ancient Chalcatzingo,* edited by David C. Grove, pp. 132–158. University of Texas Press, Austin.

1994 Observaciones sobre su pensamiento cosmogónico y la organización socio-política. In *Los olmecas en Mesoamérica,* edited by John E. Clark, pp. 223–237. Citibank and Editorial Equilibrista, Mexico City, and Turner Libros, Madrid.

Aranda Monroy, Raúl Carlos
1997 El culto a los volcánes en el sur de la Cuenca de México durante el Preclásico: Evidencias arqueológicas de Xico. In *Graniceros: Cosmovisión y meterología indígenas de Mesoamérica,* edited by Beatriz Albores and Johanna Broda, pp. 141–155. El Colegio Mexiquense, Zinacantepec, Mexico, and Universidad Nacional Autónoma de México, Mexico City.

Arnauld, Marie Charlotte
1986 *Archéologie de l'habitat en Alta Verapaz (Guatemala).* Etudes mésoaméricaines 10. Centre d´Etudes Mexicaines et Centraméricaines, Mexico City.

Arnauld, Marie Charlotte, Alain Breton, François Lartigue, and Yvon Le Bot (editors)
1993 *Representaciones del espacio político en las tierras altas de Guatemala.* Cuadernos de Estudios Guatemaltecos 2. Centro de Estudios Mexicanos y Centroamericanos, Mexico City and Guatemala City.

Arochi, E. Luis
1976 *La pirámide de Kukulcan: Su simbolismo solar.* Orión, Mexico City.

Arroyo, Barbara
1995 Early Ceramics from El Salvador: The El Carmen Site. In *The Emergence of Pottery: Technology and Innovation in Ancient Societies,* edited by William K. Barnett and John W. Hoopes, pp. 199–208. Smithsonian Institution Press, Washington, D.C.

2002 Appendix I: Classification of La Blanca Figurines. In *Early Complex Society in Pacific Guatemala: Settlements and Chronology of the Río Naranjo, Guatemala*, edited by Michael W. Love, pp. 205–235. Papers of the New World Archaeological Foundation 66. Brigham Young University, Provo, Utah.

2003 Early Formative Interaction on the Pacific Coast of Guatemala: A Ceramic Perspective. Electronic document, http://www.famsi.org/cgi-bin/print_friendly.pl?file=01091.

2007 The Naranjo Rescue Project: New Data from Preclassic Guatemala. Electronic document, http://www.famsi.org/reports/06109/index.html.

n.d. Entre cerros, cafetales y urbanismo: investigaciones en Naranjo, Guatemala. Publicación especial. Academia de Geografía e Historia de Guatemala, Guatemala City.

Arroyo, Barbara (editor)

2007 Informe final de la temporada 2005–2006 del Proyecto Arqueológico de Rescate Naranjo. Report submitted to the Dirección General de Patrimonio Cultural y Natural, Guatemala City.

Arroyo, Barbara, Karen Pereira, Margarita Cossich, Lorena Paiz, Edgar Arévalo, Mónica de León, Carlos Alvarado, and Fabiola Quiroa

2007 Proyecto de Rescate Naranjo: Nuevos datos del Preclásico en el valle de Guatemala. In *XX Simposio de Investigaciones Arqueológicas en Guatemala, 2006*, edited by Juan Pedro Laporte, Bárbara Arroyo, and Héctor E. Mejía, pp. 861–874. Ministerio de Cultura y Deportes, Instituto de Antropología e Historia, Asociación Tikal, and Fundación Arqueológica del Nuevo Mundo, Guatemala City.

Aulie, H. Wilbur, and Evelyn W. de Aulie

1978 *Diccionario Ch'ol—Español, Español—Ch'ol*. Instituto Lingüístico de Verano, Mexico City.

Aviles, María

2000 The Archaeology of Early Formative Chalcatzingo, Morelos, Mexico, 1995. Electronic document, http://www.famsi.org/reports/94047/index.html.

Awe, Jamie J., and Nikolai Grube

2001 La Estela 9 de Cahal Pech. *Los investigadores de la cultura maya* 9(1):55–65.

Báez-Jorge, Félix

1983 La cosmovisión de los zoques de Chiapas. In *Antropología e historia de los mixe-zoques y mayas: Homenaje a Frans Blom*. Universidad Nacional Autónoma de México, Mexico City.

2008 *Entre los naguales y los santos,* 2nd ed. Universidad Veracruzana, Xalapa, Mexico.

Bailey, Marco-Antonio

1980 Les Groupes cérémonials C-Sud et C-Nord. In *Cawinal*, vol. 2 of *Archéologie de sauvetage dans la vallée du Río Chixoy*, edited by Alain Ichon, Marie-France Fauvert-Berthelot, Christine Plocieniak, Robert Hill II, Rebecca B. González Lauck, and Marco-Antonio Bailey, pp. 143–171. Centre National de la Recherche Scientifique, Institute d'Ethnologie, Paris.

Balcárcel, Beatriz

1995 Abaj Takalik: Arquitectura y simbolismo del Templo 12. Licenciatura thesis, Department of History, San Carlos University, Guatemala.

Batres, Leopoldo

1902 *Exploraciones de Monte Albán: Inspección y conservación de los monumentos arqueológicos de la República Mexicana*. Editorial Gante, Mexico City.

Baudez, Claude-François

1994 *Maya Sculpture of Copan: The Iconography*. University of Oklahoma Press, Norman.

Beals, Ralph L.

1973 [1945] *Ethnology of the Western Mixe*. Cooper Square, New York.

Becquelin, Pierre

1969 *Archéologie de la région de Nebaj (Guatemala)*. Mémoires 2. Institut d'Ethnologie, Paris.

Becquelin, Pierre, Alain Breton, and Veronique Germis

2001 *Arqueología de la región de Nebaj, Guatemala*. Cuadernos de Estudios Guatemaltecos 5. Centro

Francés de Estudios Mexicanos y Centroamericanos, Escuela de Historia–Universidad de San Carlos de Guatemala, Ministerio de Asuntos Exteriores de Francia, Guatemala City.

Benson, Elizabeth P.

1981   Some Olmec Objects in the Robert Woods Bliss Collection at Dumbarton Oaks. In *The Olmec and Their Neighbors: Essays in Honor of Matthew W. Stirling,* edited by Elizabeth P. Benson, pp. 95–108. Dumbarton Oaks Research Library and Collection, Washington, D.C.

Benson, Elizabeth P. (editor)

1968   *Dumbarton Oaks Conference on the Olmec.* Dumbarton Oaks Research Library and Collection, Washington, D.C.

1996   *The Olmec World: Ritual and Rulership.* Art Museum, Princeton University, Princeton, N.J.

Benson, Elizabeth P., and Beatriz de la Fuente (editors)

1996   *Olmec Art of Ancient Mexico.* National Gallery of Art, Washington, D.C.

Berdan, Frances F.

2008   Concepts of Ethnicity and Class in Aztec-Period Mexico. In *Ethnic Identity in Nahua Mesoamerica: A View from Archaeology, Art History, Ethnohistory, and Contemporary Ethnography,* edited by Frances F. Berdan, John K. Chance, Alan R. Sandstrom, Barbara L. Stark, James Taggart, and Emily Umberger, pp. 105–132. University of Utah Press, Salt Lake City.

Bernal, Ignacio

1969   *The Olmec World.* Translated by Doris Heyden and Fernando Horcasitas. University of California Press, Berkeley.

Bernal, Ignacio, and Andy Seuffert

1979   *The Ballplayers of Dainzú.* Akademische Druck- und Verlagsanstalt, Graz, Austria.

Bernal-García, María Elena

1989   Tzatza: Olmec Mountains and the Ruler's Ritual Speech. In *Seventh Palenque Round Table, 1989,* edited by Merle G. Robertson and Virginia M. Fields, pp. 113–123. Pre-Columbian Art Research Institute, San Francisco.

Beverido Pereau, Francisco

1987   Breve historia de la arqueología olmeca. *La palabra y el hombre* 64:161–194.

Beyer, Hermann

1930   A Deity Common to Teotihuacan and Totonac Cultures. In *Proceedings of the Twenty-Third International Congress of Americanists.* Science Press, Lancaster, Pa.

Blake, Michael T., Brian S. Chisholm, John E. Clark, and Karen Mudar

1992   Non-Agricultural Staples and Agricultural Supplements: Early Formative Subsistence in the Soconusco Region, Mexico. In *Transitions to Agriculture in Prehistory,* edited by T. Douglas Price and Anne B. Gebauer, pp. 133–151. Prehistory Press, Madison, Wis.

Blake, Michael T., Brian S. Chisholm, John E. Clark, Barbara Voorhies, and Michael W. Love

1992   Prehistoric Subsistence in the Soconusco Region. *Current Anthropology* 33:83–94.

Blanton, Richard E.

1998   Beyond Centralization: Steps toward a Theory of Egalitarian Behavior in Archaic States. In *Archaic States,* edited by Gary M. Feinman and Joyce Marcus, pp. 135–172. School of American Research Press, Santa Fe, N.Mex.

Blanton, Richard E., Gary M. Feinman, Stephen A. Kowalewski, and Peter N. Peregrine

1996   A Dual-Processual Theory for the Evolution of Mesoamerican Civilization. *Current Anthropology* 37:1–14, 65–68.

Blom, Frans, and Oliver La Farge

1926   *Tribes and Temples; A Record of the Expedition to Middle America Conducted by the Tulane University of Louisiana in 1925,* vol. 1. Middle American Research Institute, Tulane University, New Orleans, La.

Blomster, Jeffrey P., Hector Neff, and Michael D. Glascock

2005   Olmec Pottery Production and Export in Ancient Mexico Determined through Elemental Analysis. *Science* 307:1068–1072.

Boehler, Wolfgang, Guido Heinz, and Andreas Marbs

2001   The Potential of Non-Contact Close Range Laser Scanners for Cultural Heritage Recording. Paper presented at the International Scientific Committee for Documentation of Cultural Heritage International Symposium Proceedings, Potsdam, Germany.

Boehler, Wolfgang, Monica Bordas Vicent, Guido Heinz, Andreas Marbs, and Hartmut Müller

2004   High Quality Scanning and Modeling of Monuments and Artifacts. Paper presented at the Proceedings of the International Federation of Surveyors Working Week, Athens.

Boggs, Stanley

1950   "Olmec" Pictographs in the Las Victorias Group, Chalchuapa Archaeological Zone. *Notes on Middle American Archaeology and Ethnology* 99:85–92.

Bove, Frederick J.

1981   The Evolution of Chiefdoms and States on the Pacific Slope of Guatemala: A Spatial Analysis. Ph.D. dissertation, Department of Anthropology, University of California, Los Angeles.

1989   Dedicated to the Costeños: Introduction and New Insights. In *New Frontiers in the Archaeology of the Pacific Coast of Southern Mesoamerica,* edited by Frederick J. Bove and Lynette Heller, pp. 1–13. Anthropological Research Papers 39. Arizona State University, Tempe.

n.d.a   Plain Stelae of the Guatemala Pacific Coast: An Interpretation. Report submitted to Foundation for the Advancement of Mesoamerican Studies, Crystal River, Fla. Electronic document, http://www.famsi.org/reports/98001/section03.html.

n.d.b   The People with No Name: Some Observations of the Plain Stelae of Pacific Guatemala (and Chiapas) with Respect to Issues of Ethnicity and Rulership. In *The Southern Maya in the Late Preclassic,* edited by Michael W. Love and Jonathan Kaplan, in press.

Brady, James E.

2003   In My Hill, in My Valley: The Importance of Place in Ancient Maya Ritual. In *Mesas and Cosmologies in Mesoamerica,* edited by Douglas Sharon, pp. 83–91. San Diego Museum Papers 42. San Diego Museum of Man, San Diego, Calif.

Brady, Liam M.

2006   Documenting and Analyzing Rock Paintings from Torres Strait, NE Australia, with Digital Photography and Computer Image Enhancement. *Journal of Field Archaeology* 31:363–379.

Brinton, Daniel G.

1894   Nagualism. A Study in Native American Folk-Lore and History. *Proceedings of the American Philosophical Society* 33: 11–73.

Broda, Johanna, and Druzo Maldonado

1997   Culto en la cueva de Chimalacatepec, San Juan Tlacotenco, Morelos. In *Graniceros: Cosmovisión y meterología indígenas de Mesoamérica,* edited by Beatriz Albores and Johanna Broda, pp. 175–211. El Colegio Mexiquense, Zinacantepec, Mexico, and Universidad Nacional Autónoma de México, Mexico City.

Brown, Kenneth L.

1977   Valley of Guatemala: A Highland Port of Trade. In *Teotihuacan and Kaminaljuyu: A Study in Prehistoric Culture Contact,* edited by William T. Sanders and Joseph W. Michels, pp. 205–396. Pennsylvania State University Press, University Park.

Brown, Linda

2005   Planting the Bones: Hunting Ceremonialism at Contemporary and Nineteenth-Century Shrines in the Guatemalan Highlands. *Latin American Antiquity* 16:131–146.

Bruehl, Gust

1888   Archaeological Remains in Costa Cuca (Guatemala). *Science* 12:156.

Brumfiel, Elizabeth M.

1994   Factional Competition and Political Development in the New World: An Introduction. In *Factional Competition and Political Development in the New World,* edited by Elizabeth M. Brumfiel and John W. Fox, pp. 3–13. Cambridge University Press, Cambridge.

Bullard, William R., Jr.

1963 A Unique Maya Shrine Site on the Mountain Pine Ridge of British Honduras. *American Antiquity* 29(1):98–99.

Cabrera, Rubén, Noel Morales, and Ignacio Rodríguez

1984 Los problemas de conservación arquitectónica en Teotihuacan: Análisis y criterios. *Arquitectura mesoamericana* 3:23–37.

Campbell, Lyle

1979 Middle American Languages. In *The Languages of Native America: Historical and Comparative Assessment,* edited by Lyle Campbell and Marianne Mithun, pp. 902–1000. University of Texas Press, Austin.

Campbell, Lyle, and Terrence Kaufman

1976 A Linguistic Look at the Olmec. *American Antiquity* 41(1):80–89.

Carmack, Robert M., and Lynn Larmer

1971 *Quichean Art: A Mixteca-Puebla Variant.* Museum of Anthropology, University of Northern Colorado, Greeley.

Carrasco Vargas, Ramón

2005 The Sacred Mountain: Preclassic Architecture in Calakmul. In *Lords of Creation: The Origins of Sacred Maya Kingship,* edited by Virginia M. Fields and Dorie Reents-Budet, pp. 62–66. Los Angeles County Museum of Art, Los Angeles.

Carter, Nicholas

2008 The "Emblem" Monuments of Structure J at Monte Albán, Oaxaca, Mexico. Master's thesis, Institute of Latin American Studies, University of Texas, Austin.

Caso, Alfonso

1947 *Calendario y escritura de las antiguas culturas de Monte Albán.* Mexico City.

1978 *El pueblo del sol.* Fondo de Cultura Económica, Mexico City.

Chimalpáhin, Domingo

1998 *Las ocho relaciones y el memorial de Colhuacan.* 2 vols. Consejo Nacional para la Cultura y las Artes, Mexico City.

Chinchilla Mazariegos, Oswaldo

2001–2002 Los barrigones del sur de Mesoamérica. *Precolombart* 4/5:9–23.

Christie, Jessica J.

2005 The Stela as a Cultural Symbol in Classic and Contemporary Maya Societies. *Ancient Mesoamerica* 16:277–289.

Ciudad Ruíz, Andrés

1984 *Arqueología de Agua Tibia.* Ediciones de Cultura Hispánica, Instituto de Cooperación Iberoamericana, Madrid.

Clancy, Flora S.

1985 Maya Sculpture. In *Maya: Treasures of an Ancient Civilization,* edited by Charles Gallenkamp and Regina Elise Johnson, pp. 59–70. Henry N. Abrams, New York.

1990 A Genealogy for Freestanding Maya Monuments. In *Vision and Revision in Maya Studies,* edited by Flora S. Clancy and Peter Harrison, pp. 21–31. University of New Mexico Press, Albuquerque.

Clark, John E.

1996 Craft Specialization and Olmec Civilization. In *Craft Specialization and Social Evolution: In Memory of V. Gordon Childe,* edited by Bernard Wailes, pp. 197–199. University Museum of Pennsylvania Press, Philadelphia.

1997 The Arts of Government in Early Mesoamerica. *Annual Review of Anthropology* 26:211–234.

2004 The Birth of Mesoamerican Metaphysics: Sedentism, Engagement, and Moral Superiority. In *Rethinking Materiality: The Engagement of Mind with the Material World,* edited by Elizabeth de Marrais, Chris Gosden, and Colin Renfrew, pp. 205–224. McDonald Institute for Archaeological Research, University of Cambridge, Cambridge.

2007 Mesoamerica's First State. In *The Political Economy of Ancient Mesoamerica: Transformations during the Formative and Classic Periods,* edited by Vernon L. Scarborough and John E. Clark, pp. 11–46. University of New Mexico Press, Albuquerque.

2008 Teogonia olmeca: Perspectivas, problemas y propuestas. In *Olmeca, balance y perspectivas: Memoria de la Primera Mesa Redonda,* vol. 1, edited by María Teresa Uriarte and Rebecca B. González Lauck, pp. 145–183. Universidad Nacional Autónoma de México, Mexico City.

n.d. Western Kingdoms of the Middle Formative. In *Early Maya States,* edited by Loa Traxler and Robert J. Sharer. University of Pennsylvania Press, Philadelphia, in press.

Clark, John E., and Michael Blake

1994 The Power of Prestige: Competitive Generosity and the Emergence of Rank Societies in Lowland Mesoamerica. In *Factional Competition and Political Development in the New World,* edited by Elizabeth M. Brumfiel and John W. Fox, pp. 17–30. Cambridge University Press, Cambridge.

Clark, John E., and David Cheetham

2002 Mesoamerica's Tribal Foundations. In *The Archaeology of Tribal Societies,* edited by William A. Parkinson, pp. 278–339. International Monographs in Prehistory, Ann Arbor, Mich.

Clark, John E., and Richard D. Hansen

2001 The Architecture of Early Kingship: Comparative Perspectives on the Origins of the Maya Royal Court. In *The Maya Royal Court,* edited by Takeshi Inomata and Stephen D. Houston, pp. 1–45. Westview Press, Boulder, Colo.

Clark, John E., and Ayax Moreno

2007 Redrawing the Izapa Monuments. In *Archaeology, Art, and Ethnogenesis in Mesoamerican Prehistory: Papers in Honor of Gareth W. Lowe,* edited by Lynneth S. Lowe and Mary E. Pye, pp. 277–319. Papers of the New World Archaeological Foundation 68. Brigham Young University, Provo, Utah.

Clark, John E., and William Parry

1990 Craft Specialization and Cultural Complexity. *Research in Economic Anthropology* 12:289–346.

Clark, John E., and Tomás Pérez Suárez

1994 Los olmecas y el primer milenio de Mesoamérica. In *Los olmecas en Mesoamérica,* edited by John E. Clark, pp. 261–275. Citibank and Editorial Equilibrista, Mexico City, and Turner Libros, Madrid.

Clark, John E., and Mary E. Pye

2000 The Pacific Coast and the Olmec Question. In *Olmec Art and Archaeology in Mesoamerica,* edited by John E. Clark and Mary E. Pye, pp. 217–251. Studies in the History of Art 58. National Gallery of Art, Washington, D.C.

Clewlow, C. William

1974 *A Stylistic and Chronological Study of Olmec Monumental Sculpture.* Contributions of the University of California Archaeological Research Facility 19. University of California, Berkeley.

Clewlow, C. William, and Christopher R. Corson

1968 New Stone Monuments from La Venta, 1968. In *Papers on Mesoamerican Archaeology,* pp. 171–182. Contributions of the University of California Archaeological Research Facility 5. University of California, Berkeley.

Clewlow, C. William, Richard A. Cowan, James F. O'Connell, and Carlos Beneman

1967 *Colossal Heads of the Olmec Culture.* Contributions of the University of California Archaeological Research Facility 4. University of California, Berkeley.

Codex Borbonicus

1988 *Códice borbónico: Manuscrito mexicano de la biblioteca del palais bourbon (libro advinatorio y ritual ilustrado) publicado en facsímil,* edited by Francisco del Paso y Troncoso. Siglo Veintiuno, Mexico City.

Codex Borgia

1980 *Códice Borgia,* edited by Eduard Seler. Fondo de Cultura Económica, Mexico City.

Codex Mendoza

1992 *Codex Mendoza,* vol. 3, edited by Frances F. Berdan and Patricia Rieff

Anawalt. University of California Press, Berkeley and Los Angeles.

Coe, Michael D.

1957   Cycle 7 Monuments in Middle America: A Reconsideration. *American Anthropologist* 59(4):597–611.

1961   *La Victoria: An Early Site on the Pacific Coast of Guatemala.* Papers of the Peabody Museum of Archaeology and Ethnology 53. Peabody Museum, Cambridge, Mass.

1962   *Mexico.* Frederick Praeger, New York.

1965a   Archaeological Synthesis of Southern Veracruz and Tabasco. In *Archaeology of Southern Mesoamerica,* part 2, edited by Gordon R. Willey, pp. 679–715. Vol. 3 of *Handbook of Middle American Indians,* edited by Robert Wauchope. University of Texas Press, Austin.

1965b   The Olmec Style and Its Distribution. In *Archaeology of Southern Mesoamerica,* part 2, edited by Gordon R. Willey, pp. 739–775. Vol. 3 of *Handbook of Middle American Indians,* edited by Robert Wauchope. University of Texas Press, Austin.

1966   *The Maya.* Thames and Hudson, London.

1972   Olmec Jaguars and Olmec Kings. In *Cult of the Feline: A Conference in Pre-Columbian Iconography,* edited by Elizabeth P. Benson, pp. 1–22. Dumbarton Oaks Research Library and Collection, Washington, D.C.

1974   Comments on Prof. Sanders' Paper. In *Reconstructing Complex Societies,* edited by Charlotte B. Moore, pp. 116–118. Supplement to the Bulletin of the American Schools of Oriental Research 20. American Schools of Oriental Research, Cambridge, Mass.

1978   *Lords of the Underworld: Masterpieces of Classic Maya Ceramics.* Princeton University Press, Princeton, N.J.

1981   San Lorenzo Tenochtitlán. In *Archaeology,* edited by J. A. Sabloff, pp. 117–146. Vol. 1 of *Supplement to the Handbook of Middle American Indians,* edited by Victoria Reifler Bricker. University of Texas Press, Austin.

1999   *The Maya.* 6th ed. Thames and Hudson, New York.

2005   *The Maya.* 7th ed. Thames and Hudson, London.

Coe, Michael D., and Richard A. Diehl

1980   *In the Land of the Olmec.* University of Texas Press, Austin.

Coe, Michael D., Richard A. Diehl, and Minze Stuiver

1967   Olmec Civilization, Veracruz, Mexico: Dating of the San Lorenzo Phase. *Science* 155:1399–1401.

Coe, William R.

1965   Tikal, Guatemala, and Emergent Maya Civilization. *Science* 147:1401–1419.

Coggins, Clemency C. (editor)

1992   *Artifacts from the Cenote of Sacrifice, Chichen Itza, Yucatan: Textiles, Basketry, Stone, Bone, Shell, Ceramics, Wood, Copal, Rubber, Other Organic Materials and Mammalian Remains.* Harvard University, Peabody Museum of Archaeology and Ethnology, Cambridge, Mass.

Cole, Kelleigh W.

2006   The Acropolis at Kaminaljuyú: A Study in Late Classic Occupation. Master's thesis, Department of Anthropology, Brigham Young University, Provo, Utah.

Collins, Lori D., and Travis F. Doering

2006   Integrated Spatial Technologies: High Definition Documentation of the Miami and Royal Palm Circles. *Florida Anthropologist* 59:161–177. Special issue: *The Miami Circle: Fieldwork, Research and Analysis II.*

Córdova Tello, Mario, and Carolina Meza Rodríguez

2007   Chalcatzingo, Morelos. Un discurso sobre piedra. *Arqueología mexicana* 15(87):60–65.

Correa Villanueva, Yolanda, Raúl Marco del Pont Lalli, Luis Rubén Rodríguez Zubieta, and Margarita Aguilar Rivero

1986   *Estudio socioeconómico para la posible reubicación de los asentamientos de la zona arqueológica La Venta, Tabasco.* Instituto Nacional de Antropología e Historia e Instituto de Cultura de Tabasco, Mexico City.

Covarrubias, Miguel

1957   *Indian Art of Mexico and Central America.* Alfred A. Knopf, New York.

Craig, Jessica H.

2005   Dedicación, terminación, y perpetuación: Un santuario Clásico Tardío en San Bartolo, Petén. In *XVIII Simposio de Investigaciones Arqueológicas en Guatemala, 2004,* edited by Juan Pedro Laporte, Bárbara Arroyo, and Héctor E. Mejía, pp. 275–282. Ministerio de Cultura y Deportes, Instituto de Antropología e Historia, and Asociación Tikal, Guatemala City.

Cyphers, Ann

1993   Women, Rituals, and Social Dynamics at Ancient Chalcatzingo. *Latin American Antiquity* 4:209–224.

1996   Reconstructing Olmec Life at San Lorenzo. In *Olmec Art of Ancient Mexico,* edited by Elizabeth P. Benson and Beatriz de la Fuente, pp. 61–71. National Gallery of Art, Washington, D.C.

1997   Los felinos de San Lorenzo. In *Población, subsistencia y medio ambiente en San Lorenzo Tenochtitlán,* edited by Ann Cyphers, pp. 227–242. Universidad Nacional Autónoma de México, Mexico City.

1999   From Stone to Symbols: Olmec Art in Social Context at San Lorenzo Tenochtitlan. In *Social Patterns in Pre-Classic Mesoamerica,* edited by David C. Grove and Rosemary A. Joyce, pp. 155–181. Dumbarton Oaks Research Library and Collection, Washington, D.C.

2004a   Escultura monumental olmeca: Temas y contextos. In *Acercarse y mirar: Homenaje a Beatriz de la Fuente,* edited by María Teresa Uriarte and Leticia Staines Cicero, pp. 51–73. Universidad Nacional Autonóma de México, Mexico City.

2004b   *Escultura olmeca de San Lorenzo Tenochtitlán.* Instituto de Investigaciones Antropológicas, Universidad Nacional Autonóma de México, Mexico City.

Cyphers, Ann, Alejandro Hernández-Portilla, Marisol Varela-Gómez, and Lilia Grégor-López

2006   Cosmological and Sociopolitical Synergy in Preclassic Architecture. In *Precolumbian Water Management: Ideology, Ritual, and Power,* edited by Lisa J. Lucero and Barbara W. Fash, pp. 17–32. University of Arizona Press, Tucson.

Cyphers, Ann, and Judith Zurita-Noguera

2006   A Land that Tastes of Water. In *Precolumbian Water Management: Ideology, Ritual, and Power,* edited by Lisa J. Lucero and Barbara W. Fash, pp. 33–66. University of Arizona Press, Tucson.

Dahlin, Bruce H.

1978   Figurines. In *Artifacts and Figurines,* edited by Payson D. Sheets and Bruce H. Dahlin, pp. 134–211. Vol. 2 of *The Prehistory of Chalchuapa, El Salvador,* edited by Robert J. Sharer. University of Pennsylvania Press, Philadelphia.

Dean, Carolyn

2007   The Inka Married the Earth: Integrated Outcrops and the Making of Place. *Art Bulletin* 89(3):502–518.

Dehouve, Danièle

2007   *La ofrenda sacrificial entre los tlapanecos de Guerrero.* Universidad Autónoma de Guerrero, Plaza y Váldes, and Centro de Estudios Mexicanos y Centroamericanos, Mexico City.

Delgadillo Torres, Rosalba, and Andrés Santana Sandoval

1989   Dos esculturas olmecoides en Tlaxcala. *Arqueología* 1:53–60.

Demarest, Arthur A.

1986   *The Archaeology of Santa Leticia and the Rise of Maya Civilization.* Middle American Research Institute, Tulane University, New Orleans, La.

2004   *Ancient Maya: The Rise and Fall of a Rainforest Civilization.* Cambridge University Press, Cambridge.

Demarest, Arthur A., and Robert J. Sharer

1986   Late Preclassic Ceramic Spheres, Culture Areas, and Cultural Evolution in the Southeastern Highlands of Mesoamerica. In *The Southeast Maya*

Periphery, edited by Patricia A. Urban and Edward M. Schortman, pp. 194–223. University of Texas Press, Austin.

Demarest, Arthur A., Roy Switsur, and Rainer Berger

1982   The Dating and Cultural Associations of the "Pot-Bellied" Sculptural Style. *American Antiquity* 47(3):557–571.

Díaz Vázquez, Rosalba

2003   *El ritual de lluvia en la tierra de los hombres-tigre: Cambio sociocultural en una comunidad náhuatl (Acatlán, Guerrero, 1998–1999).* Consejo Nacional para la Cultura y las Artes, Mexico City.

Di Castro, Anna, and Ann Cyphers

2006   Iconografía de la cerámica de San Lorenzo. *Anales del Instituto de Investigaciones Estéticas* 89:29–58.

Diehl, Richard A.

2004   *The Olmecs: America's First Civilization.* Thames and Hudson, London.

Doering, Travis F., and Lori D. Collins

2007   The Mesoamerican Three-Dimensional Imaging Project. Electronic document, http://www.research.famsi.org/3D_imaging/index.php.

2008   The Kaminaljuyú Sculpture Project: An Expandable Three-Dimensional Database, Final Report. Electronic document, http://www.famsi.org/reports/07007/index.html.

Doering, Travis F., Lori D. Collins, and Dan Perreault

2006   Guatemala Three-Dimensional Laser Scanning Project. Technical project report submitted to the New World Archaeological Foundation, Brigham Young University, Provo, Utah.

Drucker, Philip

1943   *Ceramic Sequences at Tres Zapotes, Veracruz, Mexico.* Bureau of American Ethnology Bulletin 140. Government Printing Office, Washington, D.C.

1952   *La Venta, Tabasco: A Study of Olmec Ceramics and Art.* Bureau of American Ethnology Bulletin 153. Government Printing Office, Washington, D.C.

1955   *The Cerro de las Mesas Offering of Jade and Other Materials.* Bureau of American Ethnology Bulletin

157. Government Printing Office, Washington, D.C.

1981   On the Nature of Olmec Polity. In *The Olmec and Their Neighbors,* edited by Elizabeth P. Benson, pp. 29–47. Dumbarton Oaks Research Library and Collection, Washington, D.C.

Drucker, Philip, Robert F. Heizer, and Robert J. Squier

1959   *Excavations at La Venta Tabasco, 1955.* Bureau of American Ethnology Bulletin 170. Government Printing Office, Washington, D.C.

Durán, Diego

1984   *Historia de las Indias de Nueva España e Islas de la Tierra Firme.* 2nd ed. 2 vols., edited by Ángel María Garibay K. Editorial Porrúa, Mexico City.

Earle, Timothy K.

1997   *How Chiefs Come to Power: The Political Economy in Prehistory.* Stanford University Press, Stanford, Calif.

Ekholm, Gordon F.

1964   *A Maya Sculpture in Wood.* Museum of Primitive Art, New York.

Ekholm-Miller, Susanna

1973   *The Olmec Rock Carving at Xoc Chiapas, Mexico.* Papers of the New World Archaeological Foundation 32. Brigham Young University, Provo, Utah.

Estrada Belli, Francisco

2002   Putting Santa Rosa on the Map: New Insights on the Cultural Development of the Pacific Coast of Southeastern Guatemala. In *Incidents of Archaeology in Central America and Yucatán: Studies in Honor of Edwin M. Shook,* edited by Michael W. Love, Marion Popenoe de Hatch, and Héctor L. Escobedo, pp. 103–128. University Press of America, Lanham, Md.

2006   Lightning, Sky, Rain, and the Maize God: The Ideology of Preclassic Maya Rulers at Cival, Peten, Guatemala. *Ancient Mesoamerica* 17(1):57–78.

Evans, Susan T.

2003   *Ancient Mexico and Central America: Archaeology and Culture History.* Thames and Hudson, New York.

Fábregas Puig, Andrés A.

1969　El nahualismo y su expresión en la región de Chalco Amecameca. Master's thesis, Escuela Nacional de Antropología e Historia, Mexico City.

Fahsen, Federico

1999　Sistemas de escritura maya. In *Los mayas: Ciudades milenarias de Guatemala,* edited by Gaspar Muñoz Cosme, Cristina Vidal Lorenzo, and Juan Antonio Valdés, pp. 57–63. Talleres de Edelvives, Zaragosa, Spain.

2000a　From Chiefdom to Statehood in the Highlands of Guatemala. In *Maya: Divine Kings of the Rain Forest,* edited by Nikolai Grube, pp. 87–95. Könemann, Cologne.

2000b　Kaminal Juyú y sus vecionos. In *XIII Simposio de Investigaciones Arqueológicas en Guatemala, 1999,* edited by Juan Pedro Laporte, Héctor L. Escobedo, and Ana Claudia Monzón de Suasnávar, pp. 57–83. Ministerio de Cultura y Deportes, Instituto de Antropología e Historia, and Asociación Tikal, Guatemala City.

2001　Análisis de los monumentos y textos de estilo maya de Abaj Takalik. Manuscript on file with the Proyecto Nacional Abaj Takalik, Guatemala.

2002　Who Are the Prisoners in Kaminaljuyú Monuments? In *Incidents of Archaeology in Central America and Yucatán: Studies in Honor of Edwin M. Shook,* edited by Michael W. Love, Marion Popenoe de Hatch, and Héctor L. Escobedo, pp. 360–374. University Press of America, Lanham, Md.

n.d.　Estudio epigráfico de los monumentos de Kaminaljuyu, Guatemala. Manuscript on file with the Proyecto Arqueológico Miraflores, Guatemala City.

Fahsen, Federico, and Nikolai Grube

2005　The Origins of Maya Writing. In *Lords of Creation: The Origins of Sacred Maya Kingship,* edited by Virginia M. Fields and Dorie Reents-Budet, pp. 75–79. Los Angeles County Museum of Art, Los Angeles.

Feuchtwanger, Franz

1989　*Cerámica olmeca.* Editorial Patria, Mexico City.

Fialko, Vilma

2005　Diez años de investigaciones arqueológicas en la cuenca del Río Holmul, región noreste de Petén. In *XVIII Simposio de Investigaciones Arqueológicas en Guatemala, 2004,* edited by Juan Pedro Laporte, Bárbara Arroyo, and Héctor E. Mejía, pp. 253–268. Ministerio de Cultura y Deportes, Instituto de Antropología e Historia, and Asociación Tikal, Guatemala City.

Fields, Virginia M., and Dorie Reents-Budet (editors)

2005　*Lords of Creation: The Origins of Sacred Maya Kingship.* Los Angeles County Museum of Art, Los Angeles.

Foster, George

1944　Nagualism in Mexico and Guatemala. *Acta americana* 2(1–2):83–103.

Frei, Erwin, Jonathan Kung, and Richard Bukowski

2004　High-Definition Surveying (HDS): A New Era in Reality Capture. *International Archives of Photogrammetry, Remote Sensing and Spatial Information Sciences* 36(8):262–271.

Freidel, David A., and Linda Schele

1988　Kingship in the Late Preclassic Maya Lowlands: The Instruments and Places of Ritual Power. *American Anthropologist* 90(3):547–567.

Freidel, David A., Linda Schele, and Joy Parker

1993　*Maya Cosmos: Three Thousand Years on the Shaman's Path.* William Morrow, New York.

Fuente, Beatríz de la

1973　*Escultura monumental olmeca: Catálogo.* Instituto de Investigaciones Estéticas, Universidad Nacional Autónoma de México, Mexico City.

1977　*Los hombres de piedra: Escultura olmeca.* Universidad Nacional Autónoma de México, Mexico City.

1981　Toward a Conception of Monumental Olmec Art. In *The Olmec and Their Neighbors,* edited by Elizabeth P. Benson, pp. 83–94. Dumbarton Oaks

Research Library and Collection, Washington, D.C.

1995a   El arte olmeca. *Arqueología mexicana* 2(12):18–25.

1995b   Tetitla. In *La pintura mural prehis-pánica en México, Teotihuacan*, edited by Beatriz de la Fuente, pp. 258–311. Universidad Nacional Autónoma de México, Mexico City.

1996   Cruz del Milagro Monument 1: Seated Figure with Crossed Legs. In *Olmec Art of Ancient Mexico*, edited by Elizabeth P. Benson and Beatriz de la Fuente, pp. 166–167. National Gallery of Art, Washington, D.C.

Furst, Peter T.

1968   The Olmec Were-Jaguar Motif in the Light of Ethnographic Reality. In *Dumbarton Oaks Conference on the Olmec*, edited by Elizabeth P. Benson, pp. 143–174. Dumbarton Oaks Research Library and Collection, Washington, D.C.

Gage, Thomas

1958   *Travels in the New World*, edited by J. Eric S. Thompson. University of Oklahoma Press, Norman.

Galinier, Jacques

1987   *Pueblos de la Sierra Madre. Etnografía de la comunidad otomí.* Instituto Nacional Indigenista, Mexico City.

Gallegos Gómora, Miriam Judith

1989   Excavaciones en la estructura D-7 en La Venta, Tabasco. *Arqueología*, 2nd series, 3:17–24.

García, Edgar Vinicio

1997   Excavaciones en el acceso a la ter-raza 3, Abaj Takalik. In *X Simposio de Investigaciones Arqueológicas in Guatemala, 1996*, edited by Juan Pedro Laporte and Héctor L. Escobedo, pp. 167–191. Ministerio de Cultura y Deportes, Instituto de Antropología e Historia, and the Asociación Tikal, Guatemala City.

Garibay K., Ángel María

1989   Magos y saltimbanquis. Appendix III to *Historia general de las cosas de Nueva España*, by Bernadino de Sahagún, pp. 904–909. Editorial Porrúa, Mexico City.

Gillespie, Susan D.

2000   The Monuments of Laguna de los Cerros and Its Hinterland. In *Olmec Art and Archaeology in Mesoamerica*, edited by John E. Clark and Mary E. Pye, pp. 95–115. Studies in the History of Art 58. National Gallery of Art, Washington, D.C.

2008   History in Practice: Ritual Deposition at La Venta Complex A. In *Memory Work: Archaeologies of Material Practices*, edited by Barbara J. Mills and William H. Walker, pp. 109–136. School of Advanced Research Press, Santa Fe, N.Mex.

Girard, Rafael

1966   *Los mayas: Su civilización, su historia, sus vinculaciones continentales.* Libro-Mex Editores, Mexico City.

1969   *La misteriosa cultura olmeca: Últimos descubrimientos de esculturas pre-olmecas en Guatemala.* 3rd ed. Imprenta Eros, Guatemala City.

Gómez Rueda, Hernando

1995   Exploración de sistemas hidráuli-cos en Izapa. In *VIII Simposio de Investigaciones Arqueológicas en Guatemala, 1994*, edited by Juan Pedro Laporte and Héctor L. Escobedo, pp. 9–18. Ministerio de Cultura y Deportes, Instituto de Antropología e Historia, and Asociación Tikal, Guatemala City.

Gómez Rueda, Hernando, and Liwy Grazioso Sierra

1997   Nuevos elementos de la iconografía de Izapa: La Estela 90. In *X Simposio de Investigaciones Arqueológicas en Guatemala, 1996*, edited by Juan Pedro Laporte and Héctor L. Escobedo, pp. 223–235. Ministerio de Cultura y Deportes, Instituto de Antropología e Historia, and Asociación Tikal, Guatemala City.

González Lauck, Rebecca B.

1987   Informe técnico parcial. Proyecto Arqueológico La Venta. Temporada 1985. Archivo Técnico. Coordinación Nacional de Arqueología. Manuscript on file with the Instituto Nacional de Antropología e Historia, Mexico City.

1988   Proyecto Arqueológico La Venta. *Arqueología*, 1st series, 4:121–165.

1989   Recientes investigaciones en La Venta, Tabasco. In *El Preclásico o Formativo: Avances y perspectivas,* edited by Martha Carmona Macías, pp. 81–90. Instituto Nacional de Antropología e Historia, Mexico City.

1990   The 1984 Archaeological Investigations at La Venta, Tabasco, Mexico. Ph.D. dissertation, Department of Anthropology, University of California, Berkeley.

1994   La antigua ciudad olmeca en La Venta, Tabasco. In *Los olmecas en Mesoamérica,* edited by John E. Clark, pp. 93–111. Citibank and Editorial Equilibrista, Mexico City, and Turner Libros, Madrid.

1996   La Venta: An Olmec Capital. In *Olmec Art of Ancient Mexico,* edited by Elizabeth P. Benson and Beatriz de la Fuente, pp. 73–81. National Gallery of Art, Washington, D.C.

1997   Acerca de pirámides de tierra y seres sobrenaturales: Observaciones preliminares en torno al Edificio C-1, La Venta, Tabasco. *Arqueología,* 2nd series, 17:79–97.

2000   La zona del Golfo en el Preclásico: La etapa olmeca. In *El México antiguo, sus áreas culturales, los orígenes y el horizonte Preclásico,* vol. 1 of *Historia antigua de México,* edited by Linda Manzanilla and Leonardo López Luján, pp. 363–406. Instituto Nacional de Antropología e Historia, Mexico City.

2004   Observaciones en torno a los contextos de la escultura olmeca en La Venta. In *Acercarse y mirar: Homenaje a Beatriz de la Fuente,* edited by María Teresa Uriarte and Leticia Staines Cicero, pp. 75–106. Instituto de Investigaciones Estéticas, Universidad Nacional Autónoma de México, Mexico City.

2007   El Complejo A de La Venta, Tabasco. *Arqueología mexicana* 15(87):49–54.

González Lauck, Rebecca B., and Felipe Solís Olguín

1996   Olmec Collections in the Museums in Tabasco: A Century of Protecting a Millennial Civilization (1896–1996). In *Olmec Art of Ancient Mexico,* edited by Elizabeth P. Benson and Beatriz de la Fuente, pp. 145–152. National Gallery of Art, Washington, D.C.

Goodall, Rosemary, Jay Hall, Rene Viel, F. Ricardo Agurcia, Howell G. M. Edwards, and Peter M. Fredericks

2006   Raman Microscopic Investigation of Paint Samples from the *Rosalila* Building, Copan, Honduras. *Journal of Raman Spectroscopy* 37:1072–1077.

Gossen, Gary H.

1975   Animal Souls and Human Destiny in Chamula. *Man* 10(3):448–461.

1994   From Olmecs to Zapatistas: A Once and Future History of Souls. *American Anthropologist* 96(3):554–570.

Graham, Ian

1979   *Yaxchilan,* vol. 3, part 2 of *Corpus of Maya Hieroglyphic Inscriptions.* Peabody Museum of Archaeology and Ethnology, Cambridge, Mass.

1982   *Yaxchilan,* vol. 3, part 3 of *Corpus of Maya Hieroglyphic Inscriptions.* Peabody Museum of Archaeology and Ethnology, Cambridge, Mass.

Graham, Ian, and Eric von Euw

1977   *Yaxchilan,* vol. 3, part 1 of *Corpus of Maya Hieroglyphic Inscriptions.* Peabody Museum of Archaeology and Ethnology, Cambridge, Mass.

Graham, John A.

1977   Discoveries at Abaj Takalik, Guatemala. *Archaeology* 30:196–197.

1979   Maya, Olmecs, and Izapans at Abaj Takalik. *Proceedings of the International Congress of Americanists* 8:179–188. Paris.

1980   Abaj Takalik, the Olmec Style and Its Antecedents in Pacific Guatemala. In *Los olmecas: The Parent Civilization of Mesoamerica.* University Gallery, College of Fine Arts, University of Florida, Gainesville.

1981   Abaj Takalik: The Olmec Style and Its Antecedents in Pacific Guatemala. In *Ancient Mesoamerica: Selected Readings,* edited by John A. Graham, pp. 163–176. Peek Publications, Palo Alto, Calif.

1982   Antecedents of Olmec Sculpture at Abaj Takalik. In *Pre-Columbian Art History: Selected Readings,* edited by

Alan Cordy-Collins, pp. 7–22. Peek Publications, Palo Alto, Calif.

1989   Olmec Diffusion: A Sculptural View from Pacific Guatemala. In *Regional Perspectives on the Olmec,* edited by Robert J. Sharer and David C. Grove, pp. 227–246. Cambridge University Press, Cambridge.

1992   Escultura en bulto olmeca y maya en Abaj Takalik: Su desarrollo y por-tento. In *IV Simposio de Investigaciones Arqueológicas en Guatemala, 1990,* edited by Juan Pedro Laporte, Héctor L. Escobedo, and Sandra Villagran de Brady, pp. 353–361. Ministerio de Cultura y Deportes, Instituto de Antropología e Historia, and Asociación Tikal, Guatemala City.

2005   Reading the Past: Olmec Archaeology and the Curious Case of Tres Zapotes Stela C. Paper presented at the Mesa Redonda Olmeca, Mexico City.

Graham, John A., and Larry Benson

2005   Maya and Olmec Boulder Sculpture at Abaj Takalik: Its Development and Portent. In *Archaeology without Limits: Papers in Honor of Clement W. Meighan,* edited by Brian D. Dillon and Matthew A. Boxt, pp. 345–367. Labyrinthos, Lancaster, Calif.

Graham, John A., Robert F. Heizer, and Edwin M. Shook

1978   Abaj Takalik 1976: Exploratory Investigations. In *Studies in Ancient Mesoamerica,* edited by John A. Graham, pp. 85–109. Contributions of the University of California Archaeological Research Facility 36. University of California, Berkeley.

Graham, John A., and James B. Porter

1989   A Cycle 6 Initial Series? A Maya Boulder Inscription of the First Millennium B.C. from Abaj Takalik. *Mexicon* 11(3):46–49.

Grove, David C.

1970   *The Olmec Paintings of Oxtotitlan Cave, Guerrero.* Studies in Pre-Columbian Art and Archaeology 6. Dumbarton Oaks Research Library and Collection, Washington, D.C.

1972   El Teocuicani: "Cantor divino" en Jantetelco. *INAH Boletín* 3:35–36.

1973   Olmec Altars and Myths. *Archaeology* 26:128–135.

1981   Olmec Monuments: Mutilation as a Clue to Meaning. In *The Olmec and Their Neighbors: Essays in Memory of Matthew W. Stirling,* edited by Elizabeth P. Benson, pp. 49–68. Dumbarton Oaks Research Library and Collection, Washington, D.C.

1984   *Chalcatzingo: Excavations on the Olmec Frontier.* Thames and Hudson, London.

1987a   *Ancient Chalcatzingo.* University of Texas Press, Austin.

1987b   Comments on the Site and Its Organization. In *Ancient Chalcatzingo,* edited by David C. Grove, pp. 420–433. University of Texas Press, Austin.

1989   Chalcatzingo and Its Olmec Connection. In *Regional Perspectives on the Olmec,* edited by Robert J. Sharer and David C. Grove, pp. 122–147. Cambridge University Press, Cambridge.

1993   "Olmec" Horizons in Formative Period Mesoamerica: Diffusion or Social Evolution? In *Latin American Horizons,* edited by Don S. Rice, pp. 83–111. Dumbarton Oaks Research Library and Collection, Washington, D.C.

1996   Archaeological Contexts of Olmec Art outside of the Gulf Coast. In *Olmec Art of Ancient Mexico,* edited by Elizabeth P. Benson and Beatriz de la Fuente, pp. 105–117. National Gallery of Art, Washington, D.C.

1997   Olmec Archaeology: A Half Century of Research and Its Accomplishments. *Journal of World Prehistory* 11:51–101.

1999   Public Monuments and Sacred Mountains: Observations on Three Formative Period Sacred Landscapes. In *Social Patterns in Pre-Classic Mesoamerica,* edited by David C. Grove and Rosemary A. Joyce, pp. 255–295. Dumbarton Oaks Research Library and Collection, Washington, D.C.

2000   Faces of the Earth at Chalcatzingo, Mexico: Serpents, Caves, and

Mountains in Middle Formative
Period Iconography. In *Olmec Art and
Archaeology in Mesoamerica,* edited
by John E. Clark and Mary E. Pye, pp.
277–295. Studies in the History of Art 58.
National Gallery of Art, Washington,
D.C.

Grove, David C., and Jorge V. Angulo

1987　A Catalog and Description of
Chalcatzingo's Monuments. In *Ancient
Chalcatzingo,* edited by David C. Grove,
pp. 114–131. University of Texas Press,
Austin.

1992　Ideology and Evolution at the Pre-State
Level. In *Ideology and Pre-Columbian
Civilizations,* edited by Arthur A.
Demarest and Geoffrey W. Conrad, pp.
15–36. School of American Research,
Santa Fe, N.Mex.

2002　Middle Formative Domestic Ritual at
Chalcatzingo, Morelos. In *Domestic
Ritual in Ancient Mesoamerica,* edited
by Patricia Plunket, pp. 11–19. Cotsen
Institute of Archaeology Monograph
46. Cotsen Institute of Archaeology,
University of California, Los Angeles.

Grove, David C., and Rosemary A. Joyce (editors)

1999　*Social Patterns in Pre-Classic
Mesoamerica: A Symposium at
Dumbarton Oaks, 9 and 10 October 1993.*
Dumbarton Oaks Research Library and
Collection, Washington, D.C.

Grube, Nikolai, and Linda Schele

1991　Tzuk *in the Classic Maya Inscriptions.*
Texas Notes on Precolumbian Art,
Writing, and Culture 15. Department
of Art and Art History, University of
Texas, Austin.

1996　*New Observations on the Loltun Relief.*
Texas Notes on Precolumbian Art,
Writing, and Culture 74. Department
of Art and Art History, University of
Texas, Austin.

Guernsey, Julia

2006a　Late Formative Period Antecedents
for Ritually Bound Monuments. In
*Sacred Bundles: Ritual Acts of Wrapping
and Binding in Mesoamerica,* edited
by Julia Guernsey and F. Kent Reilly
III, pp. 22–39. Ancient America
Special Publication 1. Boundary

End Archaeology Research Center,
Barnardsville, N.C.

2006b　*Ritual and Power in Stone: The
Performance of Rulership in
Mesoamerican Izapan Style Art.*
University of Texas Press, Austin.

n.d.　A Consideration of the Quatrefoil
Motif in Preclassic Mesoamerica. *Res:
Anthropology and Aesthetics,* in press.

Guernsey Kappelman, Julia

2000　Late Formative Toad Altars as Ritual
Stages. *Mexicon* 22:80–84.

Guernsey, Julia, and Michael W. Love

2005　Late Preclassic Expressions of Authority
on the Pacific Slope. In *Lords of
Creation: The Origins of Sacred Maya
Kingship,* edited by Virginia M. Fields
and Dorie Reents-Budet, pp. 37–43.
Los Angeles County Museum of Art,
Los Angeles.

2008　Cerámica y piedra: Correspondencias
entre escultura pública y artefac-
tos domésticos en la Costa Sur de
Guatemala. In *XXI Simposio de
Investigaciones Arqueológicas en
Guatemala, 2007,* edited by Juan
Pedro Laporte, Bárbara Arroyo, and
Héctor Mejía, pp. 953–969. Ministerio
de Cultura y Deportes, Instituto de
Antropología e Historia, Asociación
Tikal, and Fundación Arqueológica del
Nuevo Mundo, Guatemala City.

n.d.　Sculptures from Argelia, Coatepeque,
Quetzaltenango. Manuscript on file,
Department of Art and Art History,
University of Texas, Austin.

Guernsey Kappelman, Julia, and F. Kent Reilly III

2001　Paths to Heaven, Ropes to Earth: Birds,
Jaguars, and Cosmic Cords in Formative
Period Mesoamerica. *Ancient America*
3:33–52.

Gutiérrez Mendoza, Gerardo

1996　Patrón de asentamiento y cronología
en el sur de la Huasteca: Sierra de
Otontepec y Laguna de Tamiahua.
Licenciatura thesis, in archaeology,
Escuela Nacional de Antropología e
Historia, Mexico City.

2002　The Expanding Polity: Patterns of the
Territorial Expansion of the Post-Classic

Señorío of Tlapa-Tlachinollan in the Mixteca-Nahuatl-Tlapaneca Region of Guerrero. Ph.D. dissertation, Department of Anthropology, Pennsylvania State University, University Park.

2007   *Catálogo de sitios arqueológicos de las regiones Mixteca-Tlapaneca-Nahua.* CIESAS, Mexico City. CD-format and internet. Foundation for the Advancement of Mesoamerican Studies, Crystal River, Fla. Electronic document, http://www.famsi.org/spanish/research/gutierrez/index.html.

2008   Four Thousand Years of Communication Systems in the Mixteca-Tlapaneca-Nahua Region: From the Cauadzidziqui Rock Shelter Murals to the Azoyú Codices. In *Mixtec Writing and Society. Escritura de Ñuu Dzau,* edited by Maarten Jansen and Laura van Broekhoven, pp. 67–103. Royal Netherlands Academy of Arts and Society, Amsterdam.

Gutiérrez Mendoza, Gerardo (editor)

2008   Exploraciones en la plataforma principal del sitio de Contlalco, Guerrero. Report submitted to the Instituto Nacional de Antropología e Historia, Mexico City.

Gutiérrez Mendoza, Gerardo, Mary E. Pye, Alfredo Vera Rivera, and Juana Mitzi Serrano Rivero

2006   Las pinturas rupestres de Cauadzidziqui, Ocampo: Una revisión del fenómeno "olmeca" en el oriente de Guerrero. In *Las regiones histórico-culturales: Sus problemas e interacciones. II Mesa Redonda: El Conocimiento Antropológico e Histórico sobre Guerrero, 2006.* CD-format. Instituto Nacional de Antropología e Historia, Mexico City.

Guzmán, Eulalia

1934   Los relieves de las rocas del Cerro de la Cantera, Jonacatepec, Morelos. *Anales del Museo Nacional de Arqueología e Etnografía,* 5th series, 1:237–251.

Hammond, Norman

1988   Cultura Hermana: Reappraising the Olmec. *Quarterly Review of Archaeology* 9(4):1–4.

2001   The Cobata Colossal Head: An Unfinished Olmec Monument? *Antiquity* 75:21–22.

Hansen, Richard D.

1990   *Excavations in the Tigre Complex, El Mirador, Petén, Guatemala.* Papers of the New World Archaeological Foundation 62. Brigham Young University, Provo, Utah.

1991   The Maya Rediscovered: The Road to Nakbe. *Natural History* 100(5):8–14.

1993   Investigaciones del sitio arqueológico Nakbe: Temporada 1989. In *III Simposio de Investigaciones Arqueológicos en Guatemala 1989,* edited by Juan Pedro Laporte, Héctor Escobedo, and Sandra Villagrán, pp. 43–56. Museo Nacional de Arqueología y Etnología, Guatemala City.

1998   Continuity and Disjunction: The Pre-Classic Antecedents of Classic Maya Architecture. In *Function and Meaning in Classic Maya Architecture,* edited by Stephen D. Houston, pp. 49–122. Dumbarton Oaks Research Library and Collection, Washington, D.C.

2001   The First Cities: The Beginnings of Urbanization and State Formation in the Maya Lowlands. In *Maya: Divine Kings of the Rain Forest,* edited by Nikolai Grube, pp. 50–65. Könemann, Cologne.

Hansen, Richard D., and Stanley P. Guenter

2005   Early Social Complexity and Kingship in the Mirador Basin. In *Lords of Creation: The Origins of Sacred Maya Kingship,* edited by Virginia M. Fields and Dorie Reents-Budet, pp. 60–61. Los Angeles County Museum of Art, Los Angeles.

Hayden, Brian

1995   Pathways to Power: Principles for Creating Socioeconomic Inequalities. In *Foundations of Social Inequality,* edited by T. Douglas Price and Gary M. Feinman, pp. 15–86. Plenum, New York.

Heizer, Robert F.

1966   Ancient Heavy Transport, Methods and Achievements. *Science* 153:821–830.

1967 Analysis of Two Low Relief Sculptures from La Venta. *Studies in Olmec Archaeology* 3:25–55.

Heizer, Robert F., John A. Graham, and Lewis K. Napton

1968 The 1968 Investigations at La Venta. *Studies in Ancient Mesoamerica IV* 5:127–205.

Hellmuth, Nicholas

1987 *Monster und Menschen in der Maya-Kunst.* Akademische Druck- und Verlagsanstalt, Graz, Austria.

Holland, William R.

1961 El tonalismo y el nagualismo entre los tzotziles. *Estudios de cultura maya* 1:167–181.

Houston, Stephen D.

1998 Classic Maya Depictions of the Built Environment. In *Function and Meaning in Classic Maya Architecture,* edited by Stephen D. Houston, pp. 333–372. Dumbarton Oaks Research Library and Collection, Washington, D.C.

2004 Writing in Early Mesoamerica. In *The First Writing: Script Invention as History and Process,* edited by Stephen D. Houston, pp. 274–309. Cambridge University Press, Cambridge.

2006 An Example of Preclassic Mayan Writing? *Science* 311:1249–1250.

Houston, Stephen D., and David Stuart

1989 *The* Way *Glyph: Evidence for "Co-essences" among the Classic Maya.* Research Reports on Ancient Maya Writing 30. Center for Maya Research, Washington, D.C.

1996 Of Gods, Glyphs and Kings: Divinity and Rulership among the Classic Maya. *Antiquity* 70:289–312.

1998 The Ancient Maya Self: Personhood and Portraiture in the Classic Period. *Res: Anthropology and Aesthetics* 33:73–101.

Houston, Stephen D., and Karl Taube

2000 An Archaeology of the Senses: Perception and Cultural Expression in Ancient Mesoamerica. *Cambridge Archaeological Journal* 10(2):261–294.

Houston, Stephen D., Karl Taube, Ray Matheny, Deanne Matheny, Zachary Nelson, Gene Ware, and Cassandra Mesick

2005 The Pool of the Rain God: An Early Stuccoed Altar at Aguacatal. *Mesoamerican Voices* 2:37–62.

Ichon, Alain

1977 *Les sculptures de La Lagunita.* Centre National de la Recherche Scientifique, Institut d'Ethnologie, Paris.

1979 *Rescate arqueológico en la cuenca del Río Chixoy 1. Informe preliminar.* Mision Cientifica Franco-Guatemalteca, Centre National de la Recherche Scientifique. Institut d'Ethnologie, Paris.

1984 Le Groupe A de La Lagunita. In *La Période Formative à La Lagunita et dans le Quiché Méridional, Guatemala,* edited by Alaine Ichon and René Viel, pp. 3–51. Centre National de la Recherche Scientifique. Institut d'Ethnologie, Paris.

1992 *Los Cerritos-Chijoj: La transición Epiclásica en las tierras altas de Guatemala.* Centre National de la Recherche Scientifique, Institut d'Ethnologie, Paris.

Ichon, Alain, and Marie Charlotte Arnauld

1985 *Le Protoclassique à La Lagunita, El Quiché, Guatemala.* Centre National de la Recherche Scientifique, Institut d'Ethnologie, Paris.

Ichon, Alain, and Rita Grignon Cheesman

1983 *Archéologie de sauvetage: 5. Les sites Classiques de la Valle Moyenne du Río Chixoy.* Centre National de la Recherche Scientifique, Institut d'Ethnologie, Paris.

Ichon, Alain, and Rene Viel

1984 *La Période Formative à La Lagunita et dans le Quiché Méridional, Guatemala.* Centre National de la Recherche Scientifique, Institut d'Ethnologie, Paris.

Iglesias Ponce de León, María Josefa, and Andrés Ciudad Ruíz

1999 El altiplano occidental. In *Época precolombina,* edited by Marion Popenoe de Hatch, pp. 265–288. Vol. 1 of *Historia general de Guatemala,* edited by Jorge Luján Muñoz. Asociación de Amigos del País, Fundación para la Cultura y el Desarrollo, Guatemala City.

Ivic de Monterroso, Matilde

1999   Regiones arqueológicas de Guatemala. In *Época precolombina*, edited by Marion Popenoe de Hatch, pp. 165–170. Vol. 1 of *Historia general de Guatemala*, edited by Jorge Luján Muñoz. Asociación de Amigos del País, Fundación para la Cultura y el Desarrollo, Guatemala City.

2004   Las figurillas de La Blanca, San Marcos. In *XVII Simposio de Investigaciones Arqueológicas en Guatemala, 2003*, edited by Juan Pedro Laporte, Bárbara Arroyo, Héctor Escobedo, and Héctor Mejía, pp. 417–427. Ministerio de Cultura y Deportes, Instituto de Antropología e Historia, and Asociación Tikal, Guatemala City.

Jaime Riverón, Olaf

2004   *Análisis de la cadena operativa de materiales elaborados en piedra verde del sitio arqueológico La Venta*. Proyecto Arqueológico La Venta. Centro Instituto Nacional de Antropología e Historia Tabasco, Villahermosa, Mexico.

Jiménez García, Elizabeth, Guadalupe Martínez Donjuán, and Aarón Arboleyda Castro

1998   Arqueología. In *Época prehispánica*, vol. 1 of *Historia general de Guerrero*, edited by Elizabeth Jiménez García, Guadalupe Martínez Donjuán, Aarón Arboleyda Castro, and Raúl Vélez Calvo, pp. 23–140. Instituto Nacional de Antropología e Historia, Gobierno del Estado de Guerrero, and JGH Editores, Mexico City and Chilpancingo, Mexico.

Joesink-Mandeville, L. R. V., and Sylvia Meluzin

1976   Olmec-Maya Relationships: Olmec Influence in Yucatan. In *The Origins of Religious Art and Iconography in Preclassic Mesoamerica*, edited by Henry B. Nicholson, pp. 87–105. UCLA Latin American Center Publications, Los Angeles.

Jones, Christopher

1986   A Ruler in Triumph: Chocolá Monument 1. *Expedition* 28:3–12.

Jones, Sian

1997   *The Archaeology of Ethnicity: Constructing Identities in the Past and Present*. Routledge, London.

Joralemon, Peter David

1971   *A Study of Olmec Iconography*. Studies in Pre-Columbian Art and Archaeology 7. Dumbarton Oaks Research Library and Collection, Washington D.C.

1976   The Olmec Dragon: A Study in Pre-Columbian Iconography. In *Origins of Religious Art and Iconography in Preclassic Mesoamerica*, edited by Henry B. Nicholson, pp. 27–71. UCLA Latin American Center Publications, Los Angeles.

1996   In Search of the Olmec Cosmos: Reconstructing the World Views of Mexico's First Civilization. In *Olmec Art of Ancient Mexico*, edited by Elizabeth P. Benson and Beatriz de la Fuente, pp. 51–59. National Gallery of Art, Washington, D.C.

Joyce, Rosemary A.

2003   Making Something of Herself: Embodiment in Life and Death at Playa de los Muertos, Honduras. *Cambridge Archaeological Journal* 13:248–261.

Joyce, Rosemary A., and John S. Henderson

2002   La arqueológia del Periodo Formativo en Honduras: Nuevos datos sobre el "estilo olmeca" en la zona maya. *Mayab* 15:5–17.

Justeson, John S., and Terrence Kaufman

2008   The Epi-Olmec Tradition at Cerro de las Mesas in the Classic Period. In *Classic Period Cultural Currents in Southern and Central Veracruz*, edited by Philip J. Arnold III and Christopher A. Pool, pp. 159–194. Dumbarton Oaks Research Library and Collection, Washington, D.C.

Justeson, John S., and Peter Mathews

1983   The Seating of the *Tun*: Further Evidence Concerning a Late Preclassic Lowland Maya Stela Cult. *American Antiquity* 48(3):586–593.

Kaplan, Jonathan

1995   The Incienso Throne and Other Thrones from Kaminaljuyu, Guatemala. *Ancient Mesoamerica* 6:185–196.

1996   El Monumento 65 de Kaminaljuyú y su ilustración de ritos dinásticos de gobierno del Preclásico Tardío. In *IX Simposio de Investigaciones*

Arqueológicas en Guatemala, 1995, edited by Juan Pedro Laporte and Héctor L. Escobedo, pp. 451–460. Ministerio de Cultura y Deportes, Instituto de Antropología e Historia, and Asociación Tikal, Guatemala City.

1999 Rulership and Ideology at Late Preclassic Kaminaljuyú: A Comparative Study. Ph.D. dissertation, Department of Anthropology, Yale University, New Haven, Conn.

2000 Monument 65: A Great Emblematic Depiction of Throned Rule and Royal Sacrifice at Late Preclassic Kaminaljuyú. *Ancient Mesoamerica* 11(2):185–198.

2002 From Under the Volcanoes: Some Aspects of the Ideology of Rulership at Late Preclassic Kaminaljuyú. In *Incidents of Archaeology in Central America and Yucatán: Studies in Honor of Edwin M. Shook,* edited by Michael W. Love, Marion Popenoe de Hatch, and Héctor L. Escobedo, pp. 311–357. University Press of America, Lanham, Md.

Kaplan, Lucille N.

1956 Tonal and Nagual in Coastal Oaxaca, Mexico. *Journal of American Folklore* 69(274):363–368.

Kaufman, Terrence

1974 *Idiomas de Mesoamérica.* Editorial José de Pineda Ibarra and Ministerio de Educación, Guatemala City.

1976 Archaeological and Linguistic Correlations in Mayaland and Associated Areas of Meso-America. *World Archaeology* 8:101–118.

Kaufman, Terrence, and John Justeson

2008 The Epi-Olmec Language and Its Neighbors. In *Classic Period Cultural Currents in Southern and Central Veracruz,* edited by Philip J. Arnold III and Christopher A. Pool, pp. 55–83. Dumbarton Oaks Research Library and Collection, Washington, D.C.

Kaufman, Terrence, with the help of John Justeson

2003 A Preliminary Mayan Etymological Dictionary. Electronic document, http://www.famsi.org/reports/01051/index.html.

Kaufmann, Carol

2003 Sistine Chapel of the Early Maya. *National Geographic* 204(6):72–77.

Kidder, Alfred V.

1961 Archaeological Investigations at Kaminaljuyu, Guatemala. *American Philosophical Society Proceedings* 105:559–570.

1965 Preclassic Pottery Figurines of the Guatemalan Highlands. In *Archaeology of Southern Mesoamerica,* part 1, edited by Gordon R. Willey, pp. 146–155. Vol. 2 of *Handbook of Middle American Indians,* edited by Robert Wauchope. University of Texas Press, Austin.

Kidder, Alfred V., Jesse D. Jennings, and Edwin M. Shook

1946 *Excavations at Kaminaljuyu.* Carnegie Institution of Washington Publication 561. Carnegie Institution of Washington, Washington, D.C.

Kintz, Ellen R.

1990 *Life under the Tropical Canopy: Tradition and Change among the Yucatec Maya.* Rinehart and Winston, Fort Worth, Tex.

Kirchhoff, Paul

1943 Mesoamérica: Sus límites geográficos, composición étnica y caracteres culturales. *Acta americana* 1:92–107.

1966 Mesoamerica: Its Geographic Limits, Ethnic Composition and Cultural Characteristics. In *Ancient Mesoamerica: Selected Readings,* edited by John A. Graham, pp. 1–14. Peek Publications, Palo Alto, Calif.

Knight, Charles L. F., and Christopher A. Pool

2008 Formative to Classic Period Obsidian Consumption at Tres Zapotes, Veracruz. Paper presented at the 73rd Annual Meeting of the Society for American Archaeology, Vancouver.

Kolb, Michael

1996 Comment on "Agency, Ideology, and Power in Archaeological Theory." *Current Anthropology* 37:59–60.

Konica-Minolta

2007 VIVID 9i Three Dimensional Digitizer Technical Specifications. Non-Contact 3D Laser Scanner. Electronic document,

http://www.minolta3d.com/products/
vi9i-en.asp#specs.

Kubler, George

1961　On the Colonial Extinction of the
Motifs of Pre-Columbian Art. In *Essays
in Pre-Columbian Art and Archaeology*,
edited by Samuel K. Lothrop, pp. 14–34.
Harvard University Press, Cambridge,
Mass.

1962　*The Art and Architecture of Ancient
America*. Penguin Books, Baltimore, Md.

1990　*The Art and Architecture of Ancient
America: The Mexican, Maya, and
Andean Peoples*. 3rd ed. Yale University
Press, New Haven, Conn.

Lacadena García-Gallo, Alfonso

2008　La escritura olmeca y la hipótesis del
mixe-zoque: Implicaciones lingüísti-
cas de un análisis estructural del
Monumento 13 de La Venta. In *Olmeca,
balance y perspectivas: Memoria de la
Primera Mesa Redonda*, vol. 2, edited
by María Teresa Uriarte and Rebecca
B. González Lauck, pp. 607–626.
Universidad Nacional Autónoma de
México, Mexico City.

Lee, Thomas A., Jr.

1969　*The Artifacts of Chiapa de Corzo,
Chiapas, Mexico*. Papers of the New
World Archaeological Foundation 26.
Brigham Young University, Provo, Utah.

1989　Chiapas and the Olmec. In *Regional
Perspectives on the Olmec*, edited by
Robert J. Sharer and David C. Grove, pp.
198–226. Cambridge University Press,
Cambridge.

Leonard, Daniel, and Karl Taube

2007　The God C Variant: A Reappraisal.
Paper presented at the 72nd Annual
Meeting for the Society for American
Archaeology, Austin.

Lesure, Richard G.

1999　Figurines as Representations and
Products at Paso de la Amada, Mexico.
Cambridge Archaeological Journal
9:209–220.

Lévi-Strauss, Claude

1966　*The Savage Mind*. University of Chicago
Press, Chicago, and Weidenfeld and
Nicolson, London.

Lister, Robert H.

1971　Archaeological Synthesis of Guerrero.
In *The Archaeology of Northern
Mesoamerica*, part 2, edited by Gordon F.
Ekholm and Ignacio Bernal, pp. 619–631.
Vol. 11 of *Handbook of Middle American
Indians*, edited by Robert Wauchope.
University of Texas Press, Austin.

Litvak King, Jaime

1975　En torno al problema de la definición de
Mesoamérica. *Anales de antropología*
12:171–195.

Looper, Matthew G.

2003　*Lightning Warrior: Maya Art and
Kingship at Quiriguá*. University of
Texas Press, Austin.

López Austin, Alfredo

1967　Cuarenta clases de magos del mundo
náhuatl. *Estudios de cultura náhuatl*
7:87–117.

1984　*Cuerpo humano e ideología: Las con-
cepciones de los antiguos nahuas*. 2 vols.
Universidad Nacional Autónoma de
México, Instituto de Investigaciones
Antropológicas, Mexico City.

1994　*Tamoanchan y Tlalocan*. Fondo de
Cultura Económica, Mexico City.

2001　El núcleo duro, la cosmovisión y
la tradición mesoamericana. In
*Cosmovisión, ritual e identidad de los
pueblos indígenas de México*, edited by
Johanna Broda and Félix Báez-Jorge, pp.
47–65. Consejo Nacional para la Cultura
y las Artes and Fondo de Cultura
Económica, Mexico City.

López Bruni, Ricky

2006　*Ciudades sagradas mayas, Petén,
Guatemala*. Editores Fundación G & T
Continental, Guatemala City.

Lothrop, Samuel K.

1926　Stone Sculptures from the Finca
Arevalo, Guatemala. *Indian Notes*
3(3):147–171. Museum of the American
Indian, Heye Foundation, New York.

Loughlin, Michael, and Christopher A. Pool

2006　Olmec to Epi-Olmec in the Eastern
Lower Papaloapan Basin. Paper pre-
sented at the 71st Annual Meeting of the
Society for American Archaeology, San
Juan, Puerto Rico.

Love, Michael W.

1999a Ideology, Material Culture, and Daily Practice in Pre-Classic Mesoamerica: A Pacific Coast Perspective. In *Social Patterns in Pre-Classic Mesoamerica,* edited by David C. Grove and Rosemary A. Joyce, pp. 127–153. Dumbarton Oaks Research Library and Collection, Washington, D.C.

1999b La cultura olmeca en Guatemala. In *Época precolombina,* edited by Marion Popenoe de Hatch, pp. 191–200. Vol. 1 of *Historia general de Guatemala,* edited by Jorge Luján Muñoz. Asociación de Amigos del País, Fundación para la Cultura y el Desarrollo, Guatemala City.

2002 *Early Complex Society in Pacific Guatemala: Settlements and Chronology of the Río Naranjo, Guatemala.* Papers of the New World Archaeological Foundation 66. Brigham Young University, Provo, Utah.

2004 Etnicidad, identidad y poder: Interacción entre los mayas y sus vecinos en el altiplano y costa del Pacífico de Guatemala en el Preclásico. In *XVII Simposio de Investigaciones Arqueológicas en Guatemala, 2003,* edited by Juan Pedro Laporte, Bárbara Arroyo, Héctor L. Escobedo, and Héctor E. Mejía, pp. 449–460. Ministerio de Cultura y Deportes, Instituto de Antropología e Historia, and Asociación Tikal, Guatemala City.

2007 Regional Research in the Southern Highlands and Pacific Coast of Mesoamerica. *Journal of Archaeological Research* 15:275–328.

n.d. Early States in the Southern Maya Region. In *Early Maya States,* edited by Loa P. Traxler and Robert J. Sharer. University of Pennsylvania Press, Philadelphia, in press.

Love, Michael W., Donaldo Castillo, and Beatriz Balcárcel

1996 Investigaciones arqueológicas en El Ujuxte, Retalhuleu 1995–96: Informe preliminar. Instituto de Antropología e Historia, Guatemala City.

Love, Michael W., and Julia Guernsey

2007 Monument 3 from La Blanca, Guatemala: A Middle Preclassic Earthen Sculpture and Its Ritual Associations. *Antiquity* 81:920–932.

Love, Michael W., Julia Guernsey, Sheryl Carcuz, and Molly Morgan

2006 El Monumento 3 de La Blanca: Una nueva escultura del Preclásico Medio. In *XIX Simposio de Investigaciones Arqueológicas en Guatemala, 2005,* edited by Juan Pedro Laporte, Bárbara Arroyo, and Héctor E. Mejía, pp. 51–62. Ministerio de Cultura y Deportes, Instituto de Antropología e Historia, Asociación Tikal, and Fundación Arqueológica del Nuevo Mundo, Guatemala City.

Lowe, Gareth W.

1977 The Mixe-Zoque as Competing Neighbors of the Early Lowland Maya. In *The Origins of Maya Civilization,* edited by R. E. W. Adams, pp. 197–248. University of New Mexico Press, Albuquerque.

1989 The Heartland Olmec: Evolution of Material Culture. In *Regional Perspectives on the Olmec,* edited by Robert J. Sharer and David C. Grove, pp. 33–67. Cambridge University Press, Cambridge.

1998 *Los olmecas de San Isidro en Malpaso, Chiapas.* Instituto Nacional de Antropología e Historia, Mexico City.

Lowe, Gareth W., Thomas A. Lee Jr., and Eduardo Martínez Espinosa

1982 *Izapa: An Introduction to the Ruins and Monuments.* Papers of the New World Archaeological Foundation 31. Brigham Young University, Provo, Utah.

Lucero, Lisa J.

2006 *Water and Ritual: The Rise and Fall of Classic Maya Rulers.* University of Texas Press, Austin.

Maler, Teobert

1911 *Explorations in the Department of Peten, Guatemala. Tikal.* Memoirs of the Peabody Museum of American Archaeology and Ethnology 5, no. 1. Peabody Museum, Cambridge, Mass.

Malmström, Vincent Herschel

1997   *Cycles of the Sun, Mysteries of the Moon: The Calendar in Mesoamerican Civilization.* University of Texas Press, Austin.

Marcus, Joyce

1992   *Mesoamerican Writing Systems: Propaganda, Myth, and History in Four Ancient Civilizations.* Princeton University Press, Princeton, N.J.

1998   *Women's Ritual in Formative Oaxaca: Figurine-Making, Divination, Death, and the Ancestors.* Memoirs 33. University of Michigan Museum of Anthropology, Ann Arbor.

1999   Men's and Women's Ritual in Formative Oaxaca. In *Social Patterns in Pre-Classic Mesoamerica,* edited by David C. Grove and Rosemary A. Joyce, pp. 67–96. Dumbarton Oaks Research Library and Collection, Washington, D.C.

Marcus, Joyce, and Kent V. Flannery

1996   *Zapotec Civilization: How Urban Society Evolved in Mexico's Oaxaca Valley.* Thames and Hudson, London.

Marroquín Alvarez, Elizabeth

2005   El manejo del agua en Tak'alik Ab'aj: La evidencia de canales prehispánicos. In *XVIII Simposio de Investigaciones Arqueológicas en Guatemala, 2004,* edited by Juan Pedro Laporte, Bárbara Arroyo, and Héctor E. Mejía, pp. 997–1008. Ministerio de Cultura y Deportes, Instituto de Antropología e Historia, and Asociación Tikal, Guatemala City.

Martin, Simon, and Nikolai Grube

2000   *Chronicle of the Maya Kings and Queens: Deciphering the Dynasties of the Ancient Maya.* Thames and Hudson, London.

Martínez Donjuán, Guadalupe

1984   Teopantecuanitlán, Guerrero: Un sitio olmeca. *Revista mexicana de estudios antropológicos* 28:123–132.

1986   Teopantecuanitlán. In *Arqueología y etnohistoria del estado de Guerrero,* pp. 55–80. Primer Coloquio. Instituto Nacional de Antropología e Historia and Gobierno del Estado de Guerrero, Mexico City and Chilpancingo, Mexico.

1994   Los olmecas en el estado de Guerrero. In *Los olmecas en Mesoamérica,* edited by John E. Clark, pp. 143–163. Citibank and Editorial Equilibrista, Mexico City, and Turner Libros, Madrid.

1995   Teopantecuanitlán. *Arqueología mexicana* 2(12):58–62.

2008   Teopantecuanitlán: Algunas interpretaciones iconográficas. In *Olmeca, balance y perspectivas: Memoria de la Primera Mesa Redonda,* vol. 1, edited by María Teresa Uriarte and Rebecca B. González Lauck, pp. 333–355. Universidad Nacional Autónoma de México, Mexico City.

McDonald, Andrew J.

1983   *Tzutzuculi: A Middle-Preclassic Site on the Pacific Coast of Chiapas, Mexico.* Papers of the New World Archaeological Foundation 47. Brigham Young University, Provo, Utah.

McGee, R. Jon

1990   *Life, Ritual, and Religion among the Lacandón Maya.* Wadsworth, Belmont, Calif.

Medellín Zenil, Alfonso

1971   *Monolitos olmecas y otros en el Museo de la Universidad de Veracruz.* Corpus Antiquitatum Americanensium, Mexico 5. Instituto Nacional de Antropología e Historia, Mexico City.

Medina Hernández, Andrés

2001   La cosmovisión mesoamericana: Una mirada desde la etnografía. In *Cosmovisión, ritual e identidad de los pueblos indígenas de México,* edited by Johanna Broda and Félix Báez-Jorge, pp. 67–163. Consejo Nacional para la Cultura y las Artes and Fondo de Cultura Económica, Mexico City.

Mendieta, Gerónimo de

1993 [1870]   *Historia eclesiástica indiana,* edited by Joaquín García Icazbalceta. Editorial Porrúa, Mexico City.

Michels, Joseph W.

1979   *The Kaminaljuyú Chiefdom.* Pennsylvania State University Press, University Park.

Michels, Joseph W., and William T. Sanders

1973   *The Pennsylvania State University Kaminaljuyú Project: 1969, 1970 Seasons.* Occasional Papers in Anthropology 9. Pennsylvania State University Press, University Park.

Milbrath, Susan

1979   *A Study of Olmec Sculptural Chronology.* Studies in Pre-Columbian Art and Archaeology 23. Dumbarton Oaks Research Library and Collection, Washington, D.C.

Miles, Suzanne W.

1965   Sculpture of the Guatemala-Chiapas Highlands and Pacific Slopes, and Associated Hieroglyphs. In *The Archaeology of Southern Mesoamerica,* part 1, edited by Gordon R. Willey, pp. 237–275. Vol. 3 of *Handbook of Middle American Indians,* edited by Robert Wauchope. University of Texas Press, Austin.

Miller, Mary E.

1986   *The Art of Mesoamerica from Olmec to Aztec.* Thames and Hudson, New York.

1999   *Maya Art and Architecture.* Thames and Hudson, London.

Miller, Mary E., and Simon Martin (editors)

2004   *Courtly Art of the Ancient Maya.* Fine Arts Museums of San Francisco, San Francisco, and Thames and Hudson, New York.

Miller, Mary E., and Karl Taube

1993   *The Gods and Symbols of Ancient Mexico and the Maya: An Illustrated Dictionary of Mesoamerican Religion.* Thames and Hudson, New York.

Millet Cámara, Luis Alfonso

1979   Rescate arqueológico en la región de Tres Zapotes, Veracruz. Licenciatura thesis, Department of Anthropology, Escuela Nacional de Antropología e Historia, Mexico City.

Molina, Alonso de

1977   *Vocabulario en lengua castellana y mexicana y mexicana y castellana.* Editorial Porrúa, Mexico City.

Montgomery, John

2002   *Dictionary of Maya Hieroglyphs.* Hippocreme Books, New York.

Mora-Marín, David

2001   The Grammar, Orthography, Content, and Social Context of Late Preclassic Mayan Portable Texts. Ph.D. dissertation, Department of Anthropology, State University of New York, Albany.

Morán, Francisco

1689–1695   Arte en lengua choltí, que quiere decir
[1929]   lengua de milperos. Typewritten manuscript on file at Tozzer Library, Harvard University.

Morley, Sylvanus G.

1938   *The Inscriptions of Peten,* vol. 1. Carnegie Institution of Washington Publication 437. Carnegie Institution of Washington, Washington, D.C.

1946   *The Ancient Maya.* Stanford University Press, Stanford, Calif.

Moscoso Pastrana, Prudencio

1990   *Las cabezas rodantes del mal: Brujería y nahualismo en los altos de Chiapas.* Miguel Angel Porrúa, Mexico City.

Navarrete, Carlos

1972   Fechamiento para un tipo de esculturas del sur de Mesoamérica. *Anales de antropología* 9:45–52.

1974   *The Olmec Rock Carvings at Pijijiapan, Chiapas, Mexico and Other Olmec Pieces from Chiapas and Guatemala.* Papers of the New World Archaeological Foundation 35. Brigham Young University, Provo, Utah.

Navarrete, Carlos, and Rocío Hernández

2000   Esculturas preclásicas de obesos en el territorio mexicano. In *XIII Simposio de Investigaciones Arqueológicas en Guatemala, 1999,* edited by Juan Pedro Laporte, Héctor L. Escobedo, Ana Claudia de Suasnavar, and Bárbara Arroyo, pp. 589–624. Ministerio de Cultura y Deportes, Instituto de Antropología e Historia, and Asociación Tikal, Guatemala City.

Navarrete Linares, Federico

2000   Nagualismo y poder: Un viejo binomio mesoamericano. In *El héroe entre el mito y la historia,* edited by Federico

Navarrete and Guilhem Olivier, pp. 155–179. Universidad Nacional Autónoma de México and Centro Francés de Estudios Mexicanos y Centroamericanos, Mexico City.

Neff, Hector, Deborah M. Pearsall, John G. Jones, Barbara Arroyo, Shawn K. Collins, and Dorothy E. Freidel

2006   Early Maya Adaptive Patterns: Mid-Late Holocene Paleoenvironmental Evidence from Pacific Guatemala. *Latin American Antiquity* 17:287–315.

Newsome, Elizabeth A.

2001   *Trees of Paradise and Pillars of the World: The Serial Stela Cycle of 18-Rabbit-God K, King of Copán.* University of Texas Press, Austin.

Niederberger, Christine

1986   Excavación de una área de habitación doméstica en la capital "olmeca" de Tlacozotitlán: Reporte preliminar. In *Arqueología y etnohistoria del estado de Guerrero,* pp. 83–103. Instituto Nacional de Antropología e Historia, Mexico City, and Gobierno del Estado de Guerrero, Chilpancingo, Mexico.

1987   *Paléopaysages et archéologie pré-urbaine du Bassin de Mexico.* 2 vols. Centre d'Etudes Mexicaines et Centraméricaines, Mexico City.

1996   The Basin of Mexico: A Multimillennial Development toward Cultural Complexity. In *Olmec Art of Ancient Mexico,* edited by Elizabeth P. Benson and Beatriz de la Fuente, pp. 83–93. National Gallery of Art, Washington, D.C.

2000   Ranked Societies, Iconographic Complexity, and Economic Wealth in the Basin of Mexico toward 1200 BC. In *Olmec Art and Archaeology in Mesoamerica,* edited by John E. Clark and Mary E. Pye, pp. 169–191. Studies in the History of Art 58. National Gallery of Art, Washington, D.C.

2002a   Antiguos paisajes de Guerrero y el papel de su fauna en las creencias míticas. In *El pasado arqueológico de Guerrero,* edited by Christine Niederberger and Rosa M. Reyna Robles, pp. 17–75. Consejo Nacional para la Cultura y las Artes, Instituto Nacional de Antropología e Historia, Centro Francés de Estudios Mexicanos y Centroamericanos, and Gobierno del Estado de Guerrero, Mexico City.

2002b   Nácar, "jade," y cinabrio: Guerrero y las redes de intercambio en la Mesoamérica antigua (1000–600 BC). In *El pasado arqueológico de Guerrero,* edited by Christine Niederberger and Rosa M. Reyna Robles, pp. 175–223. Consejo Nacional para la Cultura y las Artes, Instituto Nacional de Antropología e Historia, Centro Francés de Estudios Mexicanos y Centroamericanos, and Gobierno del Estado de Guerrero, Mexico City.

Norman, V. Garth

1973   *Izapa Sculpture*, part 1, *Album.* Papers of the New World Archaeological Foundation 30. Brigham Young University, Provo, Utah.

1976   *Izapa Sculpture*, part 2, *Text.* Papers of the New World Archaeological Foundation 30. Brigham Young University, Provo, Utah.

Ochoa, Lorenzo, and Olaf Jaime

2000   *Un paseo por el Parque-Museo de La Venta.* Gobierno de Tabasco, Consejo Nacional para la Cultura y las Artes, Mexico City.

Ochoa, Patricia

1996   Acrobat Effigy Vessel. In *Olmec Art of Ancient Mexico,* edited by Elizabeth P. Benson and Beatriz de la Fuente, p. 189. National Gallery of Art, Washington, D.C.

Ohi, Kuniaki, and Miguel F. Torres (editors)

1994   *Piedras-Hongo.* Museo de Tabaco y Sal, Tokyo.

Ohi, Kuniaki, Nobuyuki Ito, Shione Shibata, Sho Nakamori, and Hiroshi Minami

1994   Trabajos de conservación y exploración arqueológica en D-III-1 (Edificio de la Obsidiana Incrustada) de Kaminaljuyu, Guatemala, 1992–1993. In *VII Simposio de Investigaciones Arqueológicas en Guatemala, 1993,* edited by Juan Pedro Laporte and Héctor L. Escobedo, pp. 155–162. Ministerio de Cultura y Deportes, Instituto de Antropología e Historia, and Asociación Tikal, Guatemala City.

Oliveros, José Arturo

1994   Imagen precolombina de Huracán. *Arqueología mexicana* 2(7):66–69.

Orellana, Sandra L.

1981   Idols and Idolatry in Highland Guatemala. *Ethnohistory* 28:157–177.

Orr, Heather

1997   Power Games in the Late Formative Valley of Oaxaca: The Ballplayer Sculptures at Dainzú. Ph.D. dissertation, Department of Art and Art History, University of Texas, Austin.

2003   *Stone Balls and Masked Men: Ballgame as Combat Ritual, Dainzú, Oaxaca.* Ancient America 5. Center for American Studies, Barnardsville, N.C., and Washington, D.C.

Orrego Corzo, Miguel

1990   *Reporte 1: Investigaciones arqueológicas en Abaj Takalik, El Asintal, Retalhuleu 1988.* Ministerio de Cultura y Deportes, Instituto de Antropología e Historia, Guatemala City.

1995   Costa sur de Guatemala: Importante evidencia sobre la presencia de la cultura maya, para los períodos Preclásico Tardío y Clásico Temprano. In *The Emergence of Lowland Maya Civilization: The Transition from the Preclassic to Early Classic,* edited by Nikolai Grube, pp. 7–15. Verlag Anton Saurwein, Markt Schwaben, Germany.

1997   *Reporte 2: Investigaciones arqueológicos en Abaj Takalik, El Asintal, Retalhuleu 1989–1990.* Ministerio de Cultura y Deportes, Instituto de Antropología e Historia, Guatemala City.

1998   Problemática de multiplicidad de estilos y patrones culturales en Abaj Takalik: Preclásico Medio y Tardío (800 a.C.–250 d.C.). In *Taller arqueológico de la región de la Costa Sur de Guatemala,* edited by Christa Schieber de Lavarreda, pp. 53–70. Proyecto Nacional Abaj Takalik, Ministerio de Arqueología y Deportes, Instituto de Antropología e Historia, Guatemala City.

Orrego Corzo, Miguel, and Christa Schieber de Lavarreda

2001   Compendio de monumentos expuestos en Abaj Takalik. Proyecto Nacional Abaj Takalik. In *XIV Simposio de Investigaciones Arqueológicas en Guatemala, 2000,* edited by Juan Pedro Laporte, Ana Claudia Monzón de Suasnávar, and Bárbara Arroyo, pp. 917–938. Ministerio de Cultura y Deportes, Instituto de Antropología e Historia, and Asociación Tikal, Guatemala City.

Ortíz Ceballos, Ponciano

1975   La cerámica de los Tuxtlas. Master's thesis, Department of Archaeology, Universidad Veracruzana, Xalapa, Veracruz, Mexico.

Ortíz Ceballos, Ponciano, and María del Carmen Rodríguez

1994   Los espacios sagrados olmecas: El Manatí, un caso especial. In *Los olmecas en Mesoamérica,* edited by John E. Clark, pp. 69–91. Citibank and Editorial Equilibrista, Mexico City, and Turner Libros, Madrid.

1999   Olmec Ritual Behavior at El Manatí: A Sacred Space. In *Social Patterns in Pre-Classic Mesoamerica,* edited by David C. Grove and Rosemary Joyce, pp. 225–254. Dumbarton Oaks Research Library and Collection, Washington, D.C.

2000   The Sacred Hill of El Manatí: A Preliminary Discussion of the Site's Ritual Paraphernalia. In *Olmec Art and Archaeology in Mesoamerica,* edited by John E. Clark and Mary E. Pye, pp. 75–93. Studies in the History of Art 58. National Gallery of Art, Washington, D.C.

Ortíz Ceballos, Ponciano, María del Carmen Rodríguez, Ricardo Sánchez, and Jasinto Robles

2007   El bloque labrado con inscripciones olmecas: El Cascajal, Jaltipan, Veracruz. *Arqueología mexicana* 14(83):15–18.

Palka, Joel W.

2002   Left/Right Symbolism and the Body in Ancient Maya Iconography and Culture. *Latin American Antiquity* 13:419–443.

Panofsky, Dora, and Erwin Panofsky

1956   *Pandora's Box. The Changing Aspects of a Mythical Symbol.* 2nd ed. Bollinger

Series LII. Princeton University Press, Princeton, N.J.

Parsons, Lee A.

1981   Post-Olmec Stone Sculpture: The Olmec-Izapan Transition on the Southern Pacific Coast and Highlands. In *The Olmecs and Their Neighbors: Essays in Honor of Matthew W. Stirling*, edited by Elizabeth P. Benson, pp. 257–288. Dumbarton Oaks Research Library and Collection, Washington, D.C.

1983   Altars 9 and 10, Kaminaljuyu, and the Evolution of the Serpent-Winged Deity. In *Civilization in the Ancient Americas: Essays in Honor of Gordon R. Willey*, edited by Richard Leventhal and Alan Kolata, pp. 145–156. University of New Mexico Press, Albuquerque.

1986   *The Origins of Maya Art: A Study of the Monumental Sculpture of Kaminaljuyú, Guatemala and the Southern Pacific Coast.* Studies in Pre-Columbian Art and Archaeology 28. Dumbarton Oaks Research Library and Collection, Washington, D.C.

1988   Proto-Maya Aspects of Miraflores-Arenal Monumental Stone Sculpture from Kaminaljuyú and the Southern Pacific Coast. In *Maya Iconography*, edited by Elizabeth P. Benson and Gillet G. Griffin, pp. 6–43. Princeton University Press, Princeton, N.J.

Parsons, Lee A., and Peter S. Jenson

1965   Boulder Sculpture on the Pacific Coast of Guatemala. *Archaeology* 18(2):132–144.

Paso y Troncoso, Francisco del (editor)

1953 [1892]   Manual de ministros de indios para el conocimiento de sus idolatrías y extirpación de ellas. In *Tratado de las idolatrías, supersticiones, dioses, ritos, hechicerías y otras costumbres gentílicas de las razas aborígenes de México*, vol. 1, edited by Jacinto de la Serna, pp. 40–368. Ediciones Fuente Cultural, Mexico City.

Patton, James L.

1987   The Architecture and Sculpture of Polol, El Peten, Guatemala. Master's thesis, Department of Anthropology, San Francisco State University, San Francisco.

Pereira, Karen

2008   Plain, but Not Simple: Monuments at Naranjo, Guatemala. Master's thesis, Department of Anthropology, University of Florida, Gainesville.

Pereira, Karen, Bárbara Arroyo, and Margarita Cossich

2007   Las estelas lisas de Naranjo, Guatemala. In *XX Simposio de Investigaciones Arqueológicas en Guatemala, 2006*, edited by Juan Pedro Laporte, Bárbara Arroyo, and Héctor E. Mejía, pp. 849–860. Ministerio de Cultura y Deportes, Instituto de Antropología e Historia, Asociación Tikal, and Fundación Arqueológica del Nuevo Mundo, Guatemala City.

Pérez Campa, Mario

1998   El gran basamento circular de Cuicuilco. *Arqueología mexicana* 5(30):34–37.

Pérez de Lara, Jorge, and John Justeson

2006   Photographic Documentation of Monuments with Epi-Olmec Script/Imagery. Electronic document, http://www.famsi.org/reports/05084.

Piedra Santa, Rony, and Miguel Angel Morales

2007   Reconocimiento arqueológico en el sitio de Barranca de Galvez, San Marcos. In *XX Simposio de Investigaciones Arqueológicas en Guatemala, 2006*, edited by Juan Pedro Laporte, Bárbara Arroyo, and Héctor E. Mejía, pp. 779–789. Ministerio de Cultura y Deportes, Instituto de Antropología e Historia, Asociación Tikal, and Fundación Arqueológica del Nuevo Mundo, Guatemala City.

Piña Chan, Román

1982   *Los olmecas antiguos.* Consejo Editorial del Gobierno del Estado de Tabasco, Mexico City.

1989   *The Olmec: Mother Culture of Mesoamerica.* Rizzoli, New York.

1993   *El lenguaje de las piedras.* Fondo de Cultura Económica, Mexico City.

Piña Chan, Román, and Luis Covarrubias

1964   *El pueblo del jaguar (Los olmecas arqueológicos).* Consejo para la planeación e instalación del Museo Nacional de Antropología, Mexico City.

Pohl, Mary E. D.

2008   *Formas de escritura tempranas en Mesoamérica.* Informe Preliminar. Instituto Nacional de Antropología e Historia, Mexico City.

Pohl, Mary E. D., Kevin O. Pope, and Christopher L. von Nagy

2002   Olmec Origins of Mesoamerican Writing. *Science* 298:1984–1987.

Pohorilenko, Anotole

1990   The Structure and Periodization of the Olmec Representational System. Ph.D. dissertation, Department of Anthropology, Tulane University, New Orleans, La.

Pool, Christopher A.

1997   *Tres Zapotes Archaeological Survey, 1995 Season, Technical Report.* National Science Foundation, Washington D.C.

2000   From Olmec to Epi-Olmec at Tres Zapotes, Veracruz, Mexico. In *Olmec Art and Archaeology in Mesoamerica,* edited by John E. Clark and Mary E. Pye, pp. 137–153. Studies in the History of Art 58. National Gallery of Art, Washington, D.C.

2005   *Tres Zapotes Archaeological Project 2003. Final Report for Award # BCS-0242555.* National Science Foundation, Washington D.C.

2006   Tres Zapotes: La unidad política y la generación de espacios. Paper presented at the Encuentro Internacional de Olmequistas, Xalapa, Veracruz, Mexico.

2007   *Olmec Archaeology and Early Mesoamerica.* Cambridge University Press, New York.

2008   Architectural Plans, Factionalism, and the Protoclassic-Classic Transition at Tres Zapotes. In *Classic Period Cultural Currents in Southern and Central Veracruz,* edited by Philip J. Arnold III and Christopher A. Pool, pp. 121–157. Dumbarton Oaks Research Library and Collection, Washington, D.C.

Pool, Christopher A., and Michael A. Ohnersorgen

2003   Archaeological Survey and Settlement at Tres Zapotes. In *Settlement Archaeology and Political Economy at Tres Zapotes, Veracruz, Mexico,* edited by Christopher A. Pool, pp. 7–31. Monograph 50. Cotsen Institute of Archaeology, University of California, Los Angeles.

Pool, Christopher A., and Ponciano Ortiz Ceballos

2008   Tres Zapotes como un centro olmeca: Nuevos datos. In *Memorias de la Segunda Mesa Redonda Olmeca 2005,* edited by María Teresa Uriarte and Rebecca B. González Lauck, pp. 425–443. Instituto Nacional de Antropología e Historia, Mexico City.

Pool, Christopher A., Ponciano Ortiz Ceballos, and María del Carmen Rodríguez

n.d.   The Early Horizon at Tres Zapotes: Implications for Olmec Interaction. *Ancient Mesoamerica* 21(1), in press.

Popenoe de Hatch, Marion

1989   A Seriation of Monte Alto Sculptures. In *New Frontiers in the Archaeology of the Pacific Coast of Southern Mesoamerica,* edited by Frederick Bove and Lynette Heller, pp. 25–41. Arizona State University Anthropological Research Papers 39. Arizona State University, Tempe.

1991   Comentarios sobre la cerámica de Abaj Takalik. In *Reporte 1: Investigaciones Arqueológicos en Abaj Takalik, El Asintal, Retalhuleu 1988,* edited by Miguel Orrego Corzo, pp. 68–71. Ministerio de Cultura y Deportes, Instituto de Antropología e Historia, Guatemala City.

1993   Observaciones adicionales sobre las tradiciones Naranjo y Achiguate en la costa sur de Guatemala. In *VI Simposio de Investigaciones Arqueológicas en Guatemala, 1992,* edited by Juan Pedro Laporte, Héctor L. Escobedo, and Sandra Villagran de Brady, pp. 353–358. Ministerio de Cultura y Deportes, Instituto de Antropología e Historia, and Asociación Tikal, Guatemala City.

1997   *Kaminaljuyú/San Jorge: Evidencia arqueológica de la actividad económica en el valle de Guatemala, 300 a.C. a 300 d.C.* Fundación para la Cultura y el Desarrollo, Guatemala City.

1999   El desarrollo en el noroccidente de
          Guatemala desde el Preclásico hasta
          el Postclásico. In *XII Simposio de
          Investigaciones Arqueológicas en
          Guatemala, 1998,* edited by Juan Pedro
          Laporte, Héctor L. Escobedo, and Ana
          Claudia Monzón de Suasnávar, pp. 497–
          508. Ministerio de Cultura y Deportes,
          Instituto de Antropología e Historia,
          and Asociación Tikal, Guatemala City.

2001   Kaminaljuyú, Guatemala. In
          *Archaeology of Ancient Mexico and
          Central America: An Encyclopedia,*
          edited by Susan T. Evans and David
          Webster, pp. 387–390. Garland, New
          York.

2002a   Evidencia de un observatorio
          astronómico en Abaj Takalik. In *XV
          Simposio de investigaciones arqueológi-
          cas en Guatemala, 2001,* edited by Juan
          Pedro Laporte, Héctor L. Escobedo, and
          Bárbara Arroyo, pp. 437–458. Ministerio
          de Cultura y Deportes, Instituto de
          Antropología e Historia, and Asociación
          Tikal, Guatemala City.

2002b   La cerámica del altiplano noroccidental
          de Guatemala, La Lagunita y la tradición
          cerámica solano: Algunas comparacio-
          nes. In *Misceláneas en honor a Alain
          Ichon,* edited by M. Charlotte Arnauld,
          Alain Breton, Marie-France Favet-
          Berthelat, and Juan Antonio Valdés,
          pp. 49–63. Centro Frances de Estudios
          Mexicanos y Centroamericanos, Mexico
          City, and Asociación Tikal, Guatemala
          City.

2002c   New Perspectives on Kaminaljuyu,
          Guatemala: Regional Interaction
          during the Preclassic and Classic
          Periods. In *Incidents of Archaeology in
          Central America and Yucatán: Essays
          in Honor of Edwin M. Shook,* edited
          by Michael W. Love, Marion Popenoe
          de Hatch, and Héctor L. Escobedo, pp.
          277–296. University Press of America,
          Lanham, Md.

2004   Un paso más en entender los inicios
          de Abaj Takalik. In *XVII Simposio
          de Investigaciones Arqueológicas en
          Guatemala, 2003,* edited by Juan Pedro
          Laporte, Bárbara Arroyo, Héctor
          L. Escobedo, and Héctor Mejía, pp.

437–447. Ministerio de Cultura y
          Deportes, Instituto de Antropología
          e Historia, and Asociación Tikal,
          Guatemala City.

2005   La conquista de Tak'alik Ab'aj. In
          *XVIII Simposio de Investigaciones
          Arqueológicas en Guatemala, 2004,*
          edited by Juan Pedro Laporte, Bárbara
          Arroyo, and Héctor E. Mejía, pp. 1037–
          1043. Ministerio de Cultura y Deportes,
          Instituto de Antropología e Historia,
          and Asociación Tikal, Guatemala City.

Popenoe de Hatch, Marion, and Christa Schieber de
    Lavarreda
2001   Una revisión preliminar de la histo-
          ria de Tak'alik Ab'aj. In *XIV Simposio
          de Investigaciones Arqueológicas en
          Guatemala, 2000,* edited by Juan
          Pedro Laporte, Ana Claudia Monzón
          de Suasnávar, and Bárbara Arroyo,
          pp. 1149–1171. Ministerio de Cultura y
          Deportes, Instituto de Antropología
          e Historia, and Asociación Tikal,
          Guatemala City.

Popenoe de Hatch, Marion, Christa Schieber de
    Lavarreda, Edgar Carpio Rezzio, Miguel Orrego
    Corzo, José Héctor Paredes, and Claudia Wolley
2000   Observaciones sobre el desarrollo cul-
          tural en Abaj Takalik. In *XIII Simposio
          de Investigaciones Arqueológicas en
          Guatemala, 1999,* edited by Juan Pedro
          Laporte, Héctor L. Escobedo, Ana
          Claudio Monzón de Suasnávar, and
          Bárbara Arroyo, pp. 159–170. Ministerio
          de Cultura y Deportes, Instituto de
          Antropología e Historia, and Asociación
          Tikal, Guatemala City.

Porter, James B.
1989   The Monuments and Hieroglyphs
          of Tres Zapotes, Veracruz, Mexico.
          Ph.D. dissertation, Department of
          Anthropology, University of California,
          Berkeley.

1992   "Estelas celtiformes": Un nuevo tipo de
          escultura olmeca y sus implicaciones
          para los epigrafistas. *Arqueología,* 2nd
          series, 8:3–13.

Price, Clifford A.

1996   *Stone Conservation: An Overview of Current Research.* Getty Conservation Institute, J. Paul Getty Trust, Santa Monica, Calif.

Princeton Art Museum

1995   *The Olmec World: Ritual and Rulership.* Art Museum, Princeton University, Princeton, N.J.

Proskouriakoff, Tatiana

1950   *A Study of Classic Maya Sculpture.* Carnegie Institution of Washington Publication 593. Carnegie Institution of Washington, Washington, D.C.

1968   Olmec and Maya Art: Problems of Their Stylistic Relation. In *Dumbarton Oaks Conference on the Olmec,* edited by Elizabeth P. Benson, pp. 119–134. Dumbarton Oaks Research Library and Collection, Washington, D.C.

1971   Early Architecture and Sculpture in Mesoamerica. In *Observations on the Emergence of Civilization in Mesoamerica,* edited by Robert F. Heizer and John A. Graham, pp. 141–156. Contributions of the University of California Archaeological Research Facility 11. University of California, Berkeley.

Pugh, Marion Stirling

1981   An Intimate View of Archaeological Exploration. In *The Olmec and Their Neighbors,* edited by Elizabeth P. Benson, pp. 1–13. Dumbarton Oaks Research Library and Collection, Washington, D.C.

Pye, Mary E.

1995   Settlement, Specialization, and Adaptation in the Rio Jesus Drainage, Retalhuleu, Guatemala. Ph.D. dissertation, Department of Anthropology, Vanderbilt University, Nashville, Tenn.

Pye, Mary E., and Gerardo Gutiérrez

2007   The Pacific Coast Trade Route of Mesoamerica: Iconographic Connections between Guatemala and Guerrero. In *Archaeology, Art, and Ethnogenesis in Mesoamerican Prehistory: Papers in Honor of Gareth W. Lowe,* edited by Lynneth S. Lowe and Mary E. Pye, pp. 229–245. Papers of the New World Archaeological Foundation 68. Brigham Young University, Provo, Utah.

Quenon, Michel, and Geneviève le Fort

1997   Rebirth and Resurrection in Maize God Iconography. In *The Maya Vase Book,* vol. 5, edited by Barbara Kerr and Justin Kerr, pp. 884–899. Kerr Associates, New York.

Quiñones Keber, Eloise

1995   *Codex Telleriano-Remensis: Ritual, Divination, and History in a Pictorial Aztec Manuscript.* University of Texas Press, Austin.

Quirarte, Jacinto

1973   *Izapan-Style Art: A Study of Its Form and Meaning.* Studies in Pre-Columbian Art and Archaeology 10. Dumbarton Oaks Research Library and Collection, Washington, D.C.

2007   Revisiting the Relationship between Izapa, Olmec, and Maya Art. In *Archaeology, Art, and Ethnogenesis in Mesoamerican Prehistory: Papers in Honor of Gareth W. Lowe,* edited by Lynneth S. Lowe and Mary E. Pye, pp. 247–275. Papers of the New World Archaeological Foundation 68. Brigham Young University, Provo, Utah.

Rands, Robert

1974   A Chronological Framework for Palenque. In *Primera Mesa Redonda de Palenque, Part I, 1973,* edited by Merle G. Robertson, pp. 35–39. Robert Louis Stevenson School, Pebble Beach, Calif.

Read, Emma J., and Christopher Chippindale

2000   Electronic Drawing or Manual Drawing? Experiences from Work with Rock-Paintings. In *U.K. Chapter of Computer Applications and Quantitative Methods in Archaeology, Proceedings of the Fourth Meeting, Cardiff University, 27 and 28 February 1999,* edited by Caitlin Buck, Vicky Cummings, Cole Henley, Steve Mills, and Steve Trick, pp. 59–79. BAR International Series 844. Archaeopress, Oxford.

Recinos, Adrián

1984 Títulos de la casa Izquin-Nehaib, señora del territorio de Otzoyá. In *Crónicas indígenas de Guatemala,* edited by Adrián Recinos, pp. 71–94. Academia de Geografía e Historia de Guatemala, Guatemala.

Redfield, Robert

1941 *The Folk Culture of Yucatan.* University of Chicago Press, Chicago.

Reents-Budet, Dorie

1998 Elite Maya Pottery and Artisans as Social Indicators. In *Craft and Social Identity,* edited by Cathy Lynne Costin and Rita P. Wright, pp. 71–89. American Anthropological Association, Arlington, Va.

Reese, Kathryn V.

1996 Narratives of Power: Late Formative Public Architecture and Civic Center Design at Cerros, Belize. Ph.D. dissertation, Department of Anthropology, University of Texas, Austin.

Reilly, F. Kent, III

1989 The Shaman in Transformation Pose: A Study of the Theme of Rulership in Olmec Art. *Record of the Art Museum, Princeton University* 48(2):4–21.

1990 Cosmos and Rulership: The Function of Olmec-Style Symbols in Formative Period Mesoamerica. *Visible Language* 24(1):12–37.

1991 Olmec Iconographic Influences on the Symbols of Maya Rulership: An Examination of Possible Sources. In *Sixth Palenque Round Table, 1986,* edited by Virginia M. Fields, pp. 151–174. University of Oklahoma Press, Norman.

1994a Cosmología, soberanismo y espacio ritual en la Mesoamérica del Formativo. In *Los olmecas en Mesoamérica,* edited by John E. Clark, pp. 239–259. Citibank and Editorial Equilibrista, Mexico City, and Turner Libros, Madrid.

1994b Enclosed Ritual Spaces and the Watery Underworld in Formative Period Architecture: New Observations on the Function of La Venta Complex A. In *Seventh Palenque Round Table, 1989,* edited by Virginia M. Fields, pp. 125–135.

Pre-Columbian Art Research Institute, San Francisco.

1995 Art, Ritual, and Rulership in the Olmec World. In *The Olmec World: Ritual and Rulership,* pp. 27–45. Art Museum, Princeton University, Princeton, N.J.

1996 The Lazy-S: A Formative Period Iconographic Loan to Maya Hieroglyphic Writing. In *Eighth Palenque Round Table 1993,* edited by Martha J. Macri and Jan McHargue, pp. 413–424. Precolumbian Art Research Institute, San Francisco.

1999 Mountains of Creation and Underworld Portals: The Ritual Function of Olmec Architecture at La Venta, Tabasco. In *Mesoamerican Architecture as a Cultural Symbol,* edited by Jeff K. Kowalski, pp. 14–39. Oxford University Press, Oxford.

2002 The Landscape of Creation: Architecture, Tomb, and Monument Placement in the Olmec Site of La Venta. In *Heart of Creation: The Mesoamerican World and the Legacy of Linda Schele,* edited by Andrea Stone, pp. 34–65. University of Alabama Press, Tuscaloosa.

2005 Olmec Ideological, Ritual, and Symbolic Contributions to the Institution of Classic Maya Kingship. In *Lords of Creation: The Origins of Sacred Maya Kingship,* edited by Virginia M. Fields and Dorie Reents-Budet, pp. 30–36. Los Angeles County Museum of Art, Los Angeles.

Relación de la provincia de Coatzacualco, villa del Espíritu Santo

1984 In *Relaciones geográficas del siglo XVI,* vol. 2, *Antequera,* edited by René Acuña, pp. 113–126. Universidad Nacional Autónoma de México, Mexico City.

Richardson, Francis B.

1940 Non-Maya Monumental Sculpture of Central America. In *The Maya and Their Neighbors,* pp. 395–416. D. Appleton-Century, New York.

Rizzo de Robles, Nidia

1991 Aspectos ecológicos del Proyecto Abaj Takalik. In *II Simposio de Investigaciones Arqueológicas en Guatemala, 1988,* edited by Juan Pedro Laporte, Sandra Villagrán, Héctor

L. Escobedo, Dora de González, and Juan Antonio Valdés, pp. 31–34. Museo Nacional de Arqueología y Etnología, Guatemala City.

Robertson, Merle G.

1985   *The Sculpture of Palenque: The Late Buildings of the Palace.* Princeton University Press, Princeton, N.J.

1991   *Sculpture of Palenque: The Cross Group, the North Group, the Olividado, and Other Pieces.* Princeton University Press, Princeton, N.J.

Robinson, Eugenia, Hector Neff, Mary E. Pye, and Marlen Garnica

2005   The Formative Archaeological Cultures of the Guatemalan Highlands and Pacific Coast: Interregional Interaction and Cultural Evolution. In *New Perspective on Formative Mesoamerican Cultures,* edited by Terry G. Powis, pp. 85–94. BAR International Series 1377. British Archaeological Reports, Oxford.

Rodas, Sergio

1993   Catálogo de Barrigones de Guatemala. *U tz'ib* 1(5):1–36.

Rodríguez, María del Carmen, and Ponciano Ortíz Ceballos

2000   A Massive Offering of Axes at La Merced, Hidalgotitlán, Veracruz, Mexico. In *Olmec Art and Archaeology in Mesoamerica,* edited by John E. Clark and Mary E. Pye, pp. 154–167. Studies in the History of Art 58. National Gallery of Art, Washington, D.C.

Rodríguez, María del Carmen, Ponciano Ortíz Ceballos, Michael D. Coe, Richard A. Diehl, Stephen D. Houston, Karl A. Taube, and Alfredo Delgado Calderon

2006   Oldest Writing in the New World. *Science* 313:1610–1614.

Ruíz de Alarcón, Hernando

1953 [1629]   Tratado de supersticiones y costumbres gentílicas que hoy viven entre los indios y de esta Nueva Espana. In *Tratado de las idolatrías, supersticiones, dioses, ritos, hechicerías y otras costumbres gentílicas de las razas aborígenes de México,* vol. 2, edited by Francisco del Paso y Troncoso, pp. 21–180. Ediciones Fuente Cultural, Mexico City.

Sahagún, Bernardino de

1977   *Florentine Codex: General History of the Things of New Spain,* book 7, *The Sun, Moon, and Stars, and the Binding of the Years,* edited and translated by Arthur J. O. Anderson and Charles E. Dibble. School of American Research, Santa Fe, N.Mex., and University of Utah, Salt Lake City.

1979   *Florentine Codex: General History of the Things of New Spain,* book 4, *The Soothsayers,* and book 5, *The Omens,* edited and translated by Arthur J. O. Anderson and Charles E. Dibble. School of American Research, Santa Fe, N.Mex., and University of Utah, Salt Lake City.

1989   *Historia general de las cosas de Nueva España.* Editorial Porrúa, Mexico City.

Saler, Benson

1964   Nagual, Witch, and Sorcerer in a Quiché Village. *Ethnology* 3(3):305–328.

Sanders, William T.

1974   Chiefdom to State: Political Evolution at Kaminaljuyú, Guatemala. In *Reconstructing Complex Societies,* edited by Charlotte B. Moore, pp. 97–121. Supplement to the Bulletin of the American Schools of Oriental Research 20. American Schools of Oriental Research, Cambridge, Mass.

Sanders, William T., and Barbara J. Price

1968   *Mesoamerica: The Evolution of a Civilization.* Random House, New York.

Santley, Robert S., Thomas P. Barrett, Michael D. Glascock, and Hector Neff

2001   Pre-Hispanic Obsidian Procurement in the Tuxtla Mountains, Southern Veracruz, Mexico. *Ancient Mesoamerica* 12:49–63.

Sapio, Giovanni

1982   Proyecto Xochicalco: Informe de la primera temporada de superficie. Salvage report submitted to the Instituto de Antropología e Historia, Mexico City.

Saturno, William A.

2006   The Dawn of Maya Gods and Kings. *National Geographic* 209(1):68–77.

Saturno, William A., David Stuart, and Boris Beltrán

2006   Early Maya Writing at San Bartolo, Guatemala. *Science* 311:1281–1283.

Saturno, Willam A., David Stuart, and Karl Taube

2005   La identificación de las figuras del muro oeste de Pinturas Sub-1, San Bartolo, Peten. In *XVIII Simposio de Investigaciones Arqueológicas en Guatemala, 2004,* edited by Juan Pedro Laporte, Bárbara Arroyo, and Héctor E. Mejía, pp. 647–655. Ministerio de Cultura y Deportes, Instituto de Antropología e Historia, and Asociación Tikal, Guatemala City.

Saturno, William A., Karl Taube, David S. Stuart, Boris Beltrán, and Edwin Román

2006   Nuevos hallazgos arquitectónicos y pictóricos en la Pirámide de las Pinturas, San Bartolo, Petén. In *XIX Simposio de Investigaciones Arqueológicas en Guatemala, 2005,* edited by Juan Pedro Laporte, Bárbara Arroyo, and Héctor E. Mejía, pp. 571–578. Ministerio de Cultura y Deportes, Instituto de Antropología e Historia, and Asociación Tikal, Guatemala City.

Saunders, Nicholas

1983   The Day of the Jaguar. *Geographical Magazine* (August):401–404.

Schele, Linda, and Jeffrey H. Miller

1983   *The Mirror, the Rabbit and the Bundle: Accession Expressions from the Classic Maya Inscriptions.* Studies in Pre-Columbian Art and Archaeology 25. Dumbarton Oaks Research Library and Collection, Washington, D.C.

Schele, Linda, and Mary E. Miller

1986   *Blood of Kings: Dynasty and Ritual in Maya Art.* George Braziller, in association with the Kimbell Art Museum, New York.

Schieber de Lavarreda, Christa

1994   A Middle Preclassic Clay Ballcourt at Abaj Takalik, Guatemala. *Mexicon* 16(4):77–84.

1997   Aproximaciones a la consolidación de arquitectura de Barro. *Apuntes arqueológicos* 5(1):49–66.

2002   La ofrenda de Abaj Takalik. In *XV Simposio de Investigaciones Arqueológicas en Guatemala, 2001,* edited by Juan Pedro Laporte, Héctor L. Escobedo, and Bárbara Arroyo, pp. 459–473. Ministerio de Cultura y Deportes, Instituto de Antropología e Historia, and Asociación Tikal, Guatemala City.

2003   Una nueva ofrenda de Abaj Takalik: El Entierro no. 1 de Abaj Takalik. In *XVI Simposio de investigaciones arqueológicas en Guatemala, 2002,* edited by Juan Pedro Laporte, Bárbara Arroyo, Héctor L. Escobedo, and Héctor E. Mejía, pp. 797–805. Ministerio de Cultura y Deportes, Instituto de Antropología e Historia, and Asociación Tikal, Guatemala City.

2005   Los alcances del mundo olmeca en Tak'alik Ab'aj. Paper presented at the Mesa Redonda Olmeca: Balance y Perspectivas. Museo Nacional de Antropología, Consejo Nacional para la Cultura y las Artes, and Instituto Nacional de Antropología e Historia, Mexico City.

Schieber de Lavarreda, Christa, and Miguel Orrego Corzo

2001a   *Los senderos milenarios de Abaj Takalik: Guía del parque.* Instituto de Antropología e Historia, Guatemala City.

2001b   Mil años de historia en Abaj Takalik. *U tz'ib* 3(1):1–31.

2002   *Abaj Takalik.* Proyecto Nacional Abaj Takalik, Instituto de Antropología e Historia, and Fundación G&T Continental, Guatemala City.

2009   El descubrimiento del Altar 48 de Tak'alik Ab'aj. In *XXII Simposio de Investigaciones Arqueológicas en Guatemala, 2008,* edited by Juan Pedro Laporte, Bárbara Arroyo, Héctor L. Escobedo, and Héctor Mejía, pp. 409–423. Ministerio de Cultura y Deportes, Instituto de Antropología e Historia, and Asociación Tikal, Guatemala City.

Schieber de Lavarreda, Christa, and Jeremías Claudio Pérez

2004   Una página más en la historia de Tak'alik Ab'aj. In *XVII Simposio de Investigaciones Arqueológicas en Guatemala, 2003,* edited by Juan Pedro

Laporte, Bárbara Arroyo, Héctor L. Escobedo, and Héctor Mejía, pp. 429–436. Ministerio de Cultura y Deportes, Instituto de Antropología e Historia, and Asociación Tikal, Guatemala City.

Schieber de Lavarreda, Christa, and Marion Popenoe de Hatch

2006   Questions to be Answered at Tak'alik Ab'aj in Reference to Future Investigations on the South Coast. Paper presented at the 71st Annual Meeting of the Society for American Archaeology, San Juan, Puerto Rico.

Schultze Jena, Leonhard

1933   *Leben, Glaube, und Sprache der Quiché von Guatemala.* Verlag Gustav Fischer, Jena.

Scott, John F.

1978   *The Danzantes of Monte Albán.* Studies in Pre-Columbian Art and Archaeology 19. Dumbarton Oaks Research Library and Collection, Washington, D.C.

1980   Post-Olmec Art in Veracruz. In *La antropología americanista en la actualidad: Homenaje a Raphael Girard*, vol. I, pp. 235–251. Editores Mexicanos Unidos, Mexico City.

1988   Potbellies and Fat Gods. *Journal of New World Archaeology* 7(2/3):25–36.

Sedat, David W., and Robert J. Sharer

1972   Archaeological Investigations in the Northern Maya Highlands: New Data on the Maya Preclassic. *Studies in the Archaeology of Mexico and Guatemala* 16:23–35.

Seler, Eduard

2004   *Las imágenes de los animales en los manuscritos mexicanos y mayas.* Translated by Joachim von Mentz, with preliminary notes by Brígida von Mentz. Casa Juan Pablos, Mexico City.

Sharer, Robert J., Bruce A. Anderson, David W. Sedat, Payson D. Sheets, and Dana Anderson

1978   *Introduction, Surface Surveys, Excavations, Monuments and Special Deposits.* Vol. 1 of *The Prehistory of Chalchuapa, El Salvador*, edited by Robert J. Sharer. University of Pennsylvania Press, Philadelphia.

Sharer, Robert J., and David W. Sedat

1973   Monument 1, El Porton, Guatemala, and the Development of Maya Calendrical and Writing Systems. *Studies in Ancient Mesoamerica* 18:177–194.

1987   *Archaeological Investigations in the Northern Maya Highlands, Guatemala: Interaction and the Development of Maya Civilization.* University Museum, University of Pennsylvania, Philadelphia.

1999   El Preclásico en las Tierras Altas del Norte. In *Época precolombina*, edited by Marion Popenoe de Hatch, pp. 213–240. Vol. 1 of *Historia general de Guatemala*, edited by Jorge Luján Muñoz. Asociación de Amigos del País and Fundación para la Cultura y el Desarrollo, Guatemala City.

Sharer, Robert J., and Loa Traxler

2006   *The Ancient Maya.* 6th ed. Stanford University Press, Stanford, Calif.

Shook, Edwin M.

1951   The Present Status of Research on the Pre-Classic Horizons in Guatemala. In *The Civilizations of Ancient America*, edited by Sol Tax, pp. 93–100. Vol. 1 of *Proceedings of the 29th International Congress of Americanists.* University of Chicago Press, Chicago.

1952   Lugares arqueológicos del altiplano meridional central de Guatemala. *Antropología e historia de Guatemala* 4:3–40.

1956   An Olmec sculpture from Guatemala. *Archaeology* 9:260–262.

1965   Archaeological Survey of the Pacific Coast of Guatemala. In *The Archaeology of Southern Mesoamerica*, part 1, edited by Gordon R. Willey, pp. 180–194. Vol. 3 of *Handbook of Middle American Indians*, edited by Robert Wauchope. University of Texas Press, Austin.

1971   Inventory of Some Preclassic Traits in the Highlands and Pacific Guatemala and Adjacent Areas. In *Observations on the Emergence of Civilization in Mesoamerica*, edited by Robert F. Heizer and John A. Graham, pp. 70–77. Contributions of the University of California Archaeological Research

Facility 11. University of California, Berkeley.

n.d.   Registry of Sites for the Republic of Guatemala. Manuscript on file with Centro de Investigaciones Regionales de Mesoamérica, Antigua, Guatemala.

Shook, Edwin M., and Robert F. Heizer

1976   An Olmec Sculpture from the South (Pacific) Coast of Guatemala. *Journal of New World Archaeology* 1(3):1–8.

Shook, Edwin M., and Alfred V. Kidder

1952   Mound E-III-3, Kaminaljuyu, Guatemala. Carnegie Institution of Washington Publication 596. Carnegie Institute of Washington, Washington, D.C.

Shook, Edwin M., and Marion Popenoe de Hatch

1981   *Archaeological Study of Monte Alto, Guatemala, and Preclassic Cultures on the Pacific Coast, 1972–77.* National Geographic Society Research Reports 13. National Geographic Society, Washington, D.C.

1999   Las tierras altas centrales: Períodos Preclásico y Clásico. In *Época pre-colombina,* edited by Marion Popenoe de Hatch, pp. 289–318. Vol. 1 of *Historia general de Guatemala,* edited by Jorge Luján Muñoz. Asociación de Amigos del País and Fundación para la Cultura y el Desarrollo, Guatemala City.

Siméon, Rémi

1997 [1885]   *Diccionario de la lengua nahuatl o mexi-cana.* Siglo Veintiuno, Mexico City.

Smith, Adam T.

2003   *The Political Landscape: Constellations of Authority in Early Complex Polities.* University of California Press, Berkeley.

Smith, A. Ledyard

1955   *Archaeological Reconnaissance in Central Guatemala.* Carnegie Institute of Washington Publication 608. Carnegie Institute of Washington, Washington, D.C.

Smith, A. Ledyard, and Alfred V. Kidder

1951   *Excavations at Nebaj, Guatemala.* Carnegie Institution of Washington Publication 594. Carnegie Institute of Washington, Washington, D.C.

Smith, Virginia G.

1984   *Izapa Relief Carving: Form, Content, Rules for Design, and Role in Mesoamerican Art History and Archaeology.* Studies in Pre-Columbian Art and Archaeology 27. Dumbarton Oaks Research Library and Collection, Washington, D.C.

Spero, Joanne M.

1991   Beyond Rainstorms: The *Kawak* as an Ancestor, Warrior, and Patron of Witchcraft. In *Sixth Palenque Round Table, 1986,* edited by Virginia M. Fields, pp. 184–193. University of Oklahoma Press, Norman.

Stirling, Matthew W.

1939   Discovering the New World's Oldest Dated Work of Man. *National Geographic* 76(2):183–218.

1940a   An Initial Series from Tres Zapotes, Vera Cruz, Mexico. National Geographic Society, Contributed Technical Papers, Mexican Archaeology Series 1. National Geographic Society, Washington, D.C.

1940b   Great Stone Faces of the Mexican Jungle. *National Geographic* 78(3):309–334.

1943a   La Venta's Green Stone Tigers. *National Geographic* 84(3):321–328.

1943b   *Stone Monuments of Southern Mexico.* Bureau of American Ethnology Bulletin 138. Government Printing Office, Washington, D.C.

1955   *Stone Monuments of the Río Chiquito, Veracruz, Mexico.* Bureau of American Ethnology Bulletin 157. Government Printing Office, Washington, D.C.

1957   *An Archaeological Reconnaissance in Southeastern Mexico.* Bureau of American Ethnology Bulletin 164. Government Printing Office, Washington, D.C.

1965   Monumental Sculpture of Southern Veracruz and Tabasco. In *Archaeology of Southern Mesoamerica,* part 2, edited by Gordon R. Willey, pp. 716–738. Vol. 3 of *Handbook of Middle American Indians,* edited by Robert Wauchope. University of Texas Press, Austin.

1968   Three Sandstone Monuments from La Venta Island. In *Papers on Mesoamerican Archaeology,* pp. 35–39. Contributions of the University of California Archaeological Research Facility 5. University of California, Berkeley.

Stirling, Matthew W., and Marion Stirling

1942   Finding Jewels of Jade in a Mexican Swamp. *National Geographic* 82(5):635–661.

Stone, Andrea J.

1996   The Cleveland Plaque: Cloudy Places of the Maya Realm. In *Eighth Palenque Round Table, 1993,* edited by Martha J. Macri and Jan McHargue, pp. 403–412. Precolumbian Art Research Institute, San Francisco.

Stuart, David

1986   *The Hieroglyphic Name of Altar U.* Copan Notes 4. Copan Mosaics Project, Instituto Hondureño de Antropología e Historia, Honduras.

1987   *Ten Phonetic Syllables.* Research Reports on Ancient Maya Writing 14. Center for Maya Research, Washington, D.C.

1996   Kings of Stone: A Consideration of Stelae in Ancient Maya Ritual and Representation. *Res: Anthropology and Aesthetics* 29/30:148–171.

1997   The Hills Are Alive: Sacred Mountains in the Maya Cosmos. *Symbols* (Spring):13–17. Peabody Museum, Harvard University, Cambridge, Mass.

2007   The Captives on Piedras Negras, Panel 12. In Maya Decipherment: A Weblog on the Ancient Maya Script. Electronic document, http://decipherment .wordpress.com/2007/08/18/the-captives-on-piedras-negras-panel-12/.

Stuart, David, and Stephen D. Houston

1994   *Classic Maya Place Names.* Studies in Pre-Columbian Art and Archaeology 33. Dumbarton Oaks Research Library and Collection, Washington, D.C.

Stuart, David, Barbara MacLeod, Simon Martin, and Yuriy Polyukhovich

2005   *Sourcebook for the 29th Maya Hieroglyphic Forum, March 11–26, 2005.* Department of Art and Art History, University of Texas, Austin.

Sullivan, Timothy D.

2002   Landscapes of Power: A Spatial Analysis of Civic Ceremonial Architecture at Tres Zapotes, Veracruz, Mexico. Master's thesis, Department of Anthropology, Southern Illinois University, Carbondale.

Tarpy, Cliff

2004   Place of the Standing Stones: Unearthing a King from the Dawn of the Maya. *National Geographic* 205(5):66–79.

Tate, Carolyn E.

1980   Maya Cauac Monster: Formal Development and Dynastic Implications. Master's thesis, Department of Art and Art History, University of Texas, Austin.

1995   Art in Olmec Culture. In *The Olmec World: Ritual and Rulership,* pp. 47–67. Art Museum, Princeton University, Princeton, N.J.

1999   Patrons of Shamanic Power: La Venta's Supernatural Entities in Light of Mixe Beliefs. *Ancient Mesoamerica* 10:169–188.

Tate, Carolyn E., and Gordon Bendersky

1999   Olmec Sculptures of the Human Fetus. *Perspectives in Biology and Medicine* 42(3):303–332.

Taube, Karl A.

1992   *The Major Gods of Ancient Yucatan.* Studies in Pre-Columbian Art and Archaeology 32. Dumbarton Oaks Research Library and Collection, Washington, D.C.

1995   The Rainmakers: The Olmec and Their Contribution to Mesoamerican Belief and Ritual. In *The Olmec World: Ritual and Rulership,* pp. 83–103. Art Museum, Princeton University, Princeton, N.J.

1996   The Olmec Maize God: The Face of Corn in Formative Mesoamerica. *Res: Anthropology and Aesthetics* 29/30:39–81.

2000a   Lightning Celts and Corn Fetishes: The Formative Olmec and the Development of Maize Symbolism in Mesoamerica and the American Southwest. In *Olmec Art and Archaeology in Mesoamerica,* edited by John E. Clark and Mary E. Pye, pp. 297–331. Studies in the History of Art 58. National Gallery of Art, Washington, D.C.

2000b   The Turquoise Hearth: Fire, Self-Sacrifice, and the Central Mexican Cult of War. In *Mesoamerica's Classic Heritage: From Teotihuacan to the Aztecs,* edited by Davíd Carrasco, Lindsay Jones, and Scott Sessions, pp. 269–340. University Press of Colorado, Boulder.

2004   *Olmec Art at Dumbarton Oaks.* Dumbarton Oaks Research Library and Collection, Washington, D.C.

Taube, Karl A., and Marc Zender

2009   American Gladiators: Ritual Boxing in Ancient Mesoamerica. In *Blood and Beauty: Organized Violence in the Art and Archaeology of Mesoamerica and Central America,* edited by Heather Orr and Rex Koontz, pp. 161–220. Cotsen Institute of Archaeology, University of California, Los Angeles.

Taylor, Dicey

1978   The Cauac Monster. In *Tercera Mesa Redonda de Palenque,* edited by Merle G. Robertson and Donnan Call Jeffers, pp. 79–89. Pre-Columbian Art Research Center, Palenque, Chiapas, Mexico.

Thompson, Edward H.

1897   *The Cave of Loltun, Yucatan: Report of Explorations by the Museum, 1888–9 and 1890–1.* Memoirs of the Peabody Museum of American Archaeology and Ethnology 1, no. 2. Peabody Museum, Cambridge, Mass.

Thompson, J. Eric S.

1941   *Dating of Certain Inscriptions of Non-Maya Origin.* Theoretical Approaches to Problems 1. Division of Historical Research, Carnegie Institution of Washington, Cambridge, Mass.

1943   Some Sculptures from Southeastern Quetzaltenango, Guatemala. *Notes on Middle American Archaeology and Ethnology* 17:100–102.

1962   *A Catalog of Maya Hieroglyphs.* Civilization of the American Indian Series 62. University of Oklahoma Press, Norman.

Tilley, Christopher, and Wayne Bennett

2004   *The Materiality of Stone: Explorations in Landscape Phenomenology.* Berg, Oxford.

Townsend, Richard F.

1992   Landscape and Sacred Symbol. In *Ancient Americas: Art from Sacred Landscapes,* edited by Richard F. Townsend, pp. 28–47. Art Institute of Chicago, Chicago, and Prestel Verlag, New York.

Tozzer, Alfred M. (editor)

1941   *Landa's* Relación de las cosas de Yucatan: *A Translation.* Papers of the Peabody Museum of American Archaeology and Ethnology 18. The Peabody Museum, Cambridge, Mass.

Traxler, Loa, and Robert J. Sharer (editors)

n.d.   *Early Maya States.* University of Pennsylvania Press, Philadelphia, in press.

United Nations

2005   *Handbook of National Accounting: Integrated Environmental and Economic Accounting 2003, Studies in Methods.* Series F, No. 61, Rev. 1, Glossary, paragraph 9.42. United Nations, New York.

Urcid, Javier

1993   The Pacific Coast of Oaxaca and Guerrero: The Westernmost Extent of Zapotec Script. *Ancient Mesoamerica* 4:141–165.

2001   *Zapotec Hieroglyphic Writing.* Studies in Pre-Columbian Art and Archaeology 34. Dumbarton Oaks Research Library and Collection, Washington, D.C.

2006   Oracles and Warfare: The Role of Pictorial Narratives in the Early Development of Monte Albán (500 B.C.E.–200 C.E). Manuscript on file, Department of Anthropology, Brandeis University, Waltham, Mass.

Valdés, Juan Antonio

2003   Tres nuevos monumentos esculpidos de Kaminaljuyu. *Estudios, revista de antropología e historia,* 4th series, 2(July):93–101.

Valdés, Juan Antonio, and Federico Fahsen

2007   La figura humana en el arte maya del Preclásico. In *XX Simposio de Investigaciones Arqueológicas en Guatemala, 2006,* edited by Juan Pedro Laporte, Bárbara Arroyo, and Héctor E. Mejía, pp. 933–943. Ministerio de Cultura y Deportes, Instituto de Antropología e Historia, Asociación Tikal, and Fundación Arqueológica del Nuevo Mundo, Guatemala City.

Valdés, Juan Antonio, and Zoila Rodríguez Girón

1999   Panorama Preclásico, Clásico y Postclásico. In *Época precolombina,* edited by Marion Popenoe de Hatch, pp. 139–164. Vol. 1 of *Historia general de Guatemala,* edited by Jorge Luján Muñoz. Asociación de Amigos del País and Fundación para la Cultura y el Desarrollo, Guatemala City.

Vega Sosa, Constanza

1991   *Códice Azoyú 1: El reino de Tlachinollan.* Fondo de Cultura Económica, Mexico City.

Velásquez, Juan Luís

1999   *Los altares del sitio Las Conchitas.* Urbanizadora Las Conchitas, Coatepeque, Guatemala.

Villa Rojas, Alfonso

1947   Kinship and Nagualism in a Tzeltal Community, Southeastern Mexico. *American Anthropologist* 49(4, part 1):578–587.

Villela F., Samuel

2006   *Guerrero: El pueblo del jaguar.* Instituto Nacional de Antropología e Historia and Consejo Nacional para la Cultura y las Artes, Mexico City.

Vogt, Evon Z.

1969   *Zinacantan.* Belknap Press, Harvard University, Cambridge, Mass.

1970   Human Souls and Animal Spirits in Zinacantan. In *Échanges et communications: Mélanges offerts à Claude Lévi-Strauss à l'occasion de son 60ème anniversaire,* edited by Jean Pouillon and Pierre Maranda. Mouton, The Hague.

Wauchope, Robert

1975   *Zacualpa, El Quiché Guatemala: An Ancient Provincial Center of the Highland Maya.* Middle American Research Institute Publication 93. Tulane University, New Orleans, La.

Weiant, Clarence W.

1943   *An Introduction to the Ceramics of Tres Zapotes, Veracruz, Mexico.* Bureau of American Ethnology Bulletin 139. Government Printing Office, Washington, D.C.

Weitlaner, Roberto J.

1977   *Relatos, mitos y leyendas de la Chinantla.* Serie Antropología Social 53. Instituto Nacional Indigenista, Mexico City.

Westheim, Paul

1950   *Arte antiguo de México.* Fondo de Cultural Económica, Mexico City.

Wichmann, Søren

1995   *The Relationship among the Mixe-Zoquean Languages of Mexico.* University of Utah Press, Salt Lake City.

Wicke, Charles R.

1971   *Olmec: An Early Art Style of Precolumbian Mexico.* University of Arizona Press, Tucson.

Williams, Howell, and Robert F. Heizer

1965   Sources of Rock Used in Olmec Monuments. In *Sources of Stone Used in Prehistoric Mesoamerican Sites,* pp. 1–40. Contributions of the University of California Archaeological Research Facility 1. University of California, Berkeley.

Wisdom, Charles

1940   *Chorti Indians of Guatemala.* University of Chicago Press, Chicago.

Woodbury, Richard B., and Aubrey S. Trik

1953   *The Ruins of Zaculeu, Guatemala.* United Fruit Company and William Byrd Press, Richmond, Va.

Yoffee, Norman

2005   *Myths of the Archaic State.* Cambridge University Press, Cambridge and New York.

INDEX

Numbers in names of architectural elements and stone monuments are *italicized* here to distinguish them from page numbers.

Chahk (deity): animate stone and, 289; axes of, 291–293, 296; in Calakmul frieze, 217, 218; in Copan monuments, 296; diagnostic features of, 209, 212–213, 216, 217, 220; embodied in monuments, 210–211; fishing associated with, 209–212; in Izapa stelae, 209–214; and jaguars, 166; in Kaminaljuyu stelae, 219; lightning associated with, 289, 291–293, 296; in Monte Alto sculpture, 220, 221; and nahuals, 50; rulers' reasons for focusing on, 210, 215–216, 220–221; in San Bartolo murals, 217–219; in Takalik Abaj stelae, 216

Chahk Xib Chahk, 212

Chalcatzingo (Morelos): as ceremonial center, 77, 80; ethnic identity in, 94–95; vs. La Blanca, 156; La Venta's relationship to, 18; topography of, 17–18, 80; water shrines near, 46; vs. Zazacatla, 77, 80, 90–91, 92–93, 94–95; Zazacatla's proximity to, 78, 80

Chalcatzingo monuments: dating of, 18; distribution of, 17–18, 20; full-round, 18; Monument 1, 18, 48–49, 53, 90–91, 93, 94; Monument 4, 92; Monument 5, 92; Monument 9, 61, 62, 94; Monument 13, 92–93; Monument 22, 94, 95; Monument 31, 47–48, 49, 51, 53; Monument 32, 90; Monument 36, 90; number of, 18; Stela 21, 25n3

Chalchitán (Huehuetenango), 253, 255

Chalchiumomozco (shrine), 46

Chalchuapa (El Salvador), 9

Champerico region, 166–167, 174

Chamula, 36

Chan, Kisslan, 264, 270

Chantico (deity), 35

chert, 292

Chiapa de Corzo, 20

Chiapas: distribution of monuments in, 17, 20; nahuals in, 42. See also specific sites

Chichén Itzá, 63, 100

Chichinautzin Mountains, 80, 83

chiefdoms: in Guatemalan Highlands, 236; rise of, 149; in Salamá Valley, 236; transition to states from, 151

Chimalpáhin, Domingo, 46

Chiquirines Viejo, 156

Chixoy River, 234

Chocolá (Guatemala): distribution of monuments at, 22; Shook Altar and, 158; Stela 1 at, 155

Ch'ol, 292

Cholan Maya language, 236, 237, 255

Ch'olti' Maya, 255, 291

Ch'orti' Maya, 287, 292

Christie, Jessica J., 10

chronology of Mesoamerica, xiii, 2–3

ch'ulel (soul), of stone, 288

city living, 3–5

city-states, 122

Ciudad Ruíz, Andrés, 171

civilization, Mesoamerican: origin of, 17; role of sculpture in, xviii, 23

Clancy, Flora S., 19, 285

Clark, John E., xvii–xviii, 1–25, 71, 108, 203, 264, 270

Classic Maya monuments: dating of, 6, 283; embodiment of deities in, 210; Kaminaljuyu sculpture as precursor to, 259; meaning of postures on, 266; plain, 284–285; stela-altar pairs, 12; writing on, 23, 285–297. See also specific sites

Classic Maya stelae, 283–297; animate qualities of stone and, 286–290; as celts, 291; cliff carvings and, 286–287; dating of, 283; language used to describe, 283, 285–286; lightning stones and, 289, 291–296; materiality of stone and, 285–290; plain, 284–285, 297; shininess and, 285, 291–296; stone as embodiment of time and, 289–290; writing on, 285–297

Classic period: boundaries of, xiv; as "golden age," 1; nahualism in, 27; problems with division of, xiii, xiv, 1

clay (ceramic) sculptures: continuity between stone sculptures and, 60–64, 152, 155, 157; distinction between stone sculptures and, 152; at El Ujuxte, 155–156; at La Blanca, 152–154; in Teopantecuanitlan Sunken Patio, 55, 60–64

cleft(s): in La Venta altars, 144; in San Pedro Aytec figurine, 32, 43, 44, 45; symbolic meaning of, 89–90; in Zazacatla monuments, 83, 89–90. See also V-shaped designs

Clewlow, C. William, 102, 108

cliff carvings, 286–287

climate, and distribution of nahuals, 42–43

clouds: in Kaminaljuyu sculptures, 270; nahuals' understanding of, 37, 38

Coamizagual, 39

Coatepeque (Guatemala): distribution of sculpture around, 164–170; location of, 164; plain stelae at, 166

coati, 168, 173

Coatlicue (deity), 93

Coba, 288

Cobata, colossal head of, 104, 109

Cocijo (deity), 50

Codex Borbonicus, 37

Codex Mendoza, 32

codices, on nahuals, 35, 37, 47, 53. See also specific codices

Coe, Michael D., 7, 8, 23–24, 25, 273, 291

Coe, William R., 116, 148n6

co-essence of the souls, 33. See also nahuals; tonal

Collins, Lori D., 259–281

colonial era, nahuals in, 34, 35, 37–38

color, as clue to meaning of monuments, 146. See also painting of monuments

colossal heads: dating of, 6, 7; at La Venta, 124, 133–135; as portraits, 123–124, 127n4; at San Lorenzo, 108; at Tres Zapotes, 98, 104, 108–109, 123–124, 127n4

commoners. See nonelites

composite figures, 136–138

Conchas phase, 152, 154, 223, 224

conflict: in Guatemalan Highlands, 236–237, 257–258; in Teopantecuanitlan, 70

Contalco, 30

context, issues of, xiii–xiv, 4, 23, 24

contortionism, 43–45, 52

Copan (Honduras): Rosalila Temple at, 295; Stela 9 at, 294, 296; Stela 63 at, 294, 295; Stela C at, 294; Stela J at, 295; Temple 22 at, 288, 289

corn. *See* maize motif

cosmic trees. *See* world trees

cosmology/cosmovision: mountains in, 80; nahualism in, 27, 54; in Teopantecuanitlan Sunken Patio, 63, 67, 69–70

coyotes, 36

craft, vs. art, 150

creation stories, 219

Cruz de Milagro, 95

Cuadzidziqui Cave, 30

Cualac, 32

Cuauhtemoc (Chiapas), 224

Cuicuilco, 12, 19

cult: ruler, 151; stela, 283

cultural beliefs, in distribution of monuments, 16

cultural diversity, 3–4, 151

cultural ecological approach, 24

cupules, 245–247, 251, 256

cylinders, at Tres Zapotes, 121–122

Cyphers, Ann, 28–29, 47, 52

Dainzú, 21

dams, 209

"Dance of the Jaguar" ritual, 219–220

danzantes: dating of, 20; development of style of, 22, 26n7; distribution of, 20–21, 22

dating of monuments, 5–15; difficulties of, 5–7, 152; and distribution of monuments, 16–23; Early Preclassic, 6–9; Late Preclassic, 10–15; Middle Preclassic, 7–12; reuse and, 5, 152. *See also specific periods and sites*

death, transformation at moment of, 34, 47

dedications, 286

deer, 193

defacement. *See* mutilation/breakage/defacement of monuments

deities: manifestation or representation of, in monuments, 19, 210–211; and nahuals, 34, 35; transformations by, 34, 35. *See also specific deities and types of deities*

Demarest, Arthur A., 237

destruction of monuments. *See* mutilation/breakage/ defacement of monuments

diagonal designs. *See* V-shaped designs

Diehl, Richard A., 7

disjunction, problem of, 147

distribution of monuments, 16–23; and dating of monuments, 6–15; Early Preclassic, 16–17; Late Preclassic, 20–23, 159–161; Middle Preclassic, 17–20, 157–159; in political placemaking, 122–126; in regional centers, 158–159, 161; outside regional centers, 160, 162–170. *See also specific sites*

diversity: cultural, 3–4, 151; ethnic, 4, 94–95, 207–208, 262; of sculptural forms, 150–151, 157–161; of sculptural materials, 150, 152–157; of sculptural themes, 173–174

divinity, of rulers, 149

documentation: conventional methods of, 260–261, 269; limitations of, 261, 263; with three-dimensional laser scanning, 259–261, 262–263, 280–281

Doering, Travis F., 259–281

Dolores, Quirino, 29, 52

domestic animals, in nahualism, 36

domestic sphere and rituals: camahuiles in, 171–173; ceramic figurines in, 173, 174, 223–229; Pacific Guatemalan sculptures in, 170–174; potbelly sculptures in, 161, 170–173, 221–229; rulers' appropriation of, 225–226, 227–229; themes of sculptures in, 173–174

Domínguez Lázaro, Pablo, 29

Draco (constellation), 194, 203

dragon, Olmec, 29, 89, 92, 93, 95

drawings: based on laser scan data, 262–263, 270, 282n5; conventional documentation with, 261

Drucker, Philip, 98

duality: in transformation figurines, 46; in Zazacatla Lajas Structure, 91

duckbill masks, 74

Durán, Diego, 37, 46

eagles, in hierarchy of nahuals, 36

ear ornaments, in La Venta sculptures, 136

Early Preclassic period: city living in, 4; dating of monuments from, 6–9; distribution of monuments in, 16–17; sculptural forms in, 6–9; social transitions in, 4; temporal boundaries of, 2

earth: stone associated with, 87, 286, 287; V-shaped designs and, 89; in Zazacatla Lajas Structure, 89, 93

earth monster, 61, 119

earthen mounds. *See* mounds

economics: of nahualism, 36, 54; and production of sculpture, 157, 174, 208, 229. *See also* politicoeconomic strategies

economy: Middle Preclassic disruptions in, 98; political, exclusionary vs. collective strategies of, 99–100, 126

El Baúl: head from, 158; Stela 1 at, 273

El Chayal, 262

El Chorro rivulet, 217

El Jardín, pedestal sculptures at, 166, 167

El Jobo, Stela 1 at, 155

El Manatí, wooden sculptures at, 7

El Mesón, Stelae 1 and 2 at, 122

El Palma (Chiapas), Stela 5 at, 290

El Portón (Guatemala), 237–245; caches at, 239–240, 241; as ceremonial center, 236, 237; construction stages of, 237; cupules at, 245; earliest occupants of, 237; growth of, 236; hieroglyphic inscriptions at, 237; under Kaminaljuyu, 236; vs. Kaminaljuyu, 256–257; Laguneta stelae from, 244; layout of, 237; location of, 237; maps of, 238, 239; Structure J7-4B at, 236–244, 258n1; writing at, 237, 242–244, 257, 258n2

El Portón monuments, 237–245; broken, 241–242; dating of, 242, 256, 258n2; destruction of, 241–242, 257; distribution of, 22, 234; earliest, 236, 244; Monument 1, 237–244, 256, 257; Monument 2, 237–244;

Monument 3, 242; Monument 4, 242; Monument 5, 241; Monument 10, 240–241; Monument 11, 240–241; Monument 12, 256; Monument 22, 256; pedestal sculptures associated with stelae, 240–242; reuse and re-placement of, 242, 257; trends in, 255–257

El Quiché (Guatemala). *See* Quiché Department

El Rey, 48, 49

El Salvador, sculptures in, 166. *See also specific sites*

El Sitio, 166, 167

El Ujuxte (Guatemala): altars at, 155; camahuiles from, 171–173, 174; ceramic domestic figurines at, lack of, 226, 228–229; ceramic sculptures at, 155, 156; distribution of monuments outside, 166–167; diversity of materials used at, 155–156; domestic settings of, 170–171, 173; potbelly sculptures at, 155, 170–171, 227, 228, 229; pottery sherd from, 155–156, 157; public rituals at, 226, 227, 228–229; secondary sites of, 166–167

El Viejón, 26n7

El Zapote, Stela 1 at, 210–211

elites: as nahuals, 34, 36; overestimation of power of, 150; as patrons of sculpture, 157, 173, 174; production of sculpture by, 157, 173, 174; and representational stelae, 161; residences of, 170, 173; and rise of inequality, 149. *See also* ruler(s)

equinoxes, 63–64, 67, 68, 194

ethnic diversity, 4; in Kaminaljuyu, 262; in Pacific coast and piedmont, 207–208; in presentation of themes, 94–95

ethnic groups: definition of, 78; map of, 30

ethnic identity, in Zazacatla Lajas Structure, 93–95

eye(s): of potbelly sculptures, 221, 223–225, 230n4; in Teopantecuanitlan sculptures, 60–61; in Zazacatla sculptures, 83, 85, 89

eyebrows: in La Venta sculptures, 136; in Teopantecuanitlan sculptures, 60–61; in Zazacatla sculptures, 83, 89

faces: of ceramic domestic figurines, 223–229; in La Venta sculptures, 136; mountain, 136; of potbelly sculptures, 221–229; in Teopantecuanitlan sculptures, 64; of transformation figurines, 31, 44, 46; in Zazacatla sculptures, 83, 89, 95

Fahsen, Federico, 18, 203, 231–258, 273

fangs, in La Venta sculptures, 136, 144

Fat God, 227

fat-boy sculptures. *See* potbelly sculptures

feasting, domestic, 226

fetus representations, 135

figurines: human form represented in, 16; transformation, 27–28, 29–33, 43–46, 54n2. *See also* ceramic figurines

Finca Las Conchitas. *See* Las Conchitas

Finca Sololá: Monument 3 at, 221, 222; potbelly sculptures at, 221, 222, 224

fishing, Chahk associated with, 209–212

Flannery, Kent V., 25n4

folk tradition, camahuiles in, 171

Formative period, use of term, 2. *See also* Preclassic period

forms. *See* sculptural forms

Foster, George, 33

Foundation for the Advancement of Mesoamerican Studies, 282n3

fountain stones, 211

four world quarters: in Teopantecuanitlan Sunken Patio, 70; in Zazacatla Lajas Structure, 89–91, 93, 95

French Archaeological Mission, 235, 255

frogs. *See* toad(s)

Fuente, Beatríz de la, 109, 111, 127n2, 136, 146

full-round sculpture: dating of, 9–10; distribution of, 9–10, 18. *See also specific sites*

Furst, Peter T., 27–28

García Guerra, Bishop, 37

Geomagic software, 262, 263, 282n2

geometrical motifs, at Laguneta, 245

glyphs. *See* writing

gneiss, 16, 187

gnomons, 67, 71, 75

god(s). *See* deities; *specific gods*

God K, 212, 216, 291

goggles, 253

González Lauck, Rebecca B., 17, 129–147

Gossen, Gary H., 36, 49

Graham, Ian, 161, 182–185, 187, 195–196

Graham, John A., 101, 109, 116, 119–120, 152, 177, 181–182, 187, 261

Great Tradition, vs. Little Tradition, 150

greenstone: burial of, 52; in camahuiles, 171; location of sources, 32; shininess of, 292; trade in, 98. *See also* serpentine

group identity, placemaking in, 122

Grove, David C., 18, 46, 48, 108, 136, 138

Guatemala: distribution of monuments in, 18; map of, 232; nahuals in, 39, 42. *See also* Guatemalan Highlands; Pacific Guatemala; *specific sites*

Guatemala, Valley of: distribution of monuments in, 18; earliest occupants of, 235

Guatemalan Highlands, 231–258; ceramics in, 235, 237; ceremonial centers in, 231, 234, 236; conflict in, 236–237, 257–258; cultural styles in, 151; dating of monuments in, 151–152; destruction of monuments in, 236–237, 244–245, 255–258; distribution of monuments in, 18, 22, 231, 234; diversity of forms in, 150, 157–161; diversity of media in, 152–157; duration of Maya residency in, 235; earliest monuments in, 236; earliest occupants of, 235; excavations in, 234–235; expansion of settlements in, 235–236; history of studies of, 231, 234–235; location of, 234; maps of, 232, 233; Mayan languages in, 235, 236, 237; nahuals in, 42; natural resources of, 235, 257–258; number of monuments in, 231; plain monuments in, 18, 158; political organization in, 236; population shifts in, 237, 257; potbelly sculptures in, lack of, 256; sculptural trends in, 255–258; topography of, 234; writing in, 231, 234, 256–257. *See also specific sites*

Guernsey, Julia, xvii–xviii, 1–25, 161, 166, 173, 190, 207–230, 264, 266, 270

Guerrero: languages in, 4; nahuals in, 46–52 (*See also* San Pedro Aytec figurine); rain shrines in, 46–47. *See also specific sites*

Guillen phase, 208

Gulf Coast: distribution of monuments in, 18; nahuals in, 42. *See also specific sites*

Gutiérrez, Gerardo, 27–54, 193

hail, 37, 38

Hammond, Norman, 109

hand glyphs, 242–243

handedness, meaning of, 270

Hansen, Richard, 19

head(s). *See* colossal heads

headdresses: in La Venta sculptures, 136, 143, 144; in Teopantecuanitlan sculptures, 62; in Zazacatla sculptures, 83

healing, by nahuals, 42

Heizer, Robert, 130, 177, 187

helmets, on La Venta monuments, 134, 135

Herrera Stela, 273

Herrera y Tordesillas, Antonio de, 39

hieroglyphs: cupules as alternative to, 245; at El Portón, 237, 242–243, 258n2; at El Zapote, 210–211; progress in decipherment of, 147; at Takalik Abaj, 190, 198. *See also* writing

highland Guatemala. *See* Guatemalan Highlands

Houston, Stephen D., 49, 210–211

Huamuxtitlan Valley (Guerrero), 29–30. *See also* San Pedro Aytec figurine

Huautla Mountains, 80

Huehuetan (Chiapas), 42

Huehuetenango. *See specific sites*

Hueyapan, colossal head of, 107

Hueyapan de Mimendez: full-round sculpture in, 109; Monument 1 at, 112, 115; Monument 2 at, 109, 110

human form: in danzantes, 20–21, 26n7; in figurines and paintings, 16; in La Venta sculptures, 133–135, 137, 138, 140–145; in Maya style, 185; meaning of postures of, 266–267, 270, 272–273; proscriptions against, 16; in Teopantecuanitlan sculptures, 70–71; in Zazacatla sculptures, 83, 89. *See also* colossal heads

human sacrifice, in nahualism, 35, 46, 51

human-animal transformations. *See* nahuals

Ichon, Alain, 171, 249, 251, 253, 254

identity: ethnic, 93–95; group, 122

ideologies, political, on display in stone monuments, 208

idolatry, nahualism as, 35

inequality, social, rise of, 149

infants, in La Venta sculptures, 140, 143–144

Inquisition trials, 37, 39

inscriptions. *See* writing

isthmian script, on Tres Zapotes stelae, 120, 126

Ixchiyá River, 201

Izapa (Chiapas): apogee of, 208–209; Group A at, 209–212, 214–215; Group F at, 211, 213; map of, 211; Mound 56 at, 214; Mound 58 at, 209–210, 212, 213, 214; Mound 60 at, 209–211; secondary sites of, 167; Tres Zapotes monuments linked to, 116, 118, 121; water management systems of, 209–216

Izapa monuments: Altar 1, 214–215; Altar 2, 213, 214–215; Altar 16, 168; distribution of, 22, 210; Miscellaneous Monument 2, 118; Miscellaneous Monument 3, 213, 215; Miscellaneous Monument 24, 211–214; Miscellaneous Monument 70, 229; narrative relationships among, 211–216; pedestal sculptures, 166; potbelly sculptures, 229; rulers' role in design of, 210, 215–216; rulership theme in, 151; Stela 1, 209–214, 219, 272; Stela 3, 212–214, 270–272; Stela 4, 266, 272; Stela 5, 214, 267; Stela 6, 214–215; Stela 11, 215, 266, 272; Stela 12, 270; Stela 23, 215, 216, 217, 218; Stela 26, 214; Stela 89, 266; Stela 90, 219; stela-altar pairs, 13, 209; style of, 186; themes of, 186; water deity representations in, 208–219

Izapa River, 209, 211, 214

Izapa style: vs. Olmec and Maya style, 181–185; at Takalik Abaj, lack of, 186, 204

jade: at El Portón, 241; in Guatemalan Highlands, 235, 257–258; at Kaminaljuyu, 262; shininess of, 289

jadeite, 195

jaguar(s): and Chahk, 166, 219, 230n3; in hieroglyphic texts, 289; in Kaminaljuyu monuments, 219; in La Argelia monuments, 166; in La Lagunita monuments, 252; in pedestal sculptures, 166–167; rituals invoking, 219; symbolic meaning of, 61, 70; in Takalik Abaj monuments, 193; in Teopantecuanitlan clay sculptures, 55, 60–61; in Teopantecuanitlan stone sculptures, 61–62, 63, 70; and water deities, 219

jaguar nahuals: in Central Mexico, 46; distribution of, 42; figurines depicting, 27–29; in Guerrero, 47, 49; in hierarchy of nahuals, 35–36; monuments depicting, 28–29, 47, 49, 51; in Morelos, 47; powers of, 27, 54n1; process of transformation, 27–29, 37, 38, 45; and rain shrines, 46. *See also* San Pedro Aytec figurine

jaguar-dragon, Olmec, 29

Johnson, Scott, 166

Joralemon, Peter David, 29

Justeson, John S., 122

Juxtlahuaca (cave), 47

Kaminaljuyu (Guatemala): apogee of, 261–262; approaches to analysis of, 23–24; conflict in, 236; earliest occupants of, 235, 261; El Portón under rule of, 236; ethnic groups of, 262; influence of site, 259; La Venta's relationship to, 22, 26n6; location of, 261, 262; Maya style at, 180; Mayan languages at, 237; obsidian controlled by, 262; Olmec vs. regional style in, 22, 26n6, 177; political organization of, 261, 262; population shifts at, 237, 257; as regional center, 159; rulership theme at, 151, 259, 262, 264–267; vs. Takalik Abaj, 177, 186; writing at, 243, 256, 257, 270, 274

monuments at, 10, 18, 161, 285; as regional center, 159; stela-altar pairs at, 12, 18

Naranjo River, 168

narrative relationships, among Izapa monuments, 211–216

narrative scenes: in Izapa art, 185; in low-relief sculpture, 10; in San Bartolo murals, 219; at Takalik Abaj, 204

natural resources: of Guatemalan Highlands, 235, 257–258; of Kaminaljuyu, 262; of Zazacatla, 80

naualli, 33

Nebaj, 255

Nestepe, 107

niche figures, 138

Niederberger, Christine, 44–45

Nil phase, 180

nomads, 4

nonelites: as nahuals, 34, 36; production and use of sculpture by, 157, 161, 173, 174; rise of inequality and, 149

Norman, V. Garth, 209, 211

numerology, at Takalik Abaj, 190, 195

Nuñez de la Vega, Francisco, 37–38

Oaxaca, nahuals in, 42. *See also specific sites*

Oaxaca, Valley of: calendrical notation in, 23; carved stones in, 20–21, 25n4; conquest monuments in, 20–22; danzantes in, 20–21; distribution of monuments in, 20–22; thrones in, 15; writing in, 23

obsidian: at El Portón, 241; in Guatemalan Highlands, 235, 257–258; at Kaminaljuyu, 262; shininess of, 289, 292; sources of, 98; at Takalik Abaj, 195

offerings: at El Portón, 241; at Takalik Abaj, 194, 195; at Tres Zapotes, 117, 118

ointments, 37

Ojo de Agua (Chiapas), 10, 25n2, 61

Olmec, problems with term, xiv

Olmec art: approaches to analysis of, 146–147; transformation in, 27

Olmec culture: economic disruptions in, 98; four world quarters in, 70; human sacrifice in, 51; languages of, 4; nahuals in, 27–29, 42, 50, 51; origins of Mesoamerican civilization in, 17; origins of stone monuments in, 7, 17, 18, 195

Olmec dragon, 29, 89, 92, 93, 95

Olmec sites: dating of monuments at, 7–8; distribution of monuments at, 20. *See also specific sites*

Olmec-style monuments: altars, 138; chronological sequence of, 101, 102; cliff carvings and, 286, 287; dating of, 7–8; distribution of, 17–20; end of tradition of, 20, 22; as first monuments, 7, 17; lack of antecedents for, 7; vs. Maya style, 181–182; motivations for, 298n2; mutilation of, 203; writing and, 146–147. *See also* colossal heads; *specific sites*

Olmos, Andrés de, 35

Orellana, Sandra L., 171

Orr, Heather, 51

Orrego Corzo, Miguel, 158, 177–204

Otomanguean language, 4, 42, 53

owls, 190

Oxtotitlán (cave), 47

Pacific coast and piedmont: ethnic groups in, 207–208; map of, 208; potbelly sculptures in, 221–229; trade routes in, 207–208; water deity representations in, 207–221

Pacific Guatemala, 149–174; dating of monuments in, 151–152; distribution of sculpture in, 162–164; diversity of forms in, 150–151, 157–161; diversity of media in, 152–157; diversity of themes in, 173–174; domestic settings of, 170–174; maps of, 151, 158, 159, 160, 162, 163; sculpture outside political centers of, 162–170. *See also specific sites*

Padre Piedra, 26n7

painting of monuments: at Copan, 294–295; at La Blanca, 152, 154; at La Lagunita, 249, 253, 254; at La Venta, 134; on plain stelae, 285; at Takalik Abaj, 187; at Zazacatla, 83, 85, 86

paintings: cave, and nahuals, 47; distribution of, 25–26n5; human form represented in, 16. *See also* murals

Palenque (Chiapas): La Picota monument at, 283–284; Oval Palace Tablet at, 273; Tablet of the Cross at, 273

Panofsky, Dora, 147

Panofsky, Erwin, 147

parallax, 261

Parsons, Lee A., 12, 23, 151, 152, 160, 187, 220, 227, 230n6, 273, 280

patronage, elite, 157, 173, 174

paw-wing motif, 29

pebble caches, at El Portón, 241

Pecked and Grooved Sculptural Tradition, 245

pedestal sculptures: dating of, 11–12, 158; destruction of, 257; distribution of, 12, 161, 162; at El Portón, 240–242; identity of makers of, 167, 174; from La Argelia, 156, 166–167; thrones depicted in, 13–14

Pellicer Cámara, Carlos, 147n4, 148n5

period-ending ceremonies, 289–290

perspective, in three-dimensional works, 29

Peten (Guatemala), 285, 286–287

petroglyphs, at Takalik Abaj, 196–197

photogrammetry, 261

photographic documentation, 260–261, 269

Piedra de Sacrificios, 245

Piedra Labrada: Monument 3 at, 49–51; Monument 13 at, 49–51; stela at, 49

Piedras Negras: Altar 4 at, 288–289; Panel 12 from, 267

pigment on monuments. *See* painting of monuments

pilas, 253, 254

Pillsbury, Joanne, xiii–xv

pisotes, 168, 173

Pitahaya phase, 171

place, use and meaning of term, 4

placemaking: distribution of monuments in, 122–126; in group identity, 122; state formation as, 97, 122; at Tres Zapotes, 122–126

plain monuments: dating of, 10; definition of, 10; distribution of, 10, 18–19, 22, 166; in Guatemalan Highlands, 18, 158; meaning of, 5, 284–285; at Naranjo, 10, 18, 161, 285; painting on, 285; shininess of, 285; stucco on, 187, 285; at Takalik Abaj, 187, 190

rammed-earth technique, 156
regional centers: distribution of monuments in, 158–159,
    161; distribution of monuments outside, 160, 162–170;
    in Guatemalan Highlands, 236; La Blanca as, 159, 223;
    La Lagunita as, 236, 247–248, 252; Middle Preclassic,
    158–159; portraits of rulers in, 160, 174; potbelly
    sculptures in, 161; Takalik Abaj as, 159, 177;
    Tres Zapotes as, 97, 98, 123–124, 126.
    See also ceremonial centers
regional sculptural styles, development of, 20, 22
Reilly, F. Kent, III, 28, 29, 52, 77, 89, 95, 127n3, 270
relief carvings, on cliffs, 286–287
religion, nahuals in, 34. *See also* deities; rituals
representational stelae: distribution of, 159, 160; vs.
    potbelly sculptures, 161; rulership theme in, 151, 160
reservoirs, Izapan, 209–210, 214
residences, elite, 170, 173. *See also* domestic sphere
    and rituals
"restorations," to La Venta monuments, 147n4, 148n5
Retalhuleu (Guatemala), 166
reuse/recycling/recarving: vs. destruction, 279; in
    difficulty of dating, 5, 152; at El Portón, 242, 257;
    at Kaminaljuyu, 152, 257, 260, 267, 274–279; at
    Laguneta, 244; at Los Mangales, 246; meanings
    obscured by, 25; prevalence of, 25; at Takalik Abaj,
    152, 181, 190–191, 200–201; at Tres Zapotes, 101,
    119–120, 122, 124, 126
reverential postures, 266
rituals: period-ending, 289–290; at Takalik Abaj Altar
    46, 195; water deities in, 219–220. *See also* domestic
    sphere and rituals; public rituals
Rocío phase, 198
Rodas, Sergio, 160, 161, 230n4, 230n6
Rodríguez, María del Carmen, 148n6
round, sculpture in the. *See* full-round sculpture
Ruíz de Alarcón, Hernando, 33, 34
ruler(s): Ajaw title for, 242; burials of, 198–199; cult
    of, 151; divinity claimed by, 149; domestic rituals
    appropriated by, 225–226, 227–229; individual vs.
    coalition as, 101, 122, 126; motivations for sculptural
    choices of, 207, 208, 215–216, 229–230; as nahuals, 27,
    33, 34, 36, 47–51, 53; nahuals used by, 34, 38; placement
    of monuments by, 210; and rules for display of
    sculptures, 20, 174; throne distribution and, 15; water
    deities as focus of, 210, 215–216, 220–221. *See also*
    elites; political power
ruler(s), portraits of: distribution of, 159, 160, 174;
    interpretations of, 151; mutilation of, 203; on stelae,
    151, 160; at Takalik Abaj, 200, 202, 203, 204; at Tres
    Zapotes, 123–124, 127n4
rulership theme: claims about power in, 150;
    distribution of, meaning of, 159, 160, 174; at
    Kaminaljuyu, 151, 259, 262, 264–267, 270, 273–274;
    in masks, 19; postures depicted in, 266–267, 270;
    in representational stelae, 151, 160; at San Lorenzo,
    6–7; at Takalik Abaj, 151, 200, 202, 203, 204; at Tres
    Zapotes, 116, 119, 122, 123–124, 126; in Zazacatla Lajas
    Structure, 90–91, 92, 93–94, 95

sacred landscape, xvii, 122–123
sacred mountain, 89, 91
sacred space, xvii
sacrifice: animal, 51; human, 35, 46, 51
Sahagún, Bernardino de, 35–37, 38, 53
Saint Andrew's cross motif, 67, 72, 89, 93
Salado River, 80, 93
Salamá Valley (Guatemala), 237–247; conflict in, 236,
    237; distribution of monuments at, 234, 237; earliest
    monuments in, 236; earliest occupants of, 235;
    expansion of settlements in, 236; map of, 233; in
    Miraflores ceramic sphere, 237. *See also specific sites*
salt, 262
Samalá River, 162
San Andrés (Tabasco), 148n6
San Andrés Sajcabajá Valley (Guatemala), 247–255;
    burials in, 236; conflict in, 237; distribution of
    monuments at, 234; map of, 233. *See also specific sites*
San Antonio Suchitepéquez, 158, 242, 244
San Bartolo (Guatemala), writing at, 23, 242, 243, 258n2
San Bartolo murals: accession scene in, 255; dating of,
    258n2; vs. Kaminaljuyu monuments, 266; and La
    Lagunita sculptures, 249; meaning of postures in,
    266; water deity in, 217–219
San Diego, cliff carving at, 286–287
San Francisco River, 168, 170
San Isidro, 17
San José Mogote, 25n4
San Juan Sacatepequez, Monument *1* at, 224, 226
San Lorenzo (Veracruz): apogee of, 7; establishment of,
    4; La Venta's relationship to, 8–9, 196; origins of stone
    carving at, 16; vs. Tres Zapotes, 108, 109
San Lorenzo monuments: colossal heads, 108; dating
    of, 6–7, 16–17; distribution of, 16–17; Monument
    6, 111; Monument *8*, 53, 121; Monument *10*, 6, 29,
    95; Monument *14*, 6; Monument *16*, 43, 44, 45, 52;
    Monument *21*, 121; Monument *37*, 51; Monument
    39, 121; Monument *41*, 6; Monument *58*, 6, 121;
    Monument *61*, 6; Monument *107*, 47, 48; Monuments
    130–133, 109; Monument *ER-5*, 28; Monument *SL-36*,
    28–29; Monument *SL-90*, 28; nahual sculptures,
    28–29, 47; stone boxes, 121; stone cylinders, 121; types
    of, 6–7, 8–9
San Martín Jilotepeque, 262
San Martín Pajapan, 109
San Miguel (Tabasco), 229
San Pedro Aytec figurine, 29–33; dating of, 30;
    description of appearance, 30–32; discovery of, 27,
    29–30; interpretations of, 33, 43–46, 52; production of,
    27, 32
San Sebastian (Guatemala), 162–164; Monuments *1–6* at,
    162–164; skill levels of artists at, 163–164, 173
sanctuaries: nahual, 42, 43; rain, 46–47
Sanders, William, 23–24, 25
sandstone, 16, 134–135
sarcophagi, at La Lagunita, 171, 249, 253–255
Saturno, William A., 258n2
scepters, 138

Schele, Linda, 291, 298n4
Schieber de Lavarreda, Christa, 158, 177–204
schist, 16, 245
Schultze Jena, Leonhard, 171
science, vs. art, 23
sculptors: elite vs. nonelite, 157, 173, 174; evidence of
    individual or group of, 167, 174; skill levels of, 163–164,
    173; specialized knowledge of, 173; training of, 173;
    travel by, 196
sculptural forms: diversity of, 150–151, 157–161; in Early
    Preclassic period, 6–9; in Late Preclassic period,
    10–15, 159–161; in Middle Preclassic period, 7–12,
    157–159; rulers' reasons for choosing, 207, 208. *See
    also specific forms*
sculpture: as active vs. reactive, 208; copying of, 174;
    definitions of, 150; elites' role in production of, 157,
    173, 174; role in civilization, xviii, 23; rules regarding
    display of, 20, 174; vs. stone monuments, xvii, 150; as
    trade item, 174. *See also specific types*
secondary centers: artists in, 174; distribution of
    monuments in, 160, 162–170; of Pacific Guatemala,
    162–170; rules for display of monuments in, 174.
    See also specific sites
Sedat, David W., 235, 236, 241, 244, 245, 246, 258n2
serpent(s): ancestors associated with, 272; Chahk
    associated with, 213; at Chichén Itzá, 63; at Izapa, 213,
    270–272; at Kaminaljuyu, 270; in nahualism, 37; at
    Takalik Abaj, 200–201; at Teotihuacan, 63, 64
serpent nahuals, 42
serpentine, 16, 32
shamans, 27, 43
Sharer, Robert J., 235, 236, 237, 241, 244, 245, 246,
    256, 258n2
shiner glyph, 291–294, 298n4
shininess: lightning as cause of, 289; and Maya
    stelae, 285, 291–296; and mirror sign, 291; of plain
    monuments, 285; representations of, 291, 292, 298n4;
    of stone, 289, 291–296
Shook, Edwin M., 18, 152, 161, 162, 166, 187, 245, 255,
    256, 258n2
Shook Altar, 158, 242, 244
Shook Panel, 43–44, 45, 52
sibik tuun (soot stone), 286
Simeón, Rémi, 33
Sin Cabezas pedestal sculptures, 158
Sitaná, 166
sites, Preclassic: in dating of monuments, 6–15; maps of,
    3, 30, 78; principal, 3. *See also specific sites*
sky, in Zazacatla Lajas Structure, 89, 93
sky bands, 270–272
sky-monster masks, 116
Smith, A. Ledyard, 234, 253
Smith, Adam T., 122
social organization: monuments as source of
    information about, 149, 236; stratification in
    Guatemalan Highlands, 236
Solano ceramic tradition, 257

solar orientation: of plain stelae, 161; at
    Teopantecuanitlan, 63–64, 67, 68, 75
Solórzano, Luís, 169
solstices, 67
Sombrerete (Zacatecas), 39
Spanish conquest. *See colonial era*
spirits, in stone, 288
S-shaped designs, 47, 48, 50, 53, 69, 70
stalagmites, 86
state formation: carved stones in, 20; from chiefdoms,
    151; as placemaking, 97, 122; political power in
    early stages of, 149–150; spread of, 10, 149; at Tres
    Zapotes, 122–126
states, regional differences in, 10
stela(e): celtiform, 136, 291; dating of, 8–13; distribution
    of, 18–19; manifestation of deities in, 210–211; Mayan
    words for, 285–286; nahuals depicted on, 49; origin of
    form, 19; rulers depicted on, 151, 159, 160; small, 10. *See
    also specific cultures and sites*
stela cult, 283
stela-altar pairs: dating of, 12–13; distribution of,
    18; at El Portón, 237–244; at Izapa, 13, 209; at
    Teopantecuanitlan, 12–13, 72–73
stereophotography, 260–261
Stirling, Matthew W., 98, 111, 112, 116, 118, 119, 120, 127n4,
    133, 134, 135
stone: animate qualities of, 286–290; carving techniques
    of, 16, 21, 101, 102, 105, 116, 119–120, 121, 124, 136,
    181, 255, 274; earth associated with, 87, 286, 287; as
    embodiment of time, 289–290; materiality of, 285–
    290; Mayan words for, 283, 285–289, 298n1; natural
    shape and form of, 285; shininess of, 289, 291–296;
    symbolic meaning of, 156
stone monument(s), 1–25; as active vs. reactive,
    208; approaches to analysis of, xvii–xviii, 4–5,
    23–24; vs. clay sculptures, 60–64, 152, 155, 157; as
    communication devices, 19, 25, 129, 145–147; contexts
    of, xiii–xiv, 4, 23, 24; dating of, 5–15; deities embodied
    in, 210–211; distribution of, 16–23; documentation
    methods for, 259–261; as dynamic objects, xvii–
    xviii; elites' role in production of, 157, 173, 174; as
    interpretive tool, xvii–xviii, 23; materials used for,
    16; Mayan words for, 283, 285–286; mobility of, 23;
    mutilation of (*See mutilation/breakage/defacement
    of monuments*); origins of, 7, 16, 17, 18, 195; other
    monuments referenced by, 211; reuse of (*See reuse/
    recycling/recarving*); role in civilization, xviii, 23;
    rules regarding display of, 20, 174; vs. sculpture, xvii,
    150; vs. small carved stones, 25n4; social organization
    revealed by, 149, 236; spread of, 16; techniques for
    carving, 16; uses and meanings of, 4–5, 23, 24
stone workers. *See sculptors*
storm gods, 37
storms, 37
Stuart, David, 49, 156, 210–211, 258n2, 267, 279, 283–297
stucco: on buildings, 19; on plain monuments, 187, 285
stucco masks, 19

subjectivity, in documentation, 261, 263, 282n4
submissive postures, 266, 267, 270
Suchiate River, 214
Sun God, 295
supernatural beings: in La Argelia sculptures, 166; in La
    Venta sculptures, 136, 137, 138; in San Bartolo murals,
    218–219; in Takalik Abaj sculptures, 204; in Zazacatla
    sculptures, 86, 92. *See also* deities
supernatural world, in Zazacatla, 80, 89, 93
supra-regional centers, representational stelae at, 160
symmetry: in La Venta, 132; in Takalik Abaj, 190, 191

Tabasco. *See specific sites*
taj tuun (torch stone), 286
Takalik Abaj (Guatemala), 177–204; ballcourt at, 180–181,
    197–198, 199; burial at, 198–199; Central Group of,
    180, 186, 187, 195; ceramics at, 177, 195; city center of,
    186–195; construction stages of, 180–181, 198–200;
    decline of, 180; distribution of sculpture outside,
    162–166; El Escondite at, 217; growth of, 180, 181;
    history of studies of, 177, 187; layout of, 178, 180, 186,
    187; location of, 177, 178; Long Count dates at, 199, 203,
    204; maps of, 178, 179; name of, 177, 205n1; origins of
    stone carving at, 195; political transition at, 202–203;
    as regional center, 159, 177; Rosada Structures I and
    II at, 198; secondary sites of, 162–166; Structure 7
    at, 186, 191–195, 198–199, 203; Structure 7A at, 192,
    198–199; Structure 9 at, 187–188, 190; Structure 10 at,
    187–188, 190; Structure 11 at, 187–188, 190; Structure
    12 at, 187–190, 199–200, 202; Structure 13 at, 186,
    187–188, 190; Terrace 1 at, 187; Terrace 2 at, 179, 180,
    181, 186, 187–190; Terrace 3 at, 179, 186, 190–195, 198;
    topography of, 178–180
Takalik Abaj monuments, 177–204; Altar 8, 199; Altar 28,
    184, 190; Altar 30, 184, 190–191; Altar 36/38, 200–201;
    Altar 37, 193; Altar 46, 192, 193, 194–195; Altar 48, 198,
    199, 205n4; animal representations, 185–186, 190,
    192–193; astronomical orientations of, 194–195, 203;
    boulder sculptures, 182, 190, 192–193, 201; coexistence
    of styles of, 177, 178, 181, 190, 203–204; dating of,
    158, 177, 181, 195–196; distribution of, 20, 22, 178, 179,
    186–195; vs. Izapa-style art, 181–185, 186, 204; vs.
    La Venta monuments, 196, 201; Maya style of, 177,
    180, 181–186, 195, 198–204, 205n2; meaning of, 178,
    201–204; Monument 1, 195, 196–197, 201; Monument
    8, 188, 189, 190, 199; Monument 9, 188, 189, 190, 199;
    Monument 14, 182, 192–193; Monument 15, 182, 192,
    193; Monument 16/17, 182, 192, 193; Monument 18,
    192, 193; Monument 19, 182, 192, 193; Monument
    23, 201, 275; Monument 27, 177, 187; Monument 42,
    155; Monument 47, 185, 192; Monument 48, 192;
    Monument 50, 193; Monument 51, 192; Monument
    55, 157; Monument 58, 163, 192, 193; Monument 64,
    196, 197–198, 216–217; Monument 65, 188, 189, 190,
    199, 201; Monument 66, 185, 199; Monument 67,
    188, 189, 190, 199; Monument 68, 185, 188, 190, 199;
    Monument 69, 188, 189; Monument 70, 185, 190, 199;
    Monument 93, 193; Monument 100, 184; Monument

107, 184; Monument 108, 184, 190; Monument 109, 184;
    Monument 188, 183, 187; number of, 177, 186; Olmec
    style of, 177, 181–186, 195–198, 201–203, 205n2; pedestal
    sculptures, 166; plain, 187, 190; potbelly sculptures,
    109, 161, 171, 184, 185–186, 190, 202; primary vs.
    secondary, 204; reuse and re-placement of, 152, 181,
    190–191, 200–201; rulership theme of, 151, 200, 202,
    203, 204; shift in styles of, 177, 181, 194, 198, 201–203;
    Stela 1, 216, 217, 218, 272, 273; Stela 3, 242, 244; Stela 5,
    183, 187, 188, 190, 199–200, 266; Stela 12, 183, 187, 190,
    200; Stela 13, 192, 193–194, 198–199, 203; Stela 18, 177,
    187; Stela 50, 192; Stela 71, 201; Stela 74, 182, 192, 198;
    stylistic divisions of, 181; themes of, 195–198; types of,
    181, 185–187; water deity representations in, 216–219
Tate, Carolyn E., 43, 135
Taube, Karl A., 45, 48, 50, 51, 69, 90, 127n3, 136, 166, 209,
    212, 216, 219, 220
taxcal, 180, 198, 205n3
Tecun Uman, 37
Tenochtitlan: axe at, 45; Monument 1 at, 51; Templo
    Mayor at, 93
tenoned busts, at Tres Zapotes, 101, 109–112
Teocuicani, 46
Teopantecuanitlan (Guerrero), 55–75; apogee of, 57–58;
    Area A of, 58, 59; as ceremonial center, 77, 80;
    conflict in, 70; construction stages of, 58; discovery
    of monuments at, 56; distribution of monuments
    at, 18; ethnic identity in, 94–95; excavations at, 55;
    foreign influence in, 72–74; full-round sculpture at,
    18; geology of, 57; vs. La Venta, 136; location of, 55–57;
    looting at, 55, 56; maps of, 57, 59; meaning of name,
    55; mutilation of monuments at, 70–71, 203; Northern
    Terrace at, 71, 72; Olmec style in, 55, 58, 70, 72; plain
    stelae at, 75; as regional center, 57–58; Structure 2
    at, 71, 89, 94–95; Structure 3 at, 67, 71, 88, 89, 94–95;
    topography of, 80; vs. Zazacatla, 77, 80, 88, 89–90,
    94–95
Teopantecuanitlan Northern Esplanade, 71–74;
    limestone head in, 72, 73; potbelly sculpture in, 73–74;
    Sculpture 2 in, 13, 72–73; sculpture fragments from,
    61–62, 63, 70–71; Stela 2 in, 73; Stela 3 in, 12–13, 72–73;
    toad sculpture in, 73
Teopantecuanitlan Sunken Patio, 58–71; astronomical
    orientation of, 63–64, 67, 68, 75; as ballcourt,
    60, 67, 69, 70, 75; ballplayer gods in, 69–70, 75,
    90; calendrical associations of, 67; ceremonial
    significance of, 58, 63–64, 75; clay sculptures
    in, 55, 60–64; construction stages of, 58, 62, 64,
    67; cosmological functions of, 63, 67, 69–70, 75;
    decommissioning of, 58, 70–71; discovery of, 55;
    glyphs in, 67; layout of, 58, 59, 61, 62; map of, 59;
    materials used in, 58–60; Monuments 1–4 in, 56,
    64–71, 89–90; S-shape in, 48, 50, 69, 70; stone
    sculpture fragments from, 61–62, 63, 70–71; time-
    keeping in, 67, 71
Teotihuacan: Fat God complex at, 227; Structure 40A
    of West Plaza at, 63, 64
Tezcatlipoca (deity), 34, 291

themes, sculptural: diversity of, 173–174; ethnic diversity and, 94–95; rulers' reasons for choosing, 207, 208, 220–221. *See also specific sites and themes*

three-dimensional laser scanning, 259–261; applications for, 259–261, 280–281; vs. conventional documentation, 260–261, 269; of damaged monuments, 259; drawings based on, 262–263, 270, 282n5; equipment used in, 262, 263, 282n1; of Kaminaljuyu Monument 65, 262–273; subjectivity in, 263, 282n4

three-dimensional works, perspective in, 29. *See also* full-round sculpture

thrones: altars as, 6, 13; dating of, 6, 7, 13–15; distribution of, 15; four-legged, 13–14; in Kaminaljuyu monuments, 264, 267; representations of, 13–15; at Takalik Abaj, 190–191

Tikal (Guatemala): plain stelae at, 284–285; representation of Chahk at, 209, 210; Stela *31* at, 285

Tiltepec (Chiapas): Monuments *23* and *25* at, 224, 226, 229; niche figure at, 118; stelae at, 116

time, stone as embodiment of, 289–290

time-keeping: Maya stelae in, 289–290; at Teopantecuanitlan, 67, 71

Tlachinollan Kingdom, 47, 54n4

Tlaloc (deity), 50, 253

Tlaltecuhtli (deity), 93

Tlapa (city), 54n4

Tlapa Valley (Guerrero), 30

Tlapacoya: figurine at, 44–45; Monument *1* at, 112; vase from, 89

Tlatilco, contortionist figurine at, 43, 44–45, 52

Tlaxcala, 74

toad(s): Chahk associated with, 213; at Izapa, 213, 214–215; at Takalik Abaj, 190, 192; in Teopantecuanitlan Northern Esplanade, 13, 72–73

toad altars: distribution of, 161, 162–163, 168; at Izapa, 213, 214–215; at Las Conchitas, 168–169; at San Sebastian, 162–163, 164; in stela-altar pairs, 13

Tonacatecutli (deity), 35

tonal: definition of, 33; vs. nahual, 33

Tonalá (Chiapas), 166

Toniná (Chiapas), Monument *30* at, 286

trade: greenstone, 98; sculptures as items of, 174; in spread of sculptural styles, 196

trade routes: Guatemalan Highlands in, 234, 235, 236, 257; Kaminaljuyu in, 262; monuments marking, 197; nahual sanctuaries along, 43; Pacific coast and piedmont in, 207–208; Takalik Abaj in, 180, 181, 196, 197, 203; Teopantecuanitlan in, 58

transformation(s): animal to human, 193; by deities, 34, 35; difficulties in classifying, 29; human to animal (*See* nahuals); in Olmec art, 27; religious beliefs about, 34

transformation figurines, 27–28, 29–33, 43–46, 54n2

Tránsito (Guatemala), 72

travel: by artists, 196; by nahuals, 38

Traxler, Loa, 256

Tres Zapotes (Veracruz), 97–126; decline of, 97; excavations at, 98; factions at, 98–99; growth of, 97, 98; individual vs. coalition as rulers of, 101, 122, 126; layout of, 124–126; location of, 98; Long Count dates at, 98, 118, 119–120; maps of, 99, 123, 125; mounds at, 97, 98; Olmec style at, 98, 116; Plaza B at, 118–119, 126; plaza groups at, 100, 124–126; political placemaking at, 122–126; politicoeconomic strategies at, 99–100, 126; radiocarbon dating at, 98, 100, 108, 118, 119; as regional center, 97, 98, 123–124, 126; territorial boundaries of, 109

Tres Zapotes monuments, 116–121; basins, 121–122; boulder sculptures, 104; boxes, 121–122; chronology of, 101–108; colossal heads, 98, 104, 107, 108–109, 123–124, 127n4; dating of, 97–98, 100, 101, 116; distribution of, 123–126; full-round, 101, 108–116; maps of, 123, 125; Monument *19*, 112, 114, 125; Monument *25*, 112; Monument *27*, 112; Monument *29*, 112; Monument *33*, 116–118; Monument *35*, 109; Monument *37*, 109, 110; Monument *38*, 120, 121; Monument *39*, 120, 121; Monument *40*, 121; Monument *42*, 120; Monument *43*, 112; Monument *44*, 108, 118, 126; Monument A, 107, 108, 123–124; Monument B, 104, 121; Monument C, 104, 105, 121, 125; Monument D, 121; Monument E, 105; Monument F, 111, 112, 114; Monument G, 111–112, 113; Monument H, 109, 110; Monument I, 102, 109; Monument J, 102, 109; Monument L, 109; Monument M, 102, 103, 121; Monument M at, 109; Monument N, 121; Monument O, 112, 115; Monument P, 112, 115; Monument Q, 107, 108, 124; Monument Q at, 108; Monument R, 112, 127n2; as portraits, 123–124, 127n4; potbelly sculptures, 109; sculptural techniques of, 101; seated figures, 102, 109; Stela A, 102, 103, 108, 116; Stela B, 119; Stela C, 98, 104, 105, 108, 116, 118–120, 122, 126, 127n3; Stela D, 102, 103, 104, 108, 116, 118, 122, 267; Stela E, 105, 120–121; Stela F, 116, 117; tenoned busts, 101, 109–112, 124–125; types of, 101

tuff, 83

Tulcingo, 32

turtles, 170

tuun (stone): Maya use of term, 283, 285–289; vs. tun, 298n1

Tuxtla Chico, 29

Tuxtla Mountains, 98

Tuxtla Statuette, 74

Tuzapan figurine, 62, 63

Tzotzil, 287

Tzutzuculi, 26n7

underworld, Zazacatla Lajas Structure linked to, 86–87, 89, 91–93

underworld-monster masks, 116

University of California at Berkeley, 130, 177, 187, 205n1

University of Pennsylvania, 234–235, 237

urban living, 3–5

Urcid, Javier, 49

U-shaped designs, 198

Velásquez, Juan Luis, 167, 169
Venus symbol, 187
Veracruz. *See specific sites*
Verapaz Archaeological Project, of University of Pennsylvania, 234–235
Verapaz Sculptural Style, 245
Verbena phase, 262
verticality, 265
visual imagery, as substitute for writing, 146–147, 148n6
volcanic stone: history of use, 16; at Takalik Abaj, 177; at Zazacatla, 83
V-shaped designs: symbolic significance of, 89, 93; in Teopantecuanitlan clay sculptures, 60; in Zazacatla Lajas Structure, 82–83, 89–90, 93, 94–95

water: animals associated with, at Takalik Abaj, 186; on Izapa monuments, 209–214; in nahualism, 37, 39, 46–47
water deities, 207–221; at Calakmul, 217, 218; at Izapa, 208–219; at Kaminaljuyu, 219–220; at Monte Alto, 220; multiple aspects of, 214, 215, 219; and potbelly sculptures, 229; and public works, 216, 217; rulers' reasons for focusing on, 210, 215–216, 220–221; at San Bartolo, 217–219; at Takalik Abaj, 216–219
Water Lily Serpent, 218
water management: at Izapa, 209–216; rain deities associated with, 213; at Takalik Abaj, 217
water shrines, 46–47
weather: nahuals' control of, 27, 33, 35, 37, 42, 46–51, 53–54; nahuals' understanding of, 37, 38
Weiant, Clarence W., 98, 119
Weitlaner, Roberto J., 33
were-jaguar gods, 55
were-jaguars: babies of, 46, 92; in Teopantecuanitlan monuments, 62, 64–66; and transformation figurines, 43, 44, 46
Wichmann, Søren, 42
wind deities, 46
winds, nahual control of, 35, 37, 42, 53
Wisdom, Charles, 292
wood sculptures: as antecedents of stone monuments, 7; evidence of, 155–156
world (cosmic) trees: definition of, 80; mountains as, 80; in Tres Zapotes stelae, 116, 127n3; V-shaped designs as, 89; in Zazacatla Lajas Structure, 89–91, 95. *See also* axis mundi
worldview. *See* cosmology/cosmovision
wrist bands, 266

writing: cupules as alternative to, 245–247; destruction of monuments with, 255; at El Portón, 237, 242–244, 257, 258n2; at El Zapote, 210–211; in Guatemalan Highlands, 231, 234, 256–257; at Kaminaljuyu, 243, 256, 257, 270, 274; at La Lagunita, 257; at La Venta, lack of, 146–147, 148n6; on Maya stelae, 285–297; origins of, 23; at San Bartolo, 23, 242, 243, 258n2; at Takalik Abaj, 203, 204; at Teopantecuanitlan, 67; at Tres Zapotes, 118, 120, 126; visual imagery as substitute for, 146–147, 148n6

X symbol, 67, 68, 143, 144
Xoc (Chiapas), 74, 286, 287

Yaxchilan, Lintels *14* and *15* at, 272–273
year-stones, 289–290
Yoffee, Norman, 149–150
Young Lord statuette, 50, 152, 158

Zacatecas. *See specific sites*
Zacualpa (Guatemala), 234
Zapotec language, 42
Zapotec people, 17
zapoteños, 124
Zazacatla (Morelos), 77–95; as ceremonial center, 77, 80; construction stages of, 77, 80–82; excavations at, 80; full-round sculpture at, 18; layout of, 79; location of, 78–80; maps of, 78, 79; natural resources of, 80; Olmec style at, 77; Structure *1* at (*See* Zazacatla Lajas Structure); Structure 2 at, 80, 82, 93; Structure 3 at, 80–82; Structure 4 at, 82; Structure 5 (Megalajas Structure) at, 82; Structure 6 at, 82; topography of, 80
Zazacatla Lajas Structure, 80–95; construction stages of, 80, 82, 85–86; different stones used at, 87; dismantling of, 82, 83, 91; distribution of monuments in, 18, 87; ethnic identity expressed in, 93–95; layout of, 82–83, 85–86, 87–89, 91–92; Monument *1* in, 77, 83–85, 87, 89; Monument 2 in, 77, 83–85, 87, 89; Monument *3* in, 86–87, 93; Monument *4* in, 86–87, 93; mountains associated with, 89–93; painting in, evidence of, 83, 85, 86; Structure *1*, 80, 81, 82–85, 87–91; Structure *1-A*, 80, 85–87, 91–93; underworld associations in, 87, 89, 91–93; V-shaped designs in, 82–83, 89–90, 93, 94–95
Zender, Marc, 51
zoomorphic beings: distribution of, 161; in Zazacatla sculptures, 86
Zoque, "Dance of the Jaguar" ritual of, 219–220
Zoque language, 4

DUMBARTON OAKS PRE-COLUMBIAN SYMPOSIA AND COLLOQUIA

PUBLISHED BY DUMBARTON OAKS RESEARCH LIBRARY
AND COLLECTION, WASHINGTON, D.C.

The *Dumbarton Oaks Pre-Columbian Symposia and Colloquia* series volumes are based on papers presented at scholarly meetings sponsored by the Pre-Columbian Studies program at Dumbarton Oaks. Inaugurated in 1967, these meetings provide a forum for the presentation of advanced research and the exchange of ideas on the art and archaeology of the ancient Americas.

Further information on Dumbarton Oaks Pre-Columbian series and publications can be found at www.doaks.org/publications.

Dumbarton Oaks Conference on the Olmec, edited by Elizabeth P. Benson, 1968

Dumbarton Oaks Conference on Chavín, edited by Elizabeth P. Benson, 1971

The Cult of the Feline, edited by Elizabeth P. Benson, 1972

Mesoamerican Writing Systems, edited by Elizabeth P. Benson, 1973

Death and the Afterlife in Pre-Columbian America, edited by Elizabeth P. Benson, 1975

The Sea in the Pre-Columbian World, edited by Elizabeth P. Benson, 1977

The Junius B. Bird Pre-Columbian Textile Conference, edited by Ann Pollard Rowe, Elizabeth P. Benson, and Anne-Louise Schaffer, 1979

Pre-Columbian Metallurgy of South America, edited by Elizabeth P. Benson, 1979

Mesoamerican Sites and World-Views, edited by Elizabeth P. Benson, 1981

The Art and Iconography of Late Post-Classic Central Mexico, edited by Elizabeth Hill Boone, 1982

Falsifications and Misreconstructions of Pre-Columbian Art, edited by Elizabeth Hill Boone, 1982

Highland-Lowland Interaction in Mesoamerica: Interdisciplinary Approaches, edited by Arthur G. Miller, 1983

Ritual Human Sacrifice in Mesoamerica, edited by Elizabeth Hill Boone, 1984

Painted Architecture and Polychrome Monumental Sculpture in Mesoamerica, edited by Elizabeth Hill Boone, 1985

Early Ceremonial Architecture in the Andes, edited by Christopher B. Donnan, 1985

The Aztec Templo Mayor, edited by Elizabeth Hill Boone, 1986

The Southeast Classic Maya Zone, edited by Elizabeth Hill Boone and Gordon R. Willey, 1988

The Northern Dynasties: Kingship and Statecraft in Chimor, edited by Michael E. Moseley and Alana Cordy-Collins, 1990

Wealth and Hierarchy in the Intermediate Area, edited by Frederick W. Lange, 1992

Art, Ideology, and the City of Teotihuacan, edited by Janet Catherine Berlo, 1992

Latin American Horizons, edited by Don Stephen Rice, 1993

Lowland Maya Civilization in the Eighth Century A.D., edited by Jeremy A. Sabloff and John S. Henderson, 1993

Collecting the Pre-Columbian Past, edited by Elizabeth Hill Boone, 1993

Tombs for the Living: Andean Mortuary Practices, edited by Tom D. Dillehay, 1995

Native Traditions in the Postconquest World, edited by Elizabeth Hill Boone and Tom Cummins, 1998

Function and Meaning in Classic Maya Architecture, edited by Stephen D. Houston, 1998

Social Patterns in Pre-Classic Mesoamerica, edited by David C. Grove and Rosemary A. Joyce, 1999

Gender in Pre-Hispanic America, edited by Cecelia F. Klein, 2001

Archaeology of Formative Ecuador, edited by J. Scott Raymond and Richard L. Burger, 2003

Gold and Power in Ancient Costa Rica, Panama, and Colombia, edited by Jeffrey Quilter and John W. Hoopes, 2003

Palaces of the Ancient New World, edited by Susan Toby Evans and Joanne Pillsbury, 2004

A Pre-Columbian World, edited by Jeffrey Quilter and Mary Ellen Miller, 2006

Twin Tollans: Chichén Itzá, Tula, and the Epiclassic to Early Postclassic Mesoamerican World, edited by Jeff Karl Kowalski and Cynthia Kristan-Graham, 2007

Variations in the Expression of Inka Power, edited by Richard L. Burger, Craig Morris, and Ramiro Matos Mendieta, 2007

El Niño, Catastrophism, and Culture Change in Ancient America, edited by Daniel H. Sandweiss and Jeffrey Quilter, 2008

Classic Period Cultural Currents in Southern and Central Veracruz, edited by Philip J. Arnold III and Christopher A. Pool, 2008

The Art of Urbanism: How Mesoamerican Kingdoms Represented Themselves in Architecture and Imagery, edited by William L. Fash and Leonardo López Luján, 2009

New Perspectives on Moche Political Organization, edited by Jeffrey Quilter and Luis Jaime Castillo B., 2010

Astronomers, Scribes, and Priests: Intellectual Interchange between the Northern Maya Lowlands and Highland Mexico in the Late Postclassic Period, edited by Gabrielle Vail and Christine Hernández, 2010

The Place of Stone Monuments: Context, Use, and Meaning in Mesoamerica's Preclassic Transition, edited by Julia Guernsey, John E. Clark, and Barbara Arroyo, 2010